SURVIVING THE HOLOCAUST
The Kovno Ghetto Diary

SURVIVING
THE HOLOCAUST

The Kovno Ghetto Diary

AVRAHAM TORY

Edited with an introduction by
Martin Gilbert

Textual and historical notes by
Dina Porat

Translated by Jerzy Michalowicz

Harvard University Press
Cambridge, Massachusetts
and London, England
1990

The first published edition of this diary, translated into Hebrew from its original
Yiddish, appeared in Israel in October 1988, published by the Tel Aviv University
Diaspora Research Institute and Mosad Bialik, and edited by Dr. Dina Porat.
    Support for the English translation came from Professor Joel Elkes, and from
Joyce and Jack Brauns and the Brauns Family Trust.

This book is printed on acid-free paper, and its binding materials
have been chosen for strength and durability.

Library of Congress cataloging information is on last page of book.

CONTENTS

INTRODUCTION ———————————

On December 5, 1982, an Israeli citizen, Avraham Tory, arrived in Tampa, Florida, from Israel. With him he brought his diary from the years 1941–1944, when he had lived in Lithuania, in the Kovno Ghetto, where the Germans had incarcerated more than thirty thousand Jews. On trial in Tampa was a naturalized U.S. citizen, Kazys Palciauskas, who was accused of having entered the United States shortly after World War II on a false declaration. In July 1941, Palciauskas had been mayor of Kovno, appointed to that position by the German occupation forces, and had acted with the Germans in the mass murder of tens of thousands of Jews. At the time of his entry to the United States, he had failed to mention his wartime position to U.S. immigration authorities.

At the outset of his trial, Palciauskas denied that he had ever been mayor of Kovno. Avraham Tory had come to show that this denial was false, for Tory's diary, about to be presented to the court, was a full, often day-to-day, account, written at the time, of the fate of the Jews of Kovno, including the part Palciauskas had played in their destruction.

The diary Tory had brought to Tampa was the original, written in Yiddish in the Kovno Ghetto. Before his journey to the United States it had been authenticated by four survivors of the Ghetto. The first was Lucia Elstein-Lavon, who had been Tory's secretary in the Ghetto throughout the period during which he had written the diary. She, too, was present at the trial in Tampa. The second was Zvi Levin, a leader of the Zionist underground in wartime Kovno, and one of the very few who not only had known about the diary at the time but had regularly seen it being written. The third was Shraga Goldsmith, the head of the repair workshops in the Ghetto, who had prepared the five wooden crates in which the pages of the diary had been hidden. Goldsmith had personally dug the hiding places, and, with Tory, secreted the crates under the concrete foundations of the uncompleted three-story building that housed his repair workshop. The fourth was Esther Lourie, a painter who had made sketches of many Ghetto inmates and scenes at Tory's request. The four authentications had been made in the form of solemn declarations in conformity with the law of the State of Israel.

Confronted by the facts set out in the diary, Palciauskas admitted that he had been mayor. In April 1984, after a series of appeals, he was found guilty, and his American citizenship was revoked. Since then, the Soviet Union has sought his extradition. The case is (in 1989) before the United States Supreme Court.

Within two years of Avraham Tory's journey to Florida, he left Israel again for another trial, this time in Toronto. Once more he took his diary with him. On trial was Helmut Rauca, the former Gestapo official who had been in charge of the Jewish desk at the Gestapo headquarters in Kovno. In court, Rauca denied that he had been in Lithuania between 1941 and 1943, claiming that at that time he had been serving as a soldier in Czechoslovakia.

From Tory's diary, it was possible to identify specific days on which Rauca had entered the Ghetto, and what he had done there, including his part in the murder of 10,000 Jews during the "Great Action" of October 28, 1941, which Tory had witnessed. The court accepted the entries in Tory's diary dealing with the Great Action as proof of Rauca's part in it, as well as in other subsequent massacres. Tory also submitted to the court documents Rauca himself had signed while he was in Kovno; these were compared with Rauca's signature on his application for entry into Canada and on his Canadian bank accounts, and were judged to be the same. Rauca was found guilty, his Canadian citizenship was taken away from him, and he was extradited from Canada to Germany, where he died in the Frankfurt am Main prison hospital shortly after having been charged with the murder of more than 11,500 Jews.[1]

More than 30,000 Jews lived in Kovno on the eve of World War II. Theirs was the eighth largest Jewish community in what, from June 1941, was to become the German-occupied area of eastern Poland, White Russia, Lithuania, and the western Soviet Union—one of the principal regions of Jewish life and creativity during the interwar years, and, indeed, since long before World War I.

The Kovno Jewish community was one which prided itself upon both its religious and its secular heritage. Nor was it an isolated community; emigration and overseas education had taken Jews from Kovno to Britain, South Africa, the United States, and Palestine in considerable numbers. Avraham Tory himself had studied at the University of Pittsburgh, and had been a delegate to Zionist Congresses and gatherings in Poland, Palestine, and Switzerland. The

1. The Rauca trial was the third trial at which Tory had been a witness, the first being the trial, in November 1962 at Wiesbaden, West Germany, of Heinrich Schmitz, deputy commander of the Gestapo in Lithuania, and Alfred Tornbaum, commander of the Third Division of the German police in Kovno, with responsibility for the Ghetto area. Schmitz committed suicide in his cell before sentence was passed, after hearing Tory's testimony for two full days. Tornbaum was acquitted after the court found that there was insufficient evidence to convict him.

children of Dr. Elchanan Elkes, the head of the Jewish Council in the Kovno Ghetto, were both being educated in Britain at the outbreak of the war.

Jews are first known to have lived in Kovno in 1410, when they were brought to the city as prisoners of war by the Grand Duke Vytautas after his victory over the returning Crusaders at the battle of Gruenwald. They were active as traders between Kovno—a Lithuanian market town on the river Nieman—and Danzig, a Hanseatic League port on the Baltic Sea. At the same time, there were also Jews living across the river from Kovno, in Vilijampolé—a suburb known to the Jews as Slobodka. It was in Slobodka, which had been a Jewish village for four hundred years, that, on German orders, the Kovno Ghetto was set up in 1941.

For three decades after 1495, because of pressure by Christian merchants, Jews were excluded from the city of Kovno, and from other parts of Lithuania. Throughout those years, however, they continued to live in Slobodka. Jews returned to Kovno during the eighteenth century, but there were two further explusions from the city, in 1753 and 1761. With each of these expulsions, the suburb of Slobodka increased in size, and also in poverty.

Restrictions on Jewish residence in Kovno were abolished in 1858. From then on, the Jewish populations of Kovno and Slobodka together grew rapidly, rising from 2,000 in 1847 to 25,000 in 1897. In that year, under the rule of the Russian Czar, the Jews of Kovno constituted one-third of the city's total population. By 1908 the number of Jews had risen still further, to 32,000, and to a substantial 40 percent.

It was not only in numbers but in achievement that Kovno's Jews flourished during the nineteenth century. Jewish cultural activity made the city a center of Hebrew writing and literary criticism. In 1863, the first of several *yeshivot*—religious study centers—made Slobodka famous throughout the world of Russian and Eastern European Jewry, and beyond.

Jewish deputies from Kovno were elected to the first and second Duma, held in the Russian capital, St. Petersburg, following the 1905 revolution. In 1909 a conference was held in Kovno to work out a law for the establishment of Jewish community councils throughout Czarist Russia. Jewish schools proliferated, as did Jewish charitable institutions.

In 1915, as the German Army approached Kovno, the Czarist authorities expelled the 32,000 Jews into the interior of Russia. But with German occupation later that year about 9,000 returned.

Following the establishment of an independent Lithuania after the collapse of Czarism, Kovno—from 1919, as Kaunas, the temporary capital of the new state—saw a flowering of Jewish cultural, educational, and economic life. A Ministry of Jewish Affairs was set up in the city, as well as a Jewish National Council for Lithuania, with considerable powers of religious and cultural autonomy for the many Jewish communities throughout the country. By 1935 there were four Jewish daily newspapers in Kovno, three of them Zionist and one Bundist, all published in Yiddish. Hebrew schools and Yiddish schools existed side by side. Individual Jews rose to important positions in medicine, and in commerce. Nevertheless, there were limits to what the Jews could aspire to: for example, there were only a very few Jewish judges, and very few Jews were employed in government offices. Nor did a single Jew reach the rank of colonel in the Lithuanian Army, despite many who had served as officers since the founding of the state.

On April 10, 1922, the Lithuanian parliament (the Seimas) abolished the Ministry for Jewish Affairs and the position of Minister for Jewish Affairs. On March 8, 1926, the Jewish National Council was abolished, ending six years of Jewish religious and cultural autonomy in Lithuania.

With the Soviet annexation of Lithuania in June 1940, the days of relative security for Kovno Jewry came to an abrupt end. Jewish life as such was ruined; Jewish institutions were closed down, and Jewish religious and communal life brought to a halt, except for clandestine activity. For the Jews of Kovno, the strength which their Jewish activities and organizations gave them was suddenly and drastically undermined. With the German invasion a year later, disaster followed.

Avraham Tory was born Avraham Golub in the Lithuanian village of Lazdijai in 1909, a subject of the Russian Czar. His father, Zorach Golub, was a graduate of the Volozhin yeshiva and had qualified as a rabbi, although he had never practiced. Tory's mother, Sarah Leah, was the daughter of Jacob and Dobrusha Prusak, farmers who owned their own farm.

Tory (he was to adopt this surname in 1950, three years after his arrival in Israel) was the youngest of six brothers and sisters. His first education was at the *cheder*—a religious elementary school—then at the elementary school which had been established in his village at the end of World War I. By the time he was thirteen, bar mitzvah age, he was already a sports guide with the Maccabi Club and an active member of the General Zionist Youth Movement in Lithuania. Later he continued his studies at the Hebrew Gymnasium in Marijampolé, the district town. This was the first Hebrew high school in Lithuania in which all subjects were taught in Hebrew; Tory graduated from it in 1927. A year later, at the age of 19, he began to study law at university in Kovno.

In 1929, when Nachum Sokolow, then president of the World Zionist Organization, visited Lithuania, Tory served as his escort during the eight days of his visit. A year later Tory went to the United States, to study law at the University of Pittsburgh. Reaching Pennsylvania at the height of the Depression, he supported himself by working as a Hebrew teacher in a school for Jews who had immigrated from Hungary.

Tory remained in the United States for a year and a half. Then, after the sudden death of his father in Lazdijai, he returned at his mother's request to Lithuania, where he continued his law studies in Kovno.

Tory's travels were not over, however. In the spring of 1932, he went to Palestine as the head of the Maccabi sports team from Lithuania, participating as a gymnast in the first Maccabiah Games, which took place in Tel Aviv that April. Immediately after the games he represented the Lithuanian Jewish students at a convention of Jewish students from all parts of the world, held at the Hebrew University of Jerusalem.

Returning to Kovno to continue his legal studies, Tory was twice head of Vetaria, a Zionist student fraternity which had been founded in Kovno in 1924. He and his fellow Zionist students often encountered hostile treatment at the hands of Lithuanian students, as well as from some professors. The cry "Jews, go to Palestine!"—and violent clashes—became more frequent from year to year.

In 1933, the year Hitler came to power in Germany, Tory graduated from the faculty of law at Kovno and was awarded a degree which entitled him both to practice as a lawyer and to serve on the judiciary. In effect, however, the Minister of Justice had practically closed the courts and the district attorneys' offices to Jews, so that Jewish jurists had almost no chance of obtaining a license to practice. A fellow student of Tory's at the faculty of law, a Lithuanian named Penchila, who had received the same diploma at the same time as Tory, was appointed judge. He did Tory a "favor" and employed him as practitioner-clerk in his court chambers.

After completing his six-month apprenticeship period with Judge Penchila, Tory was engaged as assistant to Professor Simon Bieliatzkin, a leading expert on civil law and one of the few Jewish professors at the University of Lithuania.

Between 1930 and 1939, Tory's Zionist activities and beliefs were reflected in three public positions he held: as a member of the central committee of the Maccabi Sports Association; as deputy chairman of the Hanoar Hazioni Zionist youth movement; and as a member of the central committee of one of the two wings of the General Zionists, the right-wing General Zionist Union.

In March 1939, the national executive of Tory's wing of the General Zionists in Lithuania sent three of its members, among them Tory, as delegates to a convention of Eastern European Zionists in Warsaw. While in Warsaw, Tory also participated in the world executive of the General Zionist Union. Five months later, he traveled to Switzerland as a delegate to the twenty-first Zionist Congress, held that year in Geneva. It was while at the Congress that the delegates learned of the signing of the Molotov-Ribbentrop Pact of August 23, 1939, one of the provisions of which, unknown at the time, was the effective control of Lithuania by the Soviet Union.

On September 1, 1939, five days after the Congress opened, the German Army invaded Poland. As the Congress broke up, the delegates from Eastern Europe debated whether to return to their homes or to remain in Switzerland until the storm had passed. Most of the Lithuanian delegates, Tory included, chose to return.

On October 10, 1939, scarcely a month after Tory's return to Kovno, the Soviet Union and Lithuania signed an agreement whereby the Soviet Union could establish military and air bases on Lithuanian soil. These bases came under the authority of the military construction administration of the Supreme Soviet in Moscow. Tory's Zionist work and affiliations could well have led to his deportation to a Siberian or North Russian labor camp; they did lead to his being questioned several times by the NKVD (the predecessor of the KGB). But because of his knowledge of the Russian, German, Lithuanian, and Yiddish languages, he was eventually given work by the Soviet military construction administration. His job was to prepare its financial and accounting reports for dispatch to the Baltic main office in Riga. He was also able to find work at the administration for a number of his friends, among them Shimon Bregman, a refugee from Poland and an active member of the General Zionist youth movement (after the war to become a professor of geriatrics at Tel Aviv University) and Izia Dillion, the former head of the Betar Revisionist movement in Lithuania, who was shortly to be deported to Siberia, where he died.

Tory worked for five months at the military construction administration before being forced to leave on account of his alleged "dark past" as a Zionist, the "counterrevolutionary" nature of which even his competent work could not negate. In vain did he search for work. "The Soviet Russians did not know me," he later wrote, "and were suspicious of me. The Lithuanians hated Jews and rejoiced at their troubles." Tory knew from his brother-in-law, Benjamin Romanovski—a high official in the Soviet government of Lithuania—that he was on the list of those to be deported to Siberia, and expected to be arrested at any moment. "Tell us what plots you and Dr. Weizmann have concocted against the Soviet Union," he was asked, again and again, under interrogation by the NKVD in Kovno. Fearful of deportation, Tory left Kovno for Vilna, where he was in hiding during the last weeks of Soviet rule in Lithuania. Then, on June 22, 1941, the Germans attacked the Soviet Union, "and I went"—Tory later recalled—"from the frying pan into the fire."[2]

2. A. Tory-Golub, "My Personal Experiences in the Soviet Military Administration 'Glav-Vojenstroy' in Lithuania," typescript, 10 pp., no date.

Tory's diary tells the story of that "fire." Its first entry was written at midnight on the day of the German invasion. That same day, in Kovno, several hundred Jews were seized by the Lithuanian mob and murdered. On June 23, the German Army entered the city. In the diary, the story of the life and fate of the Jews of Kovno during the war years emerges in stark detail. Tory's writing, often done late at night, combines the emotion of an eyewitness to destruction with the determination of that same eyewitness to record facts, figures, and details as precisely as possible.

From the principal European Ghettos set up by the Germans, several diaries and collections of documents survive; many others are known to have been destroyed. The three largest existing sets of contemporary records are those of the Warsaw Ghetto, collected by Emanuel Ringelblum and his "Joy of Sabbath" circle, the archives of the Bialystok Ghetto, and the chronicle of the Lodz Ghetto, a daily digest of events compiled by members of the Jewish Council there. A similar collection for Lvov, carefully collected and guarded by a group of dedicated Jewish historians, is thought to have been lost. Material also survives for the Minsk and Vilna Ghettos, including diaries and documents; the same is true of a number of the smaller Ghettos. In the main, however, only a tiny fragment of what was written at the time survived the war, or has yet been recovered.

Avraham Tory's is one of the longest and fullest of the surviving diaries. It is also the only one which (with the exception of the story of the successful struggle within the Ghetto to conceal the existence of typhus) was penned without inhibition. This frankness is particularly valuable regarding the otherwise largely unrecorded discussions between the Jewish Council and the German authorities from whom that Council received its orders and instructions.

On July 10, 1941, two senior Lithuanian officials—the mayor, Palciauskas, and the city's military commander, Colonel Bobelis—announced by decree that a Ghetto was to be established across the river from Kovno in the suburb of Slobodka, known to the Lithuanians since 1918 as Vilijampolé. In 1941 about 6,000 of Kovno's 35,000 Jews lived there, most of them in conditions of considerable poverty. The majority of Kovno's Jews lived in the city itself, from which, in July and August 1941, they were expelled and sent to Slobodka. Five days before the uprooting began, all Jews were ordered to wear a yellow "Shield of David" (also known as the Star of David) on the left side, and also on the back, of their coats. Anyone not wearing such a badge would be arrested. The Jews were also ordered to create a Jewish police force to keep order within the Ghetto.

At the end of July 1941 the German authorities in Kovno ordered the Jewish Committee for the Transfer to the Ghetto to elect an Oberjude (Chief Jew) to administer its affairs in the Ghetto with the help of an Ältestenrat (Council of Elders).[3] The man the Jews elected as Oberjude, at the last assembly of the prewar Jewish community on August 4, 1941, was one of Kovno's most distinguished Jewish citizens, the physician Dr. Elchanan Elkes.

Returning from northern Lithuania, to which he had fled on June 23 in an unsuccessful attempt to cross the Soviet frontier, Avraham Tory, who was then 32 years old, became the deputy secretary of the new Jewish Council. From this position at the center of events and at the side of Dr. Elkes, Tory recorded what happened and preserved copies of German instructions and decrees. Tory also encouraged several Jewish artists, including Josef Schlesinger and Esther Lourie, to keep a visual record of life and death in the Ghetto. At the same time, using a clandestine camera, the photographer Hirsch Kadushin kept a photographic record. Tory himself also took clandestine photographs until, quite soon after the establishment of the Ghetto, his camera was confiscated.

Esther Lourie later recalled that in the early months of the Ghetto she accompanied Tory to the house of Mordechai Yatkunski, a leading Zionist who was among a thousand Jews murdered by the Lithuanian mob in Slobodka on the night of June 25, 1941. "He asked me to perpetuate the scene for posterity with my painter's brush," she recalled. "We entered the house with some danger, and I painted the horrible sight of murder."[4] During the winter of 1941, Tory took Esther Lourie to paint the remains of the Jewish hospital and orphanage which the Germans had locked and burned on October 4, 1941, killing all its inmates: patients, doctors, nurses, and orphans. Tory kept Esther Lourie's paintings for many months, until she asked for them back. He returned two hundred to her, keeping some thirty sketches and paintings. The two hundred were destroyed by the Germans when the Ghetto was burned down in July 1944: the thirty hidden by Tory survived the war. Another painter, Ben-Zion Schmidt, known as Nolik, had all but one of his paintings destroyed. Kadushin's photographs survived in the possession of Kadushin himself. Josef Schlesinger's drawings were

3. Terms such as *Ältestenrat, Judenrat, Oberjude,* as well as *Ghetto,* were archaic titles dating back to the Middle Ages, when a German prince would appoint a Hauptjude or an Oberjude to serve as his agent in the area of the town to which Jews were confined, the Ghetto, and would establish a Judenrat (Jewish Council) or Ältestenrat (Council of Elders) to exercise authority within the Ghetto walls. The prince might, for example, summon the Hauptjude and inform him that the town's Jews must make the prince a gift of a thousand guilders to finance his participation in the Crusades: the money would then be raised by the Jewish Council through taxes on their fellow Jews. The term used by the Germans in Kovno was *Ältestenrat;* it is translated throughout the diary as Jewish Council.

4. Esther Lourie, "Declaration," Tel Aviv, November 1982; Esther Lourie, *Kovno Ghetto Scenes and Types* (Tel Aviv, 1958).

hidden with Tory's diary, and survived, as did Tory's own collection of the badges, insignia, and armbands of the Council employees. Tory's own photographs were almost all lost.

Tory was determined to keep as full a record of the war as possible—in particular, a record of the German "actions" at which Jews were taken out of the Ghetto and executed at the nearby Ninth Fort, one of the nineteenth-century Czarist fortifications which encircled the city. There was one brief period, shortly after the establishment of the Ghetto, when the pressure of his official secretarial work made it impossible for Tory to write in his diary on the day itself: it was not until October 4, 1941, that he was able to set down what had happened in the three weeks since September 15. But late at night on October 28, 1941, he wrote his account of the event which had taken place that very day, the horrendous "Great Action," during which 10,000 Jews were sent to their deaths at the Ninth Fort.

Following the substantial entry for October 28, 1941, there is no surviving diary entry until January 3, 1942, although Tory did manage to preserve four documents for the intervening period, each of which is published here in its correct chronological place.

Greatly encouraged to do so by his friend Pnina Sheinzon, whom he was to marry after liberation, Tory made every effort from January 1942 to record the events of each day on the day itself, as well as to collect as many German orders and Jewish Council reports and announcements as he could. These reports included two "censuses" taken in the Ghetto in September and November 1941, as well as other statistical materials which showed that whereas the Jewish population of Kovno in August 1941 had been 30,022, repeated killings, in addition to the "Great Action," had reduced it by almost half by December 1942, when only 16,601 Jews were still alive.[5] More than 5,000 Jews deported from Germany, Austria, Czechoslovakia, France, and elsewhere in Western Europe in January 1942 were also brought to Kovno and murdered at the Ninth Fort.

Like all the captive peoples—Poles, Czechs, Serbs, Greeks, Dutch, Danes, and many more—and in even fiercer measure, the Jews were confronted by all the cruelties, uncertainties, and sudden shifts of policy of Nazi totalitarianism. More than any other captive people, they understood from the very first days of German conquest and occupation that their one hope lay in living through the years of Nazi domination, however long those years might be. *Ueberleben,* "to live through," was the aspiration of more than 50 million people; the 8 million

5. A report sent from Riga to Berlin by a senior SS officer, Karl Jaeger, on February 8, 1942, gives the number of Jews executed throughout Lithuania between August 1941 and February 1942 as 136,421; the killings in Kovno were thus some 10 percent of the total.

Jews of Europe had no alternative but to share this aspiration, and to share it with the knowledge that they were to be the first victims—that it was not intended that they should survive at all.

The several hundred Eastern European Jewish Councils, including that of the Kovno Ghetto, on whom fell the burden of administrative contact with the Germans, daily faced the question of how best to protect those within their particular Ghetto from starvation, disease, and the constant threat of murder. None of these councils were able to avoid carrying out the orders the Germans sent through to them, although, as Tory's diary makes clear, the Kovno Jewish Council devoted considerable time and energy to trying to mitigate the effect of these orders.

The Jewish Council in the Kovno Ghetto, like those in the majority of Ghettos throughout Eastern Europe and western Russia, encouraged a substantial range of acts of self-preservation and preparation for resistance in case the Germans should ever move to destroy the Ghetto altogether, a fate which, though often feared, could never be known for certain, and could seldom be anticipated by more than a few weeks or even days.

One rescue effort in Kovno was the preparation of "malines"—hiding places under buildings and in cellars—in which, in July 1944, more than a thousand Jews were to hide when the Germans finally decided, on the eve of the arrival of the Red Army, to destroy the Ghetto.

From the fall of 1942 to the summer of 1944, the Jewish Council in the Kovno Ghetto acted on a daily basis to ensure the preservation of as much of Kovno Jewry as possible: to feed, to guard, to maintain morale, to protect. We know about similar activities in other ghettos; Tory's diary is a full and sustained account of them. It therefore enables the reader to see the absurdity of the often reiterated suggestion—made by those who ignore the conditions of all Europe's captive peoples under Nazi rule—that Jews participated in their own destruction. They participated in a desperate, prolonged, and tormented struggle to survive.

The Jews, confronted with greater hatred than existed against any other captive peoples, found, in the main, in their wartime community leaders, those who were determined not to give the Germans the victory. These leaders in the unequal relationship between conqueror and conquered—Jewish leaders such as Dr. Elkes in Kovno—were often bewildered and uncertain; but as Tory's diary shows, the Kovno Jewish Council saw itself in the forefront of the battle for survival, and acted, despite the daily uncertainties, to seek the survival of everyone in the Ghetto, and of those brought into it from outside.

The Jewish Council in Kovno understood the German need for Jewish labor, and did its best to service and sustain it. The Kovno Ghetto provided a substantial workforce for the Germans throughout 1942 and 1943: 8,000 Jews left the Kovno Ghetto every morning to work outside it, and a further 2,000 remained inside to work in the Ghetto workshops. Many of the inmates believed that in work lay the way to survival. Like the Jews in the Lodz Ghetto, led by Chaim Rumkowski, or those of Vilna under Jacob Gens, the Jews of Kovno believed that their labor was sufficiently important to the German war economy for them to be allowed to survive, despite the spasmodic killings which never fully ceased. Many entries in Tory's diary reflect the debate on whether work will prevent, or merely postpone, the day of destruction.

As well as the 10,000 Jews who worked either inside the Kovno Ghetto or beyond it, there were also a further 8,000 Jews—mostly women, children, the old, and the sick—who did not work, and who were dependent for food and subsistence not only upon those who worked but also upon the arrangements the Jewish Council made on their behalf. About 2,000 of them were not even registered; courageously, the Council maintained them in the Ghetto as if they did not exist, withholding the fact of their presence from the Germans, who would otherwise almost certainly have deported and killed them. Some of these 2,000 were orphans of the "actions" of 1941. Others were old people, or refugees from other towns and villages, including Jews who no longer had the strength to hide in the countryside among hostile or indifferent peasants, and who had decided to seek safety inside the Kovno Ghetto (see the diary entries for August 2 and December 1, 1942).

Not every entry in the diary is a tragic one; when the Council succeeded in securing more food, or more firewood, spirits rose. Spririts also rose during the various cultural events Tory describes, such as the children's Purim festival concert (March 21, 1943), the Passover celebration held in the Ghetto's vocational training school (April 26, 1943), the sermon given by Rabbi Abram Grodzenski to his religious pupils, the last circle of survivors of the once famous Slobodka Yeshiva (June 5, 1943), and—for Tory the most uplifting of all—the Zionist celebrations of July 24, 1943, which he describes as "a festive occasion, pervaded with splendor."

Despite these festivities, lovingly described by Tory, the isolation of the Ghetto was almost total, not only from whatever else was left of Jewish life in Lithuania, but even from the city of Kovno itself. Tory and the Council members were privileged in this regard; they had to go into the city in the course of their official work to discuss the Ghetto's needs with the German civil authorities. This gave them an opportunity, albeit a risky one, to make contact with Lithuanian acquaintances of the prewar years.

The relations between Jews and Lithuanians are an ever-present theme and concern of Tory's diary, highlighted by the impact of the news which reached the Council that there had been individual Lithuanians who, at the Ponar killing site outside Vilna, had refused to open fire on Jews brought there to be killed. Those inside the Kovno Ghetto constantly sought help from Lithuanians beyond the Ghetto walls, and craved whatever information they could get from them about the outside world; the discussion between Rabbi Snieg and the Catholic Bishop Brizgys was a turning point in regard to learning about the outside world (April 30, 1943), as was the meeting between Professor Birsziska and the Council's deputy chairman, Leib Garfunkel (June 2, 1943).

Another recurring aspect of the diary, as of daily life in the Ghetto, is the part played by the Jewish Ghetto police, not only in keeping order from day to day, but in rounding up Jews for work camps. The diary also tells of individual Jews who had denounced other Jews to the Germans (see December 31, 1942). The Jewish Council, which sought to maintain a structure of daily life in the Ghetto, was likewise caught in a trap, fearful of provoking German retaliation or reprisals, either by failure to satisfy demands for labor or by any hint of lack of cooperation. On February 8, 1943, Avraham Tory noted in his diary, at a time of rumors of a new deportation: "We must refrain from doing anything which might arouse the suspicions of the Germans." Four days earlier he had witnessed the notorious "Stalingrad action," when Jewish police were forced to round up twenty-seven Jewish men, women, and children in the Ghetto. These Jews were taken by the Germans to the Ninth Fort and killed. Tory wrote in his diary that day: "The life of no person in the Ghetto is secure any longer. Anyone may stumble all of a sudden. All the same, our will to go on living is as strong as ever—to go on living and to leave the horrors behind."

How to reconcile German demands with Jewish survival is a question which occurs again and again in the diary, and one that could not be resolved. "The aim of this order is to appease the Germans," Tory wrote on February 4, 1943, on the day of the rounding up of the twenty-seven Jews; there then follows a return to the "period of relative calm," but the true nature of that calm, although unknown, was sensed and feared.

Tory's diary makes it clear that the slaughter which had taken place between July and October 1941 was seen in the Ghetto as an ever-present warning throughout the period of relative calm, which continued until October 1943—a warning of what might happen. At the same time, and in common with several other Ghetto Councils, the Council in Kovno took an active part in encouraging Jews to prepare to resist if the calm should come to an end. Each month saw some German violence: random shootings, arrests, incidents in which Jews were killed or deported. Through the two years from November 1941 to October 1943, the Council regarded the maintenance of Ghetto morale and of some basic standard of life and health as an important, if constantly threatened, task. Also important, in the Council's view, was the need to maintain some form of satisfactory relations with the German civilian administration; see, for example, the discussion between Tory and the deputy city governor of Kovno, Keiffler, on January 6, 1943, or Dr. Elkes's meeting with the head of the Kovno Gestapo, Colonel Jaeger, on June 9, 1943. It is clear from many of the entries, however, that no one on the Council was under any illusions as to the cruelty of the decisions which they felt impelled to take, or were ordered to take. Whenever possible, the Council would deceive the Germans in order to safeguard the Jews, as for example by concealing the true number of Ghetto inmates who were not working on German enterprises.

In the winter of 1942, Tory allowed himself a rare expression of emotion, writing in the diary: "Matters of life and death, Lord, when will this end?" A few months later, on February 12, 1943, after a meeting with a senior German official who, at a whim, could have ordered the destruction of everything the Jewish Council had created, Tory set down his thoughts on what he felt was the strength which lay behind the daily torments of the whole Ghetto: "Despite the seven compartments of hell that the Jews—as individuals and as a community—have gone through, our spirit has not been crushed. Our eyes are wide open and we are attuned to what is going on around us. We do not forget for one moment the hallowed purposes of our people."

The burdens of daily life in the Ghetto did not seem to weaken the Jewish sense of purpose. In Tory's words that day: "Everything we do, all the things we go through, seem to us a necessary evil, a temporary hardship, so that we may reach our goal and fulfill our duty: to keep on going, and to keep spinning the golden thread of the eternal glory of Israel, in order to prove to the world the will of our people to live under any conditions and situations. These goals supply us with the moral strength to preserve our lives and to ensure the future of our people."

Was it still possible, in February 1943, to imagine that Jewish life could be preserved? Tory answered this question in a diary entry later that same day. "We will hold out," he wrote, "if quiet prevails both here and outside." No one could know in that month whether "quiet" would prevail—as Hitler's armies faced serious setbacks in Russia and Tunisia—or for how long, or to what ultimate advantage if any.

The diary describes in detail the many encounters between the Council officials and the Germans. Tory himself frequently had to leave the Ghetto to go to the offices of the city governor, to put forward requests for food and supplies or to answer German complaints. His diary also gives many examples of how the German authorities not only exploited Jewish labor in Kovno itself and throughout the Kovno region for the benefit of the German war economy, but also ensured that the Jews made a contribution to the personal gain of individual Germans, who would order suits, shoes, even rings and jewelry, to be made for them in the Ghetto, always without payment. Both the Gestapo and the German civil administrators, Tory noted early in 1943, "take advantage of their tour of duty here to get rich. Every day they pack up their parcels and bundles and send them by mail to their homes in Germany."

Many of the descriptions in the diary provide important details concerning the fate of Lithuanian Jewry during the war years. Almost every day brought new dramas, often terrible ones, which Tory described as fully as his physical strength allowed; each night Pnina Sheinzon would urge him to write, or would herself take down the diary entry at his dictation. On April 5, 1943, for example, and several times on subsequent days, Tory reported on the cruel deception practiced against several thousand Jews from the surviving small Ghettos in the Vilna region, who were told that they were being relocated to Kovno, but were murdered on the way, in the pits of Ponar. On April 6, he described the fate of several hundred Kovno Jews during one of the "selections" more than a year earlier (on February 6, 1942). On April 7, he reported on a courageous act of defiance by the Jews of Panevezys, who paid with their lives for their attempt to resist deportation.

Later that same month, as the deception and slaughter continued in other areas of Lithuania, the Kovno Jewish Council sent a delegation to the Gestapo to ask about rumors that an "action" was to be carried out soon in Kovno. The answer was that such rumors were mere propaganda, no such "action" was contemplated—and that "if anything does happen, it will only be to the old and infirm." The Council leaders then summoned the heads of the various Council departments, to tell them of the latest developments. "We also decided," Tory noted (on April 19, 1943), "to conceal from them one detail: the possibility of a German 'action' against the old and the infirm." Whether morally right or wrong, the concealment was effective. The German "reassurances," Tory added, "that no action is planned against the Ghetto in the near future, spread quickly in the Ghetto, enabling those in the Ghetto to relax a little. Sparks of hope replaced the sense of despair." Nor in fact did any "action" against the old and infirm take place. But for the Council, the dilemma of what to reveal and what to withhold remained a troubled one. Tory's diary abounds with examples of how the Council tried to maintain hope in the Ghetto, yet not to give false assurances. "The sufferings of the Jews are great," Tory noted on February 28, 1943, "also strong is their will to live and to survive the bad times. This is the source of various inventions aimed at improving the quality of life somewhat. The will to live is rooted strongly in the Jewish character; those in the Ghetto are no exception in this regard, against the will of the Jew-haters."

Some of the most powerful descriptions in the diary are of Tory's encounters and talks with these "Jew-haters," as well as the long explanation given to the

Council (on June 2, 1943), by Joseph Caspi, a Jew who had been imprisoned by the Russians during the period of Soviet rule and had subsequently thrown in his lot with the Germans to fight Communism. Tory also records soul-searching discussions with another Jew, Benno Lipzer, who had likewise decided to try to work with the Gestapo. Both these men also tried to help Jews; both, in the end, were murdered by the Germans. "You entertain illusions of survival," Caspi told the Council during their discussion in June 1943. "I know that if I survive it will be only by chance."

Chance and illusion were the two dominant shadows over Ghetto life. On learning of the Ponar massacres, Tory noted; "We hear, and we refuse to believe" (April 8, 1943). Later that year, a Kovno Jew, Blumenthal, and his Christian wife Annette, who was a Belgian citizen, were told that they could go to Switzerland. "Young Blumenthal was beside himself with excitement," Tory noted (June 25, 1943). "He could hardly believe in the good intentions of the Gestapo." The Gestapo car drove off with the Blumenthals in the direction of the airfield outside Kovno. But it took them instead to the Fourth Fort, where they were murdered.

Throughout the diary, a sense of doom alternates with a sense of hope. The indispensability of Jewish labor is clear one day, but less clear the next. "The Germans want to drain the marrow from our bones," Tory wrote on April 8, 1943, "they want to use us until the last moment of our lives, when they will take us to the Ninth Fort, or to a forest, to exterminate us."

Until the evil day came, there seemed for many Jews to be one overriding injunction, to record what was happening. Tory was far from alone in this; there are several references in his diary to other accounts which were written, but which have not survived. "The details of this life are without precedent," he wrote in the summer of 1943, "not just in Jewish history, but in universal history as well. These details must not be allowed to sink into oblivion."

On October 26, 1943, the Germans ordered 2,800 Jews to assemble in the Ghetto; the young men and women were sent to slave labor camps in Estonia; the children and old people were deported to Auschwitz, where they were gassed. That same week, the Germans announced that the Kovno Ghetto was henceforth to be a concentration camp. From that time, workers who left for work-duty were under heavy guard. Once at their workplaces they were no longer allowed to leave their tasks for even a short break—as had sometimes been allowed earlier—or to barter for food.

In the months following the transformation of the Ghetto into a concentration camp, several hundred Jews were rounded up and deported to slave labor camps in the Kovno region. In order to avoid deportation, others succeeded in digging hiding places, while members of the various underground groups—including the Zionist organization Matzok, of which Tory was one of the founders and leaders—managed to escape to the forests and to join the Soviet partisans who were disrupting German communications behind the lines.

That same autumn, at the Ninth Fort, the Germans began to remove bodies from the mass graves and burn them. Jews from the Kovno Ghetto, and Jewish soldiers in the Red Army who had earlier been taken prisoner-of-war, were forced to do this work. On December 25, 1943, sixty-four of these prisoners escaped from the Ninth Fort. Tory, who was still in the Ghetto, wrote down an account of their work at the Ninth Fort and of their escape, as told to him a few days later by Captain Vassilenko, the leader of the escape.

Among the other documents which Tory preserved was a detailed report presented at a special meeting of the Jewish underground on July 8, 1942, by a Polish Catholic woman, Irena Adamovich, giving details of the fate of the Jews of Poland in the summer of 1942. Many written orders from the Germans survived as well. Each of the documents published here—about a hundred of them in all—is printed in its chronological place in the diary.

When Avraham Tory escaped from Kovno, he took with him the last testament of Dr. Elkes. The testament, a letter to Dr. Elkes's son and daughter, is published immediately after the last diary entry.

Of the actual writing and hiding of his diary, Tory recalled forty years later:

> I wrote the diary at all hours, in the early hours of the morning, in bed at night, between meetings of the Council or Matzok, when I was left alone in the room. During meetings, I sometimes wrote headings, quotes, summaries, dates, and names of places and people on scraps of paper or in notebooks, lest I forget and make mistakes. I also often wrote down the testimony of survivors who had returned to the Ghetto from the Gestapo dungeons in the Ninth Fort, from the torture chambers of Schtitz or Rauca, from the interrogation cells of the Lithuanian Secret Police, from the Central ("Yellow") Prison in Kovno, and from failed attempts to hide with Lithuanians.
>
> There was no shortage of writing paper in the Ghetto, and there were also Yiddish, German and Lithuanian typewriters. Lucia Elstein-Lavon, who then worked at the Council's secretariat, helped me with everything, with full understanding, cooperation, and care for secrecy. As time went by, I felt that Dr. Elkes was friendly and trustful of me and I therefore decided to reveal to him that I was keeping the diary. I frequently read entries to him, as well as to his deputy, Leib Garfunkel. They both showed keen interest, made remarks, and encouraged me to continue. Dr. Elkes sometimes gave me summaries of talks he held with German officials at which I was not present. Except for him and Garfunkel, and the underground leader Zvi Levin, none of the other members of the Council knew about the diary.
>
> When a quantity of material had been accumulated at my place of work

in the Council building, and since I was for personal reasons unable to hide it at my dwelling, I turned to Pnina Sheinzon, whom I had known from before the war. To my joy, she agreed to hide it, despite the grave danger she took upon herself. I would send my writings through fourteen-year-old Joel Shmukler or eleven-year-old Yankele Bergman, messengers of the Council. I occasionally delivered material personally. A number of times, when I was on the verge of collapse from exhaustion, Pnina wrote entries as I dictated to her; this explains why some parts of my diary are in her handwriting.

Documentary material and entries were added to my diary almost daily. The great quantity of material might have been discovered, or its hiding place might one day have become part of the area outside the Ghetto, because of sudden reductions in the area of the Ghetto. Outside the Ghetto, I was unable to find a single Lithuanian who was willing to hide it. I therefore turned to Shraga Goldsmith, an old friend, who had dug a hiding place beneath the cellar of Block C, a building which housed the Jewish Council's repair workshop. We packed the material which Pnina brought from the temporary hiding place in her room in synthetic waxpaper and placed it in a wooden crate lined with tarpaper. On top of the crate I placed my will, in which I wrote that if I did not survive, and if no Jewish communities were reestablished in Lithuania after the war, the material was to be handed over to the executive of the World Zionist Organization in Jerusalem. The crate was nailed shut and covered with metal sheeting, the joints were welded and it was placed in the hiding place and buried deep. I committed the location to memory, and each of us went on his way.

When the snows melted in April 1943, and the block was surrounded by large pools of water, I could find no peace until one night Shraga Goldsmith and I dug out one of the crates and found it in good order. After a few months we added other crates to it, and we continued to do so until there was a total of five crates, one in each corner and one in the center, crammed full of writing and documentary material. I placed my identical will in each crate.

In the summer of 1943, there were increasing rumors that most of the Ghetto inmates would be deported to forced-labor camps under military control. I therefore approached the priest V. Vaickus, a writer and poet who lived in the Old Quarter of Kovno, with the following request: upon the annihilation of the last of the Jews in Lithuania, he should remove the material and deliver it to the person who would then be the head of the World Zionist Organization. I gave him a photograph of the location of the hiding place and an explanation of how to reach it, and returned to the Ghetto with a feeling of relief.

Avraham Tory escaped from the Kovno Ghetto on March 23, 1944. Four days later the Germans took most of the 130 Jewish policemen from the Ghetto to the Ninth Fort, where, under torture, they were ordered to reveal the location of the hiding places in the Ghetto. A few could not withstand the torture, and revealed some of the hiding places. The 40 most senior Jewish policemen were then shot, and 1,200 of the Jews in hiding, mostly children and old people, were seized and killed, once more at the Ninth Fort. Fewer than a hundred remained in hiding.

On April 5, 1944, the Germans abolished the Jewish Council. Three months later, between July 8 and 11, as Soviet forces approached the city, the remaining 8,000 Jews of Kovno, most of them now forced to live in nearby labor camps, were deported, the women to Stutthof, the men, including Dr. Elkes, to Dachau. By the end of the war, more than three-quarters of these deportees had perished. Dr. Elkes himself died only two weeks after reaching Dachau, on July 25, 1944.

Following this final deportation from Kovno, the Germans set the buildings in the Ghetto on fire; it was this fire which destroyed Esther Lourie's two hundred sketches and paintings.

Soviet forces entered Kovno on August 1, 1944. A few days later Avraham Tory returned to the city, determined to recover as much of his diary and the accompanying documents as he could. Three of the five crates of materials he had hidden were recovered. In some cases documents survived covering periods of time for which the diary itself was lost.

In October 1947 Avraham Tory arrived in Palestine. Two years later, in common with many citizens of the new state of Israel, he changed his name, abandoning Golub (which means "dove" in Russian) and taking a Hebrew equivalent, Tory (from the biblical phrase "The voice of the turtledove is heard in the land").

In 1948, Tory's prewar work with Maccabi in Lithuania found its culmination when he became secretary general of the Maccabi World Union, a position he was to hold for twenty years. In 1952, he opened his own law offices in Tel Aviv. Thirty-seven years later, he was still practicing as a lawyer, having been an active and distinguished member of the Israeli legal profession for many years, and the secretary general of the International Association of Jewish Lawyers and Jurists since 1969.

For Tory himself, the publication after forty-five years of what has survived of his diary, and of the documents he had hidden with it, is an act of piety and remembrance for those who have perished. For readers of the diary, its publication brings an additional dimension to our knowledge and understanding of a period in Jewish history which will remain a lament for the generations to come.

Martin Gilbert
Merton College
Oxford University
April 3, 1989

Note on the Text

The original of this diary is in Yiddish, partly in Avraham Tory's own hand and partly as dictated by him to Pnina Sheinzon. It is in Avraham Tory's possession in Tel Aviv. The diary was translated into Hebrew and published in Israel in 1988. The English translation was made with reference to both the Hebrew edition and the original Yiddish, and the annotation was especially prepared for an English-speaking readership. Many of the documents Tory collected during the war years are here interspersed with the diary text in chronological order. The photographs in this book were taken in the Kovno Ghetto by Hirsch Kadushin, and the drawings were made in the Ghetto by Esther Lourie and Josef Schlesinger.

1941

The creation of the Kovno Ghetto: Jews forced to leave the city for the suburb of Vilijampolé (Slobodka) in August 1941.

JUNE 22, 1941[1]

It was a sunny Sunday morning, June 22, 1941, in the provisional capital of Lithuania.[2] Most factories and public institutions were closed. Resting in their homes, the toils of the past week behind them, the city's residents woke up to a bitter surprise: instead of the usual diet of light music, the radio was broadcasting unusual and ominous news from Moscow; last night German warplanes had carried out bombing raids on Alytus, Kedainiai, Siauliai, Kovno, and Riga, as well as on scores of army camps in the Baltic countries and in other republics of the Soviet Union. At a number of points, German troops had attacked the Red Army frontier guards, and had crossed the border into Lithuania, as they had into other territories of the Soviet Union.

War! The news spread quickly in Kovno, as in all parts of the world, this sunny morning. Meanwhile, a number of Lithuanian border towns were already engulfed in flames. Heavy bombing raids carried out by German bombers around Kovno—on the Aleksotas airport, and on the military bases in Sanciai—as well as on the central railway station of Kovno, and on other parts of the town, provided de facto confirmation of the outbreak of war.

The Lithuanians did not conceal their joy at the outbreak of the war: they saw their place on the side of the swastika and expressed this sentiment openly.

The Poles in Kovno, whose families and people had, for the last year and a half, been subject to Nazi rule across the border, did not have any reason to rejoice, whereas the Jews were overcome by despair. They had already gone through the experience of receiving refugees from the no-man's-land into which the Germans had expelled the Jews from occupied Poland, from the Memel region, and from the territories of the Reich, and they began to make preparations to flee.[3] They packed indispensable belongings into knapsacks and began searching for cars or horse-drawn carriages. Some thought it would be better to wait until the following day, when instructions from the authorities would arrive.

Long lines suddenly appeared at the grocery stores. People started hoarding supplies. Others tried to withdraw their savings from banks, but most banks were closed because it was Sunday. The traffic in town was heavy. Crowds of people flocked to the streets to listen to the war news bulletins; to hear what their friends and acquaintances thought of the events, or to meet their relatives.

From time to time, air-raid sirens swept the streets clean of the crowds. Warplanes, with swastikas painted on their wings, appeared, dropped bombs, and quickly vanished over the horizon. Immediately afterward, the streets were full of people again. In the meantime, a light drizzle began to fall from the cloudy sky.

The Jews were busy packing their belongings.

Toward evening, suspicious Lithuanian characters appeared in the midst of the nervous crowds filling the streets, serving blows to Jewish passers-by. These Lithuanian thugs voiced threats against the Jews: "Hitler will be here before long and will finish you off." That these attacks on the Jews were not accidental is attested by the fact that they took place simultaneously in different parts of town. In fact, it later became clear that the attackers were members of Lithuanian "partisan" gangs, acting on the instructions of the fifth column of the indigenous local Nazis.[4]

During the day, most Jews did not dare to change their daily routine. They went on with their routine work in hospitals, in grocery stores, and in any of the other establishments which were open on Sundays. At the same time, they followed the developments impatiently as confusion and turmoil mounted with each passing hour. In the afternoon, most military institutions began to make preparations for departure. Directors of other public institutions instructed their employees to stay put. They even threatened heavy punishment against those attempting to leave their posts.

The telephone rang incessantly. Colleagues and friends wanted to know: "What should we take with us?" "Where should we flee?" The most acute question was "How?" Trains at the train station were packed, mainly with military personnel. A number of Jews squeezed themselves in. Later the trains were filled with fleeing civilians. They departed in the direction of Latvia, Vilna, or Belorussia.

As I mentioned earlier, most Jews preferred to await instructions from the government and other public institutions. They feared to act on their own and to risk standing trial later for desertion and treason. But quite a few of them marched, bundles on their backs, children at their side, in the direction of the road leading to Vilkomir, in order to find shelter against air raids, until the storm blew over—until the fighting was over and they could return to their homes.

The mood in the city was changing from hour to hour. People were in a quandary: to flee immediately or to wait a little longer, until the situation became clear. Leaving one's place of work carried the penalty of six months' imprisonment. This turned out to be an effective deterrent.

During the night, only a few were able to sleep. German planes bombed the city without respite, driving the residents to seek refuge in air-raid shelters, if such were available. Units of the security forces had already been evacuated from the city. That night something unusual occurred in the main Kovno prison: due to the advance of the enemy, the prison commandant and wardens ran out of time to evacuate the prisoners and to transport them to Russia, as provided by their contingency plans. The majority of the prisoners were therefore left behind unguarded, although locked inside their cells.

Before long the rumor spread, by means of prisoners' code language, that the guards had disappeared. Shouts were heard: "Comrades, the guards have fled!" A resounding response came from various cells. "The guards are no longer here—break out of the cells!"

1. This entry was written at midnight on June 22, 1941, in the house of Avraham Tory's sister, Batia (Bashel) Romanovski, 8 Maironio Street, Kovno, where the family waited throughout the night for a wagon and two horses, owned by a relative, to take them to Kovno railway station, where they eventually took a train to the Russian border. Some details were added a few days later. It was Tory's habit to write an entry and then later—if possible—to add more details he had learned in the meantime.

2. Vilna (in Polish, Wilno; in Lithuanian, Vilnius) was the capital of Lithuania from the fourteenth century until the end of World War I. In 1920, when Vilna became a part of Poland, Kovno became the Lithuanian capital. Lithuanians repeatedly stressed, however, that this situation was only temporary, until such time as Vilna was returned to Lithuania. In October 1939 Vilna and the province of Vilna were returned to Lithuania within the framework of the Ribbentrop-Molotov Pact, and the Lithuanian government institutions returned there. Despite that, Kovno continued to be called the provisional capital of Lithuania.

3. Several thousand Jews from the independent province of Memel had fled to Lithuania in March 1939, after Memel (in Lithuanian, Klaipeda) was annexed by Germany. These Jewish refugees had been accommodated in Kovno, Vilna, and other towns and given extensive assistance by the Jews of Lithuania. At the same time, Jewish refugees from Germany, as well as from both zones of occupied Poland (German and Soviet), began to arrive in Lithuania; although it is difficult to estimate accurately how many arrived, they probably numbered several tens of thousands.

4. The partisan movement which began to operate behind German lines in 1942, mainly with the assistance of the Soviet Union, is not to be confused with the Lithuanians who called themselves "partisans" immediately after the German invasion in 1941, and who helped the Germans to murder the Jews of Lithuania. These so-called partisans were mostly extreme nationalists, overjoyed at the Soviet withdrawal from Lithuania, who hoped to achieve independence for Lithuania under German auspices.

JUNE 23–JULY 7, 1941

MEMOIR[1]

We feared for the fate of the men if they fell into the hands of the Germans, but we never imagined that they would murder women, children, and the elderly; and so far as the men were concerned, we never expected mass murder. The worst thing we could possibly conceive of was that the men would be drafted as slave laborers. Most elderly persons and women therefore stayed at home, while most of the men fled.

I also tried to escape, together with my sister Batia and her husband, Benjamin Romanovski, a senior official in the Soviet government of Lithuania, who had managed to secure a cart which had not yet been confiscated. While waiting for the cart, and while the bombing continued into the night, I felt a strong compulsion to pour out my heart, so I sat down and put my experiences and thoughts into writing until three in the morning.

The cart reached us long after midnight. We traveled in the direction of the railroad station, through streets bustling with vehicles and with people who were trying to escape. The station was in flames. On the tracks stood wagons filled with Russian soldiers, and with civilians, awaiting a locomotive to take them back to Russia. I myself tried to flee northward on a bicycle. The traffic was heavy. German Messerschmitts strafed the refugees and the Red Army units, which were retreating without putting up any real resistance. I felt like a hunted animal in a forest going up in flames.

I continued, on the bicycle and on foot, from village to village, with no food and almost without sleep, until German bombs destroyed the road between Vilkomir and Utena; houses, utilities, and vehicles had been destroyed for entire kilometers. Soldiers, civilians, and animals had been killed. The escape route was blocked. I had no choice but to retrace my steps back to Kovno.

Meanwhile, the Germans were joined by gangs of Lithuanians, which had sprung up in every forest and village. Most of these gangs were armed. The mass of Jewish refugees making their way back on the highways and dirt roads were easy prey for them. For three long days I wandered on the roads, living from hand to mouth, until, tired and worn out, I reached home. As soon as I returned, I wrote down what I had experienced during my attempted escape, filling about fifty pages.[2]

Upon hearing of the mass murder of Jews in the villages in the vicinity of Kovno, I sent a cart and wagon to my sisters Rivka and Aliza (Eltza), who lived with their husbands and children in Lazdijai, my native village, begging them to come to Kovno. Logic dictated that they would be safer in a large and organized concentration of Jews, but I was plagued by doubts whether this would indeed be so. However, my sisters implored me to come to stay with them, because they believed there was no safety in large towns where most people did not know each other. They later perished together with their husbands, their children, and their whole community.[3] My elder sister, Batia, who left for Russia with her family at the outbreak of fighting, returned to Vilna after the war.

After my return, I found that Jewish Kovno seemed to have disappeared. In terror of murder and torture at the hands of the Lithuanians and the Germans, the Jews hid wherever possible. The situation made action imperative; at the home of the chief rabbi, Rabbi Abraham Duber Kahana-Shapiro,[4] the beginnings of a community organization were formed. I also went to the chief rabbi's home, with my friends Israel Bernstein and Elimelech Kaplan.[5] We expressed our readiness to help as much as we could. In spite of our youth, we were willingly accepted.

1. Avraham Tory wrote these notes in the spring of 1945, while he was in Romania, and later in Italy, where he stayed from July 1945 until October 1947 while on his way to Palestine.
2. These pages were lost.
3. Avraham Tory's sister Aliza was killed in Lazdijai, together with her husband, David Kalvariski, and their five-year-old son, Zorah, during a German "action" there in August 1941. Also killed during that "action" were Tory's other sister, Rivka, her husband, Bezalel Becker, their son, Iossi, aged seven, and their daughter, Sheinele, aged five.
4. Abraham Duber (Dov-Ber) Kahana-Shapiro, born in 1870, was the chief rabbi of Kovno at the time of the outbreak of war in June 1941. He died in the Kovno Ghetto in 1943.
5. Israel Bernstein perished in Dachau shortly before the end of the war; Elimelech Kaplan was murdered by Lithuanian so-called partisans during the mass killings of August 6, 1941.

JULY 7, 1941[1]

A warm and sunny July day. Within just a few weeks the city has lost its usual aspect. Not long ago, a mere fifteen days ago, a storm rolled over the place from west to east, instantly uprooting the foundations of order in the country. The earth shook with the heavy air and artillery bombardments, as if flung about by a volcanic eruption.

Two weeks earlier, the Jews in Lithuania were citizens with equal rights. Today—and even as early as ten days ago, two days after the terrible prologue—the Jews have disappeared from the streets and from the life of the city. Now they are cooped up in cellars and other hideouts, trembling at every sound coming from the outside. They fear that death lies in wait for them around every corner.

As early as two weeks ago, bloody battles took place between units of the retreating Red Army and the attacking "brown" German troops assisted by the Lithuanian so-called partisans. The latter fired at the Soviet soldiers from rooftops and from behind the gates of houses. They were assisted by German bombers raining fire and brimstone on the retreating Red Army. The Germans were bent on cutting off the Red Army's retreat to its homeland.

On the same streets and alleys which, just a few days ago, were turned into a bloody battlefield, now a wretched procession takes place: men, women, and children bent under the weight of bundles and parcels. They are in a hurry, fleeing for their lives. On the same streets, Lithuanian partisans, armed to the teeth, march haughtily and brazenly. They appear to think that their time has arrived. They vent the rage which has accumulated in their hearts over the last year of the Soviet rule in their country, and their lust for power, by oppressing the Jews.

Soviet rule has disappeared. The Jews are left behind as fair game; hunting them is not unprofitable, because the houses and courtyards of many of them brim with riches. Slaughter the Jews and take their property—this was the first slogan of the restored Lithuanian rule. In that respect the Lithuanians are in complete accord with the Germans.

After one year of Soviet rule a hysterical voice announced on Radio Kovno: "Long live independent Lithuania!" The national anthem was played. The names of ministers in the new Lithuanian cabinet were read out. The Lithuanian national colors were hoisted again on the tower of the military museum; on a stage set up in the museum garden a ceremony commemorating those who had died fighting for Lithuania's independence in 1918 was enacted again, after the lapse of one year.

One of the first acts of what seemed to be the government of the independent Lithuania was a bloody massacre of Jewish men, women, and children. Like a pack of bloodthirsty dogs the Lithuanian partisans prowled the streets and court-yards, seizing panic-stricken Jews who had managed to find various hiding places. These Jews were dragged away in groups to unknown destinations.

Through holes in roofs and apertures in window shutters, other Jews watched the spectacle taking place on the streets: Jews, lined up in long columns, were being beaten with truncheons on every part of their bodies; the Lithuanians were spitting in their faces. Sick people were being carried by their relatives, since they were too weak to stand on their feet after the treatment accorded to them by the Lithuanians. Other Lithuanians stood on the sides of the street and mocked the Jewish tragedy.

At first the Jews did not know the destination to which their detained brethren were dragged away. Later they received the news: the detainees were transported to prisons, to the Gestapo, to German army camps, to Municipality Square, and to Independence Square.[2]

Gangs of Lithuanian partisans would surround one or two houses; some of them guarded the entrance while the rest raided the apartments. At gunpoint they would drive the occupants outside, take what was worth taking, and depart, issuing threats about the impending destruction of the Jews. Many Jews were murdered inside their apartments. Robbery and looting followed. There were cases where women were raped at the very moment when looting and murder were in progress.

In the first days of the new Lithuanian rule, when telephones were still in working order, people were warning their relatives and friends: "Don't go out! They are abducting men on the streets. Find shelter! Don't go to Vilna street today, people are being robbed there! Don't go to Slobodka, people are being massacred there!"[3]

One house was suddenly full of partisans. Curses and screams: "You damned Zhids, we've been shot at from this house; admit it, or we'll kill all of you." One partisan fires his revolver and pandemonium breaks out. They start looking for men. "Where did all the men disappear to, you damned Bolsheviks! We'll find them before long." They start dragging pieces of furniture, beds and tables; closets are being emptied of their contents. Amid the turmoil the partisans grab the valuables and vanish. They move from house to house in this fashion leaving destruction and death in their wake. In Slobodka the murder had been going on for two days. Pogrom! They shave off the beards of rabbis and yeshiva students; heads are bashed, arms are twisted.

The sound of weeping issues from the Jewish houses in Kovno. The destruction is complete. The Jews are overcome by despair. They wonder: what will happen next?

A Gestapo car pulled up at the house of Chief Rabbi Shapiro. A German in uniform entered and demanded that the rabbi accompany him. This sudden visit frightened the rabbi. He told the German that he was very sick and showed him the rubber tube coming out of the side of his stomach. However, if a public matter was involved, the rabbi advised the German to turn to three public figures of the community, L. Garfunkel and Y. Goldberg (those two had recently been released from the Soviet prison where they had been jailed even though their impeccable credentials were well known) and Dr. Rabinovitz, a man of German education and culture.[4] In those terrible days, those three used to meet in the rabbi's apartment to discuss ways and means of mitigating the German decrees. Several days before this unexpected visit they had tried to obtain an interview with the German military governor of Lithuania, Major-General Pohl, who refused to see them, arguing that civil affairs were outside the scope of his authority.

Their addresses and occupations having been written down, they were taken from their homes, without any explanation, and taken to the Gestapo headquarters in Kovno, where they were asked which of the three was a rabbi. When they answered that none of them was, Jaeger[5] ordered some rabbis to be brought to the place. Rabbi Shapiro was contacted by phone and supplied the names of the military chaplain, Rabbi Snieg,[6] and Rabbi Shmukler from Sanciai. Both were immediately brought to the Gestapo, likewise without having been told either their destination or the purpose of the summons. Rabbi Snieg was as pale as a ghost from fear. On his way to the Gestapo he recited the Viduy [the confession before death], and prepared himself for the sentence. Rabbi Shmukler was not as frightened as Snieg. Naturally, the five did not have any idea where or for what purpose they were being summoned. Upon their arrival at Gestapo headquarters they were ushered into the commander's office. "Take a seat, insofar as chairs are available." There were two chairs in the room, but the five Jews preferred to remain standing throughout. The main speaker was a general sitting on a sofa. He announced to those present:

> The present situation—and the Jews know exactly what the situation is— cannot go on. Total disorder and unrest prevail in the city. I cannot allow this situation to continue. I will issue orders to stop shooting. Peace and order must return to the city. The Lithuanians have announced that they no longer wish to live together with Jews; they demand that the Jews be segregated in a Ghetto. The choice is up to the Jews—either the present situation with the disorder and the bloodbath, or leaving the city and moving into the Ghetto.

"You must go to the Ghetto," said the general. He pointed to Slobodka on the map. "Here will be the Ghetto. There is plenty of room for you there." The Jews pointed out that Slobodka was populated by 8,000 people. It was impossible to squeeze in 35,000 Jews there. They suggested that the Old City of Kovno be included within the designated Ghetto precincts. The general replied: "As far as I am concerned, you can add even the village of Raudondvaris. You can take your belongings with you; there you will be free to establish your community life."

At this point the general announced that he was appointing those present to be the Jewish Committee in charge of the transfer of the Jews of Kovno to the Ghetto. They would be answerable to him personally. They might co-opt other people to be on that committee. The transfer plan must be executed within the shortest possible period of time. Within a month, the city must be "clear" of Jews. "There is an intense hatred toward the Jews among the Lithuanians, because all the Jews are Bolsheviks. After all, Lenin himself was a Jew."

When one of those present observed that Lenin was not a Jew, the general kept arguing; "Then he was related to Jews by marriage; but Stalin most certainly is a Jew."[7] In short: "The Jews must go to the Ghetto and the transfer must be started at once." If the Jewish Committee would assume responsibility for the transfer, the general would issue an immediate order to release three thousand of the imprisoned women and children.[8] The Jews replied that they did not have any power to take a decision on any of those matters. Thereupon they were ordered to report to him with their answer no later than 10 A.M. the following day.

The Jews complained that it was impossible to cross the street in those days, as Jews were being abducted from the streets in broad daylight. "This situation will be brought to an end immediately," the general said.

The delegation left the Gestapo building. The first thing they did was to inform their families that they were alive and at liberty. Before entering the Gestapo commander's office, Garfunkel and Goldberg had met in the hall with the Lithuanian military city commander, Colonel Bobelis,[9] who happened to leave Jaeger's office at that moment. Goldberg approached Bobelis, intending to prevail upon him to use his authority to put a stop to the shootings and abductions of Jews in the city. Bobelis said evasively: "When you are done here, call at my office." When the meeting with the Gestapo chief was over, they repaired to Bobelis's office. Bobelis was busy and asked them to return in an hour.

They both left, heading home. Riding in a horse-drawn carriage they reached Kestucio Street, where they were stopped by a roadblock set up by the Lithuanian partisans. The latter were busy abducting Jews and looting their homes. Two partisans stopped the carriage and inquired: "What religion are you?" "We are Jews," they replied. "Get out of the carriage!" the Lithuanians shouted. The partisans then set about "taking care" of them. The two Jews tried to explain that they had been imprisoned during the Soviet occupation of Lithuania and that they were due to report in an hour at the office of the military commander, Bobelis, but their explanations had no effect. They also told the Lithuanians about their public positions: Goldberg was an officer in the Lithuanian Army and chairman of the Association of Jewish Combatants in the Lithuanian War of Independence. The reply was straightforward: "It doesn't make any difference, you are Jews." They were subsequently taken to Kovno jail. There they repeated their statement about the Lithuanian military commander expecting them soon in his office. Finally they were taken under guard to the Lithuanian military command headquarters. On the way they were warned that if their statement turned out not to be true, they would meet a bitter end.

At the entrance to the headquarters the sentries confirmed that the two Jews had, in fact, called there in the morning, and that they were scheduled to meet the commander. Thereupon Bobelis saw them and spoke to them. He feigned ignorance of the whole business of transferring the Jews to the Ghetto. He told them: "You must haggle about this with the Germans." He gave Goldberg a letter certifying his rank of lieutenant in the Lithuanian army and his participation in the war for Lithuania's independence. Goldberg did not know for what purpose Bobelis gave him the letter, but he was asked to take it anyhow. Bobelis also issued an order for a Lithuanian guard to escort Goldberg and Garfunkel back home. On the way, the guard revealed that the day before 1,800 Jews had been shot in the Seventh Fort.[10] He advised them to be cautious and to keep away from the streets.

1. This entry was written on July 7, 1941. Some additions were made after Tory had a conversation with the persons involved at the chief rabbi's house at the end of the day.
2. When the prisons were no longer able to hold additional Jews, the Lithuanian partisans took those who had been seized to the main squares, where they were interned in several public buildings, including the Town Hall.

3. Vilna Street: a street where many Jews lived. Slobodka (in Lithuanian, Vilijampolé): a suburb of Kovno, located across the Vilija river in the Old City quarter. In 1941 some 6,000 Jews lived there.

4. Attorney Leib (Leon) Garfunkel, a widely respected figure in Kovno's Jewish community. Before the war, he was general secretary of the Jewish National Council of Lithuanian Jewry, a member of the Kovno municipal council, a member of the Lithuanian parliament, and first editor of *Die Yiddishe Stimme* (The Jewish Voice) and *Dos Wort* (The Word). A Socialist-Zionist by ideology, he was a delegate to several interwar Zionist congresses. During the Ghetto period, he served as deputy chairman of the Jewish Council. After liberation, he became chairman of the Association of Jewish Refugees in Italy. He emigrated to Israel, where he wrote one of the most important books on the Kovno Ghetto, *Jewish Kovno at the Time of the Destruction*, published in Hebrew in Jerusalem in 1959. He died in Israel in 1976.

   Attorney Yakov Goldberg, chairman of the Association of Jewish Soldiers in the Lithuanian Army. Goldberg had shared a prison cell with Garfunkel during the Soviet occupation. During the Ghetto period, he was a member of the Jewish Council and head of the Council's labor department.

   Dr. Ephraim Rabinovitz, a well-known gynecologist in Lithuania. He was a member of the Jewish Council during its early stages.

5. SS Colonel Karl Jaeger, commander of the Gestapo in Lithuania, and commander of Einsatzgruppe 3A, assigned to the Baltic States.

6. Shmuel-Abba Snieg, chief chaplain of the Lithuanian Army. Active in Ghetto life, he later served as rabbi to the community of survivors in postwar Germany.

7. Lenin had one Jewish grandfather (his mother's father). Stalin had no Jewish blood.

8. Approximately 6,000 Jews, half of them women and children, had been arrested indiscriminately by the Lithuanians during the first few days of the German occupation and interned in various locations in the city. The men were later murdered at the Seventh Fort.

9. Colonel Jurgis Bobelis, a Lithuanian, commander of the Lithuanian Army in Kovno and the district before the Soviet occupation and during the German occupation. One of the organizers of the mass murder of the Jews of Lithuania, he fled to Germany in 1944. Later he worked as senior translator to the United States Army High Command. He died in the United States. Even before July 7, 1941, Goldberg had personally approached Bobelis, with whom he had once taken a Lithuanian Army officers' course, asking his help, particularly in assessing German policy. Bobelis claimed to be ignorant of German intentions. He had, however, already prepared a decree for the deportation of Kovno's Jews to the Ghetto, and at this meeting on July 7, Jaeger in fact announced what had already been agreed between him and Bobelis.

10. Kovno was surrounded by a series of forts build in Czarist times to protect the city from German invasion. Between the wars these forts were used as prisons for criminals serving long sentences. During the German occupation, 1941–1944, the forts were used as both prisons and execution sites, particularly of the Jews of Kovno. The Seventh and Ninth Forts were close to the Ghetto; in time, they became widely known as symbols of mass murder, as did the Babi Yar ravine in Kiev, the Rumbuli forest near Riga, and the ditches of Ponar near Vilna.

JULY 8, 1941

At 8 A.M. a consultation was held at Rabbi Shapiro's apartment. It was attended by the five men who had been taken to the Gestapo headquarters yesterday as well as several others: Grigori Wolf, Dr. Matis, Kopelman, Gemelitzki, Rabbi Broide, and others.[1] At the conclusion of deliberations the gathering resolved to ask permission to establish direct contact with the Lithuanian authorities with the purpose of reaching some kind of compromise with them.[2]

The German promise to release at once three thousand Jewish women and children from the prison and the forts, as well as to issue an order to stop forthwith the abductions of Jews in the streets, was a decisive factor in those deliberations.

Those attending this meeting also took into consideration what the recently appointed Lithuanian finance minister, Matulionis, had told Goldberg a few days earlier; Goldberg had visited him and asked his intervention for putting an end to abductions and shootings. In this conversation Matulionis revealed to his interlocutor the prevailing mood among the Lithuanians:

The Lithuanians are divided on the Jewish question. There are three main views: according to the most extreme view all the Jews in Lithuania must be exterminated; a more moderate view demands setting up a concentration camp where Jews will atone with blood and sweat for their crimes against the Lithuanian people.[3] As for the third view? I am a practicing Roman Catholic; I—and other believers like me—believe that man cannot take the life of a human being like himself. Only God can do this. I have never been against anybody, but during the period of Soviet rule I and my friends realized that we did not have a common path with the Jews and never will. In our view, the Lithuanians and the Jews must be separated from each other and the sooner the better. For that purpose, the Ghetto is essential. There you will be separated and no longer able to harm us. This is a Christian position.

When Goldberg asked Matulionis to try to prevail on his friends in the Lithuanian government to intervene to stop the killings, the minister answered: "The wrath of the people is so great that there is no way to stop these acts. When you leave the city for good and confine yourselves in the Ghetto, things will quiet down." Then he added: "I am speaking frankly to you." The Lithuanian minister did not mention in this conversation any pressure from the Germans. This means only one thing: assaults on the Jews express the will of the Lithuanian people.

Following this discussion, those present decided that the state of affairs in the city gave us no option but to leave the city and move into the Ghetto—and to salvage what was possible. Either the present torment or the Ghetto, there was no third option.

The Jewish representatives returned to the Gestapo to report their answer. When asked to allow a meeting with Lithuanian public figures, the Germans replied with a determined no. "Which Lithuanians do you want to meet with? The Lithuanians don't want to talk to any Jew."

The Jewish representatives' requests to extend the time required for the transfer and also to expand the Ghetto area were met with the reply "Difficulties exist in order to be overcome."

The Germans failed to give clear answers to the Jewish requests. Thus only one way out was left: the way to the Ghetto.

1. Dr. Grigori (Zvi) Wolf, a well-known Lithuanian Jewish leader, belonged to a family of industrialists. In July and August 1941 he served as chairman of the committee for the transfer of Jews from Kovno to Slobodka, the body which preceded the Jewish Council.

   Dr. Eliyahu Matis, an ear, nose, and throat specialist, became one of the heads of the Ghetto's medical service.

   Michael (Moshe) Kopelman, before the war the director of the Lithuanian branch of Lloyds of London, with his offices in Kovno. In this position he had been in close contact with both the German and the Lithuanian intelligentsia in the city. Because of this, he was often sent into the city by the Jewish Council during the Ghetto years. In August 1941 he became the commander of the Ghetto Jewish police.

   Nikolai (Michael) Gemelitzki, a Kovno bank manager before the war; in August 1941 he became head of the economic affairs department of the Jewish Council. He survived the war and subsequently lived in the United States.

   Rabbi Aharon Broide, rabbi of the Carmelita neighborhood of Kovno. He was deported to Riga in February 1942.

2. Avraham Tory later recalled: "The participants in this meeting had not the faintest idea what the term 'Ghetto' entailed, what living there would be like, and, in general, what would happen to the Kovno Jewish community at large. One thing was clear: the present situation was unbearable and must come to an end without further delay. They also resolved to attempt to bargain for annexing the Old City, populated mostly by Jews, to the Ghetto; to gain more time for the transfer, etc."

3. During the Soviet domination of Lithuania between June 1940 and June 1941, Jews had been identified with the despised Soviet regime. Because many Jews had been employed in the Soviet bureaucracy during that year, Jews in general were considered to be opposed to Lithuania's nationalistic aspirations.

JULY 10, 1941

DOCUMENT:[1] *Memorandum submitted to the Lithuanian municipality of Kovno by the Jewish Committee in Kovno, concerning the suburb of Slobodka—the planned area for the Ghetto*[2]

1. In the municipality area today there are about 25,000 Jews, of whom about 5,000 already live in Slobodka. Besides the Jews, there now live in Slobodka about 10,000 non-Jews.

2. The Jews living in Slobodka are mostly poor; their houses are nearly all old, made of wood, single-story, and low.

3. It is completely inconceivable to accommodate in the apartments of the Jews in Slobodka, which are already very densely occupied, another 20,000 Jews from the city of Kovno. If this somehow is done, Slobodka will become very quickly a nest of contagious diseases as a result of such unheard-of over-crowding, and these diseases will immediately spread to the other parts of the city. It should also be considered that there exists no sewage system in Slobodka, no water pipes, no hospital, no clinic or any medical institution, and no social services. There have already been observed cases of measles, whooping cough, and typhoid fever in Slobodka.

4. The situation could be partially improved only if the non-Jews now in Slobodka were removed from there, and their apartments used for the accom-modation of the Jews. However, this is very undesirable, because it would put great hardships on the non-Jewish population of Slobodka, because most of them are connected to their homes by economic and social links—very strong ties—and it would be most inconvenient for them to move to other parts of the city. The exchange of the immovable property of Jewish houses taken over out-side Slobodka for the houses of non-Jews in Slobodka is a complicated juridical matter and will not solve this difficult problem.

5. It is evident that the concentration of all Kovno Jews in Slobodka will put them into a very hard, really intolerable condition. Moreover, the situation thus created will constitute a sanitary hazard to the total population of the city. Con-sequently the order of the mayor of Kovno and of the military commander of the city, concerning this matter, must be canceled. If this is impracticable, the following orders must be issued:

a. that expulsion to Slobodka will not apply to Jews living in the suburbs,

b. to extend the area in Slobodka allotted to the Jews by including the area known as the Old City of Kovno, up to the streets Ozeskienes, Kanto, and Telziai,

for the following reasons:

1. This area is already populated mostly by Jews.

2. In this area are situated most of the synagogues (sixteen synagogues).

3. In this area are situated most of the important Jewish medical, social, and educational institutions, which are housed in their own buildings and have their own equipment and inventory bought and supplied by Jewish means only, such as the Jewish hospital at 3 Jakstu Street, the Jewish orphanage at 15 Fire Brigade Street, the Jewish home for the aged at 15 Puskos Street, the popular restaurant at 10 Mapu Street, the Jewish Community centers at 14 Rotuse Square and 12 Luksio Street, the ritual bath at 3 Luksio Street, the Hebrew gymnasium at 25 Nieman Embankment, the Talmud Tora school at 17 Ugnagesiu Street, the Jew-ish clinic at 7 Pilies Street, the Jewish vocational school Ort at 86 Jonavos

Street, the Jewish Health Organization OZE at 1 Misku Street, the Jewish Central Bank for the Support of Cooperatives at 76 Laisves Boulevard, and others.

4. This area adjoins Slobodka and forms—in a certain respect—a single geographical area with it.

1. Avraham Tory noted later, when his diary was being prepared for publication, that this memorandum was "prepared by the Jewish Committee for the evacuation of Kovno Jews to Slobodka a few days after the committee met with Jaeger on July 7 and 8, 1941. At that time, many Jews could not resign themselves to the move to Slobodka. It was therefore decided to struggle for the renunciation of the deportation order, or at least for the extension of the area designated for the Ghetto by including in it the Old City of Kovno, where a large commercial, social, and cultural concentration of Jews lived. The Lithuanians, led by Kazys Palciauskas, then the Lithuanian mayor, objected most strongly to all Jewish pleas. The memorandum had been prepared by two advocates, Leib Garfunkel and me, in consultation with Moshe Kopelman and Nikolai Gemelitzki."

2. This decree, dated July 10, 1941, was published on the following day, signed by the military commander of Kovno, Jurgis Bobelis, and the mayor of Kovno, Kazys Palciauskas.

JULY 10, 1941

DOCUMENT:
From the Jewish Committee in Kovno
To the German SS Security Police in Kovno

Concerning the proposal to remove the Jewish part of the population of Kovno to Vilijampolé within a certain time, we take the liberty of bringing to your attention, with the highest respect, the following points:

Vilijampolé is a small suburb, in which at present live about 12,000 people, 5,000–6,000 of them Jews and 6,000–7000 of them Lithuanians. The population there lives in the most crowded and unhygienic conditions (perhaps three to five persons per room of about nine square meters). This suburb has no homes for the aged or for orphans, no hospitals, no water pipes, no sewage system, i.e. no water; nor has it any conditions at all to make possible the orderly living of about 25,000 new arrivals. The concentration together of so many people under such conditions must create a risk of disease and epidemics, which cannot be averted in advance. The non-Jewish population which owns houses, workshops, and farms in this suburb will not give them up. The larger industrial enterprises situated in Vilijampolé, such as Guma, Boston, Inkaras, and many others,[1] cannot be moved to other parts of the city. Therefore it is impossible to isolate this suburb.

The establishment of new dwelling places and trading facilities is for financial reasons impracticable. As is known, the Soviets nationalized all immovable property as well as all money in banks and savings institutions exceeding the amount of 1,000 rubles—equaling 100 Reichsmarks—while at the same time the former Lithuanian currency was declared invalid and was confiscated. Consequently, the property of everybody, including the Jews, consists only of the furniture in their apartments and a little cash, to a maximum of 500 rubles—equaling 50 Reichsmarks—per person.

The Jews in Kovno were mostly merchants, clerks, and craftsmen. The transfer of these people to the conditions existing in Vilijampolé is impossible. They would be exposed in the meantime—without work and without food—to hunger and to the danger of epidemics.

Considering the above, we urgently request you to take pity on us, to postpone the intended order for the time being, or amend it, in order to enable us to meet with the Lithuanian authorities and personalities concerned, and to find, together with them, such organizational, economic, and hygienic ways as may enable the transfer to be carried out in an orderly way, and with minimal damage to the general public.

We hope and are convinced that you, the representatives of such a cultural and strong nation as Germany, will have pity on us unfortunate ones, who have already been deprived and robbed by the Soviets, and that you will guarantee us proper human living conditions.

1. The Guma factory produced rubber, the Boston factory textiles, and the Inkaras factory shoes.

JULY 10, 1941

> DOCUMENT: *Order no. 15, issued by the Military Commander of Kovno and the Mayor of Kovno*

I

Jews who have escaped from Kovno are not permitted to return to the city. Those who return will be arrested.

Landlords, administrators of nationalized houses, or acting administrators of other houses who allow Jews who return to Kovno to settle in the houses under their administration will be punished.

2

Starting on July 12, 1941, all Jews, regardless of sex and age, residing in Kovno must wear on the left part of the breast this patch: a yellow Shield of David, diameter 8–10 centimeters.

3

The movement of the Jews in the streets, and their presence in public places, is restricted to the period between 6 A.M. and 8 P.M. Jews who are seen in public places at other times will be arrested.

4

All Jews residing within the territory of the city of Kovno must leave their dwelling places in Kovno and move to the suburb of Vilijampolé (Slobodka in Yiddish) starting July 15, and before August 15. All displaced families will be issued an evacuation order.

5

The municipal housing department, together with representatives of the Jewish community, will determine the instructions and the transfer arrangements, in order to ensure an orderly evacuation.

6

Means of transport for the transfer will be supplied by the persons to be evacuated.

7

Non-Jewish inhabitants of Vilijampolé are allowed to move to other parts of the city of Kovno. The housing department of the city of Kovno will assist them in finding dwelling places.

8

Jews who possess immovable property in other parts of the city than Vilijampolé must first of all liquidate these properties by exchanging them primarily with Lithuanians possessing immovable property in Vilijampolé who wish to move from there.

To assist these liquidation and exchange transactions an office has been established for this purpose by the municipality of Kovno.

Any real estate not taken care of according to the above instructions will be taken over by the municipality of Kovno for itself.

Jews possessing arms must hand them over immediately to the military headquarters (34 Gadiminu Street). Wireless receivers must be handed over to the housing department (at 9 Laisves Boulevard, third floor). Anyone who does not comply with these instructions will be severely punished.

9

Jews are not permitted to employ as hired labor persons of any other nationality.

JULY 14, 1941

DOCUMENT:

From the Committee for the Transfer of the Jewish Inhabitants to Slobodka (Vilijampolé)

To Kaminskas, Representative of the Mayor of Kovno

Further to our conversation with you, the committee again requests you to supply to the committee the means of transport for the transfer of the Jewish families to Slobodka.

The horses of the Jewish coachmen, which were mobilized under the Soviet regime, were never returned to their owners. This fact increases the shortage of the means of transport. Moreover, much of the means of transport than is at the disposal of the committee cannot be fully utilized, because there is no fodder, so that even today there are fewer horses available than there might have been for the removal of the property of the Jewish families to Slobodka.

In order not to delay the orderly transfer of the Jewish families to Slobodka, and in order to execute the transfer in a proper manner, we again request you to settle as soon as possible the problem of transport by supplying to the committee a sufficient quantity of means of transport and the necessary fodder for the horses.[1]

1. This request was signed by Garfunkel and Gemelitzki.

JULY 16, 1941

DOCUMENT:

From German Field Headquarters 821, Kovno

To the Mayor of Kovno

In the course of the transfer of Jews to Slobodka, apartments are often found in Slobodka which had already been designated for the German Army, or are occupied by it.

Jews must be transferred only to apartments which have not been occupied by the German Army.

Concerning those apartments occupied by, or designated for, the German Army, and their handing over to the German Army, close contact with the local German headquarters must be maintained.[1]

1. This document was signed by Major-General Pohl, the German military commander of Lithuania. On the following day it was transmitted to the Jewish Committee for the transfer of Jews from Kovno to Slobodka by the mayor of Kovno, Kazys Palciauskas.

JULY 22, 1941

DOCUMENT: Rules for the evacuation of the Jews from Kovno to the Ghetto in Vilijampolé; a summary of the talks with Tumavicius, Ranaitis, and Adolf Blumenthal and Anatoly Rosenblum[1]

1. Evacuation plan:
   Laisves Boulevard and railway station area.
   Jonavos Street
   Green Hill
   The Old City
   Panemune, Sanciai, Aleksotas.
2. Twenty-four flats, two blocks—for immediate occupation.
3. Evacuation of non-Jews from Vilijampolé to start on July 25, 1941; twenty-five families daily. The evacuation to be completed within no more than ten days.
4. Living space—6 meters—outer measurements, but all Jews must be placed within the fixed area. In certain cases—additional living space can be permitted. For the sick—additional space may be permitted by a committee of Lithuanian sanitary inspectors. In other cases (physicians, lawyers, engineers, artisans) additional space can be permitted.
5. Houses occupied by Lithuanians and all other dwelling space in Vilijampolé is registered at the Kovno municipality. Further information will be submitted without delay.
6. Transportation facilities of non-Jews can also be used. The evacuation must be completed on August 15, 1941. Data on the number of Jews must be submitted until July 25. An evacuation plan to be prepared based on the above timetable.
7. It is planned to build thirty-two flats in the uncompleted block. The municipality itself will carry out the completion or it will supply the materials and the Jews will complete the building themselves. It may be proposed to adjust the above block for public purposes (clinics, school, etc.).
8. The sale of industrial buildings to Jews for dwelling purposes is subject to the consent of the Ministry of Industries.
9. Ranaitis has learned that the number of inhabitants will be smaller than the dwelling space divided into six square meters each, and that for the artisans and other workshops separate buildings will be needed.
10. For the time being no evacuation orders will be issued without contact with the Jewish Committee. The talks were friendly but an anti-Semitic mood was felt. The threat was that the evacuation would be carried out anyway, even if Jews refused to comply with it.

1. This summary was signed by Anatoly Rosenblum, as representative of the Jewish Committee in its talks with the Lithuanian municipal authorities. A leading architect, Rosenblum was later killed during one of the "actions" in the Ghetto. His colleague Adolf Blumenthal, a pilot, had been one of the organizers of the Lithuanian Air Force at the time of the establishment of an independent Lithuanian State in 1919–1920; he was later murdered at the Ninth Fort.

JULY 23, 1941

DOCUMENT: Kovno Municipality, Instruction

Jews must evacuate their apartments in Italijos and Jonavos Streets within two days. Jews are forbidden to travel from Kovno into the province.

JULY 24, 1941

DOCUMENT: Kovno Municipality, Instruction

Jews must erect the fence around the Ghetto themselves.

JULY 27, 1941

DOCUMENT: Lithuanian Minister of Education, Instruction

All Jewish children who are in Children's Homes in Lithuania must be handed over to the Jewish Committee in Vilijampolé.

JULY 28, 1941

DOCUMENT: Order no. 1 of the Governor of Kovno

1. The Jewish population is forbidden to walk on the sidewalks. Jews must walk on the right side of the road and go one behind the other.

2. The Jewish population is forbidden to enter promenade walks and public parks. Likewise they are forbidden to use the benches.

3. The Jewish population is forbidden to use public means of transport such as taxicabs, horse carriages, buses, passenger steamers, and similar vehicles. The owners and operators of all public conveyances must display in a visible place a sign reading: "Forbidden to Jews."

4. Offenders against this order will be severely punished.

5. This order is in force as of today.[1]

1. This order was signed by the newly appointed city governor of Kovno, SA Colonel Hans Cramer, the real ruler of the Ghetto.

JULY 30, 1941

DOCUMENT:
From the Roads Department, Kovno Municipal Council
To the Jewish Community of Kovno

For fencing the Jewish area in Slobodka, I request that you send, as from July 30 this year, fifty men, and starting on July 31 this year until the termination of the work, one hundred men each day.

The men must be fit for work and must bring spades with them and must report to work at 8 A.M.

The place of reporting: near 12 Jurbarkas Street.[1]

---

1. This document was no. 2143 of the Kovno municipal council. Supervision of the erection of the Ghetto fence was under the control of J. Ratcevicius, a technician in the roads department.

JULY 31, 1941

DOCUMENT: Public Announcement no. 2 of the Governor of Kovno

1. Those of the Jewish population who escaped at the outbreak of the war, or in course of the war, and have not yet returned, are not allowed to return to Kovno. All house owners and house administrators are herewith forbidden to provide accommodation to returning Jews.

2. The Jewish population, regardless of age and sex, is obliged to wear on the left side of the breast, and on the back, a yellow Star of David, eight to ten centimeters in diameter.

3. The order of the mayor of Kovno dated July 10, 1941, on the evacuation of the Jewish population from the inner city to the suburb of Vilijampolé must be executed by August 15, 1941, at the latest. Further information will be provided by the municipal housing office.

4. The Jewish population is herewith forbidden to sell, to exchange, or to realize in any other way, their total movable and immovable property. The destruction of equipment or valuables is likewise prohibited.

5. The curfew imposed on the Jewish population as per order of the mayor of Kovno dated July 10, 1941, is extended to apply also to the areas of the suburb Vilijampolé, including the Jewish residential area.

6. The order of the mayor of Kovno dated July 10, 1941, is revoked regarding the other parts.

7. Offenses against these instructions will be severely punished.

8. The instructions of this announcement are in force as of today.[1]

1. This announcement was signed by SA Colonel Cramer. An almost identical announcement was issued on August 4, 1941, by SS Colonel Lenzen, the governor-general of the Kovno district.

JULY 31, 1941

DOCUMENT: Communication from the Kovno Municipality

The request of the Jewish Council to be received by the mayor has been rejected by him.[1]

1. This communication was signed by Mikas Kaminskas, a Lithuanian and a senior employee of the Kovno municipality, who had been nominated by the Lithuanian mayor and the German civilian authorities to be their liaison with the Jewish Council.

AUGUST 4, 1941

Only six weeks have elapsed since the beginning of the blitzkrieg of the German Army which rolled through Lithuania. Dozens of Jewish settlements, firmly rooted on Lithuanian soil for hundreds of years, have already been obliterated from the face of the earth as if they had never existed. They were replaced by mounds of poisonous earth covering large pits—fresh mass graves, without tombstones, without inscriptions or any identifying marks—in the forests and fields beyond the town and village boundaries.

In Slobodka, the Jewish houses, looted and boarded up, have already been emptied of the last corpses, which had been lying inside ever since the "bloody prologue" which took place on the night of June 25–26, 1941. No fewer than 700 Jewish martyrs were put to death that night by the Lithuanian murderers.[1] Some of them breathed their last in the flames engulfing their homes, which had been surrounded from all sides and set on fire. Only a mound of wet sand covered the hastily piled up bodies of the victims of the first pogrom: it became the new "sand hill" on the shore of the Vilija river, Slobodka's bathing spot.

At the garage of the Agricultural Cooperative Society on Vytauto Boulevard, no trace is left of fifty-two Jews, tortured and then torn to pieces during an outburst of savagery—a fiendish spectacle which for four to five hours provided entertainment to the crowd of Lithuanian onlookers on one of the first days of the war. The victims' bodies have already been haphazardly buried somewhere in a pit.[2]

Quiet has already returned to Kovno prison and to the Seventh Fort, that horrible slaughter-field. Thousands of Jews who were crammed in there in the first weeks, and squeezed into the long passageways of the fortress, have already been slaughtered by the Lithuanian "freedom fighters"; some were killed in small groups, others *en masse*. The gray fortress barracks, permanently dank, which until recently was brimming over with Jewish women and children rounded up together, has already been emptied. Night after night the Lithuanian henchmen would proceed to select their victims: the young, the pretty. First they would rape them, then torture them, and finally murder them. They called it "going to peel potatoes."[3]

Within just ten or twelve days the Seventh Fort alone swallowed up to 6,000 Jews and then fell silent. No volleys rang out, no groans of agony were heard, nor the last cry of "Shema Israel" (Hear, O Israel!). True, the unyielding wives and mothers kept coming again and again to the entrance of the fort, waiting there for hours. They refused to resign themselves to the terrible fate of their relatives and loved ones. So they waited, hoping that their loved one would appear among the prisoners led out daily from the prison for work; perhaps, despite everything, they would receive some sign of life. They stood there for days, trying to pierce the deadly silence behind the prison wall, to detect a sign of life from their relatives, who were no longer among the living. They humiliated themselves by pleading with the henchmen, and returned—disgraced and bruised—having been driven off like dogs stricken with plague.

It seemed that hunting down the Jews in the streets of Kovno subsided. Newspapers and posters featured a decree printed in large letters, issued by the Lithuanian mayor of Kovno and the Lithuanian city military commandant. The decree was issued on July 10, 1941. It stated that all Kovno Jews, irrespective of age or sex, must leave the city and move into the Ghetto; the deadline was August 15. Any Jew found in the city after that date was to be shot without warning. That was the decree—one of the first acts of the restored Lithuania, of the renewed independence. It was victory, and the Lithuanians celebrated.

From that moment on, house janitors, neighbors, and other Lithuanians were to abuse and harass the Jews constantly "in the name of the law"; they would force them to leave the city as soon as possible and would take possession of their apartments, stores, and businesses not yet seized by the Germans. Every day, hundreds of Lithuanians would simply throw Jewish residents out onto the streets and take for themselves the "liberated" apartments. Whoever went to complain to the authorities disappeared without trace.

Jews who returned to the city from the hiding places they had fled to after the German occupation of Kovno, and the survivors of the prison and the fort, were not allowed to reenter their homes or even to salvage a single stitch of clothing; some of the Lithuanian neighbors who had seized their homes were "kind" enough not to turn the owners over to the authorities as required by the "law" at that time. Hundreds of Jews in this condition could not find a place in the city in which to spend even a single night. Christians did not let them step over the thresholds of their homes, and officially Jews were forbidden to live in non-Jewish homes, even temporarily.

Jewish shops were either seized or shut down. Christian shops did not sell to the Jews. Jews were not allowed to enter the market before 10 A.M., at which time it was nearly empty. Two or three food stores were open to serve the approximately 30,000 remaining Jews, but not before 10 o'clock when nothing was left but refuse.

Jews standing in long lines in front of grocery stores were being harassed; Lithuanian storekeepers would pour water on them or drive them away. Jews standing in shop lines were rounded up for forced labor; more than once, someone was dragged off somewhere and disappeared without a trace.

Life became increasingly unbearable with every passing day. Jews had left Kovno hastily before the deadline, looking for "dwelling space and haven" in the Ghetto where, the authorities had promised, Jewish lives and property would be "safe" with a supposedly self-governing Jewish authority.

On August 1, 1941, two weeks before the deadline, 90 percent of the Jews had already moved into the area designated for the Ghetto.

No exchange of views with the Lithuanians took place. Their ministers refused to see the Jews. The new Lithuanian mayor, Kazys Palciauskas, banned the Jews from entering the municipality offices. The Lithuanian military commandant, Jurgis Bobelis, ordered the arrest of thousands of Jews, who were put to death in the forts. Jewish complaints remained without an attentive ear. Jewish bitterness found no release.

Only one Lithuanian talked to the Jews—Kaminskas, a Lithuanian municipal official who also served as liaison officer on behalf of the civilian governor of the city. But Kaminskas spoke in the language of decrees and edicts, such as: "You must set up a barbed-wire fence around the Ghetto area by yourselves"; "You must evacuate the Jonavos and Italijos streets within two days"; "You must evacuate several streets in Slobodka where some Jews moved in a few days ago from the city"; "You must squeeze in even more—the area designated for the Ghetto has been abridged further"; "You must provide so many Jews for forced labor," and so on.

Thus spoke Kaminskas, who had a part in the first wave of extermination of Jews in Kovno. He never found a good word for the Jews. In their presence his countenance was always severe and angry. He pronounced his orders in a cynically cold voice and always strove to camouflage his evil designs. He kept completely calm, both before and after the slaughter.

One day, in the second half of July, Kaminskas passed on a decree issued by the civilian governor, stating that the Jews were to elect for themselves a Chief Jew (*Oberjude*) and his deputy who, together with his advisors, would form the

Jewish Council (*Ältestenrat*) responsible for managing the internal affairs of the Ghetto. A commander of the Jewish police was also to be elected, and the names of all those officials submitted to Kaminskas within a matter of days.

The concept of "Ghetto"—originating in the Middle Ages—was confusing enough. Even less clear was the role of the Chief Jew and the role of the Jewish "self-government" that the Germans and Kaminskas spoke about. One knew in one's heart, however, that the purpose of appointing the Chief Jew and setting up the Ghetto was to humiliate, to offend, and to cause distress. According to rumors which reached Kovno from other cities, this Chief Jew was, more or less, a synonym for scapegoat, the first victim of the Jewish destiny.

As of today the Ghetto borders have not yet been finally fixed. Every day additional streets are subtracted from the originally planned Ghetto area. Jews are still hunted down. The food supply deteriorates daily, becoming unbearable. Demands issued by the authorities keep increasing, but nothing is done to ensure stability or to enable the Jews to settle their affairs. The Jewish representatives are still not allowed to go to the municipality building. Kaminskas meets members of the committee for the transfer of the Jews in a street or in a courtyard, barely listening to them. All the requests and proposals of the transfer committee are either ignored or turned down. It is in the best interest of the Jews themselves to evacuate the city as soon as possible.

On August 4, 1941, twenty-eight Jewish public figures who were still in the city assembled for the last historical meeting of the Kovno Jewish community.[4] The meeting was convened in the building of the former Jewish elementary school at 24 Dauksos Street, which in days gone by reverberated with the joyous clamor of children.

Not long ago this very school building was filled with cries of wailing and anguish. It served as the seat of the committee for the transfer of Jews from Kovno to Slobodka. Parents in distress came there trying to rescue their detained children. There came despairing women in search of husbands who had been abducted. Women who had been raped came there to weep. The first appeals for assistance from Jews in the provincial towns of Lithuania reached this building, as well as the first echoes of the prayer "Shema Israel" (Hear, O Israel) on the lips of martyrs. In those fateful moments in the struggle between unequal forces, the Kovno Jewish community chose its last community leader—its first Chief Jew.

They sat around long tables—men of various ages and of different political affiliations. They were prompted to take counsel together by their fears for the present and their sense of responsibility for the future. They were about to bring to an end one era in the history of Jewish Kovno and to unveil a new one, perhaps the last one. Nobody among those assembled harbored any illusions regarding the future, but no one could have foreseen such a rapid downfall of the Jewish community in Lithuania. The committee members described the situation in Kovno and the nearby towns in the darkest colors. Never in its history had the community faced such peril. Never had it been so helpless. All the efforts of the transfer committee members to change the course of events, to blunt their edge, had proved futile. Whenever Jews tried to protest or to ask for assistance, they ran up against a solid wall of hostility and derision. In view of the mortal danger facing them, the Jews had to leave the city in a hurry. Thousands of homeless Jews were wandering in the courtyards and gardens of Slobodka; many of them spent days and nights under the open sky. There was not enough space for everyone because the Lithuanians had not yet evacuated the area designated for the Ghetto.

The assembly was pervaded by an atmosphere of utter dejection and despair.

Dr. Grigory Wolf—a widely respected veteran community leader and the chairman of the assembly—endeavored to lift the spirits of the gathering: "More than once the Jewish people fell upon hard times in their history. More than once they teetered on the brink of annihilation. But the Jewish people also know that every time a new Haman arose planning to eradicate us, he himself met this fate. 'The glory eternal of Israel will not fail.' " Here Dr. Wolf, an old man, broke down and wept bitterly.

Thirty thousand Kovno Jews, overcome by despair and in mortal danger, eagerly looked forward to their new leader, whom the men present at the meeting were supposed to elect. He was their last hope, and their fate depended on him. Who would be the man? Veteran community leaders refused the position; they feared the burden of responsibility. There was only one candidate no one was prepared to let go, Dr. Elchanan Elkes. His moral qualities, his familiarity with the German mentality, his strong bonds with the Jewish past, were recognized by everyone as making him the most fitting man for the job. Would he succeed in carrying the burden till the end, or would he collapse under its weight? Modest man that he was, Dr. Elkes demurred. He did not have experience in public administration, he said. He had never engaged in this kind of work; after all he had practiced medicine all his life. He asked that his candidacy be dropped. Whereupon those assembled sank into the depths of despair and helplessness.

Suddenly Rabbi Shmukler, the rabbi of the suburb of Sanciai, rose to his feet and addressed the assembly and Dr. Elkes:

> The Kovno Jewish community stands on the brink of disaster. Our daughters are being raped, our men are being murdered, and death is staring into our windows. Jews! The German authorities insist that we appoint an Oberjude, but what we need is a "head of the community," a trustworthy

public servant. The man most fitting for this position at this tragic moment is Dr. Elkes. We therefore turn to you and say: Dr. Elkes, you may be our *Oberjude* for whoever wants to regard you as such, but for us you will be our community leader. We all know that your path will be frought with hardship and danger, but we will go with you all the way, and may God come to our aid. With your deep Jewish faith you will lead us and take us out of the Ghetto, this exile within exile, to our Holy Land. There, you will be our true leader. We pray you, be our community leader at this time. Be strong, for messengers on behalf of the commandment suffer no injury thanks to the prayers of the multitude. Amen.

This call came from the depth of Rabbi Shmukler's heart. His enthusiasm had an electrifying effect on the audience. Jews broke down in tears. Everyone sensed—more than understood—the momentousness of the occasion, and was prepared for whatever might happen. One by one they rose and approached Dr. Elkes, asking him to lead the community in these stormy times. Everyone promised to support him and to cooperate with him. At last Dr. Elkes rose and yielded to the gravity of the moment, being aware of the full measure of risk that his mission entailed. He said: "If you believe that by accepting I will render a service to the common good, then I accept."

The assembly welcomed Dr. Elkes's acceptance with a measure of relief and with profound gratitude. Everyone rose and congratulated him. Dr. Elkes then took his place as chairman.[5] The meeting closed with the singing of "Hatikvah" (Hope).[6] This was the last assembly of the Kovno Jewish Community.

1. On the night of June 25, 1941, 1,000 Jews were murdered in Kovno. Avraham Tory mentions 700 murdered by Lithuanians in Slobodka only; he had not yet learned the full extent of the massacre.
2. On June 27, 1941, sixty Jews were taken to the Lithuanian national cooperative garage in the center of the city and, before a watching crowd, were mostly battered to death with iron bars or killed by having hoses used for washing cars forced into their mouths and turned on.
3. Avraham Tory later commented: "Jewish women from Kovno never forgot the terror ringing in those words."
4. The meeting referred to here was the last meeting of the remaining community leaders before the transfer of the Jews to the Ghetto. Immediately afterward, a meeting took place in another room of the same building, at which those present were Zvi Levin (then chairman of the Zionist Revisionists, and later an unofficial but active member of both the Jewish Council and the underground); Berl Cohen, of the Socialist Zionists; Shlomo Goldstein, of the Zionist Hechalutz leadership; and Avraham Golub (Tory), a member of the central committee of the General Zionist Union in Lithuania. These four decided to form a Zionist underground group, which was later named Matzok (the Hebrew-language acronym of Vilijampolé-Kovno Zionist Center).
5. Dr. Elchanan Elkes, the son of Rabbi Israelmeir and Sarah Elkes, was born in Kalvarija, in Western Lithuania, in 1879. He had an extensive Jewish education and also studied medi-

cine. In 1912 he married Miriam Albin. During World War I he served as a physician in the Russian Army and was honored for distinction in his work. Between the wars he headed the department of internal diseases at the Jewish hospital in Kovno, and practiced privately as well. Besides being the physician of the Lithuanian elite, he treated the poor, was an active Zionist, and acquired wide knowledge in both the humanities and the sciences. He died in Dachau in 1944.

6. The poem "Hope" was written by Naphtali Imber in 1878, in Romania, inspired by the founding of the Jewish settlement of Petah Tikvah in Palestine. The melody was written by Samuel Cohen, a Romanian Jew who had settled in Palestine that same year. First published in 1886, the song became the anthem of the Zionist movement after it was sung at the end of one of the sessions of the fifth Zionist Congress, in Basel, in 1901. It was not formally declared to be the Zionist anthem, however, until the eighteenth Zionist Congress, held in Prague in 1933. At the foundation of the State of Israel on May 14, 1948, it was sung at the opening of the ceremony at which independence was declared. It became the anthem of the State of Israel.

AUGUST 5, 1941

DOCUMENT:
From the Committee for the Transfer of the Jews to Vilijampolé (Slobodka)
To the Governor of Kovno

According to Order no. 15 of the military commander and the mayor of the city of Kovno, the entire Jewish population of the city of Kovno is obliged to move by August 15, 1941, to Vilijampolé. In Kovno are about 22,500 Jews, apart from some 5,000 Jews who have lived for many centuries in Vilijampolé. When the order was issued, it was mentioned that the entire area of Vilijampolé, without exception, will be used for this purpose, and that the non-Jews will leave Vilijampolé.

As per available data, the total dwelling area in Vilijampolé amounts to about 70,000–75,000 square meters. This area has been inhabited up to now by about 12,000 persons (7,000 non-Jews and 5,000 Jews). In this way the population density in Vilijampolé was an average of six square meters of useful dwelling space per person. The representatives of the mayor and the military commander informed us at the time that no Jew can be allotted more than six square meters of space. In our letter to the mayor and the military commander at that time, we pointed out that according to the opinion of experts whom we had consulted, a total space of six square meters yields an average useful dwelling space of only about three and a half square meters. Therefore, an area of 96,250 square meters of settleable dwelling space is required for the Jews of Kovno—22,500 persons plus the 5,000 Jews already settled there, a total of 27,500 Jews—who will move into Vilijampolé. However, as mentioned above, the total dwelling space in Vilijampolé amounts to only 70,000–75,000 square meters.

It has now been established that the area set aside for Jews in Vilijampolé does not include the whole of Vilijampolé, but only a part thereof, which according to the data available to us yields only 40,000–45,000 square meters of dwelling space. Should the entire Jewish population of Kovno and of Vilijampolé—27,500 persons—be squeezed into this dwelling space, this would result in an average dwelling space of 1.7 square meters per person. It is perfectly obvious that such a tiny dwelling space cannot be sufficient for even the most basic purposes.

Naturally such a situation, when several thousand people must be accommodated in an extremely small space, is also dangerous from a sanitary point of view.

The center of Vilijampolé is dilapidated and dirty. The streets and yards are in an unsanitary condition, because there are no clinics, no bathing facilities, no disinfection institutions, and no disinfectants available there. Because of the unsanitary conditions in Vilijampolé, and the expected considerable increase of the population, an epidemic (such as typhoid fever or dysentery) may break out.

Considering the above, we obediently take the liberty to request that the decision concerning the limitation of the Jewish settlement area will be examined again, and that the settlement area will be extended accordingly.[1]

> 1. This appeal was signed by the chairman of the Jewish Council, Dr. Elkes, and by Michael Gemelitzki.

AUGUST 6, 1941

DOCUMENT: Public Announcement no. 5 of the Governor of Kovno

1. The Jewish population is hereby forbidden to be present at or to make purchases at the public markets, before 10 A.M. Jews who are found making purchases before 10 A.M. must expect the most severe punishment.

2. This instruction is in force as of today.[1]

> 1. This announcement was signed by Colonel Cramer.

AUGUST 8, 1941

DOCUMENT:
Order of the Governor of Kovno, transmitted through SA Captain Jordan
To the Jewish Committee[1]

All instructions concerning the Jews of Kovno must also be applied to foreign Jews as well as to the children of mixed marriages. Those must also move into the Ghetto.

1. The Jewish Committee was the committee for the transfer of Jews from Kovno to Slobodka; it comprised Yakov Goldberg, Leon (Leib) Garfunkel, Nikolai (Michael) Gemelitzki, Dr. Grigori Wolf, Rabbi Shmuel-Abba Snieg, Michael Kopelman, Dr. Ephraim Rabinovitz, and Rabbi Yakov Moshe Shmukler. The committee they established, the Ältestenrat or Jewish Council, comprised Dr. Elkes (chairman), Garfunkel (deputy chairman), Goldberg, Rabbi Snieg, Dr. Rabinovitz, and Michael Kopelman, who was also appointed chief of the Jewish Ghetto police. At a later stage, Dr. Wolf, Leon Rostovski, Rabbi Shmukler, and Zvi (Hirsch) Levin joined the Jewish Council unofficially, as advisers.

AUGUST 8, 1941

> *DOCUMENT: Jewish Council note of a communication from SA Captain Jordan*

On his instruction twenty-six Jews were killed because of purchase of foodstuffs on the highway. For an offense committed by one Jew, ten Jews will be killed.

AUGUST 9, 1941

> *DOCUMENT:*
> *From the Jewish Council in Vilijampolé*
> *To the Mayor of the City of Kovno*

A plan for the supply of foodstuffs to the Jewish inhabitants of Vilijampolé:

At the time of the present plan the total Jewish population in Vilijampolé is estimated at about 27,000 persons. According to this plan, foodstuffs will be allocated by a ration card system. This system will be strictly observed. Also according to these ration cards will be allocated such goods as at present are distributed to the other inhabitants of Kovno by means of a ration card system. The allocation of vegetables and other unrationed foodstuffs will also be distributed through the same selling points by means of the same system.

The distribution of foodstuffs will be strictly supervised by the Jewish Council.

The food ration cards will be issued to the Jews in Vilijampolé, according to the arrangements made by the authorities, by the Jewish Council.

Foodstuffs will be supplied from places fixed by the authorities to central distribution points in Vilijampolé, put at the disposal of the Council in an unprocessed condition, such as bread in the form of flour, and meat in the form of animals.

The seven bakeries in the Jewish settlement area in Vilijampolé will be operated for the production of bread.

The following foodstuff-selling stations will be established: twelve to fifteen for the sale of all kinds of foodstuffs except meat and milk, six for the sale of meat, and two for the sale of milk and milk products.

In case grain is delivered instead of flour or barley, the Nemunas mill should be handed over to the Jewish Council.

The Jewish Council should also be permitted to use the old slaughterhouse in Skerdylos Street.

All foodstuffs will be supplied by the authorities at net prices.

Unrationed foodstuffs will be purchased for the Jews of Vilijampolé at the Kovno city markets. We respectfully request the issuing of technical instructions concerning the execution of such purchases.[1]

1. This communication was signed by Dr. Elkes, Dr. Rabinovitz, and M. Oszinsky.

AUGUST 10, 1941

DOCUMENT: Order of SA Captain Jordan

Jews are forbidden to walk on the shores of the Vilija river. Jews are also forbidden to walk in the streets with their hands in their pockets.

AUGUST 12, 1941

DOCUMENT:
From the Committee for the Transfer of Jews to Slobodka
To the Manager of the Housing Department of the Municipality of Kovno

Referring to the order of the governor of Kovno concerning the transfer of all citizens of Jewish nationality to Slobodka, we ask you to instruct the house administrators in the city of Kovno to warn the Jewish inhabitants remaining within the territory of the city of Kovno that they must move by the fixed date.

Furthermore, all members of mixed families, as well as all persons of Jewish nationality who are citizens of other countries, must also be warned that they are obliged to move to Slobodka.

Jews without means will be assisted in their transfer by this committee.

AUGUST 15, 1941

DOCUMENT: Order of SA Captain Jordan

The Ghetto must be closed. It is prohibited to leave the Ghetto arbitrarily.

AUGUST 18, 1941

DOCUMENT: Order of SA Captain Jordan

The Jewish Council is obliged to provide today 500 Jews, namely, men from among the educated classes, to be brought to the authorities at the Ghetto gate.[1]

1. The Germans, and Mikas Kaminskas, the Lithuanian head of the Kovno municipality, explicitly asked for 500 Jews from the "intelligentsia" to work in the city archives in Kovno. The attraction of this offer—of intellectual work rather than hard labor, as well as of money and better food—was such that more than the required 500, 534 in all, reported at the Ghetto gate. All of them were taken to the Ninth Fort and killed.

AUGUST 24, 1941

DOCUMENT: Order of SA Captain Jordan

The Jews of the Ghetto are forbidden to keep dogs unless they are on a leash; or to let cats into the streets.

AUGUST 29, 1941

*DOCUMENT: Order of the Governor of the City of Kovno,
SA Colonel Cramer*

It is forbidden to bring newspapers and foodstuffs into the Ghetto.

AUGUST 30, 1941

DOCUMENT: Order of SA Captain Jordan

All Ghetto inmates must hand over their electrical appliances such as kitchen stoves, ovens, etc.

SEPTEMBER 1, 1941

*DOCUMENT: Order no. 4 of the Governor General of Vilna, concerning
the registration of Jewish property*

1. The entire property of the Jewish population must be registered by September 9, 1941.

2. Everybody possessing or keeping Jewish property, and everybody who disposes of or can dispose of Jewish property without being the owner, possessor, or keeper—legally or actually—is obliged to register it.

3. The registration duty therefore applies not only to the lawful Jewish owners, but also, for example, to anyone who administers Jewish property, or has accepted it for safekeeping, or has received it in any other way.

4. The registration of Jewish property must be made on a form issued by the police station concerned; after the property is registered on the form, the form must be returned to that police station.

5. Whoever conceals or removes Jewish property, or does not register it, must expect to be most severely punished.

6. For the punctual and complete registration of all Jewish property, the chiefs of the police stations are responsible to me personally.[1]

1. This order, which also applied to Kovno, was signed by Hans Hingst, governor of Vilna.

SEPTEMBER 3, 1941

DOCUMENT: Order of the Governor of Kovno through SA Captain Jordan

I

All Ghetto inmates must deliver immediately by 6 P.M. on September 4, 1941, at the latest, the following articles to the Council for their transfer to the respective authorities:

1. Any money in Russian or German currency exceeding 100 (one hundred) rubles per family.

2. All valuables, including gold, silver, precious stones, and other precious metals, or items made from such metals.

3. Securities, receipts of deposits (if there are any).

4. Valuable paintings, valuable fur products, and furs (except for sheepskins or very worn furs), good carpets, and pianos.

5. Typewriters.

6. All electrical appliances, including those which can be used for medical or professional purposes.

7. Good materials for suits and coats.

8. Cows and poultry.

9. Horses with harness; carts.

10. Stamp collections.

2

As from the day of this announcement, it is forbidden to slaughter poultry or animals.

3

All Ghetto inmates are requested to follow this delivery duty as scrupulously and conscientiously as possible, because the fate of the Ghetto depends thereon.

If this duty is not followed scrupulously and completely, it is not only the offenders who run the risk of the death penalty, but all other Ghetto inmates.

The authorities are aware that some items are buried or otherwise concealed. In view of the risk to which individuals as well as the total population are exposed, it is absolutely necessary to find and deliver these items.

The above-mentioned articles must be delivered on Thursday, September 4, between 7 A.M. and 6 P.M. at the following places: 2 Kraziu Street, 15 Puodziu Street, 49 Varniu Street, and 41 Linkuvos Street.

The time of delivery of cows, horses, carts, and poultry will be published separately.

SEPTEMBER 6, 1941

DOCUMENT:
From the Commander of the Security Police and
*   SS Einsatzkommando 3A*
To the Jewish Council, Vilijampolé

The Jewish Council is hereby summoned to hand over all blackout materials, etc., to the commandant of the Security Police.[1]

1. This document was signed by SS Lieutenant Hamann, commander of the mobile detachment of Einsatzkommando 3A, who was at that very moment in charge of the mass murder of Jews in Siauliai (Shavli).

SEPTEMBER 6, 1941

DOCUMENT:
From the Commander of the Security Police and
*   SS Einsatzkommando 3A*
To the Jewish Council, Vilijampolé

Confirming the receipt of 40 (forty) pieces of blackout material.

SEPTEMBER 7, 1941

DOCUMENT: Order of SA Colonel Cramer

The Jews are forbidden to purchase foodstuffs and other items in the city.

SEPTEMBER 10, 1941

DOCUMENT: Order of SA Colonel Cramer

All horses, cows, carriages, and harnesses, as well as poultry, belonging to the Jews in the Ghetto, must be handed over to the city governor.

SEPTEMBER 12, 1941

DOCUMENT: Order of SA Colonel Cramer

Securities, debts, and deposits left by Ghetto inmates with other persons must be registered.

SEPTEMBER 15, 1941

DOCUMENT: Order of SA Captain Jordan to the Council, Vilijampolé

Five thousand craftsman-certificates are enclosed, for the Council. These certificates must be distributed immediately to the artisans according to the list provided, and to eleven physicians as also listed. The distribution must be made in such a way that each family receives one certificate. The certificates must be distributed in such a way that every family receives one certificate for each married couple; under no circumstances should certificates be given to other family members, such as grandparents or other relatives.

SEPTEMBER 17, 1941

DOCUMENT: Order of SA Captain Jordan

All inmates of the Ghetto must forthwith leave their premises and assemble in Sajungos Square.[1]

> 1. This order was revoked at ten in the morning, after 3,000 people had already gathered at the square. They were allowed to return to their homes.

SEPTEMBER 20, 1941

DOCUMENT: Order of SA Captain Jordan

Each Ghetto family must hand over one piece of toilet or shaving soap.

SEPTEMBER 26, 1941

DOCUMENT: Order of the Commander of the Security Police, Rauca[1]

The inmates of Veliuonos Street must leave their homes today, i.e. immediately, and report to Sajungos Square.[2]

1. Master Sergeant Helmut Rauca was the Gestapo official in Kovno in charge of Ghetto affairs.
2. A thousand Jews assembled as a result of this order; they were all taken to the Ninth Fort.

SEPTEMBER 27, 1941

DOCUMENT: Instructions issued by SA Colonel Cramer, through Mikas Kaminskas

All fodder, such as oats, hay, straw, etc., in the Ghetto must be handed over.

OCTOBER 1, 1941

DOCUMENT: Order of SA Captain Jordan

As from today, 1,000 men must be provided for work during the day, and 1,000 men for work at night, at the airfield.

OCTOBER 4, 1941

On September 15, 1941, Jordan[1] delivered 5,000 "Certificates for Jewish Artisans" to the Jewish Council to distribute to Jewish skilled workers in the Ghetto. In the Ghetto those cards were nicknamed "life papers," or "Jordan certificates." Eleven such documents were designated to Jewish physicians as specified by Jordan. No documents at all were issued to other specialists who had a university education. The Ghetto Jewish population stood at that time at about 27,000 people.[2] The purpose was clear.[3]

On September 17, 1941, the small Ghetto[4] was surrounded by reinforced detachments of German guards and Lithuanian partisans. All the inmates were assembled on the Sajungos square, situated outside the Ghetto. Holders of the Jordan certificates were concentrated on the square adjacent to the hospital. Both the outpatients of the surgical hospital and the inpatients were ordered to assemble on the square. Among the latter were many wounded, who had been operated on during the previous night. Two patients collapsed and died.

Dr. Alexei Feinberg,[5] who had been hospitalized, was taken to the Ninth Fort together with children from the children's home which adjoined the hospital. Patients from the hospital for infectious diseases, together with the physicians and the hospital staff who had been found there, were ordered to stay inside. The hospital gates were locked to prevent anyone from leaving or entering.

After the deportees arrived at the square, the Lithuanian partisans started looting their apartments. Then the turn of the deportees from the hospital came. The physicians and the technical staff were removed from the building. They were lined up in columns and marched in the direction of the Ninth Fort. At that moment a car pulled up in the square and a high-ranking police officer climbed out. He handed an envelope to Captain Tornbaum,[6] who commanded the "action." Having read the contents of the letter he had just received, the German commander ordered the "action" to be called off at once. All those assembled were sent back to their homes. The truck in which Dr. Feinberg and the children had been driven off to the Ninth Fort was also called back.

This was the order which discontinued the "action." This time the people were saved. In this "action" on September 17, 1941, as the process of assembling in the square reached its climax, a number of Jews who lived in houses not far from the square broke into the hospital building, in an attempt to save themselves.

On September 26, 1941, an "action" took place in the old quarter of the Ghetto, around Veliuonos Street. The official pretext was that Jews allegedly shot at a German police officer, Kozlovski.

The whole area was surrounded by soldiers and some 1,000 Jews were removed from it. This time the deportation was final and tragic. The deported did not return.

On the same day an order was issued to lock and seal the deportees' apartments. Several days later the furniture and the belongings of the deportees were removed from the Ghetto.

In the Ghetto itself an era of deportation began. Rumors were spreading about pits being dug in the Ninth Fort and about impending new deportations. Some people said they had seen those pits with their own eyes, while others knew when the deportations would be resumed and what would be the number of the deportees.

1. Captain Fritz Jordan, a young officer in the SA (Sturmabteilung, or Storm Detachment, an auxiliary police force used by the Germans to maintain internal order), had just been appointed superintendent of Jewish affairs on behalf of the German civil administration in Kovno. A sadistic murderer, he planned and organized numerous bloody incidents in the Ghetto. He spoke coarsely, and would open the door to the Jewish Council office by kicking it. Early in 1942, after quarreling with his superior, he was sent to the eastern front, where he was killed in action.

2. The Jewish Council deliberated for a long while whether to distribute the "Jordan" certificates or to return them to the Germans. Under pressure from the tradesmen in the Ghetto,

who argued that nobody was entitled to deny them a chance to live, it was decided to distribute them, but only to the actual tradesmen in person. Distribution of the certificates began in chaos, with many people forcing their way into the Jewish Council offices. The first German roundup of Jews began at the same time. Then, inexplicably, the roundups were canceled and the Germans left the Ghetto.

3. By October 4, 1941, it was clear to many of the Ghetto inmates that those who did not have a Jordan certificate were to be killed. Even then, however, people were divided as to whether the alternative was in fact to be death. As Avraham Tory wrote in his description of the October 28 "action," "many did not understand what was happening to them."

4. When the Ghetto was established in August 1941, it was divided into two separate sections, the large Ghetto and the small Ghetto, separated by Paneriu Street, above which a high wooden bridge was built to connect the two sections. In all, 30,000 Jews were forced to live in an area which had previously been inhabited by 7,000 Jews and non-Jews. The buildings in the small Ghetto were newer than those in the large Ghetto, which was mainly in Slobodka, an old, dilapidated quarter with no sewerage or running water, and unpaved. Many important Ghetto institutions were therefore housed in the small Ghetto, including the hospital for internal medicine and contagious diseases, the children's nursery, and the old-age home.

5. Dr. Alexei Feinberg, president of the Kovno Physicians' Union before the war.

6. Captain Alfred Tornbaum was the commander of the third division of the German police in Kovno. It was this division which was assigned to the Ghetto. He often set his dog upon Jews, and he beat Jews with a lead-tipped baton. He was tried in Wiesbaden in 1962; Avraham Tory testified against him, but the court found that there was insufficient evidence to convict him.

OCTOBER 6, 1941

On October 2, 1941, Captain Jordan and his Lithuanian assistant Kaminskas arrived. They sealed off the public square near the hospital for contagious diseases and tarried at the sewage pit behind the hospital building. Before leaving they asked the commander of the Ghetto Guard to find twelve spades. When the news of this order came through to the Council and to other Ghetto inmates, serious apprehensions arose. Rumors reached Dr. Zacharin,[1] director of the surgical department, about the danger facing the hospital. From that day on he no longer slept in his home in the small Ghetto but decided to lodge in his friends' homes in the large Ghetto.

The Ghetto inmates could not understand the purpose of the request for twelve spades. Work in the hospital proceeded normally. On October 3, 1941, the hospital staff went to work as usual. On that day people were seized for work at the airfield due to the shortage of labor power.

At 10 o'clock, a Jewish worker named Gutman returned from the city. He was employed at a garage construction for the ninth squad of the German Police. His wife worked in the hospital in the Ghetto. He said that a German employee at his workplace had told him that the hospital was to be removed from the

Ghetto. The German advised him that his wife should stop going to work in the hospital and that, in general, everybody should stay away from the place.

When Dr. Brauns,[2] the hospital director, heard the news, he decided to send home all patients who were able to stand on their feet. The patients, however, refused to leave. They felt more secure in the hospital than in their own homes.

On the same day, Dr. Elkes went to the city governor's office. He wanted to talk with Jordan about rumors which were circulating in the Ghetto, but he was refused an interview. Kaminskas endeavored to dispel his fears; he told Dr. Elkes that the rumors were unfounded. There would be no deportations and no transfers. The twelve spades which had been requested the day before were designated for the front. But Kaminskas could not be trusted. During the "action" of the 500, it was Kaminskas who had said that those rounded up had been taken to work in the archives, and that they would return to their homes that same day. He always concealed the truth. His announcements to the Council had always been evasive or false. All the same, the news about the transfer of the hospital to another place seemed improbable.

On October 4, 1941, at 6 A.M., reinforced detachments of the third squad of the German Police (some fifty men) and Lithuanian partisans (about one hundred men) were seen near the bridge, known as the Viaduct, which connected the small Ghetto with the large Ghetto. These men blocked the way across to the small Ghetto. Only the night-shift airfield workers were allowed to cross over. Just a handful of people, holders of the Jordan certificates, were allowed out of the small Ghetto, and even they were allowed out only after a prolonged argument. Neither the physicians nor the hospital director was allowed in.

At that same time, ten Jews, equipped with spades, were brought to the hospital vicinity. They were given an order to dig a large pit next to the sewage pit in the hospital courtyard. They were told to hurry up with their job and, in fact, their faces were soon bathed in sweat.

At 8 A.M. the process of dragging people out of their homes and assembling them at Sajungos Square, outside the Ghetto, began. Those carrying the Jordan certificates were removed from the square and taken to the large Ghetto. Those without such documents were taken to the Ninth Fort, including a few holders of Jordan certificates who, amid the turmoil, had become caught up with the rest.

All the patients in the surgical and therapy ward were evacuated, including Dr. Feinberg and his wife, who had nursed him, and Dr. Zvi Elkes, the brother of the Council chairman.

In the maternity ward, which housed eight women, preparations got under way for the evacuation of the patients. Women who could not leave unaided remained in their beds, waiting to be carried out on stretchers.

Two Germans entered the room. They asked what type of patients were there, and why they were not ready for transfer. The women replied that they had just given birth and that their ardent wish was to get up quickly from their beds so as not to delay the operation.

The Germans wanted to see the babies who had just been born. They came up to the ledge by the window on which the six babies were lying. They stood there for a while watching the babies. The eyes of one of the Germans grew misty. "Shall we leave them?" he asked his friend. They both left the room, letting the mothers and the babies stay. This time they survived.

The Germans then started taking the children out of the children's home. Out of 153 children, only 12 were left in the Home. They were simply overlooked. The nurses were also taken away. Those children who were in swaddling clothes were taken out and placed on the ground in the stone-paved hospital courtyard, their tiny faces turned skyward. Soldiers of the third squad of the German Police passed between them. They stopped for a moment. Some of them kicked the babies with their boots. The babies rolled a little to the side but soon enough regained their belly-up position, their faces turned toward the sky. It was a rare spectacle of cruelty and callousness.

A heavy truck pulled up. First the children and then the nurses were thrown into it. The truck was then covered with a canvas cloth, and drove off in the direction of the Ninth Fort.

The hospital for contagious diseases was housed in a two-story wooden structure. In the cellar there was an office in which various documents were stored, as well as a kitchen, a washroom, and a small storage room.

Patients were housed in fifteen rooms on two floors. One of the rooms served as the doctors' office; it also contained the X-ray equipment. The hospital was furnished with modern medical equipment as well as with medicines, linen, and other articles. The physicians gathered all those items in one place, hoping to save them.

On that day there was a total of sixty-seven patients and technical staff in the hospital. In the morning they were joined by a number of healthy residents of the small Ghetto, who assumed that they would be able to find shelter there. However, the opposite happened.

As the "action" began, all the gates of the hospital were locked. The locked gates were then boarded up with thick wooden planks. The hospital watchman, who lived with his twelve-year-old son in a wooden shack in the courtyard, was pushed into the hospital building before it was locked. The Germans also brought to the hospital an old man and his wife who had stayed in their apartment and had not left for Sajungos Square. They too were forcibly pushed into the sealed-off hospital.

In the surgical hospital at 55 Paneriu Street a handful of patients had remained who could not be transferred. On German orders they too were brought to the hospital for contagious diseases and pushed into the sealed-off hospital building.

Of the ten Jews who had been ordered to dig a pit near the sewage pit in the courtyard, only two were allowed to pass over to the large Ghetto; the other eight did not return.

Opposite the hospital building, on the other side of the fence, a fur factory called Lape (Fox) was situated. From that location the hospital courtyard could be seen clearly. The factory workers there saw the ten Jews digging the pit on that day; they saw how the residents of the old people's home were lowered into it, how patients were thrown into it and then shot inside the pit; they saw how little children were thrown into the pit, as well as patients who could not stand on their feet. They also saw how the remaining residents of the small Ghetto were driven out in the direction of Demokratu Square and how they were beaten with rifle butts.

At 1 P.M. smoke could be seen rising over the hospital building; later flames shot up from it. The hospital was burning. The fire burned all day and night.[3]

Eight women patients in the maternity ward and six newborn babies, as well as some medical staff, were confined in the surgical ward and released only on Monday, October 6. On the same day, between 4 and 6 P.M., holders of the Jordan certificates were allowed to enter the small Ghetto for two hours, in order to remove from their homes such belongings as could be carried in one hand or on the back. It was only then that the maternity ward patients were evacuated from the hospital, together with their babies, and those of the surgical ward staff who had stayed there.

Firemen were not allowed to come and put out the hospital fire, which was clearly visible from all over the city. Dr. Balcunas of the municipal sanitation department reported afterward that three hours before the hospital was set on fire, fire trucks, summoned by the municipal firemen, had been positioned near the hospital to prevent the fire from spreading outside the Ghetto.

Together with the patients who lost their lives in the conflagration, all the medical equipment, as well as the medicines, archives, and the office of the health department of the hospital, was destroyed in the fire. After this event, the physicians and the staff of the health department went to great lengths to get registered as workers in the forced-labor brigades, or to acquire another trade, in order not to be identified with the medical profession. The health department's activity was discontinued. Everything was lost. Everything had to be started over again, beginning with the search for a suitable building to serve as a hospital, and the gathering of the much-needed medical equipment.

The prevailing mood among those Jews who were left was terrible. Rumors about new expulsions kept circulating. After October 4, the Jews lent their ears to every rumor. The smell of gunpowder hung in the air.

1. Dr. Benjamin Zacharin, director of the surgical department of the Ghetto hospital. He was later head of the health department of the Jewish Council. After the liquidation of the Ghetto he worked as a physician in various concentration camps in Germany.

2. Dr. Moses Brauns, director of the Jewish hospital in the Ghetto; later head of the sanitation and contagious diseases department of the Jewish Council. After the war he lived in the United States. His principal achievement in the Ghetto was to combat typhus successfully while hiding its existence from the Germans and Lithuanians, who might otherwise have obliterated the Ghetto in 1942.

3. Among those killed in the hospital was the physician Dr. Davidovich. Dr. Brauns, however, was saved. "On that day," he later recalled (in his privately printed memoirs, Los Angeles, 1985, p. 149), "my son Jack and I escaped death by an accident. As usual we went to the hospital and tried to cross the bridge over Paneriu Street before six o'clock in the morning. For 'security' reasons, my son was working in the office of the hospital of contagious diseases. He worked there every day under my supervision. At that day, on our way to the hospital, we met an inmate of the Ghetto who started a conversation with me about our situation. Because of this conversation, our arrival at the bridge was delayed by some ten to fifteen minutes. There, a Lithuanian soldier with a machine gun stood guard. He did not allow my son and me to cross. So we had to remain in the 'large' Ghetto, and we escaped death."

OCTOBER 28, 1941

MEMOIR[1]

On Friday afternoon, October 24, 1941, a Gestapo car entered the Ghetto. It carried the Gestapo deputy chief, Captain Schmitz, and Master Sergeant Rauca. Their appearance filled all onlookers with fear. The Council was worried and ordered the Jewish Ghetto police to follow all their movements. Those movements were rather unusual. The two Ghetto rulers turned neither to the Council offices nor to the Jewish police, nor to the German labor office, nor even to the German commandant, as they used to in their visits to the Ghetto. Instead, they toured various places as if looking for something, tarried awhile in Demokratu Square, looked it over, and left through the gate, leaving in their wake an ominously large question mark: what were they scheming to do?

The next day, Saturday afternoon, an urgent message was relayed from the Ghetto gate to the Council: Rauca, accompanied by a high-ranking Gestapo officer, was coming. As usual in such cases, all unauthorized persons were removed from the Council secretariat room and from the hallway, lest their presence invoke the wrath of the Nazi fiends.

The two Germans entered the offices of the Council. Rauca did not waste time. He opened with a major pronouncement: it is imperative to increase the size of the Jewish labor force in view of its importance for the German war effort—an allusion to the indispensability of Jewish labor to the Germans. Furthermore, he continued, the Gestapo is aware that food rations allotted to the Ghetto inmates do not provide proper nourishment to heavy-labor workers and, therefore, he intends to increase rations for both the workers and their families so that they will be able to achieve greater output for the Reich. The remaining Ghetto inmates, those not included in the Jewish labor force, would have to make do with the existing rations. To forestall competition and envy between them and the Jewish labor force, they would be separated from them and transferred to the small Ghetto. In this fashion, those contributing to the war effort would obtain more spacious and comfortable living quarters. To carry out this operation a roll call would take place. The Council was to issue an order in which all the Ghetto inmates, without exception, and irrespective of sex and age, were called to report to Demokratu Square on October 28, at 6 A.M. on the dot. In the square they should line up by families and by the workplace of the family head. When leaving for the roll call they were to leave their apartments, closets, and drawers open. Anybody found after 6 A.M. in his home would be shot on the spot.

The members of the Council were shaken and overcome by fear. This order boded very ill for the future of the Ghetto. But what did it mean? Dr. Elkes attempted to get Rauca to divulge some information about the intention behind this roll call, but his efforts bore no fruit. Rauca refused to add another word to his communication and, accompanied by his associate, left the Council office and the Ghetto.

The members of the Council remained in a state of shock. What lay in wait for the Ghetto? What was the true purpose of the roll call? Why did Rauca order the Council to publish the order, rather than publish it himself? Was he planning to abuse the trust the Ghetto population had in the Jewish leadership? And if so, had the Council the right to comply with Rauca's order and publish it, thereby becoming an accomplice in an act which might spell disaster?

Some Council members proposed to disobey the Gestapo and not publish the order, even if this would mean putting the lives of the Council members at risk. Others feared that in the case of disobedience the arch-henchmen would not be contented with punishing the Council alone, but would vent their wrath also on the Ghetto inmates, and that thousands of Jews were liable to pay with their lives for the impudence of their leaders. After all, no one could fathom the intentions of Rauca and his men; why, then, stir the beasts of prey into anger? Was the Council entitled to take responsibility for the outcome of not publishing the order? On the other hand, was the Council entitled to take upon itself the heavy burden of moral responsibility and go ahead with publishing the order?

The Council discussions continued for many hours without reaching a conclusion. In the meantime, the publication of the order was postponed and an attempt was made to inquire about Rauca's plans, using the contacts of Caspi-Serebrovitz[2] in the Gestapo. Zvi Levin, who was Caspi's fellow party member (they were both Revisionists), was asked to leave for the city, to call on him and ask him what he knew about Rauca's plans, and to ask Rauca to grant an audience to Dr. Elkes. Levin found Caspi packing his bags. The latter was stunned to learn about the order and exclaimed spontaneously: "Aha, now I understand why Rauca is sending me to Vilna for three days just at this time. He wants to keep me away from Kovno, especially now."

Complying with Levin's request, Caspi set out to inform Rauca that disquiet prevailed in the Ghetto and that the Council chairman wished to see him that very evening. Rauca responded favorably.

The Council members agreed that the meeting with Rauca should take place in the modest apartment of Dr. Elkes, in order to keep the meeting as secret as possible. At 6 P.M. Rauca arrived at Dr. Elkes's apartment. Yakov Goldberg, a member of the Council and head of the Council's labor office, was also present. Dr. Elkes began by saying that his responsibilities as leader of the community and as a human being obliged him to speak openly. He asked Rauca to understand his position and not to be angry with him. Then he revealed his and the Council members' fears that the decree spelled disaster for the Ghetto, since if the German authorities' intention was only to alter the food distribution arrangements, the Council was prepared to carry out the appropriate decrees faithfully and to the letter. Therefore, he went on to say, there is no need for roll call of the entire Ghetto population, including elderly people and babes in arms, since such a summons was likely to cause panic in the Ghetto. Moreover, the three roll calls which had taken place over the past three months had each ended in terrible "actions." Therefore, he, Dr. Elkes, pleaded with "Mr. Master Sergeant" to reveal the whole truth behind the roll call.

Rauca feigned amazement that any suspicion at all could have been harbored by the members of the Council. He repeated his promise that a purely administrative matter was involved and that no evil intentions lurked behind it. He added that at the beginning the Gestapo had, in fact, considered charging the Council with the distribution of the increased food rations for the Jewish labor force, but having given thought to the solidarity prevailing among the Jews, had suspected that the food distribution would not be carried out and that the food delivered to the Council would be distributed among all Ghetto residents—both workers and nonworkers—in equal rations. The Gestapo could not allow this to happen under the difficult conditions of the continuing war. Accordingly, the Gestapo had no choice but to divide the Ghetto population into two groups. The roll call was a purely administrative measure and nothing more.

Dr. Elkes attempted to appeal to the "conscience" of the Gestapo officer, hinting casually that every war, including the present one, was bound to end sooner or later, and that if Rauca would answer his questions openly, without concealing anything, the Jews would know how to repay him. The Council itself would know how to appreciate Rauca's humane approach. Thus, Dr. Elkes daringly intimated a possible defeat of Germany in the war, in which case Rauca would be able to save his skin with the help of the Jews. Rauca, however, remained unmoved: there was no hidden plan and no ill intention behind the decree. Having said this he left.

After this conversation, Dr. Elkes and Goldberg left for the Council offices, where the other Council members were waiting for them impatiently. Dr. Elkes's report of his conversation did not dispel the uncertainty and the grave fears. No one was prepared to believe Rauca's assertions that a purely administrative matter was involved. The question remained: why should the elderly and the infants, men and women, including the sick and feeble, be dragged out of their homes at dawn for a roll call by families and by workplace, if the purpose was simply the distribution of increased food rations to the workers? Even if the plan was just to transfer part of the Ghetto population to the small Ghetto—why was a total roll call needed? Was it not sufficient to announce that such-and-such residents must move into those living quarters within the small Ghetto which had been left empty after the liquidation of its residents and the burning of the hospital?

Even before Rauca ordered the Council to publish the decree, rumors originating in various Jewish workplaces in the city where there was contact with Lithuanians had it that in the Ninth Fort large pits had been dug by Russian prisoners-of-war. Those rumors were being repeated by various Lithuanians and, naturally, they reached the Council. When Rauca announced the roll-call decree, the rumors and the roll call no longer seemed a coincidence.

As the rumors about digging of pits persisted, and the members of the Council failed to give any indication of their apprehension, an atmosphere of fear pervaded the Ghetto, growing heavier with each passing day. The very real apprehensions of the Council were compounded by the fear that any revelation of its suspicions and doubts might lead many Jews to acts of desperation—acts which were bound to bring disaster both on themselves and on many others in the Ghetto.

Since the members of the Council could not reach any decision, they resolved to seek the advice of Chief Rabbi Shapiro. At 11 P.M. Dr. Elkes, Garfunkel, Goldberg, and Levin set out for Rabbi Shapiro's house. The unexpected visit at such a late hour frightened the old and sick rabbi. He rose from his bed and, pale as a ghost, came out to his guests. He was trembling with emotion.

The members of the Council told Rabbi Shapiro about the two meetings with Rauca, and about the roll-call decree. They also told him about their fears and asked him to rule on the question of whether they, as public leaders responsible for the fate of the Jews in the Ghetto, were permitted or even duty bound to publish the decree.

The rabbi heaved a deep sigh. The question was complex and difficult; it called for weighty consideration. He asked them to come back to him at 6 A.M. the next day. Dr. Elkes and his colleagues replied by stressing the urgency of the matter, since the Council had been told that it must publish the decree before that time. Each further delay was liable to provoke the ire of the Gestapo. The rabbi promised that he would not close his eyes all night; that he would consult his learned books and give them an early reply.

When the Council members returned to the rabbi's house at 6 A.M. they found him poring over books which lay piled up on his desk. His face bore visible traces of the sleepless night and the great ordeal he had gone through to find scriptural support for the ruling on the terrible question facing the Council. He lifted his head—adorned by white beard—and said that he had not yet found the answer. He asked them to come back in three hours' time. But at 9 o'clock he was still engrossed in study and put off his answer for another two hours. At last, at 11 o'clock, he came up with the answer. In studying and interpreting the sources, he had found that there had been situations in Jewish history which resembled the dilemma the Council was facing now. In such cases, he said, when an evil edict had imperiled an entire Jewish community and, by a certain act, a part of the community could be saved, communal leaders were bound to summon their courage, take the responsibility, and save as many lives as possible. According to this principle, it was incumbent on the Council to pub-lish the decree. Other rabbis, and a number of public figures in the Ghetto, subsequently took issue with this ruling. They argued that it was forbidden for the Council to publish the decree, since by doing so it inadvertently be-came a collaborator with the oppressor in carrying out his design—a design which could bring disaster on the entire Ghetto. Those bereft of all hope added the argument that since the Ghetto was doomed to perdition anyway, the Coun-cil should have adopted the religious principle "yehareg u'bal yaavor" (to re-fuse compliance even on the pain of death), and refrained from publishing the decree.

Immediately after their visit to the chief rabbi, members of the Council con-vened for a special meeting and decided to publish the decree. So it was that on October 27, 1941, announcements in Yiddish and in German were posted by the Council throughout the Ghetto. Their text was as follows:

The Council has been ordered by the authorities to publish the following official decree to the Ghetto inmates:

All inmates of the Ghetto, without exception, including children and the sick, are to leave their homes on Tuesday, October 28, 1941, at 6 A.M., and to assemble in the square between the big blocks and the Demokratu Street, and to line up in accordance with police instructions.

The Ghetto inmates are required to report by families, each family being headed by the worker who is the head of the family.

It is forbidden to lock apartments, wardrobes, cupboards, desks, etc. . . .

After 6 A.M. nobody may remain in his apartment.

Anyone found in the apartments after 6 A.M. will be shot on sight.

The wording was chosen by the Council so that everyone would understand that it concerned a Gestapo order; that the Council had no part in it.

The Ghetto was agog. Until the publication of this order everyone had carried his fears in his own heart. Now those fears and forebodings broke out. The rumors about the digging of pits in the Ninth Fort, which had haunted people like a nightmare, now acquired tangible meaning. The Ghetto remembered well the way the previous "actions" had been prepared, in which some 2,800 people had met their deaths. An additional sign of the impending disaster was that on that very same day workers in various places were furnished with special papers issued by their German employers—military and paramilitary—certifying that their holders were employed on a permanent basis at such-and-such a German factory or workplace.

This category also included the airfield workers, who had been issued suitable cards and yellow armbands to be worn on their right sleeve, as well as members of the Jewish labor brigade which worked for the Gestapo. Workers in this brigade, headed by Lipzer,[3] were particularly conspicuous since, in addition to the documents certifying their employment by the Gestapo, they were provided by Lipzer with a sign bearing the word "Gestapo" as their workplace.

The overwhelming majority of the Ghetto inmates did not have in their possession such privileged documents, or Jordan certificates. People kept flocking to streetcorners and into courtyards, making inquiries, hoping to hear something which might put them at their ease. Everyone was busy interpreting each word in the decree. Particularly ominous was the threat that anyone found in his apartment after 6 A.M. would be shot. The Gestapo also announced that, immediately after this deadline, armed German policemen would be deployed in every house and courtyard and would kill anyone to be found there regardless of the reason.

No one in the Ghetto closed an eye on the night of October 27. Many wept bitterly, many others recited Psalms. There were also people who did the opposite: they decided to have a good time, to feast and gorge themselves on food, and use up their whole supply. Inmates whose apartments were stocked with wines and liquor drank all they could, and even invited neighbors and friends to the macabre drinking party "so as not to leave anything behind for the Germans."

There were also those who, despite everything, did not lose hope and kept themselves busy, hiding away money, jewelry, and other valuables in hiding places under floorboards or in door lintels, in pits they dug that night in their courtyards, and so on. Every unmarried woman looked for a family to adopt her, or for a bachelor who would present her as his wife. Widows with children also sought "husbands" for themselves and "fathers" for their children—all this in preparation for the roll call, in the hope of being able to save themselves.

I, too, adopted as my son an eleven-year-old boy, named Moishele Prusak, who was a remote relative of mine. His parents and the other members of his family were living in my native village of Lazdijai, whereas he lived alone in Slobodka, where he studied at the yeshiva.

Tuesday morning, October 28, was rainy. A heavy mist covered the sky and the whole Ghetto was shrouded in darkness. A fine sleet filled the air and covered the ground in a thin layer. From all directions, dragging themselves heavily and falteringly, groups of men, women, and children, elderly and sick who leaned on the arms of their relatives or neighbors, babies carried in their mothers' arms, proceeded in long lines. They were all wrapped in winter coats, shawls, or blankets, so as to protect themselves from the cold and the damp. Many carried in their hands lanterns or candles, which cast a faint light, illuminating their way in the darkness.

Many families stepped along slowly, holding hands. They all made their way in the same direction—to Demokratu Square. It was a procession of mourners grieving over themselves. Some thirty thousand people proceeded that morning into the unknown, toward a fate that could already have been sealed for them by the bloodthirsty rulers.

A deathlike silence pervaded this procession tens of thousands strong. Every person dragged himself along, absorbed in his own thoughts, pondering his own fate and the fate of his family whose lives hung by a thread. Thirty thousand lonely people, forgotten by God and by man, delivered to the whim of tyrants whose hands had already spilled the blood of many Jews.

All of them, especially heads of families, had equipped themselves with some sort of document, even a certificate of being employed by one of the Ghetto institutions, or a high school graduation diploma, or a German university diploma—some paper that might perhaps, perhaps, who knows, bring them an "indulgence" for the sin of being a Jew. Some dug out commendations issued by the Lithuanian Army; perhaps these might be of help.

The Ghetto houses were left empty, except for a handful of terminally ill persons who could not raise themselves from bed. In compliance with the instruction issued by the authorities, on every house in which a sick person had been left behind a note was posted giving his name and his illness. The Council offices, as well as the offices of the Jewish Ghetto police, the labor office, and the Ghetto workshops, were also left empty; doors of offices were left ajar, as well as closets, desks, and drawers, in compliance with Rauca's order, so that nobody could remain there in hiding. The storerooms containing the Ghetto's food supplies and raw materials were left unattended on that day, as was the private property of the Ghetto inmates.

As the Ghetto inmates were assembling in Demokratu Square, armed Lithuanian partisans raided the Ghetto houses, forcing their way into every apartment, every attic, every storage room, and every cellar, looking for who might be hiding Jews. Many of these Lithuanians took the opportunity to loot. Some carried with them suitcases stuffed with goods, but these looters were subsequently arrested by the German police officers, who disarmed them and removed them from the Ghetto.

The Ghetto fence was surrounded by machine guns and a heavy detachment of armed German policemen, commanded by Captain Tornbaum. He also had at his disposal battalions of armed Lithuanian partisans. A crowd of curious Lithuanian spectators had gathered on the hills overlooking the Ghetto. They followed the events taking place in the square with great interest, not devoid of delight, and did not leave for many hours.

The Ghetto inmates were lined up in columns according to the workplace of the family heads. The first column consisted of the Council members, followed by the column of the Jewish policemen and their families. On both sides and behind stood the workers in the Ghetto institutions, and many columns of the various Jewish labor brigades together with their families, since on that day the Ghetto was sealed off. No one was allowed to go out to work. The airfield workforce, which had left for work the previous day and had stayed there for an additional shift in compliance with General Geiling's order,[4] were returned to the Ghetto after the entire Ghetto population had already been assembled in the square. Having completed two shifts of hard labor, these people hurried to and fro among the columns, tired, hungry, and dirty, in an effort to locate their families.

In the meantime, dawn broke. The grayish light of a rainy day replaced the nocturnal darkness. Old people, and those too weak to remain standing on their feet for long hours, collapsed on the ground. Others, having learned from past experience, had brought with them a chair or a stool on which they could sit and rest. Some had even equipped themselves with food before coming to the roll call, but the great majority of the Ghetto inmates remained standing on their feet, hungry and tired, among them mothers and fathers with children in baby carriages or in their arms.

Three hours went by. The cold and the damp penetrated their bones. The endless waiting for the sentence had driven many people out of their minds.

Religious Jews mumbled prayers and Psalms. The old and the sick whimpered. Babies cried aloud. In every eye the same horrible question stood out: "When will it begin?! When will it begin?!"

At 9 A.M. a Gestapo entourage appeared at the square: the deputy Gestapo-chief, Captain Schmitz, Master Sergeant Rauca, Captain Jordan, and Captain Tornbaum, accompanied by a squad of the German policemen and Lithuanian partisans.

The square was surrounded by machine-gun emplacements. Rauca positioned himself on top of a little mound from which he could watch the great crowd that waited in the square in tense and anxious anticipation. His glance ranged briefly over the column of the Council members and the Jewish Ghetto police, and by a movement of his hand he motioned them to the left, which, as it became clear later, was the "good" side. Then he signaled with the baton he held in his hand and ordered the remaining columns: "Forward!" The selection had begun.

The columns of employees of the Ghetto institutions and their families passed before Rauca, followed by other columns, one after another. The Gestapo man fixed his gaze on each pair of eyes and with a flick of the finger of his right hand passed sentence on individuals, families, or even whole groups. Elderly and sick persons, families with children, single women, and persons whose physique did not impress him in terms of labor power, were directed to the right. There, they immediately fell into the hands of the German policemen and the Lithuanian partisans, who showered them with shouts and blows and pushed them toward an opening especially made in the fence, where two Germans counted them and then reassembled them in a different place.

At first, nobody knew which was the "good" side. Many therefore rejoiced at finding themselves on the right. They began thanking Rauca, saying "Thank you kindly," or even "Thank you for your mercy." There were many men and women who, having been directed to the left, asked permission to move over to the right and join their relatives from whom they had been separated. Smiling sarcastically, Rauca gave his consent.

Those who tried to pass over from the right to the left, in order to join their families, or because they guessed—correctly, as it turned out—that that was the "good" side, immediately felt the pain of blows dealt by the hands and rifle butts of the policemen and the partisans, who brutally drove them back again to the right. By then everyone realized which side was the "good" and which the "bad" one.

When some old or sick person could not hold out any longer and collapsed on to the ground, the Lithuanians set upon him instantly, kicking him with their boots, beating him, and threatening to trample him underfoot if he did not get up at once. Drawing the last ounce of strength, he would rise to his feet—if he could—and try to catch up with his group. Those unable to get up were helped by their companions in trouble, who lifted them up, supported them, and helped them along to reach the assembly spot in the small Ghetto, to which they were marched under heavy guard.

In most cases these were old people, women, and children, frightened and in a state of shock, turned by screams and blows into a panic-stricken herd which felt it was being driven by a satanic, omnipotent force. It was a force which banished all thought and seemed to allow no hope of escape.

In especially shocking cases where members of a family were separated, when pleas and cries were heartrending, Dr. Elkes tried to come to the rescue, and at times he even succeeded in transferring whole families to the left. Among others, he intervened on behalf of a veteran public figure, the director of the hospital, a skillful artisan, and a number of activists of Zionist and non-Zionist underground circles. Unfortunately he did not succeed in transferring everyone to the left.[5]

The commander of the Jewish police, Kopelman, who stayed with Dr. Elkes near Rauca, also succeeded in saving Jews and whole families. The number of such survivors, throughout this bitter and hurried day, reached into the hundreds.

Rauca directed the job of selection composedly, with cynicism, and with the utmost speed, by mere movements of the finger of his right hand. When the meaning of the movement of his finger was not grasped instantly, he would roar: "To the right!" or "To the left!" And when people failed to obey at once he shouted at them: "To the right, you lousy curs!" Throughout the selection he did not exhibit any sign of fatigue or sensitivity at the wailing, pleas, and cries, or at the sight of the heartrending spectacles which took place before his eyes when children were separated from their parents, or parents from their children, or husbands and wives from each other—all those tragedies did not penetrate his heart at all.

From time to time, Rauca feasted on a sandwich—wrapped in wax paper lest his blood-stained hands get greasy—or enjoyed a cigarette, all the while performing his fiendish work without interruption.

When a column composed mostly of elderly people, or of women or children, appeared before him, he would command contemptuously: "All this trash to the right!" or "All this pile of garbage goes to the right!" To Dr. Elkes, when he tried to intervene in an attempt to save their lives, he would say: "Wait, you'll be grateful to me for having rid you of this burden."

Whenever Rauca condescended to respond favorably to Dr. Elkes's intercession, he would say carelessly: "Well, as far as I am concerned . . ." and then order the German policeman: "This fat one, or this short one, or this one with the glasses on, bring him back to me."[6]

Now and then Rauca would be handed a note with a number written on it, copied from the notebook kept by the German who diligently applied himself to the task of recording the number of Jews removed to the small Ghetto.

Rauca was quick to dispense "mercy" to those who, having found themselves on the left side, asked to be reunited with their families motioned to the right. In such cases he would say: "You want to be together—all right, everybody to the right!"

Everyone passing in front of Rauca would wave a document he held in his hand. This brought a scornful smile to Rauca's lips. He acted in accordance with his own criteria.

Members of the Jewish labor brigades working at Gestapo headquarters, headed by Benno Lipzer, Rauca sent to the "good" side, together with their parents and children. He also motioned to the left the entire brigade of workers employed at German military installations whose commanders had contacted Rauca earlier. He also treated benevolently single women, and even women with children or aged parents, when that woman called out that she was employed by a high-ranking German officer, or by the German police commandant or by the German Ghetto commandant and such like. Their employers also had contacted Rauca in advance of the selection.

In contrast, there were cases where he paid no heed to the Jordan certificates, regarded thitherto as secure life permits in the Ghetto, and sent their holders to the right.

The selection was a protracted affair. Hungry, thirsty, and dejected, thousands of people waited for their turn from dawn. Many had already undergone the selection process, yet the square still seemed full. No end to the torment seemed in sight. Many resigned themselves to their fate and sighed in despair: "Come what may, as long as this waiting comes to an end." Mothers clasped their little children to their broken hearts, hugging and kissing them as though aware they were doing so for the last time. As a matter of fact, it was not clear what would happen to those sent to the right, but it was clear that it was the bad side and in the Ghetto "bad" in most cases meant death.

Those who were weak—those who could not withstand the psychological tension and the bodily torment—collapsed and breathed their last even before their turn came to pass before Rauca.

Dr. Elkes stood there, his pale face bearing an expression of bottomless grief. Since 6 A.M. this sixty-five-year-old man[7] had been standing on his feet, refusing to sit on the stool that had been brought to him. Now and then, when he was overcome by a fit of weakness, those near him asked him to sit down to regain his strength, or offered him a piece of bread. He refused, murmuring: "Thank you, thank you, gentlemen; terrible things are happening here; I must remain standing on guard in case I can be of assistance." Whenever he succeeded in transferring someone from the bad to the good side, and the person saved would try to shake his hand, he would refuse, saying: "Leave me alone, leave me alone." Sometimes, when in his efforts to transfer somebody to the left side he would inadvertently step too close to the guard unit charged with keeping order at the dividing line, he would be showered with curses and threats from the Lithuanian partisans: "Get away, you old, stupid Zhid, or else you'll go together with them."

It was beginning to grow dark, yet thousands of people remained standing in the square. Captain Jordan now opened another selection place; he was assisted by Captain Tornbaum. Rauca could count on this pair without reservation.

Except for an occasional sarcastic smile, Rauca's face did not betray any emotion, whereas Jordan stood with a frozen, sullen expression on his face and watched with fear-inspiring eyes the Jews passing in front of him. At first he was a little hesitant, lest he transfer to the good side those "not deserving" it, but he regained his composure quickly and followed Rauca's example by motioning families and whole columns either to the left or to the right without hesitation.

There was, nevertheless, some difference between Jordan and Rauca. The former did not motion to the bad side anyone holding a Jordan certificate, not even family members of the permit holder, without taking into consideration their age and physical condition.

SS Captain Schmitz would show up between counts and whisper something in Rauca's ear, showing him a note he had just received from the crossing point to the small Ghetto. That note indicated the number of Jews who had already passed through the selection.

Time passed. The people waiting in the square suffered more and more; it seemed to them that the selection would never come to an end. Even those who emerged from the selection intact were in a state of shock as a result of all they had undergone in the recent days and during the long hours of waiting for their fate to be decided. There was no easing of tension even for these "fortunate" ones. Apart from that, there were many families of whom only part found themselves on the good side; either one or both parents, or a brother or a sister, or one or several children had been torn away from them. Those families succumbed to inconsolable grief.

The Jewish Ghetto policemen were instructed to keep order in that part of the square where those who had passed the selection were assembled. On that day the Jewish policemen displayed initiative, daring, and resourcefulness—they cheered up the dispirited, they lent a hand to those who collapsed on the ground or fainted, and gave them water. They even worked wonders: while lining up the survivors in a new column, they seized every opportunity of transferring individuals—and even whole families still waiting for their turn—over to the good side. They did this with cunning and deftness; they would signal by a wink, or a movement of the hand, to slip away, to jump quickly, or to crouch and crawl toward them without drawing the attention of the guards. Whenever such a person drew near them, the Jewish policemen would set upon him screaming and push him brutally to the good side, pretending that they were forcing him back to his correct place. But whenever they did not succeed in deceiving the guards, a hail of curses and blows would pour on the unfortunate policeman caught in the act.

The selection was completed only after nightfall, but not before Rauca made sure that the quota had been fulfilled and that some 10,000 people had been transferred to the small Ghetto. Only then were those who had passed through the selection, and had remained standing in the square, allowed to return to their homes.

About 17,000 out of some 27,000 people slowly left the vast square where they had been standing for more than twelve hours. Hungry, thirsty, crushed, and dejected, they returned home, most of them bereaved or orphaned, having been separated from a father, a mother, children, a brother or a sister, a grandfather or a grandmother, an uncle or an aunt. A deep mourning descended on the Ghetto. In every house there were now empty rooms, unoccupied beds, and the belongings of those who had not returned from the selection. One-third of the Ghetto population had been cut down. The sick people who had remained in their homes in the morning had all disappeared. They had been transferred to the Ninth Fort during the day.

The square was strewn with several dozen bodies of elderly and sick people who had died of exhaustion. Here and there stools, chairs, and empty baby carriages were lying about.

On his way back Dr. Elkes muttered: "It wasn't worthwhile living for more than sixty years in order to witness a day like this! Who can bear all this when you are being appealed to with heartrending cries and there is nothing much you can do? I can't bear it any longer!"

When we reached Dr. Elkes's house we found many people besieging his door. All of them wanted to know what had happened to the people who had been taken to the small Ghetto. Men and women implored him to save their parents, wives, children, brothers, sisters, or other relatives. Everyone had a moving story of his own to tell.

Deadly tired and crushed by the day's horrors as he was, Dr. Elkes listened to every one. In vain he tried to explain that he had no idea of the German plans regarding the people transferred to the small Ghetto and that he was powerless to get them out of there. Nonetheless he promised to do all he could and to intervene with the authorities to comply with their requests. He wrote down the names of those he had been asked to rescue, including details such as occupation or skill which might produce some result with the Germans.

Among the Jews transferred to the small Ghetto there were pessimists who felt that all was lost, whereas others refused to give up all hope. But everyone tried to keep his head above water in case a miracle might occur. As more and more people were transferred there, there was more conflict and even competition among them. Each family tried to take possession of a better apartment, to gather more wood for fuel, to get indispensable household utensils, and so on. Some people set about tidying up and improving apartments that had long ago been abandoned by their previous occupants, filling up holes in the wall and fixing windows to protect against wind and rain. The more industrious got together during the night to discuss how to organize their lives in the new quarters. Some even proposed to elect immediately a Council on the pattern of the Council in the large Ghetto. All night long they debated and haggled among themselves, but were unable to agree about the composition of the proposed Council, the distribution of apartments, and so on.

It was an autumnal, foggy, and gloomy dawn when German policemen and drunken Lithuanian partisans broke into the small Ghetto, like so many ferocious beasts, and began driving the Jews out of their homes. The assault was so unexpected and brutal that the wretched inmates did not have a single moment to grasp what was going on. The partisans barked out their orders to leave the houses and to line up in rows and columns. Each column was immediately surrounded by partisans, shouting "Forward march, you scum, forward march," and driving the people by rifle butts out of the small Ghetto toward the road leading to the Ninth Fort. It was in the same direction that the Jews had been led away in the "action" commanded by Kozlovski on September 26, 1941,[8] and in the "action" of the liquidation of the small Ghetto on October 4, 1941. The same uphill road led Jews in one direction alone—to a place from which no one returned.

It was a death procession. The cries of despair issuing from thousands of mouths were hovering above them. Bitter weeping could be heard from far off. Column after column, family after family, those sentenced to death passed by the fence of the large Ghetto. Some men, even a number of women, tried to break through the chain of guards and flee to the large Ghetto, but were shot dead on the spot. One woman threw her child over the fence, but missed her aim and the child remained hanging on the barbed wire. Its screams were quickly silenced by bullets.

Thousands of inmates from the large Ghetto flocked to the fence and, with tearful eyes and frozen hearts, watched the horrible procession trudging slowly up the hill. Many recognized a brother, a sister, parents or children, relatives or friends, and called to them by name. They were thrust back brutally by the reinforced guard of Lithuanian partisans, who pointed to the signs posted on the fence. In German, Lithuanian, and Yiddish the signs warned: "Death zone! Whoever approaches within two meters of the fence will be shot on the spot without warning."

Dr. Elkes and the head of the Jewish Ghetto police, Kopelman, accompanied by their assistants, arrived at the fence. No sooner was Dr. Elkes seen than the cries and pleas went up from those being marched up the hill, as well as from those crowding near the fence, inside the large Ghetto: "Dr. Elkes, help!" The cries joined into one big outburst that rose up to heaven: "Save us!"

Dr. Elkes asked that Rauca be found with the utmost urgency. He was traced before long by Kopelman's men at the German Ghetto command. Elkes addressed him immediately, asking to "allow him to remove from the small Ghetto those people who had fallen victim to error during the selection." Rauca consented, but limited the number of men and women to be removed to 100. Dr. Elkes kept in his pocket a list of people whose relatives had pleaded with him during the night and morning to save them, but their number far exceeded the figure of 100.

Accompanied by two sentries from the German Ghetto Guard, Dr. Elkes passed into the area of the small Ghetto, where he was immediately assailed by a throng of people already lined up in a column ready for departure. They begged him to save their lives. One seized his hand, another took hold of the tail of his coat, while another clasped his neck and refused to let go. Those who surrounded him knew full well that by leaving the column they endangered their lives, but they kept crying: "It is better for us to be killed here. We won't let go of you, Doctor—save us!" Within seconds the entire column faltered. For a moment it seemed that those condemned to death had rebelled. The Lithuanian guards intervened immediately, and with blows and kicks pushed people back into their places and hurried the whole column toward the road to catch up with other columns that had moved ahead.

Dr. Elkes himself was ordered by the guards to clear out at once—if not, they threatened, they would take him too to the Ninth Fort. Dr. Elkes insisted on his right to remove 100 people, as permitted by Rauca. Thereupon the Lithuanian partisans pounced upon him, hitting him with their fists. One of them brought down the butt of his rifle upon his head. Dr. Elkes collapsed on the ground, unconscious and bleeding profusely.

Jewish policemen and other Ghetto inmates (myself included) rushed from behind the fence to help. We lifted him up and carried him on our shoulders to the large Ghetto across the road, and put him inside the first house near the fence. He lay there for several days. Physicians stitched his open head wounds and nursed him, until he was able to stand on his feet again and return to his home. His efforts to save a number of Jews from the small Ghetto had almost cost him his own life.

The procession, numbering some 10,000 people, and proceeding from the small Ghetto to the Ninth Fort, lasted from dawn until noon. Elderly people, and those who were sick, collapsed by the roadside and died. Warning shots were fired incessantly, all along the way, and around the large Ghetto. Thousands of curious Lithuanians flocked to both sides of the road to watch the spectacle, until the last of the victims was swallowed up by the Ninth Fort.

In the fort, the wretched people were immediately set upon by the Lithuanian killers, who stripped them of every valuable article—gold rings, earrings, bracelets. They forced them to strip naked, pushed them into pits which had been prepared in advance, and fired into each pit with machine guns which had been positioned there in advance. The murderers did not have time to shoot everybody in one batch before the next batch of Jews arrived. They were accorded the same treatment as those who had preceded them. They were pushed into the pit on top of the dead, the dying, and those still alive from the previous group. So it continued, batch after batch, until the 10,000 men, women, and children had been butchered.

Villagers living in the vicinity of the fort told stories of horrors they had seen from a distance, and of the heartrending cries that emanated from the fort and troubled their waking hours all day and night.

About 17,500 people were left in the Ghetto, most of them orphaned, or bereft of their children, or widowed. All of a sudden there seemed to be plenty of space in the Ghetto. In every house a void had been created, pervaded with a mute terror haunting the survivors: this fate awaits you too.

The homes, the furniture, and the belongings of the victims of October 28 seemed to exude the odor of death. Hardly anyone dared touch them or make use of them. In the courtyards, storerooms, and other places, beds, furniture, and various articles were piled up, with nobody claiming them. They were removed from the houses from which entire families had been murdered without leaving a single survivor.

On the day after October 28, the Gestapo called upon the Ghetto inmates to increase the labor force and to increase even more the output at the airfield, in digging peat in Palemonas,[9] and in other places of forced labor, since it was work alone that was a guarantee of survival.

The small Ghetto remained sealed off and surrounded by a heavy guard even after all the Jews had been removed to the Ninth Fort. For a whole week nobody was allowed to enter. On the afternoon of October 29, the Jewish Ghetto policemen were ordered to conduct a thorough search of every house and of every attic in the deserted small Ghetto to make sure no Jews remained in hiding there.

The Germans gave this assignment to the Jewish police on purpose; their plan was to lead astray those Jews in hiding who, upon hearing the Jewish policemen speaking Yiddish, were supposed to be lulled into thinking they were coming to rescue them. These Jews would then leave their hideouts and fall into a trap. The Jewish policemen were alert to such possibility, especially as they were convinced that a handful of Jews had succeeded in hiding during those critical moments. Therefore they brought with them, unnoticed, Jewish police caps, armbands, and insignia, to give them to every Jew who might be found in a hideout, or might come out to meet them, in order to give him an outward appearance of being a member of the Jewish Ghetto police, and in this way enable him to accompany them and leave the small Ghetto as one of their number. Indeed, the ruse worked. Some twenty Jews were saved in this manner— they would have been killed upon being discovered by the Lithuanians or the Germans, who were waiting for them at the opening in the small Ghetto fence, but who could not distinguish them from the real Jewish policemen.[10]

After the "action" of October 28, fear and dread fell on the Ghetto. People no longer believed the Gestapo announcements that this was the last "action," that it was not to be repeated in the future, and that from now on everyone would remain unharmed, working and earning a living. Their feelings regarding the future resembled those of a man about to be called up for military service. For the time being he is free in his home, but the inevitable lurks around the corner.

Ten thousand people were driven out and put to death in this huge "action." Before that, on September 26 and October 4, as many as 2,500 people had been killed; altogether about 17,000 people remained in the Ghetto.

Rumors sprang up again about pits dug in the fort, in Aleksotas, in Palemonas, and in Alytus.[11]

1. Avraham Tory's original description of the "action" of October 28, 1941, was written immediately after the event and buried in the ground. When, in August 1944, Tory dug out what he had buried, he felt that this entry was too short, so he expanded it. This second version, published here, was thus written three years after the event. It contains details Tory had learned during the war in discussions with survivors of the "action."

2. Joseph Serebrovitz, a Jewish journalist, who wrote under the name Caspi. He had been imprisoned by the Soviet authorities in 1940 and released shortly after the German occupation. He at once offered the Germans his services against the Soviet Union. Later he tried to exert influence in the Ghetto because of his special relationship with the Gestapo. Permitted not to wear the yellow Star of David, and allowed to live in the town with his family, he was a frequent visitor to the Ghetto. In October 1941 he was sent to Vilna. He later returned to Kovno, but in July 1942 he was again transferred to Vilna. In June 1943 he once more appeared in the Kovno Ghetto; later in 1943 he was murdered by the Nazis, together with his wife and two daughters.

3. Benjamin (Benno) Lipzer, born in Grodno in 1896, in the Kovno Ghetto was head of the brigade (work group) of Jews employed by the Germans on various work details which served the headquarters building of the Gestapo in Kovno. After he had developed contacts

with the upper echelons of the Gestapo, he attempted to gain control of the Jewish police. In June 1942 the Ghetto authorized him to supervise the labor department of the Jewish Council. At the time of the liquidation of the Ghetto in July 1944, he hid in the Ghetto, but was driven from his hiding place by the Gestapo and killed.

4. General Geiling, supervisor of the construction of the large military airfield being built by the Germans in the suburb of Aleksotas.

5. In his book *Dem Goirel Antkegn* (Facing Fate), published in Johannesburg in 1952, Professor Aharon Peretz, now of Haifa, writes that he and his family were already on the "bad" side when all of a sudden, as a result of intervention of someone on the Council, he was transferred to the "good" side and saved, together with his family. This "someone" was Dr. Elkes, who pointed him out to Rauca as a specialist needed in the hospital.

6. Rauca did not mind transferring any Jew to the left, since, as was learned later on, a quota of 10,000 victims had been set for that day, and all he was concerned with was to know at any time how many had already been transferred to the right. Every so often he would turn to the German standing at his side and ask: "The number, give me the number, I want the exact number."

7. Dr. Elkes was born in 1879.

8. A month earlier, on September 26, 1941, Kozlovski, the German commander of the Ghetto Guard, had staged his own fake assassination, on orders from his superiors. That same day, 1,200 Jews had been taken to the Ninth Fort and shot.

9. Palemonas was ten kilometers from Kovno; a labor camp was set up there to dig turf in the vicinity. The work conditions and regime at the camp were so horrible that many Jews working there were killed, or died of hunger or exhaustion.

10. This paragraph ends the version of the "action" of October 28, 1941, which Avraham Tory wrote at the end of the war. The three following paragraphs are those with which he ended his initial account of the "Great Action," written immediately after it.

11. After the war, Tory commented on this sentence: "This time the pits were not designed for us. Although pits were made ready, they were designed for other Jews, Jews from Germany, Czechoslovakia, Austria. Those Jews were brought here from those distant places to spill their blood on the Lithuanian soil; to brand with the sign of Cain the Lithuanian people for their conscious and persistent collaboration with the Germans in the murder of the Jewish people."

NOVEMBER 8, 1941

DOCUMENT: Order of SS Colonel Cramer, through Mikas Kaminskas

All Ghetto inmates must hand over carriages, cabs, and sledges.

NOVEMBER 13, 1941

DOCUMENT: To the Council of the Ghetto, Vilijampolé

We, Jewish workers with the Security Police and Einsatzkommando 3, numbering 42 (forty-two) families, need wood for heating our apartments. We ask you to obtain for us—if possible immediately—a permit for receiving the heating wood.

We shall provide transport for the wood ourselves.

DECEMBER 8, 1941

DOCUMENT: SA Captain Jordan
To the Jewish Council, Kovno Ghetto

In order to ensure the exact supervision and accounting of the employment of Jewish working manpower, the precise names and addresses of Jewish working manpower must forthwith be given, wherever it is detailed by the Labor Exchange.

The weekly lists for me must be brought up to date accordingly.

DECEMBER 27, 1941

DOCUMENT: Order of SS Master Sergeant Rauca

The Jews must hand over their furs and fur products to the authorities today at Demokratu Square.

1942

A group of Jews leave the Ghetto on their way to work. In front, in the white cap, is a Jewish policeman; to the right are two armed Lithuanians.

JANUARY 3, 1942

The Council laid out regulations for activities in the Ghetto police station with organizational and art sections. Police station regulations were designed to give official status to the orchestra.[1]

1. The Kovno Ghetto contained several outstanding musicians, including former members of the Lithuanian State Opera. To provide a cover for their rehearsals, most were enlisted in the Jewish police and presented to the Germans as the police orchestra. This led to the idea of establishing a "policemen's club," within the framework of which the orchestra appeared on a regular basis, twice weekly, after its first concert in August 1942.

JANUARY 5, 1942

Kozlovski, the German Ghetto commandant, has banned demolishing houses, or parts of houses, or dismantling fences in the Ghetto.[1]

1. In the cold winter of 1942, Ghetto inmates used furniture, and even parts of wooden houses and fences, for heating, contrary to Kozlovski's order.

JANUARY 9, 1942

At the airfield, a timber beam fell on the head of a Jewish laborer by the name of Singer. He was killed instantly.

At 10 P.M. five Lithuanians broke into the house of a police official. They shot and killed two people and a little girl in the house and badly wounded the police official. The Lithuanians looted the apartment, tied up the hands and legs of everyone in the apartment, and fled.

On the same day, a woman who tried to buy groceries near the Ghetto was killed.[1]

The Ghetto court promulgated a general ruling: the property of a Ghetto inmate who has been killed or has disappeared belongs to his children or grandchildren. If there are none, it belongs to his parents; if there are none, to his brothers and sisters; if there are none, the property belongs to the Council.[2]

1. Those who were unable to buy food at their workplaces outside the Ghetto often purchased or bartered for food through the wire fence surrounding the Ghetto. For trading near the gate ("gate trading," as it was called in the Ghetto vernacular), those caught were often shot.

2. The intention of this decision was to ensure that the property of deportees devolved upon their heirs. The property of deportees who had no heirs was distributed to the needy by the welfare department of the Jewish Council. The Ghetto court (known as the short procedure labor court) had been set up in the Ghetto by the Jewish Council on October 24, 1941. Its principal purpose was to bring to trial Jews who endangered the Ghetto by deliberately avoiding their work-duties. Punishments included confiscation of the right to work in a Kovno city work group (from which it was relatively easy to barter clothes for food), and imprisonment for up to one month in the Ghetto detention house.

JANUARY 10, 1942

Three Lithuanians broke through the fence into the Ghetto. One of them held in his hand an iron bar weighing half a kilo to be used for robbery. They were arrested and transferred to the German Ghetto commandant.[1]

1. These three Lithuanians were arrested by the Jewish Ghetto police, which only had the authority to deliver them to the German Ghetto headquarters; there they not only went unpunished but were released immediately, the spoils of their robbery being divided between the Germans and the Lithuanians.

JANUARY 11, 1942

At noon, the Council chairman was summoned to the German Ghetto command. Cramer, Jordan, and Tornbaum were present. They gave an order to evacuate the area of the Ghetto around Demokratu Square by 4 P.M. in order that Jews who were expected to arrive from Germany could be put into the buildings there. Jewish Ghetto policemen and firemen helped in the transfer. A committee was established to deal with the evacuation of the inhabitants from this area and with the accommodation of the Jews from Germany. The Germans intended to take away their passports—and their fur coats. They waited for them all day long. But the Jews failed to arrive. That day, the temperature fell to 30 degrees below zero centigrade.

A German police commission, and an NSKK[1] squad (for special duties) arrived in the Ghetto to survey and select several houses for the German Ghetto guard.

Ghetto house managers were appointed by the Council.[2]

1. The National Sozialist Krafts Kompanie, the heavy transport department of the German police. In January 1942 some of its members were formed into an armed detachment charged with running the German Ghetto command headquarters.
2. The housing department of the Jewish Council appointed house managers, who were responsible, as best they could be, for the maintenance and sanitation of their buildings.

JANUARY 12, 1942

A horse-cart driver named Gempel and a woman were shot and killed.

JANUARY 13, 1942

The Ghetto command is to be located in three houses in the Ghetto on 20 Stulginskio Street.[1] The residents were forced to evacuate these houses within three hours.

> 1. The German promise in August 1941 that Jews in the Ghetto would be left alone was broken by this decision, whereby the German Ghetto Guard corps was to be located inside the Ghetto, on Stulginskio Street. Subsequently, tension mounted in the Ghetto, and inmates were afraid to go out in case they might meet wearers of German uniforms and their Lithuanian assistants. As well as the general Ghetto Guard, the Germans had also established a special Ghetto gate guard.

JANUARY 14, 1942

An order to bring all dogs and cats to the small synagogue on Veliuonos Street, where they were shot.[1]

Lithuanians dressed in partisan uniforms, and one Lithuanian woman, were caught in the act of pillage in the Ghetto. They had in their possession two coats which they had stolen from a Jewish house.

> 1. The bodies of the cats and dogs remained in the synagogue on Veliuonos Street for several months; the Jews were forbidden to remove them.

JANUARY 23, 1942

The principal of the Ghetto elementary school, Zelig Altman, was killed by a stray bullet which entered his apartment through the window. The shot came from a member of the Ghetto Guard.

JANUARY 26, 1942

It is forbidden for anybody, with the exception of doctors, labor brigades, and Council officials on duty, to be out on the Ghetto streets after 9 P.M.

The area adjoining the Ghetto fence (three meters on each side) was declared a Death Zone. Anyone approaching the fence will be shot without warning.[1]

The bodies of two children were found.

During the night, several bullets were shot at Jewish houses from the direction of the Vilija river.

1. This edict deterred neither Jews from hiding near the fence in the hope of smuggling in food nor Lithuanians from entering the Ghetto and plundering Jewish homes.

JANUARY 27, 1942

The Ghetto court promulgated a general ruling: persons married by the magistrate may get a divorce in the Ghetto court.[1] People married in a Jewish religious ceremony can still be divorced only by a rabbi.

1. This was a revolutionary decision by a Jewish court in Lithuania; reality required it, however, since there were hardly any rabbis, and no rabbinical court, left in the Ghetto.

JANUARY 29, 1942

The Council drew up regulations for the housing office.

JANUARY 30, 1942

A Lithuanian policeman shot and killed the physician Dr. Zerah Gerber on a Ghetto street. The reason: the doctor did not remove his hat in the presence of the policeman, as required.[1]

1. The German edict required that Jews remove their hats in the presence of all Germans, not Lithuanians, in uniform; after the death of Dr. Gerber, no more chances were taken.

FEBRUARY 1, 1942

The Council imposed taxes on profits made by skilled workers and free professionals.[1]

1. Until August 1942, Jews were permitted to hold money. The Jewish Council was paid by the German civil administration at the rate of 3 marks per woman and 3½ marks per man per day of labor. Some tradesmen had their own income, as did many professionals. The Jewish Council therefore decided to impose a tax on those with an income, in order to assist it in providing public services and to prevent the starvation of widows, orphans, and the aged who were not on the labor-force list, for whom no food was received.

FEBRUARY 4, 1942

A strict ban has been imposed by the Germans on taking money when going to the city, in order to prevent the buying of supplies there.

FEBRUARY 5, 1942

The third squad of the German police, commanded by Captain Tornbaum, assisted by the Jewish Ghetto police, rounded up more than 200 Jews with the purpose of transferring them to Riga. The arrests lasted until 2 A.M. The detainees were taken to the small house of study on Veliuonos Street, and from there to the train station. All of them were brought back to the Ghetto in the morning.[1]

The Ghetto court promulgated a general ruling: notary duties are to be performed by the Ghetto court, either by the chairman or by the judge on duty.

1. The Germans had demanded 500 men from the Kovno Ghetto for work in the Riga Ghetto, promising that they would return to Kovno after three months, and that living conditions in Riga would be reasonable. However, after the October "actions," people no longer believed German assurances, and many went into hiding. As a result, the Council was unable to enlist the required number of people capable of working. The 200 men were therefore returned to the Kovno Ghetto.

FEBRUARY 6, 1942

Jordan came to the Council and ordered all the Ghetto inmates to assemble on the Demokratu Square. Assisted by Schtitz[1] of the Gestapo, Jordan selected 300 people and sent them to the train station under heavy guard. He issued a threat to the Council that if the 200 remaining people were not provided by 4 P.M., reprisals would follow! The people were recruited and dispatched to the train station in the evening.[2] Before that, Rauca of the Gestapo also arrived in the Ghetto.

1. SS Master Sergeant Schtitz, one of the most brutal Ghetto rulers. In mid-1942 he replaced Rauca as the Gestapo official in charge of the Ghetto.
2. On the day after the return to the Ghetto of the 200 Jews originally destined for deportation to Riga, the Gestapo itself arrested 300 men and women, mainly young and capable of working. A further 80 were enlisted by the Jewish Ghetto police and by the Council's labor department; this was done when the Council began to realize the significance of the arrests by the Gestapo, who had taken heads of families and mothers indiscriminately. A total of 380 Jews, including 140 women, were sent to Riga. They were later to share the fate of the inmates of the Riga Ghetto; of the 380 Jews sent from Kovno to Riga, only 20 survived the war.

FEBRUARY 8, 1942

The Jewish Labor Office drew up the list of the laborers sent to Riga. The Council also issued a strict ban on appropriating the belongings of the inmates removed from the Ghetto.

The Council appointed a committee of physicians entrusted with allocation of additional food rations for the seriously ill.

FEBRUARY 9, 1942

During the night two Lithuanian youths were caught in the Ghetto with stolen goods. On the order of the Ghetto commandant they were locked up together with their two friends for several days in the Ghetto detention center.

FEBRUARY 10, 1942

The city governor ordered the Jews to hand over to him all wire-cutters for cutting metal wire.

The former commandant of the Ghetto Guard, Sergeant Wille, announced that the Jews dispatched to Riga had arrived there yesterday. They are employed there in workshops and receive wages of 0.75 marks per day.

FEBRUARY 13, 1942

Fire broke out in the Ghetto. It was not put out until several hours later.

FEBRUARY 17, 1942

New badges were introduced for various Jewish Ghetto police ranks: police chief, deputy chief, inspector, precinct commandant, deputy precinct commandant, first policeman.

FEBRUARY 18, 1942

Three Lithuanians were apprehended in the Ghetto. They were locked up in the Ghetto detention center and from there transferred to the city.

FEBRUARY 19, 1942

The German labor office issued an order to draw up (by February 25) a list of all able-bodied men in the Ghetto. A branch of the German labor office was set up in the Ghetto.[1]

Yehoshua Grinberg[2] was temporarily appointed as work-detail inspector with the Jewish police.

---

1. The German labor office was headed by SA Lieutenant Gustav Hermann, who treated the Jews of the Ghetto humanely, searching for ways to ease their lot. His office was managed by Dr. Isaac (Yitzhak) Rabinovitz (a great-grandson of the distinguished Chief Rabbi of Kovno Yitzhak-Elchanan Spector). Rabinovitz survived the war; he lives today in Tel Aviv. All labor office employees were Jews from the Ghetto.

2. Yehoshua (Ika) Grinberg, chief of the Jewish Ghetto police in the first district (or precinct). A former officer in the Lithuanian Army, he was one of the leaders of the Jewish underground, and a weapons instructor for its members. On March 27, 1944, he was tortured and executed at the Ninth Fort, along with several dozen other Jewish policemen who had refused to reveal the location of the places in the Ghetto in which Jews were hiding.

FEBRUARY 21, 1942

The Jewish Ghetto court promulgated a general ordinance: all residents of a house are collectively responsible for its electricity bill, the payment of which they may distribute among themselves.[1]

1. The Ghetto court had adopted this decision after a series of arguments between tenants over payments for electricity, which was still being supplied by the Kovno power station to the whole city, including the Ghetto. Because Slobodka was now inhabited by so many more people than before the establishment of the Ghetto, overloading was frequent, causing extended breakdowns.

FEBRUARY 23, 1942

DOCUMENT:
From SA Colonel Cramer (signed by SA Captain Jordan)
To the Jewish Council, Kovno-Vilijampolé

It has been established that Jews repeatedly carry money with them and that they enter shops in the city and buy and barter. I shall confiscate in the future all money which I find on Jews in the city.

FEBRUARY 27, 1942

The Jewish Police started operating a telephone exchange.[1]

Yankel Balkind was shot dead outside the Ghetto fence.

The Organization for the Confiscation of Jewish Books, headed by Alfred Rosenberg, has ordered all books in the Ghetto, regardless of their content or language, to be handed over.[2]

The Jewish Ghetto court promulgated a general ordinance: in cases involving breaches of discipline, appeals for pardon will not be considered.

1. The Germans agreed to a request from the Council to install a telephone exchange for approximately twenty official telephones located in the Council offices and Jewish Ghetto police headquarters in the Ghetto; this made German control easier, saving German officials unnecessary travel from the city when they wished to issue instructions. The telephone system also enabled the Germans to eavesdrop on Council conversations.

2. Some of the confiscated books were sent to Germany, to the Institute for Study of the Jewish Question in Frankfurt; others were used by the Germans for recycling into paper, of which there was then a serious shortage.

FEBRUARY 28, 1942

Today is the deadline for handing over all the books in the Ghetto, without exception, as ordered by the representative of the Rosenberg organization, Dr. Benker.[1]

The body of Joseph Czerniak, who had been shot dead in the sixth precinct of the city police, was brought to the Ghetto. According to the German police communiqué he was shot during an attempt to escape.

Leah Gilelson, twenty-two, an airfield worker, was shot dead by a German policeman during an attempt to run away from a work detail.

Jews were allowed to return to their homes on Vienozinskio and Demokratu streets.[2]

1. Dr. Benker, a representative of Alfred Rosenberg, had threatened the death penalty to anyone failing to hand in books. The Ghetto inmates, however, particularly the youth, helped by carters who worked for the Council, saved many books and hid them, including the Torah scrolls which had been brought from the city's synagogues to the Ghetto.
2. On January 11, 1942, Veniozinskio and Demokratu Streets had been temporarily removed from within the boundaries of the Ghetto.

MARCH 2, 1942

The Council asked the Ghetto inmates to donate shoes and galoshes for the airfield workers.

MARCH 4, 1942

The Council decree went into effect, making it compulsory to declare income over 300 rubles per month, so that the Council could levy taxes designed for subsidizing communal needs.

MARCH 6, 1942

The Gestapo announced that it would be possible to send letters to relatives in Riga through the Ghetto Guard.

The Jewish labor office opened courses for locksmiths.

MARCH 10, 1942

The body of a Jew by the name of Azef was found under a ramshackle timber warehouse.

MARCH 11, 1942

The Council set fees for medical examination and treatment at the Ghetto clinic and at the hospital.

MARCH 11, 1942

> DOCUMENT:
> The Commander of the Security Police and the SD,[1] Lithuania, SS Colonel Jaeger
> To the Jewish Council, Kovno Ghetto

On March 10, 1942, upon my order, twenty-four Jews were shot dead because, contrary to the instructions issued regarding Jews, they had engaged in considerable black marketeering with the Lithuanian population, and without wearing identification marks.

This information must be brought to the attention of the Jews in a proper manner.

1. SD: *Sicherheitsdienst,* or Security Service, the intelligence branch of the SS.

MARCH 12, 1942

The confiscated books were transferred to the city and stored in a former house of study outside the Ghetto area.

MARCH 16, 1942

Vigorous action was undertaken by German Ghetto Guard commander, Lot, aimed at keeping the Ghetto clean, mainly in the first police precinct. The purpose: to prevent the spread of illnesses caused by pollution in the spring when the ice melts, and with it hitherto frozen rubbish.

MARCH 17, 1942

An official announcement by the Gestapo: on March 10, twenty-four Jews were shot dead, on Jaeger's order. The reason: they did not wear the Star of David badges on their clothes, and they engaged in trade with Lithuanians, in violation of the ban.

The Council was instructed to make this incident public.

MARCH 21, 1942

Seven Jews from Germany were brought to the Ghetto to spend the night here. Recently they had lived in the Riga Ghetto, from which they were dispatched, as specialists, to Minsk.

MARCH 22, 1942

The Council resolved that work duty applies to men aged from sixteen to fifty-seven, and women from seventeen to forty-six. In the case of noncompliance, the director of the Council labor office is authorized to impose the following punishments: a fine of up to 50 marks; arrest up to ten days; invalidation of the labor card; transfer to another workplace outside Kovno; eviction from apartment and transfer to a labor camp.

Decisions taken by the director of the labor office relating to the two last punishments may be appealed, within three days, before the Jewish Ghetto Court.

MARCH 23, 1942

Two workers, Nachman Shrak and Josel Fried, were shot dead on the airfield while buying groceries. Their bodies were brought to the Ghetto.

A decree: beginning April 1, the Star of David badge is to be embroidered in yellow thread and not sewn on, as hitherto.

MARCH 25, 1942

The Gestapo chief, Jaeger, visited the Ghetto and toured the area still in the Ghetto on Paneriu Street. With him was the chairman of the Council, Dr. Elkes, and the representative of the city governor. Jaeger ordered the whole area, inhabited by 2,000 people, to be evacuated by May 1.

MARCH 26, 1942

The Jewish Ghetto court promulgated a general ruling: work at the airfield is a duty applying to each Ghetto inmate. Everyone is required to abide by it. It is however permitted for a person to discharge this duty by sending someone else in his or her place.

MARCH 31, 1942

The Jewish policemen and workers in the Ghetto institutions were sent to work at the airfield.

APRIL 1, 1942

DOCUMENT:
From SA Colonel Cramer
To the Jewish Council of the Ghetto Community Kovno-Vilijampolé

1. A collection of all metal in the Ghetto must be carried out immediately.

2. The following items are to be collected: (a) copper, (b) tin, (c) nickel, (d) lead, (e) brass, (f) bronze, (g) silver, (h) gold.

3. The collection includes all loose and built-in items such as: ashtrays, tabletops, decorative pieces, bronze items, cans and kettles, trays and table utensils, household items—especially cooking utensils—birdcages, door signs and fixtures, ledges, door handles, window handles, hooks, doors, railings, figures, carriages, reliefs, clothing, wall and door plates, as well as coins, copper roofs, wall coverings, stairtops, brass weights, all kinds of hooks, hot water bottles, musical instruments, lead pipes, unusable lead, and in general all articles of the above-named metals and alloys existing in households and workshops.

4. You are responsible for the handing over of all metal items listed. For replacements of door and window handles which are handed over you may contact the manager of the Ghetto workshops.

5. The metal collection must be completed on April 11. You must make the organizational arrangements. The Ghetto Guard has to inform me from where the metals will be collected.

6. Failure to hand over any of the items listed, or any other irregularities, will be severely punished.

APRIL 2, 1942

Owing to the increased demand for Jewish workers, the Council discontinued issuing all exemptions from work which covered more than a seven-day period.

Offices of the Ghetto institutions are closed for today. All their employees were sent to work at the airfield.

The living space per person was further reduced to 2.5 square meters.

APRIL 3, 1942

An order: all Council workers aged between sixteen and fifty-seven (for men) and between seventeen and forty-six (for women) are required to go out for work at the airfield.

APRIL 4, 1942

A rifle bullet came through the window into the apartment of a certain Feinberg, who lives at 8 Mildos Street.

APRIL 6, 1942

An announcement issued by the Gestapo: absence from work without justifiable reason will be punished by death. Inspections and searches of the Ghetto houses will be conducted by the Gestapo.

APRIL 7, 1942

The Jewish police force has been reduced. Seventy-seven Jewish policemen were dismissed on orders of the Gestapo.[1]

1. The dismissed policemen were sent to work at the airfield. Up to this time, during the period of relative calm, there had been on average 200 Jewish policemen serving in the Ghetto police.

APRIL 8, 1942

The Ghetto registration office has been separated from the Jewish Ghetto police and annexed to the statistics office.

A soup kitchen opened at 11 Ariagolos Street; Ghetto inmates must bring their own plates and crockery.

Wooden shoes for the airfield workers are being manufactured in the Ghetto.

APRIL 11, 1942

All pieces of metal should be handed over in compliance with the instruction issued by the city governor.

The funeral of the fireman Puner took place. He was busy repairing the Ghetto fence when a Lithuanian policeman shot him dead.

APRIL 12, 1942

A decree was issued by the city governor: before April 24 the Ghetto inmates are required to provide information concerning their indebtedness to various individuals as well as about their financial claims against others.[1]

1. Avraham Tory later recalled that most of the forms sent by the Germans were returned blank. Nobody wished to report to the Germans about debts which were owed to them, with the exception of isolated cases motivated by the desire for some revenge on the Lithuanians.

APRIL 14, 1942

A decree issued by the city governor requires us to supply information on gardens and fields in the city owned by the Jews in the Ghetto.

The Council submitted a memorandum to the city governor asking for increased food rations also for workers employed within the Ghetto, including the Council staff; this memorandum refers only to the workshop workers and the Jewish policemen.

APRIL 15, 1942

The Gestapo has ordered the registration of all United States nationals residing in the Ghetto.[1]

The Gestapo denied the rumors that Ghetto inmates will be taken out of the Ghetto and sent to various labor camps.

1. Earlier a number of Jews who held United States passports had attempted to use them to leave the Ghetto, but had been seized by the Gestapo and murdered at the Ninth Fort. Therefore, when this directive was received, no one registered.

APRIL 17, 1942

The Council has approved regulations concerning the activity of the public prosecutor at the Jewish Ghetto Court: the public prosecutor will perform his duties in accordance with the laws of the former Lithuanian Republic, insofar as they do not conflict with the current conditions in the Ghetto. The public prosecutor will also perform the duties of the special investigator at the control commission.

For administrative reasons the Council decided to divide the police precincts in the Ghetto into neighborhood units inhabited by 250 to 300 residents each.

APRIL 20, 1942

The Council has appointed a special commission at the statistics office which will be charged with determining the age of Ghetto inmates who do not have birth certificates in their possession. This commission will issue them with identity cards.

APRIL 21, 1942

Elementary schools in the Ghetto have been reopened. They were closed because of the shortage of firewood.[1]

The Council has approved regulations which make it mandatory for the Ghetto inmates to be registered at the Jewish police station in their neighborhood. The registration will be conducted by house managers.

1. Dr. Elkes had repeatedly pressed the German authorities to provide wood for heating the elementary schools in the Ghetto.

APRIL 21, 1942

DOCUMENT:
From SA Colonel Cramer
To the Jewish Council in Kovno-Vilijampolé

I cannot agree to all the points of your request to allocate food items for all the Jewish Ghetto laborers. The following Ghetto laborers will receive additional food rations: Ghetto workshops and Ghetto police.

The following will not for the time being receive any additional rations: Ghetto repair shop, Ghetto clothing and shoe workshops, airport laborers, Ghetto internal labor service, Ghetto transport and sanitation, Ghetto labor exchange, and Ghetto fire brigade. All future distribution of foodstuffs should be carried out accordingly.

By the order dated April 9, the following food rations have been fixed for the Jewish population: (a) nonworking Jews will receive half-rations of the portions allocated to the local population, (b) working Jews will also receive the same half-rations of all foodstuffs. Upon approval of their work performance they will receive the full bread ration.

According to an arrangement with the economic department, the allocation of foodstuffs from April 26 will be as follows: the list of compulsory labor during the period from April 11 to April 20 will serve as the basis for the allocation of food. Food for the remaining days of April will be derived from the above list of compulsory labor. The list of compulsory labor from April 21 to

April 30 will serve as basis for the allocation of food rations for the period from May 1 to May 10, and so on.

Any fluctuations in the number of workers will be balanced in the subsequent allocation of foodstuffs. As the rations are not always the same, the size of the ration per person can be announced only at the time of allocation. My previous instructions concerning the allocation of rations are canceled.

APRIL 21, 1942

DOCUMENT:
From SA Colonel Cramer
To the Jewish Council in Kovno-Vilijampolé

Center no. 724 for army provisions and the military building administration have ordered the following from the Ghetto workshops:

Clothes-brushes: 2000 pieces
Shoe-brushes: 2000 pieces
Large broom-brushes: 2000 pieces
Tar-brushes: 100 pieces.

If material for the production of these articles is still available, production must start immediately.

I have ordered further material today. Any material may be collected, pending the approval of the army commander, at department II/2 of the city governor.

APRIL 22, 1942

DOCUMENT:
From SA Colonel Cramer
To the Jewish Council, via the German Ghetto Guard, Kovno-Vilijampolé

I request you to inform me immediately if the Jew Israel Gutman, formerly living at 88 Jonavos Street, Kovno, is in the Ghetto.

APRIL 22, 1942

DOCUMENT:
From SA Colonel Cramer
To the Jewish Council, via the German Ghetto Guard, Kovno-Vilijampolé

I request you to inform me immediately if the Jew Karl Natkin, formerly living at 15 Mickeviciaus Street, Kovno, is in the Ghetto.

APRIL 22, 1942

The Council has opened a public bath in the Ghetto; this service has been urgently needed by the Ghetto residents.

APRIL 25, 1942

The labor office is seeking to set up a detention center in the Ghetto for work-shirkers.

APRIL 26, 1942

The city governor has issued a directive: Ghetto inmates are again being requested to provide information on their financial obligations to other people, as well as their financial claims against others.

The Ghetto commandant has issued an order: the evacuation of the Ghetto inmates from the area left to it on Paneriu Street must be carried out before the deadline (not on May 1, but on April 26).

The Council has established rules for the operation of the soup kitchen.

APRIL 27, 1942

A six-member special commission has been appointed to investigate the actions of policemen at 3 Veniozinskio Street.[1]

> 1. The Council appointed this commission to inquire into rumors of parties held by Jewish police officers in an apartment in the Ghetto. The rumors scandalized the police force, most members of which were former members of Zionist youth movements and loyal to their moral obligations as Jews. It was found that there had been some irregularities; those responsible were reprimanded. The Council was unable, however, to dismiss functionaries who had previously had contact with the Germans, or who knew too much about the Council's "illegal" activities.

APRIL 28, 1942

A Jewish family by the name of Krum (three persons) has been brought to the Ghetto from the Raseiniai area. They are the only survivors from a village near Raseiniai.

APRIL 29, 1942

DOCUMENT: Report of the Ghetto Workshops of the Jewish Ghetto Community in Vilijampolé, for the period from the establishment of the Ghetto until April 25, 1942[1]

On December 5, 1941, the Council of the Jewish Ghetto community in Vilijampolé was ordered by the city governor to establish workshops for the production of various articles and to set up a laundry. For this purpose were chosen the localities of the former Home of the Homeless at 107 Krisciukaicio Street.

The repair, maintenance, and furnishing works started immediately. We have received from the regional administration only small quantities of the required materials for these works, so that we were forced to buy such from the population, and had to pay a considerable amount for it. We also had to pay a great deal in wages, since the furnishing of the workshops, and particularly the laundry, required highly qualified manpower. We could only hire these workers for payment, as there exists a demand for such manpower outside of the Ghetto. Nevertheless, we have carried out the order of December 5, 1941, in accordance with the plan and the delivery time.

The first workshop was established on January 12, the department for men's clothing. For this operation were purchased twelve sewing machines and their necessary equipment, and also the required professional personnel was kept ready. Unfortunately this workshop stood idle due to lack of orders until the end of March. At the beginning of April we received the first order, for the repair of military garments. In this workshop worked 55 people—men and women—at 21 sewing machines.

Up to now we have been sent for repair:

military coats, 799
military jackets, 1500
military trousers, 400.

Of these we have already repaired:

military coats, 100
military jackets, 200
military trousers, 356.

Most of the items sent for repair had to be turned. Further similar orders have been promised.

Besides the above-mentioned department for men's wear, which only repairs worn garments, we are about to open a separate department in the same workshop, which will work at the production of new garments. From the police we have already received an order for the production of 550 new police uniforms.

We shall start this work as soon as the necessary materials and the accessories have been supplied.

On January 12, 1942, the linen sewing workshop began operation. Forty-five sewing machines and other equipment, as well as the required personnel, were available. This workshop was intended to make all kinds of underclothes, bed linen, children's clothing, aprons, working suits, etc. Orders of this nature were at first received only occasionally, and on a small scale. The first large order came from the German Army for the manufacture of cloth gloves and glove linings, and also of fur gloves. Altogether we have manufactured 2,500 pairs of gloves; this was done by a team of 70 workers. Then the workshop stood idle for two weeks, until, on February 5, we received an order for the repair of worn linen. About 20,000 pieces of such linen have so far been repaired by a team of 32 people, mostly women. Since then no new orders have been received, and the repair of the linen has been finished; but in the meantime the men's wear department has had to be enlarged, and we have transferred most of the sewing workshop team to work in the men's wear department. Only a few women remain, who are still occupied with small repair works. However, this department can be reactivated at any time and resume its original task, the manufacture of linen, even on a larger scale. Some of the released women have also been transferred to the knitting workshop, on which we shall report below.

On January 12, 1942, the brush workshop was ready to begin work. In this department there now work 15 people, men and women. They manufacture clothes-brushes, shoe-brushes, lubricating brushes, brooms, bottle-brushes, and brushes for rifles. These brushes are made of horsehair and manes. Up to now, 5,634 brushes of various kinds have been manufactured. This workshop is mechanized and very effective. With an increase of personnel, its productivity can be significantly enhanced. Just now, an order for 6,100 brushes has been received from the German Army.

On January 21, 1942, the shoemaking workshop was ready to begin work. This workshop was planned for 15 cobblers, capable of repairing old shoes and manufacturing new shoes and boots. The actual operation of this department started only on March 12, 1942, because the necessary accessories did not arrive in time. We received the first order from the regional administration, for the repair of old shoes. Up to April 9, 1942, 230 pairs of shoes had been repaired and delivered. On April 9, 1942, we received an order from the German civil police for the repair of military boots: 1,543 pairs have been brought to the workshop for repair; up to now, 385 pairs have been repaired. The work team consists now of 33 cobblers. Further orders of a similar nature have been promised.

On February 16, 1942, the Ghetto laundry workshop was also ready to start operating. Equipping this department was exceptionally difficult, because, as is well known, there is no drainage system and there are no water pipes in the Ghetto. Nevertheless, we succeeded in organizing this workshop according to the prevailing conditions in a quite modern way, i.e. with water pipes, central heating, steam supply, a dry room, and an electrical centrifuge. At present, 41 people work in the laundry, mostly women. Up to now, 31,789 items of laundry have been delivered to us, of which 25,132 pieces have already been laundered. At the beginning we received orders from the regional administration, but recently we have also received orders from the Gestapo and the Security Police, German civil police and military construction management. The present capacity is about 600 items per day, but this can be increased to 1,000 items per day with a relative increase in personnel. The laundry's full capacity is not utilized, because orders do not come in regularly or in sufficient quantities.

On February 16, a soap and candle manufacturing workshop was opened. In this department 7 men work. Up to now, 213 kilograms of candles and 820 kilograms of soap have been made from chemicals supplied to us by the regional administration. Also, small quantities of shoe polish and shoe wax have been manufactured. We have been informed that no further chemicals will be supplied, so that the closing of this department is expected soon.

On February 19, 1942, we organized a wool-shearing shop (removing sheep wool from fur waste). This work employs 70 people, mostly women. Up to now, 3,929 kilograms of fur waste have been delivered for processing. The orders were given by the Ostland Fasergesellschaft Company. The yield of this work is about 30–32 percent pure wool, 55–60 percent shorn fur pieces, and the rest waste and dust.

On March 9, 1942, a sock-knitting shop began operation. The shop was opened with 5 women and 3 knitting machines. At the beginning we received orders from the regional administration for cotton socks. The cotton was delivered to us by the orderer. When we received on April 14 a larger order from the German Army for the repair of military socks, we discontinued the manufacture of socks for the regional administration, by order. In this department 28 women work at present. We have been informed that we shall soon receive larger orders, so that an increase of this operation, up to 50 women, may be expected.

On March 10, 1942, a workshop for children's toys was established, manufacturing both soft and hard toys. The soft toys are made by hand, by women. The hard toys are manufactured by machines in a carpenter's workshop organized by ourselves. This carpenter's workshop also does a small amount of specialized work for the other workshops. In the carpenter's shop are the following machines:

4 motorized turntables

1 rotary saw and workbench, combined and motorized

1 lattice saw, motorized

1 drilling machine, with a motor under construction, and

1 polishing machine, also under construction.

Up to now, about 1,500 toys have been manufactured. In this department there are at present employed 17 men and 30 women. This workshop is very effective and can also be enlarged. Next week, it will start mass production of toys on a larger scale.

On March 10, 1942, a tinker's workshop was opened, in which at present 19 men and women are employed. The German Army has sent about 100 items (military dishes) for repair. Delivery of further quantities has been promised.

On March 18, 1942, a saddler's workshop was opened, in which at present 11 workers are employed. The German Army has sent orders for the repair of cartridge pouches and food bags. Up to now, 2,048 cartridge pouches and 1,000 food bags have been received for repair. Further, larger orders of such nature have been promised, so that this department can also be expanded and its workforce increased accordingly.

Besides the above workshops, a repair shop is also operated here, which works exclusively at repairs and equipment, mainly for the other workshops. In this workshop about 14 men are employed; the number of workers is increased or reduced whenever necessary.

A workshop for the processing of medical bandages and the like will start operating within the next few days. For the time being there is an order for 400 pieces of eye and ear protectors. Three workers are employed at this. Further, larger orders have been promised, so that this department can be increased in the near future.

The establishment of a furniture carpentry shop, a vulcanization shop, and a furrier workshop is also planned. For the furrier shop, an order of 550 police caps has already been announced.

At the end of February, a part of the camp of the regional administration was transferred, at the initiative of the regional administration, from the old municipality building to the Ghetto workshops at 107 Krisciukaicio Street. Together with the camp, a number of small workshops have also been transferred, i.e. one knitting shop, one tailor's shop, one cobbler's shop, and one repair shop for typewriters, electrical appliances, suitcases, and leather articles. The group of workers which came here from the old municipality building consisted of 38 people.

The tasks of the workshops generally involves production based upon materials delivered by those who place the orders. During the short time of the existence of the workshops, it has become evident that single workshops, due to the seasonal conditions, cannot be of a continuous nature. Therefore we have ensured that the workshops remain sufficiently flexible in their construction, in order to adapt themselves to changing demand quickly and in time.

The Ghetto workforce consists at present of 400 people, half of them women.

For the wages of the working personnel we received, on March 7, 1942, an amount of 2,000 Reichsmarks, which we have distributed among the workers, excluding the management. The wages were paid on February 28, 1942, so that each worker has received 0.71 Reichsmarks per day.

Concerning food, we have been ordered to establish a kitchen for the workforce and to supply one lunch per worker per day. The food will be provided by the regional administration. As from the 26th of this month, the workers are to receive additional rations, as is also planned for the workers of the city brigades.

At the head of the workshops is a management, consisting of five people, who were appointed according to the instructions of the regional administration by the Council of the Jewish Ghetto community. The management consists of one plant manager, one office manager, one material acquisition manager, and two foremen. The management reports directly to the Council.

Summarizing, it may be said that the Ghetto workshops include 14 departments, namely:

1. Department for men's wear—repairs
2. Department for men's wear—new garments
3. Linen sewing shop
4. Brush workshop
5. Shoemaking workshop
6. Laundry
7. Soap and candle manufacturing workshop
8. Wool-shearing shop
9. Sock-knitting shop
10. Workshop for children's toys
11. Tinker's workshop
12. Saddler's workshop
13. Repair shop
14. Workshop for processing medical bandages.

The personnel consists at present of 400 people, of whom a half are men and a half are women. A considerable number of the workers were not previously involved in their present occupation, and had to be retrained. Consequently, the performance at the beginning was lower than that which has now been achieved.

No fixed wage system has yet been established. At the beginning of March we received 2,000 Reichsmarks for distribution among the employees. We have paid this amount to the workers, excluding the management, for the working period up to February 28, 1942, so that each worker, regardless of sex, qualified or unqualified, received 0.71 Reichsmarks per day. The tally of wages has already been submitted. We have not yet received its money equivalent.

As of today, the workforce has received neither food nor any regular additional rations whatsoever. Occasionally we receive from the Ghetto Guard small quantities of foodstuffs, which we distribute equally among the workers. Up to now, each worker has received an average of a kilogram of bread or its equivalent in value in other products (such as flour, salt, or similar). As from the 26th of this month, the Council of the Jewish community in Vilijampolé has announced that the workshop workers will receive an additional ration, as allotted to all the other Jewish workers of the city brigades, and at the airport. Furthermore, the city governor has ordered us to establish a kitchen in the workshops, which will serve hot lunches five times a week, except on Saturdays and Sundays.

Each workshop department is managed by a responsible foreman, who also is a first-class expert in the relevant profession. This foreman is in charge of the technical work of his department. Furthermore, the single workshops are supervised and controlled by two members of the management. These management members function as plant managers; each of them must supervise 7 workshops.

At the head of the workshops is a management whose functions are divided among them as follows:

1. General manager, who manages the operation (Gemelitzki).
2. Office manager, who is in charge of the office, personnel, and food, as well as the secretary's office (Brik).
3. Material acquisitions manager—contact with the municipality, ration vouchers, material acquisition, transport (Kagan).
4. Plant manager—of the departments for men's wear, linen sewing, laundry, soap and candle manufacturing, sock knitting, and medical bandages (Schwarz).
5. Plant manager—of the departments for brushes, shoes, wool-shearing, children's toys, the saddler's and tinker's workshops, and the repair shop (Friedmann).

Furthermore, an administrator has been appointed on behalf of the regional administration, who supervises the activities of the workshops. Also, the stores both of raw materials and of final products are administered by the regional administration; these stores are not included in the sphere of the activities of the management.

1. This report was submitted to Dr. Elkes by Nikolai (Michael) Gemelitzki, head of the economic affairs department of the Council.

APRIL 30, 1942

Reinforced guards of Jewish police patrolled the Ghetto during the night in order to prevent the possibility of violations of public order.[1] There were no disturbances of order in the Ghetto.

An instruction: before May 4 all the fields within the Ghetto bounds must be replowed.[2] In case of noncompliance, no potatoes will be brought to the Ghetto.

1. Rumors had spread of a possible infiltration of the Ghetto by members of the Lithuanian underworld. The Jewish police took precautions accordingly. The policemen were armed with batons only.

2. Vacant land in the Ghetto, totaling 25 dunams (about six acres) in four different locations, was maintained as a public vegetable garden by some 300 women, under the direction of an agronomist, Shlomo Kelzon. Work was supervised by Misha Mudrich, and the inmates worked every available piece of land. Under the initiative of Dr. Chaim Nachman Shapiro, eldest son of Chief Rabbi Shapiro, a youth movement named Eshel (the Hebrew acronym for Organization of Garden Guards) was established. Its members guarded the crops and ensured that after they were picked they were distributed fairly. Within the framework of Eshel, young people were educated in Zionist and underground activities. The Germans favored the Jews having their own sources of supply, since this allowed them to take for themselves the meager rations which were allocated to the Ghetto. Allocation of vegetables to the inhabitants of the Ghetto was made from warehouses on Varniu Street to distribution points throughout the Ghetto.

MAY 1, 1942

The evacuation of the area near Paneriu Street has been completed.

MAY 4, 1942

The liaison officer of the labor office at the main gate, Karl Natkin, has been arrested.[1] He was taken to the Gestapo under suspicion of spying. He was denounced by a Lithuanian employee of the Metropol hotel.

1. Karl Natkin, a wealthy Jewish merchant from Berlin, had been trapped in Kovno on the outbreak of war in June 1941. He was in charge of a unit of the Jewish labor office, located near the gate. The gate itself was manned by both Germans and Lithuanians. The Lithuanians attempted to remove Natkin, because he never bribed them as he did the Germans (nor did he speak a word of Lithuanian). After interrogation, and following strenuous efforts by Dr. Elkes, Natkin was released.

MAY 6, 1942

Mrs. Levin, a Jewish convert, has been brought to the Ghetto together with her little boy. She has been residing for a long time in the city with her Lithuanian husband.[1]

The new bathhouse has been opened to the public.

1. The twenty-two-year-old Mrs. Levin had taken the Lithuanian name Maria Germana Levinaite. Her son was eight months old in May 1942.

MAY 8, 1942

Decision of the Ghetto commandant: the curfew is to begin at 10 P.M. (instead of 9 P.M. as before).

MAY 9, 1942

Karl Natkin has been released from prison by the Gestapo.

MAY 12, 1942

The secretary of the Council, Bernstein, together with Chaikin and Jutter, has been arrested.[1] The charges: operating a clandestine mail service between the Kovno Ghetto and the Vilna Ghetto. They were taken to the Ghetto detention center and from there to the Gestapo.

> 1. Dr. Israel Bernstein was the first secretary of the Council; advocate Chaikin was an employee of the Council's population registry bureau; and Jutter was one of the Council's messengers. All three were arrested when it was discovered that postal contacts had been maintained with the Vilna Ghetto over a period of six months, through a Lithuanian railway worker. It was not they who had maintained these contacts, however, but Ephraim Silberman, head of the brigade of Jewish workers at the garage near Kovno railway station. He too was arrested. After one month's imprisonment by the Gestapo, all four were released.

MAY 15, 1942

A kindergarten has been set up in the Ghetto.[1]

The labor office designated the rooms of the synagogue at 23 Krisciukaicio Street as a detention center for those shirking work.

> 1. Sonja Segal-Varshavski, a leading Kovno kindergarten teacher and the wife of Dr. Eliyahu Segal, head of the welfare department of the Jewish Council, set up a clandestine Hebrew kindergarten for orphaned and abandoned children, and for children whose parents had been taken for long-term forced labor.

MAY 16, 1942

The city governor has issued a decree to hand over all fresh-water sports gear to the authorities.

MAY 16, 1942

> *DOCUMENT:*
> *From the City Governor's Office*
> *To the Council, Kovno*

Within eight days, a detailed list must be sent to me, specifying all motorboats, racing boats, folding boats, paddleboats, sailing boats, and all other water-sports equipment formerly owned by Jews.

The list must specify the exact address of the previous owner, the last station or location of the sports equipment, as well as a detailed description of the boats.

If the sports equipment has been deposited for safekeeping with the Lithuanian population, this must also be reported in detail.

I explicitly emphasize that this information must be accurate and complete.

MAY 17, 1942

In Panemune, a German policeman has shot and killed a young Jewish worker, Chanan Aronovski, while he was at work.

A commission has been set up, charged with providing for the material needs of the employees in the Ghetto institutions and with establishing a loan fund. The same commission is also entrusted with the distribution of food rations to these employees.[1]

The airfield labor force has been increased; now it numbers 3,200 workers.

1. This commission existed only for a short time, as the Ghetto's financial economy was brought to an end in August 1942. The planned loan fund was apparently never actually established.

MAY 19, 1942

A directive has been issued by the Ghetto commandant: instead of embroidered Shields of David, the Ghetto residents are required to carry Shield of David badges made of fabric.

A short visit of Reichsminister Rosenberg and his entourage in the Ghetto.[1]

1. Alfred Rosenberg visited the Ghetto in his capacity as German minister for the occupied eastern areas. Accompanied by an entourage which comprised the German civil administration and SA elite of Lithuania and Kovno, he visited the large workshops in the Ghetto. The supervisors of the workshops displayed their products and presented them to the visitors as gifts.

MAY 20, 1942

A lice disinfection center has been opened in the Ghetto.[1]

We have been ordered to transfer Jewish workers to dig peat in Palemonas.

> 1. The lice disinfection center contributed greatly to easing the conditions of life in the Ghetto. The Germans also had a center in Kovno for delousing soldiers returning from the front; Jews from the Ghetto were employed there. Inside the Ghetto, the battle against lice and typhus was conducted with considerable ingenuity, and success, by Dr. Moses Brauns (see the Memoir dated October 15, 1942).

MAY 21, 1942

The airfield labor force has increased to 3,414 workers. Rumors about transfer of workers to other workplaces outside the Ghetto have been denied.

MAY 23, 1942

Two hundred members of the Jewish police and employees in the Ghetto institutions went out to work at the airfield.

Cramer, Hermann, Obst,[1] and a German Army general toured the Ghetto workshops and the Council.

The chairman of the Council issues regulations relating to confiscations in the Ghetto: confiscation of property or belongings in the Ghetto will be carried out only on the instruction of the chairman of the Council or as a result of an order of the Jewish Ghetto court.

> 1. Obst, an SA man, headed the food and supply department of the German civil administration of Kovno.

MAY 24, 1942

No work during the Pentecost holy days.[1]

> 1. This unexpected holiday took place because that year the Jewish festival of Shavuot (Pentecost) fell on the same day as the Christian holiday.

MAY 25, 1942

Fire in the lice disinfection center. The fire was put out with the help of firemen from the city.[1]

A second elementary school has been opened in the Ghetto.

Building-construction courses have been opened in the Ghetto.

1. Firefighters from the city rarely entered the Ghetto unless fire threatened to spread beyond the Ghetto, as in this case. Fires inside the Ghetto were put out by the firefighting department of the Jewish Council.

MAY 27, 1942

According to a directive issued by the Ghetto commandant, it is forbidden to keep unwrapped razor blades in one's pockets, in order to prevent injuries to the German policemen conducting searches on workers on their return from the city.[1] Every male is required to wear headgear when walking in the streets and to pay respects to uniformed persons by taking it off.

There was an air-raid alarm during the night; a number of bombs fell on the city of Kovno.

1. One means of expressing bitterness against the endless searches and checks at the Ghetto gate was to carry unwrapped razor blades in pockets. These razor blades often injured the searchers. The commander of the German Ghetto Guard corps (the Ghetto commandant) summoned the Jewish police chief and the head of the labor office to warn them that punishment for continuing this practice would be delivery to the Gestapo.

MAY 31, 1942

The chairman of the Council has been received by the Gestapo: he was informed that all vegetable gardens must be seeded and that it is forbidden to cause damage to the vegetable gardens. Seven German policemen of the NSKK formation visited the Council. One of them, a high-ranking officer who had recently returned from the front, heaped insults and curses on the Jews: "You are to blame for the war; just wait, the time will come when you'll eat grass."

JUNE 1, 1942

Bernstein, Chaikin, and Jutter have been released from prison. Also, thirty-two people (fifteen women and seventeen men) returned from the Gestapo and from prison.

JUNE 2, 1942

Seventy-three people were sent to dig peat in Palemonas. Some of them escaped on the way to the labor camp.

The Jewish religious class for boys and the small Ohel Moshe yeshiva have been incorporated into the Ghetto education system. Their programs of study have been expanded.[1]

A full meeting of the Council, attended also by Caspi and by Lipzer.

1. Because of the difficult circumstances, all forms of education, including religious education, were amalgamated in the Council's education department. The Ohel Moshe yeshiva was one of the only two places of prayer remaining in the Ghetto (the other was the Halvayet Hamet synagogue). All other religious study centers had to be used as living quarters because of the shortage of housing, and the other synagogues had been desecrated.

JUNE 3, 1942

The German director of the labor office, together with a representative of the Jewish labor office, I. Rabinovitz, visited the Jewish workers in Palemonas.[1]

1. Palemonas was considered to be a particularly harsh place to work. At the initiative of Dr. Elkes, Lieutenant Gustav Hermann and Dr. Isaac Rabinovitz went to examine the situation, in the hope of being able to improve it. After the visit, Hermann allowed a doctor and an administrator from the Ghetto to be sent to the camp.

JUNE 4, 1942

Forty additional men have been sent to work in Palemonas. They were accompanied by a physician and an economic supervisor.

An advisory commission has been set up at the Council. It is assigned the task of ensuring satisfactory crops in the vegetable gardens and fields within the Ghetto bounds.

JUNE 5, 1942

A directive has been issued on behalf of the city governor: house windows on Veliuonos Street, near the Ghetto fence, must be boarded up with planks. A new barbed-wire fence on this street must be set up as well.[1]

Wiedmann[2] visited the Council offices.

The Council submitted, via Caspi, a report to the Gestapo of its activities, as well as of the activities of the labor office and the economic affairs office.

1. Veliuonos Street ran along the barbed-wire fence of the Ghetto. Lithuanians sometimes infiltrated into the Ghetto from it and caused considerable damage to those Jews who lived close to the Ghetto fence, and occasionally to the Germans as well.
2. Wiedmann, an SA man, had replaced Jordan as chief of the German civil administration of the Ghetto.

JUNE 6, 1942

The Council has set up a workshop for the manufacture of wigs.

JUNE 10, 1942

The Jewish police began distributing Ghetto cards to the inmates. The cards are signed by the commandant of the Jewish police.

Corpses of Jews murdered in the Slobodka massacre last year have been pulled out of the Vilija river.

JUNE 11, 1942

The Germans have returned a small part of the books they had confiscated in the Ghetto (prayer books, school books, medical and technical books, etc.).

JUNE 12, 1942

The Council asked the city governor that the workshops in the Ghetto, which the Council set up using its own resources and labor, should remain in the future under the auspices of the Council, managed by a five-member board.[1]

Notes of a conversation with Keidan:[2]

Keidan was arrested on January 10, 1942. He was led away to prison and from there, on May 5, 1942, he was transferred to the Ninth Fort. He was released on June 12, 1942.

In a conversation with me, he related his ordeal during his imprisonment:

There were twenty-one of us. One day they came and told us to gather our belongings. We were transferred from the prison to the fort. The executions there used to take place early in the morning, between 6 and 7 A.M. We arrived at 11:30 P.M. The underground cell was cold and dank. We were put in a particularly bad cell. We were led to work at once. We carried heavy bags of potatoes on our backs. We had to run while working. There was a break and we got some sleep. We worked again until 8 P.M. At 5 A.M. the following day we went out to work again. The work was backbreaking.

The building where we were incarcerated contained sixteen or eighteen cells. Our main job was to fill with clods of earth the graves inside seven large pits. Jews from Lithuania had been thrown into three pits. Jews from Germany and from other countries had been thrown into two other pits.

In the fort we found Jews, including prisoners-of-war—a total of sixty-four people. They work like everybody else, but their food rations are larger. A special bread is made for them and it is mixed with sawdust. It causes one's stomach to swell up, followed by quick death. They receive 300 grams of bread, soup twice a day, and 30 grams of sugar and jam.

Previously they worked for the peasants. They were brought to the fort following an order to concentrate all the Jews in one place. Here they dig pits and fill them up. Previously, twenty-one Jews and twenty-three Christians had been doing this work. Those condemned to death are thrown into the pits and then shot. When they brought the German Jews here, they arranged for a special orchestra to play for the children and also a merry-go-round. These Jews worked for several days in the fields. While working in that place we found barrels filled with various papers and documents belonging to the murdered Jews. "When we get to the graves," our supervisor told us, "you'll be able to embrace your mothers, your sisters and brothers. You'll find them all there."

The big extermination operations were carried out by the Lithuanians; the smaller ones by the Germans. On May 15 we saw how the people brought in here were removed from the trucks and pushed straight into the pits. Then they were shot.

Those who conducted these operations stripped the Jews of gold and other valuables. In one bag we found socks, shaving utensils, and bars of soap. We handed those articles to the foremen.

Some of the prisoners-of-war were unable to walk—they were too weak. A Lithuanian doctor was brought in, and he injected them with a toxic drug. Thirty of them died on the following day. The remainder were shot by the supervisor. Five of the prisoners-of-war were Jews: Felman from Shavli, one from Keidan, one from Merkine, and two others. The Jews from Lithuania are in a better situation since they speak the language of the Lithuanian murderers. Other Jews come from the districts of Minsk and the Volhynia.

On Tuesday, June 3, in the afternoon, we sat down to rest a bit. All of a sudden a truck arrived packed with men and women: they had been sent previously for an interrogation and did not have any belongings on them. They knew they had been brought here to be murdered. The men—Zsuchovski, Litman, Zalmanovich, Lifschitz, Ziv, Leufer, Berman, and others. The women—Mrs. Friedland and others.

They conducted themselves properly. Only Berman cried. He carried a prayer book with him. They spent one night here; waited in line to get soup. The guards treated them as people condemned to death.

I had a suit. I sold it to the cook for half a kilo of bread. Kanzer and Reznik pounced on me and snatched the bread away. The people brought here knew they were going to die. Some of them said that before they died they wanted to eat their fill.

That Tuesday, toward evening, the commandant wrote down the names of all seventeen people. On the following day, at 10 A.M., the supervisors entered and ordered them to get dressed and go outside. They were taken outside the walls and made to form up in rows, three people to a row. Seven or eight Germans, headed by Schtitz of the Gestapo, waited for them. According to the list held by Schtitz, the Gestapo "needed" ten people. He told Shapiro, Shershevski, and me to step aside.

The women stood in a separate row. Two of them asked Schtitz to let them live. One of them was put into a room; later she was taken out and murdered, together with the Christians.

We heard volleys of gunfire emanating from the house; the Jews were murdered first and then the Christians. The Christians were bound and heavily guarded.

After this operation we were taken back into our cell. That day we were not sent out to work. While standing in the row, we were certain that our fate was sealed. At the same time, however, there was a spark of hope that nothing would happen to us. After we had stepped aside, Zsuchovski asked permission to get back his wallet and trousers.

On the following day we returned to work. Eleven days later I was taken back again to prison. Schtitz turned to me and asked my first name and the family name. This gave me courage and hope that I would survive.

On Friday morning the supervisor came in and asked: which one is Keidan? (I was nicknamed "old man.") I was ordered to drive with him to the city. I was taken back again to prison. The man who brought me to the city told me that I was free. I was told the same thing in the prison in Kovno. At half past three I was taken to the Gestapo. Schtitz warned me to refrain from disclosing anything of what I had seen. Otherwise I would meet the same fate as the others.

Having been taken to the prison, I began to cry. The hours I spent sitting in the waiting room seemed like so many years.[3]

While in Lipzer's room,[4] I asked for a slice of bread. I hadn't had anything to eat that day. Berman's legs were swollen, and he was sent to the Kovno prison hospital. (Sick Jews were not, as a rule, sent to a physician; Christian patients were.) He came back from the hospital the same day. He seemed a skeleton. They put him in our room. The following day he was unable to walk. As a result he was carried straight to the pit.

1. Avraham Tory is referring here to the "large" workshops, which employed 1,800 people in shifts and consisted of a laundry, a blacksmith shop, and metalworking, carpentry, sewing, brush, glove, and rope-making, clothing, shoe repair, and other workshops, all of which supplied goods and services to the Germans. The large workshops were under the management of Moshe Segalson, and the small workshops under the management of Ephraim Bunim; both were vital elements both in the Ghetto economy and in justifying the Ghetto's existence to the Germans. They also secretly supplied the Jewish partisans who had fled to the forests. It was not surprising that the Council, which had initiated their establishment and management, did not want them to be managed by the Germans. The "small" workshops, which employed 150 workers, did mostly reconstruction and repair work for the Ghetto itself.

2. Keidan had been a member of a work brigade called, ironically, "Jordan's grandsons." He was apparently the first Jew to return alive from the Ninth Fort during the so-called period of relative calm.

3. In Kovno there were both the Lithuanian city prison (the Yellow prison) and a prison in the Gestapo building. Keidan is speaking of his transfer from "the prison" (the Gestapo prison) to "the prison in Kovno" (the city prison). In the Ghetto there was a detention center used by the Jewish police and the Jewish court.

4. Lipzer, as head of the brigade of Jews who worked in the Gestapo building, had a room in that building.

JUNE 13, 1942

The Palemonas workers came to the Ghetto for a one-day holiday.

The Jewish labor office has arrested Dr. Poretzki. He has been detained for several days. The reason for his arrest: his refusal to go to Palemonas as a physician accompanying the labor brigade, because of hard conditions there.

JUNE 14, 1942

A brigade of workers has been mobilized for agricultural work at Marivianka. It is composed of 200 boys aged fourteen and fifteen.[1]

At 11 o'clock a parade of Palemonas workers took place near the German labor office. The parade was attended by Lieutenant Hermann, by representatives of the Jewish labor office, and by others.

1. This was the first attempt to employ boys under the minimum forced-labor age of sixteen. They were employed in farming, under the supervision of professional instructors from the Ghetto. The Ghetto was alarmed at their departure and greatly relieved when they returned safely.

JUNE 15, 1942

Moshe Rosenberg has been shot and killed near the fence. The reason: he was not wearing the yellow badge on his clothes.

Rumors in the Ghetto of "actions" in Riga and Siauliai. The Siauliai Ghetto has been liquidated.[1]

Fees have been fixed for the issuing of birth certificates and other personal papers.

Fees for treatment in hospitals and clinics have been approved.

1. The Siauliai (Shavli) Ghetto was not in fact liquidated until the summer of 1944. In Riga, German "actions" were not renewed until November 1943, when several thousand Jews were murdered.

JUNE 16, 1942

Wiedmann visited the Council. He asked: "Where is the key to the gate of the Jewish cemetery in Kovno?" He also demanded that the writing desk of the chairman of the Council be brought to his quarters.

The Gestapo has issued an order: those sentenced to several days of imprisonment will be confined in the Ghetto detention center (and not in the central Kovno prison as was the practice until now).

Hermann came to the Council. He announced that the city governor's proposal to set up large workshops in the Ghetto was to be put into effect by the Council. The workshops will be run by the district governor through a German manager.[1] The Council may maintain contacts with the manager in all matters of interest to it. This is also the view of the German director of the workshops, Government Councillor Peschel.[2]

1. The Kovno district governor was Lenzen. In addition to the Kovno district, the Lithuanian region comprised two further districts, Vilna and Siauliai. Above them in authority was the governor-general of Lithuania, Dr. Adrian von Renteln, whose headquarters were in Kovno.
2. Peschel was head of the German department of labor in Lithuania, subordinate to the governor-general, Dr. von Renteln. In the late autumn and winter of 1941, Peschel had argued with superiors that Jewish laborers in the Vilna, Kovno, and Siauliai Ghettos should be kept alive. It was believed in the Kovno Ghetto that it was largely as a result of Peschel's initiatives, the first in October 1941 and the second in December 1941, that orders had reached Kovno which resulted in a halt to the mass murder. For a certain period, Peschel was also supervisor of the large workshops in the Kovno Ghetto.

JUNE 17, 1942

A Jewish policeman, Abramson, was arrested at the Ghetto gate, after 16,000 rubles had been found on him. Thereupon the Council sent a letter to the Ghetto Guard, saying that the money belonged to the Council. As a consequence, the Jewish policeman was released.

The Ghetto Guard commandant, Tiele, completed his tour of duty. Tschich is the new commandant.[1]

An instruction has been received from the Gestapo to submit a list of all former Kovno dentists who reside in the Ghetto at present.

1. Personnel changes such as this one, which took place quite frequently at German headquarters, were always accompanied by grave fears in the Ghetto.

JUNE 18, 1942

Caspi has received the list of twenty-four dentists (one dentist drew up a list of all the dentists in the Ghetto, without the knowledge of the Council).[1]

1. On the previous day, the Council, its medical service, and its labor office had all refused to provide the list of dentists demanded by the Gestapo, because they feared the dentists' fate.

JUNE 19, 1942

The Council appointed a commission charged with supervising the wives and family members of the workers of the Council office and the members of the Jewish police going out to work at the airfield.

An instruction has been received to pave the section of Krisciukaicio Street from the main gate to the workshops.[1]

1. Krisciukaicio Street was a main artery of the Ghetto, leading from the gate to the area of the workshops. The German civil administration had ordered it to be paved with stones to make it easier for German vehicles to reach the workshops. Paving was carried out by Jews from the Ghetto.

JUNE 20, 1942

Wiedmann transferred the sum of 10,000 marks to the Council.[1]

The workers from Palemonas came to the Ghetto for a one-day holiday.

Wiedmann wrote to the Council concerning the setting up of a large furniture factory in the Ghetto.[2]

1. Wiedmann gave the Council this money so that it could pay the salaries of those Jews in the Ghetto who should have been paid by the workshops or were employed by the German civil and military workplaces. Although this sum was a fraction of any realistic salary, the Germans made no effort to explain how it had been calculated.
2. The Ghetto had many first-class carpenters and other artisans, better than most of those available among the Lithuanians. At Wiedmann's request, the Council opened a carpenters' workshop; it was managed and staffed by Jews. The only German supervision was by an architect by the name of Wintzer.

JUNE 22, 1942

The first anniversary of the outbreak of war between Russia and Germany. SA Lieutenant Borou of the Ghetto Guard shot and killed a Jewish woman, Mrs.

Gurland.[1] The reason: selling various goods on one of the Ghetto streets. One hundred fifty employees of the Council administration worked today at the airfield.

1. Her name is given in a report to the Council as Sara Kurland.

JUNE 23, 1942

Rauca of the Gestapo ordered a sculpture of a naked woman from the sculptress Gehrscheim.

The organization of garden watchers began its activities. Its purpose: to watch over the Ghetto vegetable gardens. It also undertakes cultural, national activities.[1]

Caspi gave a party at his house in the city which was attended by Rauca and other Gestapo officials.

1. The latter activities were conducted clandestinely.

JUNE 24, 1942

Zvi Levin and Goldberg made it a condition that the extension of their Gestapo permits to go outside the Ghetto be approved by the Council; Caspi had to swallow it.[1]

1. On Caspi's initiative, the German authorities gave Yakov Goldberg and Zvi Levin, members of the Council, permits to leave the Ghetto and to visit the city of Kovno unaccompanied. Goldberg and Levin asked for the Council's approval as well, so as not to be identified with collaborators, like Caspi, who had German permits only.

JUNE 25, 1942

Rumors are making the rounds that Dr. Zacharin is about to be appointed commander of the Jewish police. The Council is opposed to this idea.

Consultation at the Council concerning the large workshops. It was attended by Segalson, who has been appointed director of the workshops by the city governor.

JUNE 26, 1942

Wiedmann asked the Council to find a suitable location in the Ghetto for the large furniture factory to be set up.

The commandant of the Ghetto Guard gave his permission—for the first time in the Ghetto—for children's festivities to take place in the Ghetto school.

JUNE 27, 1942

The commander of the Ghetto Guard, Tschich, completed his tour of duty. He is to be replaced by SS Company Commander Katein.[1]

> 1. Katein, who replaced Tschich, was an SS company commander who had come from Vienna. Avraham Tory later recalled that his manner was "relatively tolerable."

JUNE 27, 1942

DOCUMENT:
From SS Colonel Jaeger
To Dr. Adrian von Renteln

During the escorting of Jewish convoys from the Ghetto and back, complaints and unpleasant remarks have frequently been made by the Lithuanian citizens.

It is my opinion that a German of the Reich is much too valuable to be used for the escort of Jewish convoys to the Ghetto.

Therefore, in the interest and prestige of Germany, I request you to appoint policemen of the Lithuanian police for the escorting of Jewish convoys.

JUNE 28, 1942

Festivities for the schoolchildren took place in the yeshiva on Yeshiva Street. An orchestra composed of well-known Kovno musicians played. The organizers asked the audience: "No applause, please." Placards with quotations in the hall read: "God consoles in the straits of pity"; "I led you out of your grave, my people." From this very same hall of the yeshiva, 534 academics had been taken out in the first "action" in the Ghetto.

JUNE 29, 1942

An order from Caspi: Zupovitz is to be suspended from his duty as the deputy commander of the Jewish police.[1]

Checks and searches for shirkers of work-duty.

The Lithuanian so-called partisans, who have been charged with watching over the Jewish workers in Palemonas, opened fire during the night on the huts where the workers sleep. Three of the workers (Arieh Strash, Haim Akerman, and Shlomo Levin) were killed instantly.

B. Lipzer has been empowered by the Gestapo to inspect the Jewish labor force in order to prevent irregularities.[2]

> 1. As part of the power struggle between Caspi and the Council, Caspi demanded that Yehuda Zupovitz, deputy chief of the Jewish police, who was trusted by the Ghetto inmates, be

dismissed. With great effort a compromise was reached, whereby Zupovitz would be inspector of one of the three police precincts into which the Ghetto was divided, while Caspi would have a certain degree of authority in the Ghetto police.

2. Benno Lipzer had persuaded Rauca that half of the Council bureaucracy and half of the Jewish Ghetto police force could be cut back, thus releasing more men for work outside the Ghetto. In a compromise with the Council, Rauca agreed to cut the police force by a quarter rather than half, in return for giving Lipzer some authority in the Council's labor department.

JUNE 29, 1942

DOCUMENT:
From SS Master Sergeant Rauca
To the Jewish Council, Kovno Ghetto

The Jew Benjamin Lipzer, born on March 22, 1896, in Grodno, now living at Kovno Ghetto, 21 Aukuro Street, is authorized to control the Jewish labor exchange, in order to remove mismanagement. His instructions must be obeyed.

JUNE 30, 1942

The bodies of the three workers murdered in Palemonas were brought to the Ghetto. All the Palemonas workers returned to the Ghetto out of fear.

A consultation took place in Caspi's apartment in the city.

Advocate Abramovitz[1] is a candidate for the post of deputy commander of the Jewish police instead of Zupovitch. Caspi issued threats against the Council in general and against Levin and Goldberg in particular.

A consultation with Dr. Elkes, attended by Caspi and Lipzer, concerning the problems of the Jewish police and the labor office. Police matters in the Ghetto will remain in future under Caspi's supervision. Lipzer will supervise all labor force matters. All this in line with the Gestapo instruction.

1. Jacob Abramovitz was a judge in the Jewish court in the Ghetto; later he was deputy chief of the Jewish police.

JULY 1, 1942

DOCUMENT:
To SS Master Sergeant Rauca
From Benjamin Lipzer

In compliance with the duties conferred upon me by you, I have contacted the members of the Council and the labor office of the Jewish Ghetto community, and after discussions with them I have come to the following conclusions:

1. After a thorough scrutiny of the personnel of all the Ghetto offices, to

reduce the personnel to a quarter of its existing strength, and to employ at this work only old people or those who are unfit for work at the airfield.

2. To change the composition of all working places in the city so that only artisans will remain permanently at the places of work where they are needed, whereas physical workers will be frequently exchanged with workers at the airport.

3. To arrange forthwith for better conditions for the workers at the airport, and also to alleviate their problems of clothes and shoes.

4. In order to stop any possible occurrence of protectionism, to annul the current passes used for temporary work.

5. To issue an appeal to the inmates of the Ghetto, reading as follows:

It is again urgently brought to your attention that all inmates of the Ghetto, namely, men aged between 17 and 60 and women aged between 17 and 47, must comply with their working duties. In order to avoid any mis-understanding, mothers of children more than 5 (five) years old must comply fully with their working duty. Women who have children less than 5 (five) years old, and who share their apartment with other women, are likewise compelled to work.

Regarding women, it must also be stressed that there will be no exceptions: wives of members of the Council, the labor office, the police, or any other institution are not exempt from work. If such cases should occur, they will be ruthlessly punished—and on an increasing scale.

Furthermore, it is pointed out for the last time that every deliberate work-refusal will be referred to the commander of the Gestapo for Lithuania, for suitable punishment.[1]

1. A note on the bottom of this document states: "Approved, Rauca, SS, July 1."

JULY 1, 1942

Rauca approved Lipzer's proposal to cut by 50 percent the staff of the Council; to replace the airfield workers with the city labor brigade workers and vice versa; to revoke the passage permits (to the city); to publish an announcement to the Ghetto residents about work-duty for men aged sixteen to fifty-six and for women aged seventeen to forty-seven. Mothers of children up to five years old are exempted from work-duty.

Personnel changes in the Jewish police command: Jacob Abramovitz has replaced Zupovitz as the deputy commander of the Jewish police. Zupovitz will be the police inspector (as a result of Caspi's intervention).

JULY 1, 1942

DOCUMENT: Order of SS Master Sergeant Rauca

The number of workers in the offices and institutions in the Ghetto must be reduced by half.

JULY 2, 1942

At a meeting of the Council, the following were present: Garfunkel, Levin, Goldberg, Snieg, Rabinovitz, and Shmukler. All of them are department heads.

Dr. Elkes announces that the number of employees in all Jewish institutions has to be reduced by half. This should not amount to amputation. Department heads must submit within a day the list of employees who will stay on and those who are to leave.

The cuts do not affect manual workers, only the office staff and employees of public institutions. The Ghetto court must be closed down. Several schools and health clinics must also be closed. The younger workers are to be laid off while the older ones who are not fit for physical work should stay. There will also be changes in the Ghetto police. The number of policemen will be reduced, but only by twenty-three men. The new lists must be submitted by eight o'clock.

JULY 3, 1942

A session of the Council. Difficulties stemming from reduction of the number of workers, particularly at the health office and the labor office. Negotiations with Lipzer concerning increasing the number of physicians in the hospital.

Jewish workers at the Heresbau plant are allowed to bring potatoes into the Ghetto.

At night an inspection took place of those to whom the work-duty applies.

The belongings of the Palemonas workers are being returned to the Ghetto. The workers themselves are not going back there anymore.

JULY 4, 1942

The Council has held a consultation with Lipzer. He informed the Council that Rauca had ordered the control commission of the Council to be dissolved.[1]

There is a collision between Caspi and Lipzer about their "dominance" in the Ghetto. Levin's and Goldberg's permits, allowing them to go to the city without guard, were not extended, because of the refusal of the Council, which opposes the idea of any exceptions. Caspi has issued strong threats against them both.

1. Rauca's instructions, dated July 4, 1942, were signed by Lipzer, in Rauca's name. According to these instructions the Ghetto court, the schools, and the counseling committee were to be dissolved as well.

JULY 5, 1942

The employees put pressure on the Council in connection with reductions of the staff. At noon the Council held a session attended by Lipzer, concerning the reduction of the number of employees. The control commission was dissolved.

The Council set regulations concerning the adoption of children. Children up to the age of fifteen may be adopted. The adopting parties must be at least twenty-five years old. Registration takes place in the department issuing birth certificates.[1]

1. These regulations were formulated because of the large number of children who were left to fend for themselves after their parents had been murdered or deported.

JULY 6, 1942

In compliance with the Gestapo decree, the Council will reduce the staff of the Ghetto institutions by 206 employees; 207 employees will stay on. The Jewish Ghetto court has been disbanded. Two schools, two food distribution stations, and two clinics have been closed down. The lice disinfection center has been closed down temporarily.

JULY 7, 1942

The pharmacist Melnik, who has been dismissed, threatens to inform if he is not reinstated.[1]

From now on, bathing in the Vilija river is permitted. If a section of the river is fenced by barbed wire beyond the designated area, it is forbidden to bathe in it.

In compliance with the Gestapo decree, the Jewish police force has been reduced by an additional twenty-three men.

The Council has issued a decree: an assembly of more than three persons (standing) is forbidden on Vytenio Street.

Wiedmann has issued a written instruction: information about the number of apartments and the number of households in the Ghetto must be provided by July 13, so as to make it possible to calculate the amount of firewood to be used in the Ghetto in the coming winter.

1. He was later reinstated.

JULY 8, 1942

DOCUMENT: SA Lieutenant Hermann, Instructions for carrying out compulsory labor duty in the Ghetto

1. All able-bodied men, and all able-bodied women aged from 17 to 46 years, are subject to compulsory work.

2. Able-bodied men are considered men aged from 16 to 60 years, unless they have been recognized by the health authority as unfit for work.

3. Male youth 14 and 15 years old are subject to compulsory labor according to their working capability, as individually determined by the compulsory labor authority. The compulsory labor authority is entitled in certain cases to recognize men above the age of 60 as fit for compulsory labor and to assign certain works to them.

4. Mothers of children up to the age of 5 are not subject to compulsory labor duty.

5. Women who are entirely occupied with housekeeping for their working family members and children are exempted from compulsory labor duty.

6. The exemption according to instruction 5 will be granted for by the compulsory labor authority under the following considerations: (a) In each household unit, only one woman can be occupied with housekeeping. (b) If there are several women in one household unit, the women not subject to compulsory labor, or the oldest woman of the household, will do the housekeeping. (c) The splitting up of existing household units will not be taken into consideration.

7. All men and women subject to compulsory labor must receive a compulsory labor certificate or labor card from the compulsory labor authority, and keep it with them at all times.

8. Men and women subject to compulsory labor duty who because of ill health are unable to perform heavy labor outside the Ghetto will be assigned to lighter work inside the Ghetto.

JULY 8, 1942

DOCUMENT: Report by Irena Adamovich[1]

Review of the situation in Vilna. Ten to sixteen people in one room. "Fictitious persons": adding two or three people to a family of a person holding the Yellow Card.[2] Some order must be now imposed because of the coming introduction of Bread Cards.

Places of work: workshops in the Ghetto employing 120 people.

Death sentences: the Jewish police carried out death sentences by hanging six Jews accused of murdering another Jew. The execution took place on orders of the Jewish police.[3] Since then the Jewish Police has been feared more than ever.

Trade in all kinds of goods is conducted in private apartments.

Health services: work at the military hospital; there is a hospital in the Vilna Ghetto which operates normally.

Three weeks ago the Germans ordered a hundred Jews to be turned over to them, to be executed as a reprisal for illicit trade activities in the Ghetto.[4]

In Vilna there are cooperation and mutual tolerance between the Germans and the Poles. Mutual hostility reigns between the Poles and the Lithuanians.

In Warsaw people have not yet tired of the war. In Vilna people are already tired. In Vilna there are hardly any arrests.

Umbrella organization[5]: Dvorzecki, Dimantman, Pinchuk, Trapido, Abba Kovner, Glazman, Milkonowicki.

Jewish Council: Fried, Yashunski, Milkonowicki, Fishman, Gutman.[6]

In June executions took place in Glebokie, Dzisna, Druja, Lida, Zeludok, and Werenow. There was resistance in those places.[7] Refugees from Werenow and Zeludok went into hiding in the forests. Some of them were shot and killed. In Lida only 1,500 Jews remain. The Lithuanians encountered resistance from the Jews employed at digging pits, who used spades to defend themselves. In Vilna, this incident sparked the notion of "death with honor."

A Jew working for the Gestapo stabbed a White Russian priest in Lida. A demand was issued to put to death a certain number of Jews as a reprisal. The Germans were handed criminals for this purpose. These criminals raised various accusations against the Jews. They were put next to the barred peephole in the prison. A number of Jews were accused of various crimes. They were lined up in a row; some were directed to the right and executed, while others were turned to the left. The latter survived.

Rebellion in Lida.

There are rumors in Druja that the Jews set the town on fire. It was a form of uprising. Self-government is being set up in White Russia where large-scale executions are taking place.

Since Passover, "actions" have been taking place in the provincial towns in occupied Poland.[8] In Lublin, 42,000 Jews have been murdered; three Jews survived. Teachers were ordered to witness the murder of the children. The Jewish population was divided into men, women, and children. Some of them were taken to the market square and put to death. Children clung to their teachers. They were thrown into pits—the living together with the dead. Five hundred children were murdered in this fashion. The teachers begged to be put to death first but their request was turned down. The dying asked to be stoned so that they would die quickly, but the Germans chose to prolong their suffering. All this was done by the Germans. Finally, an order came to stop the carnage.

In Hrubieszow there was a Ghetto with several thousand Jews. Three thousand were murdered, 1,200 hid, 1,500 found shelter in the surrounding countryside.

There were four kinds of Ghettos: closed Ghettos, Ghettos open to Jews, Ghettos open to Christians, and Ghettos with free access. Belzec is a killing center; Sobibor and Majdanek, extermination centers.

In Cracow there are now 10,000 Jews (previously there were 100,000). All the Jews in Tarnow and Mielec were killed. There is a special Ghetto for retired Jews in Cracow. Walls built of stone in the architectural style prevalent in the city surround the Ghetto. There are many informers there.

In Czestochowa many Poles enter the Ghetto. The Jews work in heavy industry. The actions of the Jewish Council are preceded by careful deliberations. Everyone is required to work. There are three kibbutzim there, but their members go hungry.[9] No executions there. In the town of Zarki near Czestochowa, close to the border with the Reich, fixed bribes are being paid to avoid punishment.

The Jewish Council in Radom was skillful and efficient. The Ghetto did not last for a long time there. The Poles also turned to the city court to settle their disputes with the Jews. At present there is a closed Ghetto in the city. When in a certain place the situation is particularly good, it happens that it leads to explosion.

In Warsaw it is forbidden to mention the word "Ghetto." Instead one is supposed to say "Jewish residence zone." We looked for Jews in the closed zone, but did not find any. In November 1940 the Ghetto was closed. One hundred and eleven persons suffering from contagious diseases were brought from Kaluszyn to Warsaw. People were ordered to leave the townlets of the region and go to Warsaw. The Jews thought then that their time had come.

Recently in Biala Podlaska and Biala (in Polesia) executions took place.

There are two Ghettos in Warsaw. They are connected by means of a street running through both of them. The street is blocked by a gate—three minutes for the passage of Jews and three minutes for the passage of Poles. There is a wall next to the Ghetto. The gate opposite the train station is used by the workers for smuggling. They smuggle people and goods in exchange for payment. Jewish children aged thirteen and fourteen pass through the roadblock and beg on the Polish side. They obtain soup and bring back with them various goods. They often stay there for the night.

Public organizations, newspapers, and such like had existed in Warsaw. Until April, the public and social life had been running a normal course. In April the Germans came with a list of names. They arrested mainly members of the Bund, shooting them on the spot. This stirred sad thoughts in the hearts of many.

I had had a long and cultural conversation with Linder, M.A.[10] On the same night he was murdered.

Warsaw is full of life. An impulsive city. There are more Jews there than ever. They have come there from Silesia and Pomerania.

A country of slaves is in the process of being created in Poland. A Pole loyal to the authorities can attain the post of deputy factory manager.

The Germans wanted to grant Poland self-government, but the Poles refused to accept the offer. The German governor, Frank, several times invited Baron Roniker[11] of the Polish Central Aid Organization and presented to him various proposals. The Baron turned them down. Frank told him that he, Roniker, probably maintained ties with the Polish government in London. Roniker replied that he had sought to achieve such ties, but, to his regret, he had not succeeded.

Municipal self-government exists in certain places in Poland. Schools are not free, however, from pressure and oppression. The nation of slaves must not merge into any other people. In the Reich they are barred from marrying German women. Sexual relations between Poles and Germans are forbidden.

1. Irena Adamovich, a Polish Catholic woman, then aged about thirty, had developed such close relations with members of the Zionist Hechalutz (Pioneers) in Warsaw that she was called "the Chalutzishe Shikse" (the pioneering gentile girl). In June and July 1942 she traveled from one Ghetto to another in German-occupied territories, passing information about life in the Ghettos. That June, in Kovno, she entered the Ghetto with a worker's brigade returning from the town, having first sewn on a yellow star. She spent a whole day meeting with members of Matzok, the Zionist underground group, in Avraham Tory's room. She was then shown the Ghetto institutions, and left for Siauliai on the following day. A few weeks later she returned to the Kovno Ghetto, bringing further information on events in Lithuania and Poland. On this second visit she delivered orally this report, which Avraham Tory appended to his diary on July 8, 1942. Irena Adamovich visited Israel in the 1960s, where she was greeted by Avraham Tory at his home in Tel Aviv and met several of her former Hechalutz acquaintances. She died in Poland.

2. In Vilna in October 1941, between 3,000 and 3,600 Yellow Cards were issued by the German labor department to Ghetto inmates employed in organizations and units located outside the Ghetto. This card, known as a *Schein,* granted immunity not only to the holder but also to wife (or husband) and up to two children aged fifteen or under. Many fictitious families were formed around those holders of certificates who did not have large enough families to make the fullest possible use of the certificate.

3. This episode took place on June 4, 1942, in the presence of the Jewish Council and thousands of Vilna Ghetto inhabitants. Six Jews were hanged; all were members of the black market underworld who had been found guilty of the murder of a Jew and the attempted murder of a Jewish policeman. The hanging took place after a judgment by the Vilna Ghetto court had been ratified by all the members of the Vilna Jewish Council on the day after the murder; Gens, the Vilna Ghetto strongman, acted quickly and without reporting to the Germans.

4. These executions were apparently never carried out.

5. A clandestine organization was established in the Vilna Ghetto in the autumn of 1941 by the Zionist parties and youth organizations. It was called The Roof or The Committee of Seven, after its members: Dr. Meir Dvorzecki; Sava Gurian of the Zionist Workers, later replaced by Israel Dimantman; Avraham Pinchuk, General Zionists (A); Chaim Trapido, General

Zionists (B); Abba Kovner, Hashomer Hazair; Joseph Glazman, Revisionists; and Shabtai Milkonowicki, Nonpartisan Zionists.

6. The members of the Vilna Jewish Council were Anatol Fried, a bank manager and assimi-lated Jew; Grisha Yashunski, a Bundist attorney who had fled from Warsaw; Yoel Fishman, a shoemaker and Bundist leader, who was a member of the Vilna community's prewar lead-ership board; Shabtai Milkonowicki, an attorney, deputy-president, and then president, of the Vilna Jewish community for many years between the wars; and G. Gochman (not Gutman as Avraham Tory wrote), an engineer. These men had been appointed to the Jewish Council of the Vilna Ghetto on September 7, 1941.

7. A total of 1,200 Jews had been murdered in Lida on June 10, and a further 5,000 on June 25. In Druja, 1,000 Jews were killed during an "action" in June. On June 14, 4,000 Jews were killed in Disna, and on June 19, 2,500 were killed in Glebokie. Resistance is now known to have occurred at least in Druja, Dzisna, Lida, and Glebokie, and in two other towns in White Russia that same month: Braslav (where 3,000 Jews were killed on June 3) and Slonim (where 10,000 were killed on June 29). The previous May, when 1,400 Jews were murdered in Zeludok, there were mass escapes to the woods from nearby Lida (12,000 killed on May 8) and from Stolbcy. On May 11, 3,000 Jews had been murdered in Werenow.

8. In 1942 the first night of Passover fell on April 2.

9. These kibbutzim were part of the prewar Hachshara system, for training young Jews for communal life in Palestine. Each of the principal Zionist youth organizations, Gordonia, Hashomer Hazair, and Dror, had an agricultural training center in Czestochowa.

10. Menachem Linder, an economist and demographer, was active in the Warsaw underground and was the founder of Icor (the Hebrew acronym for Yiddish Cultural Organization). He was murdered on April 18, 1942, a night when several dozen underground activists were murdered by the Germans.

11. Baron Adam Roniker had been head of a leading Polish social welfare organization during World War I. At the time of the Nazi occupation, he headed a similar organization, the Central Aid Organization. He also headed the Supreme Aid Organization, which brought together Polish, Jewish, and Ukrainian aid organizations.

JULY 8, 1942

Irena was in the Ghetto.

The commander of the Ghetto Guard has toured the Ghetto; he visited the hall of the Lituanika cinema, the new detention center for work-shirkers, and the apartments for the members of the Ghetto Guard near gate no. 1.

JULY 9, 1942

Mr. Michnowski and Miss Gerstein arrived in the Ghetto. Both of them some-how survived in Lazdijai. They hid in a peasant cowshed.[1]

A group of Jews were murdered in the Ninth Fort, including two boys aged fourteen.

1. Jews who had been hiding in various villages sometimes sought sanctuary in the Ghetto because they were unable to tolerate living like hunted animals. On this occasion, the two

people who arrived—the only survivors of Lazdijai, Avraham Tory's home town—had been eyewitnesses to the murder of his townspeople and of two of his sisters and their families. Both of these two eyewitnesses survived the war and now live in Israel.

JULY 10, 1942

Lipzer appointed Moshe Jatzkan as his representative. The latter is authorized to inspect all the Council departments and to obtain information on their activities.

JULY 11, 1942

A meeting of the Council was held, attended by Lipzer. It was proposed to him that the Council would retain its powers; all work-duty affairs would be brought before both the Council and Lipzer. Employees of the Ghetto administration would address only the Council; an appropriate circular has been promulgated by the Council. Only persons who have worked at the airfield will be granted cards of the city labor brigades.

Wiedmann came to visit the Ghetto and the Council offices. He was accompanied by four members of the Hitler Youth. One of the latter remarked mockingly: "Nothing can be obtained outside; the Jews have everything."

JULY 12, 1942

A flour mill has begun operating in the Ghetto.[1]

Last visits of Caspi to the Ghetto. Beider continues to hold a Gestapo pass.[2]

Every day the Lithuanians arrest dozens of Jews shopping in the city.[3]

1. Because of a labor shortage at the flour mills in the city, which had to supply flour both to the Germans and to the local Lithuanians, the Germans allowed a small, primitive flour mill to operate inside the Ghetto. There was great rejoicing at this opportunity to smuggle into the Ghetto more wheat than was officially permitted, and to mill it for the benefit of the Ghetto's inhabitants. This flour mill had previously operated illegally, under the auspices of the Council's welfare department.
2. Both Beider (who worked for Caspi) and Moshe Jatzkan (who worked for Lipzer), had Gestapo permits to leave the Ghetto and to go into Kovno unaccompanied.
3. Lithuanians pretended to be interested in buying items, or in bartering them for food; they would then take the items and hand over the Jewish owner to the police or the Gestapo.

JULY 13, 1942

Four Hebrew teachers have completed their work of sorting the books which had been confiscated in the Ghetto by the Rosenberg organization.

The Council awards prizes for good cultivation of the vegetable gardens.

Eight Jews have been brought to the Ghetto from Pilviskiai, where they had worked in the local fur factory. Apart from them, no Jews have been left there.[1]

1. In July 1941 there were 1,000 Jews in the village of Pilviskiai. Most of them were murdered in August and September 1941. Survivors who hid in farms in the region confirm that the eight who worked at the Tigras fur factory were transferred to the Kovno Ghetto.

JULY 14, 1942

A directive: inspection of parcels at the gate will be conducted by the Lithuanian policemen. The German policemen will oversee their work.

A meeting of the Council. The subject: rescuing two policemen, Krum and Shubitz, who are being held in the Ninth Fort. Until now they have saved themselves from death by giving false names.

Four Jews from Lodz have been brought to the Ghetto hospital for surgery. They had spent a long time in a labor camp.

JULY 15, 1942

Moshe Levin came to the Ghetto from Vendziogala.[1] He had been saved miraculously from the massacre there and had been hiding in the forest.

The Gestapo gave its permission to set up a criminal section attached to the Jewish police.

1. Most of the 400 Jews of Vendziogala, a small town in the Kovno district, were murdered between July and September 1941; only a few survived.

JULY 16, 1942

The Council imposed the penalty of three days' imprisonment or a ten-mark fine on twenty Ghetto inmates who failed to abide by the instruction of the sanitation department to disinfect themselves of lice.

Wiedmann issued an announcement: permission to walk on the city streets outside the Ghetto without being accompanied by a guard is issued only by the city governor or the Gestapo; all other permits are no longer valid.[1]

1. Workplaces, mainly military, had begun to issue permits to leave the Ghetto unaccompanied. This had incurred Wiedmann's wrath.

JULY 16, 1942

DOCUMENT:

From Wiedmann, City Governor's Office
To the German Ghetto Guard, Kovno-Vilijampolé, for delivery to the
Jewish Council

It must be publicly announced that workplaces in the city are not authorized to issue certificates to Jewish workers entitling them to walk through the streets without supervision.

Jewish workers are not permitted to ask their employer for such certificates, and must also draw the attention of their employer to this effect. If Jewish workers are found with such certificates on them, they will be handed over to the Gestapo for punishment.

Certificates for walking through the streets may only be issued by the city governor or the Gestapo.[1]

> 1. A note at the bottom of this document states: "For immediate action and publication. Katein, SS company commander."

JULY 17, 1942

Two women, who had been in prison, returned to the Ghetto.

In compliance with the directive issued by the German Labor Office, fifty Jewish workers from the Ghetto have been dispatched to Jonava for work there.[1]

> 1. Jonava was a town in the Kovno district with about 3,000 Jewish residents; in August 1941 about 2,500 of them were murdered. In September 1941 a deputation of the surviving Jews of Jonava traveled to Kovno to ask for help in raising 100,000 marks to pay a ransom to the Lithuanians. All those Jews remaining in military barracks in Jonava were marched to Kovno on October 4, 1941, apparently so as to add them to the inhabitants of the small Ghetto to be executed at the Ninth Fort. They arrived at midnight, however, after the "action" had been completed, and were placed in the large Ghetto. Since no Jews remained in Jonava in July 1942, Jewish workers were sent there from Kovno.

JULY 18, 1942

The Epstein family left (illegally) for the Vilna Ghetto in a truck which had arrived from Vilna.

Wiedmann forbade Lipzer—via the commander of the Ghetto Guard—to open an office or to intervene in the affairs of the Council; he may involve himself only in labor matters.

Five women, who had been imprisoned in the Ninth Fort, returned to the Ghetto.

JULY 19, 1942

Israel Berlin, fifty-two, committed suicide by hanging himself. Lately he had been apathetic to his surroundings.

JULY 20, 1942

The Council introduced changes in the status and the role of the Jewish police: from now on the Jewish police is authorized to handle the criminal and civil affairs of the Ghetto inmates. In the past those matters had been the prerogative of the Jewish Ghetto court.

JULY 21, 1942

Goldin arrived in the Ghetto from the peat labor camp, for a two-day break. He conveyed greetings from the Radvilishok camp, where Jews are employed at digging peat, and from the local Ghetto.[1]

> 1. Radviliskis (in Yiddish, Radvilishok) was an important railway junction in central Lithuania. In July 1941 there were 250 Jewish families there; most were killed that summer, after being moved to an abandoned army camp. A few remained in the Ghetto and labor camp.

JULY 22, 1942

Night inspection of work-shirkers.

Sixteen Jewish workers have been seriously injured in an accident involving two trucks. They were on their way from the Ghetto to their place of work in Kybartai.[1]

Rabbi Shmukler and Rabbi Snieg recited "Eicha" (Lamentations) in the Council office.[2]

Conversation between Wiedmann and the members of the Council concerning goods which had not been supplied to the Ghetto. Wiedmann announced that issuing demands is a nasty act. He himself knows what is to be done.

> 1. Kybartai, a small town on the German border; its Jewish community of about 200 Jews had been murdered in the summer of 1941.
> 2. That day was the eve of Tisha B'Av (the Ninth of Av—a fast day), of the year 5702 of the Jewish calendar, a day of mourning and lamentation over the two destructions of the Temple in Jerusalem (the first by the Chaldeans, the second by the Romans). It was also the day of the publication in 1492 of the edict for the expulsion of the Jews from Spain.

JULY 23, 1942

Wiedmann issued a ban on bringing wood into the Ghetto on carts belonging to Christians. A way was found to get around the ban: a Jewish cart-driver would climb onto the cart at the gate, unload the wood within the Ghetto bounds, and return the cart to the peasant waiting at the gate.

At night an air-raid alarm was sounded.

JULY 24, 1942

The Gestapo issued an order: pregnancy in the Ghetto is forbidden. Every pregnancy must be terminated. An eighth- or ninth-month pregnancy may be completed. From September on, giving birth is strictly forbidden. Pregnant women will be put to death.

An unexpected visit from Irena.[1]

The commandant of the Ghetto Guard, Katein, completed his tour of duty. The new commandant is Tiele.[2]

1. Irena Adamovich, who had earlier visited the Ghetto on July 8.
2. Tiele had been commander of the Ghetto guard corps just over a month earlier, before being succeeded by Katein.

JULY 25, 1942

The commandant of the Ghetto Guard ordered that bushes by the Vilija river be uprooted. It appears that a Christian parachutist had been hiding there.

Caspi leaves for Vilna. He came into the Ghetto to say goodbye.

JULY 26, 1942

The Lithuanians are spreading rumors that the Ghetto will be liquidated. It is said that the Jews will be transferred to Petrasun, Kacergin,[1] or other places. An atmosphere of unrest in the Ghetto.

A commission has been set up within the framework of the Jewish police, charged with defense against air bombardments. It is headed by the commandant of the Ghetto Guard.

1. Petrasiunai (in Yiddish, Petrasun) was a suburb of Kovno, the location of a paper factory, to which some of the books confiscated in the Ghetto had been taken. Kacergin was a summer resort not far from Kovno, on the Vilija river; it had been a popular resort for Jews between the wars. During the time of the Kovno Ghetto, a Jewish labor brigade from the Ghetto worked there at felling trees and loading logs on barges.

JULY 27, 1942

The Council had a talk with the German director of the workshops, Peschel, regarding food supply.
Rumors about Jews still alive in the Provienishok labor camp.[1]

  1. Pravieniskis (in Yiddish, Provienishok), a railway station twenty kilometers from Kovno in the direction of Vilna, was the location of a labor camp for criminals. The Germans took Jews to this camp from various Ghettos, employed them for a while, and then murdered them.

JULY 28, 1942

The Gestapo sent twelve Jews to the Ninth Fort (Michnicki, Izraelit, and others). They had been arrested for various offenses.

JULY 29, 1942

The Council distributed a circular letter to physicians and midwives announcing the requirement to terminate pregnancies.
A society called Aid for the Needy and Hungry in the Ghetto has been founded. The founder is Mrs. Krumer.

JULY 30, 1942

Lately, the Ghetto inmates have been somewhat relieved of concern over the food supply. The guards at the entrance gate have not been very strict. The Germans received an order to leave the control of the entrance gate to the Lithuanians, whereas the Germans are required to oversee them and refrain from taking anything for themselves. Seeing the indifference of the Germans, the Lithuanians also lost their willingness to confiscate goods passing through the gate. They could not enjoy their spoils, as every article confiscated at the gate must be brought to the German Ghetto Guard.

As a consequence, a more relaxed atmosphere pervades the Ghetto gate, and the inmates sense this. The prices of various goods have gone down and—the main thing—the inmates have something to eat. There are no hungry people in the Ghetto anymore.

Better crops of various vegetables further improved the situation. Extensive work invested in the cultivation of vegetable plots in the Ghetto now bears fruit. We can be proud of the extensive experience acquired by the Council's gardening department. The results are pleasing, particularly in view of the accusation that the Jews are strangers to agriculture. The German local authorities and the Gestapo have had to acknowledge that the vegetable gardens in the Ghetto are better cultivated than those in the city.

The Jewish genius, and the talent displayed by the Jewish people for adapting themselves to any conditions, have been given an expression in the form of cultivation of vegetable plots and fields in the Ghetto.

Before the Ghetto was set up, Kelzon, an agronomist, had been working as director of the Jewish People Bank. Now, in the Ghetto, he has rediscovered his original vocation, even though it was a calamity which forced him to take up his agricultural profession again. He started putting his professional knowledge into practice.[1]

When I asked him where his practical knowledge of the cultivation of vegetable gardens came from, as he had been working in the banking business for twenty years, he replied: "Even when I was active in banking, I followed with great interest the literature and the developments in agricultural research; now I can put this knowledge to use for the benefit of the people in the Ghetto."

The weather this year has been propitious for gardening and, as a result, we have achieved good crops.

Only now do the Kovno Jews appreciate the importance of vegetables and the cultivation of the gardens. This is why no one damages the vegetable gardens, and why unripe vegetables are not harvested. Everyone knows that the food supply to scores of people is at stake and that it should be nurtured and protected. The vegetable gardens are not fenced, owing to the shortage of planks and steel wire. It is enough to put up a sign reading Organization of Garden Watchers, on behalf of groups of youngsters who have volunteered to watch the vegetable gardens.

Unfortunately, rumors spread again last week about harsh edicts lying in store for the Ghetto after a long period of respite. The rumors say that all the Jews are to be transferred from the Ghetto to Petrasun, and that huts are being built there for that purpose.

According to other news, on July 24, 1942, all the Jews—some 1,200—were deported from Königsberg to the territories in the east, and only four or five families are left in the city.

Other news, no less worrisome: (1) Beginning on the first of the next month, money belonging to the Jews will be confiscated; each family will be allowed only 100 marks. (2) The Ghetto area will be reduced by subtracting a sizable area from it (Demokratu Street). This street was once cut off from the Ghetto in the past, but was reincorporated some time later. (3) The Lodz Jews who had been employed at the construction of the Kovno-Vilna highway and were transferred to Riga will be replaced by 500 workers from the Ghetto.

This news has caused great concern among the Ghetto inmates. As a result the merchants have raised prices of goods. People are asking: will the era of deportations and executions begin again?

Until now the Jews have not been pleased with their life in the Ghetto. The chances of improvement in the foreseeable future have looked grim. But even under the present conditions no one is willing to wander from place to place—like disembodied souls restlessly roaming the world.

To this one should add the recent changes: the appointment of Lipzer as Gestapo liaison with the Council, and the departure of Caspi. These changes caused great concern among the members of the Council. They wanted to hear those rumors being denied, to know whether they might be believed at all.

After the consultation with L.,[2] the Council asked him to find out at Gestapo headquarters how true those rumors were. The answer from there was that "those rumors are without substance and in all probability are being spread by the Lithuanians. Their purpose is to distract the attention of the Germans from the Lithuanian matters and turn it toward the treatment of the Jews. The persons responsible for spreading those rumors will be punished."

Five Jews who risked their lives by escaping from a labor camp, where they had been employed at highway construction, arrived in the Ghetto, having traveled by various routes. The inmates of this labor camp had been transferred by road to Riga, and fifty Jews escaped during the transfer. As they jumped off the trucks, they were shot at. Two of the escapees waded into the river and remained hiding there, submerged in the water up to their necks. After the first danger passed, they entered the forest and hid there. Then they traveled by roundabout paths until they reached Kovno. In Kovno, they blended into a group of Jewish workers and returned with them to the Ghetto. They had hardly any clothes on, were barefoot, hungry, and frightened; for a year and a half they had endured heavy labor at road construction and at the harbor. Recently it had been particularly difficult for them. They suffered from starvation and from backbreaking labor. Everything they owned they had exchanged for a slice of bread. They had covered themselves with threadbare clothes, which turned into rags.

The camp commandant pretended to be the friend of workers. In fact, he disposed of everyone who, for different reasons, fell behind in his work. One day twenty people were killed by injections of poison, having been told beforehand that they were exhausted and sick and needed some rest. Those who asked to be taken to a physician were taken to the forest and shot. Only four inmates were brought to the Ghetto hospital for surgery; there they remain as of now.

The Council extended assistance to the inmates of this labor camp. This assistance was of some help. But the inmates were desperate and availed themselves of every opportunity to flee, despite the risk to their lives.

Fifteen of those people are now in the Ghetto. First, they were cleaned of lice at the lice disinfection center. They have also received clothes, which enable them to conceal their condition and status in the Ghetto. They must also be protected from the evil eye. At the same time, however, they present the Council with a problem: should the Gestapo find out about their presence in the Ghetto, their fate will be one and the same—death.

Today I received a letter from a person living in a nearby townlet. He cries for help. He has been hiding for a long time, together with his family; they are hidden in a barn. One of them was taken ill and died of consumption. Two others were caught and murdered. Several others were caught but were later released, having converted to Christianity. The remainder converted also, but the peasants in the area refuse to regard them as Christians.

They cry for help. Recently, letters such as these are not uncommon. I have received many such letters. Their content is nearly identical: their authors long to live in a Jewish milieu, among Jews. They are prepared to share the Jewish fate—come what may.

The "ingathering of exiles" from the neighboring townlets to the Kovno Ghetto has begun. But nobody knows whether these people will find physical and spiritual shelter here.

Recently, close ties have been formed between the Council and Peschel, the German director of the Ghetto workshops. They are based on matters of practical interest to both parties. Needless to say, the Ghetto workshops are of crucial importance. Ever since the workshops were removed from under the control of the Council and placed under the German city governor, various enterprises need materials, machine parts, and various services provided by the Council and its institutions. The system of obtaining permits for raw materials places a heavy burden on their orderly operation. There are no private entrepreneurs who could get hold of materials and various services for the industry. In such cases the requests are passed on to the Council, which finds ways to obtain the needed materials and services from the Ghetto inmates, or in the city, or from Lithuanian acquaintances, at a reasonable price.

Thus, for example, Peschel, the German director of the Ghetto workshops, has turned to Garfunkel with an urgent request to procure for him eleven small-size spools for sewing machines. Without these parts he will not be able to complete a large order placed by the German Army. He is embarrassed, he said, since, by working through the usual channels—i.e., by placing an order through the government agencies—he cannot procure the required part. As usual, the Council did all it could and procured them. Mr. Peschel was very pleased and prepared to help the Jewish institution; this is very important.

Jewish entrepreneurship, and the ability of Jews to adapt themselves to any situation, made possible the setting up of the large workshops in the Ghetto.

But after those workshops had been set up and were operating smoothly, the German managers believed there was no longer a need for the Council. The reality has often demonstrated, however, that the Jewish talents are nonetheless crucial for the orderly operation of those enterprises.

The chief inspector at the airfield, General Geiling, visited Dr. Elkes in his apartment.[3]

Five Jews from the labor camp near Vievis[4] arrived in the Ghetto. They were given clothes and underwear.

The Gestapo has denied the unsettling rumors which again spread in the Ghetto.

A fee of fifty pfennigs has been set for an application to adopt a child.

1. Shlomo Kelzon, a Zionist activist and a leader of Jewish cooperativism in prewar Lithuania, had been appointed by the Council to supervise the public vegetable gardens in the Kovno Ghetto.
2. "L." was Lipzer, through whom the Council frequently tried to clarify rumors.
3. When no other Germans were present, General Geiling treated Dr. Elkes respectfully. His visits to Elkes were concerned with the German need for extra manpower for work at the airport.
4. Vievis, a small town on the road from Kovno to Vilna, had 350 Jewish residents before the war. Most of them had been murdered by October 1941, and Jews from other towns were taken to work at the nearby labor camp.

JULY 31, 1942

A conversation between Wiedmann and Golub, in the presence of Ghetto Commandant Tiele, who was interested in the composition of the Council.

At 10 P.M. Ghetto Commandant Tiele asked to be provided with pornographic literature.[1]

1. It was the duty officer of the Jewish Ghetto police who reported this demand to the Council.

AUGUST 1, 1942

Beider, Lipzer's right hand, has been appointed as the police sanitation official at the request of the Gestapo.

AUGUST 2, 1942

An announcement on behalf of the Council: it is permitted to add the first name and the surname of the deceased, in addition to the number written on the wooden planks serving as tombstones.[1]

Two sisters have arrived in the Ghetto from Skaudvilé.[2] They were saved by a miracle. Until now they have been hiding in peasant houses.

1. In the early period of the existence of the Ghetto, the Germans prohibited inscriptions and even names from being placed on graves, which were registered by number, but with no indication of the number at the graveside itself. They later permitted stakes bearing the numbers to be fixed by the graves. In August 1942 they agreed to permit the full name of the deceased to be written next to the number.

2. Skaudvilé, a small town in western Lithuania, almost all of whose 1,000 Jews had been murdered in the summer of 1941.

AUGUST 3, 1942

Krum and Schubitz have been brought back from the Ninth Fort. Both were sentenced to death, but as they were about to be taken out of their dungeon in the fort for execution, they did not answer when their names were called out. In this way they saved themselves from death.

Wiedmann completed his tour of duty.

AUGUST 4, 1942

Instead of ten tons of bread, the Ghetto has been supplied with two tons of rotten cabbage. Wiedmann referred us to the German director of the nutrition office, but they chase the Jews away from there; only the Germans are allowed to enter.[1]

General Wysocki, commander of the police in Lithuania, paid a visit to the Ghetto.[2] He came to see the Ghetto Guard, the workshops, the German labor office, and other establishments.

1. For six weeks, the Ghetto was given rotten sauerkraut to eat instead of bread. All requests to the Ghetto commander were fruitless, until Wiedmann agreed to instruct a representative of the Council to turn to the supply department of the German civil administration. Avraham Tory went there, accompanied by a German guard, and entered the building, in spite of the fact that entry was permitted to Germans and Lithuanians only. He was quickly driven from the building, amid much kicking and shouting.

2. SS General Lucian Damianus Wysocki, commander general of the German police in Lithuania, was commander of the SD (security service), the SIPO (security police), the ORPO (public order police), and the Lithuanian police throughout Lithuania.

AUGUST 4, 1942

DOCUMENT: Circular of the Jewish Council, signed by Dr. Elkes, concerning the introduction of the duty to keep a Ghetto pass

Beginning on August 5, 1942, each Ghetto inhabitant will have an identity card—a Ghetto pass.

As from that day, the identity of a person must be established on the basis of this identification alone. The Ghetto pass will contain the family name, first name, father's name, and the birthday or age and address of the holder.

In order to avoid misunderstandings or errors, all Council departments are obliged to ask for the identification document when examining and establishing the identity of a person, and to take down its number whenever required. This will particularly apply:

> for the submission of requests
> for the issue of confirmations, certificates, etc.
> for the payment of money
> for the issue of foodstuffs
> for the compilation of minutes, the opening of files, etc.
> for the issue of orders for apartments

and in every other case for which the establishment of the identity of the person is important. Besides these general cases, each Council department will use these identification documents in the following ways:

1. *Food Administration.* The numbers of the identification documents must be registered in the lists of customers, and other lists, of all shops and enterprises of the food administration. This must be done within one month. Furthermore, the numbers must also be entered on the firewood distribution cards.

2. *Labor Office.* The numbers of the identification cards must be registered in the card index of the labor office. When new working cards for the city, and new airport cards, are issued in future, the number of the identification card must be entered in these cards. When leave or exemption certificates are issued, the number of the identification card must be entered.

3. *Social Welfare Office.* The numbers of the identification card must be entered in the card included in the card index of all recipients of social benefits. Existing personal data must be corrected, if required, according to the identification card. Whenever benefits are issued—foodstuffs, articles, money, or similar items—the identity of the recipient must be established by means of the identification card.

4. *Health Office.* When sick persons are admitted to the hospital, their identification number must be entered in the admission register.

In the lists of sick persons sent to the food administration by the hospital, for the receipt of their food rations, the identification number of the sick person must be marked, in order to avoid any misunderstanding in the subsequent settling of the accounts of the sick person by the food administration.

5. *Police.* Whenever minutes, reports, or other important documents are compiled, the identification card must be asked for, and the number of the identification card must be marked.

The identity of the person in control of the work, as in any other cases when identification must be established, must be checked against the relevant identification card.

In the lists of arrested persons sent to the food administration for the receipt of their food rations, the identification number of the arrested person must be marked, in order to avoid misunderstandings in the subsequent settling of the accounts of the arrested person by the food administration.

6. *Registration Office.* The details in the card index of Ghetto inhabitants must be corrected according to the details in the identification cards.

Whenever birth, marriage, death, or any other certificates are issued, identification must be asked for, and the identification number marked on the certificate concerned.

7. *Housing Department.* Whenever orders for living rooms, or similar dwelling space, are issued, the identification numbers of those for whom the order is issued must be entered in the order.

8. *Office of Economic Affairs.* Whenever money is paid, or articles issued, the identity of the person to whom the payment or distribution is made must be checked by means of the identification cards.

9. *Department of Education.* At the time of admission to schools, the identification numbers must be marked in the admission registers.

AUGUST 5, 1942

The Council has made it mandatory for the Ghetto inmates to carry with them the Ghetto identity card at all times.

At night a search for shirkers of work-duty took place.

In the Ninth Fort there are now a number of Jews who had converted to Christianity: Milowicki, Schwarz—who had been living in Kovno with his Christian wife for more than twenty years; and Narak (from the Siauliai region) who had in his possession documents certifying to his being a Christian; he himself was a Lithuanian partisan in the townlet of Prienai,[1] where he had shot Jews.

1. Prienai, a small town on the River Nieman, most of whose 1,000 Jews were murdered on August 26, 1941.

AUGUST 6, 1942

At 5 P.M. Wiedmann, accompanied by Koeppen[1] who is to replace him, paid a visit to the Council. Wiedmann introduced Koeppen to the members of the Council. He also confirmed the composition of the Council: chairman, Dr. Elkes; deputy chairman, Garfunkel; advisor, Goldberg; secretary, Golub.[2]

1. Erich Koeppen was appointed Ghetto commander for a short time, between Wiedmann and Miller. He was much feared by the Jews of the Ghetto, having earlier been active in murdering Jews in the townlets of Lithuania.
2. Koeppen thus removed from the Council rabbis Snieg and Shmukler, as well as Rostovski, Levin, and Rabinovitz. All five nevertheless continued to take part in its meetings.

AUGUST 7, 1942

A letter from Koeppen confirmed in writing the composition of the Council: chairman, Dr. Elkes; deputy chairman and advisor, L. Garfunkel; advisor, I. Goldberg; secretary, A. Golub. The Council is responsible for managing the internal affairs of the Ghetto.

Rauca, accompanied by Garfunkel, toured the institutions of the Ghetto. During the tour he noticed a pregnant woman, in her seventh month. Rauca said: "This embryo must perish. If not, it will be taken away from its mother right after birth."

The first anniversary of large-scale arrests and abductions of Jews on the streets of Kovno (August 7, 1941).[1]

1. There is no reference in Avraham Tory's diary for this date to the seizure that day in the Ghetto, by Lithuanian partisans, of 1,200 Jewish men, of whom 900 were shot and 300 released.

AUGUST 8, 1942

Soon after their appointment the members of the Council—Garfunkel, Goldberg, and the secretary, Golub—visited Dr. Elkes for a preliminary consultation. Dr. Elkes said: "The fewer the number of Council members, the more duties; we must be prepared for greater sacrifices."

A commission, composed of senior German officials, toured the Ghetto and the workshops.

The commandant of the Ghetto, Tiele, announced that paying respects to Germans by a military salute is forbidden. Even policemen working at the labor office, and others, must pay their respects by taking off their cap.

AUGUST 8, 1942

DOCUMENT:
From the Ghetto Guard
To the Council of the Jewish Ghetto community in Kovno-Vilijampolé

Upon higher authority I inform you as follows:

It is hereby forbidden to all Ghetto inhabitants to pay their respects by means of a military salute. Members of the Ghetto police, the Ghetto fire brigade, and the Ghetto labor exchange, as well as all other Ghetto officials, must pay their respects in the morning by lifting their caps, and on all other occasions by standing to attention.

I take this opportunity to emphasize again that all male inhabitants of the Ghetto must cover their heads at all times.[1]

1. This order was signed "Tiele, SS company commander, German Ghetto Guard, Vilijampolé."

AUGUST 10, 1942

The Gestapo has issued a demand to provide information about the number of people who died in the Ghetto from January 1, 1942, until today (apart from those arrested or taken to the Ninth Fort).

The Council has received an official letter from the city governor approving the new composition of the Council.

AUGUST 11, 1942

The Council has opened a laundry near the office of economic affairs.[1]

1. The laundry at the large workshops, established by the Council in the very early days of the Ghetto, worked mainly for the German Army. The new laundry was needed for the Ghetto itself.

AUGUST 12, 1942

Wienkelstein, a Jew from Marijampolé,[1] has been released from the Ninth Fort. He had been hiding in Marijampolé for quite some time. Recently he was arrested by the Gestapo on a road near the Ghetto, on his way from Marijampolé.

1. Marijampolé, a town in central Lithuania, most of whose 3,500 Jews were murdered in July 1941; there were only a few survivors.

AUGUST 13, 1942

The Council has opened a mental asylum under the auspices of the health office, located in an isolated and hidden house.[1]

An extended consultation at the city governor's concerning the affairs of the Ghetto. Attending: the representatives of the Gestapo, the representatives of the German labor office, and the representatives of all the institutions at which Jews are working. This is a sign boding a stricter regime for the Ghetto and is the reason for a new wave of unrest in the Ghetto.

1. Only five or six patients were ever treated at this mental hospital—in fact, a small hut—a tiny figure in view of the suffering of the 16,000 remaining Jews of Kovno.

AUGUST 14, 1942

Two Jews from Vilna are visiting the Kovno Ghetto. They have conveyed heartfelt greetings from the Vilna Ghetto.

The city governor, Cramer, Koeppen, and a number of senior officials have visited the Council offices and the Ghetto.

Eglin has been relieved of his duties at the Gestapo. He was deprived of his privilege of walking in the city without the yellow badge.[1]

The orthopedic specialist Dr. Heuer and his family, who until now have lived in the city, have been ordered to transfer to the Ghetto.[2]

1. This privilege was granted to extremely few, and was almost always subsequently taken away.
2. Dr. Heuer, a refugee from Vienna in 1938, had become at that time a specialist physician to the Lithuanian elite. Until August 1942 he had been allowed to live in Kovno with his family.

AUGUST 15, 1942

The Jewish labor office has opened a detention center in the Ghetto, located in the synagogue at 23 Krisciukaicio Street. It is designed for those who shirk their work-duty.

AUGUST 16, 1942

A criminal section has been set up at the Jewish police, replacing the former Jewish Ghetto court.

AUGUST 17, 1942

A family of four people has moved from the Kovno Ghetto into the Siauliai Ghetto—quite an unusual occurrence.

Dr. Heuer and his family have moved from the city into the Ghetto.

AUGUST 18, 1942

The first anniversary of the deportation of 534 men from the Ghetto by the Gestapo. They did not return to their homes.

Koeppen has issued a directive: permits for going into the city will be deposited with the Ghetto Guard. Anyone going to the city will first report to the commandant and upon his return return the permit to the Ghetto Guard.

At night: defense exercises against air bombardments.

AUGUST 19, 1942

The Council has ordered the Jewish Police to lower the prices of goods in the Ghetto.

AUGUST 20, 1942

At 3 P.M. Koeppen and Keiffler[1] came to the Council and confiscated money from the cashbox (31,000 marks). They left only 5,000 marks. The Council stopped all payments for today.[2]

A demand has been issued to send 700 workers from the Ghetto to Linkaiciai,[3] to Riga, and to Lake Ilmen near Leningrad. The Council is going to great lengths to have this edict revoked.

1. Keiffler, Cramer's deputy city governor, was the supervisor of supply at the German civil administration.
2. In August 1942, all forms of education in the Ghetto were prohibited, bringing food from the city to the Ghetto was forbidden, and the Ghetto's monetary economy was brought to an end. Leib Garfunkel later recalled that the Council treasury had, officially, the sum of 35,000 marks, which was confiscated, but that the Council succeeded in hiding a further sum of 25,000 marks from the Germans and maintained a secret treasury with it. In practice, the German prohibition against financial dealings had begun with the confiscation of Jewish property immediately after the establishment of the Ghetto in August 1941, but in the year that followed the Council had collected fees, sold medicine, and used its money to bribe Germans and Lithuanians and to purchase raw materials for the workshops. The reorganization which Koeppen decided to carry out in the Ghetto affected all its inhabitants and seriously impeded the Council's ability to conduct its affairs.
3. Linkaiciai (in Yiddish, Linkeitz), a labor camp halfway between Kovno and Siauliai; the German Army had warehouses and factories there.

AUGUST 21, 1942

The city governor has given permission for Dr. Heuer to receive Lithuanian patients in the Ghetto.

Lithuanian community leaders have confirmed that there was a plan to transfer the Jews from Slobodka to some other place. This plan no longer exists.

Koeppen has announced that, beginning on August 26, a strict ban on bringing goods into the Ghetto will be enforced.

AUGUST 22, 1942

The deputy city governor, Keiffler, together with Koeppen, called on the Council. They ordered the Council not to receive money for goods and firewood.

AUGUST 23, 1942

The Ghetto inmates have put strong pressure on the Council to allow them to leave the Ghetto together with the brigades[1] in order to bring goods from outside, since after August 26 bringing goods into the Ghetto will be practically impossible.

1. "Brigades" was the name given to the labor groups in the Ghetto; these groups left the Ghetto each morning for the city or nearby workplaces and returned to the Ghetto each evening. While they were outside the Ghetto, workers in the brigades could purchase food, either for money or by bartering goods; these acts were forbidden, and could be punished by arrest and even execution.

AUGUST 24, 1942

The Council has issued a directive: every Ghetto inmate is required to hand over all medicines in his possession to the Ghetto pharmacy.

AUGUST 25, 1942

DOCUMENT:
From SA Colonel Cramer
To the Jewish Council

Order no. 1

As from August 26, 1942, a new regulation concerning the supply of food to the Jews will be enacted:

1. The ration allocated to the Ghetto inmates will be put at the disposal of the Council and will comprise per week per person: bread, 700 g.; meat, 125 g.; flour, 112.5 g.; nourishment, 75 g.; salt, 50 g.

2. The Council is in charge of the just and proper distribution, without payment, of these quantities.

3. After receipt of the weekly rations, the German manager of the Ghetto workshops must immediately be informed, so that he can check the quantitative and qualitative condition of the foodstuffs.

4. In addition to the rations mentioned above, the working part of the Jewish population will be granted an extra ration.

5. The extra rations will consist until further notice of: bread, 700 g.; meat, 125 g., fat, 25 g. per person per week.

6. The additional rations will be distributed directly at the workplaces.

7. In special cases, the additional rations, together with a list of names, will be sent to the Council, which is responsible for the speedy distribution of rations to those entitled to receive them.

8. Any arbitrary acquisition of foodstuffs is prohibited forthwith.

9. Any attempt in the future to bring any foodstuffs into the Ghetto will be severely punished.

AUGUST 25, 1942

DOCUMENT:
From SA Colonel Cramer
To the Jewish Council

Order no. 2

The Ghetto in Kovno is subordinated to the exclusive administration of the city governor. The city governor provides the Ghetto with all the necessary foodstuffs and consumer goods. The Council, as well as individuals, are not allowed to pursue on their own a provisions-supply economy. Particularly to be observed are the following instructions:

1. The nourishment of the Ghetto inmates is regulated by Order no. 1 of today. Foodstuffs will be delivered weekly at the expense of the city governor to the Council, which must distribute them to all those who are entitled to receive them without pay.

2. The supply of working clothes, shoes, etc., to the Ghetto inhabitants is also secured by the city governor. The most urgent demand for these commodities must be presented at the beginning of each month by the Council to the city governor's Ghetto administration department. The Council must guarantee an equal supply to all the Ghetto inhabitants. Working Jews will get preference as far as the distribution of work clothes and shoes is concerned.

3. Every money transaction in the Ghetto is hereby prohibited. The treasury and the cash department of the Council are forthwith disbanded. The Council is forthwith forbidden to impose any taxes or fees, to pay salaries and wages, or to ask for any payment for the commodities supplied by the city governor.

4. All public facilities in the Ghetto, such as the pharmacy, the hospital, ambulances, the bathing and delousing institution, workshops and repair shops, etc., are the property of the city governor.

All the supplies and services of these facilities to the inhabitants of the Ghetto are provided gratis. Existing schools must be closed immediately, and the personnel employed in the schools must be transferred immediately to compulsory labor. Any teaching, as well as any religious training, is forthwith prohibited.

5. The total demand for materials needed by all public facilities in the Ghetto must be presented at the first of each month, separately for each facility, to the city governor's Ghetto administration department.

6. The offices of the Council, including the departments of housing, labor, nutrition, and economy, the police and fire brigade, the health and registration offices, and the social welfare departments, will remain. The education office, however, must be closed immediately.

AUGUST 25, 1942

Koeppen and Keiffler summoned the members of the Council to the workshops. They confiscated the remainder of the money to be found in the Council's Treasury and announced orders no. 1 and no. 2; the money economy in the Ghetto is to be abolished and the Council banned from operating a money economy; it is forbidden to pray in public in the Ghetto; goods must not be brought into the Ghetto; schools will be closed down. The entire property of the Council is thereby declared as the property of the city governor.

Schtitz of the Gestapo, accompanied by Lipzer, visited the Council. Rumors about transferring Jews from the Ghetto to another place are devoid of substance. The new directives issued by the city governor will not have an adverse effect on the attitude of the Gestapo toward the Ghetto and its residents. Lipzer's duty to oversee the labor force in the Ghetto remains in force.

At 4 P.M. the Gestapo conducted searches in the houses of people occupying important posts in the labor office. The searches followed a denunciation by a letter. Large quantities of supplies found in their apartments were brought to the Ghetto Guard. As the searches were under way, Bramson and Granovski[1] were called to report to the Ghetto Guard. Suspicion arose that they were not without blame in this whole affair. Unrest prevails in the Ghetto.

1. Michael Bramson had been the principal of a Hebrew high school before the war. A former officer in the Lithuanian Army, he served as deputy chief of the Jewish police. One of the first Jews to acquire a weapon in the Ghetto, he used it to train members of the underground. Granovski was also a member of the Jewish police. Both were under German suspicion of helping to smuggle food into the Ghetto.

AUGUST 26, 1942

DOCUMENT: SS Master Sergeant Rauca, Instruction

Following a denunciation, house searches will be made at the homes of the heads of the labor office and at the homes of Council members, who are accused of having large stocks of food.

AUGUST 27, 1942

Defense exercises against air bombardments took place during the night.

The Council has asked SS Colonel Jaeger to free the engineer Murin. He was arrested while attempting to bring valuables into the Ghetto from a provincial town. The request has been approved.

The Gestapo has conducted searches in the apartments of office directors and their deputies.

A commission in charge of closing down the education office has been appointed.

AUGUST 29, 1942

Nine Jews have arrived from the Vilna Ghetto. One of them, a woman, Mrs. Schein (her parents live in the Kovno Ghetto) was arrested by the Gestapo immediately upon her arrival and led away to the fort. The reason for the arrest— unknown. Meir Lev of the Vilna Jewish police is a secret police type.[1]

Murin has been released from the Ninth Fort.

Defense exercises against air bombardments were conducted during the night.

1. In February 1942 Meir Lev (Levas) had been put in charge of the Ghetto gate in Vilna. "The behavior of the Jewish police at the gate"—one historian has written, "the searches and the beatings—made them and their commander, Levas, the most hated group among the Jews of the Ghetto." Yitzhak Arad, *Ghetto in Flames: The Struggle and Destruction of the Jews in Vilna in the Holocaust* (Jerusalem, 1980), p. 305.

AUGUST 30, 1942

The German Ghetto Guard has been disbanded. From now on the guard duty will be in the hands of the Lithuanian policemen under the command of three officers of the Vienna defense police: Litschauer, Tzach, and Feuer.[1]

1. Litschauer had earlier been chief of police in Vienna. After commanding the Kovno Ghetto Guard he was transferred to the Ninth Fort. It became known to the inhabitants of the Ghetto that he stole money and valuables in exchange for promises of leniency, which were never kept. No details on Tzach and Feuer are available.

AUGUST 31, 1942

The German architect Wintzer,[1] director of the furniture factory, came to the Council accompanied by his mistress, Countess von Ravensburg. In his view, the Ghetto is a prison camp and its inmates are prisoners. At the same time, however, he treats the Jews with understanding and courteousness. He plans to set up a pottery workshop in the Ghetto.

At night: searches for those who have shirked their work-duty.

The Council has published a leaflet for Ghetto inmates, announcing the abolishment of the money economy in the Ghetto. The Council calls upon Ghetto inmates to abide by their work-duty.

1. Wintzer, an architect by profession, headed the workshops where furniture was made for Germans who had come to live in Lithuania as part of the Germanization of the Baltic States. These workshops came under the authority of the SS Office for Germanization by Settlement. Wintzer was also a member of the SS, but he seemed to the Ghetto inhabitants to be repelled by the deeds of the Nazis, and he treated the Jews humanely. He took little interest in the workshops, preferring to occupy himself with art and with his mistress, Countess Hilda von Ravensburg, a young, intelligent, and usually drunk woman. She also treated the Jews humanely.

SEPTEMBER 1, 1942

For the first time, the Council has submitted to the Germans thirteen lists of materials and appliances for the institutions and workshops in the Ghetto for the month of September. The city governor will allow the Council to buy them and to pay for them.

A conversation between Lipzer and the Gestapo chief, Jaeger; many denunciations written by Ghetto inmates have recently reached the Gestapo.

SEPTEMBER 2, 1942

Deputy Gestapo chief Schmitz toured the Council offices, the workshops, and the vegetable gardens. He promised that the situation in the Ghetto would remain stable.

The city governor set increased food rations, including those for employees of the Council and its institutions.

SEPTEMBER 3, 1942

The Gestapo has banned Dr. Heuer from treating Lithuanian patients.

The German director of the workshops, Modzievski, inspected the quantity and the quality of the foodstuffs supplied to the Ghetto.

For the first time, the Council allotted a quarter of a kilo of tomatoes to every person in the Ghetto. Great congestion at the vegetable distribution centers.

SEPTEMBER 4, 1942

The Council is pursuing an investigation against a number of Jewish policemen suspected of uprooting vegetables from the Ghetto vegetable gardens at night.

SEPTEMBER 5, 1942

A meeting of the Council; Garfunkel voiced a view favoring the disbanding of the Council due to lack of suitable conditions to enable it to operate in a respectable fashion. He suggested the appointment of new members to another Council who could fulfill Lipzer's wishes and act in compliance with his dictates. It was decided that resignation of the members of the Council might have dangerous consequences. For this reason it is not feasible.[1]

> 1. As Avraham Tory later recalled, Lipzer's interference had reached such a level that at this meeting Garfunkel proposed that the Council resign. After a stormy debate, it was decided that such a move would involve the irresponsible placing of the Ghetto in the hands of people devoid of any public or national consciousness. The Council thus continued to function as best it could with the same membership.

SEPTEMBER 6, 1942

Representatives of the labor office visited the swimming beach in the Ghetto.[1]

Physicians Akabas and Strassberg were dismissed from their jobs because they had picked cucumbers in the Ghetto vegetable gardens.

Cramer threatens to halt food supplies to the Ghetto for a period of eight days if the Ghetto fails to provide the required number of workers for the airfield.

> 1. Jews were allowed to bathe at the riverbank running along the Ghetto for two months during the summer of 1942. On the day of this diary entry, members of the Council's labor department checked to see if any "work-shirkers" were bathing at the river.

SEPTEMBER 7, 1942

General Wysocki and Captain Binger came to visit the Ghetto Guard. Binger delivered a virulently anti-Semitic speech to the Lithuanian policemen.

SEPTEMBER 8, 1942

The Council has issued an announcement about the ban on pregnancies in the Ghetto. From now on, the Germans declare that any pregnant woman will be killed on the spot.

SEPTEMBER 9, 1942

The Germans demand 250 workers to be sent to dig peat in Palemonas.

SEPTEMBER 10, 1942

The Council has set up a special police squad to watch over the vegetable gardens in the Ghetto. This unit is headed by Padison.[1]

An "action" in the area of the former small Ghetto, recently populated by Russian, Polish, and other women. Jewish workers were mobilized to help in the transfer.[2]

1. In view of previous disastrous experiences when mobs and individuals had descended on the vegetable gardens, Peretz Padison, a Jewish police officer, was placed in command of this unit. Padison, who had served in the Lithuanian Army before the war, was one of the first members of the Ghetto underground. He now lives in Israel.
2. One of the most humiliating and complex incidents to occur in the Kovno Ghetto: Jewish workers were forced to assist in moving non-Jews who, since the end of 1941, had been living in the former small Ghetto. The Germans thus created another reason for the local Lithuanians to hate the Jews.

SEPTEMBER 11, 1942

At night: recruitment of 150 Jewish workers for work in Palemonas.

Workers are required to show up for work on holy days.[1]

The new German workshops director, Hoenigman,[2] came for an introductory visit to the Council.

Rauca of the Gestapo made an inspection at the gate to be sure that the workers do not smuggle foodstuffs into the Ghetto from the city.

1. Rabbis and public figures urged the inhabitants of the Ghetto to report to work on Jewish holy days, since people had already been killed for failure to report to work on the principal Jewish festivals.
2. Hoenigman, a senior employee of the German civil administration, had replaced Modzievski as manager of the Ghetto workshops.

SEPTEMBER 12, 1942

News has reached us that Caspi was forced to leave Vilna. Some say that he was executed.[1]

A demand to send 600 Jewish workers to the airfield in Riga.

One hundred and five workers have been sent to Palemonas to dig peat.

Doctor Shilanski has committed suicide. He was seventy-five.

1. Rumors of Caspi's execution were false. It seems that, in order to save himself from execution, Caspi suggested to the Germans that he be allowed to set up an anticommunist propaganda office in Leningrad once that city had been captured. Leningrad, although besieged for more than two years, never fell to the Germans.

SEPTEMBER 13, 1942

A meeting of the Council on the subject of schools in the Ghetto: the plan is to set up a vocational training school with an expanded program of study which would include general subjects.[1]

All administrative employees are required to work one day a week at the airfield (circular issued by the Council).

1. The official function of the vocational training school was to train youngsters for the workshops; in practice, it was an ordinary primary school, which also taught technical studies, as a means of compensating for the closing down of the Ghetto schools that August. The vocational training school survived until the liquidation of the Ghetto in 1944. A wide range of cultural activities were conducted there. The school had been founded, and was headed, by the agronomist Jacob Oleiski, assisted by Mendel Sadovski. Oleiski survived the war and emigrated to Israel, where he headed the ORT network of vocational schools. He died in 1984.

SEPTEMBER 14, 1942

"The benches are not for you, brothers," said Koeppen to Kopelman and Golub. The latter were waiting in the hallway of the city governor's offices and had sat on one of the benches in the hallway.

Koeppen demands sixty additional workers to dig peat in Palemonas.

During the night, workers were recruited for Palemonas.

SEPTEMBER 15, 1942

The first anniversary of the distribution of the Jordan permits.

Koeppen has ordered the Council to prepare a report about the Jewish labor force to be presented to an important commission from Berlin. This commission is scheduled to visit the Ghetto in a few days.

SEPTEMBER 16, 1942

Unrest in the Ghetto caused by the coming visit of an important commission from Berlin. The Council has ordered a vigorous inspection of able-bodied residents, stoppage of traffic in the Ghetto streets, and a halt to bringing supplies from the city.

Rumors about a new reduction of the Ghetto area.

SEPTEMBER 17, 1942

First anniversary of the "trial action" on Sajungos Square in Slobodka.

Litschauer, commandant of the Ghetto Guard, came for a visit to acquaint himself with the Council.

SEPTEMBER 18, 1942

The city governor has approved the request submitted by the Council to reopen the vocational training school, under the supervision of Hermann.

A commission from Berlin toured the workshops in six cars.

SEPTEMBER 19, 1942

Koeppen toured the area between Demokratu and Vienozinskio Streets. This inspection caused confusion in the Ghetto. There is fear that this area will be cut off from the Ghetto.[1]

1. This area was cut off from the Ghetto on October 5, 1942, the evacuation having begun on September 25.

SEPTEMBER 20, 1942

Rabbi Shapiro has announced that, on the Day of Atonement, workers must appear to work.[1] He sent his wishes of "Gmar khatimah tova" (May you be sealed for a good Judgment), and granted a year of life and peace to all Ghetto inmates.

Despite the ban on praying in public, many *minyanim* (a prayer quorum of ten Jews) assembled in the Ghetto. The wording of "Hazkarat neshamot" (remembrance of souls) has been printed on a typewriter by the Council because of the shortage of prayer books and orders of prayer for the holy days.

"The pits are always open and the bullets are always ready for the Jews," said Spiez, the political deputy of the military construction corporation,[2] to engineer Yellin.

1. Avraham Tory, who took down the final wording of this announcement from Rabbi Shapiro, later recalled that anyone seeing the profound expression of pain on the face of the elderly rabbi would have been brokenhearted. Shapiro also permitted the weak, particularly women and the elderly, to eat on the Day of Atonement, a day of fasting.
2. Spiez was a kind of *politruk,* or political deputy, supervising the German employees and their political conduct. The military construction corporation made considerable use of manpower from the Ghetto.

SEPTEMBER 21, 1942

Koeppen and a German physician have visited the pharmacy.[1] They announced that the pharmacy may order only fifty items of medicines in the city each month, for some 17,000 Ghetto inmates.

Two Jewish workers, Katz and Ziv, have been arrested while working in Jonava. The arrest came as a result of denunciation by a Lithuanian policeman who said that the two Jews had talked to Soviet prisoners-of-war. The two have been taken away today to the Ninth Fort.

Because of the Day of Atonement, many workers fasted today in their work-places.

Today, the Day of Atonement, the director of the workshops, Hoenigman, visited the Council to discuss the issue of clothing. Later, Koeppen and a German physician inspected our health institutions. They went in the direction of the hospital, where a prayer meeting was taking place. The praying Jews were warned only at the last moment, but succeeded in dispersing before the Germans came.

1. The Ghetto pharmacy was under the management of the pharmacist Aizik Srebnitzki, a Labor Zionist and a member of the Zionist group in the Ghetto. He was active in helping those who left the Ghetto to hide in the woods and, later, to try to join Soviet partisan units. He was also entrusted with the clandestine radio, which he hid in the cellar of the pharmacy. After the visit of Irena Adamovich in the summer of 1942, this radio was used by an inner circle of underground activists.

SEPTEMBER 23, 1942

A concert of the symphonic orchestra took place as part of the children's festivities in the hall of the former yeshiva in Slobodka.[1]

A truck carrying flour was intercepted at the Ghetto gate. Kopel Gutman[2] and a policeman by the name of Feinberg were arrested. They were sent to the Gestapo.

1. The Ghetto orchestra functioned within the framework of the Ghetto police. The former Slobodka yeshiva building had been renovated, and the concert was held despite the strong opposition of many who claimed that such a concert desecrated the memory of those Jews who had been murdered. It was with considerable excitement and emotion that the audience had gathered in the yeshiva hall for this first concert of the Ghetto. As soon as the first notes were heard—the tune of Kol Nidrei (the Day of Atonement's opening prayer)—many in the audience burst into tears.
2. Kopel Gutman was the son of Rabbi Eliezer Gutman, a dealer in Jewish religious books in Kovno. This was an extremely daring smuggling attempt, both in scope (a truck full of flour) and in the way in which it was carried out. However, the guard who had been bribed had been changed by chance, and a senior officer of the Ghetto Guard happened to be at the gate.

SEPTEMBER 24, 1942

The policemen Grossman and Lifschitz have been arrested and taken to the Gestapo in connection with interception of a load of flour at the Ghetto gate yesterday.

SEPTEMBER 25, 1942

Evacuation of the area between the Demokratu and Vienozinskio streets has begun.

SEPTEMBER 26, 1942

At night: recruitment of workers for Palemonas.
The first anniversary of the "action" on Veliuonos Street.

SEPTEMBER 27, 1942

A special squad has been set up within the framework of the Jewish police. This unit is charged with watching the Ghetto gate and the detention center at 23 Krisciukaicio Street.

SEPTEMBER 28, 1942

Dr. Grigori Wolf, a former member of the Council and a well-known Jewish public figure in Kovno, died at 3 A.M. He was Isser Ber Wolf's son.[1]

Hermann is inspecting the situation of mobilization of workers in the Ghetto. Two Ghetto firemen were forced to go to Palemonas.

1. Isser Ber Wolf had been president of the Kovno Jewish community before the war.

SEPTEMBER 29, 1942

A labor squad of fifty workers left for Vilkaviskis.[1]

The commandant of the first police precinct, Grinberg, the policeman Reibstein, and a former policeman, Krieger, were taken to the Gestapo. They had been arrested in connection with interception of the load of flour at the Ghetto gate. Grinberg returned to his home in the evening. Reibstein and Krieger remain under arrest.

The city governor has issued Order no. 6: the deadline for the evacuation of residents from Vienozinskio Street has been extended until October 5, 1942, at noon.

Katz and Ziv have been released from the fort.

1. Vilkaviskis, a district capital in western Lithuania; most of its 3,000 Jewish residents were murdered between July and September 1941.

SEPTEMBER 30, 1942

During the night fifteen workers were recruited for Palemonas.

OCTOBER 1, 1942

Evacuation of residents from the Demokratu area has begun in compliance with the city governor's order.

The policeman Reibstein, together with Kopel Gutman, Krieger, and their families, was taken to the Fort. All of them were executed the same morning.[1]

Regulations have been set for the criminal section of the Jewish police. This section replaces the Jewish Ghetto court.

1. They were actually executed on October 17, 1942.

OCTOBER 2, 1942

Lithuanian policemen shot and wounded Leib Kaplan, aged 17, and Mrs. Kanzer. The incident occurred along the Ghetto fence.

OCTOBER 2, 1942

> *DOCUMENT:*
> *From SA Colonel Cramer, City Governor, Kovno*
> *To the Jewish Council*

Again and again, I am approached by firms which employ Jews, and which request the release of materials which are in the possession of a certain Jew employed by them. In each case, these materials have been offered by that Jew himself.

I hereby comment in this respect as follows:

Oral and written orders have been issued repeatedly, to the effect that all articles, moneys, and materials still in the personal possession of Jews must be handed over. Apparently some Jews have failed to comply with these orders. Therefore I ask the Council, for the last time, to arrange for the immediate and complete confiscation of the above articles.

Last day: October 10, 1942. Whoever possesses any such articles after this date will be punished.[1]

1. This document was signed by Koeppen, over Cramer's official stamp.

OCTOBER 3, 1942

The city governor has issued Order no. 7, according to which money, materials, and various belongings must be handed over to the authorities.

Simchat Torah (the rejoicing of the law): in the hospital there were *hakafot* (dancing with the scrolls of the Torah).[1]

> 1. Inside the hospital building, Jews gathered to celebrate the Simchat Torah festival, while the Jewish police stood guard outside, and at the Ghetto gate.

OCTOBER 4, 1942

The first anniversary of the "action" in the small Ghetto.

Following the conversation with Rauca concerning Ghetto affairs, Hermann, director of the German labor office, said "How can a person speak this way about helpless and defenseless people?"

OCTOBER 5, 1942

The evacuation of the Demokratu-Vienozinskio streets has been completed, and the Ghetto area abridged. At ten o'clock, Koeppen ordered the Ghetto fence to be moved to the new Ghetto border within two hours.

Two Jews were arrested with foodstuffs in their possession. The commandant sent them to the Gestapo. Koeppen's comment: "Why send them to the Gestapo? They should be shot right there."

OCTOBER 6, 1942

Medical report about the condition of the Jewish workers digging peat in Palemonas: they are covered with lice and wounds. The camp commandant refuses to send workers for medical treatment in the city. "In the camp you are either healthy or dead," he said.

Obst, and Chief Inspector Kerlitze, came to the Ghetto to announce the imminent delivery of 800 cubic meters of firewood.

OCTOBER 7, 1942

Five bags containing groceries, and one coat, have been found near the fence. It appears that the bags were left behind by Jewish workers when they crawled under the fence.

The Gestapo conducted searches of Jewish houses at Puodziu and Krisciukaicio Streets. The Jews whose houses were searched are suspected of black-marketeering. Two Jewish women, together with their husbands and children, were transferred to the Gestapo.

OCTOBER 8, 1942

One more Jew has been brought to the Gestapo on the suspicion of the crime of trading along the Ghetto fence. The Gestapo decision is being awaited concerning the four Jewish policemen, as well as Kopel Gutman, who were arrested on the charge of bringing a truckload of flour into the Ghetto.

Four barges carrying the load of firewood for the Ghetto came along the Vilija river.

OCTOBER 9, 1942

Koeppen has completed his tour of duty. He is being replaced by Miller.[1]

Nine firemen were arrested at the Ghetto fence in the act of smuggling in foodstuffs.

1. Lieutenant Miller, a member of the SA, replaced Koeppen as Ghetto chief acting for the German governor of Kovno. He served in Kovno until late 1943, when the period of relative calm came to an end. A young man with an ever-immaculate uniform, peculiar and unpredictable, he despised the Gestapo and dealt humanely with the inmates of the Ghetto and with the Council, particularly when no other Germans were present. Nevertheless, he sometimes acted pompously and cruelly.

OCTOBER 10, 1942

The Council asked Ghetto inmates to provide information on horse-drawn carts that the Jews had left behind in the city.

Machines, work tools, and money must be turned over to the authorities (Koeppen's order).

The German director of the furniture plant, Wintzer, visited the Council in the company of his mistress, Mrs. Ravensburg.[1]

The Vocational Training School opened courses in baking.

1. Avraham Tory, who was present during this visit, later recalled that Wintzer and the Countess von Ravensburg avoided speaking derisively to the Jews or using anti-Semitic expressions. This was so rare when Germans met Jews that it was the talk of the Council for many days.

OCTOBER 11, 1942

Seven workers from Vilna arrived in the Ghetto from Palemonas. Four are staying here; three went back.

OCTOBER 12, 1942

A meeting of the Council: a commission has been appointed, charged with recruiting 300 workers for Riga.

The city governor has issued an instruction to hand over single shoes.

In the morning a demand was issued to recruit 300 workers for work at the airfield in Riga. Later the demand was rescinded.

OCTOBER 14, 1942

During the night a Lithuanian woman by the name of Kelvaitite was arrested in the Ghetto. She was turned over to the Lithuanian Guard.

OCTOBER 15, 1942

The demand to send workers to Riga is still in force. Until October 16 one may sign up voluntarily.

"This is unheard of: Jews in the ordnance corps," a German officer exclaimed upon seeing Kopelman and Golub, who went there on Ghetto matters.[1] They were chased away.

A commission of Lithuanian doctors visited the Ghetto to inspect the sanitary conditions.

1. Michael Kopelman, chief of the Jewish police, and Avraham Golub (Tory), the Council secretary, attempted to obtain from the German Army ordnance corps items which were unavailable from the German civil administration or from the city governor.

OCTOBER 15, 1942

MEMOIR: Report by Jack Brauns[1]

The purpose of the visit of the Lithuanian doctors was to discover, confirm, and report to the German authorities the presence of contagious diseases in the Ghetto, and to confirm an epidemic of typhus.[2] Following the burning of the contagious disease hospital on October 4, 1941, the term "contagious disease" was struck from the Ghetto dictionary. From that moment, Dr. Moses Brauns undertook the responsibility of not reporting contagious diseases to the Lithuanian Board of Health, as was required, and personally treated every case of contagious disease in the Ghetto.

The Lithuanian Board of Health was aware that the basic ingredients of a typhus epidemic were present in the Ghetto: overcrowding, unsanitary conditions, no bathhouse, and hunger—and they were right. People had to live in a space of three square feet per person. Water had to be taken from individual wells, and cesspools were used to dispose of excrement.

Because the winter of 1941 had been so harsh, many of the outhouses had been dismantled and their wood used for firewood. The cesspools were therefore exposed and overflowing. No new cesspools could be dug due to the frozen ground. It was a nightmare for Dr. Brauns to imagine what would happen in the spring of 1942, when all the icebergs of excrement would begin to melt. That spring new cesspools were dug, and several protective measures were taken to protect the water wells and to keep the newly dug cesspools the prescribed distance from the wells. On April 22, 1942, the first public bathhouse was opened in the Ghetto, built by the inmates. Hunger, leading to undernourishment, a permanent feature of life in the Ghetto, was an ever-present possible factor in the outbreak of any epidemic.

In the summer and fall of 1942, the German Army sustained enormous casualties on the eastern front. Thousands of wounded soldiers were transferred by train to Germany. Many of them were infected with typhus. To combat the spread of the disease in Germany itself, the German authorities established in Kovno a delousing center for wounded German soldiers; it was situated at 4 Vytauto Street. Wounded soldiers were taken off the trains and transported to the center. Their heads were shaved. They were bathed, and their clothes were disinfected. All this work was carried out by Jewish workers brought daily from the Ghetto. After this was completed, the soldiers were taken back to the trains by Lithuanian workers. An epidemic of typhus, with a high mortality rate, broke out among the Lithuanian workers at the delousing center.

Following this outbreak of the disease, a secret meeting was held at the Jewish Council, attended by Dr. Elkes, Garfunkel, Goldberg, Dr. Zacharin, Dr. Berman, Dr. Gerstein and Dr. Brauns. Those present discussed the experience of October 4, 1941, when the Germans had burned down the infectious disease hospital in the Ghetto, killing all its patients, doctors, and nurses; the knowledge of the recent mass murder of Russian prisoners-of-war who had been suspected of being infected with typhus; and the rumors of typhus in the Ghetto itself.

There was indeed typhus in the Ghetto. It came from three sources: from the inmates who had to work at the delousing center; from the Ghetto workshops, where articles of clothing received were supposed to have already been disinfected, but where live lice were often found in the clothes; and from inmates transferred from other camps (Zezmer—nine cases). Typhus is transmitted to man in the feces of lice when a puncture wound is contaminated by scratching. Dried lice feces may also infect mucous membranes in the eyes and the oral cavity.

At the time of the visit of the Lithuanian doctors, twenty-nine people in the Ghetto were infected with typhus. The disease was renamed "influenza." Without causing any suspicion, Dr. Brauns gave special instructions to each of the affected families. He was able to remove the children, who were most at risk, from the crowded quarters of each patient's family, and send them to other, though of course equally crowded, quarters of relatives and friends. With the help of the Jewish Council, Dr. Brauns was able to increase the distribution of soap, wood, and food rations to the typhus patients and their families. The patients stayed in their own quarters, cared for by their own families, and were visited twice a day by Dr. Brauns. Sporadic searches by the Gestapo of the living quarters in the Ghetto failed to discover the existence of these typhus patients.

The visiting doctors from the Lithuanian Board of Health in October 1942 were expecting to find an epidemic of typhus, and while they were in the Ghetto they confronted Dr. Brauns with their suspicions. He was aware that the real danger to the Ghetto did not come from the lice but from the attitude toward the disease of German authorities and the Lithuanian Board of Health.

Dr. Brauns's reputation as an expert in contagious diseases was unquestionable. So, too, was his integrity. At stake was not only his own family's life for not having reported any infectious diseases to the Lithuanian Board of Health, but also the destruction of the entire Ghetto population.

During the visit of the Lithuanian doctors, Dr. Brauns explained to his colleagues of the prewar years that the high mortality rate among the Lithuanian workers had most likely been caused by the vaccination of the workers during their incubation time, and by the use of improper vaccine (the vaccine used was prepared from live lice), while the Jewish workers were not vaccinated.

The Lithuanian doctors accepted Dr. Brauns's explanation and left the Ghetto. The dark clouds passed, and the true story—that Dr. Brauns had treated, and was to continue to treat, seventy cases of typhus—never became known to either the Lithuanians or the Germans.

Of the seventy cases treated, without adequate medication, by Dr. Brauns, only three died (4.3 percent mortality). The fatality rate in untreated groups of patients, with classic typhus exanthimaticus rickettsia prowazekii, is usually from 10 to 60 percent.[3]

1. This memoir was prepared in 1988 by Dr. Moses Brauns's son Jack, who was with Dr. Brauns in the Ghetto and survived the war at his father's side. The extreme secrecy of the facts set out here, and the danger to the whole Ghetto if the Lithuanians or the Germans had found out about them, made it impossible at the time to do more than commit them to memory.

2. This was typhus exanthimaticus rickettsia prowazekii.

3. Other contagious diseases were also present in the Ghetto. One was dysenteria shigellosis (bacillary dysentery)—this prevalent disease seemed to disappear completely after the burning of the hospital, probably because people were afraid to ask for medical help. A second was typhoid abdominalis, paratyphus A and B, of which eighty cases were treated with no fatalities. In the autumn of 1942 an epidemic broke out and was traced to a water well, and the small medical laboratory in the Ghetto confirmed the presence of typhoid bacilli in the water. The well was closed and treated. Inmates were advised that two dead cats had been

found in the well. After the treatment, the well was reopened. A third contagious disease was infectious hepatitis (one case). There was also scarlet fever—a few mild cases before the burning of the hospital on October 4, 1941. There were later sporadic cases of scarlet fever with a mild course without the tendency to an epidemic outbreak. Finally, there was diphtheria, of which thirty cases were treated. In spite of difficulties in obtaining antidiphtheria serum, the morbidity of the disease was mild and no fatalities occurred.

OCTOBER 16, 1942

The Gestapo issued an instruction: all those working in the city must return to the Ghetto at the end of their work day and are banned from spending the night in the city.

The recruitment of 300 workers for Riga has begun; workers will be allowed to take their belongings with them.[1]

Today Kopelman came back from the city together with Lipzer. The latter had never been seen in the Ghetto at such an early hour. I thought, therefore, that he brought some news with him. We met for a conversation. Lipzer, his spirits up, announced that three policemen would be released today from the fort and returned to the Ghetto. The other policeman—Reibstein—together with the two Ghetto residents, Kopel Gutman and Krieger, would be sent to Riga (with the group of 300 workers). This group will be sent to do forced labor at Riga airfield, in line with the instruction issued by the German commandant of the Kovno Ghetto.

Lipzer was very satisfied with the outcome of this complicated affair, which had lasted for a long time and endangered the lives of six young men. He came especially to the Ghetto to bring the good tidings. He asked us not to tell anyone about this. Lipzer himself would like to meet with Feinberg's parents to pass on to them the good news about the release of their only son, who today will be back home.

How well I recall that ill-fated evening when Kopel Gutman, the son of Rabbi Gutman—a well-known rabbi in Kovno and owner of a publishing house—together with a young policeman, Feinberg—were arrested at the Ghetto gate as they were bringing a truckload of flour into the Ghetto.

That evening Lipzer had visited the Council office. Kopel Gutman's family and Feinberg senior waited for him outside. As he came out they pleaded with him tearfully: "Save our children; without them our lives have no meaning." A most moving scene.

This was a depressing affair, since they were caught in the act for everyone to see. They used an old permit allowing them to bring coal into the Ghetto in order to bring a truckload of white flour concealed under planks. Officially, the truck was carrying a load of firewood, but even this was against the regulations, since the permit was only for bringing in coal.

Apparently this ruse had been arranged in advance with the Lithuanian sentry guarding the gate, who was bribed to turn a blind eye. Unexpectedly, however, a disaster struck: as the truck was crossing into the Ghetto, the Lithuanian inspector in charge of the Guard arrived at the gate. In actual fact, he also could have been "bought," but no such precaution had been taken. Pandemonium broke out: the truck was thoroughly searched and during the examination of the permit the ruse was exposed. As a result, Kopel Gutman was arrested and brought to the Ghetto command headquarters. Later Feinberg was also arrested.

On the following day, after the Gestapo set upon Kopel Gutman, beating him about the head, and after a vigorous interrogation of Feinberg, it turned out that Gutman had bought the flour from the Lithuanian owner of a flour mill. The purchase was negotiated on behalf of a group of Jewish policemen from the first police precinct. This was why policeman Feinberg was in the truck.

Some time later, two other policemen were arrested: Grossman and Lifschitz. In addition, Yehoshua Grinberg, chief of the first police precinct, and the policeman Reibstein were also summoned for an investigation. The latter was arrested, whereas Grinberg was released, having been cleared of his alleged involvement in the smuggling of flour. Krieger, fence merchant and speculator, was also arrested in connection with this affair.

When Rauca of the Gestapo was informed of this development, he voiced threats against the policemen from the first precinct in the Ghetto: "You too, Brutus?" he screamed at them. "Men entrusted with keeping the law are engaging in smuggling? They must be taught a lesson; all of them must be shot."

With the sentence of death hanging over the heads of the Jewish policemen, the Council resolved to dispatch a delegation to the deputy Gestapo commander of Lithuania, Schmitz, to ask for clemency. Schmitz told them that he would oppose imposing a heavy punishment on the policemen involved.

The policemen were detained in the Ninth Fort for a prolonged period of time and their fate caused concern in the Ghetto. As a result, Lipzer arrived hurriedly in the Ghetto as early as 10 A.M. in order to pass on the good news that the three policemen would be released and returned to the Ghetto. The rest were to be sent to work in Riga.

It was good news for the first three, but for the other three it was not much of a consolation. In spite of that, members of their families were glad. Kopel Gutman's brother told Lipzer: "Well, let him go to Riga, I would very much like to see him already on the train, going to Riga with the others. May he leave the Ninth Fort; just to slip away from the claws of Asmodeus." He spoke as if he had a premonition.

Lipzer stayed in the Ghetto throughout the day. Kopelman left for the city one more time to check the reliability of Lipzer's information. Lipzer then came to the Council to bring the good tidings to the heads of the Jewish community.

On this occasion Lipzer brought Rauca's leather coat to the Ghetto to have it cleaned of oil stains. The coat was sent to one of the Ghetto workshops. Friends of Grossman, Lifschitz, and Feinberg were summoned to the council to hear the good news from Lipzer. They were happy and waited impatiently for the return of the stray sons.

And indeed, the three policemen returned to the Ghetto in the afternoon and were received with open arms by their families and friends. They were pale, their eyes had sunk deep into the sockets, and their bodies were weary and emaciated.

At about the same time news reached the Ghetto that Krieger and the policeman Reibstein had been seen being led away to the Ninth Fort. The fear over their fate was aroused again. After all, Lipzer had announced unequivocally on behalf of the Gestapo that these three were to be sent to work in Riga. Why then were they sent back to the fort?

This is probably a mistake, Lipzer said. They were supposed to return to the Ghetto to get their belongings and to set on their way to Riga together with the others. His words carried a great deal of conviction. Only few dared to doubt them. On the basis of this information, their relatives were asked to get ready the belongings of the three, as well as the clothes of their wives and children, in preparation for the departure for Riga, as whole families went there.

1. This was the beginning of the second deportation to Riga. As a result of the first deportation in February, there were many families now divided between Kovno and Riga who wished to be reunited. The Council also encouraged the registration of volunteers for transfer to Riga, in order to try to avoid the indiscriminate arrests which had accompanied the first deportation. At the same time, the Council took advantage of this second transport to Riga to punish Jews who had evaded forced labor, and hooligans. The Jewish police were charged with holding them, according to a list, at the Ghetto detention center until departure. Some nevertheless managed to avoid deportation; other Jews were then sent in their place.

OCTOBER 17, 1942

This morning brought the bitter surprise: at 7 A.M. a Gestapo car arrived. The wives of Krieger and Reibstein, together with their children, were taken urgently to the Ghetto command. A woman and her two little children were also taken there; her husband had been arrested on charges of black-marketeering and was imprisoned in the Ghetto detention center near the junction of 71 Krisciukaicio Street.

Schtitz also ordered Erich Kohn to be taken there. Kohn was a sick man. He had been in the hospital for a long time and had to be taken to the Ghetto command headquarters on a stretcher. Kopelman pleaded with Schtitz to leave the man in peace on account of his illness. He said: "Why should he be troubled; after all, he is unable to run away." Erich Kohn was returned to the hospital.

Schtitz told the women and children that they were going to join their husbands and fathers on a journey to Riga. He put them in the car which drove off in the direction of the Ninth Fort. There they were executed that same morning. The German Ghetto commandant, Litschauer, attended the execution.

Taking people to the Ninth Fort and then murdering them brutally was unheard of until now. It boggles the mind. Why lie? Why didn't they say: "These people are condemned to death?" Or, as has always been the case, not say anything? And the most ominous question of all: why do the children have to die for the real or imaginary offenses of their parents, or women for the sins of their husbands? Ever since human beings stopped eating the flesh of their own species, such horror has been unheard of. And all this because a number of people made a wrong step: not to get rich, but to bring home some flour!

We at the Council, and the whole Ghetto, have been deceived in a satanic fashion. Lipzer, who has always been so sure of himself as an omniscient person, a person with access to inside information, was disappointed. After all, Schtitz, his Schtitz, had promised him that the three men would go to Riga together with their wives and children. And now—such a great disappointment. Lipzer regards himself as having been deceived all along. From now on he is not going to believe anyone. Now he fears for his own life.

Today thirteen Jews died in the Ninth Fort, including five little children. A black day for the Ghetto. A very sad day.

OCTOBER 21, 1942

A German engineer, Chech,[1] inspector of Riga airport, arrived in Kovno in order to take with him to Riga those 500 Jewish workers from the Kovno Ghetto who had been recruited to be transferred to Riga.

Jewish Ghetto police, fire-brigade men, and employees of several of the Council's departments accompanied the 500 recruits (who had been kept at the Jewish police detention house in the Ghetto) to their homes, to enable them to collect some of their belongings before being sent to Riga.

---

1. The engineer Chech, a German Army officer, treated the workers humanely. It was he who agreed to exempt the sick from deportation, the first time this had happened in the fourteen months of the Ghetto's existence. He transferred children to their parents in Riga, watched them on the way, and brought Dr. Elkes confirmation from their parents that they had arrived safely.

OCTOBER 23, 1942

Koeppen instructed members of the Council to appear before him, but only Garfunkel was admitted to his office at the city governor's office.

The Lithuanian sanitary committee requires us to submit to them information on all contagious disease in the Ghetto.

At 1 P.M., 369 Jews, together with their families, including children, were transported to Riga for work. They were transported by train from the railway sidings at Kovno airfield to Riga.

Depression in the Ghetto after the departure of the men.[1]

> 1. On the face of it, everything had gone well. The men traveled with their belongings, and either with their families or to join their families in Riga. The Council had succeeded in preventing a manhunt by the Germans. But people had once again left the Ghetto unwillingly, and no one knew when they would return, if ever. Worst of all, Jewish policemen had rounded up other Jews, at times using force, and had delivered them to the Germans. In spite of all the promises, therefore, and the favorable news which had reached the Kovno Ghetto about Riga, the mood in the Ghetto was not good. The transport arrived in Riga on October 24, 1942, but after a few days the deportees were once again uprooted from their families, with whom they had been so briefly reunited, and were moved to labor camps outside Riga to work at the military airport there.

OCTOBER 24, 1942

During the night armed Lithuanian policemen set upon a Jewish house near the fence with the purpose of robbery.

OCTOBER 25, 1942

Two senior officials of the general government of Lithuania and one official from Minsk are visiting the Ghetto in the company of Cramer. They came to the Council and toured the workshops. They seek to get to know the structure of the Ghetto, its labor force and so forth.

OCTOBER 26, 1942

Koeppen has completed his tour of duty. "He's got more fear than love of the fatherland," said Hermann about him.[1] Miller is replacing him. He announced this to the Council over the telephone via the Ghetto Guard.

> 1. Koeppen, like Jordan before him, was sent to the eastern front. He had made no secret of his terror of being sent there (Jordan had been killed on the eastern front).

OCTOBER 28, 1942

The first anniversary of the "great action" in the Ghetto.

Seven bargeloads of firewood have now been supplied to the Ghetto along the Vilija river.

OCTOBER 29, 1942

Miller visited the Council offices.

A woman who had lived by herself was found lying dead on the floor of her room.

OCTOBER 30, 1942

Dr. Segal and Goldberg[1] had a conversation with the Lithuanian director of the Red Cross, Dr. Ingelevicius. There was an exchange of information, but no practical results have issued from this conversation.

A letter from Stockholm reached the Council, inquiring after the Jews who had been transferred from Hamburg last year and were supposed to arrive in Kovno. The German authorities forbade replying to this letter.[2]

The German commandant of the labor camp in Palemonas came for a visit to the old municipality building, where he delivered derisive and hateful comments against the Jews. He said: "When I need to kill even a hundred Jews, I do it with pleasure; I don't mind killing even a thousand Jews"—and other "gems" in this vein.

1. Dr. Eliyahu Segal, head of the Council's welfare department, and Jacob Goldberg, head of the labor department. Although they met with the head of the Lithuanian Red Cross, whom they had known personally, he failed to respond to their requests.
2. It is not clear who sent this letter from Stockholm. It was the Gestapo which would not allow the Council to reply to it, since the Jews from Hamburg had in fact been murdered at the Seventh Fort, and had never reached the Kovno Ghetto.

NOVEMBER 1, 1942

A solemn assembly, occasioned by the signing of a pledge by all the Jewish policemen, took place in the hall of the yeshiva.[1] A concert took place, also attended by the members of the Council and the police command.

1. In the former yeshiva hall, converted to a concert hall, each of the Jewish policemen signed an oath, pledging loyalty to the Jewish inhabitants of the Ghetto and promising to fulfill their

duty to the utmost of their ability. This ceremony took place a week after the deportation to Riga. Avraham Tory—who drafted the oath which was administered on November 1, 1942—later described the chief of the Ghetto police, Michael Kopelman, as "a uniquely honest, decent person, who took the job only because the Council begged him to do so."

NOVEMBER 4, 1942

DOCUMENT: Instruction from Lieutenant Miller

The milk of the six cows in the Ghetto must be handed over to the German Ghetto Guard.

A garage for cars should be established in the Ghetto.

NOVEMBER 4, 1942

DOCUMENT:
From Lieutenant Miller
To the Jewish Council in Kovno-Vilijampolé

Beginning on November 5, 1942, the following instructions concerning the keeping of cattle (six cows) and the use of fodder are enacted:

1. Cattle will, as hitherto, be fed and specially cared for by you.
2. The products—milk—must without exception be handed over to the German Ghetto Guard and to the Lithuanian security units, namely to Guard Master Litschauer. Mr. Litschauer is entitled to order an examination of the condition of the milk (bacteria). You must contact Mr. Litschauer concerning this Order.

NOVEMBER 7, 1942

DOCUMENT: Order from SA Colonel Cramer, City Governor, Kovno

The Ghetto workshops, the furniture and carpentry workshop, and the pottery workshop, must be amalgamated under a unified administration called Great Ghetto Workshops, under the administration of the city governor.

NOVEMBER 7, 1942

The furniture factory, located outside the Ghetto adjacent to the Ghetto barbed-wire fence, is to be merged with the big workshops inside the Ghetto.[1]

Firewood supply for the Ghetto has been discontinued.

1. The furniture factory was managed by the German architect Wintzer; Jews who worked there could go in and out of the Ghetto through a small gate, whose keys were held by Wintzer.

NOVEMBER 8, 1942

A meeting at the Council; members of the management of the big workshops participated.

Important decisions were taken, such as the annexation of the furniture factory to the large workshops. The policy on how the large workshops are run will be laid down only with the consent of the Council.[1]

Eighteen workers returned from the labor camp at Palemonas.

1. The Jewish management of the large workshops was headed by Moshe Segalson.

NOVEMBER 9, 1942

Visit of Miller, accompanied by Gilow, the new German manager of the large workshops, to the Council offices. The pottery workshop will from now on be under the authority of the large workshops.

NOVEMBER 10, 1942

Miller has permitted the Council to maintain telephone contact with the city of Kovno through the German Ghetto guard. Until today, direct telephone contact between the Council and the city of Kovno was strictly forbidden.

Talks between representatives of the Council and the Lithuanian commander of the Ghetto guard, Petkunas, on Ghetto problems, and on a possible transition period in case of the liquidation of the Ghetto—either by radical changes at the front or at the end of Nazi occupation.

After the area around Demokratu Square was excluded from the Ghetto, the Council reduced the Ghetto police precincts from four to three.

For the next three days, Jewish workers whose workplaces are in the city will be checked while at work.

NOVEMBER 10, 1942

DOCUMENT:
From SA Colonel Cramer, City Governor, Kovno[1]
To the Jewish Council, Kovno-Vilijampolé

It has been repeatedly reported that Jews in compulsory work units are engaging in gossip concerning the manufacture of the Ghetto workshops and other matters. I hereby forbid any propaganda by the Jews, and I shall order a most severe punishment for any further cases.

Arrange for the earliest possible distribution of my order.

1. This order was signed on Cramer's behalf by Lieutenant Miller.

NOVEMBER 11, 1942

Kopelman, the head of the Jewish Ghetto police, was called to the Gestapo for a talk about his former tutor, who had helped the Kopelman family in the Ghetto for a long time. Kopelman was released but his tutor, a woman, was punished by two weeks' imprisonment. An easy punishment.

An announcement by Hermann: Jewish workers are obliged to work in the places indicated on their labor cards. It is strictly forbidden to go from one place of work to another without being escorted by police.

NOVEMBER 12, 1942

DOCUMENT: Communication from Lieutenant Miller

The 18-year-old Blecher wanted to barter his boots to a Lithuanian policeman, and was killed by the same.

NOVEMBER 12, 1942

The body of a Jewish worker, Blecher, age eighteen, was found at the airport construction site; he had been caught by a Lithuanian partisan who was guarding the Jewish workers. This partisan took off Blecher's shoes, shot him dead, and hid his body. The Gestapo did not allow us to bring the body to the Ghetto; it was buried outside the Ghetto.

NOVEMBER 13, 1942

Letters from those who had been transported from the Kovno Ghetto to Riga reached the Ghetto today. They are all alive and are working in Riga.[1]

Members of the Council held talks with Segalson, the Jewish manager of the large workshops, on matters relating to the management of the workshops. The Council asked that all important matters concerning the workshops be brought before all the members of the workshop management, and not be solved by Segalson alone.

1. The same German who had accompanied the deportees to Riga had returned with many letters; these letters, with their proof that the deportees were alive and safe, brought considerable relief to the families of the deportees, to the Council, and to the Jewish police.

NOVEMBER 14, 1942

Warning from the city governor: Jews are forbidden to walk along Laisves Boulevard in Kovno, either in groups or singly.[1]

A Jewish worker at the airfield construction site was crushed and killed by a small truck. His name was Pine Galperin.

The six cows that we had here in the Ghetto have been taken away. The Ghetto is left without milk, even for the babies.

Professor Mazylis[2] visited the Ghetto hospital and called upon Dr. Elkes, in order to give his advice about a particular operation. This is the first such visit in the Ghetto by such a well-known Lithuanian professor. "To come to the Ghetto is for me like traveling to a far and unknown country," said Mazylis.

1. Laisves (Freedom) Boulevard was the city of Kovno's main thoroughfare; Jews walking along this street each day on their way to work had "offended" the Germans and the Lithuanians by their mere presence.
2. Professor Pranas Mazylis, a noted gynecologist, was one of the few Lithuanians who assisted Jews, and particularly Jewish children, by helping to hide them.

NOVEMBER 15, 1942

DOCUMENT: Master Sergeant Rauca, Order, issued from Gestapo Headquarters, Kovno

The members of the Council—Garfunkel, Goldberg, and the secretary Golub—must be arrested, together with the Ghetto inhabitant Meck, who was caught when he attempted to cross the fence, and on this occasion fired several shots in the presence of the commandant of the Ghetto Guard, Fleischmann.

Furthermore, twenty additional Ghetto inhabitants must be arrested as hostages and detained in the Ghetto prison.

NOVEMBER 15, 1942

At 5 P.M. the commander of the Ghetto Guard, Fleischmann, detained a young Jew by the name of Meck as he was trying to escape from the Ghetto by crawling under the fence. Meck immediately fired a gun into the air three or four times. He was arrested on the spot and taken to the German Ghetto Guard. In reprisal, the Gestapo arrested, and brought to the headquarters of the German Ghetto command, three members of the Council—Garfunkel, Goldberg, and Golub (Dr. Elkes, the chairman of the Council, was ill and confined to bed). At their headquarters, they threatened to kill us. We were taken the same evening, under heavy guard, from the Ghetto commander's headquarters to Gestapo headquarters in Kovno, together with Meck.

Inside the Ghetto, a further twenty Jews were arrested as hostages and imprisoned in the Ghetto detention center.[1]

1. During the arrest of the twenty hostages, the Jewish police detained the sick, the insane, and several Jewish criminals. Meck's accomplice was never betrayed, although Meck himself suffered terrible tortures. All the hostages were released, as were the Council members and the Council secretary; it was Avraham Tory's opinion at the time that the Gestapo wanted to prove to its superiors in Berlin that its control over the Kovno Ghetto was complete. Tory later recalled: "The Gestapo deputy commander, Schmitz, told the arrested—Garfunkel, Goldberg, and me—in the cellar of Gestapo headquarters in Kovno, 'For this game you will all be publicly hanged in the Ghetto, unless we are able to get Meck to tell us the name of the second Jew who was with him when he tried to escape from the Ghetto.' We refused."

NOVEMBER 16, 1942

B. Lipzer published a proclamation on behalf of the Gestapo, saying: "People who spread false rumors in the Ghetto about the twenty-seventh (rumors that on November 27 the Gestapo would carry out an 'action,' following Meck's failed escape from the Ghetto) will be punished. There will be no more 'actions.' Everybody must work—and maintain quiet and order."

The detained Council members were released from Gestapo custody and brought back into the Ghetto at 10 A.M.

NOVEMBER 17, 1942

DOCUMENT:
From SA Colonel Cramer, City Governor, Kovno
To the Jewish Council, Kovno-Vilijampolé

It is henceforth forbidden to use horses within the Ghetto, except for the acquisition of materials.

Funeral hearses and all other types of wagon must henceforth be pulled by the Jews themselves.

NOVEMBER 17, 1942

Gestapo officers searched Meck's apartment most carefully and discovered a treasure—2½ kilograms of gold, diamonds, and valuables.[1] The Gestapo ordered Meck to be hanged publicly in the Ghetto. The Jewish police have been ordered to erect the gallows and to carry out the hanging.

The Jewish police have found two young men in the detention house, both originally from Poland, who have agreed to carry out the hanging. In return, they will be released from detention.

All the Ghetto inmates were instructed by the Gestapo to hand over any weapons they might possess, bringing them to a pit at Puodziu street. Only one old gun was surrendered in this way.[2]

1. Before the war Meck's parents had owned a watchmaker's shop in Kovno; Meck had brought all their stock into the Ghetto in August 1941. All the jewelry discovered was taken by Schtitz. It was he who later ordered the execution of Meck's mother and sister, who had witnessed the robbery.

2. Two days after this order was issued, not a single weapon had been thrown into the pit. To prevent further German reprisals, the Council therefore handed over the single gun which the Germans found in the pit. The incident was then closed.

NOVEMBER 17, 1942

DOCUMENT: Gestapo Order

Meck will be publicly hanged in the Ghetto. The gallows are to be erected in the Ghetto and the execution is to be performed by the Jewish Ghetto police.

NOVEMBER 18, 1942, 12 P.M.

DOCUMENT: Gestapo Order

Meck shall remain hanging on the gallows for twenty-four hours.
All Ghetto inhabitants must hand over guns.

NOVEMBER 18, 1942

At noon today, the public hanging of Meck took place in the Ghetto, directly opposite the Council building, in the presence of Gestapo officers, German and Lithuanian policemen, German Ghetto Guard and police, representatives of the city governor, and the Jewish police. The Jews were forced to come to the site of the execution. Meck's body was to remain hanging on the gallows for twenty-four hours.[1]

1. Several eyewitnesses later recalled that Meck, who was difficult to recognize because of the torture to which he had been subjected, and which he had resisted, told the two young Jews from Poland—who had been caught stealing in the Ghetto—when he was about to be hanged: "Brothers, I forgive you. I know you were forced to do it. Give my love to my mother and sister."

NOVEMBER 19, 1942

DOCUMENT: Gestapo Order

The mother and the sister of the hanged Meck must be taken to the Ninth Fort for execution.

NOVEMBER 19, 1942

Goldberg (member of the Council) telephoned Gestapo headquarters. The twenty Jewish hostages detained in connection with the Meck case have been released. At ten this morning, however, Meck's mother and sister were detained by Schtitz, and taken by him to the Ninth Fort, where they were killed.

At noon Meck's body was taken down from the gallows.[1]

1. Meck was buried in the Ghetto cemetery.

NOVEMBER 20, 1942

The Council set up a special group to safeguard the transport of potatoes into the Ghetto.

NOVEMBER 22, 1942

Lipzer discovered a wireless set in the Ghetto. It belonged to Sergei, a Jewish policeman. Lipzer broke it into pieces on the spot.[1]

1. Sergei had obtained a permit to repair the wireless kept by Srebnitzki in the cellar of the pharmacy. After Lipzer broke it, the radio was repaired; it continued to serve the Ghetto underground clandestinely.

NOVEMBER 25, 1942

The Ghetto police have now completely renovated the building of the Slobodka yeshiva and adapted it to serve as a concert hall for the police orchestra, despite strong protests from religious and other circles.

NOVEMBER 26, 1942

The Gestapo has ordered the Council to submit a list of Ghetto inhabitants who are living outside the Ghetto, and of those who do not return every day from the city to the Ghetto.[1]

1. According to Avraham Tory, no such list was provided, because of the Council rule not to give any lists to the Germans. Even the list of dentists which the Germans had asked for in June 1942 had not been handed over.

NOVEMBER 27, 1942

The German manager of the Ghetto workshops has sent, as a gift, toys produced by the Ghetto inmates—to Reichsmarshall Hermann Göring, for distribution to

German children as Christmas presents. Before the toys were dispatched, an exhibition of them before the city governor was arranged.

NOVEMBER 28, 1942

There has been a denunciation to the Gestapo that Jewish wagoners transporting fodder from the village of Vilky to the Ghetto are also smuggling many other products into the Ghetto. The Gestapo therefore strengthened the guard at the Ghetto fence.

From inside the Ghetto, warnings were sent to the wagoners before they reached the Ghetto gate, so that during the search of the wagons and wagoners, nothing was found.

NOVEMBER 29, 1942

An institute for delousing and destroying various insect pests was recently opened in the Ghetto; 4,000 were designated to be checked by the institute.[1]

1. That is, more than a quarter of the Ghetto population.

NOVEMBER 30, 1942

Keiffler instructed the Council to submit invoices for work done by Jews from the Ghetto in various workplaces, indicating that the payment should be made to the city governor.

DECEMBER 1, 1942

A Jewish woman who has been in hiding in a peasant's stable since the winter of 1941 with her husband—both from the village of Vidiskiai[1]—came into the Ghetto with a work group that had been working in town.

1. Vidiskiai, a small town near Ukmerge; the few Jewish families who lived there were almost all murdered on September 5, 1941, together with the Jews of Ukmerge.

DECEMBER 3, 1942

The Council has organized transportation inside the Ghetto, using small two-wheeled wagons drawn by men; this has had to be done because of the absence of any other transportation, all of which is forbidden in the Ghetto.

A private association named Tsedaka—Charity—has been established with the aim of assisting the needy.

A permit has been obtained to bring firewood into the Ghetto for several work groups. Under this pretext, more firewood was also brought in for other inmates of the Ghetto.

Ernest Geist, a musician and composer who lived in the Ghetto for a prolonged period and then, being half-Aryan, was allowed to live in the city, was brought back into the Ghetto today by the Gestapo, and was taken to the Jewish police detention center in the Ghetto, upon order of the Gestapo.

DECEMBER 3, 1942

DOCUMENT: Gestapo Order

The Jewish musician and composer Geist, who first lived in the city and has been returned to the Ghetto today, must be detained in the Ghetto prison and be kept at the disposal of the Gestapo.[1]

> 1. Geist, a German who was married to a Jewish woman named Lydia, was shot by the Gestapo on December 10; his wife poisoned herself.

DECEMBER 4, 1942

DOCUMENT: Lieutenant Miller, Order

The Jew Schaffer must be punished by five days in prison, because of his failure to carry out the required salute of lifting the cap.

DECEMBER 4, 1942

One Jew was imprisoned for five days, and another Jew for one day, for not taking off their caps when they passed Miller in the street.

DECEMBER 5, 1942

The news of a wave of "actions" against Jews in Poland (mainly in Warsaw) has depressed the Ghetto inhabitants.[1]

Chanukah celebration at the Jewish police headquarters with members of the Council participating.

> 1. The deportations from Warsaw had begun on July 22, 1942; this diary entry is the first in which Avraham Tory mentions these deportations, during the course of which as many as 6,000 Jews were deported from the Warsaw Ghetto every day, until a total of 300,000 had been deported to Treblinka, where most of them were killed by gas. During the same four-month period, a further 250,000 Jews from the Warsaw region were deported to Treblinka and killed.

DECEMBER 6, 1942

Provocative behavior by a Lithuanian police guard near the Ghetto fence led to mass shooting. The Lithuanians told the German Ghetto Guard that Jews had shot at them. Unrest prevailed until the matter was clarified.

Children's Chanukah festivities took place at the main hall of the hospital.[1]

1. It was the kindergarten teacher Sonja Segal-Varshavski who organized this party for the kindergarten children. There were several Chanukah parties that year, including one held by the members of the Zionist group Matzok which was attended by both Dr. Elkes and Garfunkel.

DECEMBER 7, 1942

The Minister of Health of the Reich visited the Ghetto, accompanied by the city governor. The minister inquired about the state of sanitation in the Ghetto.

The Council resolved that the sending of people out of the Ghetto will have to be agreed upon by all members of the Council.[1]

1. This decision placed equal responsibility on all members of the Council.

DECEMBER 8, 1942

A Jew by the name of Rizan entered the Ghetto, after having been hidden near Vidiskiai by a peasant. His wife reached the Ghetto a week ago. They had slept in hiding with their clothes on for fifteen months.

DECEMBER 9, 1942

Lithuanian partisans volunteered to be sent to Lublin, allegedly to participate in "actions" against Jews there.

DECEMBER 10, 1942

Schtitz of the Gestapo took the musician Geist out of the Ghetto to the Ninth Fort, where he was killed right away.

A young girl by the name of Zisling has come to the Ghetto from the labor camp in Vievis.

After having disappeared from the Ghetto in 1941, Miss Bloch, who was in hiding at a farm in Latvia where she worked, has now come back to the Ghetto.

DECEMBER 11, 1942

Miller has issued a permit to purchase a hundred cubic meters of firewood for the institutions inside the Ghetto.

Today, Miller himself canceled an earlier German order that Ghetto inhabitants going outside the Ghetto should deposit their permits with the German Ghetto Guard.

DECEMBER 12, 1942

DOCUMENT:

From Benjamin Lipzer, Representative of the German Criminal Police and the Security Police for Jewish Compulsory Labor
To the Chief of the Police of the Jewish Community, Vilijampolé

By order of the criminal police, the present chief of the Jewish criminal police, Levin, must be dismissed by the fifteenth of this month.

The vacated position must be assigned to the former chief of the Jewish criminal police, Bramson.

I request you to ensure the punctual carrying out of this order.

DECEMBER 13, 1942

The German commandant of the Ghetto today attended a concert given by the Jewish police orchestra.

News has reached the Ghetto that a public fast has been proclaimed throughout the Jewish world, in view of the annihilation of the Jews in Europe by the Nazis and their collaborators.[1] The news of this fast greatly impresses the Ghetto inmates, and encourages them.

> 1. The Jewish community in Palestine had declared a three-day period of mourning; sympathetic groups had convened at the same time in both London and New York. See also the diary entry for December 19, 1942.

DECEMBER 14, 1942

Miller found ten marks on one of the Jewish women working in the workshops. He confiscated the money and punished her with three days' imprisonment.

DECEMBER 15, 1942

I visited the Lithuanian priest, Vaickus, in the priests' seminar in Kovno. The subject of our conversation: the rescue of the Jewish library belonging to Abba Balosher.[1]

News reaches us of protests in the parliaments of England and the United States, and in the Soviet Union, against the persecution of the Jews.[2]

1. Abba Balosher, a well-known Kovno Zionist, an intellectual and a scholar, and active in the cultural life of the Ghetto, had been asked by the Council to record the history of the Ghetto. His large library had been left behind in the city at the time of the creation of the Ghetto. The priest Vaiskus was respectful and friendly, but in spite of his efforts, the library was not saved. Balosher's history (if indeed he wrote it) has not survived. Balosher was killed during the so-called children's action on March 27, 1944.
2. The date of this paragraph must be in error; it was on December 17, 1942, that the public statement about the "bestial crimes" being committed against the Jews was issued simultaneously by the British, U.S., and Soviet governments.

DECEMBER 16, 1942

The Jewish police guard at the furniture factory just adjacent to the Ghetto was withdrawn; from now on, Lithuanian police will guard the factory.

DECEMBER 17, 1942

Electric light has been cut off in the Ghetto.

DECEMBER 18, 1942

Garfunkel reported at the meeting of the Jewish Council on the inner problems of the Ghetto; Golub reported on the problems of relations with the city governor and the Ghetto Guard.[1]

1. Garfunkel and Avraham Tory presented these reports to a meeting of the leadership of the Zionist group Matzok.

DECEMBER 19, 1942

The three Jewish policemen who had been under arrest, by order of Captain Binger, since December 15, were released.

Electric light has been renewed in the Council building, the workshops, at the Ghetto Guard, and in the German labor office in the Ghetto.

A Jewish worker named Fisher was shot dead at the Ghetto gate by a Lithuanian policeman for trying to bring some food into the Ghetto.

Following the protests abroad, there is fear in the Ghetto of new decrees.

DECEMBER 20, 1942

The Jewish dentist Dr. Kvitner, who worked at the Gestapo, and his wife were both arrested. Because of his special tasks at the Gestapo, various speculations spread in the Ghetto.[1]

> 1. Dr. Kvitner had gone each day from the Ghetto to Gestapo headquarters in Kovno, with no contact with the Council, and without reporting to the Council on his return. He was originally from Germany.

DECEMBER 21, 1942

DOCUMENT:
From SA Colonel Cramer, City Governor, Kovno
To the Jewish Council in Kovno-Vilijampolé

I forthwith prohibit smoking to all Jews, whether they leave the Ghetto individually, in groups, or in columns, or stay in the area of the city of Kovno, or, naturally, beyond it.[1]

> 1. As with all Cramer's orders at this time, this one was signed by Miller, using the stamp of the city governor.

DECEMBER 21, 1942

Order no. 12 of the city governor: Jews are forbidden to smoke cigarettes while outside the Ghetto.

City Governor Cramer visited the workshops with senior German officials.

DECEMBER 22, 1942

Rumors reach us of the establishment of a Jewish independent state in Palestine with President Chaim Weizmann heading a five-member government. Great joy in the Ghetto.[1]

Dr. Kvitner and his wife were released by the Gestapo. They were ordered to work at the military airfield as ordinary workers.

The Council received a letter from the labor camp in Zezmer.[2] The workers there are begging for clothing, foodstuffs, etc.

> 1. This rumor was of course false. In May 1942, however, in New York, Zionist leaders had approved a plan to work for the creation of a Jewish commonwealth in Palestine. It was approved by the Zionist Action Committee in Jerusalem in October. Perhaps the approval in Jerusalem caused the rumor.
>
> 2. Ziezmariai (Zezmer) was a small town fifty kilometers from Kovno. The 200 Jewish families who lived there were murdered in August 1941. At the labor camp which was then estab-

lished nearby, Jews from other towns and villages worked at building a road from Kovno to Vilna. The camp was technically affiliated with the Vilna Ghetto, but it received help from the Council of the Kovno Ghetto.

DECEMBER 23, 1942

Electric light has been renewed in the Ghetto for several hours each day.

DECEMBER 25, 1942

Tamshe[1] and Golub visited the Lithuanian commander of the Ghetto Guard. Natkin and Golub then visited the German commander of the Ghetto Guard and paid our respects on behalf of the Council.

Because of Christmas, the Council offices and the Council institutions were closed.

1. David Tamshe was both an officer in the Jewish Ghetto police force and an instructor of members of the Jewish underground in the use of weapons. He was later murdered at the Ninth Fort along with forty other policemen who had refused to reveal the hiding places of Jews in the Ghetto.

DECEMBER 26, 1942

A large Chanukah gathering in the Ghetto of the members of the Jewish students' fraternity Vetaria.[1]

A fundraising party for the needy in the Ghetto hospital on behalf of the medical institutions in the Ghetto. Literary works written in the Ghetto were read aloud.

1. Vetaria was a student group not associated with any particular Zionist party.

DECEMBER 27, 1942

Kazimirovsky, a Jew from the Vilna Ghetto, visited the Jewish Council and conveyed greetings from Vilna. News of the massacre in the Warsaw Ghetto was confirmed.

DECEMBER 28, 1942

A circular letter and pamphlets from the Council ask Ghetto residents to refrain categorically from arranging any festivities in connection with the New Year.

An X-ray apparatus has begun to function in the Ghetto.[1]

A year ago today the fur "action" was carried out.[2]

1. Dr. L. Goldstein had moved his X-ray machine into the Ghetto in August 1941, when the Ghetto was established. But for more than a year he had not been able to use it, and by the end of 1942 he gave it to the Ghetto hospital.
2. On December 27, 1941, the Germans demanded that the few furs remaining in the Ghetto after the general looting of property in September 1941 be handed over to them. A few people assembled in great terror at Demokratu Square, where the big "action" had taken place, but the Germans simply collected the furs.

DECEMBER 31, 1942

Katz[1] and his wife came back to the Ghetto. They are wanted by the Gestapo. The Jewish Ghetto police detained them; the Council instructed the Ghetto police not to deliver them to the Gestapo, and told them to change their names.

Consultations on how to reorganize the Council's labor department.

Today is the eve of the Christian and civil New Year. The year 1942 comes to an end. We are on the brink of the new year 1943. As in previous years, the Lithuanian newspaper appeared in an enlarged form and is full of summaries, evaluations on the events of the past year, and forecasts for the new year.

I was in town yesterday and learned that in spite of the war and the misery of millions, big preparations are being made to celebrate New Year's Eve as before. For example, yesterday I was in the Opera theater building in Kovno; not, however, to secure tickets for the Opera—God forbid—which is performing tonight. We are in a Ghetto. Here we have our own worries and our own interests quite at variance with the festivities of New Year's Eve. Our women once wore ball dresses and we—the men—wore tuxedos, evening clothes, etc. Insofar as some, or any, of this festive dress is left in the Ghetto, it is for sale, or for exchange for food. Regular clothing or footwear can easily be exchanged for food; but to sell a tuxedo or an evening gown, and their accessories—this is a big problem. So we took advantage of the incoming New Year, when a good friend of mine thought she might be able to exchange her fancy ball gown. Now, in the Ghetto, it is useless to her, but perhaps some of the Kovno theater staff might be interested in buying it in exchange for some foodstuff, or for money. Various Jewish artisans from the Ghetto—dressmakers, hairdressers, etc.— work in the theater building, so we joined a group of workers from the Ghetto and went today to the theater with a view to offering our merchandise.

When I entered the entrance hall of the theater and walked along the adjacent corridors, it looked so strange to me, so far away. Now I am in a theater—at a time of "actions," terror, slavery, forced labor, hunger, and food rations; at a time when a pair of wooden shoes, a pair of plain trousers, or a jacket is a dream for many—not only for many Jews but for millions of non-Jews who are starving and suffering in concentration camps and prisons.

It is in such days that I have seen—in the theater in Kovno—rehearsals of plays, preparations for luxurious gala parties, gossips, women in splendid clothes. It all seemed so strange to me. Here, in this theater, are many people who have no idea what war means; they know nothing about its cruelties and distress.

We in the Ghetto have no possibility, nor have we any inclination, to celebrate on these "festive" days. We are surrounded by a barbed-wire fence. Thousands of evil men are watching our every step, looking at our every movement; they "care" that we should not forget for a moment that we are slaves here. Our very condition of life cuts us off from the New Year celebrations of the outside world.

For us, the year 1942 was a year of annihilation, slavery, terror, and the evil spirit. Every day we became more bereaved and poorer. Today we can only lament, and preserve our mourning in memory of the tens of thousands of our brother martyrs who died sanctifying God's name, the victims of a "crime"— to be a Jew.

Who among us thinks today of festivities? Who is able to put on festive dress instead of mourning dress? A few of the Ghetto inmates with bad consciences, lawless ones, or the "new rich" are longing for a glass of wine, accompanied by song and dance.[2] That is why the Council published today a circular prohibiting any festivities on the eve of the New Year, or any participation in such festivities.

"Owing to the unprecedented tragedy which is afflicting the multitude of children of Israel," the announcement issued by the Jewish leadership read, "we must refrain from celebrating the incoming of the New Year. We hope that each one of us will exhibit prudent and responsible conduct."

This announcement met with understanding among the Ghetto Jews. Indeed, the New Year was a quiet day in the Ghetto, without festivities or a celebration.

Today we faced a difficult problem, a matter of life and death in the literal meaning of the term. The chief of the Ghetto police, Kopelman, is in trouble: he asked for a secret meeting. He asked me to accompany him to Dr. Elkes's office to discuss the steps to be taken as a result of his situation.

The problem is as follows: in the aftermath of the Meck case, two Ghetto inmates, Shimon Katz and his wife, escaped from the Ghetto through the barbed-wire fence. They resided in the city clandestinely and were in hiding for a long time. It appears that the man was somehow involved in the illicit business of Meck. After the incident with Meck and Gelson, the Gestapo ordered the Jewish police to submit forthwith a list of the Ghetto residents as well as a list of residents who had left for work and failed to return to the Ghetto.

Because of the presence in the Ghetto of clandestine agents of the Gestapo, the Jewish police had to submit a list which included a number of names of Jewish escapees—altogether eight people—including Katz and his wife.[3] As it turned out, the couple made their way back to the Ghetto. They could not hide in the city any longer: the Germans had discovered their traces, and they had no choice but to return to the Ghetto.

Today a search took place in the Ghetto for able-bodied inmates, and the Jewish police inadvertently got hold of Katz. The policemen demanded to see his labor card so that they could know where he had been working in recent months. Since Katz did not have the labor card in his possession, they placed him and his wife under arrest on the charge of shirking work duty.

At this point the problem emerged: what is to be done now? The Jewish police command long ago placed Katz's name on the list of people who had left the Ghetto. The Gestapo has demanded that such people, if caught, should be handed straight over to it. If Katz and his wife, two young people, are turned over the Gestapo, their fate is as good as sealed. Hiding them away now, however, when they are under arrest in the detention center, would mean endangering the life of the chief of the Jewish police. Kopelman is indeed in dire straits.

We sat in Dr. Elkes's office and considered all the possible options. Until now the guiding principle of the Council has been not to turn Jews over to the Gestapo. But what would happen if the news about Katz's arrest in some way reached the Germans? Kopelman is frightened. In a situation like this, it is certain that the Germans will impose heavy punishment against the members of the Jewish police.

Kopelman argues that by leaving the Ghetto Katz proved he was unwilling to share our plight. He hid away in the city with his wife, to save his and her skin, without taking into account the situation and the fate of the Jewish community. Why should we now put our lives at risk, lives of the representatives of the community and of the members of the Jewish police, for the sake of a character like Katz? Katz is one and we are many. If we must make a choice between the fate of a single person and that of many, we must not risk the life of many. This was Kopelman's view.

This argument would have made sense under normal conditions. It is true that Katz had fled from the Ghetto. He had sought to save his life, at a time when the whole Ghetto was in danger because of the Meck case. However, it cannot be said that he betrayed our community, just as those who hid away and survived in cellars and attics during deportations and mass murders did not betray us. Would we have been better off if Katz and his wife had been dead? The principle of self-defense, of protecting the life of an individual, is a positive principle. Katz may have stumbled, but we must not deliver him with our own hands into the jaws of death.

My suggestion was to release Katz—arrested on the charge of shirking work duty—from jail. From now on, he will go to work. Upon his release it should be hinted to him that he would do well to disappear from the Ghetto, or to go into hiding for a while. In the police books he should be entered as having served time in jail for work absenteeism, but not as Shimon Katz. He should be entered under the name of Levi Katz. After all there are many Jews in the Ghetto whose surname is Katz.

Once this step is taken, the police will be "in order" from the official point of view. Besides, there is no way to avoid completely some measure of risk, if we want to save Jewish lives.

Dr. Elkes concurred in my view not to deliver Katz to the Germans. His name and his residence will be changed. Kopelman accepted our view and expressed his consent. He said: "If this is what you decide, then we shall do it." But deep in his heart he was very much afraid.

Matters of life and death. O Lord! When will this end?

Dr. Kvitner, the Jewish dentist of the Gestapo, was dismissed from his job following his arrest. He was ordered to go to work at the airfield. Today he was reinstated as the Gestapo dentist. Kvitner's case is not quite clear: was he arrested because of his relations with Mrs. Miller, who is German and, like him, works for the Gestapo? Or rather was he arrested because of the workers on whom suicide pills had been found,[4] or, perhaps, because they wanted to get rid of him?

One thing is clear: Dr. Kvitner's life was in danger. He relates that during his interrogation in the Gestapo prison he addressed Schtitz, with whom he had maintained contact on a daily basis: "I am telling you, Mr. Schtitz, I did not commit any offense and I did not break any law." Schtitz's reply to him was: "And all those in the Ninth Fort—did they commit any offense?"

This was a straightforward reply. All comment is unnecessary. Throughout a life filled with savagery, Schtitz had never uttered such a truth as this. A sad and bitter truth.

1. Shimon Katz, the young man who had attempted to escape with Meck on the day when Meck was caught.
2. Avraham Tory is referring here to those few Jews who became rich while in the Ghetto, mainly from smuggling. There were even a very few who had personal contacts with Lithuanians, and some even with Germans, which extended to drinking together.
3. This one time, the Council had to set aside its principle of not turning over people or names to the Germans.
4. Many Jews had suicide pills in case they should be caught by the Gestapo and be unable to withstand torture. This particularly applied to those who had to work at the Gestapo building.

END OF DECEMBER, 1942

DOCUMENT: Avraham Golub, Last Will and Testament[1]

Driven by a force within me, and out of fear that no remnant of the Jewish community of Kovno will survive to tell of its final death agony under Nazi rule, I have continued, while in the Ghetto, to record my diary, which I began on the first day of the outbreak of the war.

Every day, I put into writing what my eyes had seen and my ears had heard, and what I had experienced personally.

As secretary of the Jewish Committee of the Ghetto, the Ältestenrat as the Nazi authorities named it, I had a unique vantage point and direct contact, almost every day, with Jewish institutions and individuals in the Ghetto, and occasionally with some of the Nazi and Lithuanian rulers, whose personal treatment had a far-reaching effect on our lives in the Ghetto, for better or for worse—everything within the framework of our final destruction, of course.

I was fully aware of what happened every day in the Ghetto. I was present at meetings of the Council, and I heard the cries of the people who were crushed by the burden of forced labor, of others who were racked by hunger pains, and of those who begged for help. I heard the weeping of women who were raped in public and humiliated despicably, and the words of those who poured out their hearts before the Council members, saying that they no longer had the strength or will to fight for their hopeless lives, devoid of any purpose or hope— lives which were nothing else but protracted physical and mental torture.

I took part in the efforts to console the young and the old, to encourage them not to surrender and to continue to struggle and to believe that they would be rescued from the Ghetto and from their bitter fate in spite of everything.

As one of the founders and leaders of Matzok, the Zionist underground group in the Ghetto, I made very effort under the prevailing circumstances, and together with my comrades, to give the Zionist youth a glimmer of hope that they would yet live to see their dream of aliya—emigration to the land of Israel— come true.

In order to illustrate actual life within the Ghetto, I also collected documents, publications, orders, warnings, notices, and commands issued by the evil regime and—not to mention them in the same breath—announcements of the Jewish Ghetto Council and its departments, as well as judgments of the Jewish court of the Ghetto, which often constituted precedents in times of emergency, the likes of which are not to be found in any law book anywhere in the world.

I collected paintings, symbols, graphics, songs, and macabre humor, which, as in a distorted mirror, reflect private and social life in the Ghetto.

I overcame the fear of death which is directly connected with the very fact of writing each page of my diary, and with the very collection and hiding of the documentary material. Had the slightest part of any of this been discovered, my fate would have been sealed.

With awe and reverence, I am hiding in this crate what I have written, noted, and collected, with thrill and anxiety, so that it may serve as material evidence— "corpus delicti"—accusing testimony—when the Day of Judgment comes, and with it the day of revenge and the day of reckoning, the calling to account.

All this I leave and entrust to the Zionist Leadership of the Jews in Lithuania, if such a body will still exist after the fall of the bloodthirsty regime. If no such body exists in Lithuania, heaven forbid, then it is my last wish that this crate, with all that is in it, should be handed over to the executive of the World Zionist Organization in Jerusalem.

Eternal shame on the Nazis and their collaborators—the Lithuanians, the Ukrainians, and the others!

REVENGE! NEVER FORGET! NEVER FORGIVE!

In the Ghetto of Kovno, December 1942
One of the tens of thousands who did not survive
Avraham, son of Zoruch and Sarah Leah Golub

1. This will was placed on top of the diary material in the first crate to be buried. An identical will, except for the date, was placed in each of the four other crates.

1943

The Ninth Fort, where tens of thousands of Jews from Kovno and elsewhere in Europe were murdered between 1941 and 1944.

JANUARY 1, 1943

DOCUMENT: Council of the Jewish Ghetto Community, Vilijampolé, Instruction[1]

It is herewith confirmed that Mr. Benno Lipzer, working with the Council, is authorized to inspect all the Council facilities and offices, as well as the Jewish Ghetto police, and to obtain any information concerning the activity of each office and its employees.

Council employees are obliged to give him the necessary information concerning their activities, and to present their official certificates upon request.

The orders given by Mr. Lipzer during Ghetto gate duty must be obeyed.

1. This instruction was signed by Dr. Elkes.

JANUARY 6, 1943

Several days ago the deputy city governor, Keiffler, head of the German municipal administration, visited the Ghetto. Among other places, he visited the horse stable of the Council's transportation department. This department is an important economic factor in the Ghetto. In the period of the great "actions," in the months of August, September, and October 1941, an order was given to transfer to the city governor's office all our means of transport—horses, carts, carriages, sleighs, etc.

After numerous applications and supplications, and thanks to the intercession of the commander of the third squad of the German police, Captain Tornbaum—who was an enthusiastic fancier of all sorts of animals—we succeeded in convincing the city governor's office to let us keep four or five horses. These horses constituted our only means of transport, serving a Ghetto population which then numbered about 27,000.

How, we asked, is it possible for us to meet even the most essential transportation needs of so large a population? The reply of the Germans was clear: "Let the Jews harness themselves to the carts and bring the supplies into the Ghetto in this way."

In those days the Ghetto was terrorized constantly. The terror did not even subside between one "action" and the next. There was no place for an orderly economic life in the Ghetto then. Human life did not count for much, and it simply was not possible to organize the life of the Ghetto residents.

After the first period of terror, the need emerged to impose some order on the economic life of the Ghetto: to set up workshops, to organize sanitation services, to create an orderly system of food supply, and much else. Without some regular and orderly means of transportation, none of these tasks could be accomplished. The five horses at our disposal were a drop in the ocean of our needs. A sixth horse, which wandered by chance into the Ghetto area, did not in any way improve the situation.

By and by, we increased the number of carts and horses, without the knowledge of the city governor's office. The Council, using its own resources, took care to supply the fodder and to keep the carts in working order. An important form of help came from the German Ghetto command headquarters. One of the commanders of the Ghetto Guard, Levitt, who was a farmer and loved horses, sent one of his subordinates to help us to purchase horses and to supply them with fodder.

As conditions in the Ghetto became somewhat more stable, our needs also grew. The Ghetto economy was working and the means of transportation expanded progressively. Large workshops, the vegetable gardens, the repair of roads and sidewalks, the supply of timber and firewood for houses—all these required the constant expansion of the means of transportation.

During this period the area of the Ghetto was reduced eight consecutive times. When some quarter was placed outside the Ghetto precincts, a large number of people—sometimes as many as two or three thousand—had to be moved urgently to the remaining area. Such evacuation called for the deployment of a large part—sometimes even most of—the means of transportation at our disposal. In sewage works we could not act according to Jordan's directives, and there was a need to harness people to the carts to pull them. This was carried out by the Council's transportation office.

The Ghetto transportation system was also used to bring into the Ghetto blocks of ice and firewood, and, quite often, for funerals. There was also a need to build new rooms for the people to live in. For that purpose balconies were closed and converted into rooms, while storerooms and stables became lodging quarters. In addition, various public institutions (houses of study, synagogues, and the like) were in need of repair.

All these needs required the constant expansion of our transportation department. Today its size is quite impressive: twenty-two horses, a large number of carts, a new stable, and a blacksmith shop. The number of horses at our disposal is still too small, however, and needs to be doubled. This means getting a permit from the city governor's office, where things are moving at a very slow pace. If we had complied with the advice and prohibitions of the German authorities, we could not subsist.

This expansion of the transportation system was not at all to the liking of the city governor's office. It began issuing edicts forbidding the use of horses for funerals, for house repairs, and for other vital needs. For tasks such as these, the Jews must harness themselves to the carts, the city governor's office told us. Horses may be used only for transporting raw materials for the workshops and foodstuffs for the Ghetto residents. The officials at the city governor's office did not ask how the transportation system had expanded from four or five horses into a sizable enterprise. They added that if there were carts and horses in large numbers in the Ghetto, a considerable part of them must be transferred to the city governor's office.

Every day, officials from the city governor's office come to the Ghetto: Miller, Gilow, and a few days ago Keiffler himself put in an appearance. All of them are looking for various "faults": apertures in the walls of the stable are too wide, the horses not groomed, cleanliness is not satisfactory. Keiffler was stunned to see two special carriages for funerals in the large courtyard of the transportation department; these carts had been left over from the bygone days. The German ruler was seething: why all that ceremony in connection with funerals and burials? If a Jew was dead, all one had to do was to throw him into the pit and the whole burial ceremony was over and done with.

The transportation arrangements in the Ghetto were not to the liking of the German senior official. He announced his intention to take over the administration of the transportation department and to entrust it to the hands of Gilow, the German director of the workshops.

This decision was extremely upsetting for us, especially since it spelled the paralysis of the Ghetto. Keiffler summoned the representatives of the Council to appear at his office at 9 A.M. on the following morning. The Council delegated Garfunkel and me to go to him.

We arrived at the city governor's office as early as 8 A.M. Miller has come back from his vacation today, and I wanted to snatch a conversation with him before the meeting with Keiffler. Miller received me. I told him about the upcoming meeting with Keiffler and asked him to try to prevail on Keiffler not to change the status quo as far as transportation was concerned. After all, he, Miller, called at the stables quite often and could therefore make sure that matters were conducted properly. Miller contacted Keiffler by telephone and announced that he would like to join our discussion.

At nine o'clock we entered Keiffler's small office, which was rather tastefully decorated. He did not bother to motion us to sit down, so we remained standing. As usual, he was smoking a cigar. He asked us very politely how things were going in the Ghetto. He did not care whether the rations that the city governor's office allocated were enough to keep body and soul together. All he wanted was to make sure that the appointed rations actually did arrive in the Ghetto, rather than disappear en route.

We answered that the rations arrive in fits and starts and with certain delays. Then followed questions about the sanitation services: How many beds were there in the hospital? How many patients, what was the nature of their illness, the mortality statistics, how many births? And, in general, were records kept of all these events in the Ghetto?

We answered that ever since last September there have been no births in the Ghetto. That was news to him: "How is it possible? Are there no children born in the Ghetto?"

"The Gestapo had strictly forbidden women in the Ghetto to give birth, and so they all had to terminate pregnancies," we answered. When the word "Gestapo" is uttered, the great Keiffler refrains from asking questions. His unwillingness to hear this dreadful name is a characteristic and known reaction.

It appears that even a figure like Keiffler does not dare to show any interest in the Gestapo's activities. He fixes us with a penetrating gaze when we tell him about the activities of the Gestapo, as if he wanted to say: "You are dealing with the Gestapo? Nothing good will come out of it. Woe to you." He moves on to questions about other problems in the Ghetto.

A stranger, eavesdropping on this conversation, would think that we were faced with a well-mannered man showing great interest in friends whom he had not seen for a long time. In fact, Keiffler's questions are correct and to the point. But if the aforementioned imaginary stranger were to peer through the keyhole at the partners in this conversation, he would behold a weird scene: Keiffler stretching himself in his armchair, puffing smoke from his cigar, from time to time looking at Garfunkel and me with eyes full of disgust and contempt. At the same time, he would see both of us standing on our feet throughout the meeting, anxiously following not only the drift of his questions but the tone of his voice, his facial expression, and his gaze penetrating the depths of one's soul. The stranger would realize then that this was not exactly a conversation between friends—that we stood in front of a beast of prey in human disguise, an aggressive, biting animal, eager to inflict pain.

We are trying to defend ourselves as best we can, to give the right answer to every question, to avert danger. This cat-and-mouse game occurs because all the statements of the person who asks the questions are false.

That is what our conversation with Keiffler and his ilk looks like. They are always on the offensive, whether openly or by means of apparently innocent questions, whereas we must find a proper and logical reply to questions whose drift is clear.

At long last, Keiffler gets to his main purpose in this conversation: cleanliness in the stables is not observed, and several of the horses have been taken sick. The transportation department will therefore be taken over by the city governor. In this way, at least, supervision of transportation will be vested in the hands of the German director of the workshops, Gilow, who visits the Ghetto very often.

Keiffler said all this quietly, composedly, and serenely, as if we were not affected by his decision at all. He did not ask, nor did he want to know, how the new arrangement would work in the Ghetto or what its impact would be on the lives of the Ghetto inmates.

JANUARY 20, 1943

Miller told us that today, between 10 and 11 A.M., he had entered the Ghetto in a car driven by a Lithuanian driver. Together with a certain lady, he occupied the back seat. The car windows were frosted over and nobody could have recognized him. As it happened, no one intercepted the car at the Ghetto gate; no one inquired about its passengers. On the contrary, the gate was flung open and the car drove into the Ghetto. There was also a city government office official in the car, who asked Miller whether there was not any inspection at the gate. Miller was embarrassed because the sentries at the gate had failed to do their duty.

Miller asked me what penalties were imposed on Jewish policemen. I replied that there were the following penalties: a warning, a transfer to another duty, degradation, and finally dismissal. "Are the policemen also punished by imprisonment?" Miller asked. Yes, I told him. "Well," said Miller, "in that case the Jewish policeman who was on guard duty at the gate today between 10 and 11 A.M. will be given a warning and put in the Ghetto jail for seven days."

I tried to explain that the Jewish policeman was not to blame. Control over the entrance to the Ghetto was, in actual fact, in the hands of the Lithuanian policemen. Miller became very angry. Earlier, before I entered the office, Segalson had told me that Miller was not in the best of moods.

Miller said that he was going to punish the Lithuanian policeman also; that from now on a Jewish policeman would stand next to a Lithuanian, to help him supervise the traffic entering the Ghetto.

Later, Miller asked me whether the workers who leave for work every morning are back in the Ghetto at 8 P.M. When I answered in the affirmative, he ordered me to convene all the heads of labor brigades in the Council office at 8 o'clock that evening. Miller would also be there and instruct those present on the marching of the labor brigades through the city streets to and from work; he would also discuss the subject of work discipline and the manner of marching of the labor brigades.

Miller then telephoned Hermann, the director of the German labor office, and asked him to attend the meeting at eight o'clock, at which Natkin would also be present, at Miller's insistence. I wrote those directives in my notebook.

Miller complained about a lot of things: in the city the Ghetto residents walk on the streets and not on the sidewalk. When he, Miller, rides in a car, he always encounters people walking down the middle of the road. This must not be allowed to happen. It is forbidden for the Ghetto residents to walk down the middle of the road. They are required to walk along the side of the road.

Miller went on to complain about Jews not wearing their Star of David in the proper manner. The yellow badge must be worn on the clothes both on the front and on the back.

I replied that we did not have in our possession the yellow fabric needed for the badges. If he signs an order for the yellow fabric, the workshops will produce sufficient quantities of the regulation yellow badges. Miller accepted my suggestion and immediately signed an order for 200 meters of yellow fabric. Gilow witnessed the conversation between Miller and me. Miller's tone of voice was domineering and commanding. This is the accepted practice when speaking to Jews when there are two Germans or more in attendance. One to one they are not so dangerous. I often speak with Miller one to one; on such occasions our conversation is polite and to the point. But when Gilow or Keiffler is also present, Miller raises his voice to show how the Jews are to be spoken to.

I know and recognize this German practice, and do not make a fuss over it. In contrast, Natkin took this seriously; when at the end of the conversation Miller told him "And now get out!" he was very agitated. I explained to him the way the Germans speak to Jews in public.

We went outside. I asked the labor department to summon the leaders of labor brigades ("brigadiers") as well as the commanders of the Jewish police, for the meeting at 8 P.M. I also gave the Jewish police the text of Miller's order about the warning, and the sentence of seven days' imprisonment for the policeman who had been on duty between 10 and 11 A.M. at the Ghetto gate. Then we waited for the hour of eight to come. No such meeting has ever taken place in the Ghetto.

Just before eight o'clock leaders of the labor brigades were assembled in the labor department; between sixty and seventy had been summoned. Police chiefs, as well as senior officials of the labor department and of the Council, were also present.

Several minutes after eight o'clock Miller and Hermann arrived. We waited for them outside and ushered them into the room, where labor brigade leaders had already been ranged in rows, military style. A table and some chairs stood in the middle of the room. When the Germans entered the room, Kopelman, the

Ghetto Jewish police chief, called out "Stand at attention!" Miller sat down at the table; Hermann sat down next to him.

Miller played the main part; he radiated contentment. His behavior gave the impression of a Polish aristocrat among his servants, who were deprived of any rights. He willingly accepted help in taking off his coat. He then accepted a lighted match offered to him to light a cigarette. He also asked for an ashtray. Then he took a sheaf of papers out of his briefcase and laid them on the table. Having done this, he began walking between the table and the rows of labor brigade leaders.

Miller opened the meeting by asking whether everyone present knew him; he asked those who knew him to raise their hands and then asked the same of those who did not. He said that it was important to him that everyone should know him. (Incidentally, whenever he ran across somebody—in the workshop, in the Council office, or in the street—he would always ask such a person whether he knew him.) Everyone, he said, is required to recognize him, even when he wears civilian clothes. And not only him. The Ghetto inmates are required to recognize four important people: Miller; Gilow, the manager of the workshops; the commandant of the Ghetto guard; and the director of the German labor office, Hermann. These are the personages the Ghetto residents may contact.

At that point Miller reached the main topic of the meeting; for the next hour he lectured those present about the way in which labor brigade leaders should lead their crews to work; how they should conduct themselves during work hours, and in what fashion they should return to the Ghetto. He proceeded to read out two new orders (nos. 12 and 13) according to which a labor brigade leader is responsible for the behavior of the members of his brigade. Workers must march to work in rows of three, and the rows must march in unison. The marching pace must be adjusted to the pace of the slowest worker in the column. Workers carrying various bundles, or food rations for the brigade, must bring up the rear. Upon encountering a German Army man, the brigade leader must salute him by taking off his cap.

A further directive, no. 14, forbids anyone to leave his labor brigade at the workplace for any reason. It is forbidden for Jews to speak with non-Jews. It is forbidden to tell outsiders about our work. It is forbidden to pass on to anyone any information about the Ghetto. Staying in the city without a guard may be approved only by Miller or the Gestapo. All other permits are deemed invalid.

Miller added some comments of his own to these directives: he knows that the Council is not always capable of carrying out the directives issued by the authorities. It was for this reason that he had decided to convene the labor brigade leaders and explain to them personally what is required of them. The execution of these orders will, as always, rest in the hands of the Council.

With regard to the general problems of the Ghetto: the supply of firewood for the winter of 1943–1944 will improve. The supply depends on the availability of transportation, which is heavily used. Some supplies will not be available. We must exert greater efforts in the field of agriculture, especially in the vegetable gardens in the Ghetto, in order to ensure a sufficient supply of vegetables for the next year. Miller opposed growing vegetable "delicacies." His preference was for "simple" vegetables such as cabbages, potatoes, cucumbers, and the like.

Other comments made by Miller: nowadays the Jewish police and the members of the Council salute the Germans in a military fashion which is reserved only for the German Army. Representatives of the Ghetto institutions are required to salute by taking their caps off. The Jews must stop talking about events in the Ghetto. There is no point in their glorifying their achievements. Miller himself will do it.

Miller then asked those present if any workers were receiving money from any source. He is required to deliver any such person to the city governor. The same applies to other Ghetto inmates. He knows that there are breaches of discipline during work, and that the pace of work remains inadequate, but he prefers not to elaborate on this at the moment. He wants, however, to see an improvement in this area starting tomorrow. If a German should ask about various materials to be found in the Ghetto, the reply must be that the Jews are forbidden to speak about the Ghetto. All such questions must be addressed to Miller. He will provide the necessary explanations.

Miller then spoke about the workshops. Thanks to Segalson, a good job was being done there. The Jewish police must extend assistance to the Lithuanian Guard at the Ghetto gate, primarily in translation into Lithuanian. The following are to be allowed to enter the Ghetto freely: Miller himself, City Governor Cramer, Governor-General of Lithuania Dr. von Renteln, and the commandant of the Gestapo, Jaeger. Other persons wishing to enter the Ghetto must show an entrance permit signed either by Miller or by Jaeger.

Finally, Miller said that all workplaces which employ Jews will receive instructions regarding how to handle them. He will instruct the police to ensure that no one stays in the city without proper authorization. He will make sure that all Jews on work details will receive warm meals at their places of work. The remaining Ghetto inmates will receive increased food rations.

Having finished his address, Miller adjourned the meeting.

This was the first meeting of its kind in the Ghetto. The Council members were as surprised as the manager of the German labor office, Hermann. His reports and explanations to Miller should be seen in a positive light. In the days of Jordan, and even under Koeppen, such a meeting with the Germans was out of the question. In those times our rulers did not speak to us at all. If they did, it was in the language of abuse and insults.

The focus of today's meeting was on clarifications concerning the existing regulations. It was quite theatrical, but this is how the German rulers usually present themselves. The Germans speak with us as humans quite often, but when they suddenly realize that the person they are talking to is simply a Jew, they raise their voices.

Until now the Ghetto inmates have maintained contact with representatives of the authorities only at their places of work, where they swallow insults and even receive blows on occasion. There has been no other form of contact between the two sides. This meeting was different in this respect. Its positive aspect stems from Miller's character. Following Miller's address, the Council issued directives to the labor office and to the Jewish police.

JANUARY 20, 1943

DOCUMENT:
From SA Colonel Cramer, City Governor, Kovno
To the Jewish Council

Re: Marching discipline of the columns of compulsory labor outside the Ghetto, in the area of the city of Kovno

1. In charge of the column is the appointed leader.

2. The marching column comprises rows of three, with distance of one meter between rows.

3. Members of the column carrying something (wood, foodstuffs, and other permitted items) must always be put at the end of the column, so that marching at the head are only Jews without loads.

4. On this depends the speed of movement of the column. The leader must take care that the column does not drag like an accordion. The marching speed must therefore conform with the slowest member of the column, but at the same time any unnecessary idling must be avoided.[1]

---

1. This order of Colonel Cramer, as well as the two that follow, was signed by Lieutenant Miller.

JANUARY 20, 1943

DOCUMENT:
From SA Colonel Cramer, City Governor, Kovno
To the Jewish Council

Re: Movements of individual Jews outside the Ghetto when working at compulsory labor, etc.

1. All Jews who must leave the Ghetto and return there alone on official duties, or who must walk alone through the area of the city of Kovno on official missions, as ordered by appointed offices, can do so only with a certificate issued by me. This certificate, as already mentioned, must be requested from my office by the compulsory-labor places concerned, which will hand them over to the Jews.

2. All column leaders at compulsory-labor places are responsible to me, to ensure that during lunch and other breaks no contact with the local population is established. Likewise, the column leaders must ensure that no Jews stroll freely in the streets during such breaks, as such strolling is done mostly for bartering. The result of this is

3. that no Jew, except in official matters, is allowed to enter into conversation with the local population and certainly not with Germans.

JANUARY 22, 1943

DOCUMENT:
From SA Colonel Cramer, City Governor, Kovno
Instruction to the Ghetto Guard, particularly gate five, concerning the
presentation and permission to all persons passing into the Ghetto[1]

The Ghetto may be entered individually or in groups, on vehicles or without, officially or unofficially, only with a permit issued by the governor of Kovno.

The only exemptions are permits issued by the security police and the Gestapo.

Furthermore, the following persons are authorized, either alone or accompanied, to enter the Ghetto without such a permit: (1) the governor-general, Dr. von Renteln; (2) the permanent representative of the Nazi Party in Kovno, Nabersberg; (3) the governor of Kovno, Colonel Cramer.

If persons arrive from other places and are not aware of the administrative regulations concerning the Ghetto, with whom they must officially negotiate, etc.—for example, with the manager of the workshops—(especially members of the armed forces), the following procedure must be adhered to, in order to make things easier (to save on fuel on the way to the office of the governor of Kovno):

The Ghetto gate guard will telephone the manager of the workshops or me, and we shall decide how to proceed.

All other persons and vehicles, not recognized by the Ghetto Guard as authorized to pass, must stop and submit to permit control. The Ghetto gate guard is instructed to take any invalid permit and inform the person concerned that he must apply for a new one. In such a case, the passing of such persons into the Ghetto is not allowed.

Nobody has the right to act in contradiction of this order, which is indispensable for the maintenance of an orderly administration.

1. This order was signed by Miller.

JANUARY 22, 1943

I went to the city early in the morning and had a talk with Miller. There was an urgent need to discuss with him the problem of the supply of raw materials to our workshops (particularly those turning out clothing, shoes, underwear, furs, and rubber boots) as well as the purchase of various materials and machinery for the house repair department, for the vocational training school, for the laundry, for the baths, and for various other enterprises.

Directive no. 2, issued by the city governor's office, makes it compulsory to submit a monthly list of materials necessary for operating various enterprises and services in the Ghetto. We do submit such lists, but recently we have received things like medicines only in small quantities, as well as ten kilograms of thick threads to be used for tying things, and bags for the food department. We have also received a small quantity of materials for the workshops and for the house repair department.

Our warehouses are practically depleted by now. Even the scraps are gone. If we do not soon receive substantial quantities of iron, iron sheets, and timber, we shall be forced to close down the house repair department. We also need sewing thread and tools for the workshops.

Orders for various raw materials have been lying on Obst's desk for months. When I remind him that they are urgently needed, he pretends to be offended: he claims to be very busy; it has been a long time since he met Miller, etc. I decided therefore to settle the matter with Miller.

A few days ago I went over the list of orders with Miller. When I saw him again yesterday, he told me that he wished to visit the workshops on behalf of which I placed the orders for raw materials.

So he came to the Ghetto. First, we went to the Council offices, where we asked Goldberg and Potruch[1] to join us. Then we began touring various enterprises. Miller was pleased with what he saw, and approved our orders. He did have some comments, though. When visiting the house repair department, for example, he saw workers making a sleigh for children. He asked: "You're fixing up a sleigh to use it for gliding on ice at the time we suffer from a severe shortage of iron? This is out of the question." I explained to him that this was not a sleigh for children to play with, but that because of the shortage of means of transport we were using sleighs to carry wood and other goods.

Afterward, Miller's attention was drawn toward a certain item on our order: materials for mending dresses for women. His comment was: "Even the German woman has nothing to wear nowadays; she is hard pressed to get even a button, and you want me to get you hundreds of buttons." I told him that the buttons are needed for mending clothes for the entire Ghetto population. Miller's answer was: "You should know that we will supply you with all kinds of necessary materials so that production can go on; so that you will be able to get up every morning at 5 A.M. and go to work. For other needs, you will not get anything."

Our labor department had been receiving used clothes and shoes. In the old municipality building had been stored huge quantities of clothing, cooking utensils, and pieces of furniture seized from the Kovno Jews, and from Jews from other provincial towns. There are no women's dresses at all in the municipal storehouses. Miller's comment: "We are at war, and everyone should wear whatever he has got in his wardrobe."

"Go back to the Ghetto now, Golub," Miller said. "Think about what I've told you. We are at war, remember. Many articles are in short supply everywhere. Germany itself is not an exception. But we shall win this war. You can count on us in this matter. Do not entertain any foolish hopes about our possible defeat. We must economize wherever and whenever possible." In the end, however, Miller supplied us with all the items we had ordered.

In actual fact, Miller's whole trip to the workshops was just a show for the benefit of Obst. As I mentioned earlier, Miller is very talkative. He likes to explain things down to the minutest detail. Quite often he even speaks out without giving it a second thought.

That very day, he gave me a permit to bring 850 cubic meters of firewood into the Ghetto, for the use of the workers at the airfield. We were also allowed to bring in blocks of ice for the hospital.

When I visited Miller yesterday, I asked his permission for a number of workers to ride in a truck to Siauliai, to bring back a certain amount of leather from the factory—formerly belonging to Fraenkel[2]—for the use of the Ghetto workers. There is simply nothing to repair shoes with; not one piece of leather with which to patch up a torn shoe.

Miller gave his permission. His question was: "Who is going to guard them?" I told him that they would leave in a truck belonging to the airfield, in the company of a German soldier from the airfield who would keep an eye on them.

Miller signed the permit and yesterday the workers left to bring the leather.

Upon my return to the Ghetto from the city yesterday, I was told that Miller was strolling about in the laundry area, where a barber shop which sells wigs is also located. I decided to join him.

I found Miller in the barber shop, where one woman is making wigs for women. There were many customers in the barber shop at this time, getting a haircut or a shave. When Miller stepped over the threshold of the shop, everyone leapt to his feet and one of them shouted "Achtung!" Miller asked "Where do you have a room for women here?" Then he cried out loud: "Memento mori! Memento mori!" (Remember the dead) and asked if there was anybody there who could understand Latin. Having received no answer to his question, he added: "In vino veritas, in vino veritas" (There is truth in wine), and left.

About thirty meters away from us, Mrs. Goldberg, a young and pretty woman, was walking along. Her husband, the engineer Goldberg, had "gone" with the five hundred,[3] and she was left alone with a baby. It looked as if Miller fancied this woman. He asked me who she was and I told him.

Miller cried out aloud: "Mrs. Goldberg!" The woman turned around and approached us, looking dejected. He asked her whether she recognized him; what was his name; how old was she; whether she had a husband; where did she work; did she have a friend; did she wish to marry anyone. She answered "no." "That's not much," Miller said. "You look like a person with a passion for life," he continued. "It is possible that I am like that," she said. "Very well," said Miller, and went on his way. "A wonderful woman," he told me.

We came to the Council offices. On the walls were posters and various announcements. One of them says that the baths are open three times a week. Miller asked: "Where are the baths?" Meanwhile, his car arrived. We got into it and drove to the baths.

At that time women were using the baths. Miller wanted to inspect the arrangements inside. He asked, therefore, that the women go into the washing rooms. He then inspected the baths and their arrangements. He is quite a character, this Miller.

Yesterday a strange incident took place at the Ghetto gate. A labor brigade leader, Reznik, was involved. His squad works in the townlet of Prienai and the workers return to the Ghetto once a week, or once in two weeks. The workers bring with them large quantities of goods, and when they leave in the morning they take with them various articles to trade them for other goods. When leaving the Ghetto, or on their way back, they drop a "little something" for the guards at the gate.

Yesterday Reznik rebelled. When leaving the Ghetto, loaded with bundles, he refused to abide by the long-standing practice. In response, the guards detained him at the gate. They were aware that such behavior might have a "bad influence" on other workers. They therefore asked him to "settle" this affair. Reznik refused to budge and threatened to call on "his" German, who would teach them a lesson.

The guards led him away to the Ghetto detention center at 23 Krisciukaicio Street to "cool off." Lipzer, who happened to be there, went berserk. He ordered ten lashes to be administered to Reznik. This is the first time this has happened in the Ghetto.

1. Moshe Potruch, a former industrialist, was head of the economic affairs department (also known as the finance department) of the Council. He died in November 1943, two weeks after the first group of partisans left the Ghetto for the Augustow Forest. It was his department which had put three wagons with horses at their disposal for a few hours, supposedly so that they could go to chop wood outside the Ghetto.

2. Jacob Fraenkel, an industrialist, had been the owner of a large fur and leather factory in Siauliai. In June 1941 it was confiscated by the Germans.

3. Goldberg was one of the 534 Kovno Jewish intellectuals murdered on August 18, 1941.

FEBRUARY 1, 1943

"Ratnikas[1] is upon you, Israel!"—people cry with one voice in recent days. The man joined the Lithuanian Ghetto Guard some time ago and has already poisoned the atmosphere in the Ghetto, both at the Ghetto gate, where he conducts meticulous searches of workers, and along the Ghetto fence. He even took it upon himself to conduct house searches of those suspected of selling foodstuffs. Since his arrival, he sets his own assignments in the Ghetto. He ignores the general directives of the commander of the Lithuanian Guard. He is not even particularly impressed with the orders issued by the German commandant, who, for his part, is not happy with Ratnikas's behavior.

With the exception of special cases, it is forbidden to conduct searches in the Ghetto without Gestapo authorization. With Ratnikas, searches have become commonplace. More than that: when he sees a woman on the street carrying a few kilograms of flour for baking bread, he takes her to the Ghetto command headquarters without delay. Natkin has his hands full until he manages to settle the affair and release the detained woman.

Ratnikas frightens many people and the German commandant does not like it; he is interested in seeing peace prevail in the Ghetto. Thus, for example, Ratnikas does not wear a uniform like other policemen of the Ghetto Guard; wearing civilian clothes, he roams the Ghetto streets like a stray dog, especially along the Ghetto fence. He shows up in places where nobody expects him, looking for victims. Legends have already been created about his character and his deeds. For instance, it is said that several times he stuck yellow badges on his clothes and passed through the Ghetto fence in order to test the reaction of the Lithuanian guards. The latter hate him with passion. He harasses them and informs on them for taking bribes and for failing to do their job properly. He even prevents them from making a little profit on the side once in a while.

For us, Ratnikas is most dangerous. As a result of house searches, quite a few Jews have been sent to the Gestapo and their fate sealed.

Both the Germans and the Lithuanians abhor him. The Lithuanian sentries are in the habit of saying: "Give it to us, otherwise it will fall into the hands of Ratnikas." They detest him, not out of moral considerations, but for practical reasons. The Germans despise him too, because he gives them unnecessary headaches. Ratnikas is making our lives bitter. If he is seen standing at the main Ghetto gate, people turn away and move to the other gate, and vice versa. If you see him from far off, you turn into another alley. He inspires the Ghetto inmates with mortal fear.

Ever since Ratnikas's arrival, the bakery owners tremble with fear; flour mill owners are afraid; pharmacy workers are worried; fear and dread have fallen on the food distribution stations. Not everything here is absolutely "kosher." In the Ghetto everything is "kosher" until policemen come and start snooping around. For example, he asks the flour mill owners where they get the flour for baking bread, when it is forbidden to keep it in the Ghetto and every Ghetto inmate receives bread once a day. And, in general, why are flour mills needed in the Ghetto, and where is the flour being bought? The owners of the mills, of course, come up with a ready excuse: the flour is needed for the Ghetto Guards, who receive grain once in a while. It goes without saying that this is a good excuse as long as one does not have to use it.

Other questions: where do the bakeries get their salt and firewood? Answers to queries like these are likely to result in grave consequences. Until now such questions have not been asked. A tacit fiction has been created: different workplaces supply various materials to produce goods in order to secure a special addition of rations to the workers. Yet fiction it remains. Everybody knows this, including the Ghetto command headquarters, but people prefer to pretend they know nothing.

This was the situation until Ratnikas arrived. He is everywhere. He turns every small offense into a serious crime. People say that we must get rid of him. In the meantime, he stirs up fresh trouble every day. People fear him, not only at the entrance to the Ghetto but in their own homes. It happens that someone keeps ten kilograms of flour in his apartment and one kilogram of butter. Something should be kept at home, because it might not be available tomorrow. When there is an opportunity, people buy things come what may. One way or the other, Ratnikas must go.

Deputy City Governor Keiffler is leaving his post today. He was involved in all the Ghetto's problems, even if only a few people knew about his existence, as he seldom came into the Ghetto. When he did come, either to the Council office or to the workshops, his arrival always spelled new trouble for the Ghetto inmates. He served as inspector of economic affairs in the Ghetto. In the days of Jordan he was always looking for ways and means of putting pressure on us. Under Koeppen's tenure, Keiffler completely ignored the Council meetings and left the Ghetto administration destitute. It was not just an economic loss but an act of political injustice, and it caused great damage to the Ghetto.

Our relations with the outside world, as well as our public activity—if it could be viewed as such—always depended on our economic situation. Should our economy suffer, we would lose an important leverage in our public activities.

Keiffler was well aware of this; it was his goal. His deportment and his way of speaking were those of a person incapable of hurting a fly. He is a dangerous man, though; a man who carries out his plans in cold blood. He used to do terrible things while looking at the ceiling and calmly continuing to smoke his cigar or cigarette. Suspicion arose that he was planning a new nasty surprise for us.

Keiffler was the most composed official of the city governor's office, where he played the part of the moving spirit. Owing to his high position he enjoyed free access on every important issue. Every problem which came up in the Ghetto waited for his decision. Today he is leaving us. We do not know whether his departure is temporary or permanent. From our point of view, it may be said: Blessed be He who has rid us of this man.

Yesterday a Jewish worker was killed during the transporting of coal in the electric power plant in Petrasiunai. He was fifty-eight. Work at this place is very strenuous; trainloads of coal arrive there and must be unloaded forthwith. The Lithuanian overseers are brutal and coarse, and treat the Jewish workers cruelly. Not for nothing have the Poles for many years been calling them the sons of Ham—brutes. In most cases, the name is quite appropriate. Their numbed brains and dull wits do not allow them to grasp our unique situation in these days of war and German rule. They make the life of the Jewish workers in Petrasiunai miserable. They scream: "You, damn Zhids, you don't like to work, do you? The times when you did not have to work are over now." The Jews are overcome by fear and despair.

A Jewish worker aged fifty-eight, who had made a good name for himself and had gone to great lengths to succeed in his job, stumbled suddenly and fell under the wheels of two railway wagons carrying coal. Thus he met his death. In Petrasiunai there are no safety precautions to prevent such things from happening.

Today another victim fell as a result of forced labor. Another victim in the Ghetto.

1. Ratnikas, an officer of the Ghetto Guard corps and the Lithuanian overseer of the Ghetto gate, was noted for his cruelty.

FEBRUARY 4, 1943

In the last three days an atmosphere of fear and trepidation has set in here in the Ghetto. Breathing has become difficult. For a relatively long period of time, the situation in the Ghetto has been "stable": "normal" arrests, various persecutions and excesses, which did not deviate from the practice established with the coming of the German troops. Troubles of this sort have become a part of Ghetto life. The most important thing, however, is that the clouds of fear concerning "actions" and destruction have not appeared on the horizon recently, as was the case in the first period of the Ghetto, when pillage and murder were the order of the day.

Now uncertainty has set in again; no one knows what the new day will bring—disaster may strike at any moment. It all began last week. Several Lithuanians were taken from their apartments in the city at night, without being allowed to take any belongings with them; this incident left a very bad impression among the Ghetto inmates.[1] Many people believe that the main reason behind this operation is the approaching war front, which causes the Germans to get rid of expendable and unwanted persons.

A number of mixed Jewish-Christian families were arrested in the city as well, including Christian women whose husbands were Jewish and other similar cases.

Yesterday afternoon Lipzer returned from the city, carrying a sealed envelope addressed to the commandant of the Ghetto Guard. This constitutes a surprising innovation in comparison with past practices. Lipzer has always been greatly valued by the Gestapo. Whenever Lipzer has been ordered to bring a Ghetto inmate for investigation to the Gestapo, or even to place a Ghetto inmate under arrest, he has always received directives in writing inside an unsealed envelope. He has always carried out every assignment to the letter. In recent days, Lipzer says, the atmosphere in the Gestapo has changed, and the attitude toward him has changed as well.

The day before yesterday, too, Lipzer delivered a sealed envelope to the chief of the Jewish police. This frightened us a great deal; this is because, in the past few days, a number of Jewish workers have been arrested in the city, and not even one of them has returned, as was the case on previous occasions.

One labor brigade leader told us the following: yesterday, three women slunk away from his brigade and entered the home of a Lithuanian in order to buy some food. This occurred not far away from their place of work. A Lithuanian policeman who caught sight of them, arrested them, and took them to the nearby police station. This was not very much to the liking of their brigade leader, Katz by name (his brother-in-law, Gutman, together with several other Jews, later paid with their lives, after having been arrested with various commodities in their possession and taken to the Gestapo). Katz applied to his German work brigade leader and told him about the incident. He asked for his help in saving the three women.

The German boss, together with the Jewish head of the labor brigade, went to the police station where the three women were being detained. The German work brigade leader asked the commander of the Lithuanian police to release them. The Lithuanian replied that he had received directives to bring to the Gestapo any worker who left his place of work, irrespective of the reason. The intervention of the German was in vain, and the three women were sent to the Gestapo.

The German commander and his Jewish companion set out for the Gestapo. The German argued there that the three women had been working outside as part of the labor brigade and that they had entered the courtyard of some Lithuanian in search of a bathroom to relieve themselves. The argument worked; the three women, together with their German and Jewish companions, left the Gestapo happily.

The women did not want to give up the parcels of food they had bought, and which they had left behind in the house of the Lithuanian. They therefore returned there to fetch the parcels. The result—they were arrested again. One of them succeeded in escaping. The other two were placed under arrest. The German superior, with the assistance of several other Germans, arrested the Lithuanian policeman and attempted to release the two Jewish women. A commotion resulted, in the midst of which another woman escaped. Only one woman was left, Mrs. Altschuler; the policeman was holding her by the arms with a strong grip and took her to the Gestapo. It was already 5 P.M., and the woman remained in detention.

Several people were arrested because of a loaf of bread. Two Jewish workers, Shimanski and Heyman, were arrested yesterday morning on their way to work as they were trying to purchase a loaf of bread. The sum of thirteen marks was found on them. They were taken to the Gestapo and have not yet been released. Yesterday a locksmith by the name of Sadovski was arrested as he was buying a newspaper. This too is forbidden.

Both the day before yesterday and again yesterday, Lipzer came back from work depressed and overcome by anguish. Many Jews were arrested yesterday both in the city and in the Ghetto. Lipzer failed to secure the release of a single one of them. And in what way was he spoken to? Rauca spoke to him in thunder and lightning. Even the intelligent and polite Schmitz spoke to him harshly. Schmitz was angry with the Jews who "lately allow themselves too much. As the most recent arrests show, bottles of liquor and large quantities of lard have been found in their possession."

Lipzer's efforts to explain to the Germans the conditions of life in the Ghetto proved fruitless. They did not let him speak. This has never happened before. No wonder Lipzer is depressed.

In order to avert a further deterioration of the situation, the Council issued an order the day before yesterday, to the Jewish police and the labor office, to close all the stores in the Ghetto. The Council also decided that those engaged in smuggling large amounts of goods into the Ghetto would be transferred from their labor brigades to more difficult workplaces, such as the German construction company Grün-Bielfinger[2] and others.

The Council has also issued an order to the Jewish police to arrest people who enter the Ghetto through the gate carrying large parcels of products and goods. The aim of this order is to appease the Germans.

The situation became even more difficult when Rauca issued a veiled warning to the Council. He said that he "knows who should be punished," and he added: "In Vilna, the Jewish leaders hand over offenders to the Gestapo, whereas in Kovno the Jewish community leaders protect such people." Rauca also told Lipzer, "the Ghetto will be in serious trouble in the near future."

The day before yesterday the Ghetto commandant inquired of the Jewish police about a certain street in the Ghetto. The inquiry aroused fears over future arrests, or even an "action" in the Ghetto. The restlessness and uncertainty which characterized the first period of the Ghetto have set in again. The fears grew yesterday as a result of the continuing arrests of Jews in the city.

Yesterday afternoon the Ghetto commandant summoned the chief of the Jewish police and the chiefs of three police precincts in the Ghetto. He told them to arrest the families of the eight Jews who had been under arrest at the Gestapo for several days and to bring them to the Ghetto police today before 8 A.M. He also passed on to them the names and addresses of Jews whose families were to be placed under arrest. He added that, for the purpose of this operation, "family" included a husband or wife, parents, children, and the parents of both husband and wife. The chief of the Jewish police, Kopelman, would be personally responsible for carrying out this order.

Among the detainees were owners of small stores in the Ghetto, whose names were supplied to the Gestapo by the new oppressor of the Jews, Ratnikas, and by a Polish youth who had been arrested in the city as he was trying to purchase a bottle of vodka. The remainder of the detainees were Jewish workers who had either tried to purchase, or had purchased, potatoes, flour, or bread. Members of their families were arrested yesterday; today they were brought to the Ghetto command.

Also yesterday, a warrant was issued for the arrest of Erich Kohn. He had been decorated with the Iron Cross for his services to Germany on the war front in World War I. It appears that it was Caspi who denounced him to the Gestapo; Caspi alleged that he had seen Kohn in the city without the yellow badge, while he was purchasing food. Previously, each time Kohn was about to be arrested, a miracle occurred and he escaped death. Some time ago he was in the hospital in poor condition. Then, he was allowed to recuperate from his illness. For some time he was spoken to politely, and even offered help in finding a suitable occupation.

Yesterday Erich Kohn came to me and asked me to find a job for him. I understood his situation and promised to find a position for him in one of our institutions.

Yesterday the Ghetto commandant ordered the arrest of Orechkin and his wife. Furthermore, Lipzer passed on an order from Rauca to find Katz and his wife, and to bring them to the Gestapo within eight days. If this is not done, the chief of the Ghetto police, Kopelman, and the head of the criminal section of the Ghetto police, Bramson, will be executed together with their families.

Katz disappeared from the Ghetto several months ago in connection with the Meck case. Rauca says he knows that Katz is back in the Ghetto. He should therefore be found and handed over to the police. A very nasty assignment.

Srebnitzki, manager of the Ghetto pharmacy, came to the Council. He was visibly shaken and scared: "Did you hear the latest news?" Wintzer, the German director of the furniture plant (at 55 Paneriu Street), and his deputy, the Countess von Ravensburg, have been arrested. They were both taken to the Gestapo. There was a Jewish labor brigade working at the factory and it supplied the couple with all kinds of goods. The couple were having a great time there. Things reached a point when their apartment, located within the factory precincts, from time to time hosted swinging parties which sometimes ended in an orgy. Jews also took part in these parties.

The foreman at the furniture factory, Makovski,[3] more than once reported the irregularities taking place in the factory to the Jewish management, but to no avail. It turns out that Wintzer also engaged in selling huge quantities of medicine. Some of this medicine reached the Ghetto and its pharmacy. This was apparently the reason for Srebnitzki's being shaken and scared.

For me the whole affair was nothing short of a revelation, and a very unpleasant one at that. Wintzer had been very much involved in Jewish matters. It is only to be expected that his arrest will result in arrests of the Jews. It is noteworthy that the German couple were expected to leave for Germany today. They had already packed their bags. The Gestapo arrested them at the last moment.

This was the end of the Wintzer affair in the furniture factory; it could not have been unexpected. Jewish workers there had developed unique relationships with the management, and even purchased various goods from it. It goes without saying that these workers are not calm or at ease today. The same applies to the Council.

Later, Segal, a worker in the electricity department, came to us. He too was very agitated. He brought urgent news. It turned out that his wife was working with Germans in the city. Her manager was a senior German military officer and he treated her with respect. Yesterday he told her: "If something happens in the

Ghetto, you will not be harmed." He was paid a visit by German policemen and handed a list of Jewish workers employed at his office. The list was accompanied by a request: "Not to be harmed."

As usual, such news aroused fears. It means that the Ghetto is heading for bad times. We asked the woman who passed on the information to us to try to get more details about future developments in the Ghetto.

Miller of the city governor's office contacted me on the telephone. He announced that a Jewish worker by the name of Sadovski had been caught in the act of buying a newspaper. The worker had been handed to the Gestapo. He asked me to warn all the leaders of labor brigades to take steps so that such incidents did not recur.

Miller also told me that another Jewish worker had been arrested; he had had the audacity to walk on the sidewalk on Laisves Boulevard. "Such a thing cannot be tolerated," Miller said. Such offenders will be handed over to the Gestapo. The chief of the Jewish police is required to issue proper warning on this subject.

Yesterday at seven o'clock a Council meeting took place in Dr. Elkes's apartment. It was attended by Lipzer and the chief of the Jewish police. There was general agreement regarding the situation in the Ghetto. It was resolved that if the situation is not to deteriorate, orders and directives will have to be obeyed strictly and to the letter. We cannot change the difficult situation, which is probably caused by the events on the war front. The Germans are irksome and might want to vent their revenge on us. We must warn the Jewish workers to refrain from buying food and not to leave their place of work until the storm blows over.

Yesterday evening the Jewish police arrested whole families according to a Gestapo list. This was not an easy task—to place old people, women, and small children under arrest. They were taken to the Ghetto detention center.

Dr. Elkes did not rest or sit idle. Perhaps some of them could be saved. At 10:30 P.M. he summoned Isaac (Yitzhak) Rabinovitz and instructed him to call on Hermann, director of the German labor office, to ask him to be present early in the morning when the German military field police come to get the detainees. Perhaps he will be able to save a few of them—those who are excellent professionals. Hermann even issued a directive that a physician and a nurse be on duty in the Ghetto detention center during the night.

The people involved knew very well what lay in store for them. Lately the following system has been introduced: a Jew is caught and taken away to the fort. Afterward the members of his family are arrested. During the night they are injected with morphine so that they will fall asleep, will not think, and will not feel pain. Nevertheless, the night in jail was terrible. Mrs. Orechkin, who was arrested together with her husband, tried to commit suicide time and again.

Today, early in the morning, we came to the Council offices. It was just impossible to sit at home any longer. Lipzer did not leave for work today. We asked him to stay in the Ghetto; perhaps he will be able to prevail on Schtitz to release a number of skilled Jewish workers.

Altogether twenty-seven people were arrested, including ten children. At 7:30 A.M. the Jewish Ghetto police began transferring them from the Ghetto detention center to the Ghetto command. They were received there by a reinforced detachment of Lithuanian policemen holding rifles with bayonets fixed. They waited for the arrival of the Gestapo.

Yesterday the Council published an appeal to Ghetto inmates which reemphasized the ban on buying newspapers, walking on Laisves Boulevard, bringing certain kinds of goods into the Ghetto, and leaving one's workplace. The Ghetto was shocked by the arrests conducted at night; in the morning the mood of "an action imminent" set in.

I went to the city and had a talk with Miller at the city governor's office. He asked me whether I knew that twenty-seven Ghetto inmates would be handed over today into the hands of the Gestapo. I replied that indeed I knew about it. I then asked him the reason for their arrest. He said that these people had been arrested because of foolish things they had done in the city. I told him that the twenty-seven were in no way connected with what was going on in the city; they are just members of the families—old people, women, and children. He responded by saying that he did not approve of this particular arrest, but that the Jews in their behavior were breaking rules and regulations.

Miller told me about one woman whom he did not want to hand over to the Gestapo. He asked her to tell him the truth. She said that she did not know anything. Then he handed her over to the Gestapo. Miller asked me to refrain from drawing hasty conclusions from these actions by the police. He asked me to pass on his warning that "the Jews should not do foolish things" when staying in the city.

I returned to the Ghetto hurriedly. On my way I saw three Gestapo cars. I was rather familiar with this sight. They had just returned from the Ninth Fort, after the executions had taken place.

On my way I met a Jewish woman, Mrs. Krut, who was in a hurry to get back to the Ghetto. Her husband had been mistakenly arrested and she was eager to return there.

At 9:30 A.M. Schtitz arrived in the Ghetto. Hermann was already there. He haggled with Schtitz over each person: "Heyman is an excellent blacksmith. Let him go." "Yes," says Schtitz, "but his wife has been liquidated this morning. He has three children. What will he do now? He won't be able to make a significant contribution anyway. It's better for him to go." The same thing occurred with the others.

Today twelve Jews held by the Gestapo, together with six Jews from the municipal jail, have been executed. Now Schtitz comes to take delivery of twenty-seven Jews from the Ghetto.

The chief of the Ghetto police announced that a boy, aged fourteen, a member of the Sadovski family, has not been found. One Jewish soul has managed to escape.

Those arrested were ordered to climb onto the truck, which was covered with canvas cloth on all sides. Erich Kohn and Orechkin helped them to get on the truck. The arrested passed between two lines of Lithuanian policemen. The last to get on the truck were Erich Kohn and Orechkin. The former stretched his hand out, as if he was leaving everything behind and willingly departing to the next world. The latter turned his penetrating gaze toward the rows of Jewish policemen, as if expecting them to save him at the last moment.

It was terrible to watch the women getting on the truck; they held in their arms babies of different ages and wrapped them in more and more sweaters so that they would not catch cold on the way.

There were four Lithuanian policemen on the truck. As the truck started moving, they ordered the Jews to take off most of their clothes. The truck then drove to the Ninth Fort and pulled up at the pit. The passengers were lowered into the pit and a volley of fire put an end to their lives.

The Ghetto is pervaded by heavy mourning, exactly as in the aftermath of the great "actions" last year. Who knows whether we are not facing a new tragic era in the Ghetto?[4]

Today Jaeger was also in the Ninth Fort. Today is an important day. A day of vacation. The Germans put to death many Jews as well as Lithuanians, Russians, and others.[5]

The homes of the murdered Jews were locked. Today a consultation was held in the home of Dr. Elkes. The sorrow and the pain which affect everyone in the Ghetto were given expression. It is possible that we are facing difficult days ahead. This makes it incumbent upon us to take strict measures in order not to give the Germans an excuse to accuse us of violating the rules.

It was decided not to hold concerts on the coming Saturday and Sunday, and to forbid the bakeries to bake white bread. It was also agreed strictly to enforce the guarding at the Ghetto gate.

There was no work today at the Jewish institutions in the Ghetto. It was simply not possible to conduct any public activity under the conditions of the prevailing mood of depression. The life of no person in the Ghetto is secure any longer. Anyone may stumble all of a sudden. All the same, our will to go on living is as strong as ever—to go on living and to leave the horrors behind.

1. One of those taken away, and then murdered, was the son of Orechkin, a non-Jewish journalist famous throughout the Baltic countries who had married a Jewish woman. When the Orechkin couple discovered that the Gestapo was searching for them, the mother attempted suicide and the father burned all his writings. The mother later repeatedly tried to leave the Ghetto in order to help her son, until she discovered that he had already been murdered.

2. This construction site was considered a particularly harsh one to work in.

3. Avraham Makovski, an attorney by profession, active in the Council's labor office and also in its social welfare department, was a member both of the Council's complaints committee and of the Ghetto court.

4. This "action" by the Germans occurred immediately after their defeat at Stalingrad, and became known in the Ghetto as the Stalingrad action. On the previous day, February 3, 1943, an announcement had been published by the German Army to the effect that, with the surrender of the Germans in the face of the enemy's superiority and difficult warfare conditions, "the Stalingrad battle is over." More than 160,000 German soldiers had been killed at Stalingrad and 90,000 taken prisoner, including the German military commander, General von Paulus, whom Hitler had appointed Field Marshal on January 31, 1943.

5. An undated note in Avraham Tory's diary states: "Several days later news reached us that, in addition to the Jews who were murdered, Lithuanians and members of other nationalities were also executed at the Ninth Fort. Not far from the Ghetto, two people had jumped out of the truck which was carrying Christian prisoners to the fort. One of them was shot dead on the spot by Schtitz. The other was wounded in the hand, but succeeded in escaping." Tory's note continues: "One day, a half-naked man appeared in the Ghetto. He wore nothing but shoes and socks. He asked the passers-by to give him clothes and galoshes. People were frightened by his looks. He probably got frightened too, and fled."

FEBRUARY 5, 1943

When the labor brigades set out today for work in the city, they were told in no uncertain terms not to leave their place of work during the day, not to buy newspapers, not to move about in the city without guard, not to buy anything in the city, and not to bring with them any parcels. Any deviation from these strict instructions is liable to end badly, not just for the offenders but for their families as well.

All the workers understood the meaning of these instructions. After all, yesterday the Ghetto paid a heavy price of forty-five victims for failing to abide strictly by them. A fresh mass grave, into which innocent children, women and old people had been thrown, was covered yesterday in the Ninth Fort. All pleas proved fruitless. The German rulers decided to demonstrate the full measure of their cruelty.

Was the punishment meted out by the Germans a single affair? Or did it, perhaps, mark an opening of a new campaign? Not only the public but its representatives, the Council members, are eager to know the answer. The Council is waiting impatiently for news from Lipzer, who has been asked to try to find out the answer from the German authorities.

When Lipzer came back from work, it was already clear that not one of those who had been caught, nor their families, was any longer among the living.

Lipzer is very depressed. He had an opportunity to talk with Rauca and Schmitz. Rauca received him in the hallway. His speech was typical: "You are the people of dogs and pigs." "You have the audacity to speak to the Lithuanians about the butchering of Germans in the near future," and such like. "We shall teach the Jews how to rejoice and how to talk. We shall raze the Ghetto to the ground. Let nobody think that because Stalingrad has fallen the Germans have lost the war. The German people are eighty-five million strong." He kept saying things like that.

Even Schmitz, who has always spoken about Jewish issues moderately and logically, today heaped curses and imprecations on Lipzer: "For what purpose do the Jews visit the homes of the Lithuanians and talk about taking joint steps against the Germans when the time comes? I don't need idle workers; I am simply not interested in them. The professionals, like those from your brigade, will be always needed." Does this mean that nonprofessional workers will be expendable?

Rauca wanted to know how the Ghetto had been affected by yesterday's executions. When told that the whole Ghetto was in a state of shock, he said: "I know what's going on in the Ghetto, and who should be 'cleaned up.'"

Lipzer tried to explain to the Germans that the whole story is nothing but a Lithuanian provocation. Jews do not visit Lithuanian homes; they think only about their work and about bread to eat. To sum it up: Jews do not concern themselves at all with political issues.

The attitude of the Germans was quite clear. The atmosphere in the Ghetto is thick with fear. The system of severe punishments will stay in effect until Tuesday. Until that day, anyone caught in the act of breaking regulations or directives will be executed, so that the rest will see and be afraid.

A fourteen-year-old boy from a labor brigade has been taken to the Gestapo today. He was caught buying bread in the city, not far away from his workplace. The boy is alone and has no family. His parents died immediately after the outbreak of the war. Lipzer told the Germans: "What do you want from the boy? After all, he is an orphan. Do you need large families with grandfathers and grandmothers? Let him go. The work-duty doesn't even apply to boys of his age. What offense did he commit? He wanted to eat?" The boy was released.

A proposal was put forward that the Council should send a delegation to Jaeger. The purpose is to revoke the draconian punishments meted out to the Jews, and to deny the false charge that the Lithuanians are putting about, that Jews visit their homes and warn them about the future consequences of the maltreatment of the Jews. The Council's position, however, is that the time is not yet ripe for sending such a delegation, as the Germans are very angry with the Jews just now. It is also a time when not only Jews but also Lithuanians, Poles, and Russians are being led away to the Ninth Fort every day. Jaeger himself visited the fort yesterday. There is no point in sending a Jewish delegation to him at this time. We should wait a few more days, see how things develop, and see what the mood of the Germans is going to be.

Yesterday the Jewish police discovered in the Ghetto the apartment of Katz, who is wanted by the Gestapo on a charge of theft.

Lipzer has issued a demand to find Katz and to hand him over to the Gestapo. The reason for this demand is that Rauca knows that Katz has returned to the Ghetto. It is not possible to hide in the city. Every day, houses there are being searched.

Additional instruction arrived yesterday: the second man connected with the Meck case must be found and placed under arrest. That man is Gelson. Gelson, however, is not in the Ghetto. When the Meck affair blew up, he left the Ghetto, and up to now he has not returned. His sister lives in the Ghetto, but the two have not been close. It is conceivable that the Gestapo will issue an order for her arrest, and even execute her. There is a general consensus that in such case she would be an innocent victim.

We are racking our brains trying to find a way out of this mess. This is not a theoretical issue but a matter of life and death. The Gestapo is looking for Gelson, who is not in the Ghetto. It is possible that tomorrow its men will again be looking for Katz, should they reach the conclusion that Katz is back in the Ghetto. They have set a deadline—eight days from today—for handing Katz over. If within that time Katz is not found, the chief of the Jewish police, Kopelman, and the chief of the criminal section of the Jewish police, Bramson, together with their families, will be taken to the Ninth Fort.

The situation is difficult. In the meantime there are three live prisoners in the Ghetto jail: Katz and his wife, and Miss Gelson. Which one of them will be the victim, and who will manage to get away from the talons of the fiend?

The Council resolved to discuss this complicated issue once again.

FEBRUARY 6, 1943

Again today, several tension-filled hours passed at the Council. It has been almost a week since the mood of fear set in in the Ghetto. Anything is likely to bring about grave consequences. We feel that they want to humiliate us, that they seek an excuse for bloodshed.

Yesterday the oppressor Ratnikas arrested a Jew by the name of Shapiro at the Ghetto gate, when the latter was trying to bring in a cart loaded with firewood. Shapiro carried a permit to bring in firewood to the Ghetto, but Jews are forbidden to buy wood as they are not allowed to keep money in the Ghetto. Officially, the Ghetto inmates may buy wood at the timber warehouse, or at the sawmill, at the official price of two and a half marks per meter; the purchase receipt must be submitted to the city governor's office. In actual fact, in order to get the wood, it is necessary to bribe either the directors or the foremen, or even certain workers, both at the timber warehouse and at the sawmill; those enterprises settle their accounts with the municipal authorities. The official accounting plays a minor part in deals of this sort.

Since there are more than 16,000 people in the Ghetto, requiring an absolute minimum of fifty to sixty cubic meters of firewood per day, many inmates engage in the traditional form of the trade. They buy the wood from the peasants in the nearby villages, who bring it on carts or sleighs from out of town. All this is done without permits or receipts. Everyone knows that firewood is being supplied to the Ghetto in this way. The most important thing from the legal point of view is to procure the permit to bring the wood into the Ghetto.

Some time ago, I spoke about this with Miller at the city governor's office. I explained that without sufficient quantities of wood our enterprises (workshops, laundry, and health institutions) could not operate: that the workers will freeze and will not be able to perform their tasks. Certain enterprises where Jewish workers are employed were willing to provide their workers with a certain amount of firewood; I asked Miller to allow these workers to bring the wood provided by the workplaces into the Ghetto.

Miller agreed to my request and added an explanation of his own: the institutions involved failed to supply the Ghetto with a sufficient amount of firewood. Consequently, I was subsequently permitted to allow the Ghetto inmates to get firewood on their own and to bring it into the Ghetto. Several times I have given Miller the letters issued by the German workplaces in which they ask the city governor's office to allow their Jewish workers to bring into the Ghetto pieces of firewood up to half a meter long, or one cubic meter per person.

Thus the question of firewood for the Ghetto was solved. The Ghetto command and the guards were aware of the existence of this general policy and did not cause any trouble. True, from time to time we did pay them for their "good behavior," but this was a time-honored practice.

That was the situation until Ratnikas joined the Lithuanian Guard. He wanted to demonstrate that he knew everything and that he would not allow carts loaded with various goods to be brought into the Ghetto. Indeed, only yesterday he prevented a cart carrying firewood from coming into the Ghetto: the wood was supposed to be paid for at the price of a hundred marks per cubic meter. Ratnikas searched Shapiro and found 117 marks in cash on his person. He sent him to the Ghetto detention center.

Shapiro was seized by fear. Under present conditions, this could mean being sent to the fort. The police chief in the Ghetto announced Shapiro's arrest, and asked his superior for instructions concerning the course of action in this case.

I rushed to the city and spoke to Miller. From what he said, I gathered that he was not planning to make a big fuss about it. He told me that he would be visiting the Ghetto and would attend to the matter. Just the day before yesterday, Miller told me that he would not hand Jews over to the Gestapo, and that he wanted the Jews to work and not to engage in foolish behavior.

Miller came to the Ghetto. He ordered the confiscation of the 117 marks found on Shapiro and in this way concluded the affair. But our fear was not dispelled. This was yesterday.

Today, a special messenger dispatched by Lipzer told us that someone from the Gestapo is due to arrive in the Ghetto at any moment, to visit the pharmacy and the hospital. The arrest of Wintzer probably came as a result of an illicit trade in medicine. Today's investigation aims at finding out whether the medicine involved found its way into the Ghetto. We are certain that this medicine will be found neither in the pharmacy nor in the hospital. But there is concern that Wintzer might have told his interrogators everything, in which case it is not just Srebnitzki who will be adversely affected, but all of us.

Ever since the arrest of Wintzer, Srebnitzki has been living in constant fear; he looks like a man crushed in soul and body. Now we are all anxiously waiting for the arrival of the man from the Gestapo.

Before long, a Gestapo car entered the Ghetto gate. It took the shortest route to the pharmacy. A man with blond hair climbed out of it and entered the pharmacy, in the company of Lipzer. Politely, he asked Srebnitzki whether he knew Wintzer, whether he had obtained medicine from him, and whether he knew who in the Ghetto had bought medicine from Wintzer. The man added that Srebnitzki should not be afraid; nothing was going to happen to him. The problem was Wintzer, not Srebnitzki.

Srebnitzki replied that he knew nothing. He also explained that the pharmacy got all its medicine through official channels, and from the Council, acting on requests which had to be approved officially. All the receipts for medicine could be found at the Council office. A few more questions, and the meeting was concluded.

The Gestapo man and Lipzer left. Srebnitzki had felt relieved by the presence of Lipzer at the meeting. If a Jew is present on such an occasion, it means that there is no reason to fear.

Having left the pharmacy, the Gestapo man and Lipzer drove to the hospital. There too they asked the same questions. One more question was asked: Where did the physicians and the patients get medicine? And another question: Had they heard about Wintzer and the medicine he had supplied to various places? The reply was that the hospital obtained medicine from the pharmacy; the physicians did not buy it. The patients get their medicine in the pharmacy according to prescriptions issued by a physician.

The next stop was the Ghetto workshops. A first aid station is located there. Here medicine is obtained via the city governor's office. The physicians there knew Wintzer well, but they had never obtained any medicine from him. On the contrary, it was they who supplied medicine to the workers at the furniture plant which Wintzer headed.

The Gestapo man and Lipzer then paid a visit to the furniture plant at 55

Paneriu Street, where Wintzer's private apartment was also located. The Gestapo man told Lipzer to order the manager of the pharmacy, the manager of the health office, and the physicians to sign a written statement saying that they had never obtained or purchased any medicine from Wintzer. He added that should this statement turn out to be false, serious consequences would follow.

Despite the fact that the visit of the Gestapo man was short, and that the investigation was carried out in an orderly and polite fashion, and that it was attended by Lipzer, serious apprehensions were aroused at the Council. The visit was a time bomb which could blow up at any moment, and could claim many victims.

Should such anxieties, apprehensions, and fears of disaster beset us every day—our situation will become truly unbearable.

The manager of the workshops, Segalson, called me on the telephone from the workshops. He asked me to come over for a talk. I set out right away. Chance had it that, at that time, the Gestapo man was there in connection with his investigation of the Wintzer affair. I waited until he left.

In the meantime, I noted the new arrangements in the manager's office—a row of tables with typewriters on them, more comfortable chairs, etc. I also saw there a young, familiar-looking man who seemed a bit strange to me: he had a thick moustache and wore spectacles. In the city he looked different; he was a salesman in the store I had been connected with for some time before the war. In the past his name was Gordon. Here I heard him being addressed as Mr. Stein. I realized that his name had been changed; or perhaps he himself had changed it for various reasons. I greeted him and we talked for a while.

I was sitting in a side room when I heard the call: "Attention!" This was the usual sign heralding the entrance of a German official, whom all those present were required to greet by standing to attention. But in this case the call was followed by howls of laughter emanating from the office. It turned out that one of the Jewish workers, a well-known clown, was moving from one room to the next in the company of Wintzer's dog, which now, after Wintzer's arrest, stays in Gilow's room. Gilow is the German manager of the workshops. Upon entering Segalson's office with the dog, the Jewish worker cried "Attention!" When the workers saw the dog, they burst out laughing.

In the meantime, Segalson bade his visitors goodbye. We entered the side room and began our conversation. He told me that Miller and Gilow were due to leave for Riga on Tuesday to see the Ghetto and workshops there. I immediately informed him that there was no Ghetto in Riga, but camps in the form of barracks, housing contingents of Jews who had been transferred to Riga from different parts of Germany, and from Lithuania as well.[1] And in general, it was not good for us that they should learn in Riga how to run our Ghetto. But then we are not asked for advice. They just up and went to Riga.

I asked Segalson to let me know as soon as Miller returned in the afternoon. I will try to explain to him that no comparison should be made between the Kovno and Riga Ghettos. In any event, this trip to Riga is not good from our point of view.

1. The Riga Ghetto had been greatly reduced after the German "action" in late November and early December 1941; it was subsequently called a *Kasernierungslager* (semimilitary labor camp), but was still inside the area of the Ghetto. In July 1943 the Germans began to remove the inmates of both sections of the Ghetto; the section which housed Jews from Riga and Kovno, and the section which housed Jews who had been brought from Germany and Austria. The Jews who were removed were deported to Kaiserwald concentration camp, outside Riga.

FEBRUARY 8, 1943

There is a somber mood in the Ghetto. No one knows the reason for this, but everyone senses that living conditions have deteriorated. No one knows what tomorrow will bring.

Lately, rumors have spread in the Ghetto that the Germans "demand 200 people" if Gelson—Meck's partner—is not handed over the Gestapo. According to other rumors, a contingent of 1,000 people is required for work in Riga. These rumors were given another boost when it became known that today Miller and Gilow had left on a four-day visit to Riga.

Leaders of the labor brigades received instructions not to allow their workers to carry large parcels with them or, in general, to carry on their person various articles for some time in the future. The Council, helped by the Jewish police, has taken strict measures against small stores, with the aim of closing them down. Without these stores and various stalls, there will be less room for black-marketeering. Also, an edict was issued to seize the goods in stock in the stores. The fence traders were informed that they must end their business there.

The Council published an appeal addressed to the Ghetto inmates, calling on them to refrain from talking in the city, especially to non-Jews; not to leave their workplaces during work hours; not to walk on the city streets without a guard, etc. We must refrain from doing anything which might arouse the suspicions of the Germans.

Lipzer brought some news which had a calming effect on the Council. When deliberations in this forum were resumed, concerning irregularities in the bakery which were committed by some of the fire brigade men, it was resolved—after a prolonged discussion—to suspend the fire brigade chief, Abramovitz, for a month and to dismiss Ashinski, Braver, and Volberg from their posts as firemen. This time the Council decided to take stern measures in order to deter others.

This morning, when I came to Obst, he was being paid a visit by a German by the name of Peter, from the supply section of the regional command headquarters of the German Army. That is where we get the potatoes for the Ghetto. The payment for those purchases is remitted via the city governor. Peter announced: "The Jews cheat; cheating is in their blood. I was in the Ghetto and saw how the potatoes are weighed on broken scales and how false weights were used." "I can believe that," commented Obst: "they cheat on me too."

Obst used the opportunity to ask me how we do in fact weigh potatoes. I replied that we weigh each sack separately and that our scales and weights are good. Peter left. He had said what he had to say and departed.

I asked Obst: "What sort of a conversation is this?" He did not answer me, but moved on to the current matters as if nothing had happened.

That is the way the Germans talk about the Jews, even among themselves, when no Jews are present. Even after a year and a half of life in the Ghetto it still manages to shock.

FEBRUARY 10, 1943

Today, the city governor, Cramer, came in person to visit the large workshops in the Ghetto. He has not visited them for some time. His visit today was of special importance, particularly in view of the disquiet prevailing in the Ghetto these days.

The large workshops give us some political leverage; they form a very important part of the Ghetto. Here, 1,400 Jewish workers show their accomplishments. They prove that the Jews are capable not only of swindling and living as parasites, but that they can work, produce, and repair machinery and machine parts which cannot be repaired in the city.

Together, the large workshops make up a formidable enterprise. The credit for this must go, above all, to the Council, which had already grasped their importance at the time of their construction. When ominous winds start blowing, when we are being accused of ancient and fictitious offenses, we hold on to the workshops which we have set up, as to our last refuge.

We say: "On the contrary, see for yourselves the work we are performing for the German Army! No other place can boast such enterprises. We do not ask to be rewarded for them. All we ask for is work and bread."

If it happens that one or two Jews are caught committing some offense, and the Germans generalize from this case to all the Jews, we point to our workshops, to the airfield, and to a great many other places where Ghetto inmates work with great success. There are many instances when our employers, some of them very important Nazis, take pride in "their Jews."

On many occasions these enterprises supported us in times of trial, such as, for instance, when the Germans wanted to transfer Jewish workers to Riga.[1] We often heard about plans to separate young able-bodied workers from the old people who were no longer able to work. On such occasions we proved to the world that the large workshops can employ even old women—in mending socks, plucking feathers, knitting woolen clothes, etc. Here, in the workshops, a great many people of retirement age are employed in productive work, the fruits of which cannot be had in the city.

In the course of time, the city governor showed great interest in the workshops. It seems that they were a surprising discovery for him. He also credited himself with their success. He brought important figures to the Ghetto from the German administration and told them: "See for yourselves what I have managed to do with the Jewish parasites. I have forced them to work for the benefit of the Reich, for the German Army, and for our victory." The city governor does not allow any harm to come to the workshops. He also refuses to introduce any changes in the Ghetto, insofar as they might have any adverse effects on the workshops.

At the time, even Jordan held on to the workshops as to a last resort. He sought to avoid being sent to the front, arguing that without him it would be impossible to run the workshops properly. His arguments, however, did not help him. He was sent to the front and was killed.[2]

In the Ghetto disquiet set in in the aftermath of the "small action" on February 4. Rumors spread about a plan to reduce the size of the operation of the workshops, and perhaps even to liquidate them. These rumors aroused grave fears in the Ghetto. As I mentioned earlier, Cramer came into the Ghetto today to visit the workshops; he showed an interest in their operation, in the products being turned out there. He also asked if there were enough orders. He is prepared to "make sure that new orders will come in, so that the work in the workshops will continue and even expand. If need be, several houses nearby can be annexed to the workshops."

This proposal aroused great interest in the Ghetto, because it dispelled the rumors which were a source of fear and anxiety.

At 3 o'clock in the afternoon, Brik[3] came to my room and invited me to a discussion with several members of the Council. The invitation was issued by the management of the workshops. The meeting was to take place at once, in fifteen minutes' time. There is an important issue which demands that a clear position be adopted. The matter concerns a theft from the large workshops which occurred ten days ago. This requires the presence of the director of the criminal section, Mr. Bramson. He and Brik have already spoken to Garfunkel, and the discussion will take place at Garfunkel's room. I had to invite Bramson on the telephone.

I set out to the police station and telephoned Bramson from there. He came over quickly and we both went to see Garfunkel. Segalson and Gemelitzki were already there. We also needed to summon Grinberg; he came immediately.

Mr. Segalson made a report about the affair: about ten days ago, the head of the saddle-production department in the workshops came to him to say that on coming to work in the morning he noticed that two parcels of leather, containing a total amount of leather 120 feet in length, were missing. This is a considerable amount of material. He immediately informed the work manager, Kelzon, who in turn passed on the news to Mr. Segalson and Mr. Gemelitzki. The question immediately arose, what steps should be taken? Should the German manager of the workshops, Gilow, be told, or not? The Jewish workshop staff did not tell the German manager, out of fear that the affair might cause a pandemonium which would be liable to reach the ears of the Gestapo. The leather belonged to the German Army, and the whole thing might end up very badly.

The Jewish staff searched for ways and means to solve the problem of the shortage of leather for saddle production—by scrupulous planning and saving, in cooperation with other departments. Parallel with these steps, the foreman informed the chief of the criminal section of the Jewish police about the theft, so that he could investigate the matter and try to apprehend the thieves.

Bramson ordered meticulous searches to be carried out in seventeen houses where he had reason to believe the stolen leather was hidden, but the searches bore no fruit. Grinberg, commandant of the first police precinct, places no great faith in the abilities of the detectives of the criminal department, and he tends to criticize their methods of work. Today at noon two policemen from the first police precinct arrested a man who was carrying an unfinished leather case. His house was searched and a whole parcel of leather was found. Grinberg sent the man and the articles found at his home to the criminal section of the police. Grinberg was certain that he was on the right track. And, in fact, examination of the unfinished leather case revealed that it was made of the same material as that which had been stolen from the workshops.

It also turned out that the detained man was working in the saddle workshop. Bramson investigated, and informed the management of the workshops about the results. Having heard Bramson's report, the members of the management became very frightened. Although they were glad that the police had caught the thief, still they were worried over the public implications of the discovery. Also, three workers from the saddle workshop were urgently summoned from their homes. It seems that these summonses are connected with the arrest of the man with the unfinished leather case in his possession.

Now the problem is this: what is to be done? To press ahead with the investigation until the fact of theft from the saddle workshop can be firmly determined, or, and perhaps better, to hush up the whole affair, that is, to cover up the shortage of leather somehow and say that it was due to an error. Perhaps an accounting error? It could also be said that the leather of which the unfinished case was made is of a different kind from that used in manufacture of saddles.

At the same time, however, it is important to find those who stole the leather, in order to punish the offenders, and also in order not to provide grounds for the German claims about the unreliability of the Jews. This step, however, entails a grave danger for the Ghetto inmates.

It was therefore decided—to our great regret—that the news of the leather theft should be suppressed. We live in times when the whole Jewish community is responsible for offenses of some of its members. We must not breach the law, not just each one of us for his own personal benefit, but for the good of the whole community.

Today the city governor's office was informed that news had reached the Lithuanian city mayor that the large library belonging to Professor Bieliatzkin is stored in the home of his maidservant in the city. According to the law, as well as to the directive issued by the city governor, each Ghetto inmate is required to declare all property he had left behind in the city. In actual fact, only a handful of the Ghetto inmates have done that. Professor Bieliatzkin has not done it either. His relations in the past with his Christian maidservant were especially good.

Having heard the news about this denunciation, we decided to discuss the matter with Professor Bieliatzkin. If the fact of the existence of his library in the city comes to light, it could cause him a great deal of trouble.

Now Professor Bieliatzkin is sitting at my desk in the Council office. He has lost his composure, and for good reason, I look at him with sorrow and pity. He, my tutor for four years in the past—how much he has changed, how he has grown old. Professor Bieliatzkin, the genius, the unique person who for many years had defended people in trouble, who always had a kind word in exchanges with anyone, however humble, who always found an ingenious solution in a complex situation in court—now he sits in front of me, seized by panic, confused, drained of courage.

Professor Bieliatzkin is already envisioning the serious consequences for his own person, and for his public position. I must put him at ease: "Things will sort themselves out, we shall find a way to get out of this mess," I say. He looks at me with sad eyes which say "Help me." I very much want to make it easy for him, to help him. It pains me to see him so dejected. I have had a talk with Garfunkel on this matter and he, too, tried to raise the professor's spirits. I am sure that Professor Bieliatzkin will not sleep tonight.

Something strange happened today. A telephone call was received at the Council, from the city, requesting the Council to send a cart, in order to load it with various goods. Neividel, the head of our transportation department, took a cart to the city and returned with a huge pile of various goods and articles. A letter from the Kovno branch of the German National Socialist Workers' Party was enclosed with the goods; the letter said that the goods had been confiscated from the Poles and were being handed over to the Jews. This is the first case of this kind in these crazy times.

Today Lipzer convened leaders of the labor brigades and read out to them an order issued by the Gestapo. It said that labor brigade leaders would be answerable for unauthorized trading and absenteeism from the place of work. If anyone is caught committing these offenses, his labor brigade leader and the members of his family will be arrested and executed. In more serious cases, several labor brigade leaders will be executed, together with their families. The guiding principle behind this order is: all are responsible for everyone and everyone responsible for all.

Yesterday was a black day for the labor brigade of Heresbau, which belongs to the administration for military construction, and by which 800 Jewish workers are employed at various workplaces. Upon their arrival at work yesterday morning, the workers were greeted by a search of their belongings by the man known to everyone by his nickname, "the Bayonet." He is the spiritual guide of the Nazis at Heresbau. He is a huge man, with bloodshot eyes and the countenance of a pirate. He conducted a thorough search of the workers' clothes. He found over 2,000 marks on one man, a certain Pagir. The man had received the money on his way to work from a peasant, as payment for a sewing machine he had sold him a few days earlier. As soon as the Bayonet discovered such a "treasure," he pounced on the offender, dealing him fearful blows all over his body, accompanied by screaming at him: "You'll be executed! Tomorrow you won't be alive!"

The Bayonet pushed the man aside and carried on the search. He found small amounts of money on several other workers, as well as a small amount of old clothing which was intended to be exchanged for various goods.

The Bayonet continued searching the remainder of the labor brigades; here and there he found something. He delivered blows right and left, and his screams rose to high heaven. Altogether, a few thousand marks turned up by the time the search was over.

Margolis,[4] who had been to Heresbau yesterday, had a very hard day, even though he is a strong and courageous man, not afraid of facing unusual situations. Yesterday, however, he was at a loss to know what to do. He went to the main office of the construction administration and, after numerous pleas, received a promise that no serious action will be taken following the search and that the Gestapo will not be informed. The searchers will split the money and other articles among themselves. Those on whom the money was found will be jailed in the Ghetto detention center.

It was also a difficult day for the Heresbau workers; a day of terror. Information arrived from other workplaces that the Jewish workers were being watched very closely. It was also learned that at the meeting of the Gestapo, attended by representatives of all those workplaces which employed Jews, these representatives were told that they must tighten up their supervision of the Jewish workers. Someone reported that it was said at the meeting that, as the fate of the Jews was sealed anyway, they should not be "played around" with.

This morning, as we came to the Council office, we saw a large poster on the wall. It was signed by Lipzer, and said that public discussions on various issues, as well as unauthorized absence from one's place of work, were forbidden. It was followed by an unexpected sentence: "Quiet prevails in the Ghetto today."

Lipzer sought to prove that his authority did not lag behind that of the Council, and that if the Jewish body posts announcements, he will do the same. This is the way of the ignorant. When I told him that his announcement should have been worded in a clearer way, Lipzer was amazed: "What was wrong with my announcement?" As I said, a numbskull.

1. Although several hundred Jews were deported to Riga from the Kovno Ghetto, far fewer were deported than the Germans originally intended, perhaps because they were needed in the workshops.

2. In his diary Avraham Tory repeats several times the story of Jordan's fate: a small, sweet revenge against the man who had been one of the organizers of the mass killings of October 1941.

3. Zvi Brik, a well-known Zionist leader in prewar Kovno, had been head of the Palestine Office in Kovno (for the distribution of British mandate certificates for Palestine) until Lithuania's annexation by the Soviet Union in June 1940. In the Ghetto, Brik was a member of Matzok and a manager of one of the large workshops. He survived the war and today lives in Jerusalem. His son, Aharon, born in Kovno, was hidden during the war, together with his mother, Liuba, by a Lithuanian peasant; today, as Aharon Barak, he is a member of the Israeli Supreme Court. In 1978 he was the principal drafter of the Israeli-Egyptian agreement at Camp David.

4. Pavel Margolis, the supervisor of the recruitment of laborers at the Council's labor office.

FEBRUARY 10, 1943

DOCUMENT:
German National Socialist Workers' Party
National Socialist House
Department of People's Welfare

The following foodstuffs, confiscated from private homes, were handed over to the Jews:

1. Cereals   ca. 120 kg
2. Flour   ca. 180 kg
3. Salt   ca. 15 kg

4. Sugar   ca. 50 kg
5. Coffee   96 packets
6. Pickled cabbage   1 ton
7. Black bread   13.5 loaves
8. Jam (diluted)   —
9. Beans   ca. 1.50 kg
10. Peas   ca. 7 kg
11. Toothpaste, shaving powder, licorice
12. Second-hand carpet   1 piece

Receipt for above mentioned items signed
[signature]
Heil Hitler
General Manager of the Working Group

FEBRUARY 12, 1943

Miller and Gilow have returned from their four-day visit to Riga. Much speculation arose in the Ghetto concerning this visit. Some said that it had been undertaken in connection with the demand to send 1,000 people from the Kovno Ghetto to Riga. It was also said that a meeting attended by many officials had been convened in Riga by the governor general of the Ostland region, to discuss the Jewish question, and that new edicts and other troubles are likely to result from it. In short, the Ghetto was pervaded by fear. This Riga trip took place at a very inopportune moment, when the German attitude to the Jews has worsened and the Gestapo have begun treating the Jews with growing strictness. Everyone in the Ghetto waited anxiously for the outcome of this trip to Riga.

This morning, Kopelman and I went to the city governor's office very early. Miller had already arrived there. He received me very politely and asked Kopelman and me to come to his office. I looked him straight in the eye and followed closely each of his movements, so as to draw certain conclusions.

This is always the way with the Germans. They do not tell you things clearly, except when they curse you and scream at you. It is therefore imperative to assess their mood properly before they open their mouths. We must understand that, from their point of view, our situation must always remain unclear; we are not to be allowed to understand anything, even if our lives are at stake. Anything that happens to us must occur like a bolt from the blue. We are to remain always in a state of anticipation, without understanding what is going on around us.

However, it is impossible for us to live in a state of permanent nervous tension. Despite the seven chambers of hell that the Jews—as individuals and as a community—have gone through, our spirit has not been crushed. Our eyes are wide open and we are attuned to what is going on around us. We do not forget for one moment the hallowed purposes of our people.

Everything we do, all the things we go through, seem to us as a necessary evil, a temporary hardship, so that we may reach our goal and fulfill our duty: to keep on going, and to keep spinning the golden thread of the eternal glory of Israel, in order to prove to the world the will of our people to live under any conditions and situations. These goals supply us with the moral strength to preserve our lives and to ensure the future of our people.

Kopelman and I were standing in Miller's office. He kept pacing from wall to wall and from window to window. He gave us a look as if he had made up his mind as to what to say to us, and how to say it. Did he like what we had done? Had we carried out properly the instructions we had received? De jure, all we do should appear as not quite up to the mark, because we are swindlers and treacherous. The Jews are treacherous—that is the axiom.

Now Miller is speaking to us: we must ensure that the arrangement recently introduced, in the marching of the labor brigades to work, will also be obeyed in the future. There is room for improvement. Thus, we were led to conclude, things are all right in our department and Miller is satisfied with our arrangements.

Miller went on to say that the Jewish police must constantly supervise the behavior of the labor brigades in the city. Should the Jewish policemen keep shoplifting during their stay in the city, Miller has just one word to say to them: "Gestapo." This should be enough. Then he said, offhandedly: "Recently I have seen other Ghettos and I know how things should be run." Then, wondering if he had, perhaps, said too much, he added: "In the final analysis, I know very well what to do. Here, it is I who set the rules." And again: "You must make sure that the recently introduced arrangements are observed."

Kopelman left, and I remained with Miller alone. Now he is more relaxed. From our conversation about other Ghetto matters, such as gardening and the report about the activities of the Council I had submitted to him, as well as about private matters (a new ring for his wife), I gather that Miller has not brought bad tidings from his trip and that, compared with other Ghettos, we are all right. The tone of his voice was proof of that.

Our conversation was interrupted by a telephone call from the office of city governor, Cramer, who asked Miller to see him. "I must go now, Golub, to present a report of my trip to the Brigadier." [1]

I returned to the Ghetto, where all the Council members were awaiting the results of my conversation with Miller. On my way back I met Goldberg. He told me that Segalson from the workshops had informed him that, having returned from the journey to Riga with Miller, Gilow had been irksome all morning and was looking for faults everywhere. I told him about my impression of the conversation with Miller, and put him at his ease. I contacted Dr. Elkes, who asked to see me. I told him that the results of the journey to Riga can be regarded as positive.

In the meantime, a telephone call from Dr. Rabinovitz of the German labor office was received at the apartment of Dr. Elkes. He reported to Dr. Elkes about his conversation with Hermann. Hermann had contacted Miller, who told him that he, Miller, was proud of our Ghetto and of all that he had created here. Thus it turned out that my assessment was correct. We all rejoiced. A heavy stone was lifted from our hearts. All the ominous rumors in connection with the journey to Riga were laid to rest.

The commissioner in charge of recruiting workers for the Ostland region came to the Ghetto yesterday, accompanied by the director of the German labor office, Hermann, and by Obst. He showed particular interest in the deployment of the labor force both inside and outside the Ghetto. He demanded that skilled workers should be employed only in their own trades. The work on the railroad and at the bridges over the Nieman river is of great importance to him. Locksmiths and technicians must be employed there. He inspected the workers' roster and their division into different categories of work. He also toured the Ghetto workshops. He liked the departments working for the German Army, such as the department where army uniforms were sewn, and the saddle department. In contrast, he regarded as expendable the departments specializing in manufacturing toys for children, or in special orders for senior officials. He said that those departments serve the regional governor and the city governor, not the Army.

Segalson, the Jewish manager of the workshops, saw fit to come out in defense of orders from German officials. He "explained" that the coats being processed in the workshops had, as a matter of fact, been confiscated from the Jews, and that after being mended they were sent to the German store in Kovno for sale. A good excuse. They can be satisfied—Cramer and other German senior officials—who show up here with pride and arrogance: the Jew Segalson rescued them from an unpleasant situation. Incidents such as these, when a Jew is required to spare a German notable embarrassment of one kind or another, occur quite often.

The Ghetto workshops were very much to the liking of the distinguished visitor. The Jews, it turned out, are not doing a bad job. This visit, too, produced positive results. The main one was the remark of a member of his entourage who said that skilled workers must be employed at their trades and not in menial work. For the latter, Jews from the Reich may be brought in. This would mean that removing the Jews from here is no longer on the agenda. This casual remark had a calming effect on us.

Yesterday and today were quiet, after two weeks of tension. It is true that the workers return from the city empty-handed, but it is of no importance. We will hold out if quiet prevails both here and outside.

Yesterday the Gestapo released Pagir, who had been arrested after 2,000 marks had been found on him at his work place at Heresbau. One more woman was also released. This means that in the Gestapo, too, the Jews are no longer treated with severity. That is better. The pressure on us has been relaxed somewhat.

Furthermore, the affair of theft from the large workshops has also been satisfactorily resolved. Segalson informed his German superior about the affair and, more important, there is no shortage of leather for saddles. We have managed to pull ourselves out of a bad fix. Would that the coming days would be quiet also. We need some peace.

1. Cramer had recently been promoted from colonel to brigadier-general.

FEBRUARY 13, 1943

I went to see Miller this morning. He informed me that he would be coming to the Ghetto at three o'clock in the afternoon. The problem on the agenda is the food supply to the Ghetto inmates. Miller will be coming with Obst, and with the director of the administration and food supply department, Mr. Viertel. Miller asked me to prepare all the data and documents pertaining to the subject we are going to discuss.

Later I spoke with Obst. I asked his permission to transfer to the Ghetto four tons of potatoes for the use of the soup kitchen. He pondered my request for a moment and then gave his permission. This is the first time we are getting something for our kitchen from the city governor's office. Until now it was the responsibility of the Council to supply the needs of our soup kitchen from its own very limited resources. I was very pleased with this accomplishment and returned to the Ghetto to make preparations for the visit of Miller and company.

At about three o'clock, Miller, Obst, and Viertel arrived in the Council offices. They asked me to accompany them to the workshops. I took with me the papers they had asked to see. The three Germans, as well as Segalson and I, assembled in the workshops office.

Miller informed us that from now on Mr. Viertel would be responsible for the food supply to the Ghetto. The new director asked to see immediately the information about the workshop kitchen. What, for instance, was cooking in the kitchen today? He wanted to see the menu.

Segalson told him that ever since the workers stopped bringing groceries from the city into the Ghetto, and various goods are no longer confiscated at the Ghetto gate, the Ghetto Guard no longer supplies food and, as a consequence, there is no food to be cooked. It is simply impossible to prepare a meal from the ration of 120 grams of flour and 7.5 grams of coffee per week. At best, meals are prepared two or three times a week.

We moved on to another subject: do the workers eat the food they get in the kitchen, or do they take some of it home? We replied that there are workers who take some of the food home for their families; others desist from eating all the soup and give it to their children, or to an elderly father, etc.

Thereupon Viertel told us in the strongest terms that such an arrangement is out of the question. The Germans are interested in keeping the food rations for workers only, so that soup can be prepared five times a week. The workers, however, must eat this food on the spot. It is forbidden to take food out of the workshops and bring it home. If one worker does not want to eat the food from the kitchen, it must be given to another worker. He, Viertel, is going to be strict regarding this matter. Woe to anyone who contravenes this directive.

Miller added to this. "From the humane point of view," he said, "I understand that a worker wants to share his food with his children or his parents. That's very nice. However, the worker must produce products of reasonable quality, and when he gives up some of his food ration, he won't be able to make a proper contribution to the productive effort of other workers. It is not dissimilar to a woman who is suckling an infant and who is being given nutritious food especially for that purpose."

Viertel sums up the discussion: "I am going to appoint a special man who will ensure that my directives will be carried out in practice."

I brought up another subject for discussion: additional food rations for workers who do not receive food at their workplace, that is, workers in the house repair department, transportation workers, and others. The Jewish policemen also work very hard day and night, as well as firemen and workers of the labor office.

Viertel tells us that he has not been aware of these problems. He will make sure that, first of all, workers in the large workshops receive increased food rations. Later he will devote himself to the other problems we have brought to his attention.

The next issue on the agenda is the question of nutrition, as far as the general Ghetto population is concerned. I said that food supplies fall short of the official quota. Thus, for example, eight tons of bread and three tons of meat are due, but have failed to arrive.

Here Miller interjected to say that the Lithuanians who are required to supply food to the population believe that, as far as the Ghetto is concerned, they can do anything they want. And, in fact, they do as they please: they are late with food supplies, or do not supply food at all; they say, wait a while longer, and postpone the supply from one day to the next. This cannot continue. Here, in the Ghetto, people are working; the Jews are toiling for the benefit of the German Army. It seems only proper that they should be supplied with food in sufficient quantity, and on time. In this case there must be equality of rights: every worker must be provided with the food ration which was set for him.

I stood near Segalson and listened to Miller. When speaking, he seemed to forget that he was a Nazi, and spoke like a logical human being. The expression "equality of rights" as referring to the Jews, was heard by us for the first time under German rule. Are we really hearing new voices? Do they really consider our problems out of a humane approach? Or was it just a slip of the tongue on the part of Miller? In any event, the expression "equality of rights," referring to the Jews, inscribed itself in our memory.

I understand the unwillingness of the Lithuanians to toil for the Germans. The Lithuanians are not dependent on the Germans for their food rations. They have ties with their villages, which supply them with plenty of food; therefore, they do not make a connection between their work and their food rations.

The Germans have a long score to settle with the Lithuanian people; the account grows longer with each passing day. This is probably the reason that the question of "equality of rights" cropped up in the conversation. As used by Miller, this expression stems not so much from the love of Mordechai as from the hatred of Haman. Nowadays, the Germans do not love the Jews more, but they hate the Lithuanians more than they used to.

I brought up again the question of the general food supply to the Ghetto: lately we have not received sugar or fats. Viertel promised to improve the situation in that respect. However, instead of fats he will give us horsemeat, perhaps even pork.

Another subject in the discussion: sowing our fields and vegetable gardens. So far we have not received all the seeds, and it is time we received them. Viertel regarded the problem of seeds as very important. He wanted to know how the whole vegetable venture operates in the Ghetto. We told him that we have a comprehensive sowing plan which can be obtained at the city governor's office. We need implements and seeds. Also we need hoes and suchlike. He told me to come back to him on the coming Tuesday to talk about this matter.

At this point Miller remarked that the German obligation to supply the needs of the workers hinges on one condition—greater work effort and larger output. The labor force should be expanded by adding younger people to it. Every additional worker is important. He, Miller, will make sure that more medicine is available in order to reduce work absenteeism due to illnesses. He will also speak with the employers about supplying the workers with one hot meal a day. Should an employer refuse, his workers will be transferred to other places. Furthermore, the workers should be supplied with socks and shoes, particularly during the winter. To sum it up: he will make every effort to ensure that each worker achieves maximum productivity.

Throughout this conversation, which lasted about an hour, I kept looking at Viertel—a German with a red neck. His figure and deportment are fear-inspiring; he will use strong-arm tactics, he said, he will stand on guard, etc. As I looked at him, images which I will not forget flashed through my mind; last summer, when I called on him concerning the food supply to the Ghetto, he grabbed me by the neck and dragged me, not just out of his office, but all the way to the sidewalk. He kicked me out of the building, plain and simple. This same Viertel sits with me today for the second time. We are discussing the same subject: the food supply for the Ghetto. He even went so far as to promise to increase the food rations for the Ghetto inhabitants generally.

Something has changed among the Germans, after all. Even Viertel says: "Amen!" In all probability he just cannot help it.[1]

1. Following the German surrender at Stalingrad, there was a discernible change in German attitudes in many Ghettos and labor camps; this change was to last for several months. The German surrender at Stalingrad had been a moment of national humiliation and potential danger for Germans throughout the occupied territories of Europe.

FEBRUARY 14, 1943

The Council has decided that starting today (Sunday), work at the Council institutions will begin at 11 A.M. on Sundays, and not at 8 A.M. as is usual on every other day of the week. The reason for this decision is to enable the workers to stay for a few hours at home, to attend to their private matters, to take a shower and to rest a little. Sunday is usually a quiet day. In public institutions people work seven days a week. They should have a few hours for themselves.

Some time ago we decided that no work would be done on Saturday afternoons at the public institutions in the Ghetto; now this is being completed by starting the work on Sunday at 11 A.M. In the city governor's office and other municipal institutions no work is being done on Sunday.

On my way to the Council offices, I ran into a special messenger.[1] He asked me to set out for the Council at once. Schtitz of the Gestapo should arrive there at any minute. On the way, I met several policemen who told me that Lithuanian policemen had shown up in the Ghetto early in the morning, and that Schtitz was coming in their wake. What had happened? During the night a live cow had been smuggled into the Ghetto through an opening in the fence near Mesininku Street. It was slaughtered here. The cow was stolen, and this is why the Lithuanian criminal police were involved. In the barn situated by the Ghetto fence, remains of the slaughtered cow were found. A barrel of beer and several dozen empty beer and vodka bottles were discovered there as well. It should be remembered that the barn was fitted out with electric light, which means that it was used for smuggling goods through the Ghetto fence.

At no. 3 Mesininku Street lives a Jew by the name of Lipshes. He is known to our police as a black-marketeer and smuggler. The Jewish Ghetto police have warned him several times to discontinue his activities. After the execution of forty-five Jews ten days ago, the Ghetto police drew up a list of people suspected of engaging in illicit trade. In order to forestall further executions, the Ghetto police sent these people to do hard labor as part of a special labor brigade which was assigned to bridge construction.

Lipshes was on that list and went out to work every day. It appears, however, that he managed to run his black-market business at night, after returning from his daily work. Today it happened: Lipshes stumbled. The matter is already in the hands of the Gestapo, and the whole Ghetto is agitated and worried. Lipshes is a "troublemaker for Israel," say the Ghetto inhabitants. "These days not even a small parcel is smuggled through the Ghetto gate. The Jewish police make sure it won't be. And at a time like this, Lipshes saw fit to take up this ignominious business and, by doing so, to risk the lives of his family and perhaps even the lives of others in the Ghetto."

The Ghetto inmates remember well the bitter experience of ten days ago, and they are afraid. They do not want to see the Gestapo putting in an appearance on our streets. The Ghetto inmates who live on Mesininku Street are moving out into other areas; they fear that all the inmates of this street will be arrested. Lipshes was not at home and went into hiding.

I entered the Council office. The atmosphere was thick with apprehension. We were informed that Schtitz had already gone, leaving behind an order to find Lipshes. The Jewish police are looking for him. Another warning has been issued to the workers in the city to refrain from smuggling goods through the Ghetto gate. It has also been decided to concentrate all Ghetto inmates suspected of black-marketeering in the Ghetto detention center. During the day they will go out to work and at night they will be locked up in the detention center, in order to prevent them from hanging around the Ghetto fence.

While all this was happening, Dr. Elkes called me on the telephone and asked me to come over at once, which I did. He seemed very worried. He told me that two days ago a senior physician from the city health office had visited the Ghetto and informed him that there was an illegal tavern at no. 3 Mesininku Street. He had been told about the tavern by a nurse who lived at this address; she asked him to take her out of there because her life was in danger. It turns out that this house served as a black-market center on a permanent basis. Moreover, Lithuanians pass through the Ghetto fence and Lipshes drinks "your health" with them. This nurse is now under arrest in connection with the Lipshes affair. Dr. Elkes regards the immediate release of the nurse as a very important matter. He had not had the time to transfer her to another apartment because Garfunkel had recently been taken ill. Should something befall this nurse, it would weigh heavily on Dr. Elkes's conscience.

I promised Dr. Elkes to do everything possible to secure the release of the nurse. I immediately approached Grinberg, the commander of the first police precinct. "You've placed under arrest the nurse who lives in Lipshes's house," I told him. "You must release her at once." He told me not to be agitated. The case is known to him. He, Grinberg, knows everybody in his precinct, and he knows wheat from chaff. He had already asked the commander of the Jewish Ghetto police not to enter the arrest of the nurse into the books. She has nothing to do with the case. She has already been released. I passed this information on to Dr. Elkes. It put him at ease.

The Jewish police had meanwhile succeeded in locating Lipshes and had placed him under arrest, together with two accomplices. Someone told Lipshes that during the interrogation by the Gestapo he must tell them that he acted alone. This might save the lives of his family.

I remained in my room. Potruch, head of the economic affairs department, came to me and told me that someone from the Jewish police telephone exchange had been in his office and wanted to take the office telephone, in compliance with Lipzer's orders. I asked Potruch to leave the telephone in his office.

A short time later Lipzer came to my room. He was accompanied by his personal assistant, Aronstamm,[2] and by Katz from the telephone exchange. Lipzer was very upset. He asked me why I did not allow him to take the telephone from Potruch. I explained to him that only the Council is authorized to confiscate a telephone from one of its offices. "Really?" says Lipzer. "If you or one of your friends needed a telephone, you would have got hold of it already, whereas I am being put off from day to day." I did not respond. I did not tell him that neither I nor my friends have telephones in our apartments, and that we do not request them.

Lipzer: "You've got two telephones in the Council; one in the economic section and one in the labor section. You'll soon receive a directive to take this one away." He pointed at the telephone on the wall of the Council secretariat room.

"When we receive such an order, we shall take away this telephone. Until today we have not received such an order," I replied.

Out of his wallet Lipzer pulls a paper issued to him by Dr. Elkes. It read: "I am entitled to visit and inspect the Council offices." Lipzer adds: "I don't believe you; I don't believe the Council. I have no faith in your 'papers.' Do you know why I asked Rauca of the Gestapo to certify this paper? Because I don't believe you." Here Lipzer points with his finger at Rauca's signature, and at the Gestapo stamp on his certificate. He wants to make a point about his being above us which entitles him to give us orders. He says: "Your papers are of no use to me whatsoever. I shall take off my cap neither to Golub nor to Goldberg nor to Garfunkel. If I take off my cap to Elkes, it's my own business, because that's what I feel like doing."

I sat back in my chair and listened throughout. I did not say anything. I knew that it was pointless to argue with him. One must let him talk; to disburden himself of the profanity which had accumulated in his mouth, particularly in the presence of his bodyguard Aronstamm and the telephone operator Katz. He talks to me this way because he wants everybody to hear, to know who Lipzer is.

As I was listening, I kept thinking about Lipzer, out of whose mouth coarseness, arrogance, and ignorance were pouring. At this moment he was publicly forsaking all the norms of proper conduct and appeared the way he really was. He not only demands of us a share in decisions on public matters, but wants us also to be his good friends.

Several times I wanted to tell him frankly: "Go away, you ignominious creature!" But, as it happens, he has free access to the Gestapo, where the fate of dozens of people is frequently decided. Moreover, we need the man, we cannot do without him. Something may happen each day. We must keep him close to us, and create the impression that he is one of us. We must praise him, bow to his whims, turn a blind eye to his crooked ways.

Lipzer does not just want all this from us; he forces us to pay him our respects. "What do you give me?" he asks us, quite often. "I do everything I can for the Ghetto, for the Council. And what do I ask in return? A little respect."

There was an argument once about an honorary title in the Jewish police for him. He wanted to be an "honorary commander" of the Jewish police. Not an honorary member, but an honorary commander. He demanded from Dr. Elkes a letter on behalf of the Council authorizing him to inspect the Council offices. The document was to be issued in Yiddish; Lipzer promised he would not abuse it. He wished to keep it for himself and for posterity. Dr. Elkes had no choice but to acquiesce, and to issue the document to him.

One morning Lipzer stayed in the Ghetto. He came to me and did not let up until I issued the document he wanted. Afterward, he went to the Gestapo and had Rauca sign the document, and make it official by stamping it with the Gestapo stamp.

Lipzer also insisted on his own office in the Ghetto, near the Council, to conduct his own private business. He got a room and once came there with a woman. By chance, Abraham Levin, a Council employee, entered the room. Lipzer showed him the woman and the document issued by Dr. Elkes and signed by Rauca with the Gestapo stamp. Then he asked Levin: "So, what do you say, Levinke? Isn't she a pretty woman? How do you like the letter?" This is Lipzer for you.

However, Lipzer's intrusion today into the Council offices, and the conversation with me, were too much, even for a character like Lipzer. He knows there is nothing he has asked for that he did not get. For him there was never a problem of "too much" or "too expensive." On occasion he asked me to write a speech for him—and got what he asked for. Often I went with him to visit his house. I did this, not because of my private interest—I have never asked him for anything—I did it in compliance with Dr. Elkes's request, for the benefit of the Council and of the Ghetto.

Lipzer regarded me as his personal friend. He told me so many times. All this was done for practical reasons. He obtained from me everything he asked for. I even wrote for him the speech which he delivered on the occasion of his becoming an honorary member of the Jewish police. Despite all that, today he broke into my office, not even alone, but in the company of two policemen, in order to frighten me.

Finally, Lipzer left; the conclusion of our meeting was not the way he had planned it. He had got used to getting anything he wanted. I would have yielded, if it was just a matter of one telephone. This time, however, I refused because it was a matter of principle.

I recall that many times I have been told that I give in to Lipzer too much; that I say yes to all his requests. Even his wife, who is not stupid by any means, told me once that I give in to her husband "even when you think that he is wrong. Why do you do that? Why don't you say just once: 'No!' " I told her: "Mrs. Lipzer, I can promise you that when it becomes necessary, when an important matter is at stake, a matter of principle, I will be able to say no. But I don't believe it is worthwhile to enter into argument with Lipzer over a thousand petty matters and thereby strain relations with him."

Lipzer's wife did not believe my assertion about my ability to say no as far as important matters were concerned. Today she could see for herself that I had not been bragging just for the sake of it. The issue today was the honor of the Jewish institution, the Council. Lipzer must understand that peace and quiet in the Ghetto depends on the respect given to the Council. The Council employees must sense its authority; they must know that the Council stands guard, defending them and their jobs.

I acted the way I did without paying heed to the danger that a man like Lipzer might cause me. He is capable of doing things even he might regret later.

I went to Dr. Elkes and told him of my meeting with Lipzer today. Elkes agreed that I had acted correctly. He, Dr. Elkes, will invite Lipzer and have a talk with him in the presence of the Council members. He will talk to him even if this might open a rift in their relations. Rauca should not be involved in the internal affairs of the Jews. The Council must uphold its authority.

Afterward I spoke with Garfunkel. I told him about Lipzer's behavior. Garfunkel said that this was bound to have happened sooner or later. "You should be praised for your courage, Golub," he said.

This was the reaction from Elkes and Garfunkel. Goldberg reacted differently. He came to the Council offices in the afternoon and told me that he had dined with Lipzer at his home and that my name had been mentioned. Lipzer is very angry. His wife too, regards herself as having been offended. He should have been given the telephone he asked for.

Goldberg went on to say that I had reared and nurtured Lipzer. Dr. Elkes signs everything. Goldberg is not being consulted; there is no good contact between us. Elkes has been ill for the last eight months.[3] He behaves like President Hindenburg: he signs every paper brought to him. People say that Golub is running the affairs of the Ghetto.

This is a new tune. It turns out that Goldberg too is offended. It appears that these days he and Lipzer are partners, mates in trouble. Later, I was informed that Goldberg drew sustenance from my quarrel with Lipzer.

We have gotten used to everything. We know who is mourning and who sings with joy among us; we know our friends and our enemies. We have enough strength and responsibility to lead the Ghetto. Others may laugh or weep— nothing in the Ghetto will be changed by that. The Council carries on, following the path of responsibility and dignity.

1. One of the child messengers who acted both as message carriers and as lookouts to alert the Council when Germans were approaching. About ten youngsters served the Council in this capacity, often carrying messages which were too sensitive for the telephone because of German eavesdropping.
2. Tanchum Aronstamm was Lipzer's right hand and bodyguard and the member of the Jewish police who was responsible for the enlistment of forced labor. After the disbanding of the Jewish police in March 1944, the Germans appointed him head of the public order service. In both positions, he was greatly feared in the Ghetto.
3. In January 1942, when the Germans announced that Jews from Vienna would be brought to the Ghetto, preparations were made by the Jewish Council for their reception (housing, hot coffee, and so on), and the arrival of their train was awaited all night long in bitter cold. Dr. Elkes, who was among those waiting, caught a severe cold; later he suffered from rheumatoid arthritis, from which he did not fully recover for more than a year.

FEBRUARY 15, 1943

At 10 A.M. Schtitz, accompanied by Lipzer, came to the Ghetto. Schtitz entered the Ghetto command headquarters and Lipzer went to his room. Schtitz ordered Lipshes, who was arrested yesterday on charges of smuggling a cow into the Ghetto, to be brought to him.

Afterward Schtitz went to unseal the apartments of the Ghetto inmates who had been taken to the fort on February 4. He summoned the commander of the first police precinct, Grinberg. Together with Lipzer they went to see the apartments.

Schtitz asked, first of all, where were the apartments of the rich located? Grinberg told him that there were no rich people in the Ghetto. Schtitz replied that Orechkin was a speculator and, therefore, he wanted to see his apartment first.

Only Schtitz could raise such an accusation against Orechkin. Only a Gestapo man could dare to call Orechkin—an upright man and a well-known journalist—a speculator. Each Ghetto inmate knew that Orechkin was an honest man and had never engaged in black-marketeering.

The three entered Orechkin's room with its four bare walls. They found some belongings, clothes and a little furniture. Schtitz offered the belongings to Lipzer and Grinberg, to divide between them. He took for himself the better-looking clothes and put them in his car. In the end the belongings given to Lipzer and Grinberg were handed over to the Jewish police for distribution among the poorer policemen. Other articles were transferred to the welfare office. In actual fact, those articles belong to the Council, which distributes them, as usual, to the most needy among the Ghetto inmates. Today, it appears, Lipzer decided otherwise.

From Orechkin's apartment the party moved on to the apartment which had belonged to Leites.[1] It was the same thing over again: Schtitz took the better-quality belongings to his car. The remainder were distributed by Lipzer as he saw fit.

His car loaded with valuables, Schtitz drove to the Gestapo building. From there he took Lipshes for interrogation. The Lipshes affair proceeded rather quietly. Schtitz was not angry. On the contrary, he was quiet and at ease. No searches were conducted for Lipshes's accomplices. At the end there was a surprise; Lipshes returned to the Ghetto the same evening. He had been beaten and bruised, but was alive and free.

"Hast thou killed and also taken possession?" (I Kings 21:19), so cried Dr. Elkes upon hearing about the searches that Schtitz had conducted in the apartments of the murdered Jews. And, indeed, Schtitz has murdered and also taken possession. It seems, however, that he was not in any way excited by his job— not yesterday nor today. He has turned into a beast; perhaps he was born this way? Human feelings are alien to him. He completed his job and returned to the city.

At 1:30 P.M. I left for the city with Segalson, to meet with Viertel concerning the increased food rations for workers in the Ghetto.

It was raining. Snow fell and turned into water. A cold wind was blowing and penetrated our bones. A long line of peasant carts on their way from the country to the city stretched across the Slobodka bridge. A group of Russian prisoners-of-war pushing an army refuse cart were marching on the other side of the road. They were guarded by armed German soldiers bringing up the rear.

The residents of Kovno are familiar with this picture. Every day, long rows of Russian prisoners, in small or large groups, march to or from work. Some of them pull a cart loaded with various materials or refuse. The cart is surrounded on all sides by prisoners who look as if they had never been free men. They cast desperate glances at the passersby. With their eyes they beg for something to eat—potatoes, a slice of bread—or a lighted cigarette butt.

The Russian prisoners exchange glances with the Jewish workers who go to the city to work and return back to the Ghetto in the evening. The Jewish workers—absorbed in their own troubles, clad in rags, and with not a penny in their pockets—look for some way to extend a little help to the Russian prisoners. How do they do it? One of them drops a little piece of bread on the ground; another throws a lighted cigarette in their direction, and such like. Everyone trudges ahead. One of the Russian prisoners bends down and picks up the piece of bread, another grabs the burning cigarette. A smile of gratitude glitters in their eyes.

During the great "actions" in October 1941, the Jews envied the Russian prisoners. Although their work was unbearable, in the long run their lives were secure. Lately it appears that their fortunes have improved somewhat; their faces are brighter and their gaze more human. Not far away from here, their immense homeland is waging a struggle of life and death. It keeps on fighting the Germans with considerable success.

The fate of our people is different. We are far away from our country, at best. Our fate has not yet been finally decided. We do not know which nation will be prepared to come to help us. It seems that strangers will not rescue us. All this talk about a war on behalf of the whole of humankind is just talk. Everyone fights for himself, for the sake of his own future. That is why our future is shrouded in darkness. Will the free Jewish State, capable of serving as a haven for its people, be established after this terrible war?

As my glance ranges over the thousands of Russian prisoners passing us by, I forget the purpose of my coming into the city. I become absorbed in thoughts about the future of our people. Segalson, who sits beside me, asks me whether I did not forget to take with me the toys which Viertel wanted. He brings me back to reality. In the meantime, heavy clouds have covered the sky and the snow falls on our faces and clothes. The chill and the dampness penetrate our bones. It is cold and damp outside, and within our hearts it is not much better.

At last we reached the city governor's office and entered Viertel's room. He has already prepared an order for an additional supply of food for the workers in the large workshops: two tons of lentils, one ton of flour, 400 kilograms of artificial honey, 20 kilograms of tea, and several hundred kilograms of pork.[2] This is for 1,300 workers for a period of one month. Compared with what we used to get, this is a huge quantity of food.

We listened and kept silent. We were Jews and must not be overly impressed. We keep silent when bad news is brought to us. So we kept our mouths shut and did not display any signs of joy as we beheld the huge quantities of food for the workers.

On our way back to the Ghetto we were marveling at the Purim presents given to us by the Germans before Purim. It appears that they need the Jews; they need the working and producing Jewish hands. After all, hungry people cannot produce a thing.

We have not yet received additional rations for the Ghetto workers. I must supply Viertel with clear and authorized information. He also promised to supply us with seeds for our vegetable gardens.

I entered Miller's office. He asked me whether Steinbrecher, who is in charge of the distribution of medicine, had visited the Ghetto today. He was supposed to come to the Ghetto today to examine the supply of medicine in the Ghetto.

Steinbrecher came to the Ghetto a little later. He paid a visit to the pharmacy and promised to supply a sizable quantity of medicines. Someone told him about the existence of a large quantity of medicine in the Ghetto. An example: an acquaintance of his needed a certain drug and could not find it in the city. A Jewish worker brought him the drug from the Ghetto. Srebnitzki explained to Steinbrecher that this may happen once in fifty years. All drugs in the Ghetto were confiscated by the physicians. Steinbrecher believed Srebnitzki's story and promised more medicine in the future.

Today we have also received four tons of washing powder and 8,000 bars of soap for the Ghetto.

On the eve of the Lithuanian national holiday, which falls on February 16, the guard in the Ghetto has been reinforced.

1. Leites was one of the forty-five Jews who had been murdered at the Ninth Fort during the "Stalingrad action" on February 4, 1943.

2. The meat usually supplied to the Ghetto was horsemeat; too often it was rotten and had to be buried. When pork was supplied, as in this case, Berl Friedman, who was in charge of the workshops' kitchen, exchanged it for horsemeat with the Lithuanian dealers.

FEBRUARY 16, 1943

Today the Lithuanians celebrate their independence day.[1] No trace has been left of Lithuanian sovereignty. All the same, the Germans fear demonstrations. That is the reason for the reinforced detachments of police guards patrolling the city and the Ghetto. The two Ghetto commandants, who alternate their jobs every twenty-four hours, remain in the building of the Ghetto command. The number of mobile guard patrols has been doubled.

I am at a loss to work out the connection between Lithuanian independence day and the reinforced guard in the Ghetto. Is there anyone capable of surmising that we, the Jews in Lithuania, harbor positive feelings toward Lithuania and its independence? Should it not be clear that all that was connected with Lithuania no longer exists? One may, perhaps, recall the Jewish autonomy during the first decade of the independent Lithuania.[2] There is no doubt that we cherish warm memories of the flourishing, nationally conscious Jewish community in Lithuania. All this, however, belongs to the past. The best Lithuanian Jews are no longer with us. They were erased without a trace. They were exterminated by murderers on Lithuanian soil. The handful of remaining Jews are overcome by grief and sorrow. Like Rachel grieving over her sons, they grieve over their martyred brethren.

One may speak of feelings of hatred and revenge with regard to everything that has to do with Lithuania. One may speak of the curse with which, in his heart, each one of us curses this Lithuania, which with its own hands has exterminated Lithuanian Jewry. Curse upon Lithuania and upon its sons, who, during the most trying times for the Jewish people, stabbed them in the back.

This is the reason why the reinforced police detachments in the Ghetto on the eve of the Lithuanian independence day seem so strange to me. When I went to the city last Wednesday and saw the Lithuanian national flags fluttering in the wind—the only demonstration allowed by the Germans—different thoughts passed through my mind: the flags were hoisted on houses built with Jewish labor and sweat. Where are they now, the former owners of those houses, who for many years had been loyal Lithuanian citizens? These days, Lithuanians live in Jewish houses; they use the Jewish furniture and wear the Jewish clothes. The Old City of Kovno is packed with people. Jewish houses and apartments have not remained vacant, but their rightful owners are not alive. The Jews who relate in their own unique way to all they have built and created are missing. What else does the future have in store for us? And what will the few surviving Jews do here?

Today the Lithuanians are forbidden to rejoice, to demonstrate. They are forced to hide their emotions. Now they begin to sense their new situation. That is the fate of Jew-haters. I have no other feelings for them these days.

These were the thoughts which passed through my mind as I beheld the Lithuanian flags hoisted on the Jewish houses of Kovno.

In the morning, Miller and Hermann came to the Council offices. During the long talk they had with the members of the Council, Miller explained—speaking to the point, in moderate and correct tone—that in Germany the main effort is now being focused on labor. All limitations on sex and age have been removed. The same applies to the Ghetto. The entire labor force must focus its efforts on production and be exploited to the utmost in accordance with the ability, the age, and the physical condition of the workers. Each Ghetto inmate can contribute to the general effort. For that purpose there is a need to concentrate all available and reliable information about each Ghetto inmate. In the Riga

Ghetto, for example, the limitations of sex and age no longer apply. The same system must be introduced into the Kovno Ghetto. In the Riga Ghetto the men live apart from their families.[3] There is no intention to introduce a similar arrangement here, as it is not thought likely to bring about increased productivity. All will remain the way it has been up to now. He, Miller, will ensure better nourishment for the Ghetto inmates, particularly for the workers. This is conditional upon an increase in the number of workers, including young people and women.

Hermann added that in some places the working day lasts only until 2 P.M. This must not be allowed to continue. The workers must be employed for a whole day. It will also be necessary to increase the daily quotas for those working on a quota basis.

On the coming Sunday, all Ghetto inmates will fill out questionnaires which Hermann has composed. The data will include the name of the worker, his occupation, workplace, sex, age, work card number, and other details. These questionnaires will help in the better deployment of the labor force.

Registration of this kind was conducted last year, but it was not accurate. People thought then that the survey was connected with an "action," or with deportation from the Ghetto. For this reason the Ghetto inmates gave misleading information concerning their occupation, age, etc. We must explain to them that, this time, the survey is in connection with the distribution of the labor force only, and that no one may shirk the work-duty. Even mothers with children must go out to work. The situation in Germany is no different. Those who refuse to work will go to jail.

The conversation was conducted at the desk of the chairman of the Council. On one side sat Miller and Hermann, on the other Garfunkel, Goldberg, Levin,[4] and I. Such a meeting between Germans and Jews is forbidden by Nazi law, but Miller asked us to join him at his desk.

Miller opened the meeting by asking of Levin: Who is he and what is his job? This was the first time he had met Levin. Miller asked about Dr. Elkes and expressed his dissatisfaction at his absence from the meeting. He said—partly to himself and partly to those assembled—that he needed people capable of carrying out things and not old people who are also sick. We explained to him that Dr. Elkes was an important figure and enjoyed great authority among the Ghetto inmates, and that he took part in all discussions. He knows everything and nothing is done without his consent.

The two Germans left. We went to see Dr. Elkes to inform him of the new questionnaires. The meeting with Elkes was also attended by Lipzer. In light of the recent tension in our relations with Lipzer, Dr. Elkes saw fit to announce that a special meeting would take place soon concerning the relationship between Lipzer and the Jewish representative body. For now, everyone is required to work as part of the common effort. It was decided to charge the Council's population registration office with conducting the survey.

In the afternoon I went to the city to meet with Viertel. I gave him a list of workers who did not receive food in the city, and a list of workers in the Ghetto whose food supply remained inadequate. Altogether 1,500 people work in the Ghetto and 600 in the municipal labor brigades. Those numbers were too large in Viertel's view. He promised to study the matter and to make a decision accordingly.

1. The Lithuanian Council, founded in September 1917 while the country was under German occupation, proclaimed Lithuanian independence on February 16, 1918. In September 1918 German forces withdrew, and Lithuania was an independent republic until its annexation by the Soviet Union in June 1940.

2. Jewish autonomy was incorporated in the Lithuanian constitution in 1922; it encompassed independent Jewish culture, language, social welfare, and taxation. Several Jews served as ministers and deputy ministers in the various Lithuanian governments. After 1926, however, Jewish autonomy was systematically curtailed.

3. In Riga, approximately 4,000 men and 200 women had survived the large German "actions" which had taken place there in late November and early December 1941; they were forced to live in separate labor camps. Other Jews, however, who had been deported from the Reich to Riga, still lived together. In July 1943 they too were deported to separate camps.

4. Zvi (Hirsch) Levin had been an unofficial member of the Council since August 6, 1942, the day on which the Germans reduced the size of the Council. The fact that Levin was present at the meeting between Miller and Hermann was evidence of the more relaxed atmosphere these two Germans had established between themselves and the Council.

FEBRUARY 18, 1943

Yesterday a discussion took place concerning the problem of the children's department. Recently a dispute had broken out between Dr. Zacharin, head of the health section, and Dr. Segal, director of the welfare office. The point at issue was, who was going to take care of fifteen or sixteen orphaned children, the sole survivors of the children's ward of the hospital that had been set on fire by the Germans in 1941.

The elderly (who are not sick) are officially classified as chronically ill patients. The fiction of the hospital, its protective function, if you will, has been a vital necessity ever since the Germans set the hospital on fire because of the contagious diseases there. In that fire, 180 children and babies met their deaths.

By a miracle, between eight and ten children survived the conflagration. We could not leave these children without any children's home or orphanage, just as we could not leave the elderly without a home for the aged. It was clear to everyone, however, that if we established such special institutions for children and the elderly, the Germans would transfer all the residents of such institutions to the Ninth Fort without any hesitation.

The Council sought to reduce as much as possible, and even to close down, those institutions ostensibly devoted to social work. More than once the Ghetto inmates came to the Council arguing that some kind of place should be created for the lonely orphaned children who had remained after numerous "actions." If we had not lived under such horrifying conditions, when terror raged in the Ghetto, no one could have argued with this plea. In the Council's view, however, under the prevailing circumstances, the well-being of these children made it essential to disperse them among many families and not concentrate them in one place under the auspices of a single institution.

Later, when the emotions surrounding this issue cooled, the Council decided to seek the adoption of these children by foster parents. For that purpose an information campaign was launched. There were parents in the Ghetto whose children had been killed or had gone to holiday resorts shortly before the war and had not returned. There were also young couples without children in the Ghetto. The aim therefore was adoption of single children by foster families. If successful, the adoption would put an end to the phenomenon of children without families and provide them with a loving and caring environment.

This solution affected children between the ages of thirteen and fifteen. For children between the ages of one and four, special steps had to be taken. It was dangerous to set up a children's home for them. It was therefore decided to house them in the children's ward of the hospital. In case of an investigation, this would provide us with a ready excuse: these are sick children who are temporarily in the hospital.

Some formal arrangement, however, had to be found. Since a special children's ward already existed in the hospital, a practically new ward was opened: a ward for orphaned children under the supervision of Dr. Zacharin.

In the course of time, a status quo evolved in which the orphaned children were de jure under the care of the welfare office, but de facto they were under the care of the health office.

In the meantime, the children found their protector in the person of Margolis, head of the section for recruitment of workers to the labor brigades. He is a very vigorous man. Since his duties require him to be present for many hours during the day at the Ghetto gate, he can procure many foodstuffs and other commodities. Thus he took upon himself to provide supplies to the orphans' ward. As the person responsible for the supplies to the children, he wanted to ensure that the goods did, in fact, reach the children.

Dr. Zacharin is a responsible person, but for various reasons he is not popular. Margolis's supervision of the distribution of food to the children aroused his ire. Once he came to me to clear up the formal aspect of the arrangement: who was in charge of the orphaned children's ward, he or Dr. Segal? I told him that officially the children were in the charge of the welfare office, which employs, among others, children's nurses. As far as the supervision of food for the children was concerned, when significant quantities of food for children had accumulated at the Council, we transferred them to the woman running the orphans' ward, without giving thought to informing Dr. Zacharin about it.

A meeting was called concerning the supply of food to the orphaned children. It was attended by Dr. Zacharin, Dr. Segal, Margolis, and others. Dr. Zacharin announced that Dr. Segal was present as a guest and that he was not entitled to take part in the discussion. He demanded a clear Council decision to determine which institution was in charge of the orphaned children. He emphasized that until that moment, he would be in charge of the orphans. He asked where had all the people in charge been during the cold winter months. Why had they not supplied firewood or food? Why did they come now, when the cupboards are brimming with food?

Dr. Segal replied that he had supplied the orphans with food throughout the period in question according to the abilities of the welfare office. In his view the institution best equipped to take care of those children is the welfare office. Consequently, he believes that the responsibility for and the supervision of those children—including medical supervision—should rest with the welfare office.

On this occasion Dr. Berman[1] and Dr. Segal reviewed the activity of Dr. Golach.[2] She is an ambitious woman, and disputes often develop on her account. For the most part these disputes involve a woman responsible for nutrition in the hospital; she receives supplies from Margolis, who instructs her to distribute them to orphaned children only. Sometimes she receives another, or a contradictory, instruction which leads to arguments which are very difficult to settle. As a result of these disputes, Dr. Zacharin ordered the dismissal of this woman—who is in charge of nutrition in the hospital.

Thus, the fundamental question is: Where does the orphaned children's ward belong? Both Dr. Zacharin and Dr. Segal must be clear about this.

Lipzer has also intervened in this dispute. As was his habit, he had not consulted anyone at the Council. He sent a letter to the head of the health section saying that he, Lipzer, requests that Mrs. Sovacki, an employee of the health section, will continue working in her post and that he hopes that his request will be honored. The letter was signed "B. Lipzer, on behalf of the German Security Police and head of the Jewish brigade at the Gestapo."

Having received this letter, Dr. Zacharin was very much offended. Dr. Elkes was also very angry at Lipzer's letter and its contents. This was another case of his intervention in the affairs of the Council without prior consultation with its leaders. Dr. Elkes reached an agreement with Lipzer that a final compromise would be reached at the coming meeting of the Council.

We were informed that Lipzer had written another draft of the letter to Zacharin. It had been worded as an order: "On behalf of the Gestapo I order that Mrs. Sovacki will remain in her post." Acting on the advice of one of his men, he sent the more moderately worded letter.

Dr. Elkes told Lipzer that after the Ghetto period he will not use the title "Acting on behalf of the German Security Police and the Gestapo." What does he need all this publicity for? Dr. Elkes believes that these titles do not bring Lipzer the respect he seeks. Lipzer realized the significance of this dispute and asked Dr. Elkes to arrange the matters so that his name and position would not be dishonored. Dr. Elkes promised to fulfill his request.

Garfunkel visited the hospital and its orphaned children's ward today. He came to the conclusion that the two institutions should be separated. He suggested turning the orphaned children's ward over to the welfare office, and placing our trust in God who judges all men.

During the discussion we were informed that a few days ago a baby was brought to the hospital and left there by people who refused to give their names. The baby had just been born. It is being taken care of, but there is no guarantee that it will survive. If it survives, a name has already been prepared for it: the second Gideon.

One year ago a newborn baby was found near the Ghetto gate. It was transferred to the hospital. It was nursed, "and his name in Israel was Gideon." This was the first, biblical Gideon. We hope that the third Gideon will not be late in coming.

Today a meeting took place at the Council on the subject of gardening. The city governor's office suggested that we cultivate all the arable areas within the Ghetto bounds. However, we lack gardening tools, seeds, etc. I took it upon myself to procure those articles from Viertel at the city governor's office.

The big question is, where do we get horses to plough twenty-seven hectares of land? Another problem: keeping an eye on the fields and harvesting the crops. We would like to avoid our experience from last year, when only a small part of the crops was harvested.[3] This failure was a stain on the name of the gardening section, notwithstanding its numerous achievements. This year we must make special efforts to avoid another failure. We passed on this resolution to the vegetable garden workers, and in particular to the director of the gardening section, the agronomist Kelzon.

1. Dr. Moshe Berman headed the hospital which was established in the Ghetto at the end of 1941, after the Germans burned down the contagious diseases hospital. He was also an active member of the Council's health department. Before the war he had been head of the Lithuanian military hospital and personal physician to the Lithuanian chief of staff, General Zukauskas.

2. Dr. Rosa Golach, a pediatrician in the Ghetto.

3. In the summer of 1942, hungry Ghetto inmates seized the crops before they were fully ripe.

FEBRUARY 19, 1943

"Alarm! The West is in danger." This is the headline of today's Kovno news-paper, which printed the full text of Goebbels's most recent speech. Ghetto inmates who read it were overcome by anguish. In his speech Goebbels said, among other things: "The Jews are the root of evil in the world; they are the devil which pushes the West toward its downfall; they are the carrier of ruin and destruction within the body of Western civilization; they are the instigator of chaos in the world. The crocodile tears shed abroad over the persecution of Jews in German-occupied territory will not deter Germany from carrying out its plans and ideas. On the contrary, Germany will pursue its course with more vigor— by any available means, if necessary—in order to implement its plan for the total extermination of Jewry." [1]

Jew-hatred has not until now been expressed so clearly, absolutely, and shamelessly. It is noteworthy that, this time, Jew-hatred was expressed without any hostile reference toward the United States or England, as if Goebbels had decided to leave the door open for a possible reconciliation with those two powers.

How many times have we heard such speeches? How many times has our total extermination been foretold? We have almost become used to speeches of this kind. But such cruel talk still manages to produce a shocking effect on us each time it is uttered anew. Every time we hear it, our wounds—which have had no time to heal—are ripped open, and we once more see before our eyes the "actions," the executions, the Ninth Fort, the mass graves. Who can forget all this?

Today's conversation with Lipzer, which took place at Dr. Elkes's office, was overshadowed by the impression of the new danger facing us. Those assembled take it seriously, even though they do their best to regain their strength.

We talked about the relationships between Lipzer and the Council, or, more precisely, about Lipzer's attitude toward the main Jewish institution in the Ghetto. Reflections on today's speech formed a part of this conversation. Lipzer is a small-time politician whose comprehension of the meaning of the speeches of leaders and politicians is even smaller than his political skills. But he has heard enough about the threats against the Jews. After all, he works for the devil himself. Every day Jews are taken to his place of work where they are subjected to torture—which at the Gestapo has a tangible meaning. Many Jews leave that place to their final destination. Lipzer is often present when this takes place. He is there in the capacity of "their man." But he also knows that the Gestapo often content themselves with screams and imprecations. He also knows that speeches by great men do not always affect those doing the dirty job at the Gestapo. They often show apathy when hearing speeches spouting fire and brimstone. There-fore, says Lipzer, there is nothing new here. These are just words. However, it is difficult to believe that Goebbels is just chattering away. One cannot belittle the man or his speeches.

Today's speech was more explicit than those in the past. Things were stated clearly. Today we know what the martyrs of October 28, 1941, did not know, and what we ourselves were ignorant of for a long time: that our enemy is on the decline and that every day something may happen which can change the whole situation. Our redemption may come quite unexpectedly.

In the evening, when we sit around the table in the small office of Dr. Elkes, each of us is pledged to speak forthrightly. On these occasions, says Dr. Elkes, we must not talk about concrete issues, but hold a general discussion instead. Certainly there is enough to discuss. In the course of time a great deal of material has accumulated concerning the system of relations among our community leaders, and we must discuss the nature of those relations as they affect our activities. The question of first importance is that of relations between Lipzer and the members of the Council. Lately, these relations have become strained. This review is in order, so as to prevent the recurrence of a dispute between us and Lipzer such as the argument over the telephone, or of further differences of opinion regarding matters on which the Council must make decisions.

At the meeting, Garfunkel said that Lipzer should have been courageous enough to listen to the views of others. He does not have to agree, but he must listen, and not boil over when he hears the views of others. Lipzer must tell us the following: What is his attitude to the Council? Does he, Lipzer, regard himself as standing above the Jewish institution? If that is the state of affairs, we must know it. And if he does not regard himself as standing above the Council, a way must be found to coordinate our activities, to work out the modus operandi of our partnership. In this case, he must take into consideration our sensibilities and views. We must unburden ourselves, in order to tighten our relations and promote our friendship.

Lipzer replied to our queries. He proclaimed that he does not stand above the Council, even if it is his job to tell his employers every day about events in the Ghetto and at the Council. He does not take advantage of his power in order to enslave anyone. He wants to cooperate. He does not agree with the assessment that he acts contrary to the Council's views.

Garfunkel then said that there is no point in settling scores between Lipzer and the Council. The Council has drawn up a list of wrongs and injustices perpetrated by Lipzer in the past, but we should talk about the future, not about the past. He mentioned the case of Hirsch Levin as an example of Lipzer's attitude toward friends. Lipzer had been angry with Levin and banned him from entering the Council offices, threatening to arrest him if he failed to comply, etc. This had been caused by differences of opinion over some trifle. In the end, the two had reached a compromise.

Dr. Elkes summed up the discussion by expressing his hope that today's conversation will clear the air; that it will create conditions for cooperation in the difficult days that lie ahead. This is imperative, especially in the light of the great danger facing us, about which we heard today. We must stand united and must know how to evaluate each person's actions.

To me it seems that our arguments did not penetrate Lipzer's mind. He is simply incapable of grasping them. In most cases he does not even understand that he is wronging someone. Lipzer has reached an age at which he cannot be changed for the better. We sense this at every moment and at every step. Lipzer remains Lipzer.

This problem forms part of the Ghetto's problems, and not an insignificant one at that.

1. This speech had been broadcast to the German people on February 18, 1943.

FEBRUARY 22, 1943

On Saturday (the day before yesterday) I got up early and went to see Miller. Our people in the Ghetto again fear for their lives, on account of Goebbels's speech. After such a speech, the need arose to find out, or, more correctly, to sense the mood, in the city governor's office.

When I met with Miller in his office, I saw a man at peace with himself, who is not trying to find fault with us. I reached the conclusion that for the time being things remained the same. He also granted me whatever I asked from him: a permit to obtain seeds and a permit to get back those vegetable garden tools which today are being used by Christian farmers. Miller also agreed to meet with Dr. Elkes at the Council offices.

Dr. Elkes has been ill now for eight months; for eight months he has not come to the Council offices. For that reason he has not yet met Miller. Miller has several times commented on this, which is why I organized this meeting. Dr. Elkes will be waiting for Miller today at the Council offices.

When Miller asked, just before I took my leave, whether the ring he had ordered was ready, I was a hundred percent certain that Goebbels's speech would not spell immediate disaster.

I went to see Viertel. There, too, I did not notice any change for the worse. Last Saturday he asked me to see him today. He wishes to have a suit made in the Ghetto. All these gentlemen make sure that their needs are supplied at the public expense. It seems that patriotic speeches intended for the Western capitals and for German citizens at home do not arouse the interest of German officials in the occupied lands.

When I arrived at the city governor's office Viertel was already waiting with the cloth for his suit. He handed the cloth to me. He even forgot his promise to give me the seeds for our vegetable garden today.

It is not just the gentlemen I have mentioned who apply themselves to supplying their personal needs. All the German officials do that. The situation is no different at the Gestapo, or at any of the institutions and enterprises managed by the Germans. They take advantage of their tour of duty here to get rich. Every day they pack up parcels and bundles and send them by mail to their homes in Germany.

When I returned from the city on Saturday and passed on my impressions of the meetings with senior German officials, there was a sense of relief. The members of the Council could relax a little. If this is the situation, one can hope for better days.

Today Miller came over for his talk with Dr. Elkes in the Council office. Dr. Elkes apologized for having been unable to meet Miller earlier on account of his illness. Miller showed interest in the nature of Dr. Elkes's illness and asked him whether he was able to attend to his affairs. On this occasion Miller showed Dr. Elkes his leg; he too suffers from some pains.

The conversation then moved on to general subjects. He, Miller, knows that sizable quantities of firewood are in the possession of many of those in the Ghetto; even more so than in the city. The same applies to other goods. This year he has turned a blind eye to many things in the Ghetto. Next year, however, he will not allow anything to be brought through the Ghetto gate. He himself will supervise the supply of food to the Ghetto.

Miller advised Dr. Elkes, as a physician, to pay attention to the sanitary conditions in the Ghetto. Dr. Elkes must also explain to the German director of the drug section at the city governor's office the need to increase the supply of medicine to the Ghetto in order to prevent epidemics. Should an epidemic break out, the Ghetto will have to be closed.

As the conversation was coming to an end, Dr. Elkes thanked Miller for his visit. "I do it willingly—it was my pleasure," said the guest. Miller had been put at his ease. The chairman of the Council had been introduced to him.

Yesterday, the labor office in the Ghetto began the registration of the Ghetto inmates according to family cards. The head of each family, or someone from the family, must report to the labor office and register all members of the family. The Germans want to know how many family members go out to work, and whether there are any family members who are not working.

Until now, the German labor office had a roster of workers only, and not of the whole Ghetto population. Now Hermann wishes to obtain a complete picture of the Jewish population, which is why all family members must register.

We in the Council know what the new register would look like; it is not to our liking at all, since there are many families in the Ghetto consisting of a woman with three small children, but with no worker in the family. In the eyes of the Germans, such families are expendable, as they cannot contribute anything from the German point of view. There are also families composed of parents over sixty, or with sick persons and invalids among them; they cannot go out to work either. Apart from these, there are people in the Ghetto whom we did not see fit to include among the workers—teachers, artists, and other respectable figures we deemed not to be suitable for menial work.

In order to prevent a gloomy outcome, we decided first of all to "make up new families." If, for instance, there are two young working men living in the same apartment, while in the adjoining apartment lives a woman with two children, they will be put in one apartment; that is, a new family of five people will be created, two of whom work and the remaining three of whom do not. But it was clear to us that even after combinations of this sort there will still remain families who are considered "negative" from the work point of view.

Today we had a meeting at the Council on this subject. The question was: What should we do in order to improve the roster of workers? The first conclusion we reached was that we must include in the labor force men and women who have not been working until now, but are capable of working. Thus, for example, there are many women in the Ghetto who do not work. The reason: until now the Germans asked mainly for men, and needed very few women. We did make an effort to send many women to work, but we were not very successful. We even introduced alternating working days: some of the women work three days a week and others for the remaining days of the week. This system was introduced in order to enter more women into the work records.

The German officials demanded all the time that we send men to work at those enterprises engaged in production for the German Army, and that we employ the women within the Ghetto. Finally we decided to set up a commission entrusted with the task of transferring the men working within the Ghetto to various workplaces in the city, and to find work in the Ghetto for women. The plan was also to enlarge the workshops in the Ghetto, and to put teenage boys and girls to work there.

In the afternoon I went to see Obst. I submitted to him a report about the quantity of potatoes we had received recently: close to 100 tons. This news upset Obst very much. He shouted: "The calculation is wrong. We sent you 150 tons. That's what the master sergeant of the Ghetto command told me. You are cheating me. The workers stole the potatoes. The weights and scales in the Ghetto are rigged. You, the Jews, are always cheating me. Where did the 50 tons disappear to?"

I tried to explain to Obst that we had not received more than 100 tons of potatoes, and that each quantity we receive is weighed and recorded properly. Obst refused to accept my explanations. He said he is going to tell Miller about it.

In point of fact, the Council has nothing to do with it. The master sergeant himself is required to supervise the quantities of food reaching us. He must weigh the potatoes and hand us the receipt, which we must then sign, for every quantity of food we receive.

I wanted to take my leave, but Obst kept me longer. Again shouts, screams, and curses. At last I succeeded in parting from him, and left. For the record, I told the Council that our brethren the Jews failed to subdue their urge, when taking delivery of potatoes in the Ghetto, to put some aside for themselves. However, the representatives of the Council weighed and recorded assiduously and accurately the quantity of potatoes which reached our own warehouse.

Yesterday Lipzer put in an appearance at the Council offices; after the unpleasant exchange between us regarding the telephone, we concluded a truce. He came to ask a little favor: he needs a small structure adjoining his house which would include a toilet. I immediately passed his request to our house repair section. Today a telephone has been installed in Lipzer's apartment. We are weary of disputes with him. Yesterday evening I visited Lipzer at his home in order to make the point that we remain on good terms with each other.

A new psychosis pervades the Ghetto. The inmates are building hiding places in their homes. It seems that the pessimists with their fears of new "actions" have gained the upper hand. I also applied myself to this task, even though I do not believe it will save me in time of trouble. Calamities wear different disguises, and never fail to catch us off guard.

Thus I contacted our Feivchik[1] and asked him what should be done to save oneself in case of disaster. Feivchik has some advice: there are unused sewer pipes in the Ghetto which run halfway under Krisciukaicio street. Those pipes lead outside the Ghetto. In time of trouble it would be possible to escape through them to a safe place. However, one needs a cellar with a hidden exit. I have been thinking about this for a long time; who knows whether I will be able to do it. In the end, either fate or chance will determine my future.

Jankel Verbovski[2] is a well-known figure in the Ghetto. As a representative of our labor office, he is always busy at the Ghetto gate. He helps the workers to smuggle various articles through the gate, and mediates among various people active on the scene. A woman friend of mine, who often passes through the Ghetto gate, bent, as she is, under the weight of packages and bundles, is very grateful to Verbovski for his assistance. She invited him over to her place for a glass of tea.

Verbovski came with his wife. Both of them are young and charming people. His wife—a former student of the Yavneh High School[3] in Kovno—works as a nurse in the first aid station at the German military hospital. She found the job without any help from her husband. The work in the military hospital is strenuous but interesting. The hospital receives sick and wounded soldiers from the front; they tell interesting stories, adorned by personal impressions.

The soldiers do not view themselves as heroes, as enthusiastic fighters on behalf of the Fatherland. They all want to live. They talk a lot, these soldiers from the front. They disregard the poster to be found at every corner, saying: "Watch your tongue! Jews work here!" They are sure that the Jews will not denounce them if they say something less than superlative about the German Army. The Jewish employees of the hospital are well treated, even by the hospital management.

Drinking tea, the nurse relates how the Lithuanian cafeteria manager saves gold. He sells chocolate, wine, and other goods which belong to the military hospital for high prices. He uses the money to buy valuables. All this is done at the expense of the German wounded and the German war effort.

The cafeteria manager does not discriminate against the Jewish workers either: he sells them cigarettes, spirits, and other goods cheap. The Jewish workers at the military hospital are fed well, and even manage to bring a little food back to the Ghetto, where they sell it or give it away. It is a good job.

Lately there has been some talk about dismissing the Jewish workers and replacing them with Christian women. The latter could also give some pleasure to the wounded soldiers. It would be a pity if this place became out of bounds for Jewish workers. Our labor office makes a great effort not to lose such workplaces. But when faced with political principles, and with laws preferring workers of Aryan origins, there is nothing we can do.

1. Feivchik: Shraga Goldsmith, a building technician, the head of the small repair workshops in the Ghetto, and a personal friend of Avraham Tory. It was he who made the crates in which Tory hid his diaries and documents. After the war he lived in Israel, where he died in 1986.

2. Jacob (Jankel) Verbovski, an employee of the Ghetto labor office; he had a reputation for his quick and competent assistance to those passing through the Ghetto gate. He survived the war, and today he lives in the United States.

3. The Yavneh High School was a Hebrew religious secondary school; such high schools existed in several towns in prewar Lithuania. They were under the auspices of the Mizrachi Zionist religious movement.

FEBRUARY 24, 1943

An order was published in today's newspapers about drafting five age-groups in Lithuania. The order mentioned the danger of Bolshevism from which the Germans had "saved" Lithuania on June 22, 1941. This danger again looms large over Lithuania and over all Europe.

In connection with this order, rumors have spread that the Lithuanians will be granted some kind of autonomy—one-half or one-third. As of now these rumors have not been verified by any German official body. An order was published— nothing more.

The city is rife with tension. Today I had an opportunity to speak with some acquaintances of mine in the city. They told me about great excitement among the Lithuanian youth and the tendency to avoid the draft. Several clandestine organizations have been set up which have gained the allegiance of a great many young Lithuanians. They are being supplied with weapons and sent to the forest. The young men know that the military draft spells certain death for them.

Yesterday, Miller and Hermann came to the Council office. They were very angry: "Why does the registration of the Ghetto inmates take so long?" In their view the Council is not active enough. Here in the Ghetto, they declare, a kind of little Paris has evolved. The Germans fight at the front, and spill their blood, so that the Ghetto inmates can live in peace. The women in the Ghetto sit idle, while the Jewish policemen wander to and fro without doing anything. Workers come late to the Council offices, etc., etc.

We could counter again and again each German charge of our "sins," but it is of no use. We must hear Miller out to the end and not say a word. The implied message of Miller's accusations is: more and more people must be recruited for work. Having unburdened himself in this fashion, he left.

During his visit yesterday, Miller complained to Segalson about the Council: "Not enough is being done at this institution. Golub is the only alert person there. People in the Ghetto work very little." Segalson promised Miller to bolster the workforce in the workshops by adding 500 women to it. This will increase the women's labor force. This is the need of the hour.

Today a Council meeting took place. It was attended by Lipzer. He related a conversation among four Gestapo men about the Ghetto. The Gestapo also complained that the Jewish workforce leaves much to be desired; that the women whose husbands have been executed in the Ninth Fort lack the will to work; that the elderly—men and women—are incapable of working. For this reason, a large group of unproductive people has been created, which places a burden on the Ghetto and gets these people a free lunch. These people should have been gotten rid of long ago; it would make things easier in many respects for the remaining Ghetto inmates.

Similar "revelations" were enunciated by Rauca to the representatives of the Council just before the mass executions of October 28. On that occasion he enumerated the great benefits which the "evacuation" of eight to nine thousand of its inmates would bring to the Ghetto.

Since then, under the pressure of problems of everyday life, the plans for the extermination of many of our brothers and sisters, our parents and elderly, have been hidden behind a thin sheet of oblivion. As a result of the rulers' renewed talk about the need to get rid of our women and elderly, whom fate has punished in such a cruel fashion, horrifying images from the gloomy past again appear before our eyes. Has so little blood been spilled in the Ghetto?

Lipzer explained to the Gestapo fiends that women in the Ghetto are, in fact, very busy; indeed, they are not despairing at all, since they are not aware of the death of their husbands—1,800 men in the Ninth Fort—and that they hope to see them in the near future. For that reason, these women wish to plunge themselves into work. The elderly people in the Ghetto also work, at easy jobs of course. They help in cooking food, washing underwear, and cleaning houses, so that the young people can go to work outside. Lipzer tries to explain to the Gestapo that it is not worthwhile to kill those people, because it will cause incalculable damage to the morale of the Jewish workforce.

The problem is that we are not dealing with people whose actions are guided by logic. We are dealing with wild beasts, with savages who are bent on killing, exterminating, and destroying Jews. Mass murder is their raison d'être.

At last Obst has responded favorably to my repeated requests to allocate to our soup kitchen the foodstuffs which have been confiscated at the Ghetto gate. Miller gave his consent a long time ago. Yesterday Obst informed me that from now on the Ghetto command headquarters would send to our soup kitchen the food confiscated at the Ghetto gate. There is one condition, though: the food is for the Ghetto workers only. It must be consumed on the spot and the workers must not take it to their homes. The Council representatives will be responsible for implementing these instructions. Today, in fact, we actually received the confiscated food and transferred it to the kitchen.

I met Miller today, in the afternoon. I presented him with a gift—a cigarette case made of pure silver. He did not waste time thinking about it, but put it straight into his briefcase. Miller has become used to getting presents from us, despite his uniform and his Nazi fanaticism. With regard to his position in the Nazi hierarchy, he belongs to the second generation of leaders. His advice to his superiors would probably be to avoid the Jews like the plague. But how much are the sanctimonious preachings of the Nazi officer worth, compared with the cigarette case made of pure silver that I gave him today?

FEBRUARY 25, 1943

The day was filled with talk and conversations. Early in the morning a Ghetto policeman came to my apartment with a message that Cramer and three other Germans had arrived in the Council offices and that I must set out to go there at once. A few minutes later I was there.

In the large room belonging to the office for economic affairs and the office for food supply, I found Cramer, Gilow, and two other Germans in civilian clothes whom I did not know. Cramer's attitude toward them, and their own stern and penetrating gaze, indicated that we were dealing with important figures in the German establishment, or "top beasts" as we called them in the Ghetto.

Cramer told his guests that the office for economic affairs in the Ghetto is responsible for the management and supervision of all the buildings in the Ghetto, and that the office for food supply is in charge of distributing food to the Ghetto inmates (he showed them a food card). Prior to their visit here, the members of the delegation had toured the labor office and shown an interest in the system of registration of the workers, and their numbers.

Having left the building, the Germans read all the public announcements.[1] There were announcements about the registration of all Ghetto inmates, about the blackout, and about courses for sewing and gardening which were being opened at the vocational training school. The delegation then went to the workshops, and to the German labor office.

From the conversation between Cramer and his guests, we could draw favorable conclusions from the visit. He told them that 300 workers had recently been removed from the Ghetto on the assumption that there was no work for them. As a matter of fact, everyone in the Ghetto is working. Cramer thinks he will expand the workshops by adding workers to their staff.

The Jewish police sealed off the streets through which the German visitors passed, and issued a ban on traffic there. The reason for this action was to prevent the Germans from thinking that there were idle people in the Ghetto.

Soon after the visitors had left the Ghetto, Schtitz of the Gestapo arrived. He entered the Ghetto command headquarters. His arrival in the Ghetto is always a source of fear of new "actions." He stayed there half an hour, and then left.

Such visits, especially when accompanied by sealing off streets, create tension in the Ghetto. People keep asking: What is the reason for the visit? What do they want? Cramer rarely puts in an appearance here; he is almost never seen in the Council offices.

Some time later, news reached the Ghetto about Hitler's speech to the members of the Nazi party.[2] In this speech he explicitly called for the extermination of the Jewish race in this war, and called upon other nations to follow the German example in this regard. The news certainly did nothing to put the Ghetto inmates at their ease. Open talk about the extermination of the Jews, coming from Hitler himself, and in the wake of a similar call issued by Goebbels in his speech, aroused a new wave of fear in the Ghetto. People see themselves teetering on the brink of an abyss of destruction. Many in the Ghetto are inclined to see a connection between the visit of the German delegation to the Ghetto today and Hitler's speech.

I received a telephone call from Miller at noon. He told me that he had issued a permit to purchase 200 meters of fabric to make yellow badges. Furthermore, he approved the purchase of scraps of yellow fabric for the same purpose. He also voiced a complaint: instead of buying scraps of yellow fabric from the German-owned Ostland Faser textile mill, we had purchased 500 meters of an ordinary, newly manufactured cloth. He considers this a scandal. After all, he, Miller, clearly wrote—black on white—"scraps of material." Why, then, did the German plant sell new fabric to the Council? And why did the Council buy it from them?

I explained that the regional governor's office had issued us a permit for the purchase of 200 meters of yellow fabric. As for the permit issued by Miller for the purchase of scraps of material, we had received an offer from Ostland Faser of 500 meters of fabric. The German manufacturer is responsible for this offer; it is he who owes an explanation—not the Council. Up to now we have not yet received this fabric. The German manufacturer must decide what sort of fabric we are going to receive.

Miller had another complaint: he himself had been cheated. Engineer Chaitin had been working recently in his apartment. He was repairing it. Miller was very pleased with the job and issued Chaitin a special pass enabling him to go from the Ghetto to his apartment without an escort. Chaitin became a member of his household. Today, however, something happened which should cause concern. Miller's wife saw twenty marks in Chaitin's possession and promptly informed her husband. Miller immediately set about interrogating the Jewish engineer about the source of the money. Chaitin replied that he had acquired it by selling a pair of trousers. Miller then asked him what he needed the money for? Chaitin said: "My child is sick in bed; I wanted to buy some meat and bread for him."

Chaitin's replies made Miller angry: "I placed my trust in Chaitin and he deceived me. If he had told me that he needed money to cure his sick son, I would have made an effort to have the child taken to the hospital; I would also have approved an increased food ration. But to sell a pair of trousers? In Germany everyone wears his old clothes; a German would not sell his trousers even for 1,000 marks. What is money, after all? Dirt. The most important thing is to have belongings and clothes which can be used. The Council keeps asking me for old clothes for the Ghetto inmates, and here comes Chaitin and sells a pair of trousers. In the future he is not going to get any old clothes."

This was not the end of Miller's complaints against Chaitin: he had not properly repaired the electric lamps in the bedroom, and he had broken the radio receiver. Moreover, Chaitin had taken advantage of his access to Miller's apartment to have sex with Jewish women working there. Finally, Miller got tired of talking and complaining, and broke off the conversation.

Half an hour later Miller telephoned again to inform me that at 5 P.M. he is coming to the Council offices. Members of the Council, and office directors, should be summoned to the meeting. He, Miller, wants to talk about a few matters.

Soon afterward I received a telephone call from Segalson: Viertel had sent his men to see whether it is possible to buy flour in the Ghetto. He, Segalson, is to accompany them. The stores should be told to hide the flour, and leave a small quantity of bread in stock. I immediately passed on the news to all concerned. One bakery, however, did not hide as much as it should have; a considerable amount of bread was found there. The visit is probably connected with the plan to bake bread in the Ghetto.

At 5 P.M. Miller arrived in the Ghetto. He hung about a while at the Ghetto gate and then came to the Council offices. He seated himself on the sofa and began to tell again the story of Chaitin and his "sin"; this time, however, Miller was more restrained. He emphasized the personal element in the story: Chaitin had deceived him, Miller, personally, but Miller had decided not to hand him over to the Gestapo. He will allow him to complete the repair of his apartment. Afterward he will make sure Chaitin is assigned a more difficult job.

Then Miller addressed the subject of the war: the few setbacks suffered by the Germans at the front are temporary. In the spring, a large offensive will be launched and the Russians will be on the run again. The Germans will recover the territories lost in the winter. There is no doubt that the Germans will win the war. Those who have visited Germany recently know the state of affairs in that country. Everyone is now required to play his part in winning the war. A transportation worker, for example, loading onto a train the sacks of flour destined for the civilian population, is making his contribution to victory. Everything is important and vital for the proper conduct of the war. He, Miller, is responsible for the Ghetto and is duty-bound to do everything possible here to organize a large labor force to play its part. Consequently, everyone must carry out his directives. The Jews, too, must engage in the productive effort; after the war they will be granted a piece of land—a territory of their own where they will be able to live like other nations.

Should we take Miller's words as a comment on Hitler's declaration? Does he intend to reassure us, so that we will get down to work? Who knows? Miller continues: "If the Jews work, sow the fields and the vegetable gardens, build and produce, then I, Miller, will make sure that they are supplied with food, clothing, and such like. You must sow the fields in such a way that every visitor will marvel at them." The last point was addressed to Kelzon and Girshovitz, who had been called to the room to report on the progress of sowing and tilling the fields.

Miller then moved on to the subject of the Jewish police. He thinks there are too many policemen in the Ghetto. At the Ghetto gate he saw workers who were tired and exhausted after the day's work; the policemen, on the other hand, seemed healthy and strong. He understands that the policemen must be strong, and must stay healthy, in order to discharge their duties. However, are there not too many of them? Kopelman explains to him the arrangements of police work, and voices his opinion that the Jewish police force is maintained at its minimum level, given the needs. Miller comments that after the registration of the Ghetto residents is completed, the best of them will be diverted for work and production.

Miller spent half an hour at the Council. He spoke politely and with restraint. He motioned all those who had been summoned to sit down; then he called on them to get down to work. To a great extent he lifted the heavy burden of the negative impression left by Hitler's declaration. Having finished his address he rose, and left.

At 1 P.M. we held an important meeting concerning problems in the hospital. Those present were Dr. Elkes, Dr. Zacharin, Dr. Brauns, Dr. Berman, Garfunkel, and I.

Dr. Zacharin delivered the opening remarks: the hospital cannot accommodate all the patients. Under the existing conditions, due to lack of space, therapy is administered in the surgery room in the presence of many patients. Moreover, each room houses twelve to thirteen patients lying very close to one another. It is impossible to clean and ventilate the rooms. As a consequence, two people, a nurse and a surgery patient—Tobianski—contracted typhoid fever. This situation must not be allowed to continue. It is necessary to set up a special ward for contagious diseases in the hospital; it would be best to have a separate section for that purpose.

Officially there are no people suffering from contagious diseases in the Ghetto. We suppress facts of this nature, even from the Ghetto inmates. Should, God forbid, such news reach the Germans, they would resort to severe measures at the expense of the entire community. But after three cases of typhoid fever in the hospital, we must apply ourselves seriously to thinking about the steps to be taken. Nothing, of course, must leak outside, but the affected patients must be isolated. How this should be done? This is the crux of the problem. The Germans are capable of "erasing" whole neighborhoods, even the entire Ghetto, if they as much as sniff the existence of contagious diseases in the Ghetto.

Finally we came up with the decision: a special place should be found within the hospital for patients with contagious diseases, in order to avoid further victims. Indeed, we are overcrowded in the Ghetto; but when need arises, we always manage to find a necessary space.

1. Announcements were posted on the walls of the Council building so that the inmates of the Ghetto could read them.

2. This speech, sent by Hitler from his headquarters on the eastern front, had been read on February 24, 1943, at a gathering in Berlin of veteran members of the Nazi Party.

FEBRUARY 28, 1943

Miller has been in a very bad mood for several days. He hangs about the Ghetto gate at the time the workers return from work. He is eager to see what the workers bring back with them from the city. He issued an order to confiscate everything—large or small—found on their bodies. He personally took part in the search of Jewish women. "I don't want to starve you," he shouted, "but Jewish workers bring back with them from the city all kinds of goods, eggs and butter and even lemons, things that I myself have not seen in a long time, not to mention the German soldiers at the front."

Miller is particularly interested in the source of money for the purchases made by the Jewish workers in the city. In recent days the Germans confiscated some 5,000 German marks at the gate. No wonder. Lately, prices of various goods have soared. And where does the money come from? Jews sell their last possessions for high prices. If four or five thousand workers return from work, it is no wonder if several thousand marks are found among them.

This Jewish trade makes Miller angry. The Germans have abolished the money economy in the Ghetto, in order to paralyze its commercial links with the city. Nevertheless, the Jews sell their belongings and use the money to buy goods of various kinds.

Miller has resolved to liquidate the black market once and for all. This is to be done by confiscating every article that the workers bring back from the city. He also telephoned the Council to announce that as long as the Jews keep selling their clothing and belongings, he is not going to distribute clothes to the workers. The third measure calculated to stop the illicit trade is: anyone caught selling or trading his belongings will be handed over to the Gestapo.

The first victim of the new policy of punishments was a Jewish woman working in Miller's own household, by the name of Schlachzeite. She had obtained two eggs and half a kilogram of butter from a German woman. She put them in her basket. Miller's wife wanted to see what was in the housemaid's basket and found the eggs and the butter. The Jewish woman was questioned about the source of the food. She was taken to the Gestapo and released after a prolonged interrogation.

This woman was saved by a truly heavenly miracle. She refused to disclose the name of the woman who had given her the eggs and butter and, instead, gave the name of another woman whose husband was a senior Gestapo official. She, in turn, "confessed" to giving the eggs and butter to the Jewish housemaid, who was thus saved from certain death.

We must warn the Jewish workers again not to sell or buy anything, and not to receive any gifts. Jewish policemen and officials from our labor office visited the labor brigades and issued repeated warnings to the workers not to engage in trade.

Despite all the draconian measures taken by Miller and Ratnikas, the Jews find ways and means to smuggle goods into the Ghetto. It is difficult to describe those methods. The most common ways of hiding goods are in work tools, in containers with double walls, in underwear, in shoe heels, and even under the yellow badge.

The sufferings of the Jews are great; also strong is their will to live and to survive the bad times. This is the source of various inventions aimed at improving their quality of life somewhat. The will to live is rooted strongly in the Jewish character; those in the Ghetto are no exception in this regard, against the will of the Jew-haters.

Not that we lack troubles. Seven Jewish workers were taken to the Gestapo yesterday. They work at Lietukis, in the grain warehouse.[1] They are guarded by a soldier, a member of the Russian White Guard,[2] Petrushenko. The Jews are not particularly fond of men like him—Russians who sold their homeland for a mess of pottage; they deal blows to the Jewish workers. Nor is their attitude to their own brethren, the Russian prisoners-of-war on German soil, much better. Everybody hates Petrushenko and his friends. However, in return for a gift, one can get practically anything from them.

Each of the Jewish workers employed at Lietukis used to bring three or four kilograms of rye back with him to the Ghetto. He would bring it into the Ghetto to the flour mill, and would be paid in flour. Then he would exchange the flour for bread.

This has been going on for a long time. The guard would get something to keep his mouth shut. In the great warehouse no one could detect the disappearance of several dozen kilograms of rye or wheat. But one day Petrushenko rebelled. As a result, several Jewish workers were taken to the Gestapo. There things took a bad turn: the Jews had been robbing a military grain depot, and they would have to pay for it with their lives. Shortly afterward, however, it turned out that Petrushenko himself used to tell the workers: "Take it!" And if a guard, armed with a rifle, says take it—the Jews took some wheat or rye. This time it ended well. They were released after being beaten, and are spending a week in prison (Lipzer assisted in securing their release).

Miller asked for another woman to serve as his housemaid. Schlachzeite had abused his trust. No woman wants to work in Miller's household. People are afraid of him. We must, however, send him someone. At last a woman was found. We warned her not to take anything from her master's house and to refrain from buying anything in the city.

Yesterday, in a telephone conversation with me, Miller threatened again to uproot the black market. Boiling with rage, he added that he would not grant our request to provide ten horses to plough the fields and pave the road. Take Jewish women, he said, there are plenty of them in the Ghetto—harness them to the carts. Prisoners-of-war are also used in this way.

The day before yesterday, when I visited Miller in the city, he told me not to ask anything from him; I should postpone my requests to some other time. He is not able, he said, to consider my requests today.

Miller reiterates his assertion that he is being cheated constantly; he sees for himself what kind of things the Jewish workers hide away as they return from the city. Such goods are not to be found at his home. By chance he came across fourteen Jewish workers employed at moving the furniture and other belongings of Poles who had recently been expelled from Kovno. These workers stole everything they could lay their hands on. Some time later I was informed that the Germans were in charge of moving the belongings of the Poles, and that it was those Germans who took crates full of goods to their apartments. Miller questioned the Jewish workers in the presence of their German supervisors. When interrogated, the Jewish workers revealed the iniquities of the Germans: this one filched a piano; that one grabbed a suitcase packed with underwear and bedsheets; a third got hold of a basket brimming with various articles, etc.

When this testimony was over, Miller said: "And now Jews, what did you steal? If you won't tell me, I'll kill you right here. I'll send you to the Gestapo." The Jews kept arguing that they had not taken anything. Miller was very angry with them. Later he told me that the Jews had cheated him again.

One day Miller positioned himself at the Ghetto gate to supervise the searches—for goods bought in the city—conducted on the workers returning from work. He kept looking at one Jewish woman who apparently was to his liking. He told her to step aside and talked to her for three-quarters of an hour. During that time he was oblivious to the searches at the gate. He asked for her address and that same evening he visited her in her apartment.

This happened on Saturday night. The next day, again thunder on the telephone; he, Miller, will not give even one pair of shoes to the workers. Let them go to work barefooted; as long as the workers sell clothes in the city, he will not give them anything.

Yesterday at 3 P.M. Cramer put in an appearance in the workshops. On Saturday the working day lasts until 2 P.M. Previously Cramer had asked us not to release the workers at the appointed time: he was going to tour the workshops in the company of an important guest. He wished to show the guest around the workshops and to inspect the work being performed there. On that day the workers were not dismissed until 4:30 P.M.

Rabbi Abraham Duber Kahana Shapiro, the Chief Rabbi of Kovno and Lithuania, died yesterday morning. The Ghetto inmates are used to meeting death at every step and it does not frighten them anymore. Under such circumstances, the death of a man who dies at a ripe old age in his bed is not thought of as a tragedy at all. Yesterday, however, it was an exceptional case: the man who died was the Chief Rabbi of the Kovno Jews, a distinguished representative of the Lithuanian rabbinate, a man who had once been a serious candidate for the position of chief rabbi of Jerusalem. Rabbi Shapiro was more of a *Gaon* than a *Tzaddik*,[3] more a representative of Jewry than a rabbi; more a symbol than a living person. His death marks the end of an era in the Kovno rabbinate and in the life of orthodox Lithuanian Jewry.

Rabbi Shapiro's life was irrevocably bound up with various decisions concerning the questions which faced Lithuanian Jewry in general, and the Jews of Kovno in particular. One day he was awakened late at night and asked to rule on the matter of life and death for the 27,000 Jews then in the Kovno Ghetto. It is doubtful whether another rabbi would have been capable of doing it. In compliance with his ruling, on that cold and dark day October 28, 1941, 27,000 Jews left their homes for Demokratu Square to face their fate: who would live and who would die.

Rabbi Shapiro has been ill for many years and had long since stopped being involved in the life of his community. He left it to others. Before leaving the city for the Ghetto in August 1941, he had been in bed in his room, unwell, busy writing the memoirs of his rich life. In the Ghetto his presence was hardly felt. But when his decision was needed, he would rise to the occasion, get up from his sickbed, and issue a ruling to the leaders of the Ghetto community. Afterward he would retreat to his seclusion again. Yesterday his soul returned to its creator.[4]

A great number of people turned up for Rabbi Shapiro's funeral. Long rows of people followed his coffin, led by yeshiva students and people who had been close to him. Jewish policemen kept order on the streets through which the funeral procession passed.

No eulogies were delivered—neither at his home nor at the cemetery. From the silence of the scores of people accompanying Rabbi Shapiro on his last journey, the sound of *Kaddish*—the mourners' prayer—rose, spoken by his son, Dr. Nachman Shapiro.[5] Then Rabbi Shmukler lyrically and movingly recited *El male rachamim* for the soul "of our teacher and rabbi, rabbi and Gaon, Abraham Duber Kahana, who has passed away." The last clods of earth fell on the fresh grave, and the large crowd began flowing back to the Ghetto. The rabbi of Kovno has passed away, and with him an era in the life of a magnificent rabbinate among the Jewish communities of Lithuania.

1. Lietukis was the Lithuanian national wholesale trade corporation.

2. The White Guard was the name given to those Red Army soldiers who, after their capture by the Germans, had volunteered to serve as armed auxiliaries under German command.

3. A Gaon was a man whose attainments were intellectual, a man of genius; a Tzaddik was a man whose attainments were more righteous—an understanding for the needy and the underdog. For Eastern European Jewry, the archetypal Gaon was Elijah of Vilna (1720–1797); the archetypal Tzaddik was the Ba'al Shem Tov (ca. 1700–1760), founder of Chassidism, or Rabbi Nachman of Braslov (1772–1811).

4. Avraham Tory later recalled, "During one of my visits to Rabbi Shapiro in his dwelling in

the Ghetto, I found him sitting in his bed, busy writing. He wore half-finger knitted woolen gloves to enable him to write. I asked him: 'Rabbi, may I ask what is it you are writing?' He replied: 'My son, thousands of women in the Ghetto are *agunoth* (women whose husbands have disappeared without divorcing them) and thousands more will be *agunoth* when the war ends. According to the existing religious laws, those women will be condemned to remain widows until the end of their days, for such a tragedy of destruction has never before been visited upon us in history. This is why I am writing a paper on how to free those women from the status of *agunoth* as a result of this war.' At that time Rabbi Shapiro had written some 300 pages on the question. I was too shy to ask Rabbi Shapiro's permission to copy this huge opus, and, unfortunately, it disappeared without trace."

5. Dr. Chaim Nachman Shapiro, Rabbi Shapiro's eldest son, was an expert on Semitic languages—primarily Hebrew and Hebrew literature. Before the war he had taught at the University of Lithuania in Kovno. His published work included an important research project entitled "A History of the New Hebrew Literature"—which contained both a monograph on Avraham Mapu (a native of Kovno) and a considerable amount of research on Hebrew literature. He was active in the Zionist leadership in the Ghetto, and the focus of cultural activity in the Ghetto, where he founded the Council's cultural department and served as its head until his death. He was also the principal of the vocational school set up by the Council.

In the Ghetto, Dr. Shapiro had begun to translate Avraham Tory's diary into Hebrew (this version has not survived).

Later in 1943, the Germans announced that special visas had been obtained for Chief Rabbi Shapiro's family to go to Switzerland. The chief rabbi was already dead; his widow, Chaim Nachman, and Chaim Nachman's wife and fifteen-year-old son were taken out of the Ghetto to the Ninth Fort, where they were killed the same day.

MARCH 3, 1943

DOCUMENT:
From SS Lieutenant Miller, on behalf of the Governor of Kovno
To the Jewish Council in Kovno-Vilijampolé

1. I hereby order that all items of clothing supplied in the past from the stock of Mr. Ernst, which have remained locked up on my instructions, remain untouched and shall not be issued. The Council is responsible to me for this. A list of all items in stock must be sent to me immediately.

Note: As long as these items of clothing are used for bartering, no issue will be authorized. You must also fight against such sales by the Jews.

2. In order to provide Jews working under special and unavoidable labor conditions—such as bad weather, rain, cold, etc.—with the necessary garments, you must immediately establish an exchange center. I know that many Jews still wear very good clothes. In this way these clothes can be given to Jews who need them for their work. All other considerations must be disregarded. The number of people employed at compulsory labor will be gradually increased.

3. I order that the general administration of the Ghetto be transferred imme-

diately to women and frail persons. Furthermore, about 50 percent of manpower must be reduced in the offices of the Council, the labor exchange, the Ghetto police, and particularly in the workshops which supply the needs of the Ghetto, and wherever else it is still feasible.

MARCH 4, 1943

Miller has been away in Vilna on a tour which lasted several days. He returned yesterday and, by telephone, summoned the members of the Council to a meeting with him at 4 P.M. We awaited the meeting anxiously. Miller's trips to other Ghettos do not bode well for us. In every Ghetto there is always some fault to be found which he brings to our attention as an example. He is fond of telling us: "You fare well in the Ghetto. You're better off here than the Jews in other Ghettos."

At four o'clock in the afternoon Miller arrived at the Council offices. He stretched himself out on the sofa, and, from his briefcase, produced a new order, no. 15, which contained three sections.

Section 1: The authorities will no longer supply the workers with clothes and shoes, as long as the workers keep trading clothes for goods in the city.

Section 2: A trading center will be set up in the Ghetto where various belongings can be exchanged. Those who have goods for trade will bring them to the trading center. Clothing articles brought to the trading center will be distributed to the needy workers.

At this point, Miller interjects to say that in Vilna there is such a trading center. I volunteer that a money economy is allowed in the Vilna Ghetto, whereas it has been abolished in the Kovno Ghetto. What will the people trade their belongings for? Miller asks me: "And how do you know about the situation in Vilna?" I reply: "In the past, workers have come here from Vilna, and they have told me about it." Miller: "How much money do the Jews in Vilna have at their disposal? Workers there earn nine marks a week for their labor, whereas here you get much more—in both money and goods."

Section 3: The administration and clerical staff at the Council institutions will be reduced by 50 percent. The same applies to the Jewish police and the workshops.

Again I have a question: "Apart from their normal work, the workshops perform the service of mending clothes and shoes for the entire working population of the Ghetto. It is the only workplace where clothes and other indispensable articles belonging to the Ghetto inmates can be fixed. How can we reduce the workforce in such a place?" Miller is prepared to modify his proposal; the reductions will affect only the clerical and administrative staff.

In Vilna, Miller goes on, the regime is much stricter. The Jewish police there make sure that no black-market trading takes place. He wants to see Jewish policemen here assigned this task.

Later, on my return from the city to the Ghetto, I was informed about a very unpleasant affair. Yesterday a Jewish worker by the name of Berman[1] was arrested at the Ghetto gate. He works in the Fifth Fort at sorting ammunition. It turns out that a grenade part was found in his knapsack. Today Berman was taken to the Gestapo.

As I was passing through the Ghetto gate I was stopped, for the first time, by Ratnikas. He searched me, looking for money. I told him that I carried no money on me, except for a 50 pfennig coin. His reply was: "A Jew is not to be trusted; they are all liars." "Why do you think that?" I asked him. "Have you really never met a Jew who was telling the truth?" "No, it never happened to me. They always cheat," he replied. "Look," I said, "here, you've just searched a Jew like me for money and didn't find any. And I told you beforehand that this was what was going to happen. Yet you keep insisting that all the Jews are liars."

It is difficult to persuade Ratnikas: he is an evil man by nature. In the meantime he saw a fountain pen in my pocket and took it. "No!" I said. "I have the right to keep this fountain pen in my pocket." "Here," he says, "I am taking this pen and that's about the end of your right." He holds the pen, looking contented and proud. "I'll get it back," I say, "Miller will take care of that, it's a wasted effort." Unwillingly he gives me the pen back.

Now it is Ratnikas's turn to deliver a speech: "See, the Jews go so far as to carry grenade parts in their pockets. I understand when they bring food from the city to the Ghetto, but weapons? What do they need weapons for? When they asked the man on whom the grenade part was found whether he had anything forbidden on him, he said he did not. Then they searched him and found the grenade part. All Jews are liars."

This affair of a grenade part found in the pocket of a Jew is a sad story. Arms in the Ghetto spell danger for its inmates, especially now when a compulsory draft has been declared for all Lithuanians, when the land is rife with discontent, and when rumors circulate about the formation of a Lithuanian partisan movement to fight the Germans. These days the Germans display great sensitivity to any hint of a weapon which could be directed against them. It goes without saying that any weapon in the Ghetto poses a grave danger to us.

At a meeting which took place in the evening in Dr. Elkes's apartment, Lipzer said that the Gestapo is very angry at the Ghetto because of finding a grenade part on a Jewish worker. In general, the Gestapo has become increasingly hostile to the Ghetto in recent days.

The renewed tension and fears which pervade the Ghetto have triggered another wave of looking for hiding places and shelters for the time of trouble. Each coming day may bring a disaster. Therefore, we are better off with shelters prepared in advance. Today I went with "Ika" Grinberg to inspect the hiding places.

1. This was Yerachmiel Berman, one of the Communist activists in the underground in the Kovno Ghetto, and a member of the Anti-Fascist Association, who had attempted to smuggle into the Ghetto not a hand grenade but a rocket launcher. After repeated intervention by the Council, Berman was released; he returned to the Ghetto several weeks later. He was a member of a committee called the Black Command, which collected funds from wealthy residents of the Ghetto for the needs of the underground. On April 14, 1944, he left the Ghetto with several other resistance fighters. Most of them were killed in a battle with the Germans shortly after leaving the Ghetto. During the battle, Berman killed four members of the Gestapo, managed to evade capture, and returned to the Ghetto. Later he again left the Ghetto and succeeded in joining the partisans.

MARCH 16, 1943

Today at the Council we discussed the question: What steps should we take to foil the evil designs of the authorities against us? We searched our memories for people from the good old days to instruct us at this trying moment in our lives; people brave enough to justify our existence and to make themselves heard in the centers of power where our fate is being decided. At the same time, we know that if a decision affecting us is to be made at the top, by the German leadership, no one here, in Lithuania, will be able to help us.

Lately we have been inclined to connect our fate with the growing demand for Jewish labor. The orderly activity of many enterprises vital for the war effort depends, to a considerable degree, on the Jewish skilled workers. The Ghetto has eight to nine thousand productive and creative workers, who contribute their part to the German war effort.

It should be recalled that the huge work of construction at Kovno airfield, performed for a year and a half, was done in greater part by engineers, technicians, locksmiths, construction workers, and thousands of ordinary workers from the Ghetto. Nearly 4,000 Jews worked day and night, sometimes in three shifts, at the airfield, until its construction was completed. This is good for us.

Whenever we were faced with some "action" or deportation, or even a reduction of the Ghetto area, the German managers of various enterprises and services employing Jews immediately swung into action. They asked the top leadership not to touch "their Jews" because of their indispensability for the war effort. Many Jewish workers were saved from death because of the need for their skills. At the same time, however, there is no doubt that many executions were carried out for "ideological" reasons—on account of considering the Jews an inferior race which must be destroyed—because of orders from Berlin. The local authorities could not revoke these orders; at the most, they could carry out the evil decree with lesser severity and fewer victims.

The local German officials here credit themselves with the achievements of the Jewish labor force—our achievements—regarding them as their personal contribution to the war effort. They are being rewarded with promotions and medals, as well as with serving far away from the front, which means a life of affluence and peace of mind.

Where does Cramer's fair treatment of us stem from? We know that for a whole year this man kept boasting that he had never spoken with a Jew or shaken a Jew's hand. Cramer praised Jordan and regarded him as a symbol of German might on the home front. That is the way the Jews should be treated and that is the way they should be killed.

In the course of time, Cramer changed his attitude. Now his existence depends on the Ghetto. He keeps inviting senior officials from Berlin to show them the success of "his" Ghetto. Here he has set up the workshops. Here 1,400 Jews work for the German Army. Here the Jews perform work which is not done in the city. He demonstrates to his high-ranking guests that he, Cramer, is indispensable in the Ghetto, and that without him everything would fall apart. We, the Jews, are not among those who are decorated with medals. For the time being, however, our work blunts the edge of possible attacks against us.

We sit in the Council office, knitting our brows and racking our brains, trying to figure out what we should do. We tremble at the prospect of the transfer of 3,000 Jews from Vilna to our Ghetto. The transfer is effected by an order from Berlin and there is nothing we can do about it. But perhaps this is a local or regional problem? Perhaps the Gestapo has decided to reduce the area of the Riga Ghetto, to liquidate the Vilna Ghetto, in order to crowd as many people as possible into our Ghetto, and to turn our life here into a nightmare? Or, perhaps, they plan to liquidate our Ghetto?

The Jews here recall that in the bygone days when we were still citizens with equal rights, many of them had friends among the Germans who lived in Kovno. Some of these now occupy high-ranking posts in the German administration. Thus, for example, General Jost,[1] now the police chief in Lithuania, had been a friend of several Jews who now live in the Ghetto. Perhaps we should find a way to approach him? But this is not easy. In actual fact, until now we have not been able to reach him.

There are also a number of local Germans occupying important positions of power who could help us, if they would remember their Jewish friends from the days before the flood. Until now they have not done a thing for us. They go to great lengths to avoid Jews. When one of them by chance runs into a former Jewish acquaintance, he backs off and quickly puts a distance between himself and the "danger." All our Christian friends and acquaintances have forgotten us. We remain alone, isolated and forgotten.

Today Lipzer entered the Council offices. It was 11 A.M. and his sudden appearance heralded some news for us. He revealed to us that Rauca and Jaeger of the Gestapo had spoken to him today. They told him that 4,000 Jews from Oszmiana had been due to arrive in the Ghetto, but they would not be coming. The plan had been canceled. Jaeger added that "his" Ghetto (that is, our Ghetto) is clean of lice and he does not want to have people teeming with lice here. This means that there will be no changes in the Ghetto. We were very glad to hear it. Everything will remain the way it has been. This too is for the best.

Lipzer told us that yesterday Jaeger returned from Riga. On the same day a meeting took place at the Gestapo, attended by Hermann, Miller, and Viertel. At this meeting it was agreed that no more Jews should be moved into our Ghetto. In answer to a question from Lipzer, Jaeger said that there had not been any "actions" in Riga.[2] Again, we were very pleased to hear such good news.

Miller telephoned to announce that he would be coming to the Ghetto today at 2 P.M. He came to the Council and informed us that the transfer of the 3,000 Jews to the Ghetto (Lipzer had spoken of 4,000) is not going to be carried out. This announcement led us to a conclusion that on this question the decision had been made in Berlin and not by the local authorities. We had known about the cancellation beforehand from Lipzer, so we did not betray any signs of satisfaction. It seems that Miller was disappointed by the display of indifference on our part upon hearing the news he had brought to us. He could not forbear and asked us: "Aren't you happy that there has been a change in our plans?" "Of course we are happy," we replied.

Then we spoke about current problems. He took me for a drive in his car. I showed him the small workshops for mending clothes and for the manufacture of household utensils, the house repair department, the vocational training school, the bakery, the soup kitchen, and several other establishments. He also asked about various institutions which we did not visit; then he left.

1. Major-General Dr. Heinz Jost was the chief of police in the Office of Eastern Affairs, headed by Dr. Alfred Rosenberg.
2. The deportations from the Riga Ghetto to Kaiserwald did not begin until July 1943.

MARCH 18, 1943

Yesterday I had to perform an unusual task. Several days ago, Miller told me that the deputy chairman of the Nazi Party in Kovno, Lange,[1] wanted us to make a gold ring for him. Miller told him that I would place an order for the ring in the Ghetto. This is why I must go to his office at 20 Putvinskio Street. The office is located in a big house where the officials of the Lithuanian State Bank had lived before the war. Currently it houses the offices of the Nazi Party. There is a big sign on the building reading "House of the National Socialists in Kovno."

I entered the building hesitating whether I should wait or keep moving. There was a woman in uniform sitting in a neat and tidy office. Above her desk hung a portrait of the man on whose account rivers of blood have been flowing in Europe, and who is the main culprit for the sufferings of European Jewry. At the back there was a Nazi flag, and on the walls hung pictures of the Nazi Party leaders.

I asked the woman about Mr. Lange's whereabouts. She replied that he was not in. She advised me to go up to the third floor and see Mr. Werner. I found Mr. Werner occupying a spacious and tidy office on the third floor. I told him that I was looking for Mr. Lange and that the woman clerk on the ground floor had referred me to him. Werner said there had been a mistake.

He asked me whether I had brought some tools with me and then led me into a large room. It contained a large-size map where movements of various armies on the war fronts had been charted. Werner said he wanted to frame this map and hang it in a proper place. I said that I would send him a worker who would frame the map for him. On my way out I saw a sign on one of the doors; it read "Race Affairs Section." I caught a glimpse of two prominently displayed propaganda posters on the wall. One of them bore the slogan "Victory or Bolshevism," whereas the other featured a drawing of a Russian soldier with typically Semitic features. Both posters were unmistakable in their symbolic portrayal of the enemy: "Jew Bolshevism." The enemy that must be destroyed.

As a representative of the Jewish Ghetto institution, I must perform all kinds of tasks, such as visiting the seat of evil of the Nazis in Kovno; yet even there I learned something.

1. Lieutenant Rudolf Lange, the leader of the Nazi Party in Kovno, was in charge of measures against any Communist activity in the city, as well as of intelligence and counterintelligence.

MARCH 21, 1943

Today is Purim.[1] Hitler has promised that there will be no more Purim festivities for the Jews. I do not know whether his other predictions will come true, but this one is yet to be fulfilled. Here in the Ghetto we are celebrating Purim in a new style. None other than our little children, our Mosheles and Shlomeles, give the lie to Hitler's predictions by celebrating Purim with all their innocence and enthusiasm.

The children—pupils of the pioneer of National Hebrew education in the Ghetto, Mrs. Segal—have been preparing the Purim festivities for many weeks. They have been learning the Purim songs, the dances, and the games. They have been pervaded by the festive Purim atmosphere for several weeks now: who is to going to play the part of Mordechai the Jew, who is to play Haman; who is going to enact the story of Queen Esther and Vashti, etc. The children have been telling their parents about all their Purim preparations, and the parents—if there are parents left alive—let themselves be drawn in by the festive atmosphere.

The distinguished educator Mrs. Segal has been involved in these preparations more than anybody else. After all, these are her children, the children of her kindergarten, whom she has been looking after since the first day of the Ghetto. She pays no heed to bans and prohibitions. Although the Jewish school has been officially closed on orders from the Germans, this order has yet to reach this courageous and distinguished educator.

Every day, children gather in her own small room, where she teaches them the Hebrew alphabet, to say "Shalom" in Hebrew, and to sing Hebrew songs. She implants in their hearts a love for the Jewish people and a longing for their homeland—the land of Israel. She does all this by means of games, songs, and stories from the past. She does not let any opportunity—primarily the religious and national holidays—pass by without using it to tell the children about the history of the Jewish people and their religious and national heritage.

Mrs. Segal has been busy for some months now in preparations for the Purim festivities for her pupils. Several weeks ago she came to see me asking for sheets of paper of different colors, which I obtained specially for her. As the preparations for the Purim festivities were being completed we received depressing news: March 21 (the date of Purim) was declared by the Germans as the Day of Heroes. On that day the Germans will commemorate their war heroes. It is therefore going to be a day of mourning both in the Reich and in the occupied territories.

Mrs. Segal came to me in a very depressed state: "Mr. Golub, what shall we do? They say that it is forbidden to rejoice on that day." I told her: "It is indeed forbidden to rejoice on that day, but only as far as the German are concerned. Among us, this is going to be the Purim day and the children will be able to celebrate to their hearts' desire. From now on this is how it is going to be: a day of mourning and grief for them will be a day of joy and celebration for us. You can rest assured, Mrs. Segal, that everything will be all right and your pupils will be able to celebrate the Purim holiday."

Today is Sunday. The spring sunshine fills the Ghetto air with light and warmth. The Ghetto inmates are not working today. The Germans are busy commemorating the souls of their war heroes and, as a result, they did not come to the Ghetto. Our children stroll about freely on the Ghetto streets. They run about this way and that and their faces reflect a festive mood. They are very busy today. Their teacher has instructed them to assemble in the hall at noon. Mothers, and guardians of children, are also in a hurry to be present at the opening of festivities. At 1 P.M. members of the Jewish representative body also come to celebrate with the children. They are all here: Dr. Elkes, Garfunkel, and myself. Goldberg did not come. He does not belong to our circle. He is made of different stuff.[2]

Almost a hundred children are present in the hall, which resounds with their unrestrained laughter. Their joy is unmistakable. Finally, the festivities begin. A group of the youngest children appears on the stage. Mrs. Segal delivers a short opening speech. She says that the debate over whether to celebrate the Purim holidays publicly in the Ghetto was won by those who wanted to carry on with the festivities. It is good for the children to forget, even for a moment, their gray, fear-filled life in the Ghetto.

The event is inaugurated by a song, sung in Hebrew:

> Do not ask the old
> nor the young men.
> We small ones
> also know what Purim implies.

Games and recitations follow.

Needless to say, the main part of the program was the play about Queen Esther, King Ahasuerus, Mordechai the Jew, and Haman. A boy named Reuben mounted the stage; he wears royal robes, with a crown on his head and a golden scepter in his hand. He introduced himself to the audience, "I am King Ahasuerus," and seated himself on the throne. Then it was the turn of Shulamit[3]—a pretty and charming six-year-old girl. She entered the stage with dancing steps, wearing a pink dress and with a jewel-studded crown on her head. This, of course, was Queen Esther in full splendor. She bowed to King Ahasuerus and to the audience. Then the other members of the troupe mounted the stage.

The audience followed the play staged by children with great interest and open joy. Little charming Shulamit, leading all the dancers, was the audience's favorite. When the play was over, the children were treated to "Haman's ears" biscuits and other sweets, not to mention the thunderous applause for their wonderful performance. The veteran teacher, Mrs. Segal, also received her share of applause.

Mothers and guardians of the children sat in the audience, enjoying the performance on the stage. They wiped single tears from their eyes. But these are the tears of joy at the sight of their sons and daughters who, at this moment, give free expression to their youthful exuberance.

After this part of the program was over, three groups of children mounted the stage. Each group presented its own songs and plays. David Helerman accompanied them on the piano, playing with understanding and cheerfulness. He is a veteran Maccabi activist, an old member of the national student association Vetaria in Kovno, and a famous musician as well.

The festivities lasted a long time. The audience was becoming hungry, but everyone stayed until the program was over. We recalled the folk adage that all the holy days will disappear with the passing of time, but that Purim will remain for ever and ever, so that our enemies will not be comforted. Today the wonderful Ghetto children gave this saying another lease on life.

1. The day on which Jews celebrate the defeat of their enemy Haman at the court of the Persian king Ahasuerus, in the fifth century B.C.
2. Goldberg did not belong to the Zionist circle either in Kovno or in the Ghetto.
3. This was Shulamit Sheinzon (the daughter of Avraham Tory's friend Pnina Sheinzon, whom he would marry after the liberation of Kovno). Today she lives in Israel. Pnina Sheinzon's first husband had been murdered at the Seventh Fort during the first days of the German occupation of Kovno.

MARCH 23, 1943

The Jews are like a thorn in the flesh of the Germans, and even of the Lithuanians. When the Jews go to work or return home, they have to pass through certain streets and alleys in the city. The Germans, however, cannot come to terms with this fact. It irritates them: why do the Jews hang around in the city? Why do these lepers mix with our population? After all, they were put in the Ghetto to set them apart from the rest. Others wonder: they thought the Jews had already disappeared from the country. Not long ago Hitler announced that the Jewish race would be annihilated—why, then, are there so many Jews on our streets?

The Lithuanians are also astonished when they see Jews on their way back from work in the evening, trudging along, weary and exhausted, carrying a loaf of bread and some groceries. "The Jews buy everything for the purpose of speculation, and the Lithuanians have nothing to live on"—thus complain many Lithuanians to their German patrons.

In view of the above, it is no surprise that the Jewish workers who are seen on the streets of Kovno meet with growing hostility. Also, checks at the Ghetto gate have become stricter, and Jewish workers coming back from work undergo increasingly thorough searches. The police confiscate the goods found on them.

Miller himself came a number of times to see how the inspection is being conducted at the Ghetto gate. He himself even searched the bags of several workers. On one occasion he found a kilogram of marmalade on a woman. He asked her where she had taken it from. The woman replied that she had received it from a Lithuanian woman who had been her good friend for many years. On another occasion Miller found a kilogram of meat on a worker. Again, he wanted to know how he had gotten hold of it. The man replied that he had sold his last spare pair of trousers to purchase the meat.

At the same time, Ratnikas is taking up his position at the gate and frightens the Jews coming back from the city with his searches and questionings. Miller walks up to him and asks him: "Do you speak German?" "Yes, a little," replies Ratnikas in broken Yiddish. "Well," says Miller, "you, the Lithuanians, keep complaining that you can't buy a thing because the Jews buy up everything. And from whom do the Jews buy? Where did this Lithuanian woman get a kilogram of marmalade to give to her Jewish woman friend? I myself don't have such an amount of marmalade at home. It seems that this Lithuanian woman keeps a large quantity of marmalade at home. Now, let's talk about the meat. When a Lithuanian buys himself a pair of trousers for one kilo of meat, he is a war criminal pure and simple. Also, it seems to me this was not his last kilo of meat. So don't complain. You have yourselves to blame."

That is the way the Lithuanians are. On the one hand they want to batten themselves on the Jewish tragedy, and on the other hand they complain to the Germans that the Jews buy up everything.

The Ghetto inmates working in the city have to pass through the streets of Kovno. They march in tight formation and must keep up a brisk pace, but they keep their eyes open. Thus, they may see a Lithuanian, a stranger, passing by, who, on a closer look, turns out to be a friend from the past, with whom they had earlier deposited their belongings. And this "friend" of theirs does not return anything. He fails to answer the questions and inquiries that his Jewish friend addresses to him. He refuses to return the property which does not belong to him. That is why the Lithuanians are not happy to see the Jews on their city streets.

Yesterday, Miller and the German Ghetto commandant visited the Council. The purpose of the visit was to discuss the improper way in which the labor brigades march through the city. The workers march in small groups maintaining a very slow pace. They give an impression of strolling at their leisure. They are preceded and followed by other groups of workers taking up whole streets. This must not be allowed to happen. This situation is particularly offensive on Duonelaicio Street, frequented by SA Colonel Cramer; Kestucio Street, where Miller puts in an appearance every day; and Putvinskio Street, where the building housing the offices of the Nazi Party is situated. Cramer has already commented several times on the fact that on their way to and from work the Jewish workers stroll at a leisurely pace which creates a bad impression. Small groups of workers must march together in closed and tight formation.

The German Ghetto commandant, whom Miller brought with him, will, from now on, keep an eye on the way the workers march to and from work. An odd situation has been created: on the one hand they put pressure on us to increase our labor effort, and on the other they do not want to see us on the streets. They want us to be completely out of sight.

Yesterday Miller was busy tackling another problem: he wanted to obtain the addresses of the three Jewish workers employed in Cramer's household and in his garden. Having obtained these addresses, both Miller and the German commandant who had come with him conducted searches in their homes. They found nothing. It turns out that Mrs. Cramer has lost all her medicine. Of course, there is no doubt as to who is to blame for the theft. Shortly afterward, Miller called for the engineer Chaitin, who had been employed repairing his house. Miller then accused the Jewish engineer of storing his goods at Miller's house. Miller issued an order to place Chaitin under arrest, to lock him up for three days in the Ghetto detention center, and to "serve" him ten lashes every day of his incarceration.

Miller asked us to submit to him a complete list of our staff, men and women listed separately by age. He wishes to have a clear picture of the people employed at the Council. His purpose is clear: he strives to reduce the number of white-collar jobs in the Ghetto and to bolster the productive labor force.

Today I went to the city governor's office. Miller told me about his meeting with three young women in the Ghetto. He had asked them about their jobs. One said she was working night shifts in the workshops. After questioning her at some length he realized she was lying. The second woman said she was a housewife and was taking care of her children. In her family eight people were working, which is why she had to stay at home. This is rubbish, said Miller. Let them set up kindergartens. Such a young woman must work. That is the situation in Germany. It seems that there are many unemployed women in the Ghetto. For instance, there was a Jewish woman, Haimovitch by name, who worked in Miller's household. She was taken ill some time ago and no longer comes to work. The work this woman does during one day, a German woman can finish in two hours. Jewish women are lazy; they don't know how to work (he reminded me, in passing, to bring him another woman tomorrow; she should be strong and healthy).

I could not possibly explain to Miller that before the war our women had never performed such strenuous labor in the capacity of hired hands; in times such as these they are particularly hard pressed to get enough food to survive. Nor could I tell him that we are not very eager to set up a kindergarten in the Ghetto. We do not want to deliver our children to destruction. In October 1941, more than 160 children and babies then in the hospital were executed.

Two Jewish workers employed in Kovno at the garage for automobile repairs had their coats stolen. The garage manager called the German criminal police, but the coats were not discovered. A coat is a very important piece of clothing in the Ghetto. Many workers wear one to cover their threadbare jackets and torn trousers. Without an overcoat a worker looks somewhat like a person with no clothes on. Also, in winter, it is very cold without one.

It happened that these two workers took coal and firewood to Miller's house. They told him about their coats being stolen and asked for a permit to get new ones. There are many articles of clothing of this kind which were seized from the Jews and then stored in the clothing warehouse of the city governor's office. Miller referred the workers to me, so that I would then talk this whole thing over with him.

The two workers came to me asking for mercy. The stolen coats were the only ones they had. There are some coats in the Council storeroom. We would willingly give two of them to the workers. This, however, requires a special instruction issued by Miller who, as is well known, has forbidden issuing clothes to Jewish workers so long as they keep selling them in the city. I promised the two workers to talk to Miller about this.

Today I asked Miller whether he would allow me to issue two coats from the Council's clothing storeroom to the workers whose coats had been stolen. His reply: the Jews swindle the Lithuanians and the Lithuanians swindle the Jews. There is nothing he can do about it. I said that these two men had found themselves in a difficult situation. They cannot continue working without coats. My explanation was met by Miller with an idea: special work-clothes should be made for the Jewish workers. Then the workers would stop selling their clothes in the city and would not need additional clothing. The problem is that it would be difficult to obtain the large quantity of fabric needed to make special work-clothes.

When I heard Miller's ideas I lost my desire to haggle with him about two coats. In my view, the offer to dress our workers in special work-clothes amounts to turning them into prisoners-of-war. There is no need to underline the Ghetto slavery even more. This was the end of my discussion with Miller concerning the two stolen coats.

Last week the registration of the Ghetto population by means of a card index of families was completed. We had known the results beforehand and kept them secret. After the "actions" we wanted to conceal the existence of 3,000 of the Jews in the Ghetto. The Gestapo showed great interest in the question of how many inmates had been left in the Ghetto after all the executions. According to its calculations, no more than 14,000 people should have remained. We were afraid to disclose that there were more people in the Ghetto; perhaps the Gestapo had orders to leave only a certain number of people, and would carry out a new slaughter.

Not for nothing did Rauca—during the "action" of October 28, 1941—keep demanding of his men: "Give me the number of people." He kept saying this all day long: "I need to know the number of people already selected." It appears that he had orders then to exterminate nearly 10,000 Ghetto inmates. What did the Germans do? They counted each group that was led to Demokratu Square and from there to the Ninth Fort. Once an hour Rauca was informed of the number of those condemned to extermination. Nearly 10,000 people condemned to death—that was his count as he left Demokratu Square.

Even after the lapse of several months, Rauca kept showing an interest in the correct and complete count of the murdered Jews. We, for our part, insisted that no more than 13,000 to 14,000 people were left in the Ghetto. However, we could not hold out for long, because we received food rations according to the number of people we said lived in the Ghetto. As a result, nearly 3,000 people were left without food. What did we do? We distributed three to four food rations a week instead of seven. We bided our time, waiting for the danger to pass, before we revised the estimate of the number of the Ghetto inmates. We said that due to a mistake in the calculations there were 16,000 people in the Ghetto. By giving this number we concealed the existence of a further 1,000 people. There was talk among the Gestapo of too many women living in the Ghetto. This is why we decided to subtract 1,000 women from the estimate we supplied to the authorities.

Now, with the completion of the census of our population and with its results deposited in our labor office, the problem has emerged anew: What number should we tell the Germans? We are still in a position to fix the results in line with our interests. The question we are facing is: Whom should we include and whom leave out?

Recently we have been hearing rumors about possible "purges" in the Ghetto. It is possible that they would want to remove the elderly from the Ghetto—the "nonproductive" elements. On a number of occasions Cramer has said that there are no old people in his Ghetto. This is why we must conceal them. Furthermore, the results of our census show the relatively large number of children in the Ghetto. This, too, is not desirable from the German point of view. And what about the women? The imbalance in this area has not decreased. The relatively large proportion of women is due to the loss of their husbands. Yet they have young children, which is why we cannot send them to work.

Thus, we sat at the Council and examined the situation: What steps should we take? What carries lesser risks? In the first days of the German occupation, young men were led away to the fort. Whose turn is it now? The women? The elderly? The children? The feeble? Which category is most imperiled? Who should be hidden from the enemy's view?

We pondered the question from every possible angle. Tomorrow, the director of the German labor office, Lieutenant Hermann, will come to collect the results of the census. We must take a decision. Finally, we decided to reduce the number of the elderly in the census as well as the number of children. Women will be included in the workers' roster and will be issued worker-cards. Thus we will be able to avoid an increase in the declared number of Ghetto inmates. As a matter of fact, we will once more conceal 1,000 people. The young and the healthy will manage somehow. After all, for good or for bad, fortune plays games with us. Until the redemption comes.

MARCH 28, 1943

The German demand for an increase in the number of workers has forced us to co-opt into the labor force people who previously had been exempted from labor duty. The first of these to join the ranks of workers were youngsters aged sixteen and seventeen. Now they are required to work like adults.

Sometimes it is difficult to watch as these boys and girls, still children, go out to work. They should be in school. The Ghetto environment is not exactly conducive to their development; there are no schools here or youth movement activities. In compliance with the directive of the authorities they must abide by labor duty with all unpleasantness it entails: workers' complaints about the conditions in the workplace; pounding hearts when buying goods in the city contrary to the ban; an occasional instance of bad conduct on the part of a Jewish labor brigade leader when they pass through the Ghetto gate, etc.

It is true that twenty months of life in the Ghetto have hardened their characters, but although they no longer play the part of the spoiled child of the Yiddishe Mama, they are children nonetheless. Undernourishment, which is part and parcel of life in the Ghetto, has left its mark on them: they are pale, thin, and physically underdeveloped.

Several days ago a Jewish youth, aged sixteen, entered my office at the Council. He had received a summons to report for work at the airfield. Until now he has been working as a messenger for the bakery. This is certainly not the best possible workplace, but at least he stays warm during winter. His parents were murdered at the Ninth Fort. Apart from him, only his two sisters survived: one aged twenty and the other aged eight.

When he worked at the bakery he received an additional slice of bread every day. If he is transferred to the airfield, he is going to lose it. From now on he will have to make do with *jushnik*—a thin, watery, altogether repulsive soup— and a meager food ration. He will not be able to buy food in the city as he has nothing to sell or trade; he has no money, either. Nor does he have proper shoes to walk all the way to the airfield, his new workplace.

The lad asked me to help him to find a job somewhere closer, where workers get one kilogram of potatoes free. I asked our labor office to find a more suitable workplace for the young man.

Since the job market in the Ghetto is saturated, it is time for women between the ages of forty-seven and fifty to go to the city to work. It is not easy for them. Women at this age are busy doing housework; in many cases they serve five or six working people. They cook for them, wash and mend their clothes, bring firewood from outside, etc. If they work outside the Ghetto, how will they manage to do their household chores after a full working day?

The Germans also want women with children to go out to work. Until now they have been exempted from labor duty. The Germans offered to set up daytime kindergartens for children whose parents work, but there is no one to take care of them. In Germany, we are told, there are many such kindergartens. In Germany mobilization is total nowadays; the German women work at armament factories, replacing men fighting on the front. These factories have their own daytime kindergartens for children and babies, housed in spacious rooms and attended by a team of nurses. The children stay there all day, filling the day with songs and games. During the midday break, the women workers are given the opportunity to see their children in the kindergarten.

So the Germans want to set up similar kindergartens here. The conditions in the Ghetto are different, however; first of all, we have Jewish mothers who have had to leave their children in the care of strangers. But there is another reason, even more important: the Germans do not like the children of the Jews. It may be recalled that there was a kindergarten in the Ghetto where 165 children were looked after. On one gloomy day nearly all of them were murdered by the Germans. Only ten survived the carnage.

The Jewish mother in the Ghetto takes her own food to feed her children. She risks her life by running to the city to buy a glass of milk or an egg. When a wave of fears of an impending disaster sweeps over the Ghetto, mothers hide their children in various strange hiding places until the storm blows over.

One should also mention children who lost their mothers, and whose fathers must look after them. In some cases fathers have been exempted from labor duty to take care of their babies. In one such case, a mother of three children went to work. After the end of the workday she tried to buy a loaf of bread in the city and was arrested by the Gestapo. As it happened, this was the German day of mourning over the loss of Stalingrad. On that day they arrested forty-five Jews for buying goods in the city and led them to the Ninth Fort, where they were subsequently murdered. She was a young woman—Altschuler was her name—whom I knew well. On that day she was arrested because of the "crime" of buying a loaf of bread, and was then murdered by the Germans. She left behind a husband and three little children. Now he must look after them without knowing how to go about it.

Today we held a meeting at the Council on the subject of establishing a daytime kindergarten for children who have no one to look after them. Our office for social work, the health office, and the Ghetto police drew up a detailed plan for the operation of the new institution. The project involves a small number of children. The trouble is that an accidental visit of Schtitz in the Ghetto could cost us dear. The Germans would not tolerate the existence of such an institution in the Ghetto, and we, for our part, are not enthusiastic.

Since I had to be in the city today, I took the opportunity to take a ride on one of the carts which go to the city to bring bread. We get our bread from three bakeries in the city. Previously we had been supplied with bread by the big Parama bakery, the most modern bakery in the city of Kovno. It was owned by a Lithuanian cooperative. It turned out good-quality bread. When the indigenous Germans, who had been expelled to Germany during the period of Soviet rule in Lithuania, returned to the country, the new German authorities gave them houses and businesses, including bakeries, which previously had been owned by Jews. The new owners of the bakeries were also required to supply bread to the Ghetto.

Two Germans, Amon and Feifer, "inherited" the two big Jewish bakeries in the city—the bakery of Polak and the Konditoria of Markus. Now the quality of bread under the new owners is terrible. We argue that the bread is inedible, but the new owners are not impressed with our arguments.

There is a Pole-turned-German in Kovno by the name Boguslawski. He also supplies the Ghetto with bread. A Jew who had arrived in Kovno from Memel, after its occupation by the Germans in March 1939, established a modern bakery here. I do not know where he is now, but his bakery survives and Boguslawski inherited it.

Now Boguslawski is interested in buying gold and other valuables. He asks every customer whether he wants to sell him gold rings, watches, necklaces, etc. He is willing to pay cash. Elsewhere, Germans who had returned from Sanciai also took possession of businesses which had previously been owned by Jews. For example, the well-known Jewish factory for meat products which belonged to David Rosemarin is now in the hands of a German, Rheinhart. The old David Rosemarin was an observant Jew, and his stores were closed on Saturdays. He died at the right time, leaving behind two sons in the Ghetto. Both of them are excellent professionals in the area of various meat products. These two sons have for years been begging Rheinhart to take them as unskilled workers to work in the factory built by their deceased father. But Robert Rheinhart is a pure Aryan and cannot employ Jews in his "German" establishment.

The famous flour mills of Soloveitchik and Oszinski, the oil and soap factory of Potruch, and many others are now in the possession of the Germans. They empty the warehouses and batten on the merchandise which had been accumulating there for years. Other businesses built by Jews now employ their former owners as hired hands.

There is a pottery workshop in the Ghetto. Kovno City Governor Cramer is very proud of it. He never fails to show it to his visitors and can spend twelve hours a day there himself. Cramer looks with great interest at how the Jews turn clay and mud into beautiful vessels of various kinds. The pottery workshop is actually a Jewish business with a tradition going back many generations during which Jews lived in this house and made pottery. Now, after numerous "actions," only a handful of members of this large family remain. Some of them reopened the workshop after making all the necessary repairs there.

Yesterday I went with Dr. Elkes and his wife to see the work arrangements in the renovated pottery workshop. The chief worker and professional expert there is a heavy-set, awkward Jew with long hair. His face is wrinkled and his eyes have a penetrating, angry look. With great concentration he works bent over his potter's wheel, with which he turns a shapeless lump of clay into a beautiful piece of pottery. His big and clumsy hands stand in sharp contrast to the precise and pretty shapes he turns out on his implement. It was interesting to follow the changes effected in the lump of clay, which submitted itself to the determination and will of the craftsman until it assumed the final and desired shape of a beautiful vessel.

Dr. Elkes knows this veteran potter. He used to be his physician. Dr. Elkes says that pottery making is a type of hard work which often causes its own diseases.

This pottery workshop, which had been owned by Jews for many years, was turned into a German commercial enterprise under the city governor. It employs several Jews—or parasites, as the Nazis call them. One of those "parasites" is the Jewish potter whom we saw engaged in creative work.

1. Jews employed in the Council's vegetable garden received a free portion of potatoes.

MARCH 30, 1943

As I set out for the city today I was prepared for plenty of curses and abuse, but I had no choice. This is what I am in the Ghetto for. I must be prepared to listen to contemptuous and abusive remarks. And when the Gentile boss is seized by a fit of temper, I must be prepared to be severely beaten. In the eyes of any master sergeant, of any petty official wearing a brown uniform, of any upset Lithuanian partisan, all your papers and certificates count for nothing when you are a Jew wearing the yellow badge.

I use my papers very rarely. I do it only when the bosses I meet seem to be psychologically stable, not angry or drunk. Or when I need to obtain important papers or directives for the Ghetto. But when something is happening at the Ghetto gate, or during work, or at a meeting with lieutenants or plain thugs—I leave my papers in my pocket. For some reason, I know that in such situations papers will be of little avail.

On one occasion, when the workers were returning home, I witnessed a German guard slapping Margolis on the face. Margolis's papers and certificates of all kinds did not help him. Or take Aronstamm, who inspires with fear thousands of Jewish workers at the Ghetto gate. He was once severely beaten by the Germans within the Ghetto itself. Workshop manager Segalson was also brutally beaten, thrown on the ground, and kicked by a German officer of the Ghetto command, during a selection of Jewish workers for the purpose of transferring them to Riga. Yet Segalson was well placed as head of the "Jordan brigade" (or "brigade of Jordan's grandsons," as it was nicknamed then), which was under Jordan's special protection.[1]

Oleiski and Grinhaus—the "envoys" of the Ghetto at the airfield—have also received their share of blows.[2] Natkin, the director of the Ghetto gate labor service, who maintains excellent relations with the Germans and takes part in their drinking feasts on a regular basis, has also been severely beaten by his partners in parties. Lurie, who applies himself diligently to his duties as director of the airfield section, has also received his share of blows.[3] Dr. Elkes himself was beaten severely on a number of occasions. After the "great action" they almost broke his head. On another occasion he was beaten when the Germans allowed two hours for removing belongings of the Jews from the small Ghetto. Dr. Elkes failed to exercise due caution; he was not compliant enough for the taste of the Lithuanian partisan who had blocked the way to the large Ghetto. This Lithuanian proved his prowess by beating the chairman of the Council all over his body. Nor did the enemy baton spare my humble self. Without the taste of the master's rod, our stay in the Ghetto would lose a great deal of its meaning. Needless to say, the terror does not bypass the masses of the Ghetto inmates either. They are exposed to a rain of blows and curses on a regular basis. Nor does all this include the contempt, the screams, the abuse, etc.

I remember an incident in July 1941. Several of us, Jewish activists, met in the Jewish Committee building on Dauksos Street. At that time Gemelitzki, also a member of the Jewish committee, was passing on the street. In his pocket he was carrying documents and certificates issued by the German banks and trading houses with which he was associated. He also had in his possession a letter (in German and Lithuanian) issued by the commandant of the city of Kovno, saying that the bearer was a member of the Jewish Committee and that he should not be hampered in fulfilling his duties. Gemelitzki was also a personal friend of the German governor-general of Lithuania, Major General Jost. All these documents, and his association with Jost, were of no avail to him when a German soldier pounced on him in the street and beat him brutally. Gemelitzki arrived in the offices of the Jewish Committee, his body bruised and lacerated.

The reason for the beating: Gemelitzki had failed to salute the German soldier by taking his cap off in a proper fashion.

This incident occurred in the first days of the German occupation, when our experiences and relations with the occupier were rather scanty. Thus, at one of the committee meetings, we argued whether to include the injured Gemelitzki in the delegation to be dispatched to the local commandant so that he would see for himself how his soldiers behave toward us. Now we have become used to incomparably worse behavior. Even though it happens nearly every day, we feel, again and again, the yoke of exile and the enslavement of the Ghetto.

I was seized by this familiar feeling when I set out for the city today. I was certain, however, that I would be able to withstand the pressure from Obst and Miller. My fears were not without substance.

The story begins with the shipment of 3,054 kilograms of meat for the 17,000 Ghetto inmates. This meat reached the Ghetto in December last year, following a period of several months without meat. The meat, however, turned out to be rotten; eating even a tiny bit of it induced vomiting. We therefore asked the German supervisor of the workshops, and Miller himself, to come and see the meat for themselves and tell us whether it was edible or not. They came and, indeed, agreed with us that the meat was not edible. Thereupon we contacted the German merchant from Maistas (the meat products company) and told him about the condition of the meat we had received. He had his own opinion on the subject. He told us that the meat was edible, especially if Jews were meant to eat it. That is what was written in his papers.

This conversation started a dispute, which Miller and the German merchant conducted over the telephone for several days. Finally, we were left with no choice but to throw the meat away and bury it, so as to safeguard public health. We acted on the recommendation of physicians from our health service, who examined the meat and instructed us to bury it at once. The examining physicians issued a medical statement certifying the urgent need to dispose of the rotten meat.

It was then that the scandal broke: How did we dare to bury the meat without a special directive from Miller? We argued that Miller himself had seen the meat and ruled on its inedibility and that, in the meantime, it had started to putrefy. But our arguments were to no avail. Miller himself kept insisting that we should have asked his permission to bury the meat. He kept cursing and berating us until he regained his composure. In the end, Miller told us that we would get a new shipment of meat. He had already reached an agreement with Maistas on this matter.

We waited and waited, but the meat failed to arrive. A small amount reached us, but as part of the regular weekly rations. Needless to say, we were not reimbursed for the rotten meat. This is how things stood until Viertel replaced Obst as head of the food supply section at the city governor's office.

The two men were at odds. I presented my weekly report to Obst in which I stated that we were owed 3,000 kilograms of meat—the last shipment of which had proved inedible. Having received my report, Obst told me: "Go to Viertel; he is in charge of food supply now. Ask him for the meat you claim you are entitled to."

I went to see Viertel. The new man in charge asked me: "How come you didn't get this meat before?" I replied that we had received rotten meat which had had to be disposed of. "If there is an argument," said Viertel, "you should go back to Obst. He is responsible for this mess; let him clean it up."

What Viertel did was to write a letter to Miller, saying that Obst must clear up this matter and find a solution.

Having received this letter, Obst was furious with Viertel. I happened to be in Viertel's office at that time. He told me: "Go to Miller. I wrote a letter to him five days ago concerning the meat." I went to see Miller, who, in turn, sent me to Obst, who vented all his fury on me. Obst heaped curses and imprecations on the Ghetto institutions and, having exhausted himself, quieted down and then went out of his office to see Miller. I waited in the hallway, like a man awaiting sentence in a murder trial.

Some time later I was again called to Obst's room. He told me to inquire at Maistas what shipment of meat was involved—the rotten meat which we had buried, or, perhaps, some other shipment? He intimated that if what I had told him was not true, my future looked grim. Then I took my leave.

I started work at once. I asked the director of the nutrition department, Herman Fraenkel,[4] to go immediately to Maistas to clear up this matter of the rotten meat. Fraenkel went there twice. He called on the German merchant Steiner, of Maistas, who told him in no uncertain terms that no meat had been shipped to the Ghetto to replace the damaged shipment, nor was he going to make any such shipment. The reason, he said, was that he believes that the meat sent to the Ghetto was good enough for us. It is true that the meat gave off some smell, but this, in itself, does not mean that it was inedible.

After the visit to Obst, we stopped caring whether we would get new meat to replace the bad meat. We just wanted to forget the whole story. We sent off a letter to the city governor in which we explained our position. Knowing Obst, I feared that he would feel compelled to raise the subject again, as had happened on a previous occasion when we had received a shipment of potatoes weighing less than the weight written in his notebook.

This was the reason for my going to the city today. To my surprise, however, the whole affair ended on a happy note. Obst was not at all upset. He heard me out for an hour and accepted my explanation. Thus, the affair of the rotten meat was concluded—at our expense, needless to say.

I met Miller at the city governor's office today. He was at ease and did not repeat his harsh words from yesterday.

1. This refers to the special brigade of Jews from the Ghetto who worked for the Germans in Kovno itself, supplying services such as repairs and maintenance.

2. Oleiski and Dr. Grinhaus had established personal contact with General Geiling, the supervisor of construction at the airport. They also acted as liaison between General Geiling and Dr. Elkes. Because of their almost daily march from the Ghetto to the airfield construction site at Aleksotas, and their close friendship, Oleiski and Grinhaus were known in the Ghetto as "the two pairs of feet."

3. Before the war, Wolf Lurie had been a government attorney at the Kovno district attorney's office. During the period of the Ghetto, he argued that work at the airfield should be done properly, however hard it might be. When Council members took their turn at this work, Tory himself was in favor of not doing it as effectively as one might, by only pretending to work hard, as an act of quiet resistance. Lurie insisted that the work had to be done properly, so as not to lead to reprisals. On July 7, 1944, just before the final liquidation of the Ghetto, Lurie, his wife, and their only child—a son—tried to commit suicide by taking poison, rather than face deportation and death. The son died in terrible pain, but the parents remained alive. Later that day they were both shot for refusing to leave their home.

4. Herman Fraenkel, who for a short period in June 1943 stood in for Goldberg as head of the labor office, had been head of the Council's nutrition department since the establishment of the Ghetto. During the period of confiscation of Jewish property, before and immediately after the move to the Ghetto, he was one of those entrusted by the Council to supervise and to hide as much gold and valuables as possible for use by the community in the future. He perished in Dachau. His son, Shlomo Shafir, survived and became a scholar and editor in Israel.

APRIL 2, 1943

Yesterday at 3 P.M. I was summoned from my home to go to the Council. Miller wanted to speak with me over the telephone. I entered the Council offices and picked up the receiver. Miller was upset, having waited for me a long time by the telephone. It is scandalous, he said, that no member of the Council was in the office in the afternoon. He would issue a special directive on this matter.

I explained that there was an official on duty in the Council office at all times. Whenever a member of the Council is needed, the official on duty summons him from his home which, in any event, is not far away from the Council offices. I reminded Miller that he himself gave his consent to this arrangement. Miller responded by shouting at me: "You are all sluggards! You don't work at all! Your lunch break lasts from two till five in the afternoon and this is far too long. I'll lock you up in jail. I hereby order that at least one member of the Council—Elkes, Garfunkel, Goldberg, or you—be present at the Council office at all times. One of you will eat his meal from one till three, the others from three till five, and so on."

After a short break in our telephone conversation—Miller had left me at the receiver while he spoke with other people—he continued: "The Jewish labor office must be open on Sundays as well. There is vital work to be done for the German Army and there is no one to talk to. This is out of the question. All of you sleep until nine in the morning and take three hours to eat lunch. This irregularity must be brought to an end."

I try to explain to Miller the work schedule of the Jewish labor office. As in every other office in the Ghetto, work goes on seven days a week, including Sundays. "Yes," he says, "in the middle of the day, one of the members of the Council must be present in the office. You keep forgetting what you've been told. If you don't mend your ways in the future, you'll suffer the consequences." Having said what he had to say, he slammed down the receiver.

After such a reply, I stayed in the office yesterday until five in the afternoon. I thought that Miller would telephone again. When upset, he is capable of telephoning the Council offices several times a day. Today he came to the Council offices. He repeated his warnings from our telephone conversation yesterday. This time I emerged unharmed from the conversation.

As a rule, most of our clashes with senior German officials amount to a storm in a teapot. But under the sad conditions in which we live in the Ghetto, these clashes—which occur almost every day—cause us needless tension and unceasing torment.

APRIL 5, 1943

A month ago, on March 3, Miller had made a telephone call to summon the members of the Council and the commander of the Jewish police, Kopelman, for a meeting. At the appointed hour Garfunkel and I stood waiting in the Council offices. Dr. Elkes has not been attending meetings of the Jewish body on account of his illness. Goldberg was ill at the time, and it was impossible to locate the commander of the Jewish police. By chance, the deputy commander of the Jewish police, Abramovitz, was in the Council offices at the appointed hour. Garfunkel asked him to attend the meeting with Miller, in place of Kopelman.

Miller arrived at four o'clock. He spoke about various current problems for half an hour. In the end he said that he had an important announcement to make which was to be kept secret by those present. They could, however, divulge it to Dr. Elkes and to Kopelman.

After Garfunkel, Abramovitz, and I had pledged to keep the announcement secret, Miller said that an additional 3,000 Jews were about to be brought to the

Ghetto. In reply to the question of where these Jews would be coming from, he said that he did not know as yet, but added that all of them would be fit for work. Afterward he gave orders for us to prepare detailed plans for the accommodation of these 3,000 people, and to submit these plans to him in writing by four o'clock on the following day.

The members of the Council who had been present at the meeting had pointed out that the Ghetto had already been truncated twice, and that it was now necessary to add a number of houses to it in order to ensure minimal sanitary conditions; to allow the Ghetto the use of the building of the Lituanika cinema situated within the Ghetto precincts, as well as the use of several additional buildings in the vicinity of the Christian cemetery.

In reply to these proposals, Miller said that there was no additional area available for the expansion of the Ghetto. At the same time, however, he instructed us to include these proposals in the plan for housing the additional 3,000 people in the Ghetto.

That evening a meeting of the Council was held at Dr. Elkes's home. Both Lipzer and Kopelman were invited. It was decided to submit to Miller a detailed plan for the accommodation of the 3,000 Jews according to proposals put forward by Garfunkel, Abramovitz, and me in a meeting with him. A committee was appointed, charged with drawing up the plan; the committee members were Garfunkel, Kopelman, and me.

On March 4 I submitted the plan to Miller, who showed great interest in it. Immediately afterward, Miller went to Cramer to show him the plan.

That day news had reached the Council that a German, a certain Matias, who employed a brigade of Jewish workers and was known for his friendly and respectful treatment of the Jews, had secretly informed a number of Jewish women employed at his place that he had received news about an "action" which was to take place by the end of March. This "action," he said, was to affect the old people in the Ghetto. Matias added that several days earlier he had paid a visit to the Ghetto and spoken with the commandant of the Ghetto Guard, who had also told him about this possibility.

On March 6 I went to see Miller again, and asked him once more about the 3,000 Jews. Miller replied that for the time being the matter could wait. At the same time, he repeated his request to keep the whole thing secret so as to avert disquiet in the Ghetto. I then told him that there was already serious disquiet in the Ghetto on account of persistent rumors about an "action" against old people. Miller vehemently denied these rumors.

On March 9, Garfunkel spoke to the German director of the workshops, Gilow, in connection with the six houses on Krisciukaicio Street to be vacated so as to expand the large workshops. Garfunkel argued that in order to expedite the evacuation of the six houses it was necessary to include in the Ghetto area

A Ghetto streetcorner: announcements on the walls, business conducted unobtrusively, rumors exchanged.

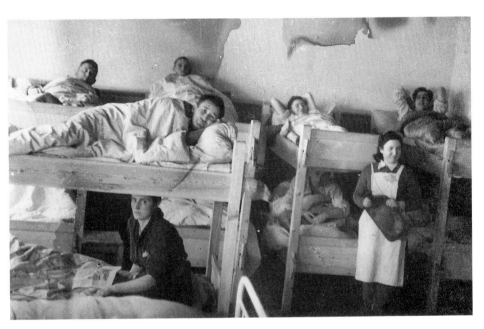

The Ghetto hospital. Because of the shortage of nurses, the sick were tended by relatives. The hospital, set up at the end of 1941, had 80 beds, and in spite of poor conditions, such as a lack of running water, it provided extensive medical care.

Yehoshua (Ika) Grinberg and Pnina Sheinzon inside the Jewish Council building. Grinberg, a senior officer in the Jewish Ghetto police, was also a leader of the underground and trained underground members in the use of explosives. Pnina Sheinzon had come to the Council building to collect a section of Tory's diary.

Left to right: Moshe Levin, chief of the Jewish Ghetto police and a member of the underground, and his deputies Yehuda Zupovitz and Tanchum Aronstamm. Zupovitz, formerly an officer in the Lithuanian Army, secretly drilled those who planned to escape to the forests and join the partisans. Aronstamm, much feared by the residents of the Ghetto, was later appointed by the Germans to be head of the police force after the Ghetto had been turned into a concentration camp and the Jewish Ghetto police had been disbanded. On the far right are Dr. Shmuel Grinhaus and Jacob Oleiski, liaison officers with General Geiling, the head of airport construction; Oleiski was also the founder of the Ghetto vocational school.

Clandestine children's care: orphans kept in the hospital as if they were sick.

A wagon loaded with food is detained at the Ghetto gate—just outside the picture at right—and taken to the German Ghetto commandant under the orders of the Lithuanian or German police.

At the Ghetto vegetable garden. Right to left: the agronomist Shlomo Kelzon, head of the vegetable and fruit department of the Ghetto; Leib Garfunkel, deputy head of the Jewish Council; Avraham Golub (Tory); Moshe Potruch of the economic department; and an employee of the vegetable garden.

The Ghetto pharmacy.

In the clandestine bakery: weighing the flour before baking

For two months during the summer of 1942, Jews were allowed to bathe in the Vilija river alongside the barbed-wire fence that enclosed the Ghetto.

Two Jewish policemen and three of their prisoners outside the Ghetto detention center.

A collection of prewar pottery. Pots were used to bribe Germans and Lithuanians. It was in some of these pots that Esther Lourie hid many of her sketches; they were destroyed when the Ghetto was burned in July 1944.

A meeting of the Jewish Council in 1943. From left to right: the Council secretary Avraham Golub (Tory), Leib Garfunkel, Dr. Elkes, Yakov Goldberg, Zvi Levin.

The Ghetto fire-fighting brigade. In the center is its commander, Moshe Abramovitz. Despite the fact that most buildings in the Ghetto were constructed of wood, few fires broke out.

A view of the Kovno Ghetto in the winter of 1942.

Dr. Elchanan Elkes, his wife, Miriam, and their son, Joel, in 1939.

A family in the Ghetto.

An artisan school in the Ghetto: two instructors in the knitting class.

The Ghetto laundry. This was the first of many workshops set up by the Jewish community so that the Ghetto would constitute a "productive element" in the eyes of the Germans. The laundry service was provided mainly for the German Army; a second laundry, for use by the inmates of the Ghetto, was not opened until August 1942.

A member of the underground makes notes as he listens to the news on the only radio set in the Ghetto. On the right (with his gun on the table) is Jacob Ratner, who was later to join the partisans in the forests outside Kovno.

A work detail returns to the Ghetto. Some of the bundles may contain food bartered from Lithuanians. Jews caught smuggling food into the Ghetto were taken to the office of the German Ghetto commandant, who released most of them after he and his fellow officials had taken their pick of the smuggled goods.

In the spring of 1942 a detailed calculation of the number of calories needed for survival was submitted to the German authorities in Kovno. To everyone's surprise, the Germans allowed a slight improvement in the food supplies reaching the Ghetto, enough that the Council was able to set up a public soup kitchen, where several hundred people received hot soup every day. The soup was known as yoshnik—pig swill.

Rabbi Ephraim Oshri, a distinguished Talmud scholar. His armband says "Head of the delousing sanitation department."

The partisan leader Chaim Yellin.

Avraham Golub (Tory) and Pnina Sheinzon after their return from taking Pnina Sheinzon's young daughter, Shulamit, to a hiding place outside the Ghetto.

Yehuda Levit at the mouth of a well which was the entrance to one of the many hiding places—in walls, behind furniture, beneath cellars—prepared as a precaution against a German attempt to deport all the Ghetto inmates. Most of the hiding places were discovered, and their occupants deported, during the final "action" in July 1944.

A young couple with their two-year-old child, born "illegally": the Ghetto commandant had forbidden all pregnancies in the Ghetto, the punishment for pregnancy being death for mother and child.

Jews being forcibly evicted from the Kovno Ghetto in 1942.

The possessions of Jews who had been deported or murdered. After such bundles had been picked over by the Germans and the Lithuanians, they were sent to the Jewish Council's welfare department, which distributed clothing, shoes, and cooking utensils to the needy.

The wagoner Teinovitz and his cart, which was used for sewage disposal. Beside the cart is Teinovitz's son Meir, a member of the Jewish underground in the Ghetto, and one of the first to escape into the forests at the end of 1943.

The journalist Dr. Volsonok, the artist and head of the Ghetto graphics workshop P. Gadiel, and Avraham Tory.

The original caption of 1943 reads: "An 'apartment house' in the 'rich quarter' of the Ghetto, Varniu Street."

At the creation of the Ghetto in August 1941, the Transfer Committee managed to move to the Ghetto more than 100,000 volumes from various private and public Jewish libraries. In February 1942 the Germans ordered Ghetto inmates, on pain of death, to hand over all books and other printed matter. Here some books are being rescued, to be hidden in the Ghetto.

The Jewish Council's boy runners, who delivered the Council's messages throughout the Ghetto. They also warned the various clandestine groups when the Germans were coming, and warned those who were trying to smuggle food into the Ghetto when a guard was near. At bottom right is Avraham Tory's personal friend Yankele Bergman. For three years he risked his safety by carrying Tory's diary entries, documents, and other materials from the Council offices to their hiding place.

Lucia Elstein (later Lavon), who was Tory's assistant at the Jewish Council and who succeeded Tory as Council secretary, with Advocate Shimberg, the assistant secretary, and the Council runner Yankele Bergman.

A Lithuanian woman and her sons pass the corpses of Jews murdered in Kovno in the first days of the war.

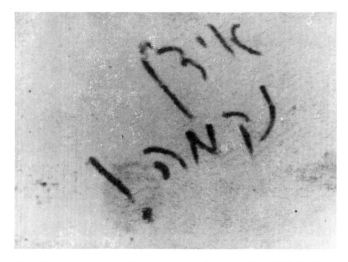

*Entering a room in the Ghetto, the photographer Hirsch Kadushin
saw a man dying of starvation and bleeding severely. The man wrote
on the wall in his own blood, "Jews, revenge!"*

Jews inside the Ninth Fort, immediately after their arrival there.

The cover designed in the Ghetto for Tory's collection of German standing orders. The drawing depicts the goddess of Justice on a cracked pedestal. The text is couched in heavy irony: the words "Eileh Hachukim" come from the Bible and mean, in literal translation, "these are the laws"; the words "Nussach Ashkenaz" come from the prayer book and mean "for Ashkenazi Jews." Here the juxtaposition of these words refers to the German style of justice. The year is given as 1943 (5723). The small print says: "Collected and edited by A. Golub. Illustrated by P. Gadiel." The bottom line says in Hebrew: "Ghetto of Slobodka, 1941–43."

Heinrich Schmitz, deputy commander of the Gestapo in Lithuania.

Hans Cramer, the German City Governor of Kovno.

Demokratu Square, where the Germans selected 10,000 Jews for death in the "Great Action" of October 28, 1941.

A sketch by Josef Schlesinger of the public hanging of Meck, November 18, 1942. The Gestapo ordered the Jewish Ghetto police to carry out the execution, and to leave the body on the gallows for twenty-four hours.

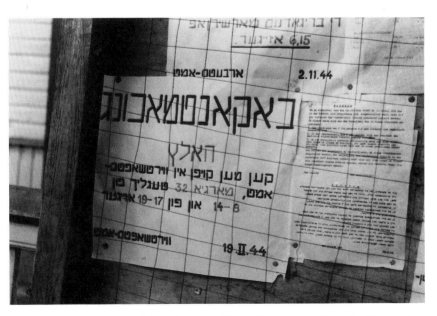

Announcements were posted throughout the Ghetto; these are on the wall of the wood storehouse belonging to the Jewish Council. The top announcement states: "Working parties (brigades) march out at 6:15. Works department, February 2, 1944." The poster at lower left reads: "Announcement: wood can be bought at the economics department, 32 Margio Street, daily from 8–14 and 17–19 o'clock. Economics department, February 19, 1944."

The Lithuanian priest Bronius Paukstys, who helped many Jews, including Avraham Tory, to escape from the Ghetto. After the war he was sentenced by the Soviet authorities to ten years in solitary confinement. He is seen here wearing a suit that Tory managed to send him after he completed his sentence.

Irena Adamovich, the Polish woman who brought news of the fate of the Jews of Poland to the leaders of the underground in the Kovno Ghetto.

Dr. Moses Brauns, a hero in the battle against typhus: by Josef Schlesinger, 1943.

Shulamit Sheinzon: by Esther Lourie, 1943.

Hela Aronovski Voschin, the Polish woman who gave birth to a daughter in the Ghetto.

Esther Lourie: self-portrait, 1943.

Professor Simon Bieliatzkin, chairman of the Jewish Court in the Ghetto: by Esther Lourie, 1942.

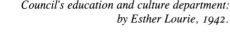

*Dr. Chaim Nachman Shapiro, head of the Jewish
Council's education and culture department:
by Esther Lourie, 1942.*

*Aizik Srebnitzki, one of the underground
leaders in the Ghetto:
by Josef Schlesinger, 1943.*

Josef Schlesinger: self-portrait, 1943.

*Rabbi Abraham Shapiro, Chief Rabbi
of Lithuania: by Esther Lourie, 1942.*

Benno Lipzer, head of the Jewish labor brigade
at Gestapo headquarters in Kovno.

Michael Kopelman, chief of the Jewish
Ghetto police:
by Josef Schlesinger, 1943.

Shraga Goldsmith ("Feivchik"), head
of the Jewish Council repair workshops:
by Josef Schlesinger, 1943.

Zvi Levin, one of the leaders of the
Ghetto underground:
by Josef Schlesinger, 1943.

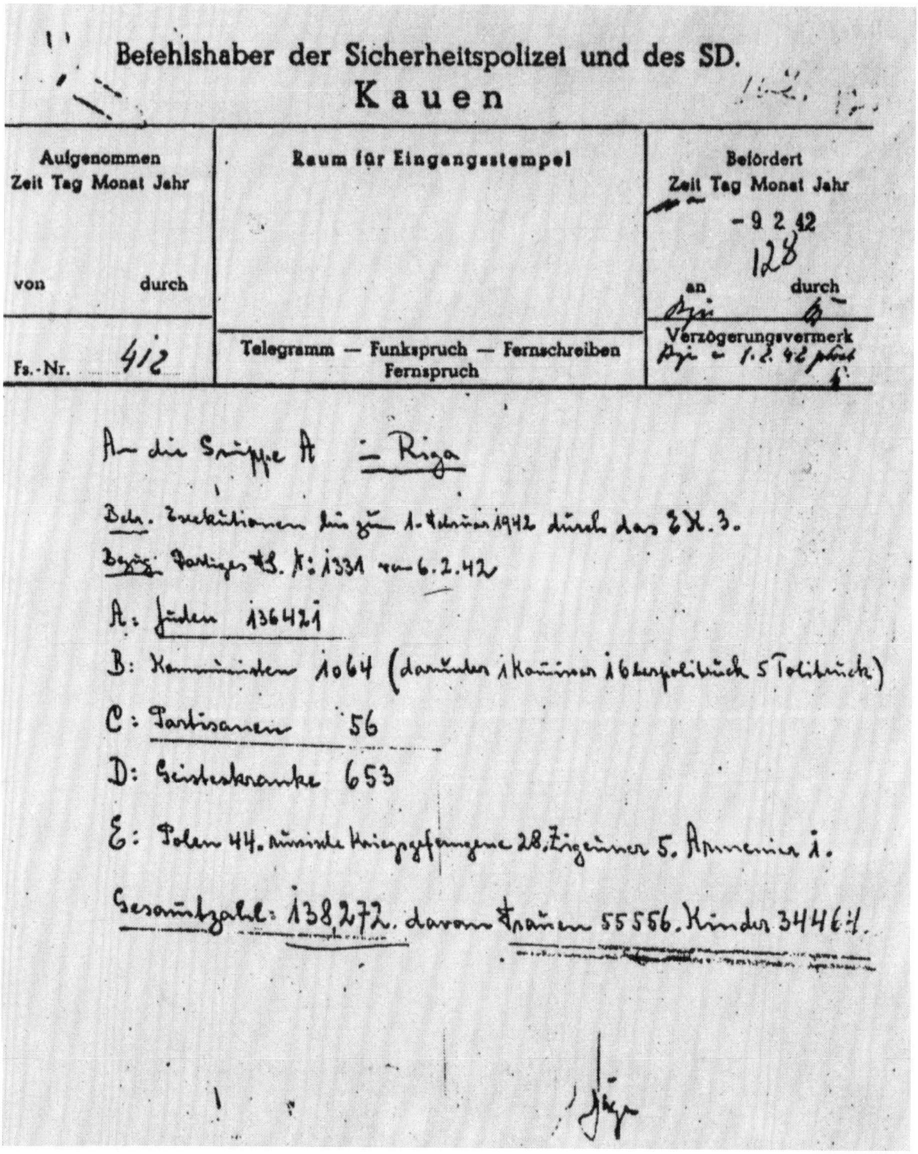

Aufgenommen Zeit Tag Monat Jahr	Raum für Eingangsstempel	Befördert Zeit Tag Monat Jahr
		- 9 2 42
von durch		an durch
Fs.-Nr. _412_	Telegramm — Funkspruch — Fernschreiben Fernspruch	Verzögerungsvermerk

[handwritten message]

An die Sruppe A — Riga

Betr. Exekutionen bis zum 1. Februar 1942 durch das EK.3.
Bezug: Vorlage №3. № 1331 vom 6.2.42.

A: Juden 136421
B: Kommunisten 1064 (darunter 1 Kommissar 16 Kerpolitruck 5 Politruck)
C: Partisanen 56
D: Geisteskranke 653
E: Polen 44, russische Kriegsgefangene 28, Zigeuner 5, Armenier 1.

Gesamtzahl: 138272. davon Frauen 55556. Kinder 34464.

Report from Jaeger, head of the Gestapo in Lithuania, to his superior in Riga, February 9, 1942, stating that to that date 136,421 Jews had been killed. In addition, he lists 1,064 Communists, 56 partisans, 653 insane persons, 44 Poles, 28 Russian prisoners-of-war, 5 Gypsies, and 1 Armenian. Of the 138,272 total, 34,464 are children.

AUSWEIS

FÜR JÜDISCHE HANDWERKER

DER GEBIETSKOMMISSAR IN KAUEN – STADT i. t.

GEZ. JORDAN

SA – HAUPTSTURMFÜHRER

A Jordan Certificate; on September 15, 1941, the District Komissar for Kovno, Fritz Jordan, gave the Jewish Council 5,000 of these certificates for distribution to artisans and workers, as well as to 11 physicians. In the German "actions" which followed, those with certificates were not seized, but thousands who had no certificates were taken to the Ninth Fort and killed. Later, the certificates proved worthless as life-saving instruments.

A U S W E I S.

Hiermit wird bescheinigt, dass

.... *Simonas Zundeliovičius* ....

wohnhaft. *Varniu, 32, Block B, Wohnung 13*

im Arbeitsamte im Auftrage der Arbeitsstelle

LUFTWAFFE-BAUAMT, KOENIGSBERG/PR./,FRONTBAU-

LEITUNG 3/I fuer den Flugplatz beschaeftigt

ist.

Seine Familie besteht aus....Personen.

Luftwaffe-Bauamt
Koenigsberg/Pr./
Frontbauleitung 3/I

A Ghetto permit: "This is to confirm that Simonas Zundeliovicius of Varniu 32, Block B, Flat 13, is employed by the Works Department on behalf of workplace: Airforce Building Section, Koenigsberg /PR/, War Building Directorate 3/1 at the airport. His family consists of five persons. Airforce Building Section, Koenigsberg /PR/, War Building Directorate 3/1."

A page of Avraham Tory's diary, written in Yiddish; this entry is the one for December 31, 1942.

A Ghetto permit: "Concentration Camp Kovno, Workshops, Night Permit no. 2326. Name and first name Rabinaviciene Fruma. Address Bajoru 10. Working card no. 8077."

"From the SS to the Ghetto Council, May 6, 1942. Maria Germana Levinaite, born July 15, 1919, in Rokischkis, is living in the city illegally and must be taken into the Ghetto. Her eight-month-old child, whose father is Stasys Ciemnalonskis of Kovno, will also be brought to the Ghetto in the next few days."

the four houses near the Christian cemetery which, in actual fact, were situated within the Ghetto boundary.

At this moment the telephone rang. It was Miller. Gilow told him that a member of the Council happened to be in his office, to which Miller replied that he would join us in a short while.

Miller appeared as promised and joined the conversation at once. Segalson, the Jewish manager of the workshops, also took part. Miller used the opportunity to reveal that the arrival of the 3,000 Jews in the Ghetto had again become a possibility. From the hints he dropped, it was possible to gather that it concerned Jews from the Vilna area.

When Garfunkel mentioned the housing plan submitted to him by the Council on March 5, Miller replied categorically that the authorities did not intend to expand the Ghetto. In reply to Garfunkel's question as to whether anyone apart from those present knew something about the plan for the 3,000 Jews which was supposed to be kept secret, Miller said it was known also to Hermann, the director of the German labor office in the Ghetto. Replying to another question by Garfunkel, Miller said that the Jews were expected to arrive in the Ghetto within five to six weeks.

On March 11, Miller paid another visit to the Council and spoke about current problems. He again referred to the 3,000 Jews, saying that the Council must make all the preparations needed to accommodate them, but again in the utmost secrecy.

At that time, Schtitz of the Gestapo, who was in charge of the "political discipline" in the Ghetto, visited the Ghetto. Schtitz entered the Ghetto command headquarters building and from there contacted Miller by telephone. From their telephone conversation, we gathered that the question of the 3,000 Jews was at issue.

Miller subsequently left the Council office and set out for Lipzer's office, where Schtitz arrived a short while afterward. The conversation between them made it clear that Miller would be going to Vilna and Schtitz to Riga.

As the conversation between Miller and Garfunkel on March 9 revealed, Hermann, who was known for his fair treatment of the Ghetto, also knew about the 3,000 Jews. Dr. Elkes therefore set out to meet him. He asked Hermann to speak frankly, and to remove the veil of secrecy surrounding the plan. Elkes pleaded with Hermann to speak as one human being to another.

Hermann, who had a high regard for Elkes, revealed to him the following: there was an order from the very highest level to liquidate the Vilna Ghetto.[1] Some of the inmates of the Vilna Ghetto, Hermann added, would be sent to the Ghetto at Kovno and some to the Ghetto at Riga. The old people and the infirm would be liquidated. Hermann also told Elkes that there was a plan to liquidate a number of the old people in the Kovno Ghetto. This, however, was opposed by City Governor Cramer, on the grounds that it might interfere with the smooth running of the labor system in the Ghetto. For that reason this plan had been put off. "Put off but not abrogated?" asked Dr. Elkes.

"To be honest with you," said Hermann, "I must say that this plan was put off for a period of time. But nothing bad is going to happen in the coming days."

Hermann also revealed that, as far as the Vilna Ghetto was concerned, there had been a plan to bring to the Kovno Ghetto men only, without their families. Cramer had opposed this plan, arguing that when Jewish workers live with their families their production output is better. It had therefore been decided to bring the Jews to the Kovno Ghetto together with their families. The Germans intended to bring here to Kovno those families whose members were fit for work, and to send to Riga those who were unfit for work. At Dr. Elkes's request, Hermann promised to find out the reason for the liquidation of the Vilna Ghetto.

That evening, Mr. Szitelni,[2] the head of the Jewish labor brigade at the labor camp at Palemonas, where a number of Jews from the Kovno Ghetto are employed, put in an appearance at the Council offices. Szitelni announced that he had visited the Vilna Ghetto several days earlier and had found a bleak mood there among the inmates. The authorities had ordered the Jewish Council in the Vilna Ghetto to distribute 15,000 identity documents to the Jewish Ghetto inmates, each document having an attached slip on which was written the document number. Seeing that there were nearly 21,000 Jews in the Vilna Ghetto, it was thought that no certificates would be issued to the old people; that had given rise to serious apprehensions.

On March 11, I called again on Miller at his room in the city governor's office. Miller told me that he was going to Vilna in order to get to know the people, and that we should make all preparations "as though they were coming." In answer to the question of whether the buildings mentioned in the Council plan would be placed at its disposal, Miller said that housing would indeed come within the framework of this plan. He promised to supply more details after his return from Vilna.

On March 15, Miller told me that there was nothing new concerning the 3,000 Jews.

On March 16, at 11 A.M., Lipzer appeared at the Council offices. He revealed that he had learned from Jaeger, the head of the Gestapo in Lithuania, and from Rauca, that on March 14 a meeting had taken place at the Gestapo which had also been attended by Hermann and Miller. At this meeting it had been decided not to bring Jews from the Vilna region to the Kovno Ghetto. The Jews in question were from the Oszmiana Ghetto.

Several hours later, Miller arrived at the Council offices to inform us of the decision not to transfer more Jews from other places to the Kovno Ghetto. He took credit personally for this decision. "Aren't you pleased?" he asked. "Yes, we are pleased," was the reply of the members of the Council.

On March 19, Dr. Elkes held another meeting with Hermann, who revealed that there had been a plan to liquidate the Vilna Ghetto in order to transfer there several thousand Poles from Kovno. But, as an agreement to that transfer had not been forthcoming from Berlin, the plan had been abandoned. Hermann expressed the opinion that no more "actions" against the Jews were now to be expected, and that there was an express order not to kill Jews who were fit for work.

On March 31, Cramer and Miller arrived at the German labor office in the Ghetto. They asked to see the director of the Council's labor office, as well as Goldberg and me. In the presence of Cramer, Miller informed me that, after all, Jews from Vilna would be coming to the Kovno Ghetto (now he spoke of 5,000 Jews) and that preparations had to be made for their accommodation. Cramer confirmed this. At the same time, no exact date was mentioned for their arrival. Miller warned us that no additional buildings would be placed at the disposal of the Council.

Following this announcement, Garfunkel ordered the head of the housing department, Pesach Meshkutz,[3] to draw up secretly a plan for the housing of the 5,000 Jews from Vilna.

On April 2, Dr. Elkes met with the German director of the workshops, Gilow, informing him that the arrival of the 5,000 Jews from Vilna was expected. Gilow asked whether an announcement to that effect had been received in writing. When Elkes replied that the Council had been informed about it by word of mouth alone, he said: "In that case there is no certainty at all about it."

On April 3, Miller told me that the 5,000 Jews would not be arriving all that soon, and that in all probability it would take another five or six weeks.

On April 6, Jewish workers from the railroad workshops spoke with several railway engineers who had arrived from Vilna. These revealed that on April 5 they had taken a train with eighty railway cars, laden with Jews, from the train station in Vilna. They took these cars to Ponar, about five or six kilometers from Vilna; there, all the Jews were murdered.

On April 4, so Lipzer told us, Gestapo officers had left the Gestapo building in Kovno in the direction of Vilna; they had gone to take part in the "action." They returned to Kovno on April 5, their clothing stained with blood.

Thus it became clear that the murdered Jews were the ones who had been due to arrive in the Kovno Ghetto. Several days later Szitelni again came into the Kovno Ghetto and revealed the following details: about five or six weeks before, an announcement had been made by the authorities in the small Ghettos around Vilna, such as Oszmiana, Sol, etc., that the Ghettos there would be disbanded and their inmates transferred to other Ghettos. On that occasion several thousand Jews had been registered for transfer to the Kovno Ghetto. At the beginning of April, these Jews had been taken to the Vilna Ghetto and housed there. On April 4 they were transferred to railway cars and taken to Ponar, where they were murdered. There are rumors that a number of Jews, principally from the Ghetto of Sol, had put up resistance to the murderers, and that a small number of them had succeeded in escaping; the rest were murdered.

Some time later, Schtitz visited the Ghetto and revealed to Dr. Elkes and to Kopelman that the Jews who had been selected for transfer to the Kovno Ghetto had made a pact with local White Russians, and had launched an attack on the Germans. As a result, eight Germans had been killed and about forty wounded. That is why, said Schtitz, these Jews would not be coming to the Kovno Ghetto.[4]

1. As became clear later on, this order actually concerned the liquidation of several smaller Ghettos in the Vilna district, not the Vilna Ghetto itself.
2. Maurice Szitelni, a refugee from Belgium, was Jewish camp leader at the Palemonas labor camp until he was succeeded by Leo Nachumson, whereupon he became Nachumson's deputy.
3. Meshkutz had been Avraham Tory's Hebrew calligraphy teacher in the Hebrew high school in Marijampolé. On April 4, 1944, he was arrested with all the other members of the Council and taken to the Ninth Fort. On the following day, nine of the internees were suddenly released; Meshkutz was one of them. He was subsequently killed in Dachau, after the evacuation of the Kovno Ghetto in the summer of 1944.
4. The final paragraphs here were added after the bulk of the entry was written.

APRIL 6, 1943

Today the rumor spread in the Ghetto that the Jews who were to have been brought here from the Vilna area have been executed. This rumor spread quickly. Fear has again seized the Ghetto. They keep asking themselves: "Is this rumor true? Were they really murdered in cold blood?" Having heard this terrible news, many thought in their heart of hearts that our own fate was sealed, that we had no chance to survive anywhere else. We must stay where we are and await our fate. Only a miracle can save us.

The source of this terrible rumor was Lipzer, who today came earlier than usual and revealed at the Council that a truck with Gestapo from Kovno returned yesterday from the Vilna area. Bloodstains on their clothing and on their weapons indicated that they had returned from an "action." Lipzer told us about it yesterday, but he did not have any details then. He now revealed that there had been a travel order put up in the Gestapo garage, giving Ponar as the destination.

Five of the Kovno Gestapo, five men who specialize in spilling blood, left for Ponar. Our Jewish workers in the garage can guess the destination of the Gestapo by the kind of equipment they assemble for the journey to the Ninth Fort, to provincial towns, or to some other city—equipment which means an "action." For it is the Jewish workers who have to bring them the machine guns, bullets, and other equipment. They have to equip them from head to toe with the necessary clothing and arms. The garage workers also know how the travel order is written. In most cases it reads: "Special Assignment." This time, however, the travel order simply read "Action." The place—Ponar—was also significant.

When the five Gestapo returned, their machine guns and combat rifles were blackened with burned cordite. Their clothes were stained with blood, and the good-quality booty which they had brought back with them—such as overcoats, leather jackets, and fur coats—proved that an "action" had, in fact, taken place.

At the same time it was impossible to know whether the people who had been murdered were Jews or Christians. Recently, many Christians—Poles and Lithuanians—have also been executed. This morning, however, the Jewish workers at the railroad workshops heard from an engineer that yesterday the "passengers" of eighty-eight railway cars packed with Jews were executed in Ponar. This was confirmed by another engineer. Since it had been said that 5,000 Jews were to be sent to the Kovno Ghetto, there was only one conclusion: these Jews had been executed at Ponar.

Today I read a letter from Riga. In fact, this is not so much a letter as a tragic document of our Jewish community in one of the Ghettos. How well I remember the events of February 6, 1942, when the Ghetto inmates here in the Kovno Ghetto, including the old and the young, were summoned once again to assemble at the infamous Demokratu Square. The purpose: Jordan needed 500 people for work in Riga. Previously, Jordan had tried—with the assistance of the then Ghetto Guard, composed of men of the third squad of the German police—to take out of their homes at night people whose names were on lists prepared in advance. However, many people had disappeared from their homes for the night, so that only a few hundred had been found and transported to the train station at two o'clock at night.

When Jordan was informed of this on the following morning, he became furious. He gave orders for the whole Ghetto population to assemble in Demokratu Square. Many people grasped that their participation in this gathering would not do them any good; consequently, they kept looking for hiding places until the storm blew over. They did not want to go through the tragedy of October 28, 1941, again.

What did Jordan do? He hand-picked 300 people from among those assembled on the square. Afterward he entered the Council offices and announced: "If 200 people are not placed at my disposal by four o'clock this afternoon, an 'action' will take place in the Ghetto this very day."

An urgent Council meeting was held. The meeting was pervaded by a premonition of great disaster lying in store for the Ghetto, should we fail to recruit the 200 extra people immediately as demanded by Jordan. At about the same time, we were promised by the third squad of the German police that, in fact, the 200 people were intended to work in Riga and that no "action" was planned. We therefore unanimously decided to recruit the 200 people at once, in compliance with Jordan's demand.

At four o'clock in the afternoon Jordan, and Rauca of the Gestapo, arrived at the Ghetto gate. The heads of the Jewish labor office asked the Germans for a reprieve of several hours so as to enable them to fill up the quota by recruiting bachelors, and younger and healthy people without large families, in order to limit the damage to families as much as possible. Apparently the Germans did not place much faith in this request, for even though they gave their permission to recruit the 200 people missing from the contingent to Riga, they stayed at the Ghetto gate. The presence of the Germans at the gate proved that the situation was serious.

Under German terror, the officials of the Jewish labor office recruited the 200 missing people, and supplied them with food and clothing, all of which was then loaded on five carts. In the midst of all the confusion they also collected for them the sum of 20,000 marks. (Earlier Dr. Elkes had spoken in his home with a German Army officer who had arrived from Riga. He gave Dr. Elkes his word of honor as a German Army officer that he would take all the 500 workers safely to Riga. The officer gained Dr. Elkes's trust, and Dr. Elkes decided to give him the money to be distributed among the recruited workers on their arrival in Riga. The German Army officer also promised Dr. Elkes to bring back with him from Riga letters from the recruited workers to their families in the Kovno Ghetto. The officer did, in fact, abide by his promise.)

When the quota of workers to Riga had been filled, Dr. Elkes, acting upon numerous requests addressed to him, attempted to release a number of people seized by Jordan earlier in the morning at Demokratu Square. Among them were the fathers of families with many children, or two parents torn away from their children leaving them without protection, as well as skilled workers who were much needed at various workplaces in the Ghetto. At last Jordan yielded, to the extent that he agreed to release fifteen of those who had been recruited in the morning.

I still have before my eyes the vivid picture of the cries of the recruited workers. They were led in two batches to the train station under heavy German military guard. A thin sheet of snow covered the streets of Kovno. The Lithuanian and German residents strolled about at their leisure on the sidewalks. At the dark hour of the night they had seen groups of Jews marching under the guard of armed German soldiers. This was an unusual sight. The city inhabitants were unaccustomed to the sight of Jews at such a late hour. Especially as they did not look like people going to work.

Behind the marching recruits and their German guards was a line of five carts loaded with bundles of clothing, food, and various belongings. To the eyes of the city's inhabitants, the slowly marching Jews, accompanied by such a heavy guard, looked like prisoners-of-war being led to a concentration camp.

The most terrible scenes occurred at the train station of Sanciai, a suburb of Kovno, where railway cars were waiting to take the Jewish workers to Riga. There, the 300 people "picked" by Jordan in the morning were locked inside sealed boxcars designed for transporting cattle and other commodities. Their faces, bearing expressions of astonishment and apprehension, and filled with longing for their homes and freedom, could be seen from the little windows. They started crying out in loud voices: "Get us out of here!"

When the second contingent was brought to the train station at night, and the guards started pushing them into the cars, the recruited workers resisted by refusing to enter the cars. But their efforts were of no avail. A number of blows on their heads and several shots in the air were enough to push them all into the waiting boxcars. Sounds of anguish could again be heard coming from the small, barred windows.

When Kopelman set about removing the fifteen Jews whom Jordan had said could be released, hundreds of Jews started pushing against the doors. A German soldier standing guard began shooting over the heads of the pushing Jews, and slammed the boxcar doors shut.

Seeing that there was no way in which we could possibly remove those Jews whose names were on the list to be brought back to the Ghetto—the cars were far too crowded to get them out in the few moments available to us—we decided to try to save at least some of those who were standing close to the doors. But there was too little time. Only seven people managed to get out of the boxcars by taking advantage of the confusion.

In the dead of night, a Jewish worker, about thirty-five years old, managed to slip away. He approached me, asking me to give his regards to his wife. She lives in the Ghetto, he said, on Krisciukaicio Street: "She has no idea that I have disappeared all of a sudden. Please also take greetings to my three children."

Suddenly I had an idea; I cast a look around and saw the German soldier who had been standing guard before the recruits were pushed into the cars. When he stood with his back to us, I told the Jewish worker with the wife and three children: "Come over here quickly! See these carts loaded with belongings of the work recruits? Jump on one of them and the trip to Riga is over and done with." He said to me: "But I have with me a bundle with things I bought at my workplace; they will recognize me instantly." "Just throw away your knapsack and come over here," I said. I did not wait for his reply but pulled him toward me and slowly led him to the cart. At that moment he looked like a Jewish worker who had brought the belongings of the Riga recruits on the cart. He was saved.

I was very excited by this, and again drew up closer to the train. In the darkness, I caught sight of another Jew (Leib Telzak) who was coming up to the group of Council workers accompanying the carts. He was bolder than his predecessor. He asked us in a whisper: "Jews, how can I save myself? Give me some advice." My advice was quick and to the point: "Throw away your belongings quickly, and crawl toward the second cart." In this way a second Jew was saved.

When we saw that we would not be able to save additional Jews from the train, we climbed on the cart so as to return to the Ghetto. My head was full of depressing thoughts. Our eyes kept seeing terrible scenes: eyes peering through the barred windows; Jews trying to break out when the boxcar doors were flung open briefly, and then pushed brutally back inside by the soldiers of the guard. We were upset that we did not manage to save more Jews.

These scenes of February 6, 1942, come alive before my eyes when I read the balance sheet of murder drawn up by Israel Kaplan, a Ghetto inmate, who was taken to Riga on that day together with 500 other Jews.

Israel Kaplan was a teacher in the Ghetto. He used to record events in the Ghetto.[1] Now and then he would come to me with the aim of setting straight details of some event or conversation. This same Kaplan had called my name through the boxcar window, crying for help. I approached the car twice, but was unable to find a way to get him out. Ever since then, I have felt guilty over my failure to rescue him.

Kaplan has been in Riga since February 6, 1942. Whether it was by chance or not, I cannot tell, but some time ago a truck left Kovno for Riga. It carried our old friend Shalom Meirowitz—or Benjamin the third, as many in the Ghetto used to call him on account of his frequent wanderings even in these difficult times.[2]

Shalom Meirowitz returned from Riga safely. The day before yesterday he brought to us regards from the Lithuanian Jews who had been transported there on February 6, 1942, as well as those sent there on October 23, 1942. Various restrictions are imposed on the two groups. Those of the first group work together with Latvian Jews, and are subject to the authority of the Jewish Council of Jews from Germany. The star of Julius Kohn,[3] who was notorious in our Ghetto, is in the ascendant there. Now we hear that he is in Riga. Another community figure who recently has come into prominence in Riga is the informer Granovski. He used to work at the Jewish labor office in the Kovno Ghetto. He was the man responsible for searches conducted by the Gestapo among the leaders of the Council.

It was revealed to us that the rumors about an "action" in Riga were grounded in fact; following an attempt by a number of Jewish policemen and other Ghetto inmates to cross the Baltic Sea to Sweden, 150 people were murdered, including forty-one Jewish policemen. The escape attempt failed. It turns out that the Jews who tried to cross the border were armed. When the Germans caught up with them, the Jews put up resistance and killed a number of German soldiers. As a reprisal, the Germans murdered 150 Jews, including some Jews from Kovno.

Israel Kaplan sent us a detailed report. In the period from February 6, 1942, until April 1, 1943, many Jews who had earlier been brought from Lithuania died. Only a handful of them died of natural causes. Most of them were killed when trying to trade their belongings for food, or during an attempt to slip away from the camp. Some were killed by stray bullets, some died of hunger, or from exhaustion caused by hard labor, or from illness. The list of our dead included in Kaplan's report adds up to a bloody testimonial from the Riga section of our "battlefront." The name of Shamai Schatz was also on this list. He and I had been friends since our youth and had studied together at the Hebrew gymnasium in Marijampolé. He grew up in poverty, but succeeded in escaping it. He was a Zionist and an active member of our Zionist circles. During the fateful night of February 5, 1942, when the third squad of the German police forcibly removed people from their homes and concentrated them in the synagogue on Veliuonos Street for the purpose of taking them to the train station, I met Shamai Schatz just after midnight, at one o'clock in the morning. Our encounter took place on Linkuvos Street. Together with his wife, he was being marched along by two Germans, and by two Jewish policemen who marched behind them.

I got very upset when I saw him. He and those with him looked like people being led to their deaths. Shamai saw me and began to stare at me. Then he cried: "Avraham, look how they lead us! This is my wife!" That was the last time I heard him. The German accompanying him dealt him a blow on his head and silenced his cries.

I set out in the direction of the synagogue on Veliuonos Street, where the detainees were concentrated. This was a few moments before they were marched to the train. It was already night when they started taking them out of the synagogue building. One of the detainees tried to break away under cover of darkness. Shamai and his group were being brought in there at about the same time. I saw him again and turned my eyes toward him. I wanted to tell him: "I'll try to do something for you." I approached one of our police chiefs, Bukantz,[4] asking him to save Shamai Schatz. At that moment shots were fired from all sides. The Germans had surrounded the area, and whenever someone tried to break away from the ranks to find some hiding place, he was fired at from all sides. Crossing the street meant exposing oneself to mortal danger. I stood behind a wall until I regained my composure.

That night Shamai's life was saved, which made me very glad. But in all probability his fate was sealed. The next day he was one of those "picked" by Jordan from those assembled on Demokratu Square and sent off by train to Riga, where he became a policeman. He wrote relatively hopeful letters. Some time later the unsuccessful attempt to escape to Sweden took place, concurrently with a revolt of Jewish policemen. The latter, including Shamai Schatz, were murdered.

Israel Kaplan mentions him among the martyrs. The names of the young Jews in the Riga group who were put to death were recorded on four sheets of coarse paper. On these four sheets Israel Kaplan also wrote us his report of the grim events. From each line, and from each name, blood trickles into the huge cup of Jewish suffering. That cup filled up long ago; the blood spilling from it has turned into rivers and lakes.

The spilled Jewish blood cries for revenge; the memory of Amalek[5] shall be blotted out from under God's sky. The people of Israel shall live forever, until the end of all generations.

1. The educator Israel Kaplan was a central figure in the cultural and educational life of the Ghetto until his deportation to Riga. After the liberation, he became the editor of the important journal *Fun Letzen Churben,* published in Germany by the Historical Committee of Liberated Jews in the American Zone. The material he had written about the history of the Ghetto was lost.

2. The first Benjamin was the biblical Jacob's youngest son; the second was Benjamin of Tudela, the medieval Jewish traveler. The third is the hero of "The Travels of Benjamin the Third," a satire written early in the twentieth century by the Yiddish author Mendele Mocher Sforim.

3. Julius Kohn had been one of the Kovno Jews sent to Riga. While in Kovno, he had been a member of a labor brigade which worked at the airfield. He did not survive the war.

4. Leizer Bukantz, a central figure in the Jewish police, was killed at the Ninth Fort in March 1944, together with other policemen who refused to reveal hiding places in the Ghetto.

5. The Amalekites were the first enemies the Israelites encountered after crossing the Red Sea. The Book of Exodus relates that Joshua fought against the Amalekites under the inspiration of Moses, who was supported by Aaron and Hur, and that he mowed them down with the sword. Amalek was not destroyed, however, and at the end of this war Moses was ordered to write in a document, as a reminder, that the Lord would one day blot out the memory of Amalek from under the heavens. In commemoration of the victory, Moses built an altar which he called Adonai-Nissi, and proclaimed that "The Lord will be at war against Amalek throughout the ages."

APRIL 7, 1943

On Sunday, four to five thousand Jews were murdered at Ponar, near Vilna. Until yesterday we fed only on rumor, speculation, and conjecture; today these became a grim fact. We have received news about the murders from various sources.

Lipzer was our main source. He spoke on this matter at the Gestapo with Schtitz, Schmitz, and others. They revealed to him that on Sunday four to five thousand Jews were executed at Ponar. Everyone he spoke with put forward a different rationale, or excuse. The first said that the Jews had done "swinish things"; they had set upon the Lithuanian policemen who were taking them out of the wagons at Ponar. Six Lithuanian policemen were killed in the revolt. The Gestapo themselves faced danger. This is why they gorged themselves on food and guzzled liquor upon their return to their camp.

Life is not easy these days. Thus, for instance, a Gestapo man was killed and several others were badly wounded in Panevezys. The Panevezys Ghetto inmates who dared to put up a fight against the Germans paid with their lives for the attempt; however, the Gestapo man who had been killed did not come back from the dead.

Today the Gestapo raised their glasses to celebrate getting out alive. When wine started flowing into their throats, they began talking. Schmitz told Lipzer that the Jews murdered at Ponar were the old and the sick. This description, however, does not square well with Schtitz's revelation about resistance; after all, old and sick people could not kill six Lithuanian policemen. Schmitz adds: "As a matter of fact, this event should not be of interest to us here in Kovno. Let them do in Vilna whatever they want. Nothing like this is going to happen in our Ghetto. All this is behind us."

What is the situation really like? We have heard reassuring announcements. But the question is, what do they intend to do? Recently we have been told that here, in Lithuania, the bad times are behind us. But then we were informed that several thousand Jews from the Vilna area would be arriving here. We made the necessary preparations to house them. At every opportunity we asked Miller when these thousands of Jews would be arriving. We hoped for the best, but feared the worst. And then disaster struck: a total extermination of thousands of Jews. Having put up strong resistance, they were murdered at Ponar—the notorious extermination center.

Today Schtitz warned Lipzer: "it is possible that the Jews who escaped from Ponar will arrive here. In heaven's name, in such cases you must immediately inform the Gestapo." We say: Let them come. Let them come unharmed. We shall know how to hide them from the enemy. We wonder how the Germans could turn to us with such humiliating suggestions; how can they ask us to render them such an ignominious service?

Today before noon, as we were sitting in the Council offices, we were shocked to hear apparently casual remarks coming from two Jewish youths from Siauliai. They arrived here as workers in a German truck from the Siauliai Ghetto, to take delivery of various materials and medicines. The German who brought them is a good man. He escorted them and left them here for the whole day.

These youths gave us a report about the Siauliai Ghetto. They related the saga of torment and hunger, of frequent "actions." They conveyed regards to us from their fellow inmates and wanted to know what life was like in our Ghetto.

We told them that life here was no different than in any other Jewish place these days. Only the details differ: here there is a yellow badge whereas there a labor card; here an Ältestenrat (Council of Elders), there a *Judenrat* (Jewish Council); there a Lithuanian tyrant who comes into the Ghetto, gorges himself on food, and departs, here a Lithuanian by the name of Ratnikas who makes our life miserable. Here there was a larger Jewish community and, consequently, the troubles loomed larger, whereas in a smaller community the toll of victims was not as large.

The youths from Siauliai sit with us and unfold the story of our martyred brethren, of hard times and countless instances of cruelty. All of a sudden they interrupt their story: "Jews from Lida, Oszmiana, and other townlets in the Vilna vicinity will be arriving in your Ghetto." It turns out that Lithuanian policemen from Siauliai on active duty in Vilna revealed this to them. These policemen saw with their own eyes the Jews being transported on carts; they should have arrived already. If they do not appear in the near future, it will be a bad sign. The question is, did these youths from Siauliai know about the fate and the end of these Jews? Did they know but not dare to tell us frankly? It is difficult to know.

The assembled members of the Council looked into each other's eyes. Then we knew: these were the Jews whom we have been told were due to arrive here, but they will never arrive, because they were exterminated by the Germans. Our conversation with the Siauliai youths took place before midday, before we learned the details of the conversation between Lipzer and the heads of the Gestapo.

In the afternoon, news reached us from various sources, all of which confirmed the rumors which had spread in the Ghetto in recent days: in early April 1943, after a break of eighteen months, a large-scale massacre took place in Lithuania—5,000 Jews were exterminated with the assistance of the Lithuanian police. Was it an isolated "action," or are we faced with a resurgence of a wave of murders? The Ghetto is pervaded by gloom and despair. Are we the next in line? Only God knows.

APRIL 8, 1943

The news about the extermination of 5,000 Jews at Ponar has been received in the Ghetto with fear and anguish. No words can express the feelings of each one of us. Suddenly we see ourselves teetering on the brink of an abyss. Any slight breeze, any wrong move on our part, may cause us to lose our balance and fall into the void.

We have received information from various sources about the shocking scenes of the massacre at Ponar. The engineer who drove the train carrying scores of

Jews to the slaughter relates with anguish the details of the executions. The train with seventy or eighty locked and sealed boxcars was brought to Ponar. Waiting for it there was a large contingent of the auxiliary units of the Lithuanian police. The Lithuanian policemen wore black uniforms, and were supervised by Germans of the Gestapo. A Gestapo reinforcement from Kovno was also brought in.

In a field nearby, a barrel of vodka had been put at the disposal of the policemen; they helped themselves to their favorite drink throughout. The drink helped them to carry out their assignment.

The train stopped. The Jews were taken out of it in small groups of twenty to eighty people and ordered to march forward. They were surrounded by German and Lithuanian policemen, beasts of prey in human disguise, ready for action. The policemen would then open fire, turning their rifles and machine guns on the stunned victims. The air quickly became thick with fire and smoke. Under the hail of bullets, the victims started running about in distress. They fell down, individuals and groups, in the field.

When the anguished cries of the victims, running in all directions under the rain of bullets, reached the ears of those who were still in the sealed boxcars, they were seized by panic and the terror of death. Through the apertures in the boxcar walls—so the engineer continues—one could see the tense faces of throngs of frightened people. They saw annihilation lying ahead—the end. Those first to get down from the cars were at a loss to know in which direction they should go, but were mowed down by a hail of bullets. The others, following behind them, made desperate attempts to flee. In one car, the intended victims succeeded in making a hole in the wall, jumped out, and started running in all directions. Some of them got away. These were the ones about whom Schtitz warned Lipzer that should they arrive in the Kovno Ghetto they must be handed over to the Gestapo.

The fields of Ponar became the scene of a spectacle of horror. A deep and wide pit was dug into which the fallen victims were thrown like so many corpses. The fields of Ponar were strewn with the bodies of thousands of martyrs. In the thick of the deluge of gunfire, several Jews rose up and defended themselves with stones which they picked up from the ground. They also pounced with sticks on the murderers. They even tried to snatch weapons from the hands of some of them. The Jews succeeded in beating to death some of the Lithuanian "hired" killers. In the ensuing pandemonium, the Lithuanian policemen fired at each other and also at the Germans of the Gestapo.

The horrible scenes keep coming alive before the eyes of the engineer: the field swarming with people running in all directions, searching for shelter; the dead and the wounded being thrown into the pit. One image inscribed itself on his memory with particular force: a blond Jewish girl, seventeen or eighteen, who fell down into a puddle of blood right next to the engine. She was lying there, her face turned skyward.

News of the horror has already reached many in the city. Even the Germans describe the killing as a heinous murder. We keep hearing terrible details from the workers at the railway workshops, and from workers in other workplaces who heard them from witnesses of the slaughter. We hear, and we refuse to believe, even though we know that the victims were thousands of Jews from the Vilna district.

Those Germans who maintain good relations with the Jewish workers said yesterday and today that Vilna Jews are not expected to arrive at the Kovno Ghetto. They will not be coming for the simple reason that they are no longer among the living.

This massive loss of human life has had a profoundly disturbing effect on us. On the one hand, the Germans keep demanding more and more Jewish skilled workers. City Governor Cramer keeps paying frequent visits to the labor office in the Ghetto, with the demand for more Jewish workers. He wants them to occupy vital positions in the German war economy. On the other hand, thousands of Jews are being packed into sealed boxcars and led to slaughter.

I, for one, believe that this whole business of the shortage of workers, the need to employ as many Jewish workers as possible—which is enthusiastically endorsed by German officials—and the slogan "Work is a decisive factor in our survival," all these have been bankrupt for quite some time. They are a lie. The Germans want to drain the marrow from our bones; they want to use us until the last moment of our lives, when they will take us to the Ninth Fort, or to a forest, to exterminate us. Ponar serves as confirmation of this. Why should we oblige them by taking part in this bloody game? Why should we help the Germans by supplying the labor force at a time when the Gestapo holds a sharp sword suspended over the heads of the workers? Why should we stay alive only to become witnesses to the inevitable epilogue: the day on which the work will end and the sharp sword will fall on our necks?

Ponar has taught us once more that neither work for the Germans, nor slavery, nor submission, will be of any avail when our turn comes. Our irrevocable sentence, signed and sealed, has already been passed somewhere in Kovno. Even if we can work wonders and miracles, we will not be able to change it. Neither Hermann nor Miller, not even Cramer and Jaeger, will come to our aid when we finally face extermination.

There was a time when we thought that our fate would be decided when the Germans had been defeated in the field; when they would find themselves in constant retreat, facing the prospect of withdrawal from our territory. Then and only then, would they seek to vent their wrath on us, so as not to leave any living trace of their crimes against our people. The events at Ponar have proved to us that the Germans are capable of exterminating us even before the downfall of their armies at the front.

But there is also another possibility. This mighty wall whose name is Gestapo—the concentration camps, the instruments of destruction at the disposal of our enemy—their combined might would not be a match against the Almighty. All of a sudden a mighty storm will issue from the heavy clouds which now cover our sky. With a hail of fire, thunderbolts and lightning, it will crush the war machine and the German apparatus of oppression in the blink of an eye. The enemies of the Jews, and of the whole of civilized humanity, will fall and be buried under the avalanche of their own strongholds, which will have suddenly collapsed, and with them will be buried the sentence they have passed on the remainder of our people.

Such an end to the enemies of our people cannot be excluded; more than once, Jewish history has seen justice being done. Until then we shall extend our hands toward the sky and cry for help. Oh lord, where are you?

APRIL 9, 1943

Yesterday I looked for an opportunity to see Miller alone. I wanted to speak to him about the 5,000 Jews exterminated at Ponar. After all, he was the first to tell us about the 3,000 Jews who had been scheduled to arrive here in Kovno; later it was 5,000 Jews. Even when we believed their arrival was very near, we were told to keep the plan secret. In point of fact, this whole affair was unclear: if the plan was meant to be implemented in the near future, why all the secrecy?

Now it has all become clear. The lives of the 5,000 Jews were hanging in the balance. The tip of the scales moved this way—to life—and that way—to death. One day they were almost here, and several days later there was quiet. One day the plan was a reality, and the next it became outdated. The murder at Ponar and its circumstances remain veiled in secrecy. It was this secret which I wanted to decipher in an open, humane conversation with Miller. I know Miller well, and I know his treatment of the Ghetto. I know that when he is not angry, and is alone with me in the room, he is capable of speaking as one human being to another. Yet it is difficult to find such a moment with Miller. I had already come twice to see him, but he had not been alone in his office. I had entered his room, settled some small current issues, and departed.

The Ghetto is in anguish. At the Ghetto gate, thousands of Jewish workers look into one another's eyes. They talk about one thing only: the slaughter at Ponar and—what next? In the Council offices, in the large workshops, in dwellings and courtyards, the same subject pervades all conversations: Ponar.

Today I must speak with Miller. I must know what he has to say. When I entered his office, Miller already had his overcoat on. He was on his way out. Nevertheless he agreed to see me, and seated himself behind his desk.

First, I asked him to sign a letter addressed to a German veterinarian, asking him to examine the horses in the Ghetto. Miller is very fond of horses and always shows an interest in and an understanding of their condition. "Of course," he said, "the horses must be examined." He signed the letter and returned it to me. "What else?" he asked. "Sir, something weighs heavily on my heart and I would like to speak openly to you."

"What is the problem?" asked Miller in a quiet, peaceful voice.

"There is a great deal of apprehension in the Ghetto," I replied. "For the last several days there have been persistent rumors that Jews from the Vilna district, who were to have arrived here, were murdered en route. This is what Lithuanian workers revealed to our workers at various workplaces. Do you have something clear to say on this subject?"

Miller got up from his chair, cast a glance in my direction, and immediately lowered his eyes. He listened to me, and all the while he kept looking at the thick carpet under his feet. He listened and did not say a word. He let me talk until I finished, as if he wanted to hear all I knew about the subject. When I finished, he said, visibly astonished: "Those damn Lithuanians know more than I do." He broke off for a moment and added: "I have been told that 5,000 Jews will be arriving here in the Ghetto. The rest is in the hands of the Gestapo." There was something like an apology in this remark. He repeated: "Yes, the Gestapo."

I said: "It seems that the fate of 5,000 Jews is unknown to you. Perhaps you know when these Jews will be arriving at the Kovno Ghetto?" Miller's reply to my question was: "When, and whether, they will come is a Gestapo matter."

Miller washing his hands of the whole affair of the 5,000 Jews, and shifting the responsibility for their fate over to the Gestapo, was tantamount to an unspoken admission. It seems that under his Nazi uniform there is some spark of humanity.

Standing by the door, just before leaving the office, his eyes cast downward, Miller said: "In any event, your people have no reason to worry. Here in the Ghetto nothing like this is going to happen. I give you my promise."

Having returned to the Council offices, I revealed to my colleagues the content of my conversation with Miller. We were all of one mind: the Ponar massacre was not an isolated incident, but a chapter in the extermination of the Jews. Not for nothing did the Gestapo celebrate upon their return from Ponar; they celebrated their success in implementing a demonic plan by leading 5,000 Jews to the death pit at Ponar. They themselves emerged unharmed and intact from it.

This time, they have succeeded in their designs. But the time will come when they will have no reason to celebrate.

APRIL 10, 1943

Jewish Ghetto police have informed us that a Gestapo car had passed through the Ghetto gate. A few moments later the car pulled up at Lipzer's office. Schtitz entered the office in the company of several Germans.

We were seized by panic. What was Schtitz doing in the Ghetto today? On what business was the Gestapo in the Ghetto? Perhaps they had come to see the Jewish ophthalmologist who treats them on a regular basis? But the ophthalmologist had not been summoned to the Council offices. After the Ponar massacre the people in the Ghetto feel completely powerless. The very same Gestapo men carried out that horrifying slaughter.

We telephoned the Jewish police headquarters and asked its commanders to check if something had happened in the Ghetto, or was going to happen. The Germans stayed in Lipzer's room for half an hour, and from there went to the workshops.

At last it became clear that the Germans had come here to attend to their own private matters. Schtitz has a little garden next to his house in which he wants to grow flowers. Schtitz—a mass murderer by profession, a dog in human disguise who cannot live without spectacles of slaughter—this Schtitz wants to grow flowers.

Schtitz is bound with organic ties to the Ghetto. Here he looks for and finds his victims. He has a secret list in his possession from which he picks his victims, according to a certain criterion.

When one of the people on the list is taken ill—as happened with Erich Kohn—Schtitz leaves him alone until the man recuperates. He keeps a close watch on the progress of recuperation of "his patient." In the case of Erich Kohn, Schtitz very much wanted to know when he would be discharged from the hospital. Kohn, for his part, was very touched by the interest shown by Schtitz in the state of his health. Nothing happened to him after he had been discharged from the hospital. And then, one day, what had to happen did happen, and Erich Kohn was led away to the Ninth Fort.

Today we were informed about a new hobby of Schtitz's: growing flowers. After a trip to the Ninth Fort, after the massacre of 5,000 Jews at Ponar, after washing his hands stained with the blood of his victims—he would like to stroll among flower beds and smell their reinvigorating scent.

Today, Schtitz came to the Ghetto to take delivery of wire for the fence surrounding his garden. Having attended to his business, he went to see the workshops.

The Germans are very fond of paying visits to the workshops, where implements and wares are being manufactured which everyone needs even when war is going on. Here they can obtain a pair of boots. Jewish cobblers, first-class professionals, turn out top-quality boots for the murderers of the Jewish people. The Germans sit in our homes and use the dishes which we bought with the sweat of our brows. They live as though in a dream and do their best to avoid being sent to the front. They live off their hatred of the Jews.

The Ghetto workshops, which the Germans describe as enterprises producing primarily for the German war machine, serve, above all, a small group of senior Nazis. They come here often. They want their clothes made here, their shoes mended, their underwear washed; and to purchase toys for their children. They leave the Ghetto carrying parcels and suitcases packed with all kinds of goods.

Schtitz is not the last one to visit the workshops. He looks at the workers with eyes full of contempt and disrespect. He probably says to himself: sooner or later all of you dogs will fall into my hands. In the meantime, he orders and takes for himself various goods and articles. When German officials get what they ask for, they leave the Ghetto.

If, prior to their arrival, we had known that they were coming only to plunder and loot, we could not have cared less. But until we are certain of this fact, we are at the point of giving up the ghost. Schtitz in the Ghetto fills us with fear, and for good reason.

At six o'clock this evening, I sat in the home of one of my friends. It is Saturday and the Council offices are closed. Unannounced, a Jewish policeman entered the room and summoned me to see Dr. Elkes urgently. It seemed that something unusual had happened.

I set out to see Dr. Elkes. Already with him were Garfunkel, Kopelman, Goldberg, Hirsch Levin, Rabinovitz, and the leader of the Palemonas labor brigade, Szitelni. When I saw Szitelni there, I immediately understood the reason for my being summoned: there is news from Vilna.

The Ghetto is still in anguish over the murder of 5,000 Jews at Ponar. All of us want to know more details about the event. Szitelni had been in Vilna. He now revealed to us the horrifying details of the slaughter at Ponar.

According to Szitelni, 4,000 to 5,000 Jews were killed at Ponar. The mood in Vilna is gloomier than in Kovno. All Jews were removed from the townlets in the Vilna district. Two thousand of them were brought to the Vilna Ghetto. These Jews took everything they had in their homes—in the townlets in the Vilna district, where they had lived under relatively normal conditions—and brought their belongings to Vilna on carts belonging to Christians. They were absorbed into the Vilna Ghetto and taught its way of life.

Szitelni brought with him the most recent news bulletin published in the Vilna Ghetto, which was mostly devoted to the 2,000 new arrivals. It related the story of the arrival of a long convoy of small peasant carts loaded high with bundles and sacks. The old, women, and children sat on top of the carts while the men walked behind them. The typical picture of the wandering Jew.

Then an announcement was posted all over the Ghetto, saying that all the Jews who had recently arrived in the Vilna Ghetto must make preparations for a new journey, this time to Kovno. They were joined by a number of Kovno Jews who had been living in Vilna for some time, and who sought to take advantage of this opportunity to be reunited with their families in Kovno.

The Vilna Ghetto police were charged with overseeing the exodus from the Ghetto of the newly arrived Jews. A detachment of twenty-six Jewish policemen, headed by Gens and his deputy Desler,[1] were ready to escort these Jews on their way to Kovno and hand them over to the Council here.

The escort reinforced the belief of the Jews that the transfer was not a fraud on the part of the Germans. After all, they were being escorted by Gens the Jew, an intimate of the Germans, who was exempted from the obligation to wear a yellow badge on his clothes, and who was authorized to carry arms. If Gens, together with twenty-six Jewish policemen, was to escort the convoy, the transfer could be regarded as a safe walk—a walk on an iron bridge.

Upon their arrival at the train station in Vilna, the 2,000 Jews, together with their belongings, were packed into freight cars. Gens and his policemen, the protectors of thousands of Jews, were loaded onto the last car. At Lentvaris[2] they were to be joined by a train with another 3,000 Jews from the neighboring townlets who were also bound for Kovno.

Carpenters came to the train station in Vilna and boarded up the boxcar doors so that they could not be opened from inside. The car with the Jewish policemen was also boarded up in this fashion.

The train started moving in the direction of Kovno and stopped near Ponar. Lithuanian policemen opened the first cars and whispered to the passengers: "Run away! In a short time they will kill all of you." The Jews began to flee, running in all directions. There was a camp nearby, set up for the Lithuanian, Latvian, and White Guard Russian policemen, under the command of German policemen. These men immediately opened fire, with all kinds of weapons, on the groups of Jews trying to get away.

In the ensuing panic, with Jews running in all directions, the Germans started shooting at the Lithuanian policemen who seemed—in their eyes—to act suspiciously. All those bearing arms were drunk and started shooting at each other. People were falling like flies.

Then came the turn of the Jews from Sol, Lida, Swieciany, Smorgon, and Oszmiana to leave the train. They were robust and strong people, ready to defend themselves with axes, which they wielded in their hands. Having climbed out of the cars, they pounced on the policemen, killing and wounding a great many of them. Finally these fighting Jews were overcome; they died the death of heroes.

The area around the train took on a ghastly appearance. It was strewn with bodies with their limbs broken and torn apart by dumdum bullets. The slaughter was perpetrated with unspeakable ferocity and savagery. The drunken German policemen, and the dogs of the White Guard, had found themselves an arena in which to settle their scores with the Jews. The Lithuanian and Latvian policemen did not sit idle either; they rained a hail of bullets on the old people, on women, men, and children, thereby casting themselves out of the human family.

Only a handful of the Lithuanian policemen refused to fire on innocent people. They paid a heavy price for their human sentiments: those Lithuanian policemen who refused to take part in the slaughter were shot then and there by the Gestapo. By their refusal to fire, these murdered policemen gained the world to come, and brought honor to their homeland, Lithuania.

Gens was entrusted with the orderly transfer of the thousands of Jews from the Vilna district to Kovno. He could be relied upon to fulfill his duties to the letter, in compliance with the instructions issued by the authorities. He had brought the Jews from the townlets to Vilna, and now he was to escort them on the last stage of their journey to Kovno. He would deliver them to the representatives of the Jewish Council in Kovno. Thereby he would complete his duty in supervising this mass transfer.

The shooting continued for a long time, until the turn of the last car came. Here were the great and terrible Gens, the terror of the Vilna Ghetto, and his escorts, the Jewish policemen.

Gens set out like a master and a sovereign, accompanied by a personal guard of twenty-six Jewish policemen and his deputy. He set out like a commander leading his troops. Strict orders, a strong hand, no superfluous words; he was on an important and secret assignment on behalf of the authorities. He must take 5,000 Jews to Kovno. What he did not know was that he himself, despite his might and splendor, would be going as a captive, imprisoned together with his staff, in a sealed boxcar like all the rest. He did not know that not only would he be unable to supervise the "little people," but he himself would be subject to strict supervision. This was part of the fiendish game, which could have ended very badly for him.

Gens was a witness to the cruel spectacle of the mass murder, from which he and his entourage were saved at the last moment by Murer[3] of the Vilna Gestapo. Now Gens goes through tragedy. He had been deceived and deeply offended. "The king is naked," said the Jewish policemen accompanying him on the bogus journey to Kovno. He is ashamed of what his German friends have done to him. This time the beast of prey has sunk its teeth in his throat. For a moment it seemed to him that his head would fall. But somehow he managed to get away from the claws of the wild beast.

Gens's head swarms with thoughts: it is not good to live next to a beast of prey; he witnessed a massacre of scores of people who were his brothers and sisters. Gens is alive, but his methods are now bankrupt.

The Gestapo say that nothing like this is going to happen in Vilna itself, as the Ponar massacre was in connection with the Kovno Ghetto. But the Vilna Jews do not swallow this nonsense. The Gestapo have told us similar things here in Kovno, but we do not place any faith in their promises either.

In the Vilna Ghetto, all concerts and other cultural and artistic activities have been canceled. The clothes and belongings of the Jews murdered at Ponar were taken back to the Vilna Ghetto. What a cynical and barbarian attitude.

Our brethren from Vilna revealed to us the details of the Ponar slaughter so that we would not be deceived when the Germans talk to us about transferring thousands of people from one place to another. We must not move; we must stay where we are. We are acquainted with Asmodeus, the king of demons, and his stratagems.[4] It is possible, however, that he might be able to surprise us with a new trick. Each time, we have to deal with a new lie.

Szitelni has brought us many letters from Vilna. They all overflow with sorrow, anguish, hopelessness, and despair. Nevertheless, each letter also contains a spark of hope that we will be able to overcome our troubles and that we shall live to see better days.

Together with Dr. Elkes we have read many of these letters. We were eager to know what people thought after such a tragedy. People keep looking for hiding places until the storm blows over; needless to say, the reassurances of the Germans are no longer believed. The situation remains dangerous.

One letter in particular affected me personally. Some time ago I wanted to save the lives of a young couple from Vilna, and later I feared that perchance I might have caused their deaths.

Here is the story in a nutshell: a close acquaintance of mine lives in Vilna; he is a brother of a person very close to me here in the Kovno Ghetto. When Hermann revealed to us that the Vilna Ghetto was to be liquidated, that part of its population was to be transferred to us, and that people unfit for work and the aged would be transferred to Riga, whereas the rest would be liquidated *in situ,* I began looking for an opportunity to pass this information on to my acquaintance in Vilna. I added an offer for him and his wife to come to Kovno as soon as possible. A day or two later I managed to send off a letter to them. I happened to run into a Pole at the home of an acquaintance of mine, a peasant by the name of Kutkevich; the Pole was to set out for Vilna on the same day. I had with me a letter written to a friend in Vilna by his sister. Then and there I added a few words in my own handwriting: "In heaven's name, come quickly to Kovno." Since I was bound by an oath of secrecy to the Council, I could not reveal to him the reason for this urgency. I also wrote to him that his sister was very ill and that he and his wife should come to Kovno at once.

When the 2,000 Jews set out from Vilna to Kovno, I was certain that my friend would take advantage of the opportunity and join them. Then I was seized by fear and panic: perhaps he had met his death as a result of his joining that convoy. From then on I could not find a moment's peace. I feared that I had caused the death of two people.

A heavy stone was lifted from my heart when I read the letter from this friend. He wrote that he had planned to go to Kovno with the 2,000 Jews, but had been refused permission to join them. In this way he was saved from certain death. The conclusion: in times like these, one must be wary of dispensing advice, even when it is motivated by good intentions.

There were other letters like this one: people wrote to their relatives about having wanted to use the opportunity to come to Kovno. Everything had been packed. At the last moment their plans were changed and they survived.

All the letters overflow with sorrow and grief, mourning and despair; and yet there is a spark of hope in every one of them. It strengthens our faith that we shall brave all the storms, and survive.

They are very sad, these letters from Vilna. Tragic is the story related by Szitelni. But our faith that the eternal glory of Israel shall not fail is as strong as ever.

1. Jacob Gens was chief of the Jewish police in the Vilna Ghetto; his deputy was Salek Desler.
2. Lentvaris, near Vilna, close to a railway junction, was a place of refuge for many Jews who had escaped from Vilna; they were sheltered there by local anti-German partisans—mostly Lithuanians.
3. Franz Murer, adjutant to the governor of the Vilna district, served as chief of the Vilna Ghetto on behalf of the local German military and civilian authorities.
4. Asmodeus (Ashmadai), the king of demons, is a figure of Jewish mythology.

APRIL 16, 1943

"We had a tough day today," Garfunkel said to me, just before we left the Council offices on our way home. He recounted the day's events.

Lipzer came to the Council offices first thing in the morning. He told us the following: the Gestapo accuses the Jews in the Ghetto; during a bombing raid on Kovno, so the Gestapo allege, signal rockets were shot from the Ghetto in the direction of the enemy aircraft. The Gestapo issued a warning that should this incident occur again, half of the Jewish police personnel will be sent to the Ninth Fort. The message is clear.

We thought: How can a serious person imagine that the Ghetto inmates, living under such harsh conditions as they do these days—particularly after the Ponar massacre, and at a time when the German leadership speaks again about the total extermination of the Jewish people in Europe—be capable of giving signals to foreign planes?

We heard this accusation against the Jews in the Ghetto and we thought: perhaps Lipzer exaggerates. The Ghetto inmates simply cannot believe a story like this. On the other hand, it is the Gestapo we are dealing with. This is why we must not say that the accusation is illogical. It seems that there is method in this madness.

We held a meeting to discuss how to get out of this mess. We called Kopelman, the chief of the Jewish police, and Natkin, our liaison with the Ghetto command headquarters, and asked them to speak to the commandant of the Ghetto and explain to him that, during an air-raid alarm, Jewish policemen patrol the Ghetto streets and enforce the ordinance about total blackout, as well as the ban on walking in the streets. Lithuanian policemen also take part in these patrols. During the last air-raid alarm no one saw any signs of signals coming from the Ghetto. It is imperative to explain this to the Ghetto commandant and to obtain from him confirmation in writing. Afterward Kopelman can go to the Gestapo and deny the accusations, adding the necessary clarifications.

Our discussion was interrupted by a telephone call from Miller, who wished to speak with me. He was telephoning from the workshops. He wanted to know whether there was a flour mill in the Ghetto; was it in working order, and who supplied grains for grinding?

I told Miller that the Ghetto flour mill is located at Linkuvos Street and that it grinds rye supplied by the Ghetto Guard. The Ghetto Guard officials confiscate the rye from the workers returning from the city. The flour mill operates only a few days a month.

Miller asked me to wait for him in the Council offices. I contacted the flour mill workers immediately, telling them to get their house in order and to ensure that no large quantity of rye would be found on the premises. I also telephoned Segalson at the workshops, to find out what was the matter. Segalson revealed to me that Schtitz of the Gestapo is also visiting the workshops and that he spoke with Miller about the flour mill.

This is very unpleasant. The Ghetto flour mill "sins" here and there. First, we have not informed the authorities through the official channels about its existence; we told them about it in a casual manner. Secondly, where do we get the rye, in view of the fact that we are being supplied with ready-made bread? Our excuse does not hold much water: quite often several dozen kilograms of rye are confiscated from the Jewish workers at the Ghetto gate. We receive this rye for our soup kitchen and grind it at the flour mill. Actually, the flour mill grinds not dozens but hundreds of kilograms of rye. It goes without saying that any information concerning these irregularities which reaches the Gestapo becomes a dangerous business.

Miller failed to put in an appearance at the Council offices. He took the Gestapo car; Schtitz and a fellow Gestapo man, Shmutlak, climbed out of their cars and entered the Council offices. Schtitz comes to the Ghetto very often, without having recourse to the Council. He is in the habit of settling his business at the Ghetto guard, at the Jewish police building, and in the Ghetto workshops. Once he arrived at the Council offices. He lingered a while in my room and asked Kopelman whether a Council meeting was being held at the time. He entered the meeting room followed by Shmutlak and Kopelman. The latter kept calling constantly: "Attention!" Dr. Elkes, Garfunkel, and Goldberg were present in the meeting room. As Schtitz entered the room they rose from their seats. I followed the "guests" into the room.

Schtitz got down to business without any delay. He said that his comrade had seen with his own eyes luminous rockets being fired from the Ghetto in the direction of the enemy aircraft. Three rockets were fired during the first attack, and two more during the second attack. His comrade had even noticed the green and purple hue of the rockets.

Kopelman tried to convince Schtitz that this was impossible. Jewish policemen had patrolled the Ghetto streets throughout the air raid and had not noticed any signals being given to the enemy aircraft. The Lithuanian policemen even fired several shots in the direction of the flares released from these aircraft. The blackout in the Ghetto during the air raid was complete.

Dr. Elkes and Garfunkel also tried to convince Schtitz that signaling enemy planes from the Ghetto was simply unimaginable.

Schtitz remained as unmoved as a rock: he insisted that his comrade had seen the thing happening. He repeated his warning, that if it happened again half the Jewish police force would be taken to the Ninth Fort.

I stood looking at Schtitz's features all the time. He stood stiff as a sculpture carved in stone. His thick fingers were tucked into his belt; as usual his face resembled a mask, his look was sharp and threatening. He reminded me of a beast of prey. He did not even raise his voice, but his appearance spoke of omnipotence and the ability to inflict pain. Having said what he had to say, he left.

Schtitz's departure left all of us in a gloomy mood. His announcement amounted to a blood libel, plain and simple. Everyone took his warning seriously. The Council placed the Jewish police on alert to see that every Ghetto street would be patrolled during air-raid alarms.

Kopelman and Natkin then went up to see the Ghetto commandant. Schtitz had already visited him and repeated his accusation, but this time in a different version: it was no longer his friend, but a German soldier and a Lithuanian, who had both reported to the Gestapo that they had seen light rockets rise from Paneriu Street—a street bordering on the Ghetto.

In all probability this is a Lithuanian invention. Some Lithuanians in the city said that the Jews in the Ghetto rejoiced at the recent Russian bombing of Kovno.[1]

The German commandant did not believe Schtitz's story either. He said that he had heard nothing about such signals. He reached an agreement with Kopelman and Natkin that in future, during air-raid alarms, Jewish policemen and members of the Ghetto fire brigade would patrol the area together with Lithuanian policemen.

Hardly had this matter been closed when we had another problem. The deputy chief of the Jewish police, Abramovitz, and Aronstamm, who is in charge at the Jewish police of recruitment for the Jewish labor force, sent a message that a Jewish woman with a small child had been brought to the Ghetto gate a short while ago. They were brought there by a German. When asked whether he carried any paper allowing him to bring the woman and the child to the Ghetto, the German said that everything was in order, and then made off.

It turned out that the woman was the daughter of a Council guard, Kolevitz. She had arrived from the Zezmer camp. According to her, she had been in the train bound for Kovno together with thousands of Jews. In Ponar she presented herself as a Christian, whereupon the Lithuanians saved her and her child. Now the two have arrived at the Kovno Ghetto where they have relatives.

The matter turned out to be not at all simple. Under Gestapo standing orders, every additional person entering the Ghetto must be reported to the Gestapo. In particular, the Gestapo has specifically warned us against receiving anyone who survived the massacre at Ponar; such persons must be handed over to the Gestapo immediately. If only the woman and the child had not been brought by a German to the Ghetto gate. Had they been able to blend themselves into the labor brigades returning from the city, it would not be a problem. No one would know about it. But since the woman and the child were brought to the Ghetto gate by a German and handed over the Ghetto police, the police are responsible for taking steps according to standing orders. In this case the situation is clear: if they are handed over to the Gestapo, they will never return. On the other hand, failure to inform the Gestapo about this would entail serious consequences. We held a discussion at the Council on how to save the woman and her child. In the end we decided to admit the child to the hospital, ostensibly for an operation the child had to undergo as a result of an inflammation of the appendix; according to this version, mother and child had both been sent here from the Zezmer camp. They would both stay in the hospital for the time needed for the operation. In point of fact, this also must be reported, but in the past we did not bother informing the Gestapo about such cases.

The woman and the child were admitted to the hospital. We hope this whole affair will end well.

Having returned home for lunch I was again summoned to the Council, together with director of the nutrition department, Rapoport. It turned out that an investigation is being pursued concerning waste at the airfield. Last year 4,000 Jewish workers were working there. This year also, many Jews work there. The person in charge of supplying food to the workers has been arrested in connection with suspected irregularities. He had at his disposal huge quantities of food for the laborers and for the workers' kitchen. He is suspected of withholding some of the food placed at his disposal.

Today a commission consisting of representatives of the German Air Force, of the labor office, and of the city governor's office arrived in the Ghetto. Its task is to assess the system of distribution of foodstuffs we receive. They questioned us about when we received the supplies, in what quantity, and to whom we distributed them.

Such investigations make our life difficult and do not bode well. In this particular case we receive the foodstuffs from the airfield for our workers there. We get less than what is due to us; nevertheless we must lay aside a certain quantity of food for the hospital, for the children's home, and for the soup kitchen. All these actions are illegal from the German point of view.

The workers who returned from the city in the evening had sad news to relate. An engineer had revealed that another train packed with Jews had arrived at Ponar, where they had been executed. Among them were Jews from Molodechna. This is horrifying. Now everybody believes it. In addition, rumors have spread that by May 25 the Baltic countries will be "cleansed of Jews."

The Jews in the Ghetto have started counting the days and the hours. We do not know what each day will bring.

After a day like this, which began with a blood libel and ended with terrible news on future "actions," there is no wonder that a Ghetto inmate is crushed and exhausted, especially if one adds all the usual daily fears. "This is too much for one day," said Garfunkel to me, and he is right. So many frayed nerves and heartbeats in one single day. And the main thing: the price paid in blood.

One day in the Ghetto.

1. Soviet bombers had struck at military targets near Kovno, including the Aleksotas airfield.

APRIL 18, 1943

Schtitz visited the Council offices the day before yesterday and accused the Ghetto of firing signal rockets during bombing raids. He added that this would cost the Ghetto heavy casualties; he even mentioned a specific number (half of the Jewish police force) of people to be sent to the Ninth Fort. As a result, the Council and the Jewish police applied themselves seriously to the task of organizing the guard in the Ghetto during air attacks.

Every night, beginning at 8 P.M., a squad of Jewish policemen is on full alert at the disposal of the Ghetto commandant. At the first sound of air-raid alarm, all the Jewish policemen take up positions in their precincts and, together with Lithuanian policemen, begin patrolling the Ghetto streets. They are on guard against any provocations, above all on the part of the Lithuanian guards or irresponsible, thoughtless Ghetto inmates.

The day before yesterday the police were placed on alert at night. It was another air raid. First the alarm was sounded, followed by the sound of the aircraft flying in the direction of East Prussia. However, some bombs fell in the Ghetto—on the sports ground[1]—as well as in the vicinity of the radio station, in Aleksotas, in the vicinity of the Maistas plants, and in several other places.

Jewish policemen and members of the Ghetto fire brigade, under the command of the German commandant of the Ghetto, patrolled the Ghetto streets. They were joined by the Lithuanian policemen, together with the chief of the Jewish police, Kopelman. Within minutes, all the lights in the Ghetto were put out. The streets were empty: only here and there could be seen the reinforced police units patrolling the area.

The Ghetto inmates were stunned by the threats voiced by Schtitz; many feared that the Germans had made these false accusations solely as a way of taking their revenge on us. All inmates had abided strictly by the blackout orders, and had made sure not to appear on the streets during the air-raid alarm.

The chief of the Jewish police, who is the main target of the serious warnings issued by the Germans, seeks to ensure that the Ghetto inmates do, in fact, abide by the instruction during air attacks; particularly in view of the serious threat against the lives of seventy-five young Jewish policemen. This is why Kopelman tours the Ghetto area without respite, making sure that all the instructions are carried out to the letter. No signs whatsoever of any signals coming from the Ghetto could be discerned, and no rockets were fired. It could be said that the Ghetto was all right that night. We thought that this time they would not dare to accuse us of any misdeeds. Indeed, the German commandant of the Ghetto confirmed publicly that everything in the Ghetto was in perfect order.

Yesterday, in the morning, the Council received a detailed report about a series of measures taken by the Jewish police during last night's bombing raid.

The report noted with satisfaction that all the necessary steps had been taken to keep order in the Ghetto, even though everyone was convinced that on previous occasions no signaling by means of rockets had taken place.

Some members of the Jewish labor brigade working for the Gestapo revealed, however, that there had been more talk at the Gestapo about rockets being allegedly shot from the Ghetto during the air attack the day before yesterday. No one believes these allegations. Are they really preparing another blood libel?

This morning the Ghetto was electrified by a rumor that the Gestapo again accuses the Ghetto of firing signal rockets during the last air attack; it is feared that the accusation was issued in advance of some future "action." On Sunday, quiet vanished as if by a magic wand; the Ghetto residents' faces reflected concern and fear. "What's going on here?" people kept asking each other. All of a sudden ominous rumors, passing from mouth to mouth, have poisoned the atmosphere in the Ghetto. This whole story about rockets allegedly being fired from the Ghetto—is it not some kind of fiendish plot? No one believes this story. Many are convinced that the Gestapo does not believe it either. They just look for victims.

It is a gloomy day in the Ghetto. The mood at the Council offices is not much different. Today we had a meeting at the Council. The prevailing view is that we must get a clear statement from the Ghetto commandant, confirming that he himself did not see any signals being fired from the ground, even though he patrols the Ghetto streets every night. The Jewish police command should draw up a detailed report surveying all the measures taken during air raids: Jewish and Lithuanian policemen together with the Ghetto commandant and the Jewish police command patrolling the Ghetto streets, a swift blackout of all houses, and the removing of passers-by from the streets. This report should be submitted to the Gestapo chiefs. They should also be told that the firing of signal rockets from the Ghetto is simply unimaginable. We must defend ourselves with all the means at our disposal against the attempts to charge us with blood libel.

We must obtain more information about the German plans concerning us. We have been informed that a wave of "actions" against the Jews is sweeping over Poland. In France, Belgium, and the Netherlands, a total "cleaning" is being prepared.[2] The German press spews fire and brimstone on the Jews every day. Every day we are reminded that the Germans brandish the sword from which we will not be able to escape.

To us, confined and crushed as we are in the Ghetto, the furious onslaught of the Nazi press against the Jews seems exaggerated. What is the purpose of this raging storm? To exterminate us? After all, we are so few in number and so weak. Any gust of wind is enough: several members of the Gestapo, together with some Lithuanian partisans, armed with instruments of destruction, are capable of putting an end to our existence.

Perhaps the real target is not us but our brethren overseas? But this also is preposterous. The time of German victories is gone and over. Only anger, bitterness, and disappointment are left to them from all their grandiose plans. They see their sworn enemy—overseas Jewry—without being able to lay their hand on it. This is why they are furious. They can, however, exterminate us in the blink of an eye.

This afternoon we gathered for a Council meeting at Dr. Elkes's apartment. The meeting was also attended by Kopelman and Lipzer. We decided to dispatch Dr. Elkes and Kopelman tomorrow, to call on Schtitz at the Gestapo, and if need be to see Jaeger also. They should make clear to the Gestapo chiefs the utter senselessness of accusing the Ghetto inmates of firing signal rockets during air raids. The Council delegation should also try to learn about plans for the Ghetto and its inmates.

We wait impatiently for the outcome of the visit of Dr. Elkes and Kopelman to the Gestapo. Even though we do not have any faith in the Gestapo's promises, and despite their having deceived us many times over, still, it is good to hear some reassuring words—even from them.

1. Avraham Tory later recalled that a part of the Ghetto vegetable garden had been cleared to form a sports ground. German soldiers, watching the Jews play soccer there, would often amuse themselves by calling out: "The team that wins will be killed last." (That is to say, when, in due course, the killings began.)

2. In March 1943 more than 10,000 Greek Jews, 7,000 German Jews, 5,000 Dutch Jews, and 4,000 French Jews were deported by train to the death camps at Treblinka, Sobibor, and Majdanek, as well as to Auschwitz. In April 1943 a further 25,000 Greek Jews, 5,500 Dutch Jews, 1,400 Belgian Jews, 938 Jews from Berlin, and 20 Jews from Avignon were deported to their deaths in Treblinka, Sobibor, and Auschwitz.

APRIL 19, 1943

The morning hours brought back memories of the first period in the life of the Ghetto, of the time when we lived in the shadow of terror, between one "action" and the next; of the time when members of the Council used to set out every day for the city to plead with the Germans for some respite for the Ghetto inmates. The Council members' comings and goings were followed by the tense Ghetto inmates with deep apprehension.

Has a new period of blood begun in the Ghetto? People again find themselves living in the shadow of terror. News reaches us from everywhere about "actions" and massacres—in Poland, in White Russia, and in the more remote territories under the German occupation.[1] In the Ghetto a waiting game is being played again: when will they take us out of here to exterminate us?

Stories abound about bands of young people fleeing from the Vilna Ghetto to the forest. They are said to be joining hidden camps of Soviet prisoners-of-war who have escaped from their captors—Lithuanian deserters, Polish guerrilla fighters, and various types of riffraff hiding in the forest. They leave the Ghetto, from which thousands of people can be taken for extermination at a moment's notice. They join the dozens of escapees who lately have virtually taken over the forests of Lithuania.

It is true that life is no safer in the forest than in the Ghetto; every day means a rendezvous with death. The Germans seldom put an appearance in the forest—very seldom. They are afraid to show their faces there. However, it also happens that when they do come to the forest in force they succeed in killing scores of people. But they also lose quite a few of their own.

Many people, above all Jews, have nothing to lose in the forest. They leave civilization and social life behind and flee to the forest to live in an abandoned barn or in a pit. In the winter they suffer hunger and cold, rain and snow. Not everyone can brave such conditions. Not everyone has a strong fist to defend himself. Not everyone can be a hero.

Many have heard about the free life in the forest, and quite a few go there. There is no difference there between the Jew and the Christian, the Russian and the German, the Pole and the Lithuanian. There is no Ghetto fence there, no yellow badge. There are no people of the likes of Rauca or Schtitz, Miller or Cramer. The people in the forest speak with the enemy in the language of force.

Feinberg is one of them. He carries within him a deep and painful wound. His wife and child lived with him in the Ghetto. One morning, Lithuanian partisans surrounded his house. The situation was hopeless. His wife said she would hide in the attic. They would not hurt a child. Feinberg himself should get away. He cast a last glance on the sleeping child, kissed his wife, and fled. From a distance he watched his wife and child being led by the henchmen to the nearby village, where Lithuanian partisans put an end to their lives.

Now Feinberg lives for one purpose only—revenge. I thought to myself: where do people like Feinberg come from? I searched my soul for the likes of him. And here they are, fighting.

Every day, life in the Ghetto becomes more difficult. In our mind's eye we keep seeing the henchmen, the Ninth Fort. The Council too has lost its faith and patience. Its members summoned up their strength and decided to meet with the enemy; let him say whether there is hope for them to live or, perhaps, that their end is near. In a gloomy mood, Dr. Elkes and Kopelman set out for the city. They were back at 11 A.M.

Dr. Elkes and Kopelman delivered their report about their visit to the Gestapo to a restricted circle of the members of the Council. They had been received by Schtitz. Before the meeting with Schtitz, Lipzer had informed them that the Gestapo believed that signal rockets had been fired from the Ghetto during the air raid. A Gestapo driver, Fritz Reiter, was a witness. He claimed that he had been in the Ghetto during the air raid and had seen with his own eyes the rockets shooting up into the sky. Rauca had also seen them.

The Council delegation submitted to Schtitz a written statement from the Ghetto police concerning the events in the Ghetto during the air raid. A dispute then developed between the two parties: Schtitz took the side of the witnesses who had seen the signal rockets being fired from the Ghetto toward the enemy aircraft. According to these "witnesses," a hundred rockets had been fired.

Dr. Elkes and Kopelman had countered by arguing that nothing unusual had taken place in the Ghetto that night, and that no one had seen signals being given to the enemy planes. The Ghetto commandant confirmed their statement.

Schtitz kept insisting that he was bound to believe the testimony of Fritz Reiter and Rauca, who had seen the thing with their own eyes. Dr. Elkes and Kopelman replied that if this, indeed, was the case, why had the Germans failed to intervene then and there? Schtitz replied that he would be in the Ghetto during the next air raid and would bring with him a heavy machine gun. Should the same thing happen again, he, Schtitz, would personally charge the enemy with his weapon. He added: "If, as you maintain, there were no shots into the air, you must not be afraid of my firing my gun."

The conversation moved on to the recurring subject: the gloomy mood in the Ghetto after the Ponar massacre and in view of the persisting rumors about numerous "actions" in the countries under German occupation. Schtitz's reply was that all these rumors are propaganda—nothing else. Indeed, it is true that many Jews have been evacuated at Ponar. "But do you know why? Because these Jews had collaborated with the White Russian gangs.[2] As a result of this cooperation, eight members of the Gestapo were killed and forty wounded. How could these Jews be allowed into the Ghetto? But, rest assured, nothing like this will happen here. The local Jews will not be hurt. All the rumors spread by the Lithuanians are nothing but propaganda."

Schtitz gives an example of propaganda: "Moscow radio has announced that on the Führer's birthday—tomorrow—the city of Kovno will be destroyed and turned into a heap of ashes.[3] You can see for yourselves what propaganda is. The Ghetto may rest assured that nothing bad will happen to it."

At this point Schtitz reveals a secret: if anything does happen, it will only be to the old and the infirm. For the time being, however, it is just a thought, a remote possibility. Such a development is not in the cards. When it does happen, no secret will be made of it. He himself will come to the Council and say: we need such and such people. Schtitz advises the Council members to issue a written and oral announcement to the Ghetto inmates, to say that all the rumors making the rounds, about "actions" and the like, are without substance. This announcement may be made in the name of the Gestapo.

At the close of the meeting, the members of the delegation asked Schtitz to allow them to meet with Jaeger. "What do you need to see Jaeger for?" asked Schtitz. "We would like to speak to him," Dr. Elkes and Kopelman replied, "about the same subjects: the situation in the Ghetto, the various rumors, etc. We would like to hear the views of the person with authority on these matters."

Schtitz: "Such a meeting is unnecessary. First, Jaeger is very busy and, second, he will not tell you more than I did."

This was the end of the meeting with Schtitz.

The Council decided to summon the department heads and the senior officials of the Council, in order to report to them about the meeting with Schtitz. It was also decided to conceal from them one detail: the possibility of a German "action" against the old and the infirm.

Soon afterward, all the senior officials gathered in the Council meeting room to hear the report about the meeting with Schtitz. Needless to say, some of his disclosures, particularly the one about the signals from the Ghetto to the enemy planes, seemed very odd. But, in general, the report was rather positive. Those assembled received the impression that the Ghetto does not face serious danger in the foreseeable future. This seems to contribute to an easing of tensions.

Today is Passover eve. I wanted to get some encouragement in order to re-call—in these days of slavery and enslavement—the miracle of the Exodus from Egypt.

Schtitz's reassurances, that no action is planned against the Ghetto in the near future, spread quickly in the Ghetto; enabling those in the Ghetto to relax a little. Sparks of hope replaced the sense of despair. On the holy day commemorating our freedom we tend to believe Schtitz's promises. We believe in the Exodus taking place for each generation. The more we are being enslaved, the greater is our faith. *Am Israel Hai* (the people of Israel live).

1. In April 1943, along with the Jews deported from Greece, Holland, Belgium, and Berlin, the Jews murdered in Eastern Europe included 4,000 from Swienciany, 2,500 from Oszmiana, 1,800 from Widze (near Vilna), and, in eastern Galicia, 800 from Trembowla (April 7), 2,000 from Buczacz (April 13), 600 from Kopyczynce (April 15), 3,000 from Jaworow (April 18), and 800 from Borszczow (April 19).

2. Peasants from White Russia (Belorussia) had begun to organize into partisan groups to fight against the German occupation, supported by arms, ammunition, and personnel parachuted to them by the Soviet Army. By the spring of 1943, these groups had begun to disrupt seriously German road and rail communications in the more remote areas. Jews were frequently found fighting as part of these groups, as soldiers, instructors, and doctors.

3. Hitler was born on the evening of April 20, 1889. Soviet propaganda erred only in the location of the "action"; it was the liquidation of the Warsaw Ghetto which had been planned for that day. Indeed, the Warsaw uprising broke out on April 19, 1943.

APRIL 21, 1943

Yesterday the Jews in the Ghetto celebrated the festival of Passover. Many Ghetto inmates celebrated the first night of Passover in full splendor. Following the Council's announcement that the Gestapo views the situation in the Ghetto as stable, they had a reason to overcome their abject mood and to celebrate the Passover festival as prescribed.

The same thing occurs over and over again in the Ghetto: all of a sudden everyone is overcome by melancholy and gloom as if we were standing on the edge of a bottomless chasm; but then some news, a hint, a scrap of information, is received from a Gestapo official, to the effect that for the time being nothing is going to happen. The Ghetto inmates cling to this temporary relief of their plight ("this too is for the best," they say to one another); let the quiet prevail even for one day, because tomorrow, something may befall us. Perhaps the redemption will arrive at a moment's notice. We live the life of the moment.

Yesterday, the first day of the Passover holy day, the Jews discarded their everyday clothes and dressed in their best attire. It was a sunny spring day and the people looked more relaxed and festive.

Many workers were absent from work yesterday. The Germans, however, pay no heed to the Jewish holy days. The director of the German labor office, Hermann, announced yesterday morning that he would come to the Ghetto and "trample underfoot" its inmates, should the workers fail to show up at work again today. There are people in the Ghetto who refuse to work on Saturdays and holy days. They cause problems for us.

The Council has decided to recruit mothers with small children for work today. Until now these women have been exempted from work-duty. They are being recruited on the condition that an elderly woman will be present in their home to look after their children. At five o'clock in the morning the Jewish police were busy taking the women out of their homes and taking them to the Ghetto gate, from where they were scheduled to go out to work.

The Council offices stayed open during the first two days of Passover. However, the working day ended at 6 P.M. in order to enable the workers to observe the Passover festival in the early hours of the evening, in case, God forbid, of blackout later due to an air raid. Such attacks have recently become quite frequent.

Yesterday, the first day of the holy day, Rabbi Shmukler passed away in the Ghetto. We are grieved by the news of his death; Rabbi Shmukler had been bound to the Ghetto and to the Council with all his soul. If the history of the Ghetto is ever written, the name of Rabbi Shmukler will be mentioned in it with affection.

I got to know Rabbi Shmukler well during the transfer of the Jews to the Ghetto in July and August 1941. He was among the first members of the Jewish Committee for the transfer. He had a warm Jewish heart, and he believed in the nearness of redemption with all his heart and soul. Whenever he met with his fellow Jews—at prayer groups in neighborhood synagogues, or in private apartments—he always found a proper quotation from our sages, or a proverb, or some other clue which proved, with signs and wonders, that the Jews would live to see better times. "You will see it with your own eyes," he used to say. He himself did not live to see the day.

If there were complaints against rabbis and the ultra-orthodox "fanatics"— and there were many such complaints—and if there were scores to "settle" with them at every step from the first day of the destruction of Lithuanian Jewry until today—there were very few complaints addressed to Rabbi Shmukler. Hundreds of Jews accompanied him on his journey to the grave. It was a mass funeral. In his eulogy, Jacob Goldberg found a proper analogy to describe our love for Rabbi Shmukler: the Germans say that their laws enjoin them to hate the Jews, whereas they hate the Lithuanians from the bottom of their hearts. With Rabbi Shmukler it was like this: not long ago, the chief rabbi of Kovno, Rabbi Shapiro, died. We followed him on his last journey as the chief rabbi and as a representative of the community, according to our ancient tradition. Rabbi Shmukler we accompanied according to the inclination of our heart.

APRIL 23, 1943

Yesterday, when I went to the city and regional government offices, I ran into several Lithuanians, my former friends, who conveyed to me their condolences; the Polish underground radio had announced that the Jewish Ghetto in Warsaw was going up in flames; the news had spread quickly in Kovno. The Germans had tried to evacuate the Jews from the Warsaw Ghetto in order to transfer them to another labor camp.[1] The Jews refused to carry out the evacuation order and decided to stay put. The Germans reacted with machine gun and cannon fire against the Ghetto, which was subsequently set on fire. The Jews defended themselves with all their might, weapons in hand, against the German fury.

This news made a great impression in the city. People kept talking about it with a great deal of emotion and shock. They viewed the German action as an abomination.

When my former Lithuanian friends revealed the news to me, they looked at me as if I were a man doomed to death. This means that a similar development is also possible here. The same rulers, the same henchmen. Some of my friends advised me to flee; otherwise it might be too late. "Flee to the forest," they said.

"You've got nothing to lose. The enemy must be resisted; the people in Warsaw were right to revolt. They were done for anyway."

Hearing the news of this horrifying event from my former Lithuanian friends, and seeing their angry faces, I felt a shiver running through my body. Outwardly, however, I showed no sign of nervousness. I understood that the Lithuanians regard the slaughter of 35,000 Jews as an ill omen for themselves also. After all, not only Jews, but Poles too, were murdered in Poland; tomorrow this horror might befall the Lithuanians in Kovno. This is why they were so excited. Many of them have been fleeing to the forest and putting up resistance to the Germans.

Thoughts like these have preoccupied us in recent days. We must flee, but where to? Who should run away? And—the main question—when? Is there really any place to run to? Should we, who are so much involved in the Ghetto life with all our heart and conscience, flee too? We are plagued by thousands of questions and we feel the thousands of threads tying us to the place.

The second question is easier and clearer, even though more ominous. Should it turn out that the Ghetto finds itself surrounded by armed policemen or soldiers; should heavy machine guns be positioned in the Ghetto and we be given an order to start marching off to some unknown destination—we will refuse to obey. I have not the slightest idea how this will be done, but I am certain we will rise up and struggle.

I recalled a conversation between Schtitz and his Jewish dentist, Kvitner. Schtitz said then that in the future an "action" in the Ghetto would not be an easy feat. There are arms in the Ghetto and the Jews can be expected to defend themselves. Such an operation would be impossible without a toll of victims.

Possibly that was a logical conclusion that Schtitz had drawn from the situation; after several cases of Jewish resistance, such a reaction must be expected. However, it is also possible that he had come to that conclusion on the basis of secret information supplied to him by some shady characters among the Ghetto residents.

There are such doubtful characters among us. Their existence was revealed last week when six or seven individuals, who once had faced grave dangers, were summoned to the Gestapo for an interrogation and then, having been interrogated, were unexpectedly released. Ever since then they have been summoned back several times to the Gestapo, ostensibly for an investigation; in fact, they pass on, or are forced to pass on, information about what is going on in the Ghetto.

It appears therefore that Schtitz also has come to a conclusion that no future operation against the Ghetto would be possible without German casualties. This is also clear to all of us: we will put up active resistance in case of an "action" in the Ghetto.

When I returned to the Ghetto, I found that the destruction of the Warsaw Ghetto had already been learned of. This news made a depressing impression on the Ghetto inmates.

Today a meeting of our underground group, Matzok, has been convened to discuss the question of what steps we should take and how. The meeting was overshadowed by the heavy impression left by the sad news from Warsaw, and the possible implications for us. This time we did not engage in theoretical discussions, or in a debate about the finer points of our future plans. Instead, we tried to assess the factual situation, and were determined to draw practical conclusions in case a situation similar to that in the Warsaw Ghetto should develop here in Kovno. The war has entered its final and decisive stage. There is not much time left for the Ghetto. For us, any moment may be too late. For this reason, we follow with great interest the attempts undertaken by neutral countries to conclude a peace agreement. However, we find it difficult to believe that, in the war between a tiger and a lion, suddenly an agreement would be reached with the two sides refraining from bloodshed and the occupation of territory. These mighty rivals do not get tired quickly. It is possible that everything around us will be destroyed even before the soldiers fall on the battlefield. There are therefore many dangers lying in store for us. We fear lest we be cut down before our enemy is vanquished.

The six of us gathered today to try to weigh all the possibilities.[2] In this battle between titans, we must prepare for eventualities by drawing up a rescue plan of our own: how should we act in the case of a partial "action" in the Ghetto, or in the case of an attempt at the total extermination of its residents, or in the case of a total evacuation of the Ghetto? What would be the right moment to hide away in various hiding places? When should we cut the barbed-wire fence for a mass escape? Should we go to the forest, or try to look for shelter in villages? How should we establish contact with the outside world? From where would come the resources necessary for carrying out our plans? When should we act alone, or should we take our families with us?

We have to clarify these problems to ourselves. Then we must search for ways and means to find some solution to the problems besetting us. Today we succeeded at least in clarifying some of those problems. How to find solutions— this we do not know yet. We have practically no resources at our disposal. For years we have tried to acquire them, but external forces have prevented us from doing so; we have been threatened, particularly by Lipzer, who kept warning us about the long arm of the Gestapo.

We must create everything from scratch, from the very beginning. We must spare no effort to procure the means necessary for our rescue. Each day may catch us unawares. Such were the bloody matters—bloody in the full sense of that term—that we discussed today at the Matzok meeting.

1. In fact, the Jews of Warsaw were being transferred to Treblinka, a death camp in which—as in Chelmno, Sobibor, and Belzec—no selection was made between the able-bodied and others, but where all but a hundred or so Jews—chosen for work tasks in the camp itself— were murdered by gas within hours of reaching the camp. More than 700,000 Jews were murdered at Treblinka within twelve months, 300,000 of them from Warsaw.
2. The six were Zvi Levin, Aizik Srebnitzki, Avraham Golub, Shlomo Goldstein, Dr. Nachman Shapiro, and Dr. Eliyahu Segal.

APRIL 26, 1943

The last days of Passover this year coincided with the Christian Easter. Public institutions and other workplaces employing Jews remain closed. This is the reason for the festive atmosphere in the Ghetto.

For the Christians in the city, this year's holy day has nothing festive about it. They live in a constant fear of bombs falling on the city from the air. Sudden air-raid alarms at night force them to rush out of their beds and hurry to their cellars, which provide a safe shelter.

The Jews in the Ghetto are "free" from this fear. During air-raid alarms they stay where they are. Those in charge of the bombing raids probably know where to drop their lethal load.

Those who hate us do not put in an appearance in the Ghetto during this festive season. We do not have to get up early in the morning and hurry to the Ghetto gate; there is no work to be done. This is why we are in a holiday mood.

In these days of relaxation, everyone is naturally drawn to his own personal interests: cultural discussions, creative thinking, and such like, which provide some mental nourishment.

Yesterday a third Passover seder was held at the vocational training school.[1] Pupils in the higher grades are organized in small groups which engage intensively in Zionist activities. The declared objective of the vocational training school—which was set up after the closing of all educational institutions in the Ghetto—was to train skilled workers for various workplaces. After a short period of education and vocational training, the school is able to graduate carpenters, construction workers, cobblers, tailors, etc.

Simultaneously with the issuing of a license for the vocational training school, the director of the German labor office, Hermann, was appointed as its supervisor. He is a relatively lenient man. On account of his numerous duties, he practically never intervenes in the affairs of the school or the activities of its students. We, on the other hand, take a very active interest in everything taking place at the school, in the curriculum and its implementation. We make sure that Jewish children will, in addition to the vocational training, receive a Zionist education in the spirit of the Jewish heritage and our national aspirations. Dr.

Chaim Nachman Shapiro is a scrupulous and loyal principal in that respect.

The third Passover night arranged for the pupils of the vocational training school took place in the hall of the workers' kitchen. Between forty and fifty young boys, aged from twelve to fifteen, were seated around long tables set for the Passover meal. Each boy had his own Passover Haggadah in front of him, from which to read and sing. The girls and the boys were dressed in their best clothes, their faces beaming, their eyes shining.

When Garfunkel and I entered the tidy, decorated room, the young people rose from their seats and gave us a hearty welcome. After we were seated, the Passover night service began.

A young man, Itzhak Shapiro, an instructor at the school, conducted the service. I know him well from numerous conversations I have had with him; we have talked a great deal about his Zionist activities, about the activities of various groups and cells, about the vocational training school and other subjects. The labor office many times has sought to "gobble him up" by sending him to work at the airfield or some other workplace. Up to now, however, we have managed to keep him for the educational work with the youngsters.

The young Shapiro opened the third Passover night meal by greeting the guests. This was followed by the reading of the Haggadah. The boy interspersed the Haggadah passages with commentaries about contemporary Egypt and the contemporary Egyptians; about the next Exodus; about building up our homeland; about the historical generation of the desert; and about the Ghetto today. He also spoke about today's youth, their hopes, and their yearnings for redemption and freedom. Here, says Itzhak Shapiro, as part of the activities of the informal nuclei of the vocational training school, we have created a "miniature temple" with Dr. Chaim Nachman Shapiro as our "high priest."

Then it was Dr. Shapiro's turn. We sat there stunned by the display of his rhetorical skills, his fluent mastery of Hebrew, his ideas brimming over with spiritual feeling, his self-confidence, and the quality of his arguments. "In what do we differ from other nations? Why are only they entitled to fight for their freedom in their own lands? Why does slavery afflict other nations only intermittently, while it is a permanent situation for us? We do not want freedom as a transient episode; we want freedom as an existing, daily reality."

In his enthusiasm Dr. Shapiro enters into an argument with the authors of the Haggadah. He presents demands of his own: freedom from generation to generation until the end of time. He takes us for a ride on eagles' wings by setting us free from the slavery of the old Haggadah and the old commentaries. He even expostulated with the heavenly hosts and listed the requests and supplications of the people of Israel.

Dr. Shapiro did not conclude his address with the traditional supplication

"Next year in Jerusalem." Instead he entered the petition "This year in the rebuilt Land of Israel!"

I then spoke a few words. I said: "This is a select audience; all those present here came of their own free will. All of them tread the same path; one vision unites them and one goal guides them. It is the idea of 'Next year in the rebuilt Land of Israel.' "

After that, Garfunkel and Oleiski delivered short speeches. Oleiski made a confession: "I have sinned. I have been in error. I have sought redemption in the ideal of universal humanity—in distant lands—and I have failed. We must have our own land, our own life. The Land of Israel is the one and only truth." How much Jewish blood has to be spilled, before everyone recognizes this truth?

Then it was the youngsters' turn: one delivered a lecture; another recited poems; a third sang a song while others sang in chorus. The program was concluded by "Had Gadiah" (Only one kid). Itzhak Shapiro then delivered the concluding remarks, which the seated youngsters drank in as if they quenched a deep thirst. At the end, the "Hatikvah" (Hope)—was sung.

The atmosphere was so enthusiastic and hearty that we were loath to disperse. Then there were dances which lasted long into the night. Outside—for this was a clandestine event—were lookouts, members of the Kovno Zionist underground, to alert us to danger. Fortunately, we were not interrupted in our joy.

Another gathering, of a totally different character, took place today. It was attended by seven people who decided to hold a meeting devoted to intellectual matters. There are people in the Ghetto who engage in literary writing. In actual fact, only a handful of writers are left; most of them have perished. The difficult conditions in the ghetto are not particularly conducive to literary work. However, there are some people among us who cannot contain their urge to write; they must put their thoughts in writing. Some of them write poems; others write stories or memoirs. Recently, after a prolonged lull in literary activity, poems of Ghetto life have been brought out, as well as stories from the history of our people; they had been secreted in various hiding places.

These seven or eight people gathered for the purpose of speaking freely to one another. In the past, those attending today's gathering, such as Dr. Kissin,[2] belonged to various intellectual circles. Today they are united by the shared language of artistic and spiritual creativity.

Burstin[3] read from his work "Yizkor" (In memoriam), relating the story of the desecrated synagogue on Veliuonos Street, inside which a large number of dogs and cats were shot. The story was entitled "Parokhet" (The curtain of the Ark of the Law). Stained with the blood of the slaughtered animals, the curtain lay among the carcasses, holy books, and torn prayer shawls.

The story contains a graphic description of people coming to the desecrated synagogue to clean it; how a small group of Jews assembled there to pray on the Seventh Day of Tabernacles, to say the prayer of remembrance for the martyrs and innocents who died for the sanctification of God's name throughout Lithuania and in other countries in Eastern Europe. In Burstin's story, the Jews conduct a dialogue with the king of the universe.

Burstin's colleagues present at the gathering were greatly moved by his story, and by the description of the desecrated synagogue. It made us relive the humiliation of that day. How well, indeed, do I remember the day on which the order was issued for everyone in the Ghetto to bring their dog and cats to the synagogue on Veliuonos Street. Animals not brought were hunted down in the streets and then taken to the synagogue, where all the assembled animals were then shot. It was a cruel and sadistic spectacle: wounded dogs and cats running about in the synagogue, wailing and shrieking.

I also recall the cold winter of 1942, when Dr. Benker of the Rosenberg Organization, set up for the confiscation of general, and especially Jewish, cultural treasures, visited the Council. He wanted to see the register of Ghetto inmates. He wanted to find the Sages, or Elders of Zion; the scholars and spiritual leaders of the Jewish community. He also wanted to see Jewish antiquities, the beloved treasures of Judaism. He had heard that Slobodka had been a center of Jewish culture, of scholars and wise men and venerated rabbis. He, and the companion he had brought with him, wanted to see the venerable Slobodka yeshiva, the synagogues and study houses, as well as the famous library of the yeshiva.

I escorted them on their tour of Jewish antiquities in Slobodka. It was a very cold day. Jews swaddled in rags could be seen on the Ghetto streets. I was flanked on both sides by the two Germans dressed in Nazi uniforms—Dr. Benker and Schiefer. They were striding forward vigorously, pistols strapped to their belts. The gleam of their yellow coat buttons, and the insignia of eagles with outstretched wings, could be seen from far off. Such was the appearance of German scientists, representatives of the superior race, the bearers of culture in the world.

They kept looking around them to see Jewish passers-by saluting them, as was compulsory, by taking their caps off. An old Jew, shivering from cold, probably failed to notice the famous scientists and forgot to take his cap off. Schiefer hurried up to him, struck him on the face, and flung his cap to the ground. Stunned by the shameful behavior of the German scientist, I carried on, trying to find the shortest route to the synagogue on Veliuonos Street.

Upon our arrival at the synagogue, I asked the two Germans to go in by themselves, but they wanted me to serve as their tour guide. I stood on the threshold without being able to move. One of them noticed it and said: "I see you are very moved, as this tour has a strong effect on your feelings. You can wait here, we will tour the place by ourselves."

I remained at the door, and followed with contempt their progress among the carcasses of dogs and cats strewn on the synagogue floor. As they stepped over the carcasses, they seemed not heroes, but dwarfs or clowns in shining uniforms.

Such were my memories as I sat with the small group of Jewish intellectuals. The meeting went on for a long time. We argued over certain passages in Burstin's story and the memories they had evoked. It was a time of freedom of the mind, and of intellectual satisfaction.

1. In the Diaspora, it was traditional to celebrate only the first two nights of the Passover festival; this third night of celebration was therefore something quite unusual.

2. Dr. Avraham Kissin, who before the war had been deputy principal of the Hebrew high school in Kovno, as well as chairman of the Union of Hebrew Teachers of Lithuania. He had also edited a journal on the subject of education. Politically he had been a member of the Zionist Socialists.

3. Michael Burstin (Michal Bursztyn) was born in Warsaw in 1897. His first novel, published there in 1931 in Yiddish, established his reputation, which three further novels (*Destiny*, 1936; *By the Rivers of Mazovia*, 1937; and *Bread and Salt*, 1934) sustained and enhanced. He fled to Lithuania from Poland as a refugee in September 1939. In the Kovno Ghetto, Burstin wrote about Ghetto life, collected popular works, and was one of the Ghetto's best-known cultural figures. He also belonged to the clandestine cultural circle that gathered twice a month in Pnina Sheinzon's room. After the deportations from Kovno in 1944, he died of hunger in Dachau. His son survived and lives in Israel.

APRIL 30, 1943

In discussions recently held by the Council, as well as in private conversations, we have reached the conclusion that we should hold talks with Lithuanian public figures in order to exchange views on the developments in the world at large, and on the current situation in Lithuania. Most important of all, from our point of view, is to hear their views about the future of the Jews in their country. Despite all that has happened, there are still a number of Lithuanian public figures—though, alas, very few—with whom we could meet to hear their views on the current situation in the world, and on the local scene.

Unfortunately, we have no contacts whatsoever these days with influential Lithuanians. Only seldom does a Lithuanian come across a Jewish acquaintance, exchanging a few words with him. Such conversations are invariably personal. Ever since the outbreak of the war, no conversation on political and public issues has taken place between Lithuanian public figures and heads of the Jewish community.

Prominent Lithuanian figures severed their relations with us in the first day of the war. All our efforts to resume contact with them proved futile. Even in the most difficult of times—the times of the various "actions"—when we were certain that all of us were going to perish, our cries for help failed to evoke any reaction on the part of the Lithuanian public figures, and contacts with them were not resumed.

We refused to believe that there were only two kinds of Lithuanians: those who took it upon themselves to help the Germans in the extermination of the Jews, and those who, once in a while, would send some food or money to their former Jewish friends out of pity. We must find Lithuanian figures with more generous hearts; people who would see fit to react to the destruction of Lithuanian Jewry from a historical point of view, and show an interest in the situation of the surviving handful of Lithuanian Jews in these insane times.

We have recently heard about Professor Vlaclovas Birsziska,[1] who served as the chairman of the Lithuanian Convention held in Kovno earlier this month.[2] It was convened according to a plan prepared in advance: the delegates, the speeches, and the decisions had all been fixed. It was attended by several hundred public figures from bygone days.

In the past, Professor Birsziska occupied the post of chairman of the Jewish-Lithuanian Friendship Society. He was a dedicated friend of the Jews. However, since the occupation began in June 1941 we have not heard from him. If it were not for last month's convention, we would have probably forgotten all about him. In his current capacity as rector of Vilna University, and as chairman of the Lithuanian convention which was convoked in compliance with the order of the German authorities, he probably has connections with the German rulers. We have therefore decided to ask him to grant an audience to one of us. However, up to now we have not succeeded in contacting him.

I am convinced that if the situation changes for the better we shall succeed in finding all our former Lithuanian friends. They, for their part, will also find a way to us in such a case. The bitter truth is that, at present, the Lithuanian leaders avoid us and do not wish to see us.

In the first days of the German occupation, the representatives of the Jewish Committee met several times with Bishop Brizgys.[3] After our expulsion to the Ghetto, when no one dared to see us, the bishop received Rabbi Snieg, who subsequently went to see him on a number of occasions, sneaking in through a side entrance.[4]

After the massacre at Ponar, and because of rumors about a new wave of "actions" against the Jews in Poland, we felt forsaken and orphaned. We decided, therefore, to ask Rabbi Snieg to see Bishop Brizgys again, in order to speak to him about our problems. To make sure that some practical results might come from this meeting, we prepared a number of questions to be discussed between the bishop and the rabbi.

Today, in the early hours of the morning, Rabbi Snieg left for the city. As on previous occasions, he did not enter the bishop's house through the main entrance—out of fear of the sentries guarding the bishop's residence—but used the hidden side door.

The bishop received the rabbi warmly. Their conversation touched upon general political issues and on those of particular interest to the Jewish community.

Bishop Brizgys spoke about the relations between the Germans and the local population in Lithuania; about the difficult situation in which the Lithuanians had found themselves last month. The difficulties were caused by heavy penalties imposed on the population because of the German failure to draft Lithuanian citizens into the German Army. After many efforts, a formula was found satisfactory both to the representatives of the Lithuanian population and to the German authorities. This formula spared the lives of many Lithuanian citizens.

The Lithuanian Convention which was convoked as a result of this agreement did, in fact, take place, even though its results could be described as a farce. The Germans thought that it would result in 25,000 Lithuanians enlisting in the German Army, but up to now only 3,000 have enlisted. At present it remains to be seen how the Germans will react to this fiasco. The wording of the official announcement about the convention, as published in the press, was reached by fraudulent means; but there was no other way.

In recent days, tens of thousands of Germans from East Prussia have arrived in Lithuania; they came from Tilsit, Istenburg, and elsewhere. The German authorities revealed this to the Lithuanians just two days before their arrival. According to the official announcement, said the bishop, the German arrivals were people who had lost their homes during air raids. It was said that they would stay here until the end of the summer. In actual fact, however, the Germans long ago deported thousands of Lithuanian peasants, and we are faced with the prospect of German colonization of Lithuania. From now on, Germans will be settling in dozens of Lithuanian villages, in order to ensure that their Lithuanian inhabitants supply grain and vegetables to the occupiers. They will also be charged with keeping the villages free from "undesirable elements."

Scores of Lithuanians who refused to join the German Army are now hiding in the countryside and in the forest. Among them are many priests who refused to go to the front, or who preached in church against the draft. This development poses a great danger to Lithuania. The bishop is very worried by it.

Today we saw a long column of carts laden with parcels and bundles of all kinds passing through the city. These probably belonged to the peasants who had been expelled from their villages.

The bishop also spoke about the relations between the Germans and the Lithuanians, and about his conversation with Major-General Jost, which, among other things, touched upon the Jewish question. When the conversation reached this subject, the senior German officer fell silent for a few moments. Then he said that the carte-blanche which had previously been given to Cramer, Jordan, and others with regard to action against the Jews had now been revoked. This led the bishop to the conclusion that there was a change for the better in the situation. The major-general added, however, that the German Army had not yet formulated a clear policy toward Jews or Lithuanians.

Brizgys also revealed to Rabbi Snieg the contents of his conversation with heads of the Gestapo. Nowadays there is no one to talk to except Schtitz and Jaeger. From his conversations with these two, he gathers that at present the Jews are not faced with any immediate danger. But, as usual in such cases, one cannot know what tomorrow will bring.

The bishop advised us to stay in touch with Schtitz and Jaeger. He then returned to the subject of relations between the Germans and the Lithuanians. In the first period of the occupation, the then governor-general, Renteln, had expressed his wish for the archbishop to pay him a friendly visit. The archbishop rejected the offer. Then, one day, an order came from the Gestapo summoning Archbishop Skvireckas[5] to report to Renteln on an appointed day. On this particular day, the archbishop was in the habit of making an official call on the German governor-general. Some days later a news item appeared in the press that "the Archbishop of Lithuania paid a friendly visit to the German governor-general of Lithuania."

After this press report, the archbishop waited at his home, expecting the German governor-general to come on a friendly visit. The visit, however, did not take place. Just a few months ago, Renteln expressed his desire to pay Archbishop Skvireckas a return visit. The latter, however, rejected the offer, explaining that he would visit Renteln in his office on official business according to an agreement reached long ago. These events reflect the state of relations between the Lithuanian clergy and the German authorities. They also shed light on the relations between the Germans and the Lithuanians in general.

Coming back to our problems, the bishop said that he had heard about the massacre at Ponar. Peasants from the neighboring villages had given a chilling description of the scene of the massacre; for many days afterward, scores of dismembered and mauled bodies, the bodies of the murdered Jews, lay in the field. According to his information, 1,500 Jews were murdered there. The bishop also knew about an "action"—following the German debacle at Stalingrad—in which the Germans had murdered a large number of Jews.

The bishop also receives information about Jews in the provincial towns. A number of priests and peasants have informed him that there are Jews hiding with them, in their homes. There are also Jews hiding in monasteries. The bishop has asked the clergymen to write down any information reaching them about the Jews. As far as the Ponar massacre is concerned, the bishop believes that there was no order from Berlin. In White Russia, from where the Jews had been brought, a large proportion of the population had been killed following a local uprising against the Germans. The Jews were among the victims. It should not, therefore, be surmised that the same thing is going to happen here.

Rabbi Snieg inquired about the possibility of hiding several hundred children from the Ghetto in monasteries. He conveyed to his host the concern prevailing in the Ghetto over the fate of old people and children left without parents or homes. The bishop replied that although the monasteries are officially subject to the authority of the church, for practical purposes they remain autonomous. Their abbots and priors do not excel in mercy and love of humankind. Even Christian children are not treated so well in the monasteries. It must also be surmised that the Christian children will not treat their Jewish counterparts well. They could be expected to reveal to their relatives the presence of Jewish children in the monastery. The bishop believes that it would be much better to hide the Jewish children in peasant cottages in the villages. There, they would be better treated and fed. He promised to give this matter more thought.

The bishop and the rabbi also discussed the question of financial aid. Dr. Elkes and his Council have resolved to set up a special fund to help those Jews whose lives are in danger, and to help Jewish children hiding with the peasants. We seek to obtain a sizable loan for this purpose. We are convinced that when the war is over we will repay the loan with the help of our fellow Jews from overseas. There is also considerable Jewish property in Lithuania which could serve as collateral for the loan. We hope that it will be possible to lend a considerable amount of money via the Vatican, which has received money from Jewish assistance funds in the United States.

The bishop revealed that $18,000 had been received from the United States on behalf of Lithuanian institutions. The Germans had laid their hands on the money and refuse to hand it over to the Lithuanians. The Lithuanian church maintains no direct contact with the Vatican; there is indirect contact via the German Catholic church.

Moving on to the general matters of war and the prospects for peace, the bishop said that according to his information, the war should be over by the end of this year. As far as peace negotiations are concerned, the bishop knows that some mediation efforts have been undertaken in Madrid, even though the Germans deny this. The Allies keep announcing that from their point of view there is only one solution: the unconditional surrender of the Axis countries.[6] He does not expect redemption or solace to come from the Vatican. In his view, the appointment of Weizsäcker, one of the best German diplomats, as Germany's envoy to the Vatican, was meant primarily to further the close relations between Italy and Germany, and not to try to open negotiations for ending the war.

At present the position of Germany is most difficult. There are no grounds to believe that another German offensive is in the offing; Germany is not even capable of pretending that it bides its time in order to launch a new offensive. The Italians and others have removed their armies from Yugoslavia and Greece in order to concentrate their forces. Italy is very much interested in an immediate peace. According to well-placed sources, the appointment of Weizsäcker as envoy to the Vatican was meant to find out about the developments in Rome.

The bishop went on to say that Germany itself is interested in peace, for the simple reason that its situation is hopeless. Some months ago, Ribbentrop wanted to visit the Vatican, but was told that the Pope cannot speak with a representative of a country which persecutes people on account of their religion and race, and which fails to observe the natural rights of human beings. The Pope's reply was published in the official organ of the Vatican, *Osservatore Romano*. This issue of the newspaper was banned from distribution in Germany, and even in Italy.[7]

No revolution has taken place in Germany because there is no one to carry it out. All the men are fighting on various war fronts. The only ones left in Germany are retired people, women, and functionaries of the Nazi Party apparatus. At the same time, however, it is also true in Germany that anything can happen. England and the United States are certain of their victory. They put off the end of the war as much as they can, on purpose. They are interested in sapping German strength. This is why even the fighting in Tunisia has been going on for such a long time. It appears nonetheless that the war will be over by the end of this year.

The bishop also mentioned the heroism of the Soviets. In his view, the English are everywhere in Moscow, even in the Kremlin. They hold all the strings in their hands. The position of Japan is also difficult. It spread its forces over thousands of miles of the war front and cannot hold out against the advantage of American weaponry and war production. This is why we must not lose hope. The speeches of Churchill and Roosevelt have strengthened the bishop's conviction that the end of the war is at hand.

At the end of the conversation, the bishop agreed to look after several articles we would like to preserve. We decided to entrust him with the knowledge of the hideaway in the Ghetto where Jewish valuables are stored.[8] Should the Ghetto, God forbid, be destroyed, there will be someone who will know where our valuables are stored. Our proposal moved the bishop greatly. He asked us not to lose hope. He is willing to help us as much as he can. He will think over once again all the matters we raised and will decide what steps he can take. He will let us know what he decides. He also asked Rabbi Snieg to send his regards to the Council members who know him, and to visit him again if necessary.

The entire conversation between the bishop and Rabbi Snieg was pervaded by his understanding of our situation. For us it was a most important meeting. We need understanding and sympathy. We want others to hear what we have to say, to listen to our arguments. We also need information about current developments in the world, and in our region. In this regard the conversation between Rabbi Snieg and Bishop Brizgys of Kovno is most illuminating. It is possible that the war is approaching its end, and that we are on the threshold of a new era for humanity, and for the Jewish people.

1. Before the war, Professor Vlaclovas Birsziska and his brother Mykolas had maintained close contact with the leaders of the Jewish community. Both of them were known for their liberal opinions. Mykolas had founded the prewar Lithuanian-Jewish Friendship Association.

2. At this convention, which took place on April 5, 1943, the Lithuanians decided—under German pressure—to support the formation of Lithuanian military units to fight against the Soviet Union, in exchange for which the authority of the Lithuanian government would be expanded.

3. In June 1941, Archbishop Skvireckas and Bishop Vincentas Brizgys, both Roman Catholics, and other Lithuanian leaders had signed a congratulatory telegram to Hitler on the occasion of the German invasion of Lithuania. In 1943 Brizgys expressed his readiness to try to help save Jewish children by hiding them with Christian families, but nothing came of it.

4. On July 9, 1941, Rabbi Snieg, Jacob Goldberg, and Leib Garfunkel met with Archbishop Brizgys, who told them he was unable to influence the Germans to revoke the order establishing the Ghetto. He was afraid, he said, that the status of the Catholics in Lithuania would suffer as a result of any such intervention on his part. He also said that any intervention by him in favor of Jews could hurt the good relations between the Germans and the Catholic Church in Lithuania.

5. Archbishop Juozapas Skvireckas, leader of the Catholic church in Lithuania, was already an elderly and sick man in June 1941; his deputy, Bishop Brizgys, took his place on most occasions. Like Brizgys, Skvireckas had been a signatory of the congratulatory telegram sent to Hitler at the beginning of the occupation, and he did not subsequently speak out against the murder of the Jews.

6. On January 24, 1943, at the end of the Casablanca Conference, Winston Churchill and Franklin Delano Roosevelt issued a declaration "placing the objective of this war in terms of an unconditional surrender by Germany, Italy, and Japan." The declaration went on to explain that unconditional surrender "means a reasonable assurance of world peace for generations," and that "unconditional surrender means not the destruction of the German populace, nor of the Italian or Japanese populace, but does mean the destruction of a philosophy in Germany, Italy, and Japan which is based on the conquest and subjugation of other peoples."

7. The Pope probably never made such a reply. It is not to be found in the *Osservatore Romano,* nor in the collections of documents published by the Vatican concerning World War II.

8. During the first days of the Ghetto, while the Germans were methodically looting and expropriating all Jewish belongings, the Council had managed to hide certain valuables, some of which were subsequently used to bribe Germans, or to raise funds urgently needed for use on behalf of the Ghetto inhabitants.

MAY 4, 1943

The radiant golden rays of the spring sunshine illuminated the morning hours of the day. The air in the Ghetto was suffused with warmth, light, and joy. The trees and plants basked in the sun.

A Jewish farmer led his plow, harnessed to two horses, over a large, wide field on Demokratu Square. Girls wearing green, red, and blue skirts were preparing narrow garden plots on the adjacent field, planting in the soil the seeds they were taking out of paper bags. It was a true spring spectacle, like the ones we used to see in a village before the war, or in a painting.

The sun fills the world with warmth and brightness. It also sends its light and warmth to us in the Ghetto. This pretty picture is sharply circumscribed, however, by the barbed-wire fence surrounding us. No painter in his artistic imagination could conjure up the combination of a fairy tale—an open landscape—and a barbed-wire fence.

This is why there is no joy in life here, no spring sunshine in our spirits, and no joy in sowing. The gray color of the Ghetto walls stops every ray of sun, every pleasant sound, every ounce of joy. And if you happen to leave the four walls of the Ghetto for the city—either to work or on some errand—the grayness of the ghetto and all that it entails keep tugging at your heart incessantly.

Here we are in the city, standing in front of a warehouse storing various materials. I have come here to take delivery of bundles of paper and cardboard cartons. The starved horse—like the mare of Mendele Mocher Sforim—stands harnessed to a dilapidated cart. It stands there, as if absorbed in its own thoughts, gazing about in the hope of spotting some straw or fodder. It has not eaten since this morning. The Jewish horse-driver from the Ghetto is absorbed in similar thoughts, and for similar reasons. Both of them are gazing at their passenger. "Lord shall redeem both animal and man," I recall the passage from the Sayings of the Fathers.

We move on to Schantz. Here we come across a large pile of timber. "There is not one piece of timber in the Ghetto," says the horse-driver. "The soup kitchen and the public bath both need firewood. If they would let us take some of the wood lying here in abundance, we would be happy."

Jewish women are employed here at stacking up the wood, which will then be sent to Germany. They gather a few logs to take them to the Ghetto. If, by chance, sympathetic sentries are posted at the Ghetto gate, they will not object to these scraps being smuggled in. If not, the wood will be confiscated.

We continue on our journey, which takes us past several German Army camps. Once again we come across Jewish women working near numerous railway cars. There are also young girls and boys among the workers. They carry bricks and sacks of gravel on their backs. They also dig earth. They are being guarded by a Russian prisoner-of-war who wears a white band on his sleeve. This Bolshevik—who once dropped bombs from aircraft or who shot at the civilian population with heavy cannons—had undergone a "revolutionary" transformation in no time; he has sold his patrimony for a mess of pottage. He has changed the red flag for a white armband. Now he is a free man.

Our workers are forced to work extremely hard; they must be watched so they will not sit idle. The Germans need the labor, but not the laborers themselves.

In the streets and alleys of Schantz, we again come across Jewish girls. They sneak into peasant cottages in an attempt to trade an old dress for something to eat.

On our way back to the Ghetto I managed to snatch a glimpse of today's newspaper. It was like night in the middle of day. The Jew is shown standing at the focus of the interest of the world. His nose is long and crooked and his nostrils black and cavernous. The nostrils are shown breathing out venom. The eyes of the Jew are sending red flames in all directions. The Jew sets the whole world on fire and the world is aflame.

Two long horns grow out of the dishevelled head of the Jew. His face beams with a demonic smile breaking into triumphal, mischievous laughter. His long tongue licks his moustache and blood drips from his beard. The Jew straddles oceans and continents, bringing fire and pestilence everywhere. The Jew rules the world. Everyone is his slave. This enslavement must be put to an end. The enemy of humanity, the eternal Jew, must be exterminated.

I have seen, many times, these pictures of the wandering Jew—in books, newspapers, and pamphlets. And each time I am seized by terror. My soul weeps. Master of the World, why? Why?

Riding our horse-cart we pass through the city streets. I gaze on the passers-by: people are walking, strolling about, stopping by cinema posters; others gaze into shop windows. In the public garden near the Military Museum, people are sitting on the park benches, warming themselves in the sun. One of them is reading a newspaper. I wonder whether he has read about the Jew endangering the whole world. He must think that it is too much to read about those Jews every day. It seems only right to put an end to their existence in this world once and for all.

I recall that in those good days which, of course, are long gone by, we were also reading with indifference and lack of interest the news about an earthquake somewhere beyond the mountains of darkness, which took a toll of many thousands of casualties; or about a flood in China, or the slaughter of millions somewhere far, far away. These people sitting here in the garden are also absorbed in their own business. At the same time, they read some news about the Jews in the Ghettos. It was then that I felt with every fiber of my body how removed we must be from the daily problems and thoughts of these people.

It was only myself alone, sitting on a horse-driven cart, whose soul was totally absorbed in the newspaper story about the Jews. All of a sudden the cart started shaking violently as it came to a road paved with uneven sharp stones. The Ghetto can be seen in the distance. All around us everything remains the way it was. I woke up from the nightmare.

The police guard is present at the Ghetto gate as usual. Ratnikas is also here. After the cart passed the inspection, we were allowed in. I remained in a state of shock for the rest of the day. I was unable to shake off the effect of the incitement against us in the newspaper, and the danger it entailed for our existence. Nor could I forget the indifference to our fate displayed by the man sitting on a bench in the Museum Park in Kovno.

MAY 7, 1943

I was informed this morning that Miller wanted to see me, so I went to the city to see him. I found him in his office. Having extended a polite greeting, he told me that the Zezmer labor camp, containing some 1,000 Jews, would be closed down. Some of the Jews are to be transferred to Pskov, in former Russian territory; the remaining 400 Jews will be brought to the Kovno Ghetto. Here in the Ghetto, additional Jewish workers are urgently needed; the city governor tried to get from Zezmer as many Jews for the Ghetto as possible, but managed to get only 400.

These Jews will be assigned jobs according to their occupations. The food problem is not difficult and will be settled in no time. The only problem is housing. How should it be solved? At this point Miller mentioned the plan submitted by us when 3,000 Jews from the Vilna district were due to arrive in the Kovno Ghetto. This plan can be used now to accommodate the 400 Jews expected from Zezmer. Miller would like to have these 400 Jews quarantined during the first period of their stay here, for reasons of sanitation. They should arrive within six to seven days.

On Wednesday, Hermann will go to Zezmer to inform the camp inmates there about their transfer to Kovno. Miller must leave urgently for Berlin for eight days. In his absence, Hermann and Gilow will be in charge of the transfer. Some difficulties are expected concerning transportation, but this problem will be solved.

I told Miller that it seems only proper that one of our people should also go to Zezmer, in order to prove to the Jews there that they are, in fact, being brought to the Kovno Ghetto. Otherwise, they may start imagining various things. As far as housing is concerned, we will take care of it. As a first step, I suggested that we accommodate the new arrivals in the building of the Lituanika cinema. Following lice and clothes disinfection, they would be gradually accommodated among us in private apartments. In the first period they would receive their meals from the soup kitchen.

Miller then asked me who it was who had issued the ban on using the premises of the Lituanika cinema for housing Jews. I replied that the order was issued by the Ghetto commandant because there were film projectors on the premises. Since then, the projectors had been removed.

Miller told me to return to the Ghetto at once. He said he would join me later on so that we might inspect the rooms of the Lituanika cinema.

I left Miller's office surprised and excited. The tone of his voice convinced me that this time the transfer plan was not a trick. True, after the Ponar massacre, it was not much of a consolation, especially now, when the Ghetto is pervaded by deep fears about our fate; when many believe that all is lost because all the Ghettos will be liquidated, following the example of the Warsaw Ghetto.

The optimists among us thought that the Germans would not exterminate all the Jews because they must take into consideration the reaction of public opinion in the West. The destruction of the Warsaw Ghetto, conducted in the face of active resistance put up by the Jews—who were given some assistance by many Poles—proved them wrong. The mood in the Ghettos is growing more somber with each passing day. Nowadays even the public figures in our Ghetto are seized with fear, and there is talk at the Council about the apparatus of destruction threatening us with imminent extermination. There is no hope for survival.

It should be noted that, in contrast to previous occasions, this time the Ghetto leadership is really worried. The mass of the people, however, are not quite overcome by despair. They remain unaware of the approaching destruction. On the other hand, we at the Council sense the approaching end.

In view of the prevailing mood, the news revealed to me by Miller about the arrival of 400 Jews in our Ghetto was nothing short of good tidings. The Zezmer camp has caused us a great deal of trouble. Lately, women, old people, and children have been taken there. The conditions in the camp are exceptionally harsh. All its inmates must leave for work every morning. No one is allowed to stay in the camp during the day. Even children aged six and above are arranged in groups and leave for work on road construction. We have managed to send assistance to the camp inmates—medicine, wooden shoes, bed linen, and the like. At the same time, however, we are forbidden to maintain any direct contact with the inmates of this camp.

Now, as it turns out, the camp will be closed down. Its inmates will be transferred to Pskov, not far from the front line. The 400 Jews due to arrive here may find themselves among the survivors. The sooner they arrive the better.

I hurried to the Council with the good news, and to make preparations for Miller's visit to the Lituanika cinema.

Miller arrived in the Ghetto shortly after me, and before I had the time to see the members of the Council. I went to the cinema building with Hirschel Levin. A few moments later Miller arrived. He looked around and decided that the place was suitable to accommodate the 400 Jews. He repeated his request that we ensure the proper sanitary conditions, and also that we find additional accommodation in case the Lituanika hall proves insufficient. I again asked Miller to allow one of us to go to the Zezmer camp, so that the Jews there would not think they were being taken away to a place from which there is no return. "You are coming with us," Miller replied. He repeated his announcement about his forthcoming trip to Berlin, which is to take eight days. After he returns, the case of the Jews from Zezmer will be taken care of.

After Miller's departure to the city, the Council appointed a committee consisting of representatives from the housing office, the social welfare office, and the Jewish police, charging it with making necessary preparations for the absorption of the 400 Jews from Zezmer.

Yesterday the secretary of our labor office, Goldman, was involved in an unfortunate incident which is not untypical in the Ghetto. He left his office at 2 P.M. and set out for the workshop where he had sent his old coat to be mended. At 3 P.M. the coat was ready (it had been turned inside out).

Goldman put on his coat and set out for home. He was not far from his home, near the Ghetto gate, when Ratnikas, the officer of the Lithuanian police at the gate, stopped him. He asked Goldman why he did not wear the yellow badge on his coat. It turned out that Goldman had forgotten to place the badge on the turned coat. Since he had been seen in the vicinity of the Ghetto gate, Ratnikas accused him of attempting to leave for the city without the yellow badge. Ratnikas then searched him and found 2,000 marks, a woman's wristwatch—which was probably made of gold—and a small notebook with various notes in it.

Ratnikas's face beamed with pleasure: he had apprehended a real blackmarketeer. Thereupon he took him to the Ghetto command headquarters, which transferred him to the Gestapo.

We were informed about the incident yesterday and were very worried. It turned out that the money found in Goldman's pocket had been collected by the Council's labor office from various labor brigades and had been earmarked for the needy in the Ghetto. At that time a money-raising drive had been launched by the Ezrah charitable society to help the destitute in the Ghetto.[1] Goldman was to deliver the money raised during the campaign to the women active on behalf of the society.

The lists in Goldman's notebook were a more serious matter. They contained information about the charitable donors, the size of contributions, and the names of the needy who had benefited from the financial assistance. There were also details about "gifts" to various German officials. As is well known, it is forbidden for Ghetto inmates to keep money, not to mention raising contributions or giving presents. The whole affair was therefore rather complicated.

Later we learned that when Goldman was being led to the Gestapo he managed to throw away the notebook containing the incriminating lists. His guard picked it up, but, having himself been promised a "gift," agreed to keep his mouth shut.

From the Gestapo, Goldman was transferred to the central Kovno prison. In his interrogation at the Ghetto command headquarters, he claimed that he had obtained the money by selling a coat and a pair of shoes to someone named Friedman, whom he had not known before; he also maintained that he did not know this Friedman's address. Trade of this kind is also forbidden, but it is better than a money-raising venture in the Ghetto. Needless to say, we at once hurried to Lipzer, asking for his help.

Today, Goldman was released from prison. He kept claiming that he had sold a few articles in order to subsist; that he had not intended to go to the city but was on his way to his home, which was located near the Ghetto gate; that his coat had been turned so that he had not had time to put the yellow badge on the turned side. He revealed that during his stay in prison he was beaten by Lithuanian policemen. How easy it is in the Ghetto to get into trouble, even if one takes great care not to stray.

At six in the evening Miller arrived at the Council offices. Pandemonium broke out: there were workers missing today at the airfield. Hermann, of the German labor office, also complained today about the missing workers. Miller warned that if workers are missing tomorrow at the airfield, he will bring in the German police, who will turn the Ghetto inside out within forty-eight hours. The German policemen will take people out of their homes.

Miller had another complaint: labor brigade leaders fail to maintain a minimal level of discipline in their brigades; they even fail to lead their workers through the city streets according to the regulations. The labor brigade leaders must therefore report at the square near the Ghetto gate on Sunday morning at 6:30 A.M. From there, they will march to the airfield as a special labor brigade. The brigade leaders will also have to work as ordinary laborers every Sunday, until such time as they manage to march their brigades through the city in the prescribed fashion.

In the evening, a young man arrived at the Ghetto from Vilna. He brought regards from the Ghetto in his native city. He also told us that the prevailing mood in the Ghetto there is still very gloomy. The Jews there are afraid of each other. They fear denunciations. Gens's conduct is that of a brutal tyrant. The authorities headed by Murer cause endless trouble for the Ghetto residents. People in the Vilna Ghetto also believe that the decisive stage in the life of the

Ghetto is rapidly approaching. They make preparations to flee to the forest and to find shelter in peasant cottages. They no longer believe the reassurances of the authorities that the Ponar incident will not be repeated.

The same mood prevails in the Kovno Ghetto. We no longer believe that work will save us. The ground under our feet does not feel secure anymore.

1. Ezrah, the assistance society in the Ghetto, had been founded by a number of Jewish women, among them Miriam Shor and Mrs. Krumer. They collected money and articles for distribution to the needy. The word "Ezrah" is derived from the Hebrew noun "help." Neither Mrs. Shor nor Mrs. Krumer survived the war.

MAY 8, 1943

Tunis and Bizerta have fallen. The news, which was broadcast on the radio, was received with joy in the Ghetto—but not without concern. No doubt, this is a formidable military achievement for the Allies. This victory brings closer the successful end of the war. London and Washington are pervaded with joy and merriment. In our mind's eye we see the victory parades. Our hearts resound with the melody of "God Save the King." In our thoughts we follow the crowds snatching the special newspaper editions in Times Square in New York, and the increased activity in the White House in Washington. Happily we drink in the news about congratulatory telegrams sent by Stalin to the British king and to the president of the United State. We imagine the envoys from various countries hurrying to convey the congratulations of their governments for the victories of the Allied powers.

We are not strangers to the emotions seizing the nations of the Free World. But today our feelings go out to the Zionist and Jewish leaders overseas. One more continent has been liberated from the rule of the evil power. No more Jewish blood will be spilled in this part of the world.

We are convinced that today the Jewish leaders in the Free World are devoting some thoughts to those of us who remain enslaved and doomed to destruction. Every day something terrible may befall us. What have we not done to ease the yoke of the evil decree? Repentance, prayer, and charity. But these were of no avail. In Rome, the Holy See published the Papal Bull in which the priests were asked to preach Christian morality to their flocks. In the name of God the Father, God the Son, and God the Holy Ghost: stop spilling Jewish blood! But the voice of the nations and of their spiritual leaders remains a voice crying in the wilderness.

Despite the savage campaign of incitement against us, and despite the danger hanging over our heads, our hearts keep nursing the spark of hope: the enemy stronghold does not seem to stand as firm as it used to. It totters and can collapse any day now. In every cellar and every hiding place, in every prison and behind all bars, the hearts of the oppressed multitudes are filled with joy and mirth. They cry out loud: "The hour of freedom is approaching fast!"

But sorrow is not tardy in gripping our souls. The henchmen are more savage than they used to be. Today we were rejoicing openly, but within our hearts we wept. If only we would not have to pay with our blood for the defeat of our enemies in Africa.

Then the news came which made everyone tremble: Schtitz had arrived in the Ghetto and set out for the Ghetto command headquarters. Shortly afterward, an order was issued to bring Mrs. Zon and her two little children to the Ghetto command headquarters. Some days ago a young man by the name of Zon was arrested and taken to the Gestapo. He was employed at the living quarters of the German women telephone operators. He took some food from the little store-room in the courtyard and was caught doing so. The supervisor caught him red-handed carrying a loaf of bread and three eggs. He was subsequently transferred to the Gestapo and confessed. He claimed to have taken some food for his two little children. And now they are taking away his wife and children. They were taken straight to the Ninth Fort and executed, together with the father of the family.

The same morning, a young man by the name of Lansewitch was murdered in the same place. He had been working in the grain warehouse, from which he took three kilograms of rye. He was arrested and taken to the Gestapo. Today he paid with his life for his deed. A huge menacing wave sweeps over us and drags its victims with it.

I remember a story my grandfather used to tell me when I was a child, in our small town. Every spring, when the sun shines brighter and warmer, the river passing by the townlet sweeps away five to six victims in its swift spring current. It happens every spring. I asked my grandfather a childish question: "If this happens every spring, then why don't the people take precautions? Why don't they avoid getting close to the river?" "This cannot be helped, my child," said my grandfather. "The spring current drags the victims into it. There is no way to avoid it." The same thing happens to us nowadays. The times we live in drag the victims with them, while we watch helplessly.

The fear in the Ghetto is great. We did not waste time in taking all the necessary precautions: instructions have been dispatched to all the labor brigades to be careful, as today is a bad day. The Gestapo has taken a whole family to the Ninth Fort. Please, be careful! Do not carry any articles or food on you. They will double-check everyone at the Ghetto gate.

I called on Miller at the city governor's office. I told him that we are not being supplied with leather for the manufacture of shoes for the workers. We cannot even mend broken shoes. The workers go on foot for ten to twenty kilometers to their workplaces every day wearing torn shoes; he went with me to see the director of the leather industries at the city governor's office. Miller told him that thousands of Jews are employed by the German war industry and they walk dozens of kilometers to their workplaces. They must be issued wooden shoes. For that purpose leather is needed. The director of the leather industries gave his consent and signed the necessary permits.

It has been a good day today, I think to myself; it also has been warm. It is Saturday. I keep telling myself that I will be back home in the Ghetto earlier. There is no work in the Ghetto on Saturday afternoon. I will meet with my friends and comrades. There is also the good news from Tunis and Bizerta.

On my way back to the Ghetto I come across a Jewish policeman. He says: "The Gestapo has taken out of the Ghetto a whole family and taken it to the Ninth Fort. Please, be careful!" My mood immediately changed for the worse. I checked my pockets to ensure they did not contain any forbidden objects.

At the Ghetto gate all was quiet. The policeman standing guard at the gate asked me whether I was carrying forbidden articles. I reassured him that I was not, and passed the inspection. I found the Ghetto and the Council offices pervaded by apprehension. Five victims—as opposed to one piece of good news, one moment of satisfaction.

MAY 11, 1943

For some time now the Council members have been discussing the need to arrange a meeting between Dr. Elkes and Major-General Jost. This is not at all easy. All our efforts to get in touch with him by means of our Lithuanian friends have failed. Recently Dr. Elkes used the services of a leader of a Jewish labor brigade to contact a friend from bygone days, the German lawyer Lukas, who is now a judge of the German court in Kovno. Lukas's neighbor is another friend of Dr. Elkes—Schtrauch. Dr. Elkes sought to use the services of Schtrauch to contact General Jost.

Lukas agreed to meet with Dr. Elkes at Marva, a suburb of Kovno. It is an estate which employs Jewish workers in agriculture. Their meeting there would not arouse undue curiosity. Both Lukas and Dr. Elkes are under constant observation. The German judge, dressed in Nazi uniform, is considered by his acquaintances to be a loyal member of the Party whose job is to enforce Nazi justice. For such a person, a meeting with Elkes would irreversibly tarnish this image and personal position.

Dr. Elkes is also under constant surveillance by German officials. As he is chairman of the Council—the position of highest authority in the Ghetto—his every movement, even a facial expression, has an impact on the Ghetto residents. A meeting between the two men in Marva would be impossible for him.

We therefore searched for a suitable meeting place between the two friends from the bygone days, which would not arouse curiosity. We thought about the vocational training school, situated on the edge of the Ghetto, but Lukas opposed the idea. In the end Lukas offered to hold the meeting in his own apartment, in the most fashionable part of Kovno, arguing that no one would suspect a German judge of inviting a Jew to his home. Since Lukas's apartment is opposite the building which houses the offices of the management of the city health department, it could be argued—should the meeting come to light—that Dr. Elkes had entered Lukas's apartment by mistake.

The meeting between the two was scheduled to take place at 12:20 P.M. The manager of the Ghetto pharmacy, Srebnitzki, was to join Dr. Elkes as a cover.

At the appointed hour we—Dr. Elkes, Srebnitzki, and I—arrived in a horse-drawn cart at the corner of Kanto and Kestucio Streets. Srebnitzki continued on his way, whereas Dr. Elkes and I entered the building in which Lukas lived. I escorted Dr. Elkes all the way to Lukas's apartment—in compliance with Dr. Elkes's express wish. I pressed the bell and the door was opened. I parted from Dr. Elkes immediately, went downstairs, and waited outside the building. After about half an hour, Dr. Elkes returned from the meeting. He seemed to be very excited by the conversation with his former friend.

Here is the account of the meeting as related by Dr. Elkes: it was lunchtime. The table was set for Dr. Elkes also. Lukas greeted him warmly and asked him to sit at the table. Dr. Elkes was seated in front of a large mirror which gave him the opportunity to observe a unique spectacle: Lukas, a judge of the German court in Kovno, dressed in the Nazi uniform, swastika on his sleeve, sat at the table opposite the Jew, Dr. Elkes, who was wearing yellow badges on his clothes on both the front and the back.

Lukas filled two glasses with wine and raised his glass in a toast: "To better times." Dr. Elkes raised his glass too, but could not bring himself to repeat his host's toast since, for Lukas, there could not be better times than these. Therefore, Dr. Elkes contented himself with a more modest toast: "To the well-being and happiness of this household." The mirror reflected this rare scene, which inscribed itself indelibly on Dr. Elkes's mind.

As for the substance of the meeting itself: Lukas's good friend Schtrauch is in East Prussia and does not come to Kovno very often. Lukas has no contact with Jost whatsoever. It is possible that Lukas will call on Schtrauch and pass on Dr. Elkes's request. Lukas knows that Schtrauch treats Dr. Elkes with respect and believes that Schtrauch will try to fulfill his request to make contact with General Jost.

Lukas does not know much about us and our problems. The information reaching him about the Jews does not contain any slander of the Ghetto. On the contrary, he has heard only good things about the Ghetto. He is willing to do all he can for us.

We went back home, to the Ghetto. The sun spread warmth and light. Spring has arrived. We were not in a hurry. Riding the cart, I dreamed: "If only they would let us ride in this cart far, far away from here, we would be happy. If only we could get away from here—from the Ghetto, from the fence, from the unceasing torment." Sweet dreams which evaporate quickly in the face of the cruel reality. Meanwhile, we had arrived at the Ghetto gate.

There was much news today, good news this time. In the afternoon Lipzer came to the Council offices to reveal that the Gestapo had held a prolonged discussion. It was attended by representatives from Riga and from Berlin, as well as by a senior Gestapo official. The subject: the Jews. After the session, which lasted several hours, Schmitz, Schtitz, and several others who had been present told Lipzer that it had been agreed that there would be no more "actions" and that no more Jews would be killed. They promised Lipzer that from now on he can live in peace, as other Jews can. The Jews must work and refrain from engaging in black-marketeering and suchlike—then nothing bad is going to happen to them.

Lipzer believes that this, in fact, is the situation, and that our future is assured. He was in good spirits and asked the Council members to bring a bottle of vodka to celebrate. Not that he forgot his own person: "See what I do for the Council; you do not appreciate my work as you should." The news quickly spread in the Ghetto, and people's faces beamed with joy. They kept saying to one another: "This means that we are going to survive and that we shall overcome all the trouble and hardships."

The same day other news spread in the Ghetto: Natkin has a Christian wife who lives in Berlin. In a letter to her husband she wrote that according to the rumors reaching her, the Jews can expect better times in the near future. Another piece of information: in Munich, or perhaps Berlin, a congress of the heads of the Nazi Party took place. They discussed the Jewish problem and differences of opinion were revealed concerning the future of the Jews in Germany and the occupied territories. It was agreed to stop the murder of the Jews.

Such news, and the various rumors, have produced a good mood in the Ghetto. We are under the impression that the miracle we have been waiting for such a long time has, perhaps, occurred. In the old quarter of the Ghetto people were kissing and hugging.

This afternoon Rabinovitz related to us his impressions of the Zezmer labor camp, which he had visited with the director of the German labor office, Hermann. Rabinovitz revealed that there are about 1,200 Jews in the camp, including 180 children and a number of old people. The inmates were brought there from Oszmiana and other small towns in the Vilna district. The management of the road construction company which administers the camp, and oversees the Jews in it, issued an instruction for the transfer of some of the inmates to Pskov and to other places. The city governor of Kovno, Cramer, is determined to have

400 Jews from the camp at Zezmer transferred to the Kovno Ghetto, owing to the labor shortage here. However, it is possible that several weeks will pass before they are transferred.

The conditions in the Zezmer camp are particularly difficult. All inmates twelve years old or older must go out to work. They are employed at road construction and live in shacks in bad conditions. Many would like to come to the Kovno Ghetto, despite the ingrained memory of the Ponar massacre. The name "Kovno" casts fear over them.

In Zezmer, details were revealed about another Jewish labor camp in Vievis. The Jewish inmates there also do hard work at road construction. Several days ago an incident took place in Vievis: a number of Jewish youths had escaped from the camp and hidden in the forest for a long period of time. When they could not hold out any longer, they decided to return to the camp. As they approached the entrance, the guards opened fire on them. The Jewish youths returned the fire, and in the ensuing battle two of them were killed. Now the camp is seized by fear. The Jews are afraid of reprisals on the part of the Germans.

Szitelni, the leader of the Palemonas labor brigade, came to the Ghetto in the evening. Apart from several Jewish workers from Kovno, the Palemonas peat-digging camp also employs Jews from the Vilna Ghetto. As a labor brigade leader, Szitelni pays frequent visits to Kovno and Vilna. He brings to us regards from the Vilna Ghetto inmates and relays news from us to them.

According to Szitelni's impressions, the mood in the Vilna Ghetto is gloomy. People are overcome by despair after the Ponar massacre. Young people are fleeing to the forest. They no longer believe German reassurances that an incident like this will not recur. Moreover, the strongman of the city governor's office there harasses the Jews by frequent house searches. Conditions in the Ghetto deteriorate daily. The German authorities are helped in their tasks by the Ghetto Council headed by Desler.[1] The Jews find themselves between the hammer of the external rule of the Germans and the anvil of the internal rule of the Jewish Ghetto chiefs. Not long ago, Jews were caught in the Ghetto carrying weapons. This proves that the inmates of the Vilna Ghetto prepare themselves for any possibility.

Rabinovitz's account of the conditions in the Zezmer camp and Szitelni's impressions of Vilna and Vievis had a sobering effect on the members of the Council who had been buoyed and comforted by the news (or rumors) about the coming salvation. It seems, however, that the pessimistic view is limited mainly to the Council, whose members are cool-headed people who tend to receive any good news with a measure of skepticism. The general population of the Ghetto has not received the news about the situation in the Vilna Ghetto, which explains the general indulging in dreams about the better days lying ahead.

It goes without saying that it is more pleasant to receive reassuring promises than to hear threats and harsh edicts. We received the news of the outcome of the consultation at the Gestapo with a measure of satisfaction. However, there is no certainty that this positive report—that the Germans have ordered a halt to the murder of Jews—will ever be implemented in practice.

1. Desler was not the chairman of the Jewish Council in Vilna, but deputy head of the Jewish police; his was a position of considerable power in the Ghetto, where he was much feared.

MAY 16, 1943

Three days ago we were instructed by Miller, over the telephone, to send fifteen—later it was forty—Jewish policemen to the city governor's office, to be placed at the city governor's disposal. Replying to my question about the nature of their assignment, Miller replied curtly: "For police work."

I passed on Miller's strange directive to the head of the Ghetto Jewish police. This is the first time we have received such an order. From time to time Jewish policemen are called on for special duties at the airfield, especially during labor shortages. Today, however, we were at a loss to work out the purpose of the summons.

At 10:30 in the evening I met Margolis, who seemed to be very worried. He asked me whether I had been told the reason for the mobilization of the fifteen policemen. In his view I should have been more persistent in trying to find out what was needed of them. I told him that as Miller had issued the order, there was nothing to be afraid of. At the same time, however, I myself was concerned. We have been punished heavily in the Ghetto. We have not yet forgotten the affair of the 534 young men.[1] Perhaps this is another such trick.

The day before yesterday the fifteen Jewish policemen marched out of the Ghetto gate and, at exactly 7:30 A.M., arrived at the city governor's office. It later emerged that they had been given a special assignment—to assist German and Lithuanian policemen in forcibly removing a number of Lithuanian residents from their homes.

Recently a substantial number of German families have arrived in Kovno, as well as in other towns and villages in Lithuania. The official explanation for the move is that the houses of these families were destroyed in air raids, thus forcing them to look for shelter in Lithuania. But, in fact, this is an instance of German colonization of a foreign country. When the Germans arrive in Kovno, the housing department at the city governor's office gives them an apartment. The apartments designated to accommodate them belong to Lithuanian families, one of whose sons, having been recruited into the German Army, subsequently defected, and is now in hiding. In other cases the apartments are situated in neighborhoods which have been preponderantly German for a long time.

When each new German family moves into an apartment placed at its disposal it moves under an escort of four policemen: one German, one Lithuanian, and two Jewish. The assignment of these four is to remove the rightful tenants (Poles or Lithuanians) from the apartment and to replace them with the new owners. They are also charged with seizing the furniture and other household utensils of the Polish or Lithuanian families whose enlisted sons refuse to report to German Army camps, and to transport these possessions to assembly points designed especially for them. In contrast, the furniture and household utensils of the families removed because their apartments are located in a preponderantly German neighborhood are not requisitioned.

The procedure of seizing the apartments is as follows: a truck with the new German tenants and the four policemen pulls up at the block in which the apartment to be requisitioned is located. The policemen then enter the apartment, announcing to its tenants that they must leave within two to three hours. They offer them the possibility of taking thirty to forty kilograms of belongings with them, provided they leave the apartment at once. No alternative housing is offered.

As a rule, the Jewish policemen are assigned the task of translation, on account of their knowledge of both Lithuanian and German. The tenants usually beg the policemen to revoke the evacuation order, or to put off its implementation for a few days, or to allow them to take away as much of their property as possible. All this is of no avail, and the apartment is evacuated. Most of the belongings are thrown out. The furniture, however, is loaded on the truck which later brings it to the assembly points in Slobodka and Schantz.

The cries and pleas of the Lithuanians are directed to the Jewish policemen, mainly because the Jews understand the language spoken by the tenants, and also because the Jews are regarded not just as translators but also as order-givers. Another assignment of the Jewish policemen is to keep an eye on the Lithuanian policemen, so that they will not steal the belongings of the older tenants.

The city governor's office is experienced in requisitioning the apartments of the Polish residents. In most cases, German policemen carry out the confiscations. They are in the habit of taking the confiscated valuables, not to the collection centers, but to their own apartments.

In the apartments where the furniture and valuables of the previous tenants were not seized, the policemen would give an order to evacuate the apartment immediately, giving the address of the new apartment as somewhere in a distant neighborhood. The policemen would immediately start removing the furniture and other valuables.

This whole business, including the part played in it by Jewish policemen, is not at all to our liking. The appearance of Jewish policemen in the houses of the Lithuanian residents whose apartments have been seized has already provoked angry reactions among the Lithuanians. Some of them thought that a special unit of Jewish policemen had offered its services to the German authorities. The Lithuanians started talking about "Jewish SS units," the "Jewish Gestapo," and "Jews who have begun to take over the city." The storm among the Lithuanians gathered force, as did their anger at the Jews.

We searched for ways to get rid of this unfortunate assignment for the Jewish policemen. Almost every day, I raised the subject with Miller. I could not bring up the argument that the Lithuanians are angry with us, as that would be of no interest to Miller. On the contrary, he could even enjoy it. I put forward other arguments: the Jewish police has duties to fulfill in the Ghetto and cannot afford to spare a considerable part of its force every day for other duties.

Miller promised me several times that within a few days the Jewish policemen will be relieved of this duty. In order to lessen the tension in the city, the Council decided that the Jewish policemen will not wear their uniforms when on duty in the city. We hope this will be interpreted as meaning that the Jewish workers are taking part in the removal of Lithuanian tenants in the same way as other workers, including Lithuanians, are employed by the Germans at jobs of various kinds.

In a few cases, however, the Jewish policemen forgot their position and behaved as if they were giving orders. These incidents all occurred on the first day of the operation. The Council ordered the Jewish policemen not to get involved in arguments between the German policemen and the tenants being evacuated.

The evacuation operation conducted with the assistance of the Jewish policemen also had an unfortunate effect on the attitude of the Lithuanian sentries posted at the Ghetto gate. They started taking revenge for the injustice perpetrated against their compatriots by the Jews. They did so on the Jewish workers who return from work in the city; they would confiscate any article found on the workers at the Ghetto gate.

It happens very often that against our will we find ourselves between the hammer and the anvil. I remember a conversation that I had with Miller three days ago. He told me that a Jewish worker had been arrested at the Ghetto gate; he had had in his possession a pair of boots that a German from his workplace had asked him to mend in the Ghetto. It is forbidden to do such a thing. "This is an instance of Jewish cleverness," said Miller. "By rendering such services the Jews seek to curry favor at the German workplaces." Miller issued an order that any Jew who takes articles with him from his workplace in order to have them repaired in the Ghetto will be locked up in jail and the articles confiscated. There must be no intimate relations between Jewish workers and German employees. The Jews are required to do their jobs and not to try their hand at other ventures. This is what Miller said. Addressing me, Miller explained: "You should understand, we must win this war; after all, it was nobody else but you who started it."

The Lithuanians vent all their fury on us for the evacuation operation. It is too dangerous to be angry with the Germans, whereas it is safe to harass the Jews even if they are only carrying out German orders.

We are thus forced to maneuver among troubles of various kinds, to bow to everyone, and not to give satisfaction to anyone. This is typical of the perennial exile we are in, of which our daily existence in the Ghetto is a perfect example.

1. See entry for August 18, 1941, note 1.

MAY 19, 1943

DOCUMENT: From Dr. Bartman, German Security Police and SD office, Kovno[1]

The Council and the Ghetto Police must grant Mrs. Hilda von Ravensburg, the bearer of this certificate, any assistance she may request.

1. Lieutenant Colonel Dr. Bartman was in charge of criminal cases in the German Security Police office.

MAY 20, 1943

There are times when, as I leave my home for the Council offices, my intuition does not tell me that anything bad is going to happen. Everything was all right yesterday when we finished work and set out for home. It is springtime, the air is fresh, the sun shines brightly, and everything around is green. One makes an effort to turn the short journey to the Council offices into a leisurely walk: to enjoy the refreshing spring day; to forget the Ghetto and all that it entails; not to think about the Council and its employees, about the fence and the gate, about the airfield and the labor brigades, about Cramer and Jaeger, about enslavement and danger.

On a morning like this, brimming with sunshine, one gazes with one's mind's eye at the distant bright horizon; in one's imagination, one travels in the distant worlds of freedom, where humans live like brothers and free men.

All this, however, lasts only a short while. You behold the Ghetto again: the Council building, the inmates with yellow badges on their clothes, their brows furrowed with worry, their questioning eyes. You climb the stairs and feel the sharp gaze of the ordinary Ghetto inmates. They are curious to know—to read from the expression on your face—what the day will bring, whether there is any news, what has just happened, whether everything is still the way it was. They know that the Council members are short on words; they are responsible, sober-minded people who speak briefly and to the point. So the curious look into our faces; perchance they will discover something from an expression, a look.

It is common knowledge that the Council members know quite a lot, but they are not loquacious; they fill their mouths with water like mutes. It is often said that the Council carries a heavy burden, that it faces constant danger. But only a few are aware of the exact nature of this burden and the danger; even they, however, do not know everything, just a fragment, a hint. No one has any idea of the incidents, the experiences, and the dangers that the members of the Council have gone through in this building; in all likelihood only a few people will know about them in the future.

Human speech is powerless to relate what has happened in this building in the past. Each day, every hour, was pregnant with danger.

In the last three or four days, the Council has again been through an ordeal in which our nerves were tried to the utmost. Tension reached the breaking point: again victims are expected. Human life is hanging by a thread. One person is behind prison bars; others remain gravely imperiled, waiting for a decision about their fate which may be made at any moment. It seems that we are in the middle of a minefield. One careless, uncalculated step, and everything can explode in our faces. As always, the dangers converge on the Council. Here, the most serious decisions must be made quickly, again and again: to talk or not, to go or to refrain from going—who, when, how?

To someone on the sidelines it must seem that all these are just innocent games. When a case is brought to a successful conclusion, it is taken for granted, as if it could not have ended otherwise. And yet how stormy and raging, how terrible and how enormous, every innocent-looking affair becomes here. In a blink of the eye one bathes in human blood; at a moment's notice, a human being is staring into the eyes of death. At one time it was the medicine affair. Only three days ago a close friend visited Dr. Elkes and revealed that Wintzer had implicated his woman friend, Freifrau von Ravensburg, who had worked with him at 55 Paneriu Street, in the medicine scandal. She also is under arrest. Now she seeks to vindicate herself. She has asked for permission to come to the Ghetto, where she hopes to find the traces of the medicine which had disappeared, and which Wintzer had acquired through illegal channels from a German pharmacist in Berlin and then brought to the Ghetto for sale.

Throughout his imprisonment, interrogation, and trial, Wintzer maintained that in November of last year he placed a big order worth 6,500 marks for medicine from Berlin. The medicine was designated for the German settlers and German physicians in Kovno, via the settlement command of the S.S. The medicine was lost, however, en route, and Wintzer does not know anything about it. This was his line of defense throughout.

Dr. Bartman, of the Gestapo, who conducted the investigation, has already visited the furniture factory at 55 Paneriu Street, as well as the large workshops, the pharmacy, the hospital, and other establishments in the Ghetto. The police suspect that since Wintzer maintained good relations with members of the labor brigade who were employed there until May of last year, and in view of the perennial shortage of medicine in the Ghetto, it could be surmised that the Jews had bought the drugs at black-market prices and brought them into the Ghetto. Dr. Bartman failed to discover any traces of these drugs, however; we, meanwhile, had forgotten about the whole case. We only heard that Mrs. von Ravensburg, who at the time had been arrested together with Wintzer, had in the meantime been released from prison, and that Wintzer himself had received a four-year sentence. Wintzer used the services of Mrs. von Ravensburg to contact the members of the labor brigade employed at 55 Paneriu Street, with whom he and she had done all kinds of illegal business, urging them not to tell anyone anything, as he had denied everything. He had in fact maintained business connections with Jews and had used their services to sell furniture and other wares, the property of the German settlement command and of the city governor's office; he had sold medicine through Jewish middlemen, making a considerable profit in the process; the furniture factory had used various materials, instruments, and expensive furniture brought there from the city governor's office and the German settlement command which had been intended for the Germans; Wintzer had continually placed orders in Germany for machinery, expensive factory equipment, paint, chemicals, and spare parts, ostensibly for a factory, but which were sold for a song. The couple had also made a pact with several Jews from the labor brigade who had their own clientele—Lithuanians and peasants—who paid for the merchandise with money, gold, and other means of payment. Needless to say, had all this come to light, Wintzer would have been given a death sentence. He was sentenced to only four years imprisonment for illegally obtaining a large quantity of medicine from Berlin, smuggling it across the German-Lithuanian border, and getting rid of it in a manner unknown to the court. Also, 25,000 marks were found on him, for which he could provide no explanation.

Despite his four-year sentence, Wintzer kept his mouth shut about the Jewish involvement in his illegal activities, for the simple reason that this would have resulted in a harsher penalty. He still hopes to reduce his sentence by not revealing the full extent of the operation which he and Mrs. Ravensburg were running at 55 Paneriu Street.

The arrest of the German couple still casts fear over several Jewish workers employed at the furniture factory. Only now they realize the full extent of the danger they would face should their involvement in this ugly business come to light. The most frightened person is the technical manager at 55 Paneriu Street, Sragovitz—a sharp businessman, formerly a Kovno furniture manufacturer, who for all practical purposes had run the factory at 55 Paneriu Street and maintained close relations with Wintzer. When Sragovitz began exploiting his connections with Wintzer, and doing whatever he pleased, the Council wanted to remove him from his position, but did not succeed in doing so because, by that time, Sragovitz was so deeply involved in the business that Wintzer blocked his dismissal. The Council did manage, however, to obtain Wintzer's approval for appointing Makovski as business manager. Makovski, we hoped, could apply brakes on the wheeling and dealing between Wintzer and Sragovitz and, in general, cut through the mess at the factory. Despite our hopes, Makovski soon ran into obstacles. In order to avoid a disaster, he wanted to sack a number of Jewish workers whose sole occupation had been black-marketeering. Wintzer refused to sack them and extended his protection to them instead.

Having blown the whistle several times, Makovski asked to be relieved of his duties, as he was convinced that the disaster would not be long in coming. All the efforts undertaken by the Council, the Jewish labor office, and the manager of the large workshops proved fruitless. These Jews refused to give up their profits and comfortable workplaces. Finally we decided to try to move the furniture plant at 55 Paneriu Street to a site within the Ghetto precincts.

Following Wintzer's arrest, all those involved with him became very worried. In particular, the affair of the medicine caused considerable distress. The true story was as follows. One day Wintzer returned from a trip to Germany. He told his Jews that he could bring medicine from Berlin, and asked the Jewish physician at the furniture plant, Dr. Nahum Katz, to prepare for him a list of all the medicine in demand in the Ghetto. Later, it came to light that a shipment of medicine, three or four boxes, addressed to Wintzer, had arrived at the border town of Eydtkuhnen. Wintzer set out to take delivery of the shipment and brought it to the furniture plant. He then forced Dr. Katz to sell the medicine at black-market prices, and took the money for himself. This is how the medicine found its way into the Ghetto; a considerable portion was purchased by the pharmacy, unaware of its origin.

A second shipment of medicine reached Eydtkuhnen from Berlin; again, it was sold in the Ghetto. This was in November or December of last year. These two shipments brought Wintzer 15,000 to 20,000 marks of easy profit. Ever since, Dr. Bartman had looked for some trace of the medicine in the Ghetto. Dr. Katz, meanwhile, had been seized by panic, fearing that he too might be implicated.

The manager of the Ghetto pharmacy, Srebnitzki, was also frightened, as he too, without doubt, would have been entangled in this affair. Since the Council is responsible for running the Ghetto, including the pharmacy, on an everyday basis, it too would certainly have been dragged into this, which could have resulted in serious consequences for all the Ghetto inmates. Dr. Bartman, however, had not conducted a thorough investigation in the Ghetto, contenting himself with a perfunctory gathering of evidence. Several months had elapsed since then; we had grounds for believing that the whole affair was no longer going to trouble us.

The news that the Gestapo prosecutor had reopened the case, and that Mrs. Ravensburg had been given permission to come into the Ghetto to search for traces of the illegally sold medicine, had a profoundly distressing effect on us. Mrs. Ravensburg was intimately involved in all Wintzer's business deals, which means that she has inside information about the details of this particular operation. She knew, for example, the identity of the buyers, as well as the price paid for various medicines. She personally smuggled the second shipment of medicine across the border. She paid numerous visits to the Ghetto and she knew everything. Her present visit therefore gives rise to concern that the whole extent of Wintzer's operation will now be exposed, and that it will blow up in our faces.

Miller has given Mrs. Ravensburg a permit to stay in the Ghetto for three days, to try to prove that the medicine was, in fact, brought into the Ghetto, that Wintzer was responsible for the whole thing, and that she herself was innocent of any illegal activity. As soon as we learned of her impending visit, we informed Srebnitzki about it; measures were taken in the pharmacy to dispose of any medicine still there. Dr. Katz and Sragovitz, both of whom had maintained close business connections with Wintzer, and who were now waiting anxiously to see what would happen, were also informed.

Our only recourse was to deny everything. Wintzer did not admit that he had either sold or given medicine to the Jews. This version must be upheld. This is easier said than done. When you are taken to the Gestapo and start counting the terrible blows landing on your body, you lose all power of resistance and start telling the Gestapo everything you know—or don't know. The Gestapo can turn you into a wild animal. Only one in a thousand is capable of withstanding the "fire test" there.

The day before yesterday, at 9 P.M., Segalson informed the Council that "Zlata"[1]—the nickname given to Mrs. Ravensburg by the workers at 55 Paneriu Street—had talked with him over the telephone and had asked to speak with Sragovitz. Yesterday, at four o'clock in the afternoon, she arrived at the large workshops and had a long talk with Sragovitz. She revealed to him that Wintzer had "spilled the beans" in connection with the medicine affair. She had not believed that he had done so, she said; he, Sragovitz, knew about her close relationship and deep friendship with Wintzer. She would not have believed it, and yet she had heard, with her own ears, the prosecutor speaking about it. It happened while she was waiting for her own interrogation in an adjacent room, separated from the next room by a thin wall. According to her, Wintzer had recently confessed that he had not sold the medicine. In his view, there were two alternatives: either the Jews working at 55 Paneriu Street had stolen the medicine from him, or, she, Mrs. Ravensburg, had sold it to the Jews. This is why she had been arrested again.

Now Mrs. Ravensburg has been given the opportunity to prove her innocence. Miller has made it possible for her to come to the Ghetto. The German criminal police have also allowed her to clarify the affair in the Ghetto. It is vital for her to find, here in the Ghetto, some of the medicine which was sold, or at least the empty tubes or packages from which it can be learned that the medicine was, in fact, brought to the Ghetto. Nobody would be arrested as a result of such a finding—not the Jews, nor she—and the whole affair would be resolved. Her advice to Sragovitz is to assemble the Jews employed at the furniture plant who were certainly involved, and to tell them to bring the medicine—if it is in their possession—secretly to an appointed place, where she will collect it. In this way everything will be all right. Both the Gestapo and Cramer have promised her that no Jew will be harmed as a result, and that nothing bad will happen to the Ghetto itself. Only Wintzer will thereby be incriminated, whereas she, as the principal witness, will be cleared and released. The German criminal police will support her. Beginning today, the Ghetto guard will take special measures to ensure that no medicine pertaining to this affair will leave the Ghetto.

Should Mrs. Ravensburg's request be refused, extensive searches will be conducted throughout the Ghetto as soon as the three days of her visit are over. Although the aim of the searches will be the medicine, it should come as no surprise—she, as a seasoned veteran, knows it—that clothing and other valuables will be found and, as usual in such cases, half of them will be taken away. Sragovitz should follow her advice. He is free to consult anyone he sees fit, including the Council. Time is short, and steps must be taken. She repeated her promise that nothing bad will happen, either to Sragovitz or to anyone else in the Ghetto. After all, Sragovitz knows that her treatment of the Jews has been fair, and that there are no reasons to fear anything.

Having heard her out, Sragovitz was seized by panic. What do you mean, he asked; you of all people should know that I had no hand in this medicine business at all. He cannot assemble the labor brigades now, he said. She should speak with Segalson. He, Sragovitz, has no influence on the Council. He advised her to speak to Segalson. He himself will arrange for the meeting. Thus Sragovitz cunningly shifted the responsibility to Segalson, who has had no connection whatsoever with this affair.

Later Zlata told the same story to Segalson: if her advice is followed, all the "top dogs"—the Gestapo, the criminal police, Cramer, Dr. Bartman, and the German prosecutor—all of them have promised her that not a single hair will fall from any one's head. If not, there will be searches and raids which certainly are not for the Ghetto's benefit.

Mrs. Ravensburg's revelations were received with complete seriousness, all the more so since yesterday morning many SS men were present at the Ghetto gate, conducting thorough searches of the Jewish workers before they left for work in the city. As a result, many workers panicked and ran back to their homes without leaving for work that day. There were thus many workers missing both at the airfield and from the labor brigades working the city.

Cramer immediately received a telephone call from the airfield, informing him that about 150 workers had failed to appear for work today. The rumor quickly spread in the Ghetto that Cramer had passed on the information about mass absenteeism at the airfield, and that shortly the Gestapo would come to the Ghetto and turn it inside out.

Very embarrassed, we sat in the Council offices, waiting for the expected Gestapo raid. The reinforced contingent of police at the Ghetto gate since early morning also gave rise to serious fears.

Many Ghetto inmates surmised that the whole brouhaha was a result of an incident involving a Jewish worker, Bas, who was arrested the day before yesterday at the Ghetto gate with eight wristwatches in his possession. Bas is a member of the labor brigade that works for the Gestapo. After being taken to the Gestapo, he confessed that only two of the eight watches were his, whereas the remaining six he had stolen from the Gestapo. On the day of his arrest he had been working in a room where he found a suitcase with watches; he had helped himself to six of them. When the news of the theft reached us, we were seized by panic: theft from the Gestapo, particularly by a Jew, was bound to have serious consequences.

When the reinforced contingent of the Ghetto guard put in an appearance at the Ghetto gate yesterday morning, many thought that it was a direct result of the theft at the Gestapo. We at the Council knew very well, however, the true reason, as we had already been informed of the conversation between Zlata and Sragovitz.

All these things together—the watches stolen from the Gestapo, Cramer's complaint to the Gestapo about Jewish workers missing from the airfield, the expected Gestapo raid in the Ghetto, and, above all, the medicine affair and Zlata's demands and threats—brought the Ghetto to the boiling point. I could not agree more with Garfunkel, who said yesterday morning that when trouble comes it comes from all directions at once. Indeed, the troubles came rolling over us like so many heavy stones.

Whatever the place, the deed, or the perpetrator—we remain personally responsible for everything and for everyone. Whether it is some foolishness or malice, mistake or premeditation, carelessness or villainy—the Council is always guilty. Its address is always known. Here at the Council sit the public's representatives; it is we who are required to pay the price.

In the course of time the members of the Council have come to resemble a sensitive membrane. Any noise, any creak, any squeak, any whistle—the membrane picks up the sound instantly. The fibers are set in motion, the whole system starts vibrating, but it does so in complete silence, straining to contain the noise within itself, so as to not leak anything outside—to the Ghetto—but to cope with the storm until the end within itself. Outwardly, everything looks and sounds as usual. All this is intended to spare the wretched Ghetto inmates the worry, the pain, the torment. They have more than enough troubles, and we are in no better situation ourselves. On the contrary, it is often necessary to suppress the trouble, not to speak, not to tell anyone, and to let the troubles sink into the oblivion of silence.

Yesterday began with a storm at the Council: threats, fears, dark schemes of this suspect creature, Zlata. Here she spoke with Sragovitz, there with Segalson; she also wants to speak with the Council. She arrived here yesterday at half past six. At the Council she was serious and businesslike. Zlata is a tall, blond German woman, about thirty years old. Her face is round, with big blue eyes and the features of a woman who has been bruised many times in her life. She still has a lot of energy, and although under arrest and expecting a heavy sentence, she is not broken.

Zlata entered, seated herself at the table, and repeated her story: Wintzer, the medicine, her alibi, the Ghetto. Once again she repeated the promise given by both Cramer and Bartman that no one in the Ghetto will be hurt. The Council should issue an announcement to the Ghetto residents, instructing them to bring the medicine to an appointed place. The legally obtained medicine will then be returned to the Ghetto, whereas she will take away only the medicine on the list. That will be the end of the whole affair.

At present, she said, not a thing can be taken out of the Ghetto. The Council can see for itself that the Ghetto is guarded by a reinforced guard. If this does not suffice, she had been told, a big raid will take place on the houses in the Ghetto. Surely this is not for the benefit of the Ghetto—is it? After all, she cooperated with the Jews at 55 Paneriu Street and she bears them no grudge. No one will be hurt. This is her plan; having checked and double-checked it, she has come to the conclusion that there cannot be a better plan. If the Council can come up with a better plan, she will be most interested to know about it. She asks the Council to give her plan its support.

There were moments when we had the impression that this conversation was about a third, uninvolved party, and not about her. She was serious, absorbed in her thoughts, but quiet. She had been here before, in the same room; she had spoken with the same people seven or eight months ago. Then she came with Wintzer, decked out in his Nazi uniform, resplendent with decorations; a loyal and proud representative of the authorities and of the Nazi Party. He used to boast then about his highly placed friends in the settlement command, the SS, and Berlin. Here, in this room, he spoke about his grandiose plans for a huge factory, hundreds of Jewish workers, equipped with modern machinery. The city governor could not place obstacles in his way, because of his excellent connections at the top.

He, the influential architect Wintzer, was then Zlata's great friend, presenting her as his right hand: "this is Freifrau von Ravensburg." She was to replace him during his absences on official journeys to Berlin. She was to be given all the powers and was to act in the capacity of the director. I remember her sitting proudly by his side, haughty, appraising with disdain and pity the pariah Jews, their brows furrowed with worry, their shabby clothes adorned with yellow badges. She was dressed with exaggerated elegance, her hair styled beautifully, very smartened up. She had no worries then, and lived her life to the full. She carried about her an air of licentiousness, debauchery, and easy affluence. Today her great friend, the architect Wintzer, once an influential man, is languishing behind bars. He will spend a long time in prison and may drag her with him. The friendship is gone, as are all the pleasures. Now she is on short leave from prison—a leave which she obtained only with difficulty. Despite all that, she does not lose her head, keeps her wits about her, and, at the same time, remains very worried. She is playing a part, and wears a mask to conceal everything from others, going to great lengths not to expose her true face. But she is no longer that proud Baroness von Ravensburg; now she is just a poor woman, drowning, and looking for rescue by embarking on a new adventure, doing her best to trick us into believing her.

The members of the Council exercise considered judgment; they listen without saying a word, without showing any signs of emotion or dejection. They neither deny her requests nor give any promises. Their attitude is "wait and see." We have to consult Miller, they say, he is the boss here. Without him nothing can be done in the Ghetto. Tomorrow one of us will speak with Miller. If he agrees, the announcement will be issued to the Ghetto residents. In any event, the Council has not been faced with such a problem before; it presents a new challenge for us. But, since she asks our assistance and we can be of help, why not? Miller must be consulted, however. "Are you absolutely certain that the medicine found its way to the Ghetto?" Dr. Elkes asks her. "Yes, I am," she replies. "Some of it was sold in the city. There is no way that none of it could have remained in the Ghetto."

Dr. Elkes asked her whether the medicine was smuggled into the city by a middleman, and whether she knows who it was who engaged in this activity. In reply, she intimated that this would be found out. At present she does not know the identity of the person who brought the medicine to the Ghetto. She only knows that it is here, and she wants to find it.

The Council reached an agreement with Zlata that it will consult Miller. She will be given an answer today, at three o'clock. In the meantime, the Council will again discuss the matter.

From the Council offices, the Baroness repaired to the workshops, where she had a talk with Dr. Nahum Katz. He had played the leading part in this whole affair and was understandably very frightened. When she began to retell her version of events, he cut her short, saying that, frankly, she cannot speak to him like that. After all, she knows how the medicine came from Germany; she knows what varieties and what quantity of medicine were involved; she knows how much was paid for it, how it reached 55 Paneriu Street, and in what manner it was subsequently smuggled into the Ghetto. She knows very well that it was she who smuggled the second shipment of medicine from Eydtkuhnen; that Wintzer himself brought most of the medicine into the Ghetto on a sleigh and that she herself smuggled the remainder. Why then does she want him to tell her all about it, if she knows the story herself? She knows very well how much money was paid for it; after all, she and Wintzer pocketed it. If she wants to drag him, Katz, into this game, if she is looking for a scapegoat, she should know that he is not going to risk his neck for her. He is going to deny everything as long as he can. And if they beat all the resistance out of him, he will tell them every single detail—not just about her and the medicine, but about all the shady operations at 55 Paneriu Street. "Let me die with the Philistines." So please, stop playing this game; stop looking for the medicine in the Ghetto. She will find nothing here; there is no medicine left in the Ghetto. She can conduct searches to her heart's content—nothing will help. Wintzer did not mention the Jews and the Jews do not mention his name. She is wasting her time arguing.

With these arguments, Katz wished to clarify the state of affairs for her, and curtail her appetite for any new adventures in the Ghetto. Let her spin these yarns to anyone she pleases, but not to him.

All the while, Gilow was receiving reports about Zlata's visit to the workshops. He followed the progress of the affair very closely, and asked for a report about each of her conversations. It was obvious that he would be glad to be rid of this problem. Possibly he had reasons of his own. Earlier, at the time of Wintzer's arrest, Gilow had shown great interest in this case. In his conversation with Segalson, Gilow mentioned the name of the physician from 55 Paneriu Street; when it was revealed to him that the physician was the son of the Jewish skilled tailor working in the workshops, making suits for Cramer and all the top figures at the city and regional commissioner's offices, he said: "More's the pity."

This was a bad omen for Katz and, by the same token, for the manager of the Ghetto pharmacy, and for the Council as well.

Before she left, Mrs. Ravensburg presented a letter to the members of the Council. The letter, from the German security police, signed by Dr. Bartman, commissioner of the police, demanded that we extend our assistance to her in embarking on this mission. She wants to save her skin. The big question is whether it can harm the Ghetto. Her story must be checked further. In particular, is it true that Cramer knows about it, that he promised not to hurt anyone in the Ghetto? Did Bartman also promise that? It was therefore decided that today we must speak with Miller and with Bartman. Since she made a practical proposal—to force the Ghetto residents to bring the medicine—we must inform Miller anyway, and ask for instructions as to whether we should do it or not. The Council decided that I will meet with Miller this morning and find out what I can; Lipzer will meet with Bartman. Afterward, the Council will discuss the matter on the basis of any new information which Lipzer and I can acquire. Until then we should wait.

As the Council concluded its discussion yesterday, Bas, the Jewish worker arrested yesterday in connection with the stolen wristwatches, was returned to the Ghetto from the Gestapo. He was lucky: one night in a cell and a severe beating. Two other Jewish workers, Bleiman and Jolk, who had seen him in the act of stealing the watches, were beaten for failing to inform on him. Now Bas will be required to work at the airfield as a punishment. This is a very light penalty; it provided some relief after the troubles of yesterday. It appears that the light sentence was given because the wristwatches were stolen to begin with, and the Gestapo was tired of raising a stink about them. The old rule "one thief covers for another" still applies. It is good that all this is now over.

This morning I left for the city to meet with Miller. In the office of the city governor I told him about Zlata's visit to the Council, about her request, about the guarantees issued by Cramer and Bartman promising not to harm the Jews in the Ghetto in connection with this affair, and about other details. I then asked Miller for his instructions.

Having heard my report, Miller was enraged: "What? She spoke with Colonel Cramer? She is still not as free as that! She has gone too far. Only I speak with Colonel Cramer. I gave her a leave of absence from prison because she asked for it; she wants to prove her innocence. Wintzer was sentenced to four years and a 10,000-mark fine. A criminal must be punished, and it does not make any difference whether he is a German or a Lithuanian or a Jew. She was also accused. It was I who sent her to Bartman, who gave her the permit to leave the prison. But she is getting arrogant and vain; I am washing my hands of her!"

Miller then telephoned Dr. Bartman and told him impatiently: "Mrs. Ravensburg turns the Ghetto upside down. She keeps talking about Cramer and me and makes threats about 'raids.' You should summon her and tell her what to say and what not to say. She had the nerve to ask me for a carriage to drive her to the Ghetto. As far as I am concerned, she can walk. I have nothing to do with this; it is a criminal case. You should speak with her. If necessary, issue the appropriate instructions to the Council."

As a result of this conversation, Miller and Cramer reached an agreement. Miller then turned to me with the words: "You heard it? This is it. Get on the telephone to Dr. Bartman and do as he says. All this must be kept secret."

Bartman then issued an order through Lipzer that as soon as Zlata puts in an appearance at the Council today, we should send her to him without entering into any conversation with her.

Shortly before three o'clock, Segalson informed the Council that Miller had told him to order the Ghetto guard not to let Zlata into the Ghetto, but to send her to Dr. Bartman instead. A few moments later, however, she again appeared at the Council and spoke to us. Dr. Elkes referred her to Dr. Bartman: "Miller has ordered us to contact Dr. Bartman concerning this matter," he explained. "Even if the Council wants to help you, it cannot disobey these orders."

This should have put an end to the whole thing. But Zlata did not leave. She was drunk. She had entered the Ghetto in an SS car and had been dropped off at the Council offices. The SS men continued on their way to the workshops. Zlata had a gun; hardly had she seated herself at the Council table when she dropped it—as if unintentionally—on the floor. Garfunkel noticed that two bullets then rolled across the floor.

Dr. Elkes and Garfunkel looked with amazement, but Zlata remained quiet, nor did she show any inclination to pick up the gun from the floor. She stayed for half an hour, repeating her request, asking the Council again to do as she wished, and promising that no one would be hurt. Dr. Elkes and Garfunkel explained once more that Miller had not given his permission and that she must go to Dr. Bartman.

Only after half an hour did Zlata pick up the gun (again as if unintentionally), place it in her leather bag, and then explain that prosecutor Paruke did not allow her to enter the Ghetto without the gun; he had been stationed previously in the Ukraine, and also in Minsk, where an unarmed German does not leave the place alive. She had told Paruke that she was not afraid, as nothing bad would happen to her here. But he had dug in his heels and had not let her go without the gun. Moreover, she was required to sign a declaration that, if something happened to her in the Ghetto, she would not be able to sue the Reich for damages. After all, the Reich is responsible for every prisoner and prisoner-of-war. As a prisoner, she is the property of the Reich and the prosecutor does not want any trouble. This is why she had no choice but to sign the declaration.

Zlata kept telling us about a German officer who had sworn on his honor that nothing bad would happen to anyone in the Ghetto if the medicine is delivered up. After all, you should know what the honor of the German officer is, she said to Dr. Elkes and to Garfunkel. Then she returned to her subject, showing a four-page-long list of the medicine brought to the Ghetto according to her own calculations. By now, her visit had begun to be a nuisance. At last she left the Council offices. As she was going down the stairs on the second floor, she caught her shoe and broke the heel. She was drunk.

From the Council building, Zlata went on to the workshops, where she spoke again with Sragovitz and with Katz. Katz repeated what he had said to her yesterday. In reply she said that the testimony of a Jew implicating her in an illegal trade in medicine in the Ghetto is not enough to convict her without Wintzer's confirmation; up to now he has not implicated her.

This conversation took place in the carpentry shop, which is located in a large room filled with machinery. There is a small room in the corner, separated from the large room by a thin partition with a glass door. Zlata and Katz talked in this small room, standing by a table. All of a sudden Zlata pulled the gun out of her bag, loaded it, rested the barrel on her left arm, and aimed it at something. Then the sound of a shot rang out, followed by a cry emanating from the large room. The bullet had passed through the left sleeve of her coat, gone through the door, and hit the leg of a lathe operator, Levish, who was busy at work there. Zlata started running, gun in hand, but Katz grabbed her arm, wrested the gun from her, and placed it on the table in the carpentry shop. Zlata then left the workshops.

Katz notified Segalson immediately. Segalson called both the Ghetto guard and the Jewish police, ordering the Jewish police to apprehend Zlata and hand her over to the Ghetto guard. He also notified Gilow and Miller.

Zlata was handed over to the Ghetto guard, where she claimed that Katz had snatched her revolver from her, and had shot at her three times. The Gestapo arrived and Miller placed Katz under arrest. The wounded Levish was admitted to the Ghetto hospital, where his wound was examined. Then both Katz and Zlata were taken to the Gestapo.

On her way to the Ghetto guard, Zlata maintained that Dr. Bartman had given her the gun, whereas in the Ghetto she had said that the SS had given it to her. She was getting confused. Thus, for example, she said that Dr. Katz had shot at her three times, whereas only one shot had in fact been fired.

But nothing helped; not even the clear and convincing testimony given by Katz. After all, he is a Jew. What difference does it make that he is intelligent and innocent? Who is going to believe him? She, on the other hand, is a "German woman." So what if she was drunk, under suspicion, and effectively under arrest? No matter how contradictory her statements, they were enough for Katz to be placed under arrest and taken to the Gestapo together with her.

Today it ended in a gunshot. One Jew is in the hospital, treated for a wound he received for no reason, whereas another one has been taken to the Gestapo, his fate unknown. Those who are guilty in the medicine affair are frightened to death. But most frightened of all is Katz's young wife. The Gestapo practice is that if the husband is guilty, his wife shares in the crime. Many Jews from the labor brigade at 55 Paneriu Street are trembling with fear, as is the Ghetto pharmacy manager. Even more frightened, however, is the Council, which is always like a bridegroom who is in mourning at his own wedding, which is always a partner in every grief. Who knows how all this will end; whether the whole thing will not be turned into a provocation, as was the case with Meck? Today grave fears have set in. This is the second time that shots have been fired in the Ghetto. No matter how innocently it began, it may turn into a most dangerous business.

Burdened with grave new fears, the members of the Council returned to their homes late in the day. A sleepless, troubled night lay in store for each one of us.

1. "Zlata" was the nickname which Jews in a small village often gave to a woman on whom they looked with disdain. Members of the Council used the nickname so that anyone hearing them talk, and especially a Gestapo eavesdropper, would not know whom they were talking about.

MAY 22, 1943

Yesterday morning a depressing silence pervaded the Council building. Everyone was highly strung. Many waited for something unforeseen to happen. The Gestapo car will perhaps pull up shortly—who will be taken away this time?

In the workshops, people were very tense. Sragovitz, the acting manager of the furniture factory, has denied any involvement in the medicine affair. At any moment, however, he may be incriminated and his life may hang by a thread. Srebnitzki stayed for a while in the pharmacy and then vanished. He is restless. Everything he did was for the Ghetto's benefit. Since it was difficult to obtain medicine, he bought it whenever the opportunity presented itself. He fulfilled a public mission, and risked his life in the process. There was nothing personal in this. Now his life is in danger. Fear weighs heavily on his heart: how to refrain from implicating another person should an investigation be opened against him. The main thing is not to involve the Council; he would take all the responsibility on himself.

At 1 P.M. Gilow revealed to us that the prosecutor believes that Katz can be released. Later, Lipzer arrived from the Gestapo, confirming this information on behalf of Dr. Bartman. He told us that Zlata now maintains that she did not bring the gun from the city but procured it in the Ghetto. It is necessary, therefore, for Dr. Elkes to send a written statement to Dr. Bartman, saying that during her visit to the Council Zlata had a gun in her possession. Dr. Elkes should also reveal all he knows about the medicine affair.

The wording of the statement was not a simple matter. Each word had to be thought over. Our spirits were lifted, however; Katz will be released from jail.

When the labor brigade returned in the evening from its work at Gestapo headquarters, its members revealed that Dr. Katz had been transferred from the Gestapo to prison. This news gave rise to renewed concern. At seven o'clock in the evening Segalson informed us that the affair had taken a turn for the worse. Miller had talked to him on the telephone and was very angry. He told Segalson: "Now everything is clear. Katz engaged in trade in medicine. Now your turn has come. If something happens, no excuse will help you. You will be held responsible for everything that happened. I believe that something illegal was going on at 55 Paneriu Street. The workshops are not above suspicion either. You will be held responsible for any act of corruption to be uncovered."

Segalson was furious. He tried to explain to Miller that there is no way he can be held responsible for everything that goes on in the workshops. There is a German manager in the place, without whose approval nothing can be done. Miller, however, was adamant: "Gilow is accountable for his actions, whereas you are in charge of running the workshops." The situation, therefore, has become quite complicated. Apparently, the investigation revealed that Katz had been involved in selling the medicine and that this medicine had indeed reached the Ghetto. That which we most feared has come to pass.

We gathered at the Council offices—Dr. Elkes, Garfunkel, Goldberg, Segalson, Lipzer, Hirsch Levin and me—for the purpose of exchanging views on this painful and complex affair. When we heard the latest news from Segalson, it was as if a bombshell had exploded in the middle of the room. The benefits resulting from the purchased medicine are nothing compared with the bloodshed lying in store for us on account of the affair and the exposure of the people involved in it. All this is because of corrupt individuals devoid of any personal and public responsibility.

Then, suddenly, as in a detective story or a film, the telephone on the Council desk began to ring. The Ghetto telephone operator said that Dr. Katz had just returned to the Ghetto. This news was not unlike a story from *One Thousand and One Arabian Nights*. We could not believe our ears.

I immediately contacted the Ghetto Guard. They confirmed the information about Dr. Katz's return to the Ghetto a short while before. The mood of the Council at once took an upward turn. Even now, however, we feared that Dr. Katz's release might be temporary. Even the temporary release of a Jew accused of committing a crime has never happened before.

Dr. Katz is a friend of mine. In recent days I had had some serious conversations with him, so I ran to see him. In Lipzer's room sat Kopelman, Margolis, and Katz. We embraced warmly. Replying to my questions, Katz told me that three people were instrumental in his release: Dr. Bartman, the prosecutor, and the prison director.

Lipzer was put at ease: "You see, it was Bartman, after all. I told you so. I spoke to him. Lipzer is always right."

Dr. Katz briefly related his story: "This gunshot event was of no significance. They all knew that it was Zlata who had fired the gun. She accused a Jew of trying to kill her. What was new in that? The main thing was the medicine affair. They put pressure on me from all sides to confess that I had a hand in selling it. They showed me Wintzer's confession. Wintzer did, in fact, confess to bringing the medicine from Germany. But where did it disappear to—Wintzer did not know. It is possible that the Jews stole it."

Yesterday Zlata confessed to everything. Wintzer also testified that Katz had prepared the list of medicine and had subsequently brought it into the Ghetto. The investigators had then told Katz: "Now everything is clear. There is no point in denying the facts. By refusing to confess, you only work against yourself. If you confess, the prosecutor will release you."

Katz knew that even if the prosecutor released him, this would not bring the affair to an end. He would still have to deal with the Gestapo. So he refused to confess. The prison director and Dr. Bartman both tried to prevail upon him to confess, saying that he would not be harmed as a result. "You tell us what happened and we will release you at once. If not—you will suffer the consequences. We know all about your deeds. The only thing we do not have is your confession."

Katz realized that he had been deceived, and decided to tell the truth, especially in view of the repeated promises that he would be released following his confession, and that the Ghetto would not be held accountable. He therefore told his interrogators how Wintzer had asked him to prepare the list of medicine; how he, Katz, brought the medicine to Kovno; how Wintzer put pressure on him to sell it; and how Wintzer made a profit of between 15,000 and 20,000 marks on the deal.

Wintzer was the big man in the factory. He had all the power and, for the Jewish workers, his request was an order. No one dared to disobey. So when Wintzer ordered Katz to do as he was told, Katz obeyed. Where did all the medicine disappear to? Katz did not answer this question. The medicine is long gone. It was all used up.

Following Katz's confession, the prosecutor ordered his release. The prison director then contacted Dr. Bartman, who let Katz out of prison. The prison director also supplied Katz with a paper which stated: "The Jew, Dr. Katz, was released from Kovno prison at 18:30. The officials involved are requested to enable him to pass from the city to the Ghetto without a guard."

"So, you are a free man," I said to Katz. "As long as the Gestapo does not arrest me," he replied. "Why do you have to worry now?" I asked. "Let's hope that this whole affair is done and over with." Later I recounted Katz's story to the Council.

We were about to go home when the Jewish police headquarters informed us that the Ghetto commandant, Tschich, had ordered the commandant of the second police precinct to bring Dr. Katz to him. Gloom filled the room again. We asked Katz not to report to the police headquarters until he received news from us. Katz then went into hiding, and the Jewish police informed the Ghetto commandant that he could not be found at his home. When, later, Natkin learned that the Ghetto commandant only wanted to check Katz's release papers, all sighed with relief.

That evening, Katz went to report at the Ghetto Guard. We decided to wait for him to return. At last, at 10:30 at night, he returned, and everybody could go home.

The situation in the Ghetto is unstable. There are ups and downs, especially in recent days. I did not go to bed before I could see Srebnitzki and shake his hand; he has been very worried lately and I was glad that he would be able to sleep in his apartment tonight. He said: "Thank you so much for coming to see me. This was my first test—see how I look. You, at the Council, are going through this every day, how can you stand it?" He is right; we will live in permanent danger until our liberation from the Ghetto comes, or until we die.

This morning the mood at the Council was good, as usual in the aftermath of a crisis. I was entrusted with delivering to the city governor's office four reports: one written by Dr. Elkes; one by the police inspector Levin, who had taken Zlata to the Ghetto guard; one written by the worker Rudeiski, a young man who had witnessed Dr. Katz wresting the gun from Zlata's hand after she had shot at him; and one written by the worker Levish, who had been wounded by the shot. I collected the materials and set out for the city.

At the last moment I had doubts about whether Dr. Elkes should have written in this statement that Zlata was drunk during her visit to the Council building. This remark could provoke the wrath of our rulers, as an insult directed against a German woman. Lipzer insisted, however, that this information should be included in the report.

Upon my arrival in the city, I delivered the four reports to Miller in the city governor's office. He read them with great interest and with approval. He then put the material in an envelope and wrote on it the name of Dr. Bartman of the Gestapo. I had then to deliver it.

It was the first time that I had visited the criminal police office. In room no. 73 I came across a young man with blond hair, wearing an SS uniform. It was Dr. Bartman. He took delivery of the material and thanked me. Recent developments had given me the impression that the whole affair was finally closed.

After I returned to the Ghetto, I received news that Miller had given an order to place Katz under arrest. The temperature at the Council rose again. I know Miller well. He does not like to be at the service of the Gestapo. It is possible that this is his whim. It happened once that Miller ordered a man to be placed under arrest after he had been released by the Gestapo. On that occasion Miller locked the man up for seven days in the Ghetto detention center.

Katz is very worried. We at the Council are also worried. I still hope that this affair will end well. The heart asks for a little peace and security. Will we ever get it?

MAY 26, 1943

Miller is going on two weeks' leave today. During his absence he will be replaced by Obst, who, among other things, conducts the Jewish account at the city governor's office. This Jewish account is the only active money account at the city governor's office, and an inexhaustible source of income for the German administration. About 7,000 Jews go out to work daily outside the Ghetto. For each day's work by a Jew, the city governor's office receives three marks for a man and two and a half marks for a woman. This makes a total of 400,000 marks. To this one should add the income from various articles impounded at the Ghetto gate or along the perimeter fence, and the expropriation of former Jewish property in the city on behalf of the city governor's office.

Obst is in charge of this account. All the income from the Ghetto workshops also flows into it. Eighteen hundred Jewish workers toil in the Ghetto day and night. They make clothes, wash underwear, repair military equipment; they even manufacture various articles for the German Army. Needless to say, all the profits go to the city governor's office.

The Jewish account keeps growing. Millions of marks have already accumulated there. There are expenses too; part of the National Socialist Party budget has to come out of it, as do some of the expenses of the city governor's office. In addition to various institutions whose expenses come out of this account, all kinds of senior figures and minor officials "handling" Jewish matters enjoy the benefits of it.

There is an old Jewish joke about Menachem Mendl, who, when asked in court about his occupation, replied that he "hangs around." The judge was not satisfied by this reply and repeated his question: the court wants to know—what is your occupation, what do you live on? "I just hang around here and there," replied Menachem Mendl. "I don't understand anything," said the judge, exasperated. Menachem Mendl explained: "Here, you are the judge and I am a Jew. If you let me hang around you, it'll be good for you and I will have something to live on."

It could be said that the Germans in Lithuania make their living by "hanging around" Jewish matters.

Obst does not want to pay too much money for firewood. So he does not buy it at all. Whenever we ask him for planks, tin, or nails, for the repair of our houses, he turns our request over in his mind ten times, with the result that the essential materials are not supplied to us. "This costs a lot of money," he says. In point of fact, the necessary expenses amount to a few hundred marks—a negligible sum compared to the millions sitting in the Jewish account. Miller, on the other hand, is not mean in these matters. "There is enough money for everything," he is in the habit of saying.

Now Miller is on leave and Obst replaces him. Obst is a difficult man to get along with. As far as his private expenses are concerned, he is not at all mean. He keeps appearing at the Ghetto workshops, placing orders for all manner of articles, such as knee boots, shoes, and suits of clothing—for himself, his wife, and his children. He also gets a part of all the goods impounded at the Ghetto gate: butter, eggs, honey, and suchlike.

The German manager of the workshops, Gilow, represents Miller within the Ghetto and in the management of the workshops. He is a corrupt man. He devotes all his efforts to one purpose: taking for himself various articles produced at the workshops. He places orders for gold rings and other valuables. Gilow hates Jews and cannot stand being in their abodes. He is also a coward. All his life he has been afraid of being sent to the front. This is why we keep counting the days until Miller's return. At least Miller has a kind word for us from time to time.

What caused us particular concern was the fact that during Miller's absence Dr. Katz would remain in detention. The situation in that respect is not clear. Katz also is worried.

Two days ago I spoke to Miller. I asked him, among other things, what was Katz's situation. Miller replied curtly: "For the time being he remains in detention." Mrs. Chaimovitz, who is employed as a cleaning lady in Miller's home, asked him several times about Katz. It is easier for her to show an interest in Katz's fate, as she does not act in any official capacity and does not represent the Ghetto inmates. She speaks with Miller at his home; on occasion she even chats with him in the kitchen. They have good relations. Miller told her almost the same thing: "For the time being Katz must remain in detention, but nothing is going to happen to him."

We learned that before going on leave Miller had left instructions to Gilow, ordering the commander of the Jewish police to release Katz from detention. We were very pleased by this good news.

Something else gave us reason for satisfaction: a Jewish dentist, Lurie, spoke today with a German priest by the name of Poltz. This priest is a good friend of Jaeger's; he also serves as liaison between the German church and the German authorities. Today Poltz told Lurie that he had learned from Jaeger that the oppression of Jews in our area has been ended. Although we no longer believe in the promises voiced by the German rulers, let alone by the Gestapo, it is better to hear this kind of news from them than to hear the news we are accustomed to.

At seven o'clock in the evening Lipzer entered the Council office with a serious expression on his face. He began at once by insisting that Garfunkel issue orders to employ a certain Meir Tainovitz as a horse driver in the transportation department. Tainovitz is known to us as one of those who trades at the Ghetto fence. Garfunkel tried to convince Lipzer that his protégé might cause trouble for us. Lipzer remained adamant, however, persisting angrily in his demand that we accept Tainovitz for work in the Council offices.[1]

Later Goldberg asked Lipzer why he was so angry. We knew the reason, but kept silent. The story is as follows: a week earlier Shlomo Goldstein[2] had joined a truck that had left Kovno for Vilna; he went with it in the guise of a worker of the technical head office. He actually went to Vilna, however, at our request, in order to meet some of our friends in the Zionist underground there. Goldstein went to Vilna and brought back their greetings to us.

Lipzer learned about Goldstein's journey; he too wanted to go to Vilna, but Dr. Elkes persuaded him not to. After the Ponar massacre, a trip by a man like Lipzer could be construed by the Gestapo as a spying mission. This is why Lipzer was angry: they do not trust him at the Council. In the meantime, Dr. Elkes arrived. Lipzer carried on with his complaints: he does everything he can for the Council, but the Jewish body does not trust him. He is kept in the dark as far as the Ghetto's problems are concerned. For example, he wanted to conduct a search of the pharmacy but was refused. He was not told that the pharmacy was implicated in the medicine affair. He wanted to go to Vilna and Dr. Elkes told him not to go. He learned that while Goldstein was in Vilna he told Gens that he, Lipzer, was merely a middleman between the Council and the Gestapo. He will not let it pass.

Dr. Elkes replied by telling Lipzer: (a) that the Council members themselves did not know the details of the medicine affair and that he, Dr. Elkes, believed that the fewer people knew about it the better; (b) that the Council did not send Goldstein on a mission to Vilna, nor did it cover the cost of his journey; and (c) that Dr. Elkes knows nothing about the conversation between Gens and Goldstein in Vilna.

After some more argument over this affair and its ramifications, Lipzer calmed down somewhat.

This dispute with Lipzer over trifles succeeded in spoiling the good mood in the Council caused by the news received in the morning about Katz's release, and the account by the German priest of his conversation with Jaeger.

1. Avraham Tory later recalled: "Later I learned that Tainovitz was involved in several daring exploits, smuggling furniture and valuables out of the Ghetto, exchanging them for arms in the city, and smuggling the arms back into the Ghetto. A simple, courageous man, willing to help."

2. Shlomo Goldstein, a Zionist activist in prewar Lithuania, was one of the four founders of the Ghetto underground group Matzok. After the war he went to the United States, where he became active in various Jewish organizations, as well as in activities in support of the State of Israel.

MAY 28, 1943

DOCUMENT:
From the German Labor Office in Kovno
To Brigadier Cramer, Governor of Kovno

In view of the noticeable shortage of Lithuanian manpower, and the still-increasing demand for urgent and important war production, the compulsory labor of the Jews becomes ever more important.

To the Jewish labor already in use must therefore be added about 300 Jews who were previously employed in loading and unloading ships, in vegetable gardens, and on municipal farms.

The following new labor brigades have now been established:

	men	*women*
The labor brigade for cutting wood	40	40
War hospital work	5	40
The department for the construction of new railroads	25	25
The Filva knitting and weaving factory	13	30
The Guma rubber products factory	40	120
The Kovno felt factory	2	22
The Krovejas transportation company	50	—
The Statyba foundry for the repair of bomb damage	60	20
Roof-felt factories	26	10
The iron foundry at Vilijampolé	10	1
Sanitation department	2	20
Soldiers' hostel	1	9

The working brigades at the airport must be increased from 800 to 1,000. The manpower working in the Ghetto workshops is busy with Christmas orders and has had to be increased from 1,250 to 1,600.

For the production of peat, eighty Jews and ten Jewesses were attached to the army accommodation administration to Kaisiadorys.

The establishment of these new brigades was partially achieved by the reduction and cancellation of less important work, but mostly by the registration of all able-bodied Jews conducted by the Council in March, and the reduction of the internal-administration personnel.

At present, Jews are employed by 110 employers, divided by percentage as follows:

1. Army and war production enterprises   68%
2. Traffic, transport, and the construction of railway bridges   9%
3. Police stations   4%
4. Administration and other civil sectors   19%

Explanations of the above items:

1. The work with the Army is carried out in close cooperation with the war production command, according to the urgency of the work. Jewish manpower employed by the Army consists mostly of craftsmen. They are employed in the following enterprises as metalworkers: workshops for the repair of anti-aircraft guns, the Metalas metal factory, the Augustaitis forge, the iron foundry at Vilijampolé, the Kutkevicius wagon-manufacturing factory, and the wire and metal-products factory. Most of the construction craftsmen are employed by the construction department of the Army and at the airport.

2. In traffic and bridge construction, the Jews are employed by the railway administration, the office for the construction of new railroads, the bridge construction company Gruen and Bilfinger, the Demag textile factory, and the Krovejas transportation company, some as locksmiths but most as unskilled workers.

3. Police stations employ Jewish craftsmen as car mechanics in garages, as locksmiths and specialist mechanics in the armory, and as cobblers and tailors in the workshops. A further eighty-six Jews are employed by the Gestapo.

4. In the civil sector, the Jews are mainly employed as construction workers in transport, in the printshop of the Kovno-Vilna publishing and printing company, and in agriculture.

At present, the unemployed Jewesses are being examined for their working fitness. Some of them will be added to the existing employed manpower.

Jews between the ages of twelve and fifteen have been registered. The strong ones among them will be added to heavy work, the weaker ones will be assigned to agricultural cultivation work.

When the workplaces are next checked, more attention must be paid to ensuring that the so-called Court Jews are assigned to more useful occupations.[1]

The recently ever increasing demand for the assignment of Jewish manpower for all kinds of work can be supplied only in a few cases. In future, as hitherto, only work of the highest urgency can be considered.

1. This derisory reference to the "Court Jews" of the eighteenth century—Jews who served as ministers and financial advisers to the German princes—overlooked the fact that in the Kovno Ghetto the Council members and the officials in the various Council departments took turns working in the labor force at Aleksotas airfield.

MAY 28, 1943

In recent weeks, anonymous persons have begun distributing in Kovno a pamphlet written in Lithuanian; its contents have given rise to apprehensions in the Ghetto. The pamphlet was printed by a group calling itself the Lithuania Liberation Organization, located in Vilna and dated May 1943. The pamphlet said: "There are clear and reliable indications that preparations are afoot for new massacres of the Jews. The previous acts of murder of the Jews brought neither honor nor benefit to Lithuania. Lithuanians will be called upon to explain to the world the fact of the participation of many of their compatriots in those criminal acts. From now on, in order not to be implicated in the crime of mass murder, Lithuanians are also called upon to refrain from carrying out the instructions of the Gestapo; when risk of their life is involved, they should flee to the forest."

The sentence stating that there were "clear and reliable indications that preparations are afoot for new massacres of the Jews" was underlined in the pamphlet.

The contents of this pamphlet have made a deep impression in the Ghetto. It indicates a change in the attitude of the Lithuanians toward the Jews. This, however, does not in any way obscure the danger pointed out by the authors of the pamphlet. We have no doubts as to who will emerge victorious from this war. At the same time, however, we have grounds to believe that the Germans will not be eager to please us by leaving us alive so that we can witness their defeat.

Up to now our only hope has been a sudden defeat of the Germans in the war. Such an end to the war offered us the only possibility for liberation. If, however, the war goes on for many months to come, while all developments point in one direction—to the German defeat—we cannot hope for a miracle. With time at their disposal they will exterminate us. This is not a question of a certain number of Jewish souls. The future of an important segment of Jewry, one which has inscribed glorious pages in the history of the Jewish people, hangs in the balance.

A few days ago, Kopelman spoke to an old friend of his, a German from Kovno by the name Garbachevski. This German is stationed in Riga, working for the German Army. The two ran into each other by chance on one of the streets of Kovno. They entered a gate leading into a courtyard so that no one would witness their conversation. The German friend told Kopelman that during the big battle near Veliki-Luki last year, when the Russians were on the point of breaking through the German front, appropriate military measures were taken by the Germans in Riga, including the evacuation of the city. Among other things, large quantities of arms and ammunition were moved from Riga to Kovno. In those fateful days, a very important figure in the German administration revealed to Garbachevski the existence of an instruction to destroy the prison and the Ghetto prior to the evacuation of the city. Garbachevski revealed this information to Kopelman so that he would know what steps to take should a similar situation develop in Kovno.

In recent days, rumors have spread in the Ghetto about deep pits being dug at the Ninth Fort and the Seventh Fort. According to these rumors, the pits are being dug in connection with the possible massacre of the Jews.

Yesterday Dr. Avraham Kishiniski[1] paid a visit to Dr. Elkes at his apartment. He now works at the Marva estate. The Lithuanian manager of the estate, who is a friend of his, had just revealed a secret to him. His friend occupies an important position in the Lithuanian criminal police. According to him, the Gestapo asked the Lithuanian criminal police to give it a list of policemen who would be willing to participate in a massacre of Jews. The list was submitted, but the Gestapo rejected it. Another list was sent to the Gestapo and, again, it was rejected. Following these two rejections, Dr. Kishiniski's friend learned that the heads of the Gestapo had decided to abandon the idea of including Lithuanian policemen in any future "actions" against the Jews. Instead, a special contingent will be brought for that purpose from the Ukraine.

Lately, the Lithuanians are advising their Jewish acquaintances to flee from the Ghetto to save their lives. Everyone knows that the Germans are not the victors in this war. They are very angry and no miracles should be expected. Some Lithuanians have learned that the Vilna Ghetto will be the first to be destroyed, followed by the Kovno Ghetto. This information comes from Professor Maszilis and others.

The official bodies with which we maintain contact vehemently deny these rumors. Lipzer calls at the Council offices every day with reassuring news: Schmitz, Schtitz, Miller, and Obst all swear on everything that is dear to them that nothing bad will happen to the Ghetto. Lipzer supplied them with a copy of the Lithuanian pamphlet warning that a massacre of the Jews is to be carried out in the near future. In response, the Gestapo chiefs showed him a crateful of such pamphlets, telling him that they are just "atrocity propaganda." The Gestapo chiefs also took Lipzer to the Seventh Fort so that he could see for himself that no pits were being dug there. Lipzer maintains that the Ghetto does not face any danger, and he believes that. Unfortunately we do not share his views and beliefs in this regard.

The news about the destruction of several Ghettos in Poland by means of gas and machine guns cannot fail to affect us.[2] Rumors about a change for the worse in the treatment of Bulgarian Jews, many of whom were deported from their country, and the information about the imposition of a levy of 4 billion lei on Romanian Jewry, prove the existence and implementation of plans whose only purpose is the extermination of Jews.[3]

It is also true that the persecution of Romanian and Bulgarian Jews can be regarded differently, that is, as indicating that large Jewish populations still exist in these countries. Looked at from this point of view, this news is reassuring to some extent.

The recent change for the better in the attitude of the Lithuanians toward the Jews was evident in a conversation that Kopelman had recently with his Lithuanian friend, a former business associate. In 1941 this friend spoke with a Lithuanian professor, Jurgutis.[4] In those days—shortly after the entrance of the Germans into Lithuania—Jurgutis occupied an important post in what was then called the government of Lithuania. It was the time of "actions" against the Jews throughout Lithuania. Kopelman's friend appealed to Professor Jurgutis to use his influence to stop the slaughter of Lithuanian Jews. The reply of the distinguished professor—a veteran Jew-hater—was that his honor did not allow him to speak with the Germans about their treatment of the Jews.

Recently, this friend of Kopelman's by chance ran into Professor Jurgutis, and spoke to him about the current situation. Jurgutis told him that in this war two disasters had been visited upon the Lithuanian people. One was the deportation of thousands of Lithuanians to the remote steppes of Russia. The second was the mass execution of Lithuanian Jews in 1941. Times have indeed changed, when even a person like Professor Jurgutis is forced to reconsider his earlier views.

The moment of decision in this war is at hand. It is as if two armored trains are rushing toward the finish line. One train will bring our death in its wake; the other one will bring liberation. Which one will reach the finish line first? No one knows.

1. Dr. Avraham Kishiniski had been a leader of the Zionist-Socialist party in prewar Lithuania. During the Ghetto days he supervised the youth work at the Marva farm.

2. During May 1943 more than 10,000 Jews were murdered in the former Polish East Galician cities of Brody (2,500 killed, May 1), Skalat (660, May 9), Busk (1,000, May 21), Stryj (1,000, May 22), Sokal (2,500, May 27), and Tluste (3,000, May 27). That same month 56,000 Jews were killed in Warsaw or deported to their deaths; more than 7,500 Jews were

deported from Holland to Sobibor and killed; and 10,000 from Salonika, 2,000 from Zagreb, and 395 from Berlin, to Auschwitz.

3. On March 17, 1943, the Bulgarian parliament rejected a German request to deport the 48,565 Jews of Bulgaria. When the war ended, the Jewish population of Bulgaria had risen to 49,172, the only country within the German sphere of influence whose Jewish population actually increased during the war. There had, however, been deportations in March 1943 from Bulgarian-occupied Greece and Yugoslavia, in which more than 11,000 Jews were sent to Treblinka and Auschwitz.

4. Professor Jurgutis, a Lithuanian economist, was subsequently imprisoned by the Germans at Stutthof, near Danzig.

JUNE 2, 1943

At the Council meeting today, Joseph Caspi was present and addressed us. He spoke clearly, without stopping. His speech bore the marks of his split personality: on the one hand a convinced Zionist Jew, and on the other a person close to the Gestapo. The Gestapo has allowed him to live in the city, exempted him from the obligation of wearing the yellow badge, and even allowed him to carry arms.

I took down Caspi's speech without his noticing me (which resulted in broken sentences). The atmosphere in the room and the tone of his voice were charged with tension. Here is what Caspi said:

It is not the Jewish intelligentsia but the educated Jews who gain esteem in times of war, above all the Jewish labor brigade.

The "Bontche Schweig"[1] type suffers. He suffered in the past and he suffers today more than anyone else. In for a penny, in for a pound—cavalry service is not like serving in the infantry. News reaches the Ghetto via Jews sent to jail, by means of letters which are written as a bill of indictment of the Council and not of the Germans. The labor office would do better than causing an avalanche of scraps of paper written on behalf of one's acquaintances. The moment will come when there will be a need to take out twenty-five innocent people. The entire staff of the labor office does not have to be present at the Ghetto gate. There are privileges in the Ghetto: it is better to work in the workshops than at the airfield. Likewise, it is better to work in the office than to go out to work at the airfield. You have to do something, achieve something in exchange for these privileges. No one is free to abandon his post or his place of work. This must not be allowed to happen. Everyone achieving something positive for us is to be blessed. Why should the labor office be seated and not the others? It is not its job to send people to jail, this is the job for the police. This decision must be revoked. There are too many employees. One can employ older people; there is the problem of the employment of the Ghetto women. Examine the situation, make changes, don't wait for the intervention of the third party. A minimum subsistence should be established for office directors. People who are irreplaceable should receive this minimum, others should be put on welfare. This arrangement should become law.

I want to give you advice. Representatives of the city labor brigades should meet with representatives of the labor office, the police, and the welfare department, in order to decide about the distribution of work in various brigades, and to decide who will go to each brigade. The personal approach should be abolished. It is a disease that must be rooted out.

It is necessary to set fines for physicians who refuse to visit patients who cannot afford to pay high fees. The physicians in the Ghetto form a privileged group. They do not go out to work at the airfield. The situation in which the Bontche Schweig cannot get anywhere is unbearable. The practice of issuing people with scraps of paper exempting them from work-duty has to be brought to an end. Delegations come to me and to Lipzer. This may cost us in blood. This situation must be brought to an end.

Only the police are authorized to make arrests. The labor office has the power to instruct the police to make an arrest. If a labor office official makes an arrest, I will personally send him to jail. This cannot go on.

The dreamers and fighters have discovered a new phenomenon, "A Jew with a gun," namely me, Caspi, a living legend who will go down in Jewish history. I will be with you at every stage, but you have to accept me the way I am.

I crave neither money nor respect from you. One way or another I am tainted by my connections with the Gestapo. I do not expect recognition from you. I am not interested in the views of Elkes or Garfunkel. I will carry on. The Ghetto does not pose a danger to the Germans. The Ghetto remains loyal to the Germans. Whatever you in the Ghetto think in your heart of hearts, that is your business. I do for you more than you can even imagine.

I am with you in mind, in prayer, and in war. Work is your duty. There is a brigade leader. When he asks for something, he makes a sacrifice. I have made the greatest sacrifices, and because of them I demand that you accept the truth as I tell it.

You entertain illusions of survival. I know that if I survive it will be only by chance. I am fighting against the rotten Jewish intelligentsia. I began my fight at the National People's Bank in the townlet of Roskiskis, my birthplace, and I have not let up since then.

My father and my grandfather were scholars. I myself am a teacher.

All my employers, the firms, all the Gestapo men and the Lithuanians, remain my good friends—my methods were correct and I did not cause you any damage.

I am being told to get my hands off the Ghetto's affairs, but I put my head into the fire myself. In the course of my life I called in at several "transit stations." As far as Eydtkuhnen I traveled with Yudl Mark.[2] From there on, I traveled with Jabotinsky.[3]

I have loved Lithuania with every fiber of my soul. Until 1933 this was the Land of Israel for me. Now all the time it seems to me that people say "hello" to me only because I have a gun, which personally makes me angry.

Who knows how things will turn out. Whether the German people will become drunk on victory or are overcome by the agony of defeat, I, with my mark of Cain, will be the first to face danger. Life is organized here in the Ghetto; it is better here than in Vilna or in any other place.

It has been quiet here. If it were not for the scandals I made, the kitchen would not have been set up until several months later than it was. For me, the most important thing is healthy skillful workers and robust young men, whose heads are filled with Jewish reasoning, and who bring benefit to the Jewish people.

I do not want to interfere in your internal affairs. Let others do it. You yourselves can decide how to deal with them.

The struggle should be more just and moral.

The labor office should function properly.

The workshops need to be expanded.

The Ghetto should dig the peat it needs by its own efforts.

The disputes between the police and the labor office should be resolved.

The problems arising at the Ghetto gate should be worked out.

Everyone, even Council officials, should eat the minimum ration.

Exemptions awarded to privileged people should be brought to an end.

The airfield workers should have an opportunity to rest.

An interoffice commission—composed of the welfare office, the labor office, and the police—should be set up for the purpose of distributing work cards for the more tolerable workplaces.

Caspi was aware of his exceptional status, entitling him to walk around free, elegantly dressed, to live in the city, and to carry a gun wherever he went. At every opportunity, however, as now, he emphasized his sharing our fate and repeatedly asked that we should accept him the way he was, with all his whims.

The question arises as to the purpose of Caspi's visit. His speech gave expression to many of our internal problems, especially the burden of forced labor.

Caspi had always been known as a sharp debater; he had moved from an extreme revisionist position to socialist-folkist, and then back again. His speech was aimed primarily at presenting himself as a Jew who had remained loyal to his people despite the services he had rendered to the Gestapo.[4]

1. Bontche Schweig was a figure in Jewish folklore who suffered greatly and was humiliated by the rich, but kept silent. He was always the underdog. In a story by J. L. Peretz, he is described as a man who never spoke up for himself, and who, when he died, was buried in a grave with no inscription, not even a tombstone.

2. Yudel (Yudl) Mark, an educator and philologist, was editor-in-chief of the Kovno Yiddish daily newspaper *Folksblat* from 1930 to 1936. A Bundist, he was strongly opposed to Zionism at that time, arguing that Jews should stay where they were born—"Where we live, there is our homeland"—and that they should work for a better life within their diaspora communities. In 1936 he emigrated to the United States, and in 1970—at the age of seventy-three— to Israel.

3. Vladimir Jabotinsky, born in Odessa in 1880, was a Zionist leader who, in 1935, formed the right-wing Revisionist movement (the New Zionist Organization), calling, among other things, for a sovereign Jewish state. In 1937 he proposed a ten-year plan to "evacuate" 1,500,000 Eastern European Jews to Palestine. He died in the United States in 1940. In his will, he expressed the desire to be buried in the land of Israel. In 1964, Avraham Tory was a member of the public committee set up to arrange for the transfer of Jabotinsky's remains to Israel. He is buried on Mount Herzl, in Jerusalem.

4. Avraham Tory later recalled of this meeting: "Caspi was most aggressive and impulsive, criticizing the way the Council's labor department was operating. He spoke in a thundering voice, warning us, and at the same time asking us to understand his determination to work with the Germans, out of his strong desire to fight Communism. He hectored his listeners, raising his voice again and again, criticizing the Jewish administration in the Ghetto. He warned and threatened, trying to give the impression of himself as a man and a Jew of high morals." Caspi and his family were murdered by the Germans in the summer of 1943.

JUNE 4, 1943

Today, a long-awaited conversation with Professor Birsziska took place. For some time now we have been considering various Lithuanian figures with whom we might still find a common language, and from whom we might hear a reliable assessment of the situation in Lithuania in general, and of the situation of the Jews in particular. Finally, we decided to contact two Lithuanian personalities: Bishop Brizgys, with whom we have been maintaining some contact, and Professor Vlaclovas Birsziska, a prominent Lithuanian figure, sympathetic to the Jews, but one we have not yet succeeded in contacting.

The name of Professor Birsziska has recently been publicized owing to his chairmanship of the Lithuanian Convention which took place several months ago in Kovno. He is in contact with Renteln, the governor-general of Lithuania. This also was an important reason for our seeking to meet with him.

At present Professor Birsziska lives in Vilna, where he is rector of the Lithuanian University. He comes to Kovno only occasionally, for a day or two, which makes it difficult to meet with him. Acting at request of Kopelman, a former Lithuanian diplomat by name of Natkevitz arranged a meeting between him and Garfunkel at the home of a Lithuanian notary in Kovno, Borkevitz.

The meeting took place in the morning; it was amicable and interesting (Birsziska embraced and kissed Garfunkel both at the beginning and at the end of the meeting).

Regarding the general situation, Birsziska said he had heard that the Germans were in the process of setting up a new army, millions strong, composed of Russians, White Russians, Ukrainians, and Russian prisoners-of-war. A Soviet general, Vlasov, captured by the Germans at Stalingrad, has been designated the commander of the new army. The Germans plan to use it to attack and conquer Leningrad at any price. The capture of Leningrad is a very important objective for the Germans. If the plan succeeds, a Russian provisional government, headed by Vlasov, will be established in Leningrad. This would amount to a major political achievement and a diplomatic victory for the Germans.

The Soviets, too, have an immediate objective: the bombardment and capture of Riga, which would block the German advance toward Leningrad.

In both of these eventualities, the front line is likely to come very close to us; this would hurt both the Lithuanians and the Jews. There can be no doubt that the army composed of good-for-nothing, right-wing Russians, which the Germans plan to set up, would sow death and destruction on its way to Leningrad and back. This army would pose a mortal danger for the Jewish community.

As for the situation in Lithuania: the spirits of the Lithuanians are low. The Kovno convention was a result of the situation in which the Lithuanian intelligentsia found itself several months ago. The Germans were angry that the Lithuanians had refused to join the German Army. In Latvia and Estonia the enlistment campaign was a success, whereas in Lithuania it failed because of the unyielding attitude of the Lithuanians.

The Germans threatened heavy punishments against the Lithuanian population. For them it was a fiasco not just from the military point of view but from a political point of view as well, especially in view of the publicity it received in the Western press. Those German authorities in Lithuania who were entrusted with the enlistment campaign sought to prove at any price that all Lithuanian resistance had been suppressed. There has also been talk about the possible abolition of the German civil administration in Lithuania, following the failure of the enlistment campaign.

Dr. Renteln, the German governor-general of Lithuania, took harsh steps. Several important Lithuanian figures were arrested and sent to a German concentration camp. One of them, a lawyer by the name of Kurpa, died there (the

German announcement gave "heart-attack" as the cause of death). Dr. Renteln did not content himself with arrests, but threatened the liquidation of the whole Lithuanian intelligentsia if the enlistment campaign was not successful. This was to be accomplished by means already used by the Germans against the intelligentsia of Czechoslovakia and Holland; they were sent to the front line in Estonia to clean up mine fields. According to the information available, some 90 percent of them were killed in the process.

Renteln sought ways of saving face, in order to preserve the German civil administration in Lithuania. The only way was to break the Lithuanian resistance. The situation was most difficult; something had to be done to appease the wrath of the Germans.

During that time Professor Birsziska stood on the sidelines, without getting involved in political disputes. In the first period of the German occupation, when large-scale "actions" were carried out against the Jews, a Jewish woman came to him seeking a letter of recommendation on some matter. He could not refuse her, and wrote a few lines on her behalf, asking the person to whom the lines were addressed to listen to her problem. Later he was called to the Gestapo. There they asked him if he was giving letters of recommendation to Jews. "Do you know who the woman is to whom you gave your recommendation? She is a spy and she was executed," he was told. A Gestapo official warned him that if he intervened again on behalf of a Jew, it would result in serious consequences for the Lithuanian University in Vilna.

Since that incident, Professor Birsziska has refrained from doing favors for anyone. He has done his best not to be conspicuous. As the situation in Lithuania kept deteriorating, however, particularly in the aftermath of the enlistment fiasco, and with the launching of the campaign of deportation and arrest of members of the Lithuanian intelligentsia, he felt duty-bound to do something. He sought to save the professors, the physicians, the lawyers, the priests, and the teachers, as well as other educated Lithuanians whose lives were in danger. This was the reason for his participation in the Lithuanian convention, which gathered in Kovno under the shadow of the threat of heavy punishments against the Lithuanian educated classes.

The Germans promised numerous concessions to the organizers of the convention, but they failed to abide by them. One of them was that the recruitment commission would be empowered to exempt many Lithuanians from military service after they came to register. This was meant to achieve a public relations coup, as it could then be said that tens of thousands of Lithuanians had signed up at the recruitment commissions. The Germans also promised to reopen the universities and other institutions of higher education which had been closed in reprisal. They also promised to approve the council elected at the Kovno convention, etc. The convention did, in fact, elect a council consisting of eighteen members; several of them resigned immediately afterward. Only twelve members were left. This council, however, was not approved, just as other promises given by the German authorities were not honored.

It is true that the Lithuanians did not exactly rush to sign up even after the convention. Instead of the 50,000 Lithuanian soldiers planned by the Germans, the recruitment commissions produced in the end only a few thousand recruits. The only achievement of the convention was the discontinuation of the campaign of arrests and reprisals.

Professor Birsziska received many letters condemning his participation in the Kovno convention and his part as its chairman. He received these condemnations with understanding. He is waiting for the day when he will be able to explain his decision to participate.

Professor Birsziska's ties with the Germans are weak; altogether he spoke to Renteln only twice. The first meeting, concerning the universities, took place at the beginning of the German occupation. The second meeting was about the convention. Renteln, says Professor Birsziska, is an evil man who hates Jews. He uses every opportunity to emphasize his attitude toward the Jews (incidentally, Renteln speaks good Russian and Birsziska spoke with him in Russian).

Professor Birsziska's present visit to Kovno was in connection with the Lithuanian educational society Shvietimas (Education) which, for all practical purposes, functions as the Lithuanian ministry of education. Until now, this society has been located in Vilna. Recently an order was received to move it to Kovno. This order worried him. The Germans do not recognize Vilna as the Lithuanian capital, or indeed as the main Lithuanian city. They concentrate all their activities in Kovno; this the Lithuanians oppose. Professor Birsziska seeks German approval to leave Shvietimas in Vilna.

The Germans seek to reduce the number of Lithuanian high schools of various kinds from fifty-seven to fifteen, and to adapt the remaining ones to the war effort. The Poles in Vilna signed up at the recruitment commissions because they knew they would not in fact be mobilized, on account of their work in enterprises working for the German Army.

There is a secret Lithuanian committee in which every political party participates except the Catholics; the Catholics, who had already been active politically before the outbreak of the war, are nevertheless represented on this secret committee. The Catholics believe that the end of the war will increase their chances to rule Lithuania; for that reason they do not seek any close ties with other political parties.

Speaking of the Lithuanians, Professor Birsziska said that Professor Kreve-Mickevitz[1] had frequently been harassed by the Germans in the first days of the German occupation. One day the Gestapo went to his house and told him that both he and his wife would be executed that same day; they were told to write their wills. Some time later the couple were placed under house arrest.

The so-called "Memoirs of Bolshevik rule in Lithuania" are now being printed under the name of Professor Kreve-Mickevitz in a German paper published in Kovno. Professor Kreve-Mickevitz was forced to write under the German threats.

Professor Birsziska has no contacts with people outside Lithuania. His information concerning the Jews is rather scanty; he has heard nothing recently about any deterioration in our situation. He has no contacts with the Vilna Ghetto. Such contacts are maintained by his brother Mykolas. As far as this brother knows, the Germans do not plan any further persecution of the Jews for the time being. Had the Lithuanians had any part in the rule of their country, says Professor Birsziska, they would have tried to ease the situation of the Jews. Under present conditions, however, the Lithuanians cannot even help themselves.

During the confiscation of Jewish books, Professor Birsziska tried to save the large Jewish Strashun library.[2] He went to great lengths to transfer its most important volumes to the university library in Vilna, but his attempts proved futile.

Professor Birsziska wanted to know whether the Ghetto keeps track of all the events and measures resulting from the anti-Jewish actions of the Germans. General Daukantas[3] was asked by Kubiliunas to gather statistical material about the Jews in northern Lithuania. Daukantas expanded his activity to cover the Jews and their problems in the entire country (from other sources we learned that Daukantas used only Lithuanian sources).

Professor Birsziska also related an incident in Vilna in which a Lithuanian priest, during his sermon, called upon his flock to refrain from taking part in persecutions of the Jews, thus following the example of Bishop Brizgys. The former Polish Bishop of Vilna was exiled to the Marijampolé monastery. He was replaced by a Lithuanian, Bishop Rainys.

Professor Birsziska also told the story of a young Lithuanian woman named Shimaite,[4] who maintains regular contact with the Jews in Vilna, including visits to the Ghetto. She revealed to him that the Jews had learned of a scheme to evacuate an area of 300 square meters around the Ghetto fence in order to form a sort of no-man's-land aimed at further isolating the Jews. This plan caused restlessness in the Ghetto. Professor Birsziska inquired about this at the office of the Lithuanian mayor of Vilna, Karol Dabulevichius, who told him that he had not heard about such a plan.

Concerning the revelations contained in the Lithuanian pamphlet about alleged German preparations for new "actions" against the Jews, Professor Birsziska believes that the source of this information was a Lithuanian organization and not the Gestapo. He himself had not seen this pamphlet. The news about the continuation of the persecution of the Jews, and its escalation, derive from the Ponar massacre. The proof of this is the recent news of the execution of another 200 Jews in the Vilna district.

As the conversation was drawing to a close, Professor Birsziska expressed an interest in the situation of the Jews from our Jewish perspective. He also asked about several of his Jewish acquaintances. He assured us of his willingness to maintain contact with us in the future by means of Natkevitz. He will let us know of any important news which reaches him.

The conversation was cordial and frank. It was a serious dialogue between two old friends meeting at a fateful historical moment.

This meeting did not bring us much in a way of consolation or hope for redemption, as Garfunkel commented on his return to the Council. But for us, the community of the oppressed and isolated, such exchanges of views are of enormous importance. This meeting revealed to us new horizons in the political-social situation in Lithuania and the neighboring countries. Knowledge of the wider problems and an understanding of their significance are as important to us as is a compass for a ship cruising in distant, unknown seas. In that respect, the conversation with Professor Birsziska was of inestimable importance to us, and we remain grateful to him for it.

1. A famous writer and socialist, Professor Kreve-Mickevitz (Mickevicius) was married to a Jewish woman. Both she and her husband survived the war.
2. The Jewish Library in Vilna, consisting of 35,000 volumes by 1940, had been founded in 1892 and was named after Matityahu Strashun, who had donated the first 6,000 volumes. Most of the books were destroyed by the Germans between 1941 and 1944; only a few thousand, which the Germans had kept, are today in libraries in Israel and the United States.
3. General Theodoras Daukantas had been the Lithuanian minister of defense before the war. In 1940 he was imprisoned by the Soviet administration. During the German occupation of Lithuania he headed a committee, "The United Struggle," which supported the Germans.
4. Ana Shimaite, an employee of the library of the University of Vilna, frequently visited the Vilna Ghetto, on the pretext of looking for library books which had been borrowed before the war but had not been returned. She maintained friendly contacts with the Jews, helping them whenever she could. After the war she visited Israel to see once more those she had known in the Ghetto. She died in Paris in 1970.

JUNE 5, 1943

The Council, the Ghetto gate, and the various labor brigades and the work at the airfield are the microcosm of Ghetto life. No less than 60 percent of the Ghetto inmates go out daily to do forced labor. The work is back-breaking. The inmates risk their lives trying to purchase goods for themselves and for their families and then smuggling them in through the Ghetto gate—all this under the watchful eyes of the German and Lithuanian policemen.

The unrelieved pressure during work, the worry over what tomorrow will bring, and the fears of extermination—all these sap the strength of the forced laborers. These people keep coming to the Council offices to seek some relief;

to seek an easier workplace, to obtain sick leave, to get a pair of wooden shoes or a suit of clothing to replace their worn-out clothes, to receive a supplementary food ration, or to obtain a better dwelling. They also come to the Council offices to hear the latest news; here the Ghetto heartbeat can be felt.

An observer from the outside would get the impression that Ghetto life focuses on the labor brigades and on the problem of food rations. Such an observer might come to the conclusion that the life of the Ghetto inmates runs entirely in the shadow of a permanent fear that the enemy is threatening to put an end to their lives. This was, indeed, the situation in the first period of the Ghetto, at the time of house raids and "actions," which lasted until October 28, 1941. Life in that period was hollow, gray, and devoid of any content, like a prison or a grave.

Little by little, however, the mood changed. The Ghetto inmates became accustomed to the Ghetto gate, to their work, and to the injustice. They tried to forget all the unpleasant things, the dangers and the yoke. Some of them even began inviting friends and colleagues for meals, for a drink of wine or vodka. Others sought an escape in study, in writing, in giving lectures, in composing poems, etc. In the course of time, Ghetto life assumed its present diversity and variety. All these activities provided the Ghetto inmates with some relief.

By law, of course, all these activities are strictly forbidden. It is forbidden to study, to assemble, to give lectures, even to pray. By the same token, it is forbidden to feast on sumptuous meals or to drink spirits. The Germans regard us as slaves, and slaves must not be allowed to enjoy life.

But the forbidden fruit tastes sweeter as oppression grows stronger. As the laws become harsher, so the desire to know and the need for spiritual nourishment grow stronger. Slobodka had been the center of Torah study, of Yeshivoth, and of Jewish religious culture, for generations. More than once I have wondered what Slobodka looks like now, in these insane times, in the times of the Ghetto. Where are all the yeshiva students from the bygone days, the *matmidim,*[1] the rabbis? For the most part they have been killed—like thousands of other Jews—for the sanctification of God's name. Only a handful have survived. They gather at night, after work, at Tifereth Bachurim, a society for fostering religious life; around the *Mussarniks,*[2] and in other small study groups, to study the Torah and to pray. They carry on. They guard the holy fire and refuse to let it die out.

Oshri,[3] a former student at the Slobodka yeshiva, is busy at all these activities. He goes to great lengths to enable the religious young men to abstain from doing forced labor on Sabbaths and holy days; he gets them jobs in the workshops and other workplaces inside the Ghetto, so that they can observe all the commandments. He gives Talmud classes to the young and to adults, he visits Tifereth Bachurim. In short, he does a great deal in the area of the religious education and for the religious way of life. If the Germans were aware of this, Oshri would long ago have been a dead man.

Oshri has a job in the Jewish administration in the Ghetto; he is manager of the lice disinfection center. This is one of the strangest phenomena in the crooked mirror of Ghetto life. His official position, however, does not prevent him from engaging in his main preoccupation—looking after the Torah students.

Oshri is my good friend. I admire him for his integrity and his steadfastness in faith. When he called on me recently to discuss the matters with which he was preoccupied, I asked him, as I always do: "Oshri, tell me, please, how are the yeshiva students doing?" He answers me politely, smiling: "Everything is all right with them. The daily page is still the daily page;[4] the yeshiva students study the Torah and the same goes for Tifereth Bachurim."

"Tell me, dear Oshri, who is the Slobodka rabbi these days? I have been interested in this problem ever since Rabbi Shapiro, and then Rabbi Shmukler who had been the Schantz rabbi, passed away."

At this point Oshri gave me a detailed account of the history of the Slobodka rabbinate; of the great controversies over the position of chief rabbi of Slobodka, and of the compromise as a result of which the Slobodka rabbinate had been separated from the yeshiva. He told me that Rabbi Skaruta is now the Slobodka rabbi; that there is no more qualified candidate than he, either for president of the rabbinical court or for chief rabbi of Slobodka.[5]

Oshri went on to speak of the problems which engage the attention of the religious public these days. One of them is the question of the *agunoth* (wives whose husbands have disappeared without divorcing them). There are thousands of agunoth in the Ghetto, and after the end of war their number is bound to increase. In many cases it is possible to establish with certainty that such and such men have died. There are also several dozen people in the Ghetto who emerged alive from the Seventh Fort, where nearly 4,000 Jews met their deaths. Many of the survivors revealed the names of men who had been shot before their own eyes. It would have been proper to call the rabbinical court into session immediately afterward so that it could have taken evidence from the witnesses and released these women from the status of agunoth.

Oshri considers this question as one of the most important challenges for the Slobodka rabbis. Since the deaths of Rabbi Shapiro and Rabbi Shmukler, there are no rabbis commanding sufficient authority to rule on questions such as these. This is why a special rabbinical court is needed.

This Saturday evening at six o'clock, between afternoon prayers and evening prayers, we will both go to visit Rabbi Avraham Grodzenski.[6] This was my agreement with Oshri.

Rabbi Grodzenski lives in the old quarter of Slobodka, in a narrow path. The building housing the Slobodka yeshiva is located there; Rabbi Grodzenski lives right next to it, in a two-story house.

The working day for the labor brigades has just ended and the path is crowded with people. Oshri tells me that, in normal times, scores of people used to gather here between afternoon and evening prayers; rabbis, yeshiva students, and ordinary devout Jews. These days the situation is different: people's faces are gloomy and dejected, their clothes shabby and tattered. They return after a hard day's work, carrying knapsacks on their backs.

Here and there one can still spot yeshiva students dressed in Sabbath attire. For them there is no difference between the Sabbath and the weekday. In a short while, however, in this very neighborhood, the police orchestra will play for Lipzer in one of the houses of Slobodka, while workers of his brigade, and his acquaintances, will try to outdo one another in sycophancy and cheap flattery.

Oshri and I trudge along a narrow alley packed with people, in the direction of a wooden house. Oshri takes the lead. He starts climbing the narrow wooden staircase; I follow close on his heels. We pass through two small rooms crammed with beds and closets, and enter a third room also overflowing with furniture and other objects. A round table, covered with red velvet, a relic of the study-house table cover, stands in the middle of the room. Books of Gemara and the Pentateuch are piled on the table.

Rabbi Avraham Grodzenski, an old man with a white beard and a pale sickly face, is seated at the table. He is dressed in Sabbath attire, skullcap on his head. He is teaching Torah. Yeshiva students, young men and old, are gathered around him in this room; others fill the second room. All their eyes are fixed on the place where the old rabbi is seated. They "swallow" each word he speaks. Both rooms are crowded and stifling. People keep wiping the sweat off their faces and from under their hats.

Our entrance caught Rabbi Grodzenski in the middle of his sermon. He stretched his hand to me as a guest. I sat down, ready to hear moral instruction from him.

Rabbi Grodzenski resumed his talk:

There is only one great marvel in the world, which is the greatness of the Torah given by the Holy One, blessed be he, to the people of Israel, by Moses our teacher on Mount Sinai. The Jews received the Torah and, even before they knew what was in it, they were quick in saying: we shall act upon it and then we shall hear it. This was something previously unheard of. The Jews believed in the master of the world; therefore they were certain that his Torah was good for the whole of Israel. No man can see God in his greatness; only to Moses, our teacher, was it given to see him face to face, as it is said: "he spoke with him face to face."

The nations of the world attach greatness and splendor to literature and art. This is because they do not recognize the importance of the Torah. Many from among the people of Israel made the same error, because of ignorance of the true greatness of the Torah. The Torah does not demand of the Jew things which he cannot fulfill; it demands of him to be what he really is: to conduct himself according to his innate abilities; not to flee from himself, not to deny his nature, he should be as God created him.

Man is inherently good; he must be on guard in order not to be led away from the straight path. One must not succumb to the evil impulse. The people of Israel were chosen by the creator of the world to be his people. This is why the master of the world demands more of the people of Israel than of other nations. The Holy One, blessed be he, gave us the Torah so that we will know how to conduct ourselves.

The people of Israel are endowed with four attributes: awe, shame, compassion, and lovingkindness. Awe is not just the fear of the God in heaven; it is a result of high respect for the greatness of God. Shame is not just to be ashamed; it means humility. Compared with the greatness of the creator, man regards himself as insignificant to the point of shame. As for the attribute of compassion: there is no limit to the Jewish compassion. All of Israel are as compassionate as it is humanly possible to be. Lovingkindness describes the relation between man and his neighbor. By virtue of all these attributes, the people of Israel could withstand all the hardships visited upon them for generations. Hardships such as the present ones have befallen our people before. The Torah says explicitly why this or that punishment was inflicted, why the First Temple was destroyed, and why the Second Temple was destroyed.

Those with faith, with good attributes, can be certain they will overcome all the obstacles raised up against them. The people of Israel as a whole will also overcome all the hardships of the present time.

With these words Rabbi Grodzenski concluded his preaching on morals.

We thanked Rabbi Grodzenski for his teaching and took our leave. Once we were in the street, Oshri said: "Rabbi Avraham has been preaching his moral instruction in the Slobodka yeshiva for thirty-five years. He kept preaching after the Soviet occupation in 1940, and now he does the same. His students wanted to send him to Palestine, but he refused to part with the place and the post that he had inherited."

In the first days of the war, Rabbi Grodzenski had sixteen students. With the outbreak of the Slobodka riots in June and July 1941, his students pleaded with him to stop teaching and to find a hiding place until the storm blew over. But Rabbi Avraham is not the kind of man to abandon his post and run away from his fate. He told them that, on the contrary, this was the right time, the time of emergency, to study the Torah. If we are doomed to die, he said, it is better to die with the book of the Torah in one's hands.

When a gang of Lithuanian partisans surrounded Rabbi Grodzenski's house, three students hid themselves in the cellar and bathroom. The partisans burst into Rabbi Avraham's room and found him teaching the Torah to thirteen students. The students were placed under arrest and taken to the Seventh Fort. The Lithuanians left Rabbi Avraham, who was limping a little, in his house; on that day they had arrested only young people.

Rabbi Avraham, surrounded by his students and followers, carries on despite the dangers and ordeals. His faith remains unshaken that the people of Israel will emerge from these times of trial. Rabbi Avraham and his students are few in number, but they remain a significant facet of the reality of Ghetto life.

At about the same time as our visit to Rabbi Avraham Grodzenski, and on the same street, in the building which had actually housed the Slobodka yeshiva before the war, a concert honoring Lipzer was taking place. One of his courtiers had composed a song of flattery for the man. The song is entitled "A Song for You"; it is nothing but bootlicking and hypocrisy. Lipzer had ordered the heads of the police orchestra to compose a melody for the lyrics, and to prepare sheet music for it, so that it could be played in this concert.

This too is an integral part of Ghetto life.

1. Matmidim are the most diligent Yeshiva students and most devoted of scholars, who study day and night, with no interruption except for the minimum of sleep.
2. Mussarniks were the followers of Rabbi Joseph Salanter (1786–1866), who taught that it was necessary for men, in addition to their relationship with God, to maintain the strictest moral behavior among themselves. Religious study was promoted through each student's comradeship with fellow students, and through the influence of a *mashgiah*—a tutor or supervisor. After studying and teaching in Lithuania for fifty years, Salanter settled in Jerusalem in 1837.
3. Rabbi Ephraim Oshri was an outstanding young religious leader in the Kovno Ghetto. He survived the war and now lives in the United States, where he has served as a rabbi in Brooklyn and written several books, among them *The Destruction of Lithuania* (New York and Montreal, 1951) and *The Book of Profound Questions and Answers* (New York, 1959). Both these books were written in Yiddish.
4. The "daily page" is a page of the Gemara, the larger and supplementary part of the Talmud. It consists of the discussions of the Mishna (the legal code edited in 200 A.D.) by the rabbis in the various Jewish religious academies in Babylon and Palestine. There are two versions of the Talmud (the combined texts of the Mishna and the Gemara)—these are the Jerusalem Talmud and the Babylonian Talmud, both of which were edited in the sixth century A.D.
5. Rabbi Moshe Skaruta perished later in the Ghetto. Today (in 1988) his daughter, Miriam Barkan, is a secretary in the office of the President of the State of Israel (Chaim Herzog).
6. Rabbi Avraham Grodzenski was the head of the Knesset Israel yeshiva in Slobodka, an admired teacher and scholar, and a central figure in the religious life of the Ghetto. Like Rabbi Skaruta, he was killed when the Ghetto was liquidated in the summer of 1944.

JUNE 6, 1943

The Ghetto population has continually decreased over the past twenty-two months. In the initial period, scores of Jews had already been murdered—individuals and groups. The Ghetto population was also reduced by arrests, and by transfer to Riga and other places. A high percentage of natural deaths has also played its part in this negative trend. Furthermore, there have been no births in the Ghetto. Giving birth is forbidden under pain of death.

Each week the Council is required to submit to the city governor a report on the number of people in the Ghetto. The authorities "encourage" the process of the liquidation of the Ghetto population.

During these difficult days, when the sky of our existence is constantly overcast, we have experienced our isolation with particular acuteness. Our souls have gone out to seek other Jews with whom we could share our grief, and in order to hear from them some words of consolation. But no one has come to us. All the roads leading to us have been blocked.

On a number of occasions, the representatives of the German authorities have announced that they were planning to bring Jews from other places to live among us in the Ghetto. Acting on those announcements, we made all the necessary preparations to accommodate the new arrivals. The German announcements, however, turned into bitter disappointments. I remember the first of them. It was a particularly cold winter day, January 11, 1942. We had been waiting for their arrival all day long, but they failed to come. It seemed that the cup of our suffering had filled up, leaving no place for the new suffering. The Jews due to arrive that day passed nearby the Ghetto—on their way to the Ninth Fort. We felt as miserable as a sick mother who, having waited many years for her son, is suddenly told that her son has died on his way to see her.

One year later we were told that 3,000 Jews, perhaps even 5,000, were to be brought to the Ghetto. Again we swung into action to prepare accommodation for the new inmates. Then the horrifying news came: 5,000 Jews had been murdered at Ponar. Our grief and disappointment knew no bounds. The authorities had deceived us once again. The scenes of the destruction at Ponar kept unfolding before our eyes like so many black flags. Images of this horror kept pursuing us day and night, at work, at home, and in the streets. Part of our souls died.

Then, about a month ago, when our mood was as gloomy as ever, Miller announced the arrival of new inmates. The announcement spoke of 400 Jews from the Zezmer labor camp. This time Miller went to great lengths to reveal to us as many details as possible about the new arrivals: their present whereabouts and the reasons for their arrival. He did this to convince us that this time no other fiendish scheme was involved, but a real plan.

There were about 1,200 Jews in the Zezmer labor camp. One hundred and fifteen of them were sent to Dno, near Pskov, and an additional contingent of able-bodied inmates is said to be due to be sent to Dno in the near future.

Unsettling rumors have reached us from the Zezmer camp itself: the young and the strong are being sent to Pskov, whereas the old and the children are in danger. Apart from that, Jewish policemen from Vilna have been arriving in Zezmer in recent days. Their appearance in the camp gives rise to fears. Not for nothing. Jews from Oszmiana are among the Zezmer inmates. It was Jewish policemen from Vilna who took part in "actions" in Oszmiana in which 800 Jews were murdered. These policemen carried out the murders with their own hands.[1] Now they come to Zezmer. The Jews who remember their deeds in Oszmiana are terrified.

The conduct of these Jewish policemen from Vilna was nothing short of infamy. They came dressed in Jewish police uniforms, truncheons in hand. Their tone of voice was commanding and severe; they announced that they needed so many "heads" for Vilna, only "heads" of skilled workers; only the young, the healthy and strong, and those fit to work would do. They would hand-pick such people themselves. As for the rest—they could not care less.

They gave an order to write down without delay the names of those they needed; they were to go to Vilna immediately. The camp inmates were terrified and refused to be registered. They did not believe the Jewish policemen from Vilna; the memory of the Ponar massacre was still fresh. The Ponar victims were dispatched to their deaths accompanied by Vilna Jewish policemen. Vilna is the city of Gens, who rules by terror inspired by his policemen.

When they realized that the Zezmer camp inmates did not trust them, the Jewish policemen from Vilna, headed by Lev,[2] made an announcement: an "action" is going to take place; those whom they select will live, whereas the fate of the others is not certain.

The Jews in the camp had heard about the Kovno Ghetto; they had received medicine, clothing, and other articles from here. Their representatives had been treated decently in the Kovno Ghetto. This was why they preferred relocation to the Kovno Ghetto over any other arrangements. In short, the Zezmer camp is pervaded by the sense of disorder and by grave apprehensions.

The representatives of the Kovno Ghetto who visited the Zezmer camp to learn about the conditions there brought back with them many notes written by the camp inmates. They all carried the same message: "Save us!" "Save us from the liquidation of the camp!" "Save us from the Vilna Jewish police!"

We made great efforts to expedite the arrival of the 400 Jews from the Zezmer camp to the Kovno Ghetto. Finally the authorities gave us permission to bring them here. We wanted badly to bring many old people and children, whose lives were endangered. We urged our labor office and our police to bring more than

400 people. This meant bringing 400 workers together with their families. We dispatched Jankel Verbovski, our "count man," especially for this purpose. He specializes in counting people "as the need dictates," that is, if a number of people are missing, he will find the way to ascertain that all the people are in fact there. In this case, his assignment would be to do the opposite: to count 400 people so that 500 or more would come.

It has now been decided that the Zezmer inmates will be brought to our Ghetto today. In order to prevent any misunderstandings, the director of the German labor office in Kovno decided to carry out the transfer without any warning; it would be effected on a Sunday, when no one goes out to work. The suddenness of the move was meant to avoid any collision with the management of the Todt organization[3] and the Zezmer camp staff.

We prepared accommodation for the new arrivals in the Lituanika cinema building and in the synagogue on Miskinio Street. Our housing office and welfare office made all the necessary preparations to accommodate the arrivals. Our labor office and the Jewish police prepared the means of transport to bring them here. We did everything we could to give them a warm and loving welcome; the event is very important to us. Just let them come.

The labor office officials and the Jewish policemen left the Ghetto early in the morning to bring the Jews from Zezmer to the Ghetto. The Council instructed them to treat these people as brothers, to help them with loading their bundles, and, most important, to bring as many people as possible.

Representatives of the Kovno city governor's office and of the German labor office also left for the Zezmer camp. Hermann ordered all the Jews in the camp to line up in a row, so that he could select the able-bodied among them. He asked each one about his age, his occupation, and the size of his family. He was looking for younger people with small families. He went to great lengths to make it clear that those suiting his needs would go to Kovno, while the others would remain at Zezmer. These detailed questions made the people standing in the row nervous. In Hermann's hands was what amounted to a decision on each person's fate: whether he was to be selected for life or for death.

Then it was the turn of our people to act; the representatives of our labor office started taking count of those selected by Hermann. Later our policemen also loaded onto trucks those who had been selected to go to Kovno. In this they followed our instructions.

Some time later, pandemonium broke out: many people pushed their way to the trucks, climbing onto them without any belongings. The disorder was usefully exploited by our people: they first of all pulled children, old people, and women onto the trucks. The last ones to get on the trucks were healthy men.

Now and then Hermann would ask the "count man," Jankel Verbovski, to tell him the number of the people already on the trucks. Each time Verbovski said that the number had not yet reached 400. This operation lasted all day.

We in the Ghetto awaited the arrival of the Jews from the Zezmer camp with pounding hearts. As long as they were not here, we could not be certain. All the members of the Council waited from before noon in front of the Lituanika cinema, located near the Ghetto fence. In order to spare the arrivals the usual inspection at the entrance to the Ghetto, we persuaded the Ghetto commandant to open a special passage in the Ghetto fence near the cinema, so that they would be able to pass quickly, with their belongings, to their new dwelling.

At one o'clock in the afternoon the first truck arrived: women and children. The news of their arrival spread quickly in the Ghetto; everyone sighed with relief.

After their reception and a short rest, the new arrivals were issued with a temporary Ghetto card. It was interesting to watch their faces and the behavior. Their first steps were uncertain and hesitant; they kept casting worried glances in all directions. Their ears were probably still resounding with sounds from the past: Vilna, the Vilna Jewish police and, of course, stories of Ponar. Little by little they were put at their ease.

Slowly, they started walking in the direction of the table standing in the cinema hall, where officials from our labor office were seated. Their names were written down. The officials kept reassuring them: "Don't worry, you are among brothers; nothing bad will happen to you here."

When questioned by one of the officials about the age of her son, one woman replied, fourteen. I looked at the boy. He did not seem to be more than eight or nine. I told her: "There is nothing to fear. Here you are among Jews. You can tell us the true age of your son." But she was adamant: "He is fourteen, I swear it." I tried to convince her by saying that if the boy was to be registered as fourteen years old, he would have to go out to work, for which he was too young. The woman seemed terrified. The boy also looked scared. He looked at me with mistrust and begged me: "I swear that I am fourteen. In the camp I worked all the time. I know how to work." I decided to cut short this argument with the mother and her son. This matter can be taken care of in the future.

Little by little people became used to the place. The warm welcome and the assistance extended to them had their effect, and they were put at their ease. In the large hall of the Lituanika cinema building, beds were put everywhere: on the stage, in various little rooms, near the banisters, even in the cellar; in some places people slept on mattresses lying on the floor. Tags with numbers were attached to each bed and mattress. Each one of our guests was told the number of his bed or mattress. On entering the cinema building, they were directed by ushers to their beds. It was seven o'clock in the evening. Exhausted by the tension of the recent days, the Jews from Zezmer—men, women, and children—were lying on beds and mattresses, their bundles at their side. Many of them were still plagued by doubts.

I approached a woman who was sitting on a mattress together with two children. I learned from her that she had left all her belongings behind in the Zezmer camp. Now she cannot even change her children's clothes. "It was good you brought us here," she said. "I shiver whenever I remember the policemen from Vilna. But what will I do now without my belongings?"

I try to reassure her: "Your belongings will be brought here from Zezmer. Now, why don't you please go to the corner over there to get bread and coffee for you and your children."

Not far away another woman was sitting. Tears flow from her eyes. I draw near her and try to comfort her. "Why do you cry?" I ask her. "I don't know. I just cry. I can't help it. I guess I should be happy today, but somehow I can't control myself."

I think to myself: "Our situation in the Ghetto is not the best. But, in this case, we play the part of hosts. This is Jewish hospitality. We are weak, and yet when we come across people weaker than we are, we invite them to our homes, give them our beds, and a piece of bread as well. This is our tradition. It is good that we have not forgotten this custom after all we have gone through."

After the last of the Jews from Zezmer had arrived, it turned out that 680, instead of the planned 400, had reached us. We were very glad. We had not believed that we could succeed in doing this. It means, however, that we must find additional accommodation; the sick must be admitted to the hospital, and the belongings of many of the new arrivals have still to be brought from the Zezmer camp.

Spirits in the Ghetto were high. To some extent we have been compensated for the agony of waiting for those Jews who were due to come to us in the past, but who did not arrive. The 680 Jews from Zezmer are the first ones to come to us. As a result, we believe that we are in for better times.

One day after the arrival of the Jews from Zezmer we were faced with a difficult problem: how to establish legal identities for the additional 280 Jews? Officially, only 400 Jews had arrived, whereas in reality we brought 680 of them. We were duty-bound to inform the authorities about the number of the Jews we had brought in. If we give the number of 400, we will be in trouble, because the director of the Zezmer camp knows that 680 of his inmates were relocated. On the other hand, if we give the true number of 680, we could be required to send 280 Jews back to Zezmer, and expect to be punished into the bargain.

Today Dr. Elkes spoke about this matter with Hermann, the German director of the labor office, who had been entrusted with bringing 400 people from the

Zezmer camp to the Kovno Ghetto. Hermann had relied on our count man, Verbovski, who kept count of the people loaded on to the trucks. The truth is that even if Hermann wanted, he could not keep an exact count in the midst of the confusion accompanying a transfer operation. Dr. Elkes told Hermann the truth about the number of people brought to the Ghetto, asking him for advice on how to resolve the problem.

When Hermann heard that instead of 400 Jews, 680 had arrived in the Ghetto, he was enraged: "Good God!" he shouted, "How did you allow this to happen?" He was responsible for this operation, he said; how would he now explain this to his superiors? Dr. Elkes tried to put him at ease: "Philosophers don't get angry," he said. "I am not a philosopher," Hermann replied.

After a prolonged argument, Hermann gave the following advice: no more than 590 should be registered; the main thing is not to go beyond 600. Also, he said, there are a great many children among the new arrivals, who should not have been brought along. In the end Hermann was pacified, thanks to the quiet and polite words spoken by Dr. Elkes, and by a gift (a brand new suit). It was agreed that 592 people will be registered.

Later we learned that the increased number of the new arrivals met with no opposition at the city governor's office or at the German labor office. Again we were very pleased. Another obstacle was removed. We will have to feed an additional hundred people from our existing supply of food rations.

Today we sent a hundred of the new arrivals to dig peat at Kaisiadorys.[4] They accepted it willingly.

During the day we dispatched several trucks to Zezmer to bring back the belongings left behind by the new arrivals. When the loaded trucks came back, there was great joy among the new residents of the Ghetto.

Today the Jews from Zezmer were given a medical checkup at our health office. The examination revealed that 117 of them are ill with typhus.

When we think about the wanderings of the Jews from the Zezmer camp, our memory calls up images of transit camps for emigrants overseas, or pictures of the arrival of the early pioneers in Palestine. At moments such as these we are seized by a desire to put an end to the wanderings of our people on their long way to their historical homeland. We have had enough. We want to be free citizens in our own country.

1. A reference to the rounding up and deportation of 406 elderly and sick Jews in Oszmiana, an "action" carried out in October 1942 by Jewish police from Vilna. The Jewish police had delivered the 406 Jews to the Germans, but—Avraham Tory was told—had not in fact killed them "with their own hands."

2. Meir Lev, who during this period was commander of the Jewish police at the Vilna Ghetto gate. He was also in charge of a special unit organized by Gens to combat the Jewish underground in the Vilna Ghetto.

3. The Todt organization, named after Dr. Fritz Todt, the creator of the autobahn system, who, as German armament minister from 1940 to 1942, had been in charge of several hundred labor camps at which Jews and other captive peoples worked in conditions of considerable hardship, many at factories belonging to leading German industrial concerns. Todt (then an SS general) died in an air crash in 1942; his organization was taken over by Albert Speer, the Reich minister for armaments and war production.

4. Kaisiadorys (Koshedar), a labor camp where peat was cut; it was near the Lithuanian town of Ziezmariai.

JUNE 9, 1943

A year and a half ago, in November 1941, at the time of one of the mass "actions" in the Ghetto, three young Jews left the Ghetto early in the morning, ostensibly for work as part of one of the city labor brigades. They were: Dr. Shlomo Nabriski,[1] a gynecologist; Dr. Baruch Voschin, a young physician; and Mr. Lechem, a teacher, whose wife was a non-Jew. As soon as these three arrived at their workplace in the city, they ran away and disappeared. They were not seen in the Ghetto again. The Gestapo, having learned of their escape, started looking for them. At that time, Caspi was deeply involved in the effort to find them. He questioned various Ghetto residents, and sniffed and poked around, but he failed to discover any traces of them. Rumors spread that the three had been hiding for some time in the house of Mr. Lechem's Christian wife, in a village in the Kovno district. Later, so it was said, she arranged a meeting for them with a German pilot who subsequently flew them to safety in Switzerland. Others were certain that the three escapees had reached the shores of Sweden in a boat. Still others maintained that Lechem's wife had fallen into Schtitz's hands at the Gestapo. According to this version, Schtitz fell in love with his prisoner and they have remained good friends to this day.

The story about Mrs. Lechem's relations with Schtitz was the one that turned out to be true. By contrast, the rumors about escape to Switzerland or Sweden, and about letters allegedly sent by them to the city, proved false. Some people envied them, while others praised their courage. About half a year ago, some people in the Ghetto said in great secrecy that the three were being hidden by their Lithuanian acquaintances. Later they were said to be making preparations to return to the Ghetto, as their further stay in the city had become dangerous. There are frequent searches of homes in the city; the war is continuing without an end in sight. By returning to the Ghetto they risk their lives. They are known. People talk about them. And the Gestapo keeps looking for them. This is why this whole matter must be approached with the utmost caution.

Dr. Schwabe, a friend and professional colleague of Dr. Nabriski, has maintained regular contact with the three escapees, and has even met with them several times in the city. She approached Lipzer, asking him to inquire at the Gestapo about the possible reaction to the return of Dr. Nabriski and his two comrades to the Ghetto. Lipzer followed up on Schwabe's request and succeeded in obtaining Rauca's consent to their return, together with a guarantee that they would be left alive. According to Lipzer, Rauca would be satisfied by a penalty of three to four weeks' imprisonment. Rauca had his own calculations. He wanted to discover the identity of the Lithuanians who had given them shelter, to learn all the details of such an escape, especially how the escapees managed to hide for such a long period of time. Dr. Schwabe passed on these guarantees to Dr. Nabriski. He, however, refused to return, despite the promise of leniency, as long as the leniency did not apply to the Lithuanians who had given them shelter and to whom they owed their lives.

Lipzer is not much impressed by such arguments, as he harbors no friendly feelings whatsoever toward the Lithuanians. It appears strange to him that Nabriski and his comrades should bring up the subject of Lithuanians at all. In the Ghetto he spoke of the return of Dr. Nabriski and others as a fact. At the Gestapo they are eager to see them. Dr. Nabriski, however, would not make a decision which would harm his Lithuanian protectors, and despite all the dangers continued to hide in the city. "Nabriski has fooled me," Lipzer claimed. All this was three months ago.

Meanwhile searches in the city mounted, becoming more and more thorough. Lithuanians desert from the German Army, fail to abide by the work-duty, engage in black-market activities, do not deliver the required quotas of food, etc. These were the reasons for the intensive campaign of house raids and searches. No place is immune: markets, streets, public restaurants, even the audiences in cinemas and theater houses, are put through searches. At times whole sections of the city are sealed off and subjected to thorough searches: in houses, apartments, attics, storerooms, cellars. They keep looking for Lithuanians who are hiding from the authorities.

Four days ago a search like this was carried out in the house of the Lithuanian family which had happened to shelter Dr. Nabriski that very night. This was not his permanent hideout. He and Dr. Voschin have been hiding in the apartment of a Lithuanian woman who worked before the war in the Jewish hospital where Dr. Nabriski also worked for several years. That night Dr. Nabriski chose to spend a night in the apartment of a good friend of the Lithuanian doctor; this friend lives in the city quarter where the search took place. Dr. Voschin, on the other hand, remained that night in their permanent hideout. Dr. Nabriski was caught and, together with members of the Lithuanian family at whose house he had slept, was taken to the Gestapo.

Voschin felt jeopardized; at any moment he, too, could fall into the hands of the Gestapo. He had to abandon his hideout, but there was no other place for him to hide. He had been hiding for twenty months in a cellar, without seeing anyone, completely isolated. The Ghetto is the only place he can go to, but can he get there?

Dr. Schwabe learned about Nabriski's arrest and about Voschin's plight. She appealed to Lipzer and to Dr. Elkes, asking them to help Dr. Nabriski and, at the same time, to make it possible for Dr. Voschin to return to the Ghetto. Lipzer was very angry; at first he refused to hear about it. Three months ago, he said, he had made all the preparations, but Nabriski had refused the offer; therefore he no longer wants to hear about Nabriski. Dr. Elkes took this whole matter very seriously and asked Lipzer to do everything possible to save Dr Nabriski. Lipzer relented and promised to plead with Schtitz to refrain from killing Dr. Nabriski. At the same time, however, Dr. Nabriski apparently promised to bring Voschin back to the Ghetto, which could well put Voschin in danger. Lipzer said unequivocally that the whole thing is very dangerous business. At the Gestapo they know everything; should Voschin come back, the Gestapo will know about it.

Voschin, however, had to abandon his hideout hurriedly, and the day before yesterday was taken to the Jewish labor brigade at 1 Janova Street; from there he was to return to the Ghetto. As it happened, that day a hundred Jews were to leave the Kovno Ghetto to Koshedar, to work at digging peat; they were recruited from among the Jews who had arrived from the Zezmer camp on June 6, 1943. This circumstance made the timing of Voschin's return to the Ghetto most opportune. According to our plan, Voschin was to blend in with the Jews from Zezmer who live in the Reservat (a special place in the Ghetto where the homeless are accommodated) and, as a new arrival from Zezmer, he was to be sent in the group of workers to Koshedar. In Koshedar his presence would not have been as conspicuous as in the Ghetto itself, which would have made his survival much more likely. The only snag in this plan was that Lipzer had to know about it. He was informed, and with great reluctance gave his consent. Supervisor Zaks of the Jewish Labor office, dispatched by the director of the labor office, Goldberg, brought Voschin to the Ghetto from the labor brigade working at 1 Janova Street. In the morning he went to Koshedar together with the hundred Jews from Zezmer. It seemed that we had succeeded in covering up Voschin's return. Lipzer spoke with Schtitz about Dr. Nabriski; he explained that as a gynecologist Dr. Nabriski could be very useful in the Ghetto. In line with the Gestapo orders, all pregnancies in the Ghetto must be terminated. At present, however, the termination of pregnancies is carried out by inexperienced physicians, which results in work absenteeism by the women undergoing treatment. If Dr. Nabriski could perform this treatment, the Jewish workforce would not suffer.

Such an argument never fails to have its effect; as a result of it, the Gestapo promised not to punish Dr. Nabriski severely. In any event, Dr. Nabriski's life was not in such serious jeopardy as we had believed. Even Hermann, director of the German labor office, had made a remark, when he first learned about Dr. Nabriski's capture: "No insurance company would be willing to insure Dr. Nabriski's life even for the highest premium."

Yesterday, at one o'clock in the afternoon, Lipzer arrived at the Council offices. He said that Schtitz had instructed him to place Jasvoin under arrest. Jasvoin is the leader of the labor brigade working at 1 Janova Street. Schtitz delegated Lipzer to make the arrest, as he himself was busy. Lipzer also revealed that the peasant who had taken Voschin to the labor brigade at 1 Janova Street from his hiding place had been taken to the Gestapo. According to Lipzer, the same peasant denounced Voschin to the Gestapo. For this reason, Lipzer said, there was no choice but to return Voschin from Koshedar and to hand him over to the Gestapo. He, Lipzer, knows all the details, though it remains unclear how he had obtained the information.

Lipzer believes that Jasvoin will be severely beaten and will have to confess everything. If Voschin is handed over, he can promise that nothing will happen to Jasvoin. If not—Jasvoin will suffer and will have to reveal the name of Zaks—who brought Voschin from the labor brigade to the Ghetto. Zaks, in turn, will reveal the part in the plan taken by Goldberg, the head of the labor office, who dispatched Zaks to bring Voschin. Dr. Schwabe, who was closely involved, will also be dragged into this, and the whole thing will blow up in our faces. Lipzer had already promised the Gestapo to find Voschin. "For God's sake," argued Lipzer, "Why should so many people suffer because of one Voschin. He didn't ask anyone's advice when he left the Ghetto; he didn't think about us. Why should we now devote so much thought to him?" Lipzer added that he had already spoken to Zaks, who told him that he would reveal everything to the Gestapo. Zaks is just an ordinary employee. Goldberg told him to bring Voschin from the brigade at 1 Janova Street, and he did as he was told. Jasvoin would not withstand the pressure either, and would certainly get into trouble. This is why Lipzer insists on bringing Voschin back. If we surrender Voshchin, no additional people will be involved.

To turn a Jew over to the Gestapo—no matter who he is or what offenses he has committed—is something we cannot bring ourselves to do. Everyone at the Council asked Lipzer why Voschin should be turned over to the Gestapo, if no such order has been given. After all, Jasvoin can simply tell his interrogators that a Jewish worker, who had not been a member of his brigade, came to him. Thereupon Jasvoin told him to go away and, as the worker refused, he removed him forcibly. He does not know where the man went. This sounds plausible.

Why should other people be involved, and why should Voschin be turned over to the Gestapo? But Lipzer did not want to listen. At the Gestapo they already know everything. Voschin must be turned over to them. If the Gestapo catch Voschin, it will be worse for him and for the Ghetto. If Voschin is turned over, he, Lipzer, can promise that Jasvoin, Zaks, Dr. Schwabe, and Goldberg will not be hurt. In any event, Voschin must be brought to the Ghetto and spoken to. Perhaps some arrangement could be found which would make it unnecessary for him to be turned over to the Gestapo.

Both Lipzer's words and behavior made it clear that we were faced with a fait accompli which we could do nothing to change. He kept his word, and on the same day (yesterday) he ordered two Jewish policemen to go by car to Koshedar to return Voschin to the Ghetto, so that Lipzer might be able to reach some kind of understanding with him before the Gestapo entered the picture. Having no choice, Grinberg and Robinson—of the Jewish police—drove to Koshedar in a specially hired car. Lipzer did not trust these two most trustworthy policemen, so he foisted upon them his own confidant, Aronstamm—the most despised Jewish policeman in the whole Ghetto police.

Having ensured Voschin's return from Koshedar to the Ghetto, Lipzer then went to the Gestapo, taking Jasvoin with him. Before long he returned, again with Jasvoin, who this time was a free man. It turned out that Schtitz did not even interrogate Jasvoin. According to Lipzer, he went to Schtitz and told him: "What do you need Jasvoin for; he is just a leader of a labor brigade who had nothing to do with the matter. An unknown Jew came to his brigade, so he kicked him out. That's all there is to it. You need Voschin and I will bring him to you tomorrow." This is why Schtitz did not even question Jasvoin, but ordered Lipzer to return the man to the Ghetto. This is what Lipzer said.

At eleven o'clock that night, Voschin was brought back to the Ghetto, and, in accordance with a special order issued by Lipzer, was jailed in the detention center at 23 Krisciukaicio Street. Lipzer has no need to worry. He can count on Aronstamm, who is fond of saying: "I need the head only. When I have the head, the legs will go wherever I want them to." In the morning we learned that Lipzer had sent Voschin to the Gestapo without further delay, even though he had promised us something different.

Yesterday Lipzer revealed to the members of the Council that during his session with Jaeger concerning Dr. Nabriski he transmitted to the Gestapo chief the Council's request for Jaeger to meet with Dr. Elkes. Jaeger agreed, and the appointment was set for today before noon. Lipzer also informed Schtitz about the scheduled meeting. He emphasized that Dr. Elkes should ask Jaeger for mercy for Dr. Nabriski; he had already briefed Jaeger about this issue. On the other hand, Dr. Elkes should refrain from speaking about Voschin, whose case is much more difficult.

Having learned of this meeting between Dr. Elkes and Jaeger, the importance of which for us cannot be overestimated, we decided to hold a special discussion. This event is of particular political significance for the Ghetto, perhaps the most important of its kind. Such meetings take place very seldom. In difficult times, on many occasions, we sought an opportunity to meet Jaeger, but we never succeeded. This time it is like a gift from heaven: it came unexpectedly and without a special effort. The meeting between the chairman of the Council and the man who occupies such a high-ranking position in Lithuania—and who holds the key to our fate—should not be wasted on petty pleas, but should be devoted instead to general matters. When the fate of 17,000 Jews hangs in the balance, there is no place for pleading on behalf of individuals. At the same time, however, when the lives of Nabriski and Voschin are at stake, it is not the right time to speak about matters affecting the Ghetto population as a whole. From the way Lipzer presented the case of Nabriski, however, it follows that Voschin is nothing but a burden for us, and an undeserved one at that. As Dr. Elkes put it: "Who can find his way in this maze; who can distinguish between truth and fiction, between good and evil?"

At ten o'clock in the morning Dr. Elkes set out for the Gestapo. It was agreed that he would speak about the general issues concerning the Ghetto, and that only at the end would he ask for mercy for both Nabriski and Voshchin.

Since it is impossible to go over Schtitz's head, Elkes saw Schtitz first. He reminded him of their conversation three months earlier, in which Schtitz had said that the Ghetto would not be hurt. Dr. Elkes had reported this conversation to the Council; the Ghetto residents had also been informed. Recently, however, unsettling rumors had again spread in the Ghetto, which is why Dr. Elkes now asked Schtitz for his permission for a meeting with Jaeger. In reply, Schtitz reassured Dr. Elkes that the rumors were groundless and asked him to find out who was the source of them, and then to give him, Schtitz, the names of the culprits. He is sure, Schtitz said, that the rumors are being spread not by a Jew but by a Lithuanian, and he is going to "liquidate" him. Having said that, Schtitz nonetheless telephoned Jaeger to report the arrival of the chairman of the Council. He then asked his superior whether Dr. Elkes could come to see him, and whether he, Schtitz, should accompany him. As a result of this conversation, Dr. Elkes and Schtitz went together to see Jaeger. During Dr. Elkes's meeting with Schtitz, Lipzer had been present, but he did not go to the meeting with Jaeger. At the meeting with Jaeger, Schtitz remained standing throughout, whereas Dr. Elkes was asked to be seated.

Jaeger began by asking what it was that brought Dr. Elkes to see him. "The fate of the Ghetto," Dr. Elkes replied. He then recounted his conversation with Schtitz three months earlier, during which the latter had promised that the Ghetto would not be hurt; as a result of this promise, the restlessness in the

Ghetto had subsided. These days, however, rumors have begun circulating again, particularly after the events in the Vilna Ghetto. People are uncertain of what the future might bring; this causes problems for work discipline. As a psychologist, Dr. Elkes understands the reasons for the disquiet, but he cannot act by himself. This is why he decided to ask for a meeting with the person in charge, so that he could hear at first hand to what extent these rumors correspond to reality.

Jaeger replied as follows: "This is utter nonsense. We Germans work to supply the Ghetto with more food and firewood for the winter—how does that fit with the rumors about 'actions'? Explain it to your people."

"Now that I hear this from the chief of security of the whole country," replied Dr. Elkes, "it will have a pacifying effect on the Ghetto residents; the heavy clouds hanging over us may disappear."

"Do you think that 'actions' make *us* happy?" asked Jaeger. "No, the 'actions' which took place were a necessary and difficult measure. We are glad to see people working. We just prosecute those engaging in sabotage and in politics against us. It does not matter to us whether a person who is a security risk is a Jew or a Lithuanian."

Dr. Elkes: "It is not that I am just curious, but it would not be natural if I refrained from asking the supreme commander in charge of security in Lithuania about the Vilna and the Siauliai Ghettos."

Jaeger replied that those two Ghettos were in the same situation.

Dr. Elkes then told Jaeger that no one in the Kovno Ghetto is engaging in politics. Everyone applies himself to his work. High-ranking Germans who have visited the Ghetto have spoken very positively about the achievements of the Ghetto residents whom they saw at work.

Jaeger confirmed that the Ghetto is indeed being praised.

Elkes: "If and when the fate of the Ghetto is being discussed, I would like to ask you, sir, to bring your influence to bear on behalf of the Ghetto and to make a decision in its favor."

Nothing like that is under discussion, Jaeger replied. Then he added, as if speaking to himself: "After all, nothing like Warsaw will happen here." He then assured Dr. Elkes that there is no plan to harm the Ghetto. "We play an open game with you. You could see that for yourselves in 1941. We were frank enough to tell you the truth."

Elkes: "If the Ghetto sky is clouded again, I would like to ask your permission, sir, to see you again."

Jaeger: "Please do. I will see you willingly."

At this point Dr. Elkes addressed himself to the question of the arrest of Dr. Nabriski and Dr. Voschin: "There is one more issue on which I would like to unburden myself. It concerns the arrest of Dr. Nabriski and Dr. Voschin. Dr.

Nabriski is a talented physician whose services are of great importance for the hospital. With his help, women will not be absent from work for prolonged periods after an abortion."

"Are there still any births in the Ghetto?" asked Jaeger.

"No, none," replied Dr. Elkes.

"It should be the same way in the future," Jaeger remarked.

Dr. Elkes went on to say that he had known Dr. Nabriski for ten years; he was an honest man and a medical specialist. There had been a great deal of tension in the Ghetto in 1941 following the "actions."

Jaeger did not let Dr. Elkes finish the sentence, but gave an order to Schtitz: "Let Nabriski go back to the Ghetto!"

"At your command!" said Schtitz.

Dr. Elkes continued: "Dr. Voschin is a young colleague of mine and he, too, if you do not know it, is an honest man."

Again, Jaeger stopped Dr. Elkes in mid-sentence: "Let this one also go back to the Ghetto!" Again Schtitz stood to attention: "At your command!" Jaeger continued: "Put this physician to work in the hospital and make sure he does not get into trouble again."

At this point Dr. Elkes began pleading with Jaeger: "I also would like to mention the people who had given shelter to the two physicians. These people acted out of humane, noble considerations. Sir, Colonel, I am speaking to you now as one human being to another: just as a judge who is about to make a decision about a sentence will take into account whether the defendant acted out of malice or out of genuine concern, so you should be aware of the fact that these people did not receive any material reward for giving shelter to the two physicians."

Again, Jaeger interrupted him: "All right—let these Lithuanians go home!" Again, Schtitz stood to attention, as a sign that he had taken note of the order.

"Thank you very much, sir," said Elkes as he was taking his leave.

"There is nothing to be thankful for," replied Jaeger. "I do it willingly."

In the hallway, Elkes ran into the Lithuanians who had sheltered the two physicians. Elkes asked Lipzer—who had been waiting in the hallway—to tell the Lithuanians that they were free and would be able to go home in a short while. Hardly had Lipzer finished giving them the news announced by Dr. Elkes, when the Lithuanians began crossing themselves. Schtitz called them into his room, leaving the door open so that Dr. Elkes could hear him saying: "Go home, go home." Leaving Schtitz's room, the Lithuanians kept kissing Dr. Elkes's hands; there is no doubt that, thanks to his intervention, they had slipped from the clutches of an inevitable death.

Schtitz then asked Elkes to follow him to his room and closed the door behind them. "Are you a Freemason?" he asked, adding that Dr. Elkes should not be afraid; his answer would not result in serious consequences. "No, I am not," replied Dr. Elkes. "I remember that when I was a student forty-five years ago, I smiled forgivingly in response to an offer to join the Freemasons." Schtitz then tried to find out from Dr. Elkes whether any of the Council members were Freemasons, but received an assurance to the contrary.

Finally, Schtitz asked a question of personal interest to him: "Who is in charge of marriage registration in Kovno?" He revealed that he had befriended a Christian woman whose husband was a Jew, Dr. Lechem. Mrs. Lechem has a child. Schtitz was interested to know whether the child was by her second, Jewish husband, or by her first husband—a Christian. Dr. Elkes promised to find out.

1. Dr. Shlomo Nabriski survived the war, to become head of the gynecology department of an Israeli hospital (at Kvar Saba), where he died.

JUNE 11, 1943

A few days ago the German director of the Ghetto workshops, Gilow, set out from Kovno to Siauliai in order to bring back various types of leather from the local leather factory (formerly belonging to Fraenkel) for the workshops in the Ghetto. After their return from the journey, the Jewish workers (Gothelff and others) who had accompanied Gilow related the story of a strange incident they had witnessed on the way back.

Between Siauliai and Kovno, their truck stopped because of minor engine trouble. The Jewish workers got out of the truck and waited for the engine to be fixed. A German soldier, who happened to be nearby, entered into conversation with them. The workers tried to avoid speaking to him, as they saw Gilow approaching them. They feared a sharp reaction from Gilow to a conversation between Jews and a German soldier.

Gilow is not just a director of the Ghetto workshops; he also occupies an important post in the Nazi Party. Cramer, the city governor, is his friend, and in general he is influential in the ruling circles. His standard response to a "sin" committed by a Jew is a slap on the face, a kick, even an arrest.

Gilow also likes getting gifts from the Jews—knee boots, new suits of clothing, coats. He is also very fond of valuables made of gold; he even gets his share of the goods seized at the Ghetto gate. He "pays back" for these presents with arrogance and violent behavior. He regards the Jews as slaves. Even his glance makes them shiver.

Since Gilow regards any attempt to contact Aryans or hold conversations with Germans as a serious crime, the Jewish workers waiting on the road signaled to the German soldier who had entered into conversation with them that they were Jews. They pointed to another German who was standing not far away, meaning that it was forbidden for them as Jews to speak with him. The German soldier, however, failed to take the hint. Instead, he began spewing out fire and brimstone against the war and against Nazi rule. Then the Jews showed him the yellow badges on their clothes, as if to say: "We are Jews, we have no rights." But the soldier was unconvinced: "What, you have no rights? Before long you'll have all the rights."

When the soldier saw Gilow's brown trousers and Nazi uniform, his anger reached the boiling point. He ran up to him: "Just what exactly do you think, you idiots from the brown gang? You are to blame for this war." Gilow's flushed red face made the soldier even angrier: "The brown pigs stuff their faces and drink themselves silly for days on end, while we, the soldiers, must fight on every front and spill our blood for the Party parasites." He picked up a heavy stone and set upon Gilow, who fled to the driver's cabin and slammed the door shut behind him. The driver had just finished repairing the engine and was ready to start the truck. The soldier threw a stone through the window but missed Gilow.

Gilow tried to pacify the soldier: "Comrade, you're mistaken. I served at the front for two years." The soldier refused to be appeased: "Your end will not be long in coming. The war is lost anyway."

The Jewish workers hurried to get on the truck, which continued on its way back to the Ghetto. This was the end of the discussion between the irate German soldier and Gilow, a functionary of the Nazi apparatus.

Gilow felt humiliated and depressed. When news of the incident spread throughout the Ghetto, many residents felt relieved: "He had it coming for his bad treatment of the Jews; now he knows that he too can be insulted."

This incident taught Gilow a lesson. Instead of abusing the Jewish workers for speaking with the German soldier, he smiled and offered them cigarettes. He had never done this before.

Since then, Gilow has lost some of his self-confidence. The soldier implanted doubt in his heart, and this doubt has been gnawing at him recently. He no longer wears his Nazi uniform on all occasions; he feels better wearing civilian clothes. He has become quieter and calmer. He is waiting until the incident with the soldier is forgotten.

For us Jews, Gilow's embarrassment is something of a consolation. After all, a simple German soldier thumbed his nose at him as Jews stood watching.

Listening to the story of the encounter between Gilow and the German soldier, I recalled a telephone conversation I once had with Hene, at the city governor's office. Hene is the head of the penal department at the city governor's office. He is also a senior official of the Nazi Party, and a great despot into the bargain. When Miller was on leave, Hene used to replace him in certain duties.

Three months ago, Hene phoned the Council offices, asking to speak with me. I knew him only by sight: a tall, fat German with dark hair and dark eyes; not at all Aryan in appearance. He was always angry. He used to walk back and forth in his room with heavy steps, dictating summaries of various resolutions to his secretary. He is in the habit of shouting at those Jews and Lithuanians who come to see him: "You engage in black-marketeering; our soldiers keep spilling their blood for you, whereas you get rich. You should be shot."

Hene regards himself as a redeemer; he saved Lithuania from both Soviet enslavement and Jewish exploitation. The Lithuanians, on the other hand, regard him as a fiend and an enemy, with whom it is impossible to speak. He is not satisfied with the Lithuanian secretaries in his office; he keeps complaining about their frequent visits to other rooms, about their talking too much on the telephone, about coffee not being brought to him on time, and similar misdemeanors. He is always angry. He is not at all a friendly man.

I picked up the telephone and heard Hene saying that he had found, on Jewish workers, various goods purchased on the black market. This was not the first time, he said. He addressed me personally: "Do you know that your Jews engage in black-market trade in the city?" "No, I don't," I replied. Hene: "Well, I am telling you that Jews from the labor brigades engage in black-market trade. From now on, I will resist it. If I run into one more case of black-market trade, I will have the head of the labor brigade and the members of the Council flogged. Do you understand?" "Yes, I do," I said, and pursed my lips.

This was the first time I had heard something like that; not even Jordan had dared to voice such a threat. We had heard all kinds of threats: hanging, shooting, decapitating, etc. These outbursts did not hurt us. But flogging? This was nothing short of hooliganism.

Hene carried on: "Do you understand?" He kept threatening flogging. He demanded that I explain to the chairman of the Council that he was serious about this warning. "Yes," I replied once more. The last on Hene's list of threats was: "*You* are going to be among the heads of the Council to be flogged."

Having heard from me about Hene's threats, the members of the Council were stunned by such brazen impudence by a Nazi official. They thought to themselves: "Have we indeed fallen so low that any Nazi bureaucrat can walk over us with his boots?" It seems that Hene has not yet gone through an encounter with a German soldier from the front, as did Gilow. More's the pity.

JUNE 14, 1943

Dr. Rabinovitz is a descendant of a good Jewish family from Kovno; he is an honest man, and in the past he was a successful businessman. These days he occupies the post of acting director of the German labor office in the Ghetto. Hermann, the German director of the labor office, visits the Ghetto once in a while, for an hour or two. He leaves instructions for Rabinovitz—instructions as to where to send Jewish workers; instructions as to where the number of workers should be reduced; comments on the discipline in the various labor brigades he has recently checked. After expressing his wish to recruit additional Jewish workers in the Ghetto, Hermann drives back to the city in his brown car.

Hermann is always busy. He is flooded from all sides with requests to provide Jewish workers. Units of the German Army, the police, the airfield construction, and the civilian administration all press on him: give us more Jewish workers. The Lithuanians evade working for the Germans; they literally run away from it. They are undisciplined and lazy. Yet there is a lot of work to be done, and workers, even paid ones, are hard to come by. The Jews are the only ones not to run away; they are also the only ones devoted to work. They are the only ones who speak German, too. But, as it happens, all the able-bodied Jews are already employed, and no additional Jews come to the Ghetto.

Recently, various branches of the German Army, as well as factories and enterprises producing for the Army, have been receiving urgent work orders. They flood the German labor office daily with demands for more and more Jewish workers. On one such occasion, when Hermann was under intense pressure to supply Jewish workers, he lost his temper and cried out: "Where should I take them from? Why don't you go and ask for Jewish workers from those who murdered 5,000 Jews at Ponar! There is no way I can get the Jews back from the Ninth Fort!"

When all is said and done, however, Hermann must find workers for those enterprises. What does he do? He resorts to "switching windowpanes": he removes the windowpanes from a place where no winds blow and installs them where their presence is felt. He keeps touring one workplace after another, removing workers from an enterprise where their presence is not absolutely necessary and transferring them to a place where they are urgently needed.

For all practical purposes, Rabinovitz runs the labor office. Among other things, he signs various papers and requests for workers coming from the Council and the Jewish labor office.

As Hermann's deputy, Rabinovitz has access to a wide range of military and civilian institutions. He pays regular visits to the Kovno branch of the Todt organization, which is in charge of a number of labor camps situated along the road between Kovno and Vilna, employing thousands of Jews (Miligan, Vievis, and Zezmer).

The director of the Todt branch in Kovno, Krecmer, is a friend of Rabinovitz's on account of their formal relations. Yesterday, Sunday, Krecmer telephoned Rabinovitz, asking him to come to see him in the city before noon. The request was urgent. Rabinovitz informed the Council about it. He was amazed at Krecmer's request, since Sunday is the only day of rest. Something serious must be afoot. We at the Council were also tense, and were eager to know what had happened.

Upon his return from the city, Rabinovitz revealed to us the reason for the urgent request for the meeting with Krecmer: it turned out that two Jewish youths, aged nineteen and twenty, had been sent from the camp at Miligan to the Todt organization headquarters to be punished. The two youths had tried to escape from the camp. Before their capture, they put up stiff resistance: one of them used a gun and the other used a heavy object. A Lithuanian guard was hit over the head with a hoe, while another guard was driven off by a knife. In the end the youths were caught. They disposed of the gun, which could not be recovered.

The director of the Miligan camp sent the youths to Krecmer in Kovno, so that he would hand them over to the Gestapo. The Jewish Council at the Miligan camp sent a letter to Krecmer, asking him not to return the two detainees to Miligan.

Krecmer told Rabinovitz that, as a matter of fact, the director of the Miligan camp had not needed to transfer the two youths to him; he could have shot them then and there. Now they remain in detention in Krecmer's garage—the garage of the Todt organization. He is certain that the Jews in the Miligan camp have arms in their possession. The two guns in his drawer, both of which were discovered in the possession of the Jews there, are proof of this. He is certain that the two Jews had a gun during their attempt to escape from the camp.

Krecmer is duty-bound to hand over the two youths to the Gestapo. If he does that, they no doubt will be murdered there. But he has resolved to refrain from doing so, because the Gestapo will then conduct searches for arms in the Miligan camp, and are certain to discover various illegal articles there. This, in turn, could cause problems for Krecmer as well.

This is why Krecmer decided to hand over the two Jewish youths to Rabinovitz. He suggested that Rabinovitz bring them to the Ghetto and place two other Jewish workers at Krecmer's disposal. But this proved to be not so simple. Officially, Rabinovitz is not authorized to bring people into the Ghetto. This can be done only by the Gestapo or the city governor's office. Furthermore, how can one force two Jews to leave the Ghetto and go instead to a military labor camp where living conditions are much harsher? Rabinovitz is also concerned over the refusal of the Jewish Council at Miligan to receive back the two Jewish youths. Who knows what the Council there is up to?

Krecmer took Rabinovitz to a locked garage in his yard. He unlocked the door with his key and showed Rabinovitz his captives. The two youths begged for mercy, denying any involvement in any crime. Since early this morning they have been asking the Jewish workers in the yard to save them. They gave the impression of being underworld figures. Krecmer intends to keep them locked up until the day is over, but no longer. If Rabinovitz is willing to exchange them for two other Jews—so much the better. If not, Krecmer will hand them over to the Gestapo.

Rabinovitz asked Krecmer why he needed two other Jews to replace the two youths; after all, once they had been murdered by the Gestapo, he would not be able to replace them with others. He, Rabinovitz, cannot hand over two other Jews from the Ghetto, who have not committed any crime, to be punished by being exposed to the harsh conditions in the labor camp. Furthermore, this camp is likely to be liquidated or evacuated.

Krecmer will give his reply later.

Krecmer has another problem on his hands: 680 Jews have recently been brought from the Zezmer labor camp to the Kovno Ghetto. In addition to the 280 who were added to the original 400 whom the Germans wished to transfer, another five Jews, together with their families, joined this contingent illegally. Krecmer wants to have these five placed under arrest and send them back to Zezmer camp. They will not be hurt, but they must return to Zezmer.

Having heard Rabinovitz's report, the members of the Council held a special meeting. We agreed that, irrespective of the characters of the two youths from the Miligan camp, they must be saved and brought into the Ghetto. Krecmer should be persuaded to send them to us without "payment" in the form of two other Jews. At the same time, we should agree to his demand concerning the five families from Zezmer: they should be sent back. If we do not do that on our own initiative, Krecmer will find ways of his own to do it. Another consideration in our decision was that we must not spoil our relations with Krecmer. After all, it is well known that at the beginning of June we brought 180 more Jews from Zezmer than we were allowed to.

Today Rabinovitz again spoke to Krecmer on the telephone. The latter accepted our offer: he will transfer to us the two Jewish youths held in his garage, whereas we will send the five Jewish families back to Zezmer.

We were satisfied with having saved the lives of two Jews. Krecmer opened the locked garage of the Todt organization and handed to us the two youths who for two days had been suspended between life and death.

JUNE 18, 1943

If a Jew is sent to the Gestapo, his fate is anyone's guess. Sometimes it does not even matter for what reason he was sent there. We know of many cases in which Jewish workers were arrested in the city near their place of work, while buying a loaf of bread or some potatoes. They were taken to the Gestapo and did not return. Once, a Jew was arrested for buying a newspaper and was subsequently executed.

There are some truly astonishing cases. On one occasion four Jewish police-men tried to bring a truckload of flour into the Ghetto. After they were caught, these four Jewish policemen, together with two of the Jewish workers also in-volved, were sent to the Gestapo. Three of those arrested were executed, to-gether with their families. The other three were released and are living in the Ghetto to this very day. These three were released following a plea for pardon from Lipzer, and appeals from a group of workers from the Jewish labor brigade working in the Gestapo building.

There are no fixed rules as far as punishing Jews is concerned. The Gestapo has carte blanche in this regard; it is empowered to act as it deems fit against Jews who have committed any "offense."

Yesterday a twenty-one-year-old Jew, by the name of Zilber, was arrested and transferred to the Gestapo. He had stolen a leather engine-belt at his place of work on an estate in the Kovno district. At present this estate belongs to a German civilian manager. Theft of state property in time of war—be it by a Jew or a German—is a capital offense. This case was even more complicated be-cause removal of a belt from an engine in time of war can be viewed as sabotag-ing the war effort.

When the fact of Zilber's arrest became known, his wife came to the Council carrying her baby in her arms. She begged us to save her husband. Lipzer, who happened to be in the Council offices at this time, said to her: "Why are you talking about saving the life of your husband; you had better start worrying about saving yourself and your baby. Do not spend the night in your apartment; if you do, they will come to take you and your baby."

We had no doubt that Zilber would be executed, but we wanted to save his wife and baby. The Ghetto residents were very annoyed with Zilber, who had put his own life and the life of his family in grave danger for the sake of a leather belt. This case is also a very dangerous one for the Ghetto as a whole.

In the morning, the Gestapo ordered the Ghetto guard to arrest Mrs. Zilber and her baby and take them to the Ghetto command headquarters. The Ghetto command men must take her there immediately.

The Ghetto is situated between the Gestapo building and the Ninth Fort. When the family of a "criminal" is placed under arrest, the Gestapo orders them to be taken to the Ghetto command headquarters; they are then taken to the Ninth Fort by the Gestapo.

The news of the arrest of Mrs. Zilber and her child spread quickly in the Ghetto; its residents were seized by fright. The last few weeks had been rela-tively quiet. The conversation between Dr. Elkes and Colonel Jaeger had pro-vided everyone with some relief. Now we are in a state of shock following the arrest of Zilber and his family. Only yesterday Zilber took a leather belt off an engine. Today he is to be sent to the Ninth Fort together with his family. This is truly an example of barbarity.

In the morning, the gray Gestapo car passed through the Ghetto gate. It seemed like a coffin coming to collect its victims: in this case, Zilber's wife and child.

The car pulled up at the Ghetto command headquarters. Schtitz of the Gestapo and three men in civilian clothes were sitting inside. Then they drove to a certain house in the Ghetto, in which a man called Gerber lived. During the search of Gerber's room they found cigarettes, bottles of wine and vodka, a gold watch, and money. They took the loot with them, locked the apartment, and set out to find its tenants—Gerber and his wife—in order to take them to the Ghetto command headquarters.

Having left Gerber's apartment, the Gestapo men set out for another "store" of this kind, where they also conducted a search. When news of the searches spread, it became clear to everyone that someone had passed details to the Gestapo of the existence of such "stores" in the Ghetto, and had supplied the Gestapo with the addresses. The Jewish police immediately warned other owners of such "stores," so as to enable them to hide their merchandise.

When the search of a third "store" failed to discover any illegal goods, the searches were called off. The Gestapo car drove back to the German Commandant's headquarters in the Ghetto. Schtitz put Zilber inside a room in the headquarters building and ordered his men to bring Zilber's wife and baby there. After a conversation with the Ghetto commandant, Schtitz told them that they were free to go home. The Gestapo car returned to the city, and Zilber, his wife and child were set free.

We at the Council had no clue to the reason for the unexpected release of Zilber. Was it because of an inexplicable fit of generosity? Later we learned what had happened. It turned out that Zilber was severely beaten by the Gestapo. Then they bound his hands and legs and threw him into the Gestapo car. Schtitz took with him an automatic gun and ordered his men to bring Zilber's wife and baby. He also ordered Zilber's work card to be sent back to the Council with a written statement saying: "Today Zilber and his family were shot because of theft and sabotage. The same fate will befall every Jew who commits such crimes."

Schtitz then got into the car to take Zilber and his family to the Ninth Fort for execution. On the way, he spoke to Zilber for the last time. He said that he wanted to help him and to give him a chance to save his life. Zilber could do this, Schtitz said, by telling him the names of Ghetto residents engaging in black-market trade; who was interested in politics; who was shirking work-duty, etc. Zilber would not have to do anything else, just tell Schtitz all the details.

Then he and his family would be transferred to a labor camp and their lives would be saved.

Zilber is not exactly a resolute man; he accepted Schtitz's offer. He told him that there were several secret stores in the Ghetto, selling goods of various kinds. He also claimed to know their addresses. Schtitz took Zilber at his word and let him point out various "stores" in the Ghetto. This operation was worth Schtitz's while: a gold watch, a substantial amount of money, sausages, cooking oil, and other goods. Two Jews were arrested following the searches.

Now Schtitz could set Zilber free. He always keeps his word. In any event, he knows Zilber's address; the man will fall into his hands sooner or later.

The trade in Jewish lives in the Ghetto is being carried on out in the open, for everyone to see. The Jews conceal their pain and shame in their hearts.

In the evening, an order was received to bring Gerber, together with his wife, to the Gestapo. They were arrested following information supplied by Zilber. Ups and downs.

JUNE 25, 1943

"I have good news for you," said Schtitz to Mrs. Blumenthal in his office at the Gestapo, whither she had been summoned from the Ghetto yesterday morning. Mrs. Blumenthal lives in the Ghetto with her husband. She is a Christian and a native of Belgium. During her studies in Belgium, she met a Jewish student by the name of Blumenthal, who fell in love with her. They got married and later came to Kovno, where her husband's parents lived. Blumenthal, the father, although a native of Kovno, held Swiss citizenship. His grandfather had been born in Switzerland and passed his Swiss citizenship on to his son. Young Blumenthal, too, was therefore entitled to a Swiss passport on account of his grandfather's nationality. On her marriage, Mrs. Blumenthal also acquired Swiss nationality.

When the war between Germany and the Soviet Union broke out, and it was decreed that the Jews of Kovno must leave their homes and move into the Ghetto, the Blumenthals pinned great hopes on their Swiss passports, thinking that these passports might save them from expulsion to the Ghetto. They also hoped that Mrs. Blumenthal's Christian faith would save them from the Ghetto. Their hopes, however, were not fulfilled. Several days after the announcement of the expulsion order, its full text was published. It transpired that expulsion applied not only to all Jews living in Lithuania, regardless of their nationality, but also to couples of mixed marriage—that is, to couples of whom one was Jewish. The non-Jewish husbands or wives were therefore faced with the alternative of either divorcing or following their husbands or wives to the Ghetto.

There were indeed cases in which mixed couples decided to divorce. In some cases the one who was Jewish decided that it would be right for the non-Jewish husband or wife to save him or herself, or at least to stay in the city in the hope that they could be reunited after the end of the war. There were, however, some Christian women who decided to link their fate with that of their Jewish husbands. They put the yellow badge on their clothing and went with their husbands to the Ghetto. Even before the exodus to the Ghetto, the residents of Kovno noticed a strange phenomenon: a young woman wearing a yellow badge on her clothing, and with a golden cross around her neck, stood in the line at a grocery store. It was Annette Blumenthal from Belgium, who, in the very first days of the war, decided to share the fate of her husband, even though she saw how thousands of Jews were led to their deaths in the Ninth Fort. She followed her husband and his parents—all of them Swiss nationals—to the Ghetto.

Mrs. Blumenthal was not the only Christian woman in the Ghetto. Another Christian woman, Hela, who also followed her husband to the Ghetto, was married to a young Jew from Kovno, a member of the Jewish police by the name of Aronovski.[1] She was a Polish Catholic. In the first days of the Ghetto, she also walked around with a yellow badge on her clothing and a cross around her neck. Later she disappeared from sight for a long time. It emerged that, after becoming pregnant, she had refused to comply with Gestapo orders to have an abortion. Despite the danger to herself and her husband, she carried the baby in her womb for nine months and gave birth to a Jewish girl.

A third Christian woman of German origin, married to a Jewish painter by the name of Burstein, has also been living in the Ghetto since the Ghetto was established.

It was profoundly moving to see yet another Christian woman in the streets of the Ghetto, clothed in rags, with a kerchief around her head, and holding a young Jewish boy—of about six or seven years old—by the hand. She had been a housemaid in a Jewish home in the city. The boy's parents were murdered during the early days of the war, but this woman succeeded in saving the couple's only child and came with him to the Ghetto. Here she looked after him with the devotion of a mother.

These four Christian women went through horrible experiences; nevertheless, they refused to be deterred by the criminal acts of the Germans. Each of them stood firm, owing to their selfless love for the men they had married, or, in the case of the housemaid, for a child. Besides love, these women also displayed a great deal of courage and spiritual integrity.

I had an opportunity to speak with Hela Aronovski.[2] During the days of the Soviet occupation we had sometimes worked together. Once I asked her openly: "Why do you keep on living in the Ghetto? You could help your husband more by returning to the city. Is it not enough that your husband risks his life by living here?" Her reply was: "A devoted wife does not leave her husband. Whatever happens to him, her fate is linked to his."

I also spoke with her husband, Liolja Aronovski, the son of a prosperous manufacturer from Kovno. He told me that on several occasions he had urged his wife to leave the Ghetto and go to the city. "If this whole thing is over soon, we'll be together again, and if not, at least you'll save your life," he told her. But his efforts to persuade her to leave the Ghetto were in vain, and she has been living here ever since. These women are the most recent embodiments of Ruth the Moabite, wife of Boaz. Also such a woman was the young Mrs. Blumenthal. She resigned herself to the hard conditions of life in the Ghetto in order to live with her husband.

The old Blumenthals and their son—Annette's husband—sought ways to put their Swiss passports and birth certificates to good use. From the time they were confined to the Ghetto, they tried, again and again, to establish contact with the Swiss consul in Berlin, to ask him to get them out of the trouble they were in. They were certain that if only they could inform the consul about the existence of Swiss nationals confined in the Slobodka Ghetto, he would intervene immediately and get them out. According to established practice, a Swiss consul is duty-bound to come to the aid of the citizens of his country. For its part, the German government is required to hand them over to the Swiss government, whose country remains neutral in this war and maintains normal relations with Germany. The Blumenthals kept dreaming about the beautiful landscape of Switzerland, its mountains and lakes. They dreamed about the country which does not discriminate between a Christian and a Jew, and where all residents enjoy freedom and equality.

The Ghetto constricts the Blumenthals. Every step here is fraught with danger. What was the purpose of holding Swiss citizenship for so many years, and why should they have held on to a Swiss passport for their son, the apple of their eye? Their decision to live in Lithuania as foreign nationals exposed them to many difficulties. They withstood them, however, believing that should the situation in Lithuania take a turn for worse, Switzerland would open its doors to them.

Once in the Ghetto, the Blumenthals were faced with the question of how to contact the Swiss consul in Berlin. Any attempt to contact the consul of a foreign country was bound to be construed as spying. A member of the Gestapo might, once in a great while, take pity on a Jew who was buying a loaf of bread with the intention of bringing it into the Ghetto, but there was no doubt as to his reaction to a Jew trying to contact the diplomatic representative of a foreign country.

The Blumenthals decided, therefore, to try something desperate: to send a letter to the Swiss consul in Berlin. In it they wrote that there were Swiss citizens in the Kovno Ghetto, and they asked the consul to help in getting them out and transferring them to Switzerland. The letter was sent via a Lithuanian acquaintance of theirs. That was thirteen months ago. The whole matter, however, came to the knowledge of the Gestapo. Rauca was handling the investigation, but apparently Blumenthal's brother-in-law, Jeglin, who worked at Gestapo headquarters at a job that was wrapped in mystery, intervened on their behalf and the investigation was discontinued. The Blumenthals were saved from certain death.

Since then thirteen months have passed. The Blumenthals thought that the whole matter had been forgotten. But the Gestapo never forgets. Some time later Jeglin—who had made possible the breaking-off of the investigation—was dismissed from his job at the Gestapo. Rauca had been taken ill and was in the police hospital in town; his affairs had been taken over by Schtitz, who reopened the Blumenthals' case.

Schtitz summoned the two elderly Blumenthals for interrogation. With an ironic smile playing on his lips, he asked them how they came to be Swiss citizens. Blumenthal senior, a decent man, who does not get excited even when the situation is not good, replied: "I have been a Swiss citizen since I was born. My father, too, was a Swiss citizen." In order to prove the truth of his statement he took out his Swiss passport, which he had preserved throughout his life, and submitted it to Schtitz. The latter thumbed through it and placed it on the table. He also took the Swiss passport of the elderly Mrs. Blumenthal and put it next to her husband's.

"The passports remain here," Schtitz told them. "Now you no longer have any need of them. Now you have Ghetto certificates. You may go back to your home in the Ghetto."

The elderly Blumenthals were seized by fright at Schtitz's action. At the same time, however, they were glad that he had set them free. They were also consoled by the fact that even though the Swiss passport was no longer in their possession, they still had their Swiss birth certificates, which were of no less value than passports.

Blumenthal the son is a labor brigade leader. One day he returned from work carrying a parcel. He was put through a search by Ratnikas. The latter found some flour, which he confiscated; he then started feeling through Blumenthal's pockets. There, he found a document which he could not interpret. The document aroused his suspicion; he ordered its owner to be taken to the Ghetto guard, where it turned out that the suspect document was a Swiss passport. The Ghetto commandant immediately reported to the Gestapo, asking how this should be handled. He received orders to arrest Blumenthal and bring him to the Gestapo offices. When Blumenthal arrived there, Schtitz was not in his office; indeed, he was drunk that day. Blumenthal was returned to the Ghetto, but the Ghetto commandant was ordered to destroy his passport. Before Blumenthal's very eyes, the commandant threw the passport into the burning stove, where it was immediately consumed. This took place several weeks ago.

Yesterday, Blumenthal's Christian wife Annette was taken to the Gestapo on orders from them. Later she reported that Schtitz had given her the "happy" news that she, her husband, and her parents-in-law would be going to Switzerland. Each one of them could take fifteen kilograms of clothing and other belongings with them. They would be flown to Berlin, on transport supplied by the Gestapo. He also asked her whether they had money enough for the journey from Berlin to Switzerland. The four of them were to present themselves at the Gestapo in the morning, and from there, Schtitz promised, they would be taken to Berlin. When the news of this became known in the Ghetto, heavy doubts were aroused. It seemed to everyone that the lives of the Blumenthal family were in danger. We could not believe the "happy news."

This morning Schtitz, together with another Gestapo man and a driver, arrived at the Ghetto command. As usual in such cases, there was an automatic weapon in the car. At the Ghetto command, the young Blumenthal couple, with two suitcases in their hands, were waiting. On Jeglin's advice, however, the parents did not appear. He had already explained to Schtitz that they were sick people and that the long journey would be too difficult for them. Schtitz was upset by this news, saying that he had received orders to send them to Berlin today. Finally he acquiesced, and agreed to delay the departure of the parents for a few more days.

Young Blumenthal was nervous and upset. He could not believe in the good intentions of the Gestapo. Although nervous, he had put on his best clothes, as if he was about to set out for Switzerland. His wife, on the other hand, was relaxed and optimistic. In the end they entered the car and Schtitz ordered the driver: "To the airfield." The car departed in the direction of the city, and not toward the Ninth Fort.

Several hours later we learned that the suitcases and coats of the Blumenthal couple had been taken to the Gestapo. No one knew about the fate of the young people. The Blumenthals did not arrive in Switzerland. It appears that they are resting now in the pit of the Fourth Fort. Upon their arrival at the fort they were told to get out of the car and they were even offered cigarettes. They were asked to take a few steps forward. Then they were machine-gunned and fell to the ground.

Blumenthal senior and his wife remained in the Ghetto. Today Jeglin had somehow managed to save them from the "journey to Switzerland." On Monday Schtitz will be coming to take them with him. How will the elderly Blumenthals spend the next four days and sleepless nights—anyone can imagine that.

Work and quiet—that is all the authorities ask from the Ghetto inmates.

People fall down under the heavy burden of work. By superhuman efforts they seek to get a moment of respite, but their efforts bear no fruit. No peace is possible in the Ghetto. Even in the days of respite between one disaster and another, we remain restless and agitated; we fear what the next moment may bring.

The Blumenthal affair is not quite over, and we already fear the coming disasters. Who will be the next victim? Which one of us is the next in line for a trip in the gray Gestapo car? Deep fear pervades the Ghetto.

1. Liolja Aronovski was among the Jewish policemen who were later murdered at the Ninth Fort for refusing to tell the Germans the location of hiding places in the Ghetto.
2. Hela (Gabriella) Aronovski survived the war. Later she married Dr. Baruch Voschin and settled in Israel. Her only daughter, Irena Savir, today is a doctor at Kaplan Hospital in Israel.

JUNE 26, 1943

In recent weeks the Council has been busy reorganizing the labor office.[1] Discussions are held every day on the question of how this should be done. Most Ghetto inmates show great interest in the labor office, which is known for the disorder reigning there. The inmates harbor many complaints against it: their requests are ignored; the treatment is impersonal; at times some of the officials insult them. The duties of the labor office include the organization of the labor force inside the Ghetto; recruitment of all able-bodied Ghetto residents for work; and supplying the ever-increasing outside need for Jewish workers. The Jewish residents of the Ghetto add up to a labor force to be reckoned with, the value of which for the German war-production effort is inestimable. The Council must ensure proper working conditions in the labor office, so that it can discharge its duties toward both the workers and the employers.

Each Ghetto inmate regards work as the sole means of making a living. When working, he can purchase foodstuffs in the vicinity of his place of work. He can have his fill of soup. He can meet his former housemaid, to whose care he entrusted various belongings. He can take care of various other errands. There are those who seek to take advantage of working outside the Ghetto by engaging in small trading, at times even in the retail trade; to listen to the news on the radio, and to talk with friends about the war and the chances of peace. All these things are impossible here in the Ghetto.

What is more, the Ghetto inmates seek not just any job but a job that will suit their needs. The Germans say that everyone must work—the location of the place of work and its conditions are of no importance to them. We in the Ghetto, however, do not look at it this way. We cannot say to the Germans that one cannot purchase foodstuffs at a certain workplace, or that working conditions there are bad, or that workers are not fed there, or that workers can be beaten there. We approach this matter from a Jewish and a human point of view as much as we can; for example, we try to exempt from work people such as weak women, mothers of little children, and teachers of children in the Ghetto.

The Ghetto inmates wait long hours in the offices of the labor office, demanding to be reassigned to a different workplace, or seeking exemption from work at the airfield, or asking not to be sent to a remote workplace. As a rule, all these demands are justified, but those who make them do not want to understand that the labor office cannot satisfy all of them. The officials of the labor office hear hundreds of complaints; they can lose their patience in the process; they lose their tempers and get worked up. On occasion, they do not provide the right answers.

The authorities' demand for new workers keeps growing with each passing day, whereas the sources of manpower in the Ghetto are practically depleted. There are also Ghetto inmates who engage in black-marketeering or fence-trade. All these must be forced to return to work. This is why the Council authorized the labor office to impose penalties on those refusing to work.

The labor office, however, was not immune to the usual illnesses plaguing all public institutions: the heads of certain departments began to behave as if they were omnipotent. The result was that without *protektzia* (favoritism) one could not get a suitable job, or be exempted from work at the airfield, or escape from unearned punishments and arrests, or obtain leave, etc.

In due course, the Ghetto inmates gradually became extremely angry with some senior officials of the labor office—Goldberg, the head of the office; Lurie, the work director at the airfield; Margolis, the head of the recruitment and punishment section; and others.

Not one of the department heads at the labor office gets along with Goldberg. The Council has advised him more than once to reach an understanding with them.

On June 24, the directive of the chairman of the Council, Dr. Elkes, was announced in the presence of the members of the Council, as well as of Lipzer. Herman Fraenkel, until now head of the nutrition department of the Council, is to be the new director of the labor office. Fraenkel's deputy is to be Dr. Grinhaus. The directive contained an expression of thanks to Goldberg for his devotion to his work, and expressed the hope that in future all the workers of the labor office would get along among themselves for the benefit of all Ghetto inmates. Fraenkel and Dr. Grinhaus expressed their thanks for their appointment and promised to act in accordance with the Council's directives.

On the face of it everything ended well. On that same day, however, Lipzer, Fraenkel, and Grinhaus presented themselves before Dr. Elkes and informed him that Lurie refused to resign from his post voluntarily. Consequently, they asked Dr. Elkes to postpone the reorganization of the labor office for a while.

The German director of the labor office, Gustav Hermann, also put in an appearance in the Council offices. He ordered Garfunkel and Goldberg, who were present in the room, to leave him alone with Dr. Elkes. Hermann then told Dr. Elkes that yesterday fifty workers had been missing at the airfield. Tomorrow, everyone must report for work. Also, Dr. Elkes had long ago been supposed to submit a list of children and elderly people unfit for work. Failure to do so amounts to an act of sabotage on the part of Dr. Elkes. If there are people missing from work in the coming days, then there will be reason to fear the worst. It is possible that people unfit for work will be killed. Dr. Elkes promised that no one would be missing from work tomorrow. He would make sure of that.

Hermann had also heard that the Council wanted to dismiss Lurie from his job, and wanted to know whether, in fact, this was the case. Dr. Elkes confirmed that indeed, this was the Council's intention. In reply, Hermann said that Lurie must not be dismissed. He needs him at the airfield.

Hermann also asked Dr. Elkes to consult him in the future whenever the Council sought to institute changes of personnel in the labor office. Hermann also said that Goldberg was not fit for his job as he was not diligent enough. Dr. Elkes promised to refrain from dismissing Lurie.

In the meantime, Miller entered Dr. Elkes's room at the Council. He began by voicing threats in connection with the fifty workers who were missing yesterday from work at the airfield. "I am going to take all 16,000 Ghetto residents out of their homes and concentrate them in one place. From there they will be sent to work. Everyone will have to work; even Garfunkel's wife and Golub's wife. I am going to turn the whole Ghetto inside out."

After Hermann and Miller left, the members of the Council expressed astonishment at the anger of the two Germans over fifty workers missing from work on one day. After all, that number of workers is missing from work for various reasons quite often. It seems that someone "staged" this whole scandal.

The conversation between Hermann and Dr. Elkes revealed several details. It turns out that yesterday Hermann, together with Margolis, drove in Hermann's car through the Ghetto streets. They were looking for work-duty shirkers. On that very day, Lurie was summoned to Hermann's office. Both of them, Margolis and Lurie, asked Hermann not to allow the Council to sacrifice them on the altar of irregularities at the labor office. It turns out, therefore, that these two went to seek justice and protection from the German ruler. When an airfield worker goes to a German to seek a redress to his grievances, or an improvement in his working conditions, he is likely to get a warning from Margolis or Lurie. We do not want the Germans to intervene in our affairs. Yesterday Margolis and Lurie did exactly that. This is the first instance of its kind in the Ghetto.

Yesterday a meeting of the Council took place in my room (as I was not well enough to go to the Council office). Dr. Elkes recounted his conversation with Hermann, who had asked that Lurie not be dismissed.

Since Hermann is the director of the labor office we must bow to his wishes, which are the wishes of the powers that be. There is only one thing we can do: to inscribe this incident in our memory. We decided to refrain from deliberating further on this subject. Lurie, Margolis, and Oleiski, together with Grinhaus, Girshovitz,[2] Jatzkan, Zundelevitz, and Natkin, will remain at their posts. Lurie and Margolis owe their jobs to the intervention of the German ruler.

While this meeting was in progress, the assistant chief of the Jewish police, Zupovitz, and the superintendent of the Jewish police, Levin, entered the room. They revealed to us that, this morning, Hermann and Margolis were again driving through the Ghetto streets and making arrests. They inspected the work-cards of the Ghetto inmates. Upon arriving at the square near the Ghetto gate, Hermann started hurling accusations against the Jewish police: "The Jewish police conceals the work-shirkers; it sabotages the recruitment of workers." Margolis, who stood next to him, did not say a word. He kept silent, even though he knew that the Jewish police makes nightly searches for work-shirkers and, in general, does everything it can in this area. Officers of the Jewish police asked the Council to reply to Hermann's accusations.

We believe that Hermann was incited by Margolis and Lurie, but there is nothing we can do about it at the present time. One thing we know, however: Lurie and Margolis have cast themselves out from our midst.

Today Fraenkel, the new director of the labor office, takes over. Lurie and Margolis will carry on at the Ghetto gate. They are assured of their power more than ever. But their friends of yesterday are ashamed of the fact that they had been standing by their side for such a long time and thereby caused damage to the Ghetto.

In this way, all the problems of the labor office were "solved." The Council recorded the results of its actions and moved on to the next subject on the agenda. All the difficulties notwithstanding, it will continue to fulfill its duties: to lead the Ghetto by the strength of the Jewish faith, according to the historical tradition of Jewish communal leaders. It will carry on in this spirit despite all the difficulties and dangers.

1. This refers to the Jewish Council's labor office, headed by the attorney Jacob Goldberg. In all, the labor office was responsible for 7,000 Jews who went to work daily outside the Ghetto and a further 1,800 who worked in the Ghetto workshops. The German labor office for the Ghetto was headed by Gustav Hermann and run, in practice, by Dr. Isaac Rabinovitz. It passed on to the Council's labor office the specific requests for Jewish labor from various German military and civilian enterprises.

2. The attorney Nahum Girshovitz had been, before the war, one of the founders of the Zionist student fraternity organization Vetaria. He was deputy director of the Ghetto housing department, and later of the labor department. In July 1944 he was deported to labor camps in Germany. He survived the war and today lives in the United States.

JUNE 30, 1943

A short while ago, Lipzer came to the Ghetto with the news that in the near future the German and Lithuanian policemen will be removed from the Ghetto. They are to be replaced by Jewish policemen.

Lipzer sounded as though he was bringing tidings of redemption, but our reaction was cautious; actually, we received the news with a great deal of concern.

At first, guard duty in the Ghetto was assigned to the German third police squad, under the command of police chief Tornbaum. The third police squad was stationed in Kovno; the Ghetto Guard was situated in the vicinity of the Ghetto fence. The Germans patrolled the perimeter fence outside the Ghetto. There were no Germans inside the Ghetto at that time.

This was the most difficult period for the Ghetto. The German commanders—Willy Kozlovski, Blasky, Krause, and others—stole, looted, and filled the Ghetto inmates with terror and fright. They conducted house searches. Under their rule Jews were deported. In compliance with Gestapo orders, they carried out fearful massacres and led thousands of Jews from the Ghetto to the Ninth Fort. They murdered dozens of Jews with their own hands. They were the first to show us what the Ghetto stood for in the Third Reich, and what it meant to be a Jew under the Nazi regime.

Those nights at the end of 1941 were long and sleepless. In the morning people were rushed to work at the airfield, and in the evening they were kept awake by the sound of shooting. This was the third police squad; their gunfire reverberated behind the windows, over the rooftops, along the fence—practically everywhere. People could not close their eyes for many nights in a row, out of fear of gunshots. Often a bullet discharged by one of the sentries would penetrate an apartment in the Ghetto, hitting one of the terrified tenants. Many Ghetto inmates slept on the floor next to their beds.

When the news came that the third police squad was to be removed from the Ghetto, it was like a golden dream. We said that such a thing was impossible. Tornbaum was the embodiment of a typical German gendarme. He expressed great interest in art, in philatelic collections, and in valuables in general. He was a sadist, fond of listening to Liszt's rhapsodies played by an artist, only to rob him afterward of his piano. He was a police dog, who forced women to undress, so that he could then conduct gynecological examinations on them while, at the same time, beating them severely. This police inspector who plundered and looted treasures from the Jews, repaying them with blows on all parts of their bodies; this broad-shouldered man in his gray uniform and shining boots, feared by his own subordinates; this Tornbaum, who had thought that his rule over us would be indefinite—how was it possible that this man would just go away and leave us alone?[1] We simply could not believe it—until a new Ghetto Guard was assigned to the Ghetto, the NSKK.

With Tornbaum's departure, a new period in the life of the Ghetto was ushered in. With the departure of the third police squad we thought that the worst was behind us. But the new overseers brought new decrees and fresh worries in their wake. They placed their headquarters right in the heart of the Ghetto. Until then, inside the Ghetto, Jews had lived among their own. Now, however, a small barracks housing thirty to forty NSKK policemen was put up in the middle of the Ghetto. Our ancestors used to say that one should not pray for the end of a cruel ruler; the policemen of the third police squad had plundered and looted, but at least we had known them and become accustomed to the quirks and idiosyncrasies of each one of them. And then, all of a sudden, a new king ascended the throne "who knew not Joseph." The new policemen were endowed with wolfish appetites, but the third police squad had robbed us of all our valuables, clothing, gold watches, and such. How would we buy off the new policemen?

At first, immediately after their arrival, our situation was unbearable—strict searches at the Ghetto gate and patrols of German policemen on the Ghetto streets. If someone failed to pay them respect by taking off his cap, he was in deep trouble at once. A long time passed before we got used to them, and somehow even managed to establish some contact with them.

The very presence of thirty to forty German policemen had a destabilizing effect on the Ghetto population. We had not gotten used to seeing German faces inside the Ghetto. In the first days of their tour of duty they presented themselves as devoted National Socialists, as dedicated members of the Party who could not be "bought" by us. They knew that the Jews of the Ghetto had maintained close contacts with the third police squad and that "gifts" aplenty had been dispensed. Nothing like that would happen with them, they promised; they would not take anything from us; they would refuse to negotiate with us.

Upon returning from work, the workers would stand for hours at the Ghetto gate waiting for the new policemen to search them and to relieve them of the few goods they had brought from the city in their knapsacks and baskets. Nor did the new policemen spare the Jewish workers heavy, random blows—both on the way to work and on their return to the Ghetto.

In the course of time, the NSKK commanders began to show an interest in the internal life of the Jewish community in the Ghetto. As a result, they started noticing things that had escaped the attention of their predecessors. In due course, the policemen greatly enjoyed the goods confiscated at the Ghetto gate; when their senior officers wished to feast on a sumptuous meal, they would take the trouble to pay a visit to the Ghetto Guard in order to eat their fill.

In time, the German policemen and their commanders came to realize that the Nazi theory and life were two different things. They realized that the Jews in the Ghetto were not as wicked and corrupt as they had read in *Der Stürmer*.[2] They noticed that there were skilled workers among the Jews who could make first-class, high-quality boots, fine clothes and leather gloves, gold or silver rings—things they could not lay their hands on in their German homeland. Here they found themselves able to get these things for nothing. They could place orders for clothes and shoes for their wives or mistresses.

The German policemen soon found that they were no longer able to contain their urges. When being offered a pair of silk stockings for their wives, or a gold watch or other such valuables without having to wait and without needing a ration card—they took with both hands, and thereby became more human. They learned to look differently at the Jews, their traits and character. The war is not yet over, they thought to themselves, and in the meantime one must enjoy life.

Natkin, a German Jew who knew a great deal about drinks, became the majordomo at the Ghetto command headquarters, and the chief supplier of all the German needs from this inexhaustible department store called "Ghetto." We were glad, just as in the old days. Thank God, the uncircumcised are taking gifts.

As the end of the war was not in sight, and as the eastern front demanded more and more human resources, the Germans became weary of spreading their front-line forces too thinly. It was still very important to guard the Ghetto, but the front now assumed growing importance for them. The Ghetto will not run away if it is guarded by local policemen.

The Lithuanians competed with the Germans in their deep hatred of the Jews. In the first days of the war they even managed to exceed German expectations as far as ill-treatment of the Jews was concerned. So it was that, one day, the German policemen vanished from the Ghetto, to be replaced by Lithuanian so-called partisans. Only four Germans were left behind in the Ghetto command headquarters to supervise the Lithuanians.

We were back where we had started. The Lithuanians regarded the Ghetto as fair game to be looted and plundered. They knew that this was open season as far as the Jews were concerned. Every one of them murdered scores of Jews. The Jews were not going to remain in the Ghetto for much longer. One day, all of them would be led to slaughter. Why, then, should their property be left to others? Every Lithuanian partisan would take advantage of every opportunity which presented itself to say: "Give me this and this and that; what's the use of these things to you, anyway?" Lithuanian guards patrolling the Ghetto would break into Jewish apartments at night, seize everything they could lay their hands on, and disappear.

In time, we started getting along even with the Lithuanians. Fixed prices ("gifts") were set for all kinds of services: this much for letting a large parcel pass through the Ghetto gate; that much for letting a carton of butter in; such and such a gift for smuggling in a sackful of flour, etc. The Lithuanian policemen, whose wages paid by the Germans did not exceed a hundred marks a month, were being paid this same sum every day by the Jews—sometimes even as much as a thousand marks a day. The Jews, it turned out, were a good business.

These Lithuanian "patriots," who befriended the Nazis, who shouted for everyone to hear that the Jews must be expelled from Lithuania, or even exterminated; these very same people did business with the Jews on a daily basis, getting rich by staying in contact with them. They feared being transferred to some other duty—guarding bridges or army camps, for example.

That is how things looked up to today. We have become used to it. Nor was it so bad. True, we have had to bear with the excesses of the Lithuanian policemen. They are cruel, money-craving, and coarse. How many troubles has Ratnikas, this sadist, caused us. He was always on the lookout for victims. He enjoyed humiliating and torturing people even more than confiscating goods at the Ghetto gate. Smailis, the Ghetto Guard chief, was not much better than Ratnikas, his fellow Lithuanian.

Now Lithuanian rule in the Ghetto is over. New times—new songs. We fear any new arrangements in the Ghetto, and we do not want them. We are being told that from now on the Jews themselves must guard the Ghetto; the Jews themselves must constrain their brethren so as to avoid collisions with German law. The Jews themselves must be responsible for everything that happens in the Ghetto. Will the Jewish policemen be issued with weapons to enable them to keep law and order?

No one asks us and no one seeks our advice. We just receive orders. Kopelman was summoned to the Gestapo, where they told him that, beginning on July 5, the German and Lithuanian guards will be removed from the Ghetto. From then on the Jewish Police will assume guard duties along the fence and at the Ghetto gate; the Lithuanians will guard the perimeter fence from outside. Apart from guarding the main gate, the Jewish policemen will also be responsible for everything that happens inside the Ghetto.

In order to enable the Jewish police to deal with their new assignments, the Jewish police force will be expanded by sixty men. The enlarged force, however, will be under the command of the Gestapo and the city governor's office. If it fails to discharge its duties, well, the Ninth Fort is not so far away.

Kopelman told the Gestapo that we do not have the proper clothing for rainy days and winter nights; also, there is no way that we can guard the Ghetto fence, prevent crime inside the Ghetto, or foil the penetration of criminals from outside, with empty hands, that is, without weapons. His arguments bore no fruit. An order is an order. The new arrangement will be in force for a month, on a trial basis, and will then be reexamined.

This new arrangement is not at all to our liking. There is too much responsibility and the prospects are few. The problem is this: when a German or a Lithuanian guard stumbled or even committed a crime, he would have a proper hearing, his statements would be listened to. Sometimes he would be believed, sometimes not. The rule was: anyone can take a false step. But should a Jewish policeman make a mistake or take a false step—he is liable to pay for it with his life. No one will listen to our explanations and arguments. And we, for our part, want to prevent new victims among us.

Guard duty by Jewish policemen in the Ghetto will invite disorder. In their searches at the Ghetto gate for packages brought from the city, the Jewish policemen will have to be strict—probably more so than the Germans or the Lithuanians; they will be called upon again and again to prove that they are acting in line with German orders. This is bound to have a negative impact on the Jewish workers returning to the Ghetto from work in the city.

To say it again, we do not like these new arrangements at all. We fear them. We are waiting for one thing only—the end of the Ghetto. Until then, any change amounts, in our view, to a new edict, a change for the worse.

1. Avraham Tory later recalled: "In 1962 I appeared before a German court in Wiesbaden as the main witness against the deputy commander of the Gestapo in Kovno, SS Lieutenant Peter Heinrich Schmitz, and also against the commander of the third department of the German police in Kovno, Alfred Tornbaum. For a whole day I recounted the tortures administered by Tornbaum, and his cruel handling of the Ghetto residents." Despite Tory's testimony, the case against Tornbaum was dismissed for lack of sufficient evidence. Schmitz committed suicide in his cell before the verdict was given.

2. *Der Stürmer* (The Stormer) was a virulently anti-Semitic newspaper published in Germany by Julius Streicher. Streicher was hanged by the Allies at Nuremberg in October 1946.

JULY 2, 1943

Yellin, the representative of Vievis camp, arrived here today. He comes to the Ghetto once every two or three weeks to collect wooden shoes, underwear, and other supplies from our welfare department.

The conditions in the Vievis labor camp are harsher than in the Ghetto. The housing conditions there endanger the health and lives of the inmates, the regime is strict, and the labor is back-breaking.

The Vievis labor camp is under the supervision of the city governor of Vilna, who is a very cruel man. About four weeks ago, the camp workers feared that all the inmates would be exterminated after two Jewish youths had refused to obey the orders of the camp guards.

Once in a while, patients from Vievis camp are admitted to our Ghetto hospital. The camp inmates also come here quite often to ask for help over some problem or other. We, for our part, extend them whatever assistance we can.

They go to the Vilna Ghetto more often than to us, however, as transportation in that direction is more readily available. The treatment accorded to them in the Vilna Ghetto is, however, less personal and more bureaucratic.

Yellin revealed to us that six Jewish workers had escaped from a labor camp situated in the Vilna district. It is a camp which employs Jews from the Vilna Ghetto. As a reprisal, sixty Jews were taken out of the camp and shot. The news spread quickly round the other camps in the area; the Jews there were overtaken by deep fear.

This news also gave rise to concern in the Kovno Ghetto. A number of Jews from the Kovno Ghetto live in the Kaisiadorys labor camp, where about 400 Jews work at digging peat. Although the living conditions there are not too bad, and the food is reasonable, a number of Jews have recently escaped the camp at Kaisiadorys and returned to the Kovno Ghetto. The Germans wanted us to find them so that they could be returned to the labor camp. After what has happened in the camp near Vilna, we are deeply concerned.

About three weeks ago, news reached us about an incident in the Vilna Ghetto in which a Jew shot and killed a Jewish policeman. In response, Gens shot and killed the Jew who had shot the policeman.

Yellin confirmed that this incident had indeed taken place, and he supplied us with details. Three weeks ago, a Lithuanian policeman arrested a Jew at the Ghetto gate; this Jew looked suspicious to him. He handed him over to the Jewish police in the Vilna Ghetto. The Jewish police put the detainee in the Ghetto prison. One day this Jew, while in his cell, pulled out a gun, shooting at a Jewish policeman who was guarding the prison. The policeman was killed on the spot. Gens was told at once. A few moments later he arrived at the prison, pulled out his gun, and killed the Jew who had shot the policeman.

The Gestapo, together with officials of the Vilna city governor's office, arrived at the scene shortly afterward and found two Jewish bodies. It turned out that the Jewish prisoner had been arrested by a Lithuanian policeman during an attempt to escape from the Ghetto to the forest. He had already obtained a gun, since without a weapon it is difficult to live in the forest. Following his arrest, this Jew had pleaded with the Jewish police to let him go, otherwise he and his family would be put to death. In an act of despair he had shot at the Jewish policeman from behind the door, hoping thereby to save himself and his family. The result: two dead Jews.

Gens acted quickly, without waiting for the arrival of the Gestapo. The latter would have shot the Jew who had killed the policeman without hesitation. But before that, they would have interrogated this Jew about the source of the gun, where he had intended to flee to, who his accomplices were, how many people were in his family, and other such questions. Such an interrogation would have left a heavy toll of casualties in its wake. Gens prevented that happening by shooting the unfortunate prisoner.[1]

Gens's actions made a profound impression in the Vilna Ghetto and also at the Vilna city governor's office. Following this incident, the Gestapo decided to supply arms to five more Jewish policemen, as a token of the trust that the Germans placed in them. Yes, the conditions in the Vilna Ghetto are different from those in ours, very different.

We have received sad news from the Siauliai Ghetto: a Jew was arrested there with twenty-seven packets of cigarettes in his possession. Searches at the Siauliai Ghetto gate are very thorough, and the penalty for an attempt to smuggle goods into the Ghetto is harsher than in our Ghetto. After the arrest of the Jew with the cigarettes in his possession, the German authorities announced that the offender would be hanged in public by members of his own Jewish community. The hanging did, in fact, take place.[2]

Thus it turns out that not only in the Vilna and Kovno Ghettos, but also in the Siauliai Ghetto, the Jews are forced by the ruler to put to death another Jew. Not for nothing did Jaeger say, in conversation with Dr. Elkes: "The conditions in the Vilna, Kovno and Siauliai Ghettos are now the same. These three Ghettos are under the same authority."

1. This incident took place on June 12, 1943, when Chaim Levin, a Jew from Swieciany, was arrested by the Vilna Jewish police at the Ghetto gate while trying to leave the Vilna Ghetto. The Jewish police having refused to release him, Levin, who had a gun, shot and killed a Jewish policeman, Moshe Gingold. Gens then arrived on the scene and demanded Levin's weapon; when Levin refused to surrender it, Gens shot him on the spot.

2. On May 31, 1943, Bezalel Mazovietzki, a Jew who worked at the bakery in the Siauliai Ghetto, was arrested by the Germans and charged with racketeering. He was later sentenced by the German authorities to be hanged. Sentences such as this had been handed down previously, but had never been carried out. The Siauliai Jewish Council intervened on Mazovietzki's behalf, but without success. On German orders, the death sentence was carried out by Jews, in the presence of all Jews of the Ghetto; a guard of armed Germans surrounded the executioners during the hanging. After the hanging, songs were written in the Ghetto describing Mazovietzki's brave walk to his death.

JULY 8, 1943

Miller came to the Council offices this morning. He has not been coming here often lately. He is in the habit of visiting the large Ghetto workshops before noon; in the evening he comes to the Ghetto gate to watch the labor brigades return from the city. He watches the searches of the returning workers and, from time to time, applies himself to searching one or two of them.

Miller is particularly fond of searching the knapsacks of young and pretty women. When he finds a kilogram of butter, or ten eggs, or a kilogram of jam, he asks: "Whom did you get these from?" As a rule, the women give him the same answer: "From some Lithuanian." In the beginning, when Miller was not yet well informed, he did not know that these women traded their own possessions for butter or potatoes. He believed that they got these products as gifts from Lithuanian acquaintances, or from Germans, at their workplaces. Later he came to a conclusion of his own: the Jewish women "sell their bodies" for food. After all, nothing in life is free. He revealed this to me in a conversation we had in his room at the city governor's office. This is why he complained about "Lithuanian pigs who profane the race."

Now Miller knows that the Jewish women buy food for money, or by trading their belongings. This led him to issue a ban on supplying Jewish workers with shoes and clothing from the Council warehouse. He was particularly angry when he found money on one of the Jewish workers. The punishment was stiff. Possession of money is strictly forbidden.

In the meantime, the Germans had decided that the Jews themselves would assume guard duties in the Ghetto and, among other things, search the Jewish workers returning from the city. Since that time, Miller has put in frequent appearances at the Ghetto gate. He orders the Jewish policemen to search the workers returning from the city more thoroughly. He himself keeps conducting searches of his own, during which he gives lectures on various subjects. In recent days he has been accompanied by the district governor of Kovno, Lenzen. The latter is a declared Jew-hater, fond of harassing the Jewish workers as they return from work to the Ghetto gate.

Yesterday Lenzen stopped a brigade of Jewish workers in Slobodka. He asked a Lithuanian peasant to bring a bucket and ordered all those who had purchased milk in the city to pour it into the bucket. On another occasion he found quantities of paper on workers from another labor brigade. To his question about the origins of this paper, he received the reply that it had been given to them at a paper factory where they had worked that day. Lenzen ordered everyone to lay the paper on the ground and moved on to inspect the packages of workers from the second labor brigade.

In the meantime a third labor brigade was approaching the scene. When its members saw Jewish workers standing in the middle of the street being searched by a German, they turned around and started looking for another route to the Ghetto. Lenzen noticed this maneuver, contented himself with confiscating the paper from the first brigade, and then started chasing after the third brigade, which obviously loathed the prospect of meeting him.

These days Lenzen comes almost daily to the Ghetto gate to ensure that the Jews do not bring foodstuffs and other articles from the city. Officially, he has no connections with the Ghetto. It is Cramer, the governor of the city of Kovno, who is in charge of the Ghetto. Lenzen is the governor of the Kovno district. This, however, does not prevent him from coming to the Ghetto gate and treating it as his own turf. In his presence, the Lithuanian policemen, as well as the German commander, display more than the usual measure of pedantry and aggressiveness toward us. As a result, more goods have recently been confiscated at the Ghetto gate.

The latest issue of the Lithuanian newspaper *Ateitis*[1] carried a long article by Lenzen on the front page. It was entitled "Slaves of the Jews." In it Lenzen wrote: "The Jews are the source of all evil. Everywhere they go, they bring trouble and destruction in their wake. The Jews are to blame for the outbreak of the Second World War. The culpability of the Jews for the war is the cause of the German decision to remove them from all spheres of life. There is no difference between the Jews in the Kremlin in Moscow, the Jews on Wall Street, the Jews of the English plutocracy, and the Jews from the Kovno Ghetto."

Of the relations between the Jews and the Lithuanians, Lenzen wrote: "Have the Lithuanians forgotten all the evils visited on Lithuania by the Jews? Have the Lithuanian peasants, artisans, and workers forgotten how the Jews used to swindle and exploit them? Have they forgotten that the Jews occupied all the high-ranking posts in the days of Soviet rule in Lithuania? Have they forgotten how in those days the Jews killed and deported scores of thousands of Lithuanians to the wilderness of Siberia?"

Lenzen went on to describe an incident he had witnessed recently on one of the Kovno streets. He had seen an elegantly dressed Lithuanian woman walk up to a brigade of Jewish workers returning from work to the Ghetto, and exchange greetings with one of the Jews. She shook his hand and her face broke into a smile. Lenzen then approached the couple, who were engrossed in conversation. When he drew close to them, they broke off their conversation; the man ran back to his brigade, which was marching to the Ghetto; the elegantly dressed lady also vanished quickly.

"It is a shame," Lenzen wrote, "that these days the Lithuanians entertain the Jews in their homes or trade with them. City residents cannot get a thing from the peasants, whereas the Jews buy everything from them. Such Lithuanians deserve to be punished. They are slaves of the Jews. They should be required to wear the yellow badge on their clothing inscribed with the words: 'Slaves of the Jews.'" At the conclusion of his article, Lenzen sounded a note of warning: "One must refrain from any contacts with the Jews. They should be driven out of every house they enter. They should be regarded as the enemy of all nations."

This article would not have made any impression on the Ghetto inmates, if it had not contained one sentence which aroused their deepest interest. Noting that the Germans had excluded the Jews from all spheres of public activity and economic life, Lenzen added: "The desire to exterminate the Jews totally has been resolutely rejected."

Many Ghetto inmates regard this sentence as an open and explicit renunciation of plans to exterminate the Jews. They are very pleased by it. Not only were they not angry with Lenzen for the incitement against the Jews in the article, but they were actually grateful for this one sentence. It was worthwhile, they said, to read this scroll of invective and incitement, just to hear from a high-ranking German that the plans to exterminate the Jews have been completely renounced.

Other Jews saw this sentence in a different light: the Germans had removed the Jews from all spheres of economic activity. There was a predisposition to exterminate them totally, but this had been rejected in the past. Today, however, it can be put into practice.

There is no way to decide which of these two interpretations is the correct one. In any event, one thing is clear: Lenzen is not exactly the sort of man to bring good tidings to the Jews.

It should be noted that yesterday—the day of the publication of Lenzen's article in a Kovno newspaper—two undercover Lithuanian policemen arrested four Jewish women on charges of buying foodstuffs. Lately, the Lithuanian policemen have refrained from harassing Jews and from arresting them. They turned a blind eye on Jewish women entering a nearby yard and trading dresses and other belongings for money or other goods. This trade was conducted in a house of a Lithuanian. Last year the Lithuanian policemen caused us a lot of trouble. They would follow the Jews at every step and take advantage of the first opportunity to arrest them and take them to the Gestapo. When the relations between the Germans and the Lithuanians became strained, and the Germans for various reasons started persecuting the Lithuanians as well, the Lithuanians simply forgot the Jews.

Well-placed Lithuanian figures had told us that the Lithuanian policemen would stop arresting Jews. In fact, in this regard, we enjoyed a period of respite. I remember Miller telling me, in a conversation I had with him in his office, that lately the Lithuanians were distancing themselves from the Germans and from German interests. We had not accepted this as a fact. I told Miller that one cannot speak of any love being lost between the Lithuanians and the Jews. But the truth remains that, for a prolonged period of time, the Lithuanian policemen accorded fair treatment to our workers in the city.

Yesterday this attitude of the Lithuanians changed for the worse. It is not a coincidence that in the last few months the Lithuanians had not arrested even a single Jew, whereas today they arrested four Jewish women and handed them over to the Gestapo.

One of the arrested women, Rachel Levin, who is an old acquaintance of mine, revealed to me the following details about her arrest: yesterday morning she set out, as usual, for work with her labor brigade in Schantz. She took with her a woman's coat to sell. Several days earlier, a Lithuanian had ordered just such a coat from her. A few hours after she started working, she left her labor brigade, took off the yellow badge so she would not be recognized as a Jew, and went to the Lithuanian, carrying with her the coat he had ordered. The Lithuanian bought the coat, paying her 1,500 marks for it.

Rachel Levin was very pleased. She had sold most of her clothes and now she had taken to selling the clothes of other women in order to give a boost to her income. On her way back to work she stopped at the house of a Lithuanian in Schantz where, several days earlier, she had left on approval a woman's blouse, some fabric for a dress, and a number of other articles of clothing. As nothing had come of this sale, she wanted to get these clothes back. She did get them, bought a kilogram of butter and a kilogram of meat, and, very contented, set off to return to her labor brigade.

On her way back to her brigade, however, Mrs. Levin was stopped by an undercover Lithuanian policeman, who escorted her to the nearest police station. On her way there, she tried to negotiate with the policeman: if he let her go she would give him money. The policeman accepted the offer and took her to the nearest police station, where they carried on with their transaction. Mrs. Levin handed him her money, the fabrics, and all that she had on her, in exchange for a promise to release her. What happened was that, despite this "deal," the Lithuanians kept her under arrest and later took her to the Gestapo. In the report that the Lithuanian policeman submitted to the Gestapo, there was no mention of the money and the fabrics; they reported only having found some butter and meat on her.

Mrs. Levin had been taken to the Gestapo once before and was very afraid. Thoughts flashed through her mind on her way to the Gestapo: they would recognize her instantly and take her straight to the Ninth Fort; they would also take her brother, and her cousin who had a baby, in whose apartment she lived.

She was taken to the building that she recognized at once: high, thick walls; gray, angry faces. Then she found herself in a closed room with a familiar figure in front of her: Schtitz, with his bloodshot eyes, speaking unintelligible German with his Swabian accent. Short questions, cold and penetrating glances, distrust and contempt. Questions: "What's your name? Where were you born? When? What was your parents' occupation? Where are they now? What do you do? Where did you take one kilogram of butter from? Tell us the whole truth."

Mrs. Levin takes a look at Schtitz. She notes the severe expression of his face; his thin, blue lips. She follows his irate glance. She is seized by panic and helplessness. Submissively, she answers Schtitz's questions: "My name is Kaganaite Sarah; age thirty-four; born in Zarasai; my parents lived here in the Ghetto and in that great 'action' of October 28 they were 'transferred' to another place; I live here by myself; I have neither family nor friends; I live in the apartment of strangers at 13 Margio Street; I sold a dress and bought one kilogram of butter. Yes, gracious sir. I forgot something: I have thirty-nine marks left. Here they are. I have told you the whole truth. I can't do otherwise."

"What do you need a whole kilogram of butter for, if you live alone?" asks Schtitz. "I wanted to share it with someone from my labor brigade," replies Mrs. Levin. "You'd better tell the truth; in a short while you will be off to the Ninth Fort. Do you have something else on you? Now take off all your clothes," growls Schtitz.

Mrs. Levin undresses completely and stands before Schtitz as naked as a newborn baby. "Spread your legs!" Schtitz orders. He then examines all the parts of her body to discover if she has hidden anything. Mrs. Levin does everything Schtitz tells her. She is not ashamed. In a short while, she is going to the Ninth Fort anyway; this is what Schtitz has told her. Only one thing is important to her: that the Gestapo will not learn of the existence of her relatives in the Ghetto and of her address.

Schtitz orders her to put her clothes back on. From his pocket he takes out the key to a box where he keeps a long whip. When Mrs. Levin sees the key, a spark of hope lights up in her. Perhaps he will content himself with a beating?

"Lie down," says Schtitz, pointing at one of the sofas. She lies down. "Not like this, on your belly."

Schtitz takes out of the box a whip used for whipping bulls. Mrs. Levin realizes that he is going to whip her. She has heard from Ghetto inmates that Schtitz does not like his victims screaming when he whips them. She says to him: "Honorable sir, please let me take a handkerchief from my coat, I need it urgently." He lets her take the handkerchief. Mrs. Levin puts the handkerchief between her teeth and lies on her belly on one of the sofas.

Six times does Schtitz raise and lower his whip on Mrs. Levin's back. Then he tells her to get up. "Now you are going to the Ninth Fort," he says. He asks to see her papers. "I didn't bring them with me," Mrs. Levin replies.

"Now, go to the cellar," Schtitz tells her, "and if I ever see your face here again, you'll go to the fort for sure." Before she leaves, Schtitz tells Mrs. Levin to straighten her dress. She thanks him, and asks him which way to the cellar. Schtitz shows it to her.

When Mrs. Levin went down—to Lipzer's room in fact, as she had been directed by Schtitz—she felt that the danger was over. She told Lipzer that the name and the address she had given to Schtitz were fictitious. Lipzer got very angry at this revelation. "I might yet be held responsible for this," he said. She was still shaking with fear when Lipzer informed her that Schtitz had sentenced her to two weeks in the Ghetto detention center as an additional punishment.

Mrs. Levin returned to the Ghetto that evening. The members of her labor brigade had already spread the news of her arrest and her family was very worried. She was sent to the Ghetto detention center that same night, together with three other Jewish women whom the Lithuanian policemen had handed over to the Gestapo earlier in the day.

When the danger was over, Mrs. Levin felt a pain in her leg. She then remembered that she had earlier been kicked in the leg by the Lithuanian policeman. Later she felt a severe pain in her back. During the beating administered by Schtitz with his whip she had not felt any pain. Now she hurts all over her body. Her heart aches also—from shame.

Is there really any connection between the arrest of the four women by the Lithuanian policemen and Lenzen's article in yesterday's newspaper? The impression that there is some connection was reinforced by additional arrests of Jews by Lithuanian policemen.

During his visit today to the Ghetto gate, Miller also warned—and even threatened—the Jewish workers, that if they dared to leave their place of work in order to buy food or to trade their clothes for various goods, they would be stripped of everything and handed over to the Gestapo.

For its part, the Council saw fit to warn the workers to refrain, temporarily, from bringing food and other articles from the city. We used the word "temporarily" because, in the long run, there is no way we can refrain from bringing vital supplies into the Ghetto, all the dangers associated with it notwithstanding.

1. *Ateitis* (Future), was a Lithuanian newspaper published, under German supervision, by pro-Nazi Lithuanians. Its first issue was in January 1943, its last in June 1944.

JULY 9, 1943

Today Dr. Elkes was summoned for a meeting with the German director of the labor office, Hermann. The conversation between them was not pleasant. Hermann revealed to Dr. Elkes that he had recently had a conversation with Schtitz. Hermann had asked for Schtitz's consent to transfer ten people from the Jewish police to the labor force, as the labor force urgently needed additional workers. Schtitz replied that the Jewish police, which had recently been reinforced by the addition of sixty new policemen to its ranks, would, for some time in the future, keep order within the Ghetto; Lithuanian policemen would be entrusted with guarding the Ghetto from outside. If this experiment was not successful, all the sixty extra policemen would return to work. We would see how all this turns out next week.

Schtitz used the occasion to accuse Hermann of giving his full backing to Margolis, whose activities in the Ghetto go beyond his powers. Margolis had wagered a bottle of wine that he was the highest authority in the Ghetto and that no one could remove him from his job.

Schtitz has further complaints against Margolis: it was he who sent Zilber—

who serves as Schtitz's informant in the Ghetto—to Kaisiadorys, ostensibly for work. Schtitz wants to see Margolis and get some clarification from him. Schtitz is not pleased that Margolis has taken upon himself the authority to arrest people and send them to jail. These powers rest exclusively in the hands of the Ghetto police. It seems that Hermann took Margolis under his wing, which is why Margolis can do what he pleases in the Ghetto.

Needless to say, these accusations did not bring out the best of moods in Hermann. He is certain that all this information comes from Lipzer. Lipzer must not forget that, after all, he is just another Jew. Schtitz's involvement in these matters might end up badly for Lipzer and for other Jews in the Ghetto. Hermann therefore asks Dr. Elkes to prevail on the Jews to stop treading dangerous paths, and to explain the controversy involving Margolis and Lipzer. Hermann is angry with Lipzer, who got him involved in this whole business. He again drew Dr. Elkes's attention to squabbles between officials of the Jewish labor office. Dr. Elkes replied that it was wrong for Lipzer to turn to Schtitz in this matter, and that it was done without his knowledge. He promised to speak to Lipzer later in the day and ask him to refrain from such actions. Dr. Elkes added that in quite a few cases Margolis has overstepped the bounds of his authority; it is this which causes him to collide from time to time with the Jewish institutions in the Ghetto.

In his work, Hermann needs people like Margolis. Although Margolis does a lot on Hermann's behalf, he also demands extensive powers for himself. He, Hermann, would speak with Margolis and ask him to refrain from overstepping the bounds of his authority.

This conversation made a bad impression on the Council. Have we stooped so low? Margolis and Lurie asked for Hermann's intervention to save their jobs. The Council recorded this outside intervention with anger and disgust; but Lipzer's behavior toward Margolis cannot be justified. Acts such as his conversation with Schtitz regarding Margolis's conduct are not to be condoned.

In the evening, Dr. Elkes saw Lipzer, and explained to him the negative consequences of his conversations with Schtitz concerning the Ghetto's internal problems. Lipzer, in turn, explained his approach to these problems: according to him, Margolis conducts himself as a dictator in the Ghetto. He does whatever he pleases. If he happens to dislike someone, he assigns him to a remote workplace. He also jails people at will. He has had several disputes with Schtitz. This is of no importance, however; nothing bad will happen to Margolis. But, as Dr. Elkes requests, Lipzer will speak tomorrow with Schtitz, in order to try to dissuade him both from seeing Margolis and from mentioning Hermann's name in the context of disputes between employees of the Ghetto institutions.

Thus, the Council has become Margolis's defender, even though some of the complaints against him have turned out to be justified. The Council remains adamant, however, in its opposition to any interference by the German authorities in our internal affairs. The Council is quite well able to call to order those among the Ghetto inmates—particularly the employees of the Ghetto institutions—who try to secure privileges for themselves at the expense of the public. This is why we condemn incidents like the conversation between Lipzer and Schtitz, just as we also oppose conversations between Margolis and Lurie, on the one hand, and Hermann, on the other. We oppose these contacts for one reason and one reason only: we do not tolerate any interference by the evil one in our internal affairs.

JULY 11, 1943

There is a great commotion in the Ghetto. I noticed it when I was on my way to the Council offices on Saturday half an hour after midday. As always, I had set out for the Council offices at the appointed hour, after spending the morning at home, where I attend to my private affairs.

At the Council offices I was accosted on the stairs by several people who asked me when the house searches would start. Will they take everything? Will they take only clothing, or also shirts and sheets? I gave them a blank stare. I had not yet heard anything about searches.

Yesterday afternoon the mood in the Ghetto was excellent. The British radio had just broadcast the news about the invasion of Sicily by the Allied armies. This news had been brought by workers returning from the city; in no time it spread throughout the Ghetto. Everyone was certain that the end is near; deep in our hearts we were very glad. Everyone regarded the invasion of Sicily as a most unusual event which might bring our own liberation closer. Optimists spoke about the surrender of Italy in the near future; about clashes between units of the Italian and German armies, and about the fiasco of the new German offensive in Russia.[1]

On this happy note the day ended. People kept waiting for the next day's news about further advances of the Allied armies. In the morning the mood was also good. The Jews kept on talking about the successful invasion of the Allied powers; about the weak resistance put up by the Germans and the Italians. The Jews, of course, were busy drawing up plans for the Allied armies.

At ten o'clock in the morning, Yitzhak Rabinovitz of the German labor office in the Ghetto was summoned to the city by Hermann. Today is Sunday, a day of rest; Hermann would not have bothered about any Ghetto business today unless it was something urgent.

Upon his return from the city, Rabinovitz revealed to us in secret (Hermann had asked him to refrain from sharing the news with anyone), that the governor of the Kovno district, Lenzen, has recently been watching very closely the workers of the city labor brigades. He inspects their parcels, confiscates the goods they purchase, and raises hell, arguing that the Jews buy up all the agricultural products of the Lithuanian peasants, leaving nothing for the residents of the city. All agricultural products flow to the Ghetto.

Lenzen's job is to ensure that the peasants of the Kovno district—the largest administrative district in Lithuania, with a population of 400,000—supply the German authorities with fixed quotas of grains, meat, and fats. Up to now, however, the peasants have supplied only a small portion of the quota. They are known for their traditional obstinacy, and it is exceedingly difficult to force them to do things they are unwilling to do. There have been numerous cases of revolts and resistance to German rule in this district.

Lenzen is furious over his lack of success with the peasants, and is busy finding excuses for the governor-general, Renteln, who keeps pestering him with demands for food supplies for the army. Lenzen is not particularly anxious to try the patience of the peasants too much. Recently there was a substantial increase in the murder of German Army officers and senior officials. Police investigations failed to bring this rash of murders to an end. So what did Lenzen do? He came to an age-old conclusion: the Jews are to blame.

Lenzen started following the Jews: he confiscates a kilogram of butter here, a liter of milk there. This is meant to demonstrate to Renteln that the agricultural output of the Lithuanian peasants in his district, which is earmarked for the German Army, in fact finds its way instead to the Ghetto, and to the Jews. The Jews undermine the German war economy; they engage in black-market trade; they buy out the foodstuffs meant for the German soldier at the front. Lenzen has therefore issued an order announcing that Jews who work far away from the city and who enter a Lithuanian village to buy agricultural products, will, when caught in the act, be shot on the spot.

Furthermore, following a meeting at the governor-general's office, Lenzen has proposed a series of measures aimed at "curbing the appetite of the Ghetto Jews." According to one of these proposals, "delicacies" such as butter, eggs, sugar, fruits, etc., will be confiscated from the Jewish houses in the Ghetto. In order to put an end to the black market, clothing, shoes, furs, and other such items will also be confiscated. The Jews will be allowed to keep only their personal clothing. When the Jews have nothing to sell or trade, the black-market trade will disappear and the authorities will be able to credit themselves with complete success in this regard.

Lenzen's proposals were extensively discussed in a series of meetings yesterday at the city governor's office. This gave rise to fears that houses in the Ghetto will be searched tomorrow and that belongings will be confiscated. Hermann revealed all this to Rabinovitz, so as to enable us at the Council to take appropriate steps. Under no circumstances should Rabinovitz disclose that it was

Hermann who told him all this; disclosure would betray Hermann and endanger him.

Later Natkin arrived, bringing more news on the same subject; he had been present during a conversation between the German Ghetto commandant and a German official. The subject was how many policemen and police officers the Ghetto commandant could spare for searches in the Ghetto. Natkin said he had been presented with the demand that he be sure a large number of Jewish policemen are available for taking part in the searches in the Ghetto.

The Ghetto was pervaded by a gloomy mood again. Do the Germans really mean to take away everything we have left, leaving us with just a shirt on our backs? If this is true, it bodes ill for our future. We must warn the Ghetto residents to refrain from buying supplies in the city for some time. For the immediate future, we will have to make do with our existing allocations. We must warn the workers not to leave their place of work during work hours and not to buy anything in the villages. We must do that if we want to avoid additional victims. Today, therefore, the Council issued an appeal to the Ghetto residents on this subject.

The Council then summoned all the labor brigade leaders. Dr. Elkes told them that we are in for very bad times if we fail to curb our impulse for purchases, at least for a time. The Council also issued a directive to the Jewish police to confiscate anything found on the workers returning from work to the Ghetto.

This announcement by the Council deepened the anxiety in the Ghetto. Everyone was now expecting extensive searches. People started packing things and hiding them in cellars and attics. Others started digging pits for the same purpose. People were kept busy dragging their belongings from one place to another until late at night. Many of them placed orders for special signs to be made for them at the furniture workshop, with the intention of putting them up on their apartment doors. On these signs they asked for a list of their jobs and rights. Lipzer ordered a sign reading: "B. Lipzer, representative of the Gestapo in the Ghetto and the chief of the Jewish Police." Dr. Zacharin was in a quandary as to what he should put on his sign. The first version read: "Commander of the Health Battalion, Doctor of Medicine, B. Zacharin, Director of the Health Office." Such a sign was bound to evoke feelings of respect toward its bearer among the Lithuanian policemen. On the other hand, it was possible that German policemen would also take part in the searches. This thought made Dr. Zacharin drop the military title of commander from his sign.

I myself was not certain that the searches would, in fact, be carried out. It seemed to me that all these rumors amounted to a warning, or a way to frighten us, so that we would be forced to discontinue purchases in the city and to stop trading our clothes for additional purchases. It was also possible that this was a typical German reaction to the Allied invasion of Sicily; the Jews must keep their heads down; they must not be allowed to rejoice at the German defeats; they must be kept busy with troubles of their own.

I shared these thoughts with Garfunkel and he agreed with some of them. He added that Dr. Elkes had possibly exaggerated to some extent the importance of the information revealed by Rabinovitz. Still, we must be prepared for the worst.

The public anxiety was exacerbated when an announcement was received that the workshop workers must go at once to their workplaces, even though today is the day of rest. It was also learned that an important German commission is expected to visit the Ghetto. Shortly afterward, nearly 800 workers assembled at the workshops. At two o'clock, three cars from the Ghetto command headquarters entered the Ghetto. They pulled up at the workshops, where Miller was waiting for them. He showed the guests around all the workshop departments and explained their operations. Among the guests were the head of the Gestapo in Estonia[2] and a general in his forties. They were accompanied by the staff of the Kovno command headquarters.

The visit of the head of the Estonian Gestapo caught the Ghetto residents by surprise. Many of us saw a connection between this visit and the expected searches in the Ghetto. Others regarded it as a sign of bad times ahead.

1. In a tank battle at Kursk between July 5 and July 13, 1943, the Germans failed to dislodge the Russians from the bulge they had created in the German lines. More than 70,000 German soldiers were killed and 2,900 German tanks destroyed; the Russians also suffered massive losses, "but," one military historian has written, "by winning Kursk they had, in effect, won the war." John Laffin, *Brassey's Battles* (London: Brassey's Defence Publishers, 1986), p. 232.

2. General Martin Sandberger, commander of the Gestapo in Estonia; his position in Estonia was similar to that of Colonel Jaeger in Lithuania.

JULY 12, 1943

Today a rumor spread in the Ghetto that the searches had already begun in the first precinct. A truck filled with Lithuanian policemen was said to have pulled up at one of the houses in the Ghetto; the policemen were said to have jumped out and begun searching the apartments, yards, and cellars. Later, it was learned that there had indeed been a truck with Lithuanian policemen who surrounded a number of houses and searched them. These houses, however, were located outside the Ghetto—on the other side of the perimeter fence.

I set out for the city to see Miller. My plan was to try to inquire about the grounds for the rumors of possible searches in the Ghetto. I learned that the rumors were devoid of substance. The Jewish workers from labor brigades keep asking me: how are things in the Ghetto? Have the searches started already?

When I told them that there were no searches, and that there probably would not be any, they sighed with relief.

Today Miller was again at the Ghetto gate when the Jewish workers returned from the city. This time they did not carry any parcels or knapsacks with them. "This is a rare sight," Miller said. "How is it possible? Who organized all this? I am not as stupid as I look"—so Miller remarked with a touch of self-mockery. He obviously realized full well what was going on. We will have to curb our impulse for buying for some time to come. At least until the storm blows over.

JULY 14, 1943

> *DOCUMENT: Regulations of the Penalty Department of the Jewish Ghetto Police*[1]

1. The Jewish Ghetto police is temporarily authorized to deal with civil and criminal matters concerning the residents of the Ghetto.

2. For this purpose, a penalty department is established at the central office of the Jewish Ghetto police, comprising three members, all police clerks, whose rank corresponds to that of precinct commander. Each member shall chair hearings in rotation. The chief of the Ghetto police or his deputy shall be chairman of the new department by virtue of his official position.

3. The penalty department shall judge according to the laws and legal procedures of the former Lithuanian Republic, insofar as these laws correspond with the conditions of the Ghetto, as well as on the bases of the Council's own directives and instructions.

4. In the event that a member of the penalty department shall be temporarily unable to discharge his duties, then another police clerk shall be appointed by the chief of the Ghetto police to take his place.

5. The penalty department shall deal with all the matters which are brought before it on behalf of the criminal division of the Jewish Ghetto police, and the precinct commanders of the police, and the other Council offices, as well as with requests and complaints by private individuals.

6. The new department's duties and minutes will be carried out and maintained by the secretary of the penalty department.

7. In matters in which the sentence is imprisonment of up to three days, and in cases in which fines of no more than fifty marks are imposed, the judgment of the penalty department is final. In other cases, those concerned who are not satisfied with the judgments may appeal within seven days to the Council's complaints committee.

8. The members of the complaints committee shall be appointed and dismissed by the chairman of the Council.

9. The complaints committee shall summon to its hearings the parties to the case and the witnesses, etc., only if it finds that this is necessary in order to reach a decision, and only if it is specifically decided upon. The complaints committee is entitled to request the penalty department to question witnesses and experts.

10. The complaints committee shall be chaired by each of its members in rotation.

11. The judgments of the complaints committee are final.

12. In criminal matters, those who are sentenced may submit requests for pardon to the chairman of the Council.

13. This addendum to the regulations of the Jewish Ghetto police comes into force as of today, and is applicable to all the matters which are currently handled by the penalty department.[2]

1. These regulations were signed by Dr. Elkes.
2. From the earliest days of the Ghetto, the Council had established a penalty department to deal with those in the Ghetto who refused to go to work, or who otherwise shirked their work-duty. This department had gradually widened its area of jurisdiction to include criminal activity within the Ghetto.

JULY 14, 1943

MEMOIR[1]

On July 14, 1943, the penalty department was reorganized. A complaints committee was set up under the auspices of the Council, which became a forum for appeals, which was authorized to hear appeals on decisions of the penalty department, and the decisions of which were final. From then on, the chief of police was the chairman of the penalty department only by virtue of his post, and was not allowed to alter the decisions of the penalty department.

All matters dealt with by the penalty department as well as by the complaints committee were heard by three judges, who served as chairman in rotation.

The members of the penalty department were: advocate Ephraim Buch, advocate Moshe Zak, and Y. Tshernes.

The members of the complaints committee were: advocate Israel Bernstein, advocate Moshe Tabatshnik, and advocate Nathan Markovski.

Typical cases before the penalty department were complaints involving residents of the Ghetto who because of age or illness were unable or refused to go to work outside the Ghetto. For example, "Chaim" took a suit from "Berl" to sell it in town for money or to barter it for food. In a transaction of this nature, Chaim would receive from Berl some of the goods or money as a "commission," which constituted a relatively large proportion, in consideration for the risk of falling into the hands of the Gestapo or the Lithuanian police during negotiations with the Lithuanians over the suit, or simply, the risk that the cruel Lithuanian would exploit the situation to steal the suit from Chaim without paying him a penny, and evict him from his home, and, as occasionally happened, inform on him to the police.

Most of the brokers were "scalpers" or opportunists, sometimes against their will, after their homes had been stripped of their entire worldly possessions, thereby forcing them to find means of survival. Brokers of the second kind were not the typical "clientele" of the penalty department. On the other hand, the scalpers were often accused of failing to return goods or their proceeds in food or money.

In its early days, the penalty department would issue judgments in the following wording:

> We find Chaim guilty of stealing Berl's possessions and sentence him to seven days' imprisonment in the Ghetto jail, according to section 591 of the Criminal Code (of the former Lithuanian Republic), and order him to pay the sum of x to Berl, or to return the suit to him. Chaim shall be exempted from imprisonment in the event that he shall return to Berl the suit or the money he owes with respect thereto within two weeks. Additional condition: that Chaim refrain from committing similar violations for a period of two months.

Another type of civil claim was mainly that of heirs of those murdered or missing in the "actions." Such claims were often extremely depressing, when heirs squabbled over the trousers or pillow of a near departed. However, there were also claims amounting to thousands of marks, in regard to a wealthy Jew who was murdered, whose relatives turned to the Ghetto court.

Typical claims were brought before the penalty department mainly after the large-scale appropriations of valuables according to the government's instructions, or after any panic in the Ghetto when Lithuanian so-called partisans, or even the official police, or Lithuanian or German soldiers, would break into homes and steal whatever they could lay their hands on. In such times, neighbors or friends would deposit with others watches, brooches, or valuables with the request that they be hidden for the duration of the "hunt" or the "action."

On occasion such persons would keep the deposited items for themselves, claim that they had been forced to surrender them, and believe that they had succeeded. However, the penalty department, after exhaustive investigation of the facts, if the prosecutor succeeded in persuading the judges that the defendant had actually received the articles for temporary safekeeping, and that they remained in his possession after the "hunt" or the "action," that is, that no one had taken the items from the defendant, then the penalty department—and prior to that the Court, while it existed—would judge the defendant guilty of theft of the possessions of others and, according to the Criminal Code, would sentence the defendant to imprisonment in the Ghetto jail, and would award the plaintiff the items deposited or their equivalent.

In such cases, penalties were more severe and fines higher, to deter anyone from exploiting emergency situations or "actions" for selfish purposes or in order to grow rich under the unique conditions of the Ghetto.

The penalty department was an integral part of the Jewish Ghetto institutions, and filled a void in the resolving of disputes between residents of the Ghetto, and at the same time set itself the moral mission of "removing the bad from inside itself."

In terms of the German authorities, the Jewish Court of the Ghetto operated mostly underground, if only because the Gestapo had expressly forbidden the existence of a court in the Ghetto. From their point of view, they—the SS and the Gestapo—were the only judiciary and executive, and any Jewish interference was viewed by them as undesirable.

It often happened that severe crimes were heard by the court, such as belonged in the realm of murder, but regardless of the severity of the crime and the public humiliation for the Ghetto, the court—and later the penalty department—upheld the rule, which was a fundamental principle of the Council, not to release from the court under any circumstances any information which might put a Jew into the hands of the Gestapo.

The Ghetto court, throughout all its permutations, fulfilled a most important function, competently, responsibly, and loyally, under extreme hardship, and contributed to the maintenance of a suitable standard of morality among the residents of the Ghetto.

A special category of cases was disputes over apartments, rooms, and residential areas and disputes between neighbors, in the first few days when individuals and entire families remained without a roof over their heads, since there was not enough residential space in the Ghetto for the 30,000 Jews who were forced to move there from Kovno. In the rush to find a room or corner to live in, severe disputes arose over the "rights" to apartments or other living areas. The housing office was unable to resolve all the disputes, and after a while they were brought for hearing by the Ghetto Court.

The overcrowding and the cooking facilities which served several families who lived together occupied the Court constantly from the beginning of the Ghetto until its end.

Illegal dealings in food and goods in certain dwellings, mainly those of scalpers, were a constant hindrance to the neighbors' rest, particularly for the airport workers, who after a long day of labor under inhuman conditions were in desperate need of a few hours of sleep, and it was in just those hours that business was conducted. Illegal commerce disturbed the rest of the workers.

The court dealt severely with lawless persons who seized the dwellings of murdered residents, or of those taken from the Ghetto to work camps, and on occasion it issued eviction orders against the seizers, in favor of the heirs of the murder victims or in favor of the sick and helpless, who were in great need of a little more living space.

1. This note was prepared by Avraham Tory immediately after the war, and later expanded by him, in order to describe the work of the Council's penalty department. The original draft of the note had been prepared by Tory in the Ghetto and accepted by the Council.

JULY 16, 1943

Yesterday Schtitz informed Dr. Elkes—via Dr. Kvitner—that he would be coming to the Ghetto at eight o'clock in the morning. He asked Dr. Elkes to come to Lipzer's room at that time; he would be waiting for Dr. Elkes there. Schtitz feels unwell; he wants Dr. Elkes to examine him.

The Nazi Race Laws forbid any such examination of a German by a Jew. But nothing is forbidden when Schtitz's health is at stake. The Nazi chiefs have a free hand in that respect. They are scrupulous in observing the regulations pertaining to the purity of the race as far as the German people are concerned, not to mention the Jews. There is, however, a world of difference between theory and practice. Every Nazi leader, large and small, maintains regular contacts with Jewish skilled workers: a seamstress making dresses for women; a cobbler who can make a pair of Prussian knee boots, etc. All this in addition to Jewish housemaids. Every Nazi everywhere does this: Jaeger of the Gestapo, General Wysocki of the German police, the German Army, the airfield administration, the civil administration, and, indeed, all other branches of the German government here.

Schtitz is in charge of Jewish affairs at the Gestapo. His attitude to the Jewish question is unyielding and cruel. He murders Jews and takes possession of their property. At the same time, he uses Lipzer to place orders in the Ghetto for toys to be made for the son of his mistress. He orders kitchen knives, rings, earrings, and other pieces of jewelry not only for his mistress and his wife, but also for numerous personal acquaintances.

Schtitz has not been feeling well recently. Although turning for help to a Jewish physician is against the regulations, the regulations do not apply to a man like Schtitz or his friends.

Now Schtitz is sitting in Lipzer's room, consulting Dr. Elkes about his health. He tells Dr. Elkes that his powers are waning; also his kidneys are not in good repair. He asks the Jewish doctor to examine him and to prescribe medicine for his illness. He wants to be healthy; he wants to be as strong as he used to be. Dr. Elkes listens seriously. He regards the man sitting in front of him, not as a cruel Nazi chief, but as a sick man in need of medical assistance.

Dr. Elkes asks Schtitz whether he sleeps well at night. Schtitz replies that, yes, he does sleep well. "Do you have dreams?" asks Dr. Elkes. "No," replies Schtitz.

Dr. Elkes is torn between his obligations as a Jew—as leader of the Jewish community in the Ghetto—and his sense of duty as a physician. But this inner conflict lasts only for a moment. The sense of duty gains the upper hand. Dr. Elkes makes a diagnosis and prescribes the necessary medicines. He is discharging his duties as a physician.

At the end of the examination Schtitz attempts to play the part of an old friend of the Jews. "Are things quiet now in the Ghetto," he asks? Dr. Elkes replies that the Ghetto is, indeed, quiet. "After my last call on Jaeger and you," he adds, "the people here sighed with relief." "I am pleased," says Schtitz, "that I could make my own contribution toward the relaxation of tension in the Ghetto. Nothing bad is going to happen in the Ghetto in the future."

Schtitz shakes Dr. Elkes's hand and thanks him for the treatment. There are no grounds to believe that he meant what he said to a Jewish doctor, chairman of the Jewish community. Today I recalled the case of Erich Kohn. Schtitz sent him for a medical examination when the man was sick. When the man recuperated, he executed him. I believe that Schtitz's time will also come. Nobody will come to his aid then.

JULY 17, 1943

Many people besiege Viertel's door. They keep standing there like beggars. They beg him for some sugar, for a little firewood, etc. They wait for hours on end until he receives them. If he comes to the conclusion that the supplicant is not trying to cheat him, he writes on a piece of paper: please supply the bearer with such and such quantity of such and such product. His generosity is reserved exclusively for the Nazi Party. I recall having heard him once dictating to his secretary: "Write down—300 lemons for the NSDAP."

I prepare myself thoroughly before every meeting with Viertel. I bring with me all the plans, the receipts, the list of all the supplies needed, for our soup kitchen, for the welfare office, for the nutrition department, and for other Ghetto institutions. I have in my possession detailed invoices of the supplies we have received in the past and the dates of their delivery. I submit requests only for the most urgently needed supplies, those needed to keep body and soul together. In my meetings with him I watch my step very closely; I remember well the occasion when he kicked me out of his office.

I am allowed to enter Viertel's room only after all the Germans waiting to see him have done so, and departed. At one time I was sitting in the waiting room, waiting my turn. When it came, Viertel's secretary let me in. Suddenly, a German who had come in after me, rose from his seat and said; "This is unheard of! The Germans come first, and only then the Jews! Let me in!" The secretary gave in to the domineering voice of the German, apologized to him, and ushered him in, passing me over, of course. Since then I know that I must wait until all the Germans have settled their business with Viertel; fifty kilograms of sweets, a thousand eggs, 150 kilograms of fish, meat, oil, vegetables, and who knows what.

I sit and wait my turn. In the meantime I read the slogans on the walls. I look at the faces of the Germans. I wonder: it would seem that they are human beings like everyone else; where, then, does their cruelty come from? What is the source of their lust for blood? Of hatred for hatred's sake?

In front of me I see a new slogan on the walls: "Don't be sorry, be proud." This is probably in connection with air raids. Another slogan reads: "The front is hard, but we are harder." This is not exactly something you would hear from a German. It certainly does not come through in their conversations. The Germans who sit here wear Army uniforms; others wear Party tags pinned to their clothes. They do not seem like people who are beside themselves with enthusiasm. It seems that they, too, are angry at everything around them; they, too, carry a pain in their hearts; they, too, want to go home; nor do they enthuse over the "victories"—and certainly not over the defeats.

At times, when these Germans are kept waiting for a long time, their patience runs out and they start complaining: Oh, yes, the front. When will all this torment end? Why does Viertel not go to the front? He would not be so severe then.

At last my turn comes and I enter Viertel's room. He is seated at his large desk. There are three telephones on it. He is getting telephone calls all the time. He speaks over the telephone and at the same time writes on the papers lying in front of him on his desk.

I take advantage of a moment when the telephone does not ring and prepare to present my requests. But Viertel speaks first. "How are things?" he asks in a soft voice, as though I were the first man to enter his office.

I begin: "Mr. Viertel, two months ago I received from you fifty kilograms of salt for our soup kitchen. The salt has run out. There is no way the soup kitchen can carry on. We also need potatoes and various vegetables. Perhaps you could supply us with potatoes, salt, and other food, so that we can cook some food for our hungry? Every day we prepare 500 meals for the Ghetto workers."

Viertel interrupts me by asking a question full of mistrust and irony: "Does your soup kitchen feed workers *also?*"

"We feed *only* workers," I reply, "workers from the workshops, the repair workshops, the laundry, and the hospital."

"Also the laundry workshops?" asks Viertel again. "They are supposed to get their meals at the Ghetto workshops."

"We have a second laundry for the Ghetto workers," I reply.

Our conversation draws to a close. Viertel writes down on a piece of paper: 500 kilograms of lentils, 250 kilograms of jam, and 50 kilograms of salt.

I thank him. Something has been achieved. Now I move on to another subject: firewood. We lack firewood to operate the laundry, the bakery of the welfare office, the soup kitchen, the hospital, the baths, and the lice disinfection department. Several weeks earlier I had submitted an estimate of the amount of firewood we need for our various institutions; the total was twenty-seven cubic meters per week. Viertel had passed on my estimates to Miller with an enclosed note: "These are theoretical calculations which cannot be verified." I had then sent Viertel another, more detailed estimate, but there had been no response.

Today I raised this problem once again: we need substantial amounts of firewood, otherwise we will not be able to support our institutions.

Viertel wants to know who is going to be responsible for ensuring that the firewood will, in fact, go to all the institutions which need it. "I do not want to have anything to do with the clever ones," he says. "You will be responsible for it personally. So you had better watch out. I am not going to be taken for a ride." He gives me a threatening look and writes down on another piece of paper: "500 cubic meters of firewood for the sanitation institutions in the Ghetto. Signed— Viertel."

I was taken by surprise; such a huge quantity of firewood at one time? I thanked him and took my leave.

At the Council offices they were very pleased with the results of my meeting with Viertel. The problem of firewood has been solved for some considerable time. On this occasion Dr. Elkes reminded me, however, that it will soon be necessary to open negotiations concerning the supply of firewood for heating the houses in the Ghetto in the winter. "Last year," he said to me, "you were also entrusted with this assignment." Firewood for heating is as important as bread. It is not an easy problem, but we will have to solve it.

Our desire, all the Ghetto hardships notwithstanding, is to remain in the Ghetto with our families, and not to be sent to a military labor camp.

Recently we have heard a great deal of talk about the transfer of the residents of various Ghettos to other places. The Ghetto is bad enough as it is; nevertheless, it is much easier to suffer the pains visited upon us in our own homes. Our own corner has become used to our sighs and moans. Let it not be a transfer.

Just let them keep on pressing down on us with the yoke of slavery—this is what we are doomed to, anyway—as long as we are in our own backyard. We are willing to bear the yoke here, at home.

JULY 18, 1943

It has been a week since the Council prohibited bringing supplies into the Ghetto. The residents seem to comply with this directive and, as a result, no supplies from the city have been smuggled into the Ghetto lately.

Every week, the Ghetto guard reports on its activities to the city governor's office. Together with these reports it has also sent in the past considerable quantities of butter, oil, eggs, meat, and other foodstuffs confiscated at the Ghetto gate. The "masters" at the municipal administration enjoy these "deliveries" very much; but in the last seven days no confiscated supplies have been coming in. The Germans have learned that, this time, the Jewish workers did, in fact, heed the warnings.

With German officialdom seemingly somewhat appeased, the council decided to permit the bringing in of small quantities of supplies from the city. In order to prevent an "opening of the gates" in that respect, the Council convened the labor brigade leaders for a meeting, at which Lipzer explained that from now on the workers must refrain from bringing in supplies in large quantities as in the past. He also revealed that he had spoken with the Gestapo, who had assured him in private that no one would be punished for bringing in a few kilograms of potatoes, a kilogram of flour, or a quarter of a kilogram of butter. The labor brigade leaders must ensure that the workers do not overstep the limit. From now on, the Jewish police will no longer carry out confiscations at the Ghetto gate. But this is on the condition that the workers exercise self-restraint.

In the Ghetto, people were glad. For many of them, refraining from bringing in supplies from the city, even for one week, had meant subsisting on starvation rations. For its part, the Jewish police, which for a whole week has been subjected to severe criticism by irresponsible elements[1] in the Ghetto because of its part in confiscations at the Ghetto gate, was also pleased with the instruction to call off the searches at the entrance to the Ghetto.

No one as much as opens his mouth when the Germans or Lithuanians carry out the confiscations. But when Jewish policemen do the same, in accordance with the Council's directives—stemming from considerations of the well-being of the Jewish public—immediately there are people who begin to raise hell. This is how things are in the Galut:[2] the Gentile can do as he pleases, whereas the Jew's hands are tied—even though he is motivated by the best of intentions.

This afternoon, Svirski[3] came to the Council. Several days earlier he had gone to Vilna, together with two Jewish workers, on behalf of the city governor's office, to bring various materials from there.

Svirski related to us the following: on Thursday last week, he and two other workers set out for Vilna in a truck belonging to the city governor's office. Their German escort accompanied them to the Vilna Ghetto gate. There they met Desler, Gens's deputy—who is also the chief of the Jewish police in the Vilna Ghetto. Desler told them that he was duty-bound to inform the Vilna Gestapo of their arrival. He also wanted to know whether the Kovno Gestapo was aware of their trip to Vilna. Svirski explained that he had been sent to Vilna with the approval of the city governor's office. He did not know whether the Gestapo had been informed of the visit or not. Both he and his two companions were working people, he explained. They go or drive to wherever they are told; they merely obey orders. Their German escort had procured for them an entrance permit to the Vilna Ghetto issued by the city governor of Vilna.

Desler then called the Gestapo on the telephone, in their presence, to impress them with his authority. The actual impression he made on them was that of a fool. His inquiry turned out to be unnecessary. During the "reception" at the Ghetto gate, they had sensed the gloomy mood. As they walked through the Ghetto streets, the mood turned gloomier with every passing moment, until it became almost unbearable.

In Vilna they learned that one week earlier the Keni labor camp in the Vilna district had been liquidated. Its inmates were Jews from small towns in the area. One day last week they were lined up in one long row and then taken to a large shed. They were locked up there, and were unable to get out.

A new Gestapo chief in Vilna, replacing Mayer, had arrived in Keni; he is a murderer and a savage of the Jordan type.[4] He surrounded the shed with armed Gestapo and set it on fire. Almost all the camp inmates, 300 Jews in all, perished in the conflagration. A handful managed to escape the flames and to reach Vilna, where they related the story.

When this barbarity came to light, a storm erupted in the Vilna Ghetto. Its residents had now witnessed the liquidation of all the Jewish settlements in the area. Everyone still remembers the Ponar tragedy. And now this horrid spectacle of Keni. One question keeps troubling their rest: why were these Jewish communities destroyed? Why did 300 Jews have to lose their lives in the flames?

The Jewish workers from the Kovno Ghetto who went on this journey to Vilna have also learned of the shooting of more than sixty Jews in another small labor camp in the Vilna area. The camp itself was liquidated.

The Jews in the labor camps in the Vilna area live in constant fear. They wait from day to day for the liquidation of their camps. They keep sending appeals for help to the Vilna Ghetto: "Bring us back to Vilna!" But the Jews in the Vilna Ghetto are themselves overcome by despair.

1. This, Avraham Tory later explained, "meant mainly the racketeers, fence traders, and black-marketeers, who were severely hit by the ban on bringing in goods, or by the confiscation of their goods."

2. The Galut (in Yiddish, Golus) is the Hebrew word for exile. In English, Jews call the lands of their wandering the Diaspora.

3. Chaim Svirski later joined those Jews who left the Kovno Ghetto for the forests to join the partisans, who had become particularly active at this time in disrupting German military communications behind the lines.

4. The new Gestapo chief was Kittel, who had arrived in Vilna in June 1943 to replace Mayer as the head of the Vilna Gestapo, Mayer having been sent to the eastern front.

JULY 24, 1943

Zionist circles in the Ghetto have been engaged for several weeks in preparations to celebrate the twentieth and twenty-first of the Hebrew month of Tammuz.[1] For the last two years we have been imprisoned in the Ghetto. In the year before the setting up of the Ghetto there was no possibility of staging large-scale Zionist rallies. Zionists of all ideological hues were hungry for a living word, for the melody of a song close to their hearts. Our underground organization, Matzok, whose existence was, for a long time, kept secret even from responsible Zionists, is at present the dominant force among Zionist circles and leaders in everything which is done in the Ghetto with even a remote connection with Zionism, members of the Zionist movement, or the Jewish national idea. Even today, Matzok acts behind the scenes, strictly observing the rules of conspiracy. Without its knowledge, however, no Zionist takes an action in the Ghetto, irrespective of ideological or party affiliation.

The members of Matzok demanded action to commemorate the twentieth and twenty-first of Tammuz. Something must be done; we must gather together, listen to the voice of the Zionist idea, listen to those who occupy important posts in the Ghetto; who in their lives and in the lives of their families remain responsible for everything that happens here. We must hear what they have to say on this important occasion. Perhaps they will have something encouraging to say, some spark of hope. After all, they are close to the center of developments, they maintain frequent contact with the fiends, they sail every day in these times of predicament in the thick of the raging storm of evil winds. Perhaps they see a ray of light. Perhaps they pick up some distant sounds of redemption drawing near. They stand on the bridge, compass in hand; they receive information at first hand.

In these days of exaltation, when memories well up in every one of us, of school days, of the activity of Zionist organizations in the national cause, of committees and congresses, of the ups and downs of the Zionist movement, of the Exile, and of the Land of Israel—in these days there is no way forward other than strengthening ourselves; than drawing from the ancient fountain, the idea of the return to Zion and the building there of a new life. How distant are these memories and yet how close to our hearts. In these moments of awakening, the heart beats stronger with joy and hope. After all, the Ghetto is a monstrous creature of our Exile. Its end will come; the Exile will not last forever. "Actions" and exterminations will not destroy the Jews, because only the last Jew would mean the end of our hope. The eternal words of our anthem "Hatikvah" (Hope) have accompanied thousands of Zionists in difficult days, in moments of danger, in long nights filled with anxiety, and now also in the time of the Ghetto.

We devoted a great deal of thought to the subject of how the twentieth and twenty-first of Tammuz should be commemorated. At first the idea was to hold a gathering of many participants, with speeches on topical subjects, but we decided not to do this, for reasons of security in the Ghetto. In the end we decided to hold a concert: Hebrew music, Hebrew songs, the recitation of Hebrew poems. Our police orchestra got down to work at once; they began rehearsals of melodies such as the song eulogizing Theodor Herzl, and other songs and melodies of the Land of Israel.

The concert took place today. The police hall was packed with notables and with the most active members of the Zionist movement left in the Ghetto. The public and the seating arrangements were different from any previous occasion. The first row of seats, always reserved for the officials of the labor office and others who have connections, was now occupied by the members of Matzok, and by veteran Zionists—the leaders and spokesmen of the Zionist public in prewar Lithuania. Behind them were seated several hundred Zionist comrades.

The atmosphere in the hall was festive. For the first time in three years our comrades saw one another at a mass meeting. Instead of pictures of Herzl and Bialik on the walls, a neatly designed evening program was handed to each of the participants. Our own Fritz Gadiel, director of the graphics workshop in the Ghetto, designed the program: it depicted a blue-white flag lowered three quarters of the way down the mast, fluttering in the wind, with black clouds above it. It was adorned by the insignia of the Committee of the Jewish community in the Ghetto, and on it was written in artistically designed letters: "Herzl-Bialik, 20th–21st of Tammuz, 1943, the Vilijampolé Ghetto."

At this point it would have been only proper for one of the leaders to rise to his feet and deliver a speech to those present; words we have been waiting for and longing for for years, words which would warm everyone's heart, which would lift them from the depths of dejection and fly them to distant, happier worlds with no barbed wire fence, not even a reminder of it.

First, the conductor and violinist S. Hofmekler gave a signal. Then the sounds of Perlmutter's "For Thou Art Dust" and Idelsohn's "For Herzl's Soul" filled the hall. Inspired by a sense of the significance of a great moment, those gathered listened to the sounds of the orchestra. Next, a Bialik poem, "The Word," was recited. Each phrase was absorbed by the audience as never before, its appreciation shown by the stormy applause. Then the orchestra played "Song of the Valley," followed by a selection of songs from the Land of Israel. The singer Mrs. Ratchko then sang with considerable talent "Two Letters" by Avigdor Hameiri and "Let Me In" by Bialik. Kupritz then recited the chapter "At the End of Days"; Zaks sang "The Harbor Song," and the violinist Stupel played—with great emotion—a Hebrew melody by Akhron. A string of Zionist dancing songs was then played, amid cries of joy from the enthusiastic audience. The concert was not over yet. But one such gathering had been enough for our people to come together in one mass, united and guided by one idea—the idea of the Kingdom of Israel.

At the end, the whole audience rose to its feet as one man and sang the "Hatikvah" to the accompaniment of the orchestra. The mighty sounds of the Zionist anthem went out great distances, to the mountains of Judaea, to the valleys of Sharon, to the Mediterranean, to the banks of the Jordan, to Mount Scopus, and to the cities and villages, farms and kibbutzim of the Jezreel Valley and the Galilee. The sounds of the anthem conveyed greetings from here, and returned from that distant land with tidings of redemption drawing near.

Our hearts were filled with joy; tears kept flowing from our eyes. Hope and courage issued from the depths of our souls, crying aloud: "Our hope is not yet lost!" The thick pillars of the yeshiva building, where the concert took place, were soon covered with drops of moisture. A mood of enthusiasm reigned in the hall. It was a festive occasion, pervaded by splendor.

Comrades shook hands and exchanged meaningful glances. It was a magnificent moment.

That night, residents of Varniu Street were wakened from their sleep at three o'clock in the morning by a noise coming from the outside. Jews jumped out of their beds, rushed to the windows, and anxiously listened to the cries for help coming from the neighboring house. "Police! Police! Help! We are being robbed, they are trying to break in! Police! Help!"

The house from which these cries were coming is near the Ghetto gate, on the road to the sawmill and the Vilija river on the other side of the fence—outside the Ghetto. The sawmill stands on a narrow strip of land between the Ghetto fence and the Vilija river; it is the only building on the free side.

A timber yard—a living contrast to the Ghetto—lies expansively and peacefully near the sawmill. Thick, huge logs lie on the ground, drying in the sun, freshened up by the summer rains, and resting majestically at their ease. Many wooden logs had lain on the ground throughout the winter, covered with a soft layer of white snow. The snow covering them had assumed the shape of rounded hillocks. As the snow melted, the first spring rain washed away the dirt and the mud. Now the logs are completely dry, waiting to deliver themselves to the saw machine at the sawmill. Their waiting in the yard will soon be over and they will be turned into planks. The planks then will be sorted into the thin and thick ones, short and long ones. Small pieces, and ends of timber from the sawn logs, will be piled up in high heaps. This is the refuse, some of which is given away to the workers, while the rest is sold in small quantities. Other pieces are arranged in step-like, high piles, separated by wedges so that they will dry faster. This is good-quality material.

The space on one side of the sawmill is taken up by fresh logs straight from the forest, some of them drier than the rest, others completely dry. They are arranged in stacks, according to the type of timber, not far away from the Ghetto fence. On the other side lie planks: one inch, one and a half inches, and two inches thick. Rounded planks, square planks, planks hewn on one side only, on two sides or on all sides; long and short planks; thin planks and thick planks. In one corner the sawdust is piled up like badly ground flour. In the large yard there are piles of timber pieces, cut into small squares which look like small lumps of coal. They are used as fuel for gas generators, instead of gasoline.

The yard is packed from one end to another with all sorts of timber, as in bygone days. Every day, carts and trucks from the city come in to take out timber, but the yard seems to be inexhaustible. Timber is brought in and taken out all the time. Every day barges made of logs—lashed together and floated down the Vilija river—arrive at the sawmill. Tractors and military trucks, some with two or even three trailers, pull in heavily loaded with rough, long logs of all kinds. Axles groan under the weight of the logs—until they are rolled into the yard.

The air and the noise are different here. There is no sound of tree branches as in the forest, no chirping of birds, no resounding echo coming from great distances. The air is saturated with black soot from the high smokestack of the sawmill, the noise of the mill, the constant hum of sawing, the dull sound of axes striking the logs. The logs need time to get used to the new place, until they are cut up, split into fours, and turned into first-, second-, and third-grade material—and refuse. They will be used to build house walls, barrack floors, shack roofing at the front, airplane wings, ships' chests, rifle butts—something either useful or fiendish.

The Vilija river licks the edges of the timber yard with its flowing waters, whispering its secrets to it. The saw-mill has been standing here for ages; the Vilija flows here from faraway places, from distant cities and countries. It has seen a great deal and can tell a great deal. It can tell about the war which is raging in the world, across the distant seas, over the roads, in the plains and beyond the mountain ranges, in cities, in villages—everywhere that man can reach. People keep fighting, spilling blood, torturing, looting. Frequently, the Vilija river itself turns red from the blood of the dying, from the carcasses which have been thrown into its waters, from the battles fought on seas, rivers, fields, and forests, from the pogroms in towns, in the Jewish neighborhoods, and in the houses of helpless Jews. But the eternally flowing current will erase the traces, wash away the stains, and wash clean the mark of Cain; it will carry the stains far far away, so that no reminder will be left of the evil in man.

The yard absorbs everything; it suffers and keeps silent. The yard does not want the war. It wants to do something but cannot move from its ordained place. The sawmill has kept on whistling in protest and spitting out thick, black clouds of smoke in disgust: pfui, you ugly world!

The sawmill was removed from the world of war. The noise of sawing did not know war. But then, one day, a strange fence struck roots near the sawmill yard; it was made of barbed wire, meshed with further, thick wire. A gate was made of the same material. A soldier armed with a rifle stands guard at the gate. What is the purpose of the rifle? What are the bullets doing in the leather belt buckled around the soldier's waist? What was wrong with the old guard at the sawmill? For years he had been guarding the sawmill, the timber, the machinery, and the house—without any rifle. Nothing had even been missing from the place.

Whom does the soldier guard? Does anyone want to attack the sawmill? No! The sentry has been posted to keep the people on the other side of the fence from running away. The barbed-wire fence has been put up especially for this purpose: not for the logs of the mill, but for the people on the other side of the fence. The bullets are for them. For on the other side of the fence is the Ghetto, with its yellow badges, edicts and "actions," with terror and suffering. The fence circumscribes the place within which human life is fair game, where the air itself exudes the odor of death, where no battle is fought and yet blood keeps flowing incessantly—innocent Jewish blood.

Animals in uniforms repeatedly break into the Ghetto, rape its residents, terrorize them, and inflict countless sufferings on them. Without any shame, the jackals keep bursting in, day and night, sowing death and destruction in their path. The Ghetto casts mistrustful and fearful glances at the fence. The fence always harbors danger.

A Gestapo man showed up in the area of the sawmill at dawn. He was drunk. He wanted to get into the Ghetto and came across a Jewish policeman who stood guard at the Ghetto. The policeman refused him entrance, as this time the Gestapo man was wearing civilian clothes. The Jewish policeman thought he was a criminal looking for easy prey. He therefore asked to see his identification, to see his identity card. The Gestapo man stood on the sawmill side of the fence and the Jewish policeman on the Ghetto side. They were watching each other through the square apertures in the barbed wire. A Lithuanian soldier stood nearby. The following conversation ensued among the three:

The Lithuanian soldier to the Gestapo man: "Entrance here is forbidden."

Schtitz: "I am allowed to enter."

The Jewish policeman: "Without identifying papers, no one can enter."

Schtitz: "And if I am from the Gestapo?"

The Jew: "Even then you must show your papers."

Schtitz: "And Schtitz?"

The Jew: "Schtitz—yes. But you are not Schtitz."

Schtitz: "I am Schtitz."

The Lithuanian soldier does not speak German and has no idea what is going on. Some drunk who does not show any papers and tries to get into the Ghetto. He clasps his rifle and asks the Jewish policeman: "Shoot?" The Lithuanian gets ready to fire into the face of the drunk who harasses them. Schtitz finds in his pocket some pin, or a tag, or some other Gestapo "talisman," and shows it. The Lithuanian soldier immediately slings his rifle back onto his shoulder and steps aside. In a regal manner, Schtitz then passes through the Ghetto gate.

As soon as he entered, he came across the Jewish policeman. He regained his composure and started shouting at him: "Why aren't you at your post? You've left it for half an hour."

The Jew: "Sir, I have been here all the time; here is my inspection book. Just ten minutes ago Guard Chief Garfunkel checked this place. It is written in the book." "All right, carry on," said Schtitz, and left the gate, approaching a Jewish house and pounding on the windows: "Open up!"

In this house lives Mr. Dvoretzki, the seventy-year-old treasurer of the Jewish burial society. At first he and his elderly wife were afraid to open the door of the house. Schtitz got nervous: "Open up!" he shouted into the night.

"Who's there?" asked Dvoretzki in a shaky voice.

"Schtitz," replied an unfamiliar voice in a Swabian dialect, from outside.

"You are not Schtitz; Schtitz does not speak such broken German," thought Dvoretzki. Then he asked the man who was shouting: "What do you want?"

Schtitz was enraged by the insolence of the Jew and shot into the air. "Open up, or else I'll liquidate all of you!" The tenants were seized with panic. The neighbors ran to the windows. The Jews thought that Lithuanians had again broken into the Ghetto through the fence to rob them. Younger people grabbed an axe, a spade, or some other nearby implement, to "welcome" the robbers.

"What do you want?" asked Dvoretzki from within his apartment. "Where does Lipzer live?" Schtitz replied. "I don't know, ask the neighbor next door, he should know," came the reply. Dvoretzki hoped to get rid of the intruder in this way.

Schtitz then knocked on the neighbor's door. Meanwhile, the Jewish police-man had rushed Lipzer to the scene. He arrived armed with a banana-shaped thick truncheon in one hand and an electric lamp in the other.

"How come you have the banana? With this you could kill a man," said Schtitz. "Who else has such bananas?" he wanted to know. "Only Kopelman and myself," replied Lipzer.

"Let's go to Kopelman," said Schtitz to Lipzer, "I wonder what he is up to now."

"Kopelman is asleep," replied Lipzer. He tried to calm Schtitz down: "Why don't we get out of here."

Lipzer ordered one of those living there to harness a horse to a cart. He then drove Schtitz out of the Ghetto and back to the city. Schtitz gave the order for Dvoretzki and his wife to be taken—together with their neighbor, Schmiten—to Gestapo headquarters. The elderly people were beside themselves with fear. Nothing like this had ever happened to them before—Schtitz in the Ghetto in the middle of the night! The three elderly people, mortally afraid, were driven on the cart to the Gestapo.

"They must be flogged," Schtitz said. But Lipzer managed to dissuade him: "They can barely stand on their legs," he pointed out.

"So how did they get here?" asked Schtitz. "They were brought on a cart," replied Lipzer. "Let them run back on foot," ordered Schtitz.

Dvoretzki recited Psalms and thanked God: this time they had gotten away with just fear. A miracle from heaven.

Just one more unnecessary glass of troubles from Schtitz—so much fear and danger he causes us.

1. On the Jewish calendar the twentieth of the month of Tammuz was the birthday of Theodor Herzl, the founder of political Zionism. The twenty-first of Tammuz was the birthday of the Hebrew national poet Chaim Nahman Bialik. In Zionist circles, the two days were combined as a joint celebration and memorial.

JULY 25, 1943

An exhibition of Esther Lourie's drawings was held yesterday afternoon; it was limited to a small circle of friends and acquaintances. The drawings represented art rich in ideas. In the very first days of the Ghetto, Esther Lourie set herself a wide-ranging aim: to preserve for posterity, by means of artistic drawings, the scenes and human types in the Ghetto, which are of value for Jewish history.

Esther Lourie had spent some time before the war in Palestine, where she engaged in intensive artistic activity. With her keen eye she grasped the new and the beautiful in the building up of the country. Her paintings achieved great acclaim. The local art critics praised her. In Palestine she absorbed the new life: the national rebirth, the awakening of an ancient and persecuted people. All this left indelible marks in her heart. For her, Palestine—the Land of Israel—became an irreplaceable value. There is the center; everything outside it must be oriented toward it.

Fate willed that Esther Lourie ended up in the Slobodka Ghetto—of all places—to witness the destruction and to go through the seven gates of hell, to absorb the reality of the Ghetto with her keen artistic perception and to preserve on canvas the historical events and indescribable scenes so that they would be saved from oblivion and passed on to posterity. This is her great historical mission in the Ghetto. If she managed to escape so many times—by miracle—from ·the jaws of death, so much the better.

In Esther Lourie's view, every artist in the Ghetto is obliged to immortalize— each according to his ability and technique—every aspect of the Ghetto reality. General, large-scale events will remain in people's memory. But singular episodes such as the sufferings of an individual are bound to be forgotten.

The Ghetto is not much different from other places, in that its life consists of details and countless singular episodes which add up to a mosaic of our existence here. The positive details embody the life of liberty and creativity, whereas the destructive and humiliating ones turn our life into one unceasing torment. This is not life, but its opposite.

Life in the Ghetto amounts to a chapter in the history of cruelty; the depriving of the Ghetto residents of their human image. It adds up to the unspeakable tragedy of the Lithuanian Jewry.

The details of this life are without precedent, not just in Jewish history, but in universal history as well. These details must not be allowed to sink into oblivion. Before being murdered, hundreds of thousands of victims of the modern dictatorship wrote their testament, in which they pledged us not to forget. This testament was written neither in ink, nor casually, but with fingers dipped in their own blood as it seeped from their dying bodies. It contained just one word: "Revenge!"

This testament is inscribed on the wall of the house of a Jew in one of the narrow alleys of Slobodka; this man, dying in a pool of his own blood, had been left on the doorstep of his house. His testament, written in his blood, enjoins on us a historical mission: to carry the cry of thousands of martyrs from one country to the next: "Revenge!"

Above all, we have been put under an obligation to remember, to record events and facts, to describe people and characters, images and important moments; to record in writing, in drawing, in painting—in any way and in every means available to each one of us.

Esther Lourie responded to this appeal without hesitation. I remember that winter day in November 1941 when even the breath in one's mouth virtually froze. It was immediately after the massacre in the small Ghetto and the fire in the hospital. I said to myself then: the horrors of destruction and the act of extermination must be recorded; the charred remains of the hospital set aflame by the oppressor, the site in which the patients—helpless children and the elderly—were thrown into the pit, the place which turned into a mass grave—all this must be preserved on canvas. After a few months, no trace will be left of the horrors perpetrated in this place.

The site of the former small Ghetto was surrounded by a barbed-wire fence guarded by the subhuman Lithuanian partisans. Individual Lithuanians hung around the place—one with a rifle slung over his shoulder, another dressed in military uniform. They entered the houses and took everything they could lay their hands on. In order to reach the place where the hospital had stood, one needed a special permit from the Ghetto guard. I found an excuse: I asked permission to collect Jewish books which had been left behind in the Jewish houses in the area. Even the Lithuanian partisans had not touched them. As soon as we procured the permit, we set out on a horse-driven pauper's cart. There were four of us: two young men, Esther Lourie, and me.

Once in the small Ghetto, we came to the burned hospital. We walked around it, pretending that we were looking for the first house in which to start to collect the books. In fact, we were looking for a site from which it would be possible to paint the remains of the hospital.

Finally we stopped at a two-story house and went inside. Various articles were lying in the hallway. The doors were broken and the cold wind kept blowing through the rooms. We climbed the stairs to the second floor and walked up to the window. Esther examined the place and found it unsatisfactory. So we went up to the attic. From its narrow window we could see the entire area. We cleared the space near the window so that a chair could be placed there, moved aside various articles that were lying about on the floor, and Esther began to work.

Various lines and shapes started coming to life in the open notebook lying on Esther's knees. One glance through the small window at the area outside, at the "orphaned" chimney, at the walls, at the piles of rubbish, and, once more, various lines and shapes appeared in the notebook. And again, and again.

Suddenly a sound reached us from one of the rooms in the attic. Perhaps a mouse, I thought. But then the sound of steps was heard; someone was walking around there. Quietly and uncertainly, I stepped inside and came across someone. I focused my gaze and saw the frightened countenance of a Gentile boy holding a satchel in his hand. Another boy was right behind him. In all probability they were looking for some treasures here. I cried out loud: "Out! Quick, get out! Or else the Germans will catch you!" The boys vanished in the blink of an eye.

Esther went ahead with her work. The cart was waiting outside. I went back down and started collecting books. Until Esther finishes drawing, I thought, I will fill the cart up with books. The streets were empty and the houses left open. I entered one house and another. The thieves had left their traces in the first house: the floors were strewn with various articles. The second house was in better shape; it seemed that its occupants had left only a short time before. The cupboards were locked; plates and glasses stood on the table as if the guests had just gotten up from their chairs and retired to the adjoining room.

Before long, the cart was loaded with books. Esther had not yet finished her work. We told her that we would take the books to the Ghetto and come back to pick her up later. It was evening when we returned to the small Ghetto. I went up to the attic; Esther had finished her work. She was hungry. We filled the cart with another load of books and set out back to the Ghetto.

At the Ghetto gate we parted from Esther with a handshake. On this cold day, we had succeeded in recording an indescribably tragic event in the Ghetto's history; a scene which is no longer recognizable.

The second time Esther and I walked along the fence on Krisciukaicio Street, inside the large Ghetto, we entered a burned-out house which had been made of wood. During the Slobodka riots, not only the old roof, the attic, and large segments of the wall had perished in the flames; the members of a Jewish family had perished with them. Only two little rooms were preserved. Family photographs still hung on the walls, including a picture of a rabbi. A cabinet full of books stood by one wall, and a sofa by the other. In the second room were made-up beds. Torn blankets lay on the floor with other articles. The blinds on one of the windows were lowered, the windowpanes broken, the curtain ripped, the table on its side. Various household utensils lay on the floor.

This destroyed house was also immortalized in Esther's drawing. It does not exist anymore—another example of Ghetto life. Each painting is a fragment of the history of boundless pain, an expression of mental and physical martyrdom.

Recently a small number of artists and cultural figures gathered to discuss the problem of art and culture in the Ghetto. Each one of them had long been dreaming of such a gathering, but the stormy life of the Ghetto had prevented its taking place.

Today these intellectuals gathered in two narrow rooms whose walls were adorned by Esther's drawings—a small part of her work in the Ghetto. Those present were assessing her work with a feeling of gratitude and with enthusiasm. Her work rekindled memories of the events in the Ghetto over the last two years.

The gathering was opened by Dr. Chaim Nachman Shapiro, the leading intellectual figure in the Ghetto. He was followed by Esther, who spoke about Jewish art in the past and in the present. Her lecture, rich in content, demonstrated that she was not just a brilliant artist but an erudite person with extensive knowledge of the domain of art. Jewish art, said Esther, was constrained by Jewish religious law. The injunction "Thou shalt make no graven image" prevented the development of religious art among the Jews—the type of art which is so esteemed among Gentiles. The long Exile, insecurity, and the absence of statehood were among the factors which explained the underdevelopment of art among the Jews.

In recent times, Esther Lourie explained, efforts have been made in Palestine to correct this situation. A Jewish center is in the process of being established there which can provide a focus for Jewish artistic creativity. For her part, Esther shaped her artistic program in line with the developments in Palestine—developments which she herself had seen. Here, in the Ghetto, situations exist which should be preserved on canvas, because artistic chapters from Ghetto life can be written only in the language of painting. Up to now, Esther has done about 200 drawings of different Ghetto characters and scenes. Here, in the Ghetto, new subjects have been brought into existence which in the future will assume universal dimensions, such as those assumed by Christian art in the past.

"What is the essence of Jewish art?" Esther asked. "Is it art created by Jewish artists, or is it art with a Jewish content?" This question is the subject of raging controversy. Some of those present argued that Jewish art is art created by Jewish artists even if their subjects are devoid of any specifically Jewish content. Others maintained that the Jewish character of art remains determined by its specific content, without any connection with the question of whether or not the artist is Jewish.

Those assembled went on to discuss the role of the Jewish artists in the Ghetto: should the bleak and unique reality here provide the cornerstone of artistic endeavor, in which case it would focus on the recording of Ghetto life with all its horrors; or should art be a creation of the free spirit, based upon the life and agonies of the artist?

The supporters of the second view maintained that art consists of free creation which, by definition, cannot be dictated by any outside factor. It originates from internal emotions and impulses.

Several hours of intense intellectual debate were spent in this fashion. Esther gained high acclaim from all those present. This was the first gathering in two years devoted to Jewish and artistic matters. The soul weeps at the sight of oppression and wanton killing, whereas the Jewish spirit continues to exist as in the past. Today the faces of those present at the gathering were lit up by Esther's works—additional proof of the refusal of the Jewish spirit to surrender at any time or in any circumstance.

JULY 30, 1943

Worrying news has reached us recently from various labor brigades. It emerges that managers of several factories and companies were asked whether they could make do without Jewish workers. In other workplaces, questions were asked such as: could the Jewish workers be put to work in army camps or barracks, and, if so, could they be guarded properly? Could they be supplied with food?

Recently, a number of German enquiry commissions have come to the Ghetto; they were composed of representatives of the Gestapo, of the governor-general's office, of the Reich mission in Riga, and of other bodies. The members of these commissions showed considerable interest in the number of the Jews in the Ghetto; the number of workers in the workshops; how many of them were skilled workers with extensive experience and how many had finished their training only recently; which departments in the workshops did useful work for the German Army and which ones are engaged in less useful work.

One of these commissions has come here with a clear purpose; it called on the rubber factories Guma and Inkaras, each of which employs 150 Jewish workers. The members of this commission wanted to know whether it would be possible to put these workers in the army camp and also ensure that they would be guarded.

These events bore out the rumors that the Jewish workers in large industrial enterprises are about to be put in army camps. Such a move leads inexorably to the liquidation of the Ghetto. This is the reason for the new fears which have gripped the Ghetto residents.

In the months which have passed since the Allied invasion of Sicily, and particularly after the overthrow of Mussolini in Italy, we have been witnessing a deterioration in the treatment of the Jews here in the Kovno Ghetto. From the first day of the landing in Sicily until the recent developments in Italy, the Ghetto expected German wrath to be vented on the Jews. The Council took the most severe measures to prevent the Jews from reacting in any way which could be construed as an expression of joy on our part.

On the day that Mussolini was removed from power,[1] the Council dispatched messengers to all the labor brigades in the city, and to all the brigades working in the Ghetto, warning the workers to refrain from entering into arguments with the Germans or the Lithuanians on political subjects, and to refrain from displays of joy, or provocations.

The situation on the Russian front—the collapse of the German summer offensive, as well as the extensive battles there which do not bode well for the Germans—has stirred some melancholy thoughts in us. As the front draws nearer to us, our fate becomes ever more precarious.

As the atmosphere in the Ghetto grew more and more oppressive, and as the rumors about plans to concentrate Jewish workers in army camps became more and more persistent, the Council decided to attempt to verify them from any source possible. But Lipzer failed in his attempts to persuade Schtitz to arrange for another meeting between Dr. Elkes and Jaeger. Lipzer has learned, however, that in recent days a discussion was held at Gestapo headquarters concerning the concentration, in army camps, of Jewish workers from numerous existing places of work. No further details have reached us on this matter.

Today Dr. Elkes spoke with Hermann at the German labor office. Hermann revealed to him, in strict confidence, the existence of an order from Riga to remove Jewish workers from the Ghetto and to concentrate them in small camps near German Army units, or near large enterprises employing Jews. The Jews will no longer be employed in small factories. The small labor brigades (there are 150 of them at present) will be wound up, and their workers distributed among larger work-units; they will both work and live there. Only the elderly, the children, and the sick will be left behind in the Ghetto.

Dr. Elkes asked Hermann about the fate of the people to be left in the Ghetto. Hermann's reply was: "Their future is bleak. Before long they will be exterminated as expendables."

According to Hermann, the plan to concentrate Jewish workers in army camps is tantamount to the liquidation of the Ghettos. This plan originated in Riga, out of political considerations. The Jews are regarded as potential spies. In critical moments they might sabotage the production process and compromise security; there was a case of sabotage in the Riga Ghetto which led to the decision to concentrate Jewish workers in specially guarded camps. The Ghettos, as concentrated Jewish communities thronging with young people, might pose danger in a critical moment. This is why the Germans want to liquidate them. The question of manpower does not play a major role in this decision, which is motivated primarily by what the Germans see as political and security problems.

In Hermann's view, the concentration of workers in army camps will throw the Lithuanian economy into confusion and cause extensive damage to the local industry. The Lithuanians are doing their best to shirk the work-duty. They can make do in the countryside. The German civilian administration and the German police cannot successfully cope with the negative attitude of so many Lithuanians toward work for the German war effort. The Lithuanians, Hermann says, are cheating the Germans right and left, top and bottom. The only positive and reliable labor force in the city is to be found in the Ghetto. Should the Jews be removed from 150 places of work, enterprises important for German military production will be brought to a standstill.

Another thing: these days, scores of Lithuanians are being sent to work in

Germany for military industry, or even sent to the front. All this is known to the city governor's office, to the governor-general's office, and to the Gestapo. The local authorities are opposed to the removal of the Jewish workers from the small enterprises. The authorities here are well aware of the situation, and of the value of Jewish labor. They have no choice, however, but to comply with orders from the top which are based on assessments of the wider political situation. Since this is a political matter, Hermann harbors grave fears.

Suspicions have also been raised about the Ghetto's connections abroad. Thus, for example, a number of foreign nationals were discovered in the Ghetto (Orechkin, Blumenthal, and others).

In practice, the implementation of the plan to concentrate the Jewish workers in army camps is impossible. The army units have at their disposal neither proper living quarters nor the necessary arrangements to ensure decent living conditions for the Jewish workers. Life in the camps affects not just one's body but one's spirit as well. Under such conditions the workers cannot perform efficiently. The local German authorities are aware of the fact that the Jews turn out high-quality products if they can live with their families under minimally human conditions. Consequently, the decision of the central authority to incarcerate Jews in camps, in which by necessity they will be exposed to dirt, hunger, and contagious diseases, leads to the conclusion that plans are afoot to liquidate the Ghettos altogether. In the past this was done by extermination in various fortresses—like the Ninth Fort; now they seek the same object by concentrating the workers in army camps.

Hermann is very pessimistic. He does not want to witness such a thing, he told Dr. Elkes. When Jewish workers are transferred to army camps, he is going to ask for a leave of absence. Within five or six weeks, the authorities are bound to realize they have made a grave mistake. But by then it will be too late. Everything will have been laid waste.

When the conversation between Hermann and Dr. Elkes came to an end, Hermann swore Dr. Elkes to secrecy. He wants to live; he has a family and a home. Should it come to light that he revealed important information to a Jew, his life would be at risk.

Dr. Elkes thanked Hermann for his candor and integrity, even though Hermann's revelations had opened up before him a void of despair and torment. In the name of his God, Dr. Elkes asked Hermann to do everything possible to forestall the disaster awaiting the Jews. Then they parted.

Dr. Elkes revealed the bad news to the members of the Council. His spirits were at their lowest. "It is possible that Hermann exaggerated somewhat in drawing the picture of the future," Dr. Elkes told us. "Nevertheless, there cannot be any doubt that the situation is serious—very serious. We may be facing disaster."

Opinions among the Council members were divided concerning the plans of the supreme German authorities, and their possible consequences. Dr. Elkes, Goldberg, and Hirsch Levin were very pessimistic; Garfunkel and I were less pessimistic. It is true that the concentration of the Jewish workers in the army camps is not going to do us any good, but I refused to believe that this plan implies another form of extermination. I do not believe this.

We decided that at this critical moment it is imperative to seek a meeting with Jaeger; after all, he promised us that if the fate of the Ghetto were ever to hang in the balance, he, Jaeger, would speak to us. Since at this moment the fate of the Ghetto is at stake, we are interested in hearing what he has to say. The atmosphere in the Ghetto was highly charged, just as it had been in the past before the "actions," as if we were on the eve of a momentous event.

Today I went to see Miller again. I went to tell him of the worrying news that has been reaching us from various labor brigades about the possible concentration of Jewish workers in army camps. Young and skilled workers will be concentrated in camps, it is said, where they will subsist on rations of 100 grams of bread a day, and 120 grams of flour a week. I wanted to ask if these rumors had any basis in fact and whether they fitted with what he had told me yesterday.

It turned out that Miller was busy getting ready to go out. He was on his way to the Gestapo; therefore I could not speak to him about the matters which trouble us.

In this atmosphere of tension which has descended on the Ghetto, many people started thinking again about escape to the city or to the countryside; to hide until the storm blows over. For my part, I began thinking again about the "storage." Should something happen to me and to my loved ones, everything I have written and collected during this terrible period will remain unknown or even lost. I felt that someone from the outside, a non-Jew, should know about the existence of this material and where it is stored. After the war, he would be able to find it, and hand it to some official Jewish organization for publication.

I devoted a great deal of thought to this, and consulted a number of people. Finally, I decided to speak to the priest Vaickus, one of the honorable people who, in the most difficult times for the Ghetto, used to show us a smiling and friendly face, and to speak encouraging words to us.

I went to see Vaickus in the city; there, in the old monastery, with its long and shadowy corridors, looking like recesses and caverns from ancient times, the air was different from that outside. The July heat did not penetrate the thick walls of the seminary. The noise of the street, the factory sirens, the clatter of the boots of the soldiers in gray uniform, the commotion of the people walking on the streets and looking at one another angrily—all this stops at the seminary wall. Peace and quiet reign inside: the slow steps of the clerics in their long, soft, black garments make them seem as if they were walking on air. Absorbed in thought, they bow their heads in greeting to a person coming toward them. A different atmosphere reigns here; it is a different world and a different people. Here they look at me quite differently from the way they do in the city; the yellow badge on my left breast does not frighten or annoy them.

I ask a man coming in my direction whether I can see the priest. "Please, wait a moment for an answer," he says. "In the meantime, please be seated."

A few minutes later the priest appears, his face open and friendly. He shakes my hand, takes my arm in his, and starts walking with me along the long corridor. We enter his tidy and spacious room. There are a desk, two chairs, and a few utensils. I say that I want to speak to him about a matter of great importance to me. He closes the door behind him.

Without any preliminaries, I begin by describing the gloomy mood in the Ghetto; the rumors about the edicts in store for us. Then I say that the time has come for me to reveal a deep secret to him. We, the Jews, have been going through an exceptionally brutal historical period. I have been recording for posterity all the terrible events through which we have gone, as they happened. We would be beside ourselves with joy if the handful of Jews who have survived up to now, were to live to see, with their own eyes, the redemption and liberation of the Ghetto, and indeed of Lithuania, so as to give testimony to all that has happened to the Jews in this land. Jewish history, and the existence of the Jewish people, will continue, no matter what happens. It is incumbent upon us to hand down to future generations the story of what befell Lithuanian Jewry.

The pulse of life still beating within our bodies and our souls is weeping, but time is short. This is why I have come to him with a final request: after the death of the last Jew on Lithuanian soil, he, the priest Vaickus, will be the one to know where to find my notes, and to pass them to the person who, after the war, stands at the helm of the world Jewry. This is a historical mission; a mission on behalf of the Jewish blood which has been spilled. The priest will certainly know how to appreciate the importance of this mission; he must certainly be aware of the importance of my visit to him.

Vaickus understood. His eyes filled with pain at the recognition of the historic mission with which he was being entrusted. He bowed his head in agreement. Then he consoled me by saying that we Jews will yet see better times and the end of our torment. People will be good again. He will not have to fulfill his mission.

I took out of my pocket a photograph of the place where the material was hidden, and explained to him how to get there. I gave him the photograph and said: "Please, put it in a safe place. This is the key to material of great importance. When the times comes, please pass it on to the right people."

We shook hands. A stone was lifted from my heart. Now, whatever may happen, nothing will be lost. The priest is a responsible person. He feels that he has been charged with a heavy responsibility; that he has been entrusted with an important secret. I left the building the same way I had reached it—the same dark corridors, the same peace and serenity, the same humane attitude. I went out into a street which was radiating summer heat, a street where the yellow badge on my chest stood out prominently.

The Ghetto looked like a Jewish village on the Day of Atonement, when the whole community, from the children to the elderly, prepare themselves for God's Judgment. Schtitz is scheduled to arrive at five o'clock this very afternoon. All the members of the Council will assemble and wait for him. The Ghetto is in the grip of mortal fear.

Later Schtitz arrived as usual with fury in his gray eyes. In a commanding voice he issued an order: all the members of the Council and all the directors of departments in the Ghetto are ordered to come to his room and to line up in a row. He will then address us.

When everyone was present in his room, Schtitz made the following announcement:

Rumors have been making the rounds about "actions" and the liquidation of the Ghetto. As a result, the Ghetto is troubled. On my own behalf, and on the orders of Colonel Jaeger, who sent me here, I hereby announce that no "actions" will take place. The Ghetto will remain. We are only talking about the concentration of workers near large enterprises, such as the airfield and similar places. These arrangements have already been put into effect in Jonava, Koshedar, Palemonas, and other places. This plan is not going to be implemented all that quickly. But nevertheless all the necessary preparations must be completed. People here say that an "action" will take place on August 1 and 2. Now I come to you on July 30 with an announcement on behalf of Colonel Jaeger: there will be no "actions." I want to emphasize once more that I come to you in Jaeger's name. All we want to do is to save one hour of running to work and back, to save clothes and shoes. If people save their strength, they work better. The army will ensure that in army camps the workers get even better food and better clothes than they get at present.

Dr. Elkes then asked Schtitz about the fate of the women and children. He wanted from Schtitz an additional assurance that the Ghetto would not be liquidated. Schtitz replied that children over twelve will be permitted to join their parents in the work camps. Younger children will stay in the Ghetto and study in vocational training schools. Kindergartens will be set up for small children so that their mothers will be able to work. The old and the sick will look after the children. But this, too, is not going to be implemented all that soon. In special circumstances, people will be transferred to other places. Other details will be revealed in due course.

Schtitz went on to warn those assembled that the Ghetto residents should not behave foolishly by running away from their workplaces. For every person running away, a quota of Jews will be executed. Jews must refrain from stirring up trouble; they must come to work.

After Schtitz had finished his address, we left the room. Dr. Elkes and Lipzer stayed behind. They asked Schtitz again about the significance of his announcement. He again reassured them that no "actions" were in prospect.

Schtitz's announcement spread quickly in the Ghetto. The situation has been somewhat clarified. The life of the moment is important in the Ghetto. The question of the expected searches in the Ghetto, and the possibility of the confiscation of food and various belongings, has not yet been resolved. One thing is clear at the moment: we are not faced with any immediate danger.

The war continues and the moment of decision is drawing near. Everyone wants to gain time, to put off the impending danger. As of this moment, the danger seems to have passed. Perhaps in the meantime the war will end. This is what we wish for right now in the Ghetto.

1. Mussolini resigned as ruler of Italy on July 25, 1943, the day after the Fascist Grand Council, meeting in Rome, passed a resolution by nineteen votes to seven inviting the king of Italy to assume control of the Italian armed forces. On the day of Mussolini's resignation, Marshal Badoglio became prime minister of Italy and King Victor Emmanuel assumed supreme command of the Italian armed forces.

AUGUST 2, 1943

This morning 200 Jewish workers have been sent to Keidan to work at airfield construction. The workers will stay there for three to four months. The Ghetto inmates have already learned of plans to concentrate the Ghetto Jews in camps in the vicinity of the places of work. This directive has been construed in the Ghetto as an edict: as a policy aimed at splitting the Ghetto population into smaller groups, which would thus be easier to liquidate—when the time comes—and would help to forestall the possible uprising of a large Jewish community.

No Ghetto inmate wishes to live in barracks, or in a military camp, far away from his family, friends, and acquaintances. Today the authorities put their plans into practice by ordering 200 Ghetto inmates to transfer to the labor camp at the airfield at Keidan.

The atmosphere in the Ghetto has become stifling. The Jews try to defend themselves with all their might and by all the means at their disposal. No one wants to be counted among the first to leave the Ghetto. Everyone wants to stay where he is.

The work at Keidan is very much like work in the labor brigades in the provincial cities. The tour of duty there lasts a week or two, sometimes longer. Once every two or three weeks one is allowed a one-day visit home. One is also permitted to bring back various supplies from the place of work. There are certain people who are willing to work in the provincial towns. This time, however, there is no certainty that it will be possible to visit one's family even once in a while; people no longer believe that they will be able to see the families they have left behind in the Ghetto. They are no longer certain that the Keidan labor camp will not be liquidated once the job has been completed, as happened with the camps in the Vilna district where the Jewish inmates were murdered.

For two days, a commission whose members included representatives of the Jewish police and the Ghetto labor office was in session, selecting candidates for work in Keidan. The commission also decided to keep all the candidates for Keidan under arrest; this was in accordance with established practice in such cases. The Jewish police took to the Ghetto detention center 180 people picked up during the last two nights.

Efforts were begun to release some of the detainees. Lipzer was the first to engage in these efforts. The commission gave him fifteen release papers without names on them. Then the requests came for the release of individuals who occupied public positions in the Ghetto. The residents regard the new directive as one of the harshest edicts against the Ghetto; they see it as the beginning of the end.

Summer is at its peak; the days of August are very hot. The vegetables have ripened and are good for eating. The air is clear. From the distance, we can hear the first sounds heralding our redemption.[1] In these hope-filled days of August, life is good—even in the Ghetto. Now, as the steps of the Messiah can be heard, people are not willing to go toward the unknown in German labor camps.

The commission entrusted with selecting workers for Keidan has gone through several difficult days. Everyone found some excuse for staying in the Ghetto: one was sick; one was a woman looking after the orphaned children of her sister; another one was supporting a large family; a fourth was an important community figure; a fifth was Lipzer's assistant. All in all, ninety people from among those initially detained by the police were released. This morning it turned out that the planned contingent to Keidan was fifty short.

Yesterday Lipzer raised an outcry. He criticized the commission and all those who pleaded with it, accusing them of having released too many people. When he learned this morning that the Keidan contingent fell short of the quota by fifty people he started shouting: "They took bribes for release papers! One man was released in exchange for 800 marks! You must tell me immediately: who took the money?!" Having been told that there was no such person, Lipzer left the Ghetto.

Less than half an hour after Lipzer's departure, Schtitz arrived: "What kind of swindling is going on here?" he asked. "Who is responsible for all this? Where is Margolis?" Zupovitz told Schtitz that the commission was composed of three people: himself, Levin, and Margolis. Margolis was at the Ghetto detention center, from which people are brought before the commission. Levin had informed Margolis about thirty workers missing from the contingent; they would be recruited at the airfield, he said.

Schtitz was somewhat reassured by this, and left on his motorcycle for the airfield at Aleksotas, where a train was waiting, with four cattle cars attached to it. A group of seventy-four women had already been sent to the airfield. When the second group of workers joined them it turned out that there were only 152 people there altogether. Schtitz fell into a rage. He at once ordered the policemen who had brought the people from the Ghetto, and guarded them on the way to the airfield, to line up in rows. Then he ordered half of the policemen— sixteen—to step forward.

Schtitz then addressed Levin: "Levin will be the first," he said, and ordered him to climb into one of the cattle cars—which stood nearby, waiting to transport the workers to Keidan. Levin got into the railway car without hesitation. He wore only his summer clothes; he had neither food nor any money with him. At that moment, however, Levin did not think about anything else; it was Schtitz who stood in front of him.

"And who are you?" Schtitz asked Flier. "I am the deputy director of the airfield department," replied Flier. "Get into the car," ordered Schtitz. Flier obeyed the order.

"And you?" he asked Dr. Levitan. "I am the physician of the manpower department," was the reply. "In!" ordered Schtitz.

The three men had come here to process the Keidan contingent, and to supply them with the necessary articles for their journey and for the camp. Schtitz ordered the sixteen policemen who had stepped forward to get into the car. Zupovitz tried to reason with him: "Honorable sir, these men have been working without respite for two nights to bring people here. We ask your permission to return to the Ghetto and to bring the missing workers back here to the airport within a few hours." "No," said Schtitz. "In that case," said Zupovitz, "I ask your permission to join my policemen." "You are staying here," replied Schtitz. "You'll go there when I order you to."

"And what are you doing here," Schtitz asked, turning suddenly to Fritz Bernstein. "I am the shift foreman," Bernstein replied. "I have to recruit the women missing from the Keidan contingent." "If you don't bring them here, you are going to go to Keidan yourself," said Schtitz. "You are responsible for it with your life."

Bernstein—a tall, good-looking Jew from Berlin—took fright. He started running to and fro around the large airfield, where some thousand Jewish airfield workers were standing, in an effort to find enough women to fill the quota of workers for Keidan.

Later, upon his return to the Ghetto, Bernstein told the same story to anyone who happened to come his way: "I am a murderer. Do you know what I did? I approached a brigade of workers, picked eight women, and sent them to the shift management. Then I went to another brigade and picked another five women. The women had no idea what they were needed for, so they went in the midday heat, half-dressed and exhausted from their work at the airfield. They thought they were being assigned to a new workplace. I picked up thirty women in this fashion. Having learned of their destination, they tried to hide and flee. Five armed German airfield policemen escorted them to the railway cars, threatening them with their rifles. The howls of these women cannot be described; they screamed as if they were being led to slaughter. "Help!" they screamed, "Save us! Don't tear us away from our families and our children!" They were forcibly pushed into the cars.

Schtitz had obtained his quota. This scene had been watched by Hermann of the German labor office, by Menzel, representing the German airfield management, and by Schtitz, who had commanded the operation.

Two hundred Jews were imprisoned in locked cars. Their panic-stricken, tearful eyes could be seen through the bars on the tiny windows; these eyes demanded justice, cried for help: "They are taking us to an army camp!" The desperate glances met Menzel's blank face, Hermann's pitiless eyes, Schtitz's arrogant expression, the look of helplessness in the eyes of the Jewish policemen who had remained standing outside the cars, the frightened face of the shift foreman, and the tormented expression on the faces of the Jewish workers at the airfield.

Four freightcars are packed with living people. Attached to these cars are a number of others, containing iron, concrete, and building materials. All these cars were to be sent to Keidan. These half-naked and starved prisoners, including many women who had been separated from their homes and children, will have to prepare the ground for the Keidan airfield. We pray that this airfield, with all its installations, will be razed to the ground in the blink of an eye when the hour of the great revenge comes.

The wagons were ready for departure when a voice—addressed to Schtitz—was heard from one of them. Schtitz recognized the voice instantly. It belonged to Bach, a fence-trader and an informer. He had something important to say to Schtitz before the departure to Keidan. The cars had already started moving.

Schtitz ordered a halt and called on Bach to get out. Once out of the car, Bach whispered something in Schtitz's ear. All of a sudden Bach called into one of the cars: "Kovenski, come over here! Say something also." The second man got out of the wagon; he was also well known as fence-trader, swindler, and informer. Both Bach and Kovenski had many times been included on the list of workers to be sent to various places of work, but each time they had managed to wriggle out by means of various tricks. This time, however, they had not managed to avoid it; they had found themselves locked in a railway car to Keidan.

The two men said to Schtitz: "Do you know why are we going to Keidan? Because we did not have enough money to pay off Margolis and the labor office. They asked for 5,000 marks. That is why we were taken, while others were released. So, where is justice? Let Schtitz answer this question."

Schtitz gazes into their faces and jots down in his notebook the names of Margolis and Aronovski. Yet he does not release the two informers. He orders them to get back into the cars and promises to check on their story.

Half an hour later Schtitz came to the Ghetto and called at the Council offices. He shouted: "Where is Margolis? I want him and the policeman Aronovski here right away!" Then he told us about "swindling," about bribes of 5,000 marks for releasing people from the Keidan contingent. This is why, he said, the quota was short of fifty people. What would happen, he asked, if he had ordered his men to shoot twenty people today at the airfield? Would it have been good? Such things must not be allowed to happen.

Dr. Elkes tries to calm Schtitz down. He asks him to have a seat on the sofa. Schtitz is boiling with anger. "What's going on in the Ghetto? Why are the people so tense?" he asks. He is shown the latest leaflet published by the Council, saying that the Gestapo has issued guarantees that there will be no "actions" in the Ghetto, and that the Ghetto will remain. People were frightened, but now they have calmed down.

In the meantime, Margolis entered the room. Schtitz rose to his feet and went up to him, his eyes bloodshot. He asked Margolis in an angry voice: "What's going on here? You released people for money. Tell me the truth: what did you do?"

Margolis went pale as a ghost; he was clearly frightened to death. In a quavering voice he said: "I didn't release anyone; I didn't have any power to do that. Others did it. I just took people from the Ghetto detention center and sent them to the airfield. I didn't receive any money."

Having heard this, Schtitz became even angrier: "I don't like being lied to. Tell me the truth. It will be better for you. Where are the 5,000 marks you got in exchange for releasing people? I know the truth." Margolis, however, went on protesting his innocence: "I didn't receive any money. I don't know what you are talking about. If it turns out that I took money from someone, you can kill me. Go ahead and search me."

Dr. Elkes noticed that Schtitz was about to have a fit, so he tried to interpose himself between the two. He asked Schtitz to have a seat. "Why should you be so annoyed?" he asked him. "I know Margolis well. I can't believe he took the money from someone. He is not the kind of man to do such a thing." At this point Schtitz interjected: "I was told that earlier today Margolis took 5,000 marks via Aronovski. Where did he hide the money? Why doesn't he hand it over to me?"

In reply Dr. Elkes said to Schtitz: "I am being lied to also, even though I am the highest authority in the Ghetto. I am sure that you were lied to too; someone wanted to get a release from work in Keidan."

Schtitz calmed down somewhat. He said to Dr. Elkes: "I will be pleased if what you say turns out to be true." He turned to Margolis: "If you don't tell me the truth right now, I will have you transferred to the main prison. You'll spend at least eight weeks there; you'll have plenty of time to decide how it really was. I have heard some bad things about you. What is it that you are doing at the Ghetto gate? You are not authorized to conduct searches."

Dr. Elkes signals to Margolis to keep quiet. Schtitz was still angry, whereas Margolis seemed to be crushed and exhausted.

"Where is Aronovski?" Schtitz shouted. "Why doesn't he come here? I want him here this instant!" Someone telephoned the police center and a few moments later Liolja Aronovski entered the room. Margolis came back to life: "You tell us, Mr. Aronovski," he asked, "did I release anyone? Was I empowered to release people from the work in Keidan?" "No, you did not," Aronovski replied. "Only Levin was authorized to release people."

Schtitz then asked Aronovski: "Did you get money for releasing people?" "No," replied Aronovski. Schtitz: "Summon two Jewish policemen. Margolis and Aronovski will be taken to the Gestapo." Dr. Elkes tried to promise that he, Dr. Elkes, would hold himself responsible for these two men. But Schtitz was adamant: "If it turns out that I have accused them unjustly, I'll be glad to release them. As things stand now, they are going to the Gestapo." These were Schtitz's last words on the matter.

Two Jewish policemen entered the room. Schtitz ordered them to escort Margolis and Aronovski to Gestapo headquarters. Then he started his motorcycle and set off.

The mood in the Ghetto again took a turn for the worse. The Council offices are packed with people who came here to beg us to release them from work in Keidan. In the morning, more people due to leave for Keidan—and their families—stirred up a commotion at the Ghetto gate. When the trucks came to take them to the train, the wailing rose to high heaven. On the streets there was weeping and shouting as if on the eve of an "action."

Walking down the street, I came across Miller riding his motorcycle. Seeing the weeping women, Miller stopped and got off his motorcycle. "You are on your way to work?" he asked me. "Yes," I replied. "Why are all these people so upset?" he asked. "Why do they keep crying? After all, nothing has happened. People are going off to work; they will be better-off there than here. The German soldiers are thousands of kilometers away from home, with death hanging over their heads every day, yet they don't weep. There is a war going on; people will be able to return to their homes after their job is completed." This is how Miller tried to reassure me.

This time the Ghetto labor office and the Jewish police had their hands full of work, particularly after the sudden detention of people to be sent to a military camp. The detainees regarded this whole business as preparation for death. After the nightly arrests, the members of the commission and the policemen came to the Council offices depressed and sad: Zupovitz of the police, Margolis, Levin, and others. They had been through the strenuous labor of rounding up Ghetto residents to be dispatched to an uncertain future. The Ghetto residents regarded them as accomplices to murder.

On top of it all, bad news came from the peat-digging camp at Kaisiadorys, where 350 Ghetto residents do forced labor. Last night, four people were murdered in the camp: the German director, a Dutch expert employed there, and two Ukrainian Nazis. Five Ukrainian camp guards ran away. A murder like this can provide an excuse for the execution of the entire camp population. The fear is that Jews might be accused of taking part in these murders, or of extending assistance to the Ukrainian partisans who in fact carried them out.

All in all, it was a day of turmoil and confusion. Two sleepless nights were followed by a tension-filled morning.

Margolis has put enormous effort into the task of recruiting candidates for work for the Germans. Today Schtitz "thanked" him for his labors. Despicable and unscrupulous characters like Bach and Kovenski are to blame for Margolis's arrest. Lipzer also has his share of blame. He has been angry with Margolis for some time. Margolis does not bow to Lipzer's every wish. At times he speaks the truth. This is the main reason why Lipzer wants him out of the Ghetto.

The fact that Hermann was fond of Margolis, and authorized him to exempt people from work, to send them on leave, to transfer them to better labor brigades, and even to arrest offenders—all this did not exactly raise Margolis's stature in Lipzer's eyes.

Today Lipzer came to the Ghetto gate. Having learned that workers were missing from the Keidan contingent, he went to Schtitz and told him that Margolis was to blame for this.

There was a great deal of tension at the Council due to these events. Everyone is fed up with Lipzer. Something must be done, so that nothing untoward will befall Margolis. I hope he will be released soon. One cannot accuse him of taking bribes. Lipzer will possibly assist in obtaining Margolis's release in order to keep his own self-respect.

It is possible that we are on the verge of a most difficult period; perhaps the ultimate and decisive era in the life of the Ghetto. This is why our hearts beat more rapidly than ever.

1. On August 1, 1943, the Allied forces in Sicily began a new offensive against the Axis line. That same day, the British, American, and Soviet governments published a note sent to all neutral governments, warning them not to give asylum to war criminals.

AUGUST 9, 1943

Today is the eve of the Ninth of Av. The mood in the Ghetto could be appropriately described as "Lamentations."[1] The Ghetto, and its handful of survivors, are headed for destruction. News keeps arriving about plans for the concentration of Jewish workers in army camps, about the expected separation of men from women, about the confiscation of goods and belongings, and about the possible extermination of children and old people. Every day, workers from various labor brigades tell us about the preparations being made in their particular brigades toward the realization of these plans. For example, in Schantz, huts are being built. At Aleksotas, the huts in the prisoner-of-war camp at the airfield are being emptied of the belongings of their former occupants; a senior German officer at the military transport depot for heavy vehicles is preparing plans for the accommodation of 5,000 Jews in the old factory in Petrasun, etc.

In recent days, the Gestapo has begun to show a keen interest in the Ghetto and its affairs. From time to time Gestapo representatives escort various German commissions on a tour of the Ghetto workshops. These commissions examine the financial and commercial affairs of these enterprises. The plan to concentrate Jewish workers near large industrial enterprises is going to be implemented. This is what Jaeger told the Council, via Schtitz.

The day before yesterday, the Ghetto was stunned by a directive ordering the German Ghetto guard to move—within two to three days—to quarters in an apartment in Slobodka outside the Ghetto bounds. This directive made a bad impression on the Ghetto and gave rise to a host of interpretations and comments.

Today I went to the city governor's office to speak to Miller. It turns out that he has not yet heard of this directive. He called the Ghetto commandant in my presence; the commandant confirmed that he has, in fact, received such an order from Captain Binger, the commander of the German police in Kovno. Lithuanian policemen will be the first to leave the Ghetto; they will be followed by the German commander. This move has long been in preparation, but its implementation was put off.

I asked Miller about a possible connection between the departure of the Lithuanian and German policemen from the Ghetto and plans for changes in the Ghetto structure, or other measures to be taken against the Ghetto residents. Miller's interpretation was as follows: the Lithuanian policemen have become too friendly with certain Jews in the Ghetto; they help them in black-marketeering. Certain Jews even have sex with Lithuanian women.

Miller replied negatively to my question about any possible connection with the planned transfer to Jewish workers to army camps. "The implementation of this plan," he said, "is not going to be carried out all that soon. This latest move has to do with difficulties besetting the war economy and industrial enterprises. I shall have a talk with Colonel Jaeger in a few days and will take over the handling of these affairs." This last sentence gives ground to our fears that Ghetto matters are being gradually taken over by the Gestapo from the city governor's office. This may signal a harsher regime for the Ghetto.

The Ghetto guard did not go to its new quarters outside the Ghetto bounds as planned. As a result, the Ghetto inmates have calmed down somewhat. Today, however, it happened: the Germans and the Lithuanians left the house they had occupied and moved into a house at 23 Paneriu Street. The Ghetto was again gripped by fear. Its inmates had already become used to the Lithuanian and German policemen. As is well known, every change is feared in the Ghetto.

News from the Vilna Ghetto has given rise to new fears; it seems that 2,000 Jews have been transferred from the Vilna Ghetto to Estonia, to do hard labor in the north of Estonia, not far from the Leningrad front. Such a move would not have been contemplated if there had not been some intention of harming the local population.[2]

Dr. Elkes spoke to Hermann, who confirmed the news from Vilna. Hermann also said that a further 2,000 Jews were to be sent from the Vilna Ghetto to Estonia.

The transfer of the Ghetto guard to its new quarters outside the Ghetto bounds—at 23 Paneriu Street—should be regarded as a precautionary measure. Recently there has been a rash of murders of the German labor camp commanders.[3] In Hermann's view, these murders are the reason for the removal of the ghetto guard to the other side of the fence. So, once again, we are waiting for the dust to settle.

In the evening we gathered in the Council office to recite Lamentations.

1. The ninth day of the Hebrew month of Av is a solemn fast day and day of mourning in the Jewish calendar. At the start of the fast, the Book of Lamentations is recited in synagogue.

2. On August 6, 1943, more than 1,000 Jews were deported from the Vilna Ghetto to labor camps in Estonia, including the camps at Klooga and Lagedi, where concentration-camp conditions prevailed. Hundreds of Kovno Jews were among the thousands murdered there, or dying of exhaustion and ill-treatment.

3. Members of the Kovno Jewish underground had killed the German commanders of five of the labor camps and labor units in the Kovno region.

AUGUST 11, 1943

DOCUMENT:
From Lieutenant Miller, on behalf of the Governor of Kovno
To all employers of Jewish manpower

The commander of the security police and the Gestapo in Lithuania has requested me to prohibit, as from Saturday, August 14, 1943, the strolling of individual Jews and Jewesses within the boundaries of the city of Kovno.

Jewish workers are only permitted to work at assigned workplaces.

The certificates of the Jewish column leaders remain valid; they are obliged, however, to lead their columns in close order from the Ghetto to the workplaces and back.

I request the withdrawal of all certificates already issued which allow Jews or Jewesses to move freely within the boundaries of the city of Kovno on official duties; these certificates are to be collected, and forwarded to me after collection. This also applies to all vehicles, such as carriages, bicycles, etc., which until now have had Jewish drivers. Henceforth, Jews and Jewesses are only permitted to carry out official missions using non-Jewish guards and drivers.

Whoever sends Jews or Jewesses out separately must expect the immediate arrest of the Jewish worker by the commander of the security police and the Gestapo.

Requests sent to my office cannot be answered, because this order is final.

For the Ghetto administration for which I am in charge, a special regulation will be issued after consultation with the commander of the security police and the Gestapo.

AUGUST 20, 1943

An atmosphere of tension has pervaded the Ghetto in recent days. Even before we learned of the plan to "liquidate" the Vilna Ghetto and the difficulties in the Vilna Ghetto itself, a rumor had started making the rounds about the planned transfer of all Lithuanian Jews to Poland. Every child in the Ghetto knows what such a move would mean.

Well-placed and reliable people at the airfield who speak on behalf of Menzel —whose decisions bind the Jewish workers at the airfield—had said that 1,000 Jewish workers are to finish their jobs on the fifteenth of this month. Later we learned that it had been decided to keep them at work for one more month. Menzel also revealed to his Jewish confidants the existence of a plan to concentrate these 1,000 workers in huts or barracks near the airfield, without any possibility of their returning to the Ghetto at the end of the day's work. The plan to concentrate Jewish workers in other military places of work, likewise without any possibility of returning to the Ghetto, is said to apply to other workers as well.

Yesterday Menzel told the Jewish engineer Luftspringer—who works at Kovno airfield—to get ready to leave for Keidan, where serious reconstruction work is under way at the local airfield. Menzel added that 800 Jews from the Ghetto would also be transferred to Keidan. When the Jewish engineer tried to explain that he could not possibly leave his family behind in the Ghetto, Menzel made a gesture with his hand as if to say: "They are all finished, anyway."

Lurie went to the airfield to find out whether these ideas of Menzel's are grounded in fact. On his return in the afternoon, Lurie revealed that 300 Jews had in fact been sent to Keidan to work there for two or three months. Nothing definite, however, could be said about plans to concentrate Jewish workers in army camps. It should be noted that at the military construction brigade there has also been talk about a new method of employing Jewish workers, which is to be revealed in the near future. This is why we are so frightened. There is no way of knowing what tomorrow will bring.

In the morning I went to the city governor's office to speak to Miller. I failed to detect any signs of impending change for the worse for the Ghetto. As usual, he signed various orders that I had placed for various supplies for the Ghetto, including fifty pairs of galoshes for our policemen; and a permit to be issued to the workers in several labor brigades allowing them to bring potatoes and a specified quantity of firewood into the Ghetto. Miller listened to Kopelman's and my proposal to increase the food rations to the Jewish policemen. He also promised to obtain the necessary approval for this request. I failed to detect any signs in him of new ideas concerning the fate of the Ghetto.

In the afternoon, Miller and Gilow came to the Ghetto gate, as is their habit, to inspect the goods brought by the Jewish workers returning from the city. They did not say a word about possible changes in the Ghetto. I got the impression that there was not a grain of truth in these rumors; at least as far as today and tomorrow are concerned.

For his part, Lipzer "felt the pulse" at the Gestapo offices. He even spoke with Jaeger in person. Jaeger reassured him that no changes are in the offing for the Ghetto. The present order will continue in the future. Despite these reassurances, however, the Ghetto is rife with fears. The residents would like to see an end to these rumors, not to mention the fear which holds them in its grip.

In recent weeks everyone in the Ghetto has been following the developments on the war front. Each day we want to know what the German and Allied powers have to say. The Ghetto inmates even have "complaints" of their own: Why has the whole of Sicily not been occupied? When will Italy surrender? And, the biggest question of them all: when will our troubles end?

People in the Ghetto keep asking questions about Cramer: what has happened to him? He has not been seen in the workshops for many weeks. Lenzen is the talk of the Ghetto these days. He is said to have replaced Cramer; whether the replacement is temporary or permanent, no one knows. Some say that Cramer is on holiday.

Responsible workers at the workshops tell strange stories about Cramer. It turns out that, several months ago, ten barrels of gasoline were brought here from the city governor's office. They were subsequently stored in a pit which then became covered over with green grass. It seems that Cramer has acquired for himself a fuel depot—in case things come to a head. One day a driver from the governor-general's office came over to ask whether there was any gasoline stored here. He received a negative reply.

In recent days, Gilow began winding up his financial affairs at the workshops. He asked for receipts for things he had received and failed to return. He does not want to get something for nothing, he said. The Jews caught his drift and submitted bills to him amounting to mere pennies. Gilow remarked that the bills were too low and asked for new, higher ones.

Yesterday Gilow came to the workshops in the Ghetto and entered the laundry heating room. He ordered the four workers to leave and locked himself in the room. Thereupon he took out sheafs of papers from his briefcase and threw them into the fire. The Ghetto jokers say that Gilow burned love letters from his mistresses, prior to the arrival of his wife from Germany.

It seems that there is something rotten in the kingdom of Cramer and Gilow. The trouble is that in most cases it is we who pay for their sins.

Cramer is—for the time being?—replaced by Lenzen, who is busy weaving a rope for our necks. Hermann told us that, and we believe it. Now, when the rumors about the transfer of Jewish workers to army camps refuse to die, Cramer's absence is keenly felt. For reasons of his personal comfort, Cramer was a supporter of the Ghetto. He needed the Ghetto, its Jews, and its workshops. He needed the Jews to work for him and to supply him with goods in abundance.

He needed the Ghetto to entrench himself in a position of power; he extolled the workshops before every German commission which visited us. It was he, Cramer, who set up these flourishing enterprises inside the Ghetto where 1,700 Jews were busy at work day and night for the German victory and for the German Army.

Now Cramer is gone. Lenzen has come to replace him. "And a new King ascended the throne and he knew not Joseph." Lenzen spells nothing but trouble for us.

AUGUST 26, 1943

Eliezer Yerushalmi, a teacher by profession, came here from the Siauliai Ghetto for a visit. At present he occupies the post of secretary of the main Jewish representative body in the Ghetto, which there is called *Judenrat*. One evening he came to my office at the Council in the company of a young man from the Siauliai Ghetto. They came escorted by a policeman. The policeman said that these were two Jews from Siauliai and that he had been assigned the task of bringing them to us. I asked them to sit down.

"Are you Golub?" Yerushalmi asked me. He seemed a tense and fear-stricken man, between forty and forty-five. His face spoke of the sufferings and traumas he had gone through. His clothes were not so clean; the wrinkles on his face, the disheveled hair, the hoarse voice, and the furtive glances he kept casting in all directions—all these confirmed my guess that this man had recently gone through Saul's torments.

"Yes," I replied.

"I've heard a lot about you," he said.

"And who are you? What do you do in the Siauliai Ghetto?" I wanted to know.

"Are you asking me officially or unofficially?" asked my guest.

"You are free to reply or to refrain from replying, as you see fit. Here you are among Jews and no one is going to hurt you. We are not going to rake you over the coals here at the Council. You can speak your mind."

"My name is Yerushalmi. I occupy the post of secretary of the Jewish Council. I have greetings for you from the director, Heller, from Leibovitz, and from other members of the Siauliai Jewish Council."[1]

This exchange took place after office hours. Yerushalmi told us about the Siauliai Ghetto, its institutions, and its relations with the Gestapo, the municipal authorities, and the Lithuanians.[2] The conditions in the Siauliai Ghetto are, more or less, similar to ours, but the housing shortage there is more severe; ten to fourteen people live in one room. The Jewish Council has an unofficial budget used to meet welfare expenses. It also operates a clandestine school. The Jewish workers do hard labor at the Linkaiciai camp, digging peat, and also in local sugar refineries. The atmosphere is relatively quiet. The fear in the Kovno Ghetto is greater; here people talk a great deal about the concentration of Jewish workers in army camps. In Siauliai they have not heard about this yet.

Yerushalmi tells his story. He also hears from us about the condition of the supply of medicines, about the hospital, and about the workshops. He wants to see all these enterprises. He has already seen some of them; he arrived here yesterday. His conclusions: "Life in the Kovno Ghetto is better. People are dressed in better clothes. But the atmosphere in our Siauliai Ghetto is more peaceful."

Yerushalmi continues:

As you have probably heard, a Jew was executed in Siauliai by hanging. It happened as follows: one day the deputy district governor, accompanied by a Lithuanian, passed through Siauliai, either back from a journey into the country or back from a business trip. Suddenly they saw a Jew running into a nearby courtyard, where he disappeared. His behavior aroused their suspicion. They walked to the place, and in the adjoining courtyard they saw twenty-seven cartons of cigarettes lying on the ground. They began a search, found the Jew, and arrested him; he was subsequently sentenced to death by hanging. The execution was to take place in public in the Ghetto.

The Jewish Council did all it could to change the verdict. It pleaded with the district governor to reduce the sentence. In reply, the district governor said that it would be interesting to watch a Jew twisting in agony on the rope. He wanted to be acquainted with the hanging procedures according to the Jewish law. He therefore gave his consent to the presence of a Rabbi at the execution.

The Ghetto Jews were forced to erect the scaffold. Jewish residents were brought from all parts of the Ghetto to attend the execution. A German from the district governor's office was also present. The latter, however, did not exactly feast his eyes on the spectacle as he had hoped. The Jew condemned to death walked to meet his fate with his head erect. He did not even weep. To the Jews who had built the scaffold, he said: "Jews, I forgive you. I know you were forced to do this." Then he took off his coat and asked someone to give it to the man from whom he had previously borrowed it. His final request was to loosen the knot on the handkerchief tied over his eyes. Then everything went in the manner of all horrid spectacles of this kind.

The representative of the district governor was disappointed: "This Jew conducted himself properly. He went to his death valiantly." The German left the scene grieving, his head bowed. The Siauliai Jews stood firm by the sheer force of their will. Later they said: "We must remember this day until the hour comes for the great revenge."

This had been the "turn" of the Siauliai Jews. The first such hanging had taken place in the Vilna Ghetto, the second here in the Kovno Ghetto, and the third in the Siauliai Ghetto.

Tense and grieving, we listened to the story of the terrible spectacle in the Siauliai Ghetto. Yerushalmi summed it up by saying: "One question keeps troubling me all these days: will we get out of this alive, or not?"

The same question troubles all of us here.

1. Mendel Leibovitz was the chairman of the Siauliai (Shavli) Jewish Council, and the leading personality in the Ghetto. He was greatly admired in the community, as were the other members of the Council, including Aron Heller, who handled the Ghetto's financial affairs. Both of them served from the establishment of the Ghetto in August 1941 until its liquidation on July 15, 1944, one week after the liquidation of the Kovno Ghetto.

2. The meeting between Eliezer Yerushalmi and Golub (Tory) and other members of the Kovno Jewish Council was the first meeting ever held between members of the Siauliai and Kovno Jewish Councils, despite the fact that they lived so near one another: Siauliai, known to the Jews as Shavli, is 120 kilometers from Kovno.

SEPTEMBER 4, 1943

Terrible news has reached us from Vilna. A few days ago we learned that people had been taken out of the Vilna Ghetto in thirty trucks. The drivers recruited for this job were told that they would be kept busy for one hour only. These rumors gave rise to great commotion in the Ghetto. An "action" in Vilna, people said, recalling Ponar.

Later it was learned that the Vilna Ghetto had been attacked by collaborators from all three Baltic States, and that the Jews are not allowed to leave the Ghetto for work in the city. No one knows what the situation is inside the Ghetto. The fact that the drivers were told that they would be working for just one hour gave grounds for the conjecture that the Jews were to be taken to Ponar. They would not have been transported to Estonia on trucks, certainly not in one hour.

Two days ago, Schtitz—accompanied by several senior Gestapo officers headed by Schmitz—left Kovno. With them went several hundred Latvian soldiers. They were summoned to Vilna to reinforce the units surrounding the Ghetto, and to assist in carrying out the plan prepared in advance. Schtitz is an expert in Jewish affairs in general, and in "actions" in particular. This meant that the situation in the Vilna Ghetto was grave. We waited anxiously for further details from there.

Yesterday new information arrived from Vilna. It turns out that several thousand people were taken out of the Ghetto; the Jewish police could not get the situation under control; the Jews hid in cellars and in the underground sewers, refusing to come out. Many Jews tried to defend themselves with weapons in hand; this resulted in an exchange of fire during which several hundred Jews lost their lives. The Lithuanians and the Germans who returned from Vilna told us more or less the same story.

For quite some time, we have regarded the Vilna Ghetto as a barrel of gunpowder. Its inmates saw themselves as prisoners, not only of the German rulers but of Gens as well. Gens added his yoke to the already harsh and strict regime imposed on the Ghetto by the Germans. For all practical purposes he acted as the representative of the Germans. He introduced a regime of terror into the Ghetto; this provoked the fierce resistance of numerous groups in the Ghetto. Some of the Ghetto inmates had arms in their possession, which they sometimes used unadvisedly. It seems that this time, too—particularly as they were overcome by a keen sense of danger and by despair—some Jews put up armed resistance to the enemy's forces. To us, this seems only a natural and logical consequence of the conditions which recently prevailed in the Vilna Ghetto.

Recently there have been many cases of young Jews from the Vilna Ghetto escaping to the forests. They have joined various groups of partisans—both Poles and White Russians. There have also been rumors that, during a German offensive against partisan forces active in the forests and villages in the Vilna district, a number of Jews were captured. That which we feared has come upon us. The demand to remove 4,000 Jews from the Vilna Ghetto, for hard labor in Estonia, we view as the beginning of the liquidation of the Vilna Ghetto. It is not a coincidence that 4,000 Jews were taken out of the Vilna Ghetto, and clearly these people were not taken out because they were lazy at work in the Ghetto. Each person in the Vilna Ghetto had his own place of work, and no employer wanted to give up his Jewish workers. This was a politically motivated measure. The internal situation in the Vilna Ghetto has again become very unstable.

Yesterday the Gestapo mission returned from Vilna to Kovno. Conversations that Lipzer had with some of its members revealed that several thousand Jews had, in fact, been taken from Vilna to Estonia. When a significant number of Jews refused to obey the transfer order and others put up armed resistance, the Germans blew up several apartment houses in the Ghetto, killing 500 people. Jews were then taken out of the Ghetto and to the nearby railway station. From there they were sent by train to Estonia.[1] The Vilna Ghetto is pervaded by tension and anxiety.

Many relatives of Jews in the Kovno Ghetto reside in the Vilna Ghetto. The two Ghettos are located in the same Gestapo district. Anything that happens today in the Vilna Ghetto may happen here tomorrow. Our sky is heavily overcast. The inmates of the Kovno Ghetto fear for their future.

Today Schtitz arrived in the Ghetto, accompanied by Lipzer. On entering the Council office, Schtitz asked, with contentment and false friendliness: "Well, how are things in the Ghetto? What do people talk about these days?" We are in the habit of giving evasive answers to such questions from the Germans, or, preferably, we try not to answer them at all. This time, however, Lipzer, who had in all probability persuaded Schtitz to come here today in the first place, and who also probably informed him about the fears permeating the Ghetto following the recent events in Vilna, addressed Dr. Elkes—who did his best to try to refrain from replying to Schtitz's questions: "Sir, Doctor, why are you silent? Don't be afraid. Why don't you tell Schtitz what the problem is?"

In order to create a relaxed atmosphere, Schtitz then asked those present to be seated. He himself took a seat at the desk. He even went so far as to allow himself to smile.

Reluctantly, Dr. Elkes replied: "Rumors have recently sprung up about the deportation of thousands of Jews from the Vilna Ghetto. Their destination remains unknown. The Kovno Ghetto inmates are very worried by this news. I am very interested in knowing what exactly happened there."

In reply to Dr. Elkes's question, Schtitz said that the Jews had been taken out of the Vilna Ghetto for work in Estonia. There is no reason to fear; it was not an "action." In such a case whole families would have been taken, and not just men. Resistance by force is meaningless. One or two Germans can be "knocked off," but the Ghetto as a whole will bear the consequences. With just one German heavy machine gun, an entire Ghetto quarter can be destroyed; two or three aircraft are enough to raze the whole Ghetto to the ground. Armed resistance is of no avail. Two or three people can escape, but scores of Ghetto inmates will suffer. Even single fighters are caught in the end, as was the case here with Dr. Nabriski.

Schtitz does not want to hear people saying that the Bolsheviks will return here before long. This will never happen. "Actions" are out of the question, so there is no reason for us to worry. The head of the Gestapo has asked him to issue a warning that rumor-mongers will be hanged. If the unrest in the Ghetto continues, he will give the order to hang one Jew. Then peace will return. Schtitz praised the Jewish policemen from the Vilna Ghetto. The Kovno Ghetto policemen, he said, do not even come close to their colleagues in Vilna. They could not even assemble 200 people for the Keidan labor camp. Should such a fiasco recur, he is going to punish the Ghetto severely.

For Schtitz, shootings and the blowing up of houses, as well as the killing of 500 as in the Vilna Ghetto, are things of the past. Today he spoke about them in a casual manner. For us, however, the recent events in the Vilna Ghetto amount to a national tragedy and a clear warning.

1. On September 1, 1943, the Germans entered the Vilna Ghetto and demanded 5,000 Jews for work in labor camps in Estonia. Exchanges of fire broke out between the Germans and members of the Jewish underground. Subsequently, the Germans rounded up 1,500 men, followed a few days later by 2,200 women. The members of the underground escaped to the forests.

SEPTEMBER 6, 1943

The danger of the transfer of Jewish workers to army camps has become more and more imminent. This morning three members of the Gestapo came to the Council. Two of them are "old acquaintances": Schtitz and Gratt.[1] Captain Gratt heads the political section of the Gestapo. The third man was unknown to us; his rank of SS captain was higher than that of his two companions.

The three men toured the workshops, visited the secretariat, and browsed through documents. They even took a look at work-cards. They eyed with a certain suspicion the rooms, the building entrances, the staircases, and the hallways. It seemed as though they were looking for secret exits or hidden cellars. They did not show any particular interest in the various production lines in the workshops; they looked for faults. They listened to reports and production statistics with marked mistrust.

Later they went out to the courtyard, and from there they took a long walk along the shores of the Vilija river, which borders the Ghetto. This area is regularly patrolled by the Ghetto guard and by the Jewish police. The Vilija river forms a bend running for two kilometers along the Ghetto perimeter. There are hardly any people to be seen there. At certain hours in the summer, a few people come to the narrow strip of the beach for a swim.

Between the Vilija and the workshops are the vegetable gardens of the Ghetto. This place is often frequented by guests from the outside world, who sing songs of praise to the work done by Jews in agriculture.

Yesterday the three members of the Gestapo examined the bank of the Vilija from all sides. On their way there, they ran into two vocational training school students. They asked them to show their work-cards. When the youths replied that they were studying at the vocational training school, that they did not have their student cards with them, and that they were on their way to take a swim in the river, the Gestapo sent them back to the Ghetto, telling them to go to Lipzer in the evening and to show him their student cards.

The extensive examination of the Vilija bank by the Gestapo was viewed negatively by the Ghetto inmates; it gave rise to new speculations about preparations for an "action" in the Ghetto.

Dr. Zacharin, head of the Council's health department, happened to be present in the Council office. He asked: "What is this visit to the shores of Vilija about? I don't like visits such as this at all." He has good reason to think this way. On October 2, 1941, Dr. Zacharin did not like the inspection of the yard in the vicinity of the hospital—which was subsequently set on fire. In these matters Dr. Zacharin can be relied on.

Walking along the shore, the Gestapo reached the sawmill. The sawmill is situated outside the Ghetto. It employs Jews who operate the sawing machinery. Trucks and carts loaded with timber keep entering and leaving the sawmill. Jewish workers buy goods near the sawmill and smuggle them with ease through the Ghetto gate. The gate is guarded by a Lithuanian policeman who is easy to "get along" with.

The first thing the Gestapo did on entering the sawmill was to inspect the workers' knapsacks, which lay in a pile in a far corner of the mill. They found eggs, even some pieces of chicken. The knapsacks were put in the Gestapo car, and the labor brigade leader was ordered to report to Gestapo headquarters tomorrow. On this occasion they "served" several workers with slaps on the face.

The Gestapo officers returned to the Ghetto through the sawmill gate and went to the German labor office, where they stayed for a long time.

In the meantime, we learned from workers at the workshops that the new Gestapo officer was a particularly tough individual. The workers did not like the three Gestapo officers' snooping around. From the German labor office we learned that the three Gestapo officials had scrutinized the records of labor brigades at the airfield, in the city, and in the Ghetto. They also inspected the work-cards and wished to know whether the names of deceased workers were removed from the files, and from whom they could obtain details on the matter. They were told that deaths were recorded at the Council's population registration department. Thereupon the three officials set out in this direction.

In the registration department they found Miss Miriam Shor of the Aid to the Ghetto Needy society. She was sitting at the desk, counting money. They started interrogating her. "Where does the money come from?" they asked. Luckily, she had only 2,000 marks. Israel Leibson, the deputy director of the population registration department, who was in the same room, had in his possession a large amount of money belonging to the Aid to the Ghetto Needy society. Miriam Shor replied that she had found the money. "Where?" was the next question. "On Varniu Street, inside this piece of paper," she replied, pointing to a dirty envelope on her desk. Instead of a third question, Miss Shor was struck on her face by one of the visitors.

Two of the Gestapo officers inspected the files of the registration department. They asked to see Lipzer's card and inspected that as well. One of them kept showing an interest in the money found on Miss Shor. "Where do you work? Show me your work-card." The investigation was thus reopened. Miss Shor took out her card and handed it to the Gestapo man. It turned out that since September 1 no records had been entered on her card, as specified by the regulations. Her interrogator became angry: "For how many days have you been unemployed?" The question was followed by another slap on her face.

That same day a policeman by the name of Sergei[2] came to see me at the Council offices. He is a dedicated man who never fails to be present whenever troubles spring up. Sergei told me that the Gestapo visitors had found money belonging to the Aid to the Ghetto Needy society fund. The workers in the registration department did not know how to get out of this mess. Perhaps someone from the Council could go there? I held a quick discussion with Dr. Elkes and Garfunkel; we decided to wait a little longer, as the situation is complicated. Money found in a Council department! Another reason to worry.

Through the Council window we saw an unusual spectacle: Miss Shor leaving the registration department building followed by the three Gestapo officers. Miss Shor was walking with her head bowed, crying. The three men were walking after her, their faces angry—as if they were ready to escort her to be hanged. A small, weak, helpless woman, captive in the hands of three strong, armed men. The contrast was striking. They were walking in the direction of the Council building. "They are coming to us," I thought.

This was, indeed, what happened. Two of the Gestapo officers entered the labor office building and went up to the first floor. Schtitz and Miss Shor remained waiting outside. In the labor office the two officers were shown Miss Shor's work-card. "This woman has not been coming to work for the last six days," they said. "Who is in charge of checking such behavior?" They were told that such matters were the responsibility of the Council. Each Council department is required to supervise its workers.

The Gestapo officers then entered the Council offices and went straight to Dr. Elkes. "Who are you?" one of them asked. "I am Dr. Elkes, chairman of the Council." "Are you a doctor?" they asked. "Yes." Thereupon they addressed Garfunkel: "And who are you?" "My name is Garfunkel. I am the deputy chairman of the Council." "Are you also a doctor?" "No."

Gratt took out Miss Shor's work-card and handed it to Dr. Elkes. The latter tried to explain that he was unaware of the whole business. He would check on it, he said, and inform them of the results.

"You mean to say that you don't know what's going on here? You have to know everything. Who is the department's director?" one of them asked. Dr. Elkes replied that no Council officials were then in the offices: they had all gone out to lunch.

The Gestapo officers showed Dr. Elkes the 2,000 marks they had found in Miss Shor's possession. They voiced the suspicion that she was bribing her boss to exempt her from work.

Dr. Elkes tried to reassure the Gestapo and to turn their minds from hostile thoughts. He told them about his own life; it turned out that for eighteen years he had served as physician to the German embassy in Kovno. He had also been the personal physician of the German ambassador to Lithuania. Perhaps they would be interested in touring the Ghetto hospital? If so, he would be most willing to serve as their guide. By and by, the Gestapo officers began to listen to Dr. Elkes. They seemed to be impressed by his story. In the meantime, it had grown late, almost three o'clock in the afternoon. The Gestapo have their lunch at this time every day. They left the Council building, taking Miss Shor's work-card with them.

We were concerned about the fate of Miss Shor. What will they do to her? At that moment, Schtitz ordered one of the Jewish policemen to take Miss Shor to the Ghetto detention center; she is to be jailed for five days.

All the Jews were relieved at the light sentence given to Miss Shor. Jewish "successes": the Germans took the money, beat up several people, put one woman in jail, and everyone is happy because it could have been much worse.

We waited anxiously for the arrival of Lipzer. He must know the purpose of the Gestapo visit. Lipzer came, but he had no information on this matter.

As usual in such cases, the Ghetto was worried. Everyone recalled the recent events in the Vilna Ghetto. There, the Ghetto had been surrounded all of a sudden; perhaps they plan to do the same thing here? Gestapo officers do not come to the Ghetto for no special reason.

In the evening, a Gestapo order was brought by Lipzer; tomorrow, seventy women and eighty men are to report at 7 A.M. for a special assignment. They will be escorted by ten Jewish policemen. The order specified neither the nature of the assignment nor where the assignment was to be. This is a typical Gestapo order: nothing is clear. Everything is shrouded in secrecy.

What is the meaning of the sudden visit of the Gestapo officers? What does the recruitment of 150 people for unspecified work in an unknown location mean? No one knows. We will wait and see.

1. Captain Joachim Gratt had been in charge of Kovno and the forts around it on behalf of the Einsatzgruppen, after the German invasion.
2. Sergei, a member of the Jewish Ghetto police, was an active member of the Zionist Revisionist party. He was one of the small number of policemen who, in March 1944, agreed to show the Germans where Jews were hiding in the Ghetto. He did not survive the war.

SEPTEMBER 15, 1943

Yesterday the Ghetto was again in a state of agitation. Everything began with another tour of the workshop by three Gestapo officials. These three did not come here just to take one look and then disappear. They came with the purpose of entrenching themselves in a position of power in the Ghetto. The three—our old "friend" Schtitz, a previously unknown German with the rank of captain,[1] and his aide-de-camp—stormed into the workshops with the air of people who owned the place. Their first question was: "Why are there sewing machines standing at the entrance to the room?" This question was addressed to the storeroom manager, Berl Friedman. "These are new sewing machines, brought here to expand the dressmaking section," he replied.

"You intended to remove these machines. From now on it is forbidden to remove anything from this place."

Next, the visitors entered the rooms where tailors, carpenters, and cobblers were toiling to supply the needs of senior officials at the city governor's office, and at the governor-general's office. Here they make suits of clothing, shoes, coats, underwear, furniture, toys, household utensils, and leather products; in short, anything in demand which cannot be obtained in the city these days. The Gestapo get all that they need here; in control, the SS say they do not get a thing. The Gestapo visitors asked the foremen: for whom do the tailors make these clothes? For whom the shoes? For whom the underwear? Who supplies the fabrics and the leather for all these products?

The foremen are well prepared to answer such questions. They gave the Gestapo clear answers: this fabric was brought by such and such in accordance with a special permit; the coat is not new, it is here to be mended. At the same time, however, they were forced to admit that the coat was being mended for Miller, whereas another coat was for Keiffler's wife; the briefcase is for an official at the governor-general's office, etc. The Gestapo officers did not believe all these explanations; they reached their own conclusions.

The Gestapo inspected one workshop after another. They kept asking what products were being manufactured in each place, for whom, and from what materials. They did not praise the achievements of the workshops. They did not like the level of cleanliness in the workshop rooms. The foreman was summoned and told: "From now on we are in charge of the workshops in the Ghetto. If we find again that the rooms are not clean, we will hang you—for all the Ghetto to see." Another member of the team remarked: "Or we will make you a simple worker." This visit of the Gestapo to the workshops has given rise to serious apprehension among the workers and the Ghetto residents in general.

The visitors had a long conversation with Gilow and Miller in the workshop offices. The conversation was not at all friendly. Afterward, the Gestapo officers ordered the workshop foremen not to remove any product from the place. Captain Goecke then announced that he was taking over the management of the workshops and of the Ghetto.

Gilow and Miller were very tense. They telephoned Cramer, and were later instructed by him to continue taking delivery of finished products from the workshops. Goods are to be stored in the building of the former Kovno municipal council. The workers were ordered to work through the night, pack the wares, and remove them from the workshops.

Trucks were now busy driving rapidly from the workshops to the building of the former Kovno municipal council and back. Every finished product was snatched as if it were on fire, and removed from the workshops. Cramer, as city governor, had lost an important position in the Ghetto; he now seeks to establish a new stronghold for himself in the municipal council building. This means that he wants to set up a small workshop to supply the personal needs of senior officials in the German civilian administration of Kovno.

At 8 P.M. members of the workshop management, headed by Segalson, came to the Council offices. During the day they had been flooded with various directives. According to one of these, issued by Cramer himself, as city governor, all the better-quality products were to be removed from the workshops. Another directive, issued by the Gestapo, prohibited their removal in the strongest terms. Keiffler first ordered the removal of certain products from the workshops; later he banned their removal. Cramer then ordered their removal. So it had gone on.

Captain Goecke's announcement that he was taking over the management of the Ghetto and the workshops caused panic in the Ghetto. People kept asking themselves about the meaning of this. "If everything in the Ghetto passes into the hands of the Gestapo," said the members of the management of the workshops, "we ought to be replaced by people on good terms with the Gestapo" (in all probability meaning Lipzer). Segalson revealed that Miller had offered him work in the new workshops being set up in the building of the former municipal Kovno council.

The members of the Council explained to the members of the management of the workshops that as long as the general situation of the Ghetto and the workshops remains unclear, it is too soon to contemplate changes in personnel. Until the dust settles, everyone should stay where he is. We must not lose our patience. If the Gestapo takes over Ghetto affairs, the Ghetto will turn into a constantly guarded camp.

The news about the takeover of the workshops by the Gestapo spread like wildfire, exacerbating the fears of the Ghetto inmates. People started talking again about the planned concentration of Jewish workers in army camps.

In recent months, life in the Ghetto has become more comfortable: the severe tone of voice and the strict official approach have disappeared; foodstuffs are again being brought through the Ghetto gate, and the economic situation of the Ghetto has also improved. Some room is even left for cultural and spiritual life. And now the Gestapo comes with the intention of breaking up everything.

The Ghetto inmates have started talking again about the "good" times in the past. We have begun imagining military labor camps and life in concentration camps. Is this how our life in the Ghetto is going to end? After all, this is not what the last chapter in Ghetto life was supposed to be—in our eyes. We thought we would leave the Ghetto to go out to freedom, to a good and interesting life—a new era in the history of nations. We did not think that our life here would end with a beast of prey pouncing on us, with efforts to break up the Ghetto and to divide it, with the deportation of its residents, and their being scattered to the four corners of the earth.

The events which took place in the Vilna Ghetto last month have also fueled our apprehensions; several thousand Jews were forcibly removed from the Vilna Ghetto and transported to Estonia to do hard labor; in the course of this "action," 500 Jews lost their lives underneath the rubble of houses blown up by the Germans with mines. At present, the Vilna Ghetto remains sealed. No one leaves it. No food is brought into it. Hunger has set in and bread prices have soared.

Thoughts of the fate of the Vilna Ghetto point to the need for caution, causing us to refrain from straying into crooked paths. We must give in to the demands of the authorities, so as not to supply them with an excuse to kill us all.

Yesterday morning, after much toil and effort, the labor office managed to assemble a new labor brigade to lay telephone cables from the city of Kovno to the former German border. This morning, 165 people were recruited for this brigade; but we are still short of the full quota of 400 workers. This quota is very difficult to fill. Everyone wants to work in the workshops, in order to insure himself against leaving for a military labor camp. The number of applicants for jobs at the workshops has reached 1,400. At the same time, the Ghetto labor office goes to great lengths to recruit workers for the new labor brigade. It is imperative that we demonstrate our ability to recruit the required number of workers without outside intervention.

These days we are witnessing the spectacle of the Ghetto inmates being dealt with as if they were beasts of burden. Whatever we produce for the authorities is not enough. In recent weeks, various branches of our rulers have been at loggerheads over power in the Ghetto: Cramer, the city governor, is unwilling to give up his monopoly on trade in Jewish slaves and thus hurt his personal interests; the Gestapo wants the same monopoly for itself. To be on the safe side, the local German civil authorities have removed the best products from the workshops and transferred them to their own warehouses. The senior officials of the German civilian administration have hurried to the workshops to place urgent orders for clothing.

Wiener, of the Nazi Party secretariat in Kovno, has asked to have the clothes he had ordered finished; those items which could not be completed should, he said, be hidden in some secret storage place. Lange, Keiffler, and Obst have each asked us to do the same.

There is a real possibility that the Ghetto will be broken up, the workshops will be liquidated, and the Ghetto inmates dispersed to distant localities. It appears that the Gestapo has received an order from its Riga headquarters to transfer Jewish workers to army camps and to liquidate the Kovno Ghetto.

Before noon, various products and materials were in the process of being transferred from the workshops to the city. Almost all the department directors of the city governor's office put in an appearance in the workshop to "get things straight" in their warehouses.

I went to see Miller, to find out what the situation was. Miller was confused. "The situation is not clear," he said. "We are in the process of relocating the workshops. I believe that the last word on this subject has not yet been spoken." Here the conversation broke off: the faces of Miller and Gilow clearly indicated that they are going through a tragedy. It seems that they have lost hold over a lucrative business and that they are extremely upset. Perhaps they will now have to go to the front?

Keiffler gave an order to settle all bills and to prepare them to be handed to the new rulers. This whole affair reminds me of a shoddy business in the process of going bankrupt: the magistrate, accompanied by policemen, enters the front door in order to take stock of all the merchandise, while at the same time the best products are being taken out through the back door.

While the snatching of products and materials from the workshops was in full swing, Schtitz and the aide-de-camp of Captain Goecke arrived in the Ghetto. For a whole hour they were deep in discussion with Hermann in the German labor office. We learned that the Gestapo officers who had visited the Ghetto recently were "experts" in everything concerning concentration camps. They had "learned" this subject in Holland, where they had confined the Jews in city blocks and put them to work polishing diamonds. The Jews had been forbidden to leave the houses. Now the Gestapo seek to put this plan into effect in Estonia. Captain Forster, a fellow Gestapo officer of Goecke, had earlier left Kovno for Vilna and Siauliai, in order to orchestrate the transfer of the Jewish workers there to military camps. Now he and Captain Goecke plan to do the same thing here. They have asked Hermann to cooperate with them in the implementation of this plan in the Kovno Ghetto. Hermann, however, voiced his view that confining the Jews in camps is not workable. The main reason, he said, is that among the local Jews there are experts in building construction, builders, specialists in making concrete, locksmiths, carpenters, and other skilled workers.

On Friday, however, a commission from Riga will arrive here to liquidate the affairs of the Ghetto. We were told the same thing at the city governor's office.

The Gestapo officials inveigh against the employees of the German civilian administration, who exploit the workshops for the satisfaction of their personal needs. Schtitz told Hermann that he had not received any favors from the Ghetto factories or services.

Having learned that the authorities have not yet made a final decision on the fate of the Ghetto, the Ghetto inmates were put somewhat at ease. Having no choice, we prefer the life of the moment.

Today we witnessed a particularly telling incident. In the thick of the grabbing of goods and materials at the workshops, Viertel telephoned the Council, ordering us to dig up five to six tons of potatoes from the vegetable gardens. He said he was coming tomorrow to take delivery of them. It turned out, however, that the potatoes will not be ready for harvest for two or three weeks. I went to see him and to explain this to him, but he dug in his heels and insisted that we fulfill his order.

In the afternoon, when it became known that the fate of the workshops has not yet been finally decided, Miller ordered us not to dig up the potatoes for Viertel. Later, Viertel arrived in the Ghetto and instructed us to give "his" potatoes to the soup kitchen at the workshops.

In the evening, Natkin telephoned us from the Ghetto gate. It turned out that an old Jew from Vilna had reached the Ghetto with one of the city labor brigades. What should we do with him? He had fled from Vilna. Following a short discussion with Dr. Elkes, I told Natkin to admit this Jew to the hospital. As his body was crawling with lice, he was first entrusted to the care of the lice disinfection center, where he was given clean underwear. Afterward he was transferred to the Ghetto.

It is seven o'clock in the evening. The power supply is weak and the electric lights are very dim. The main cable was damaged yesterday by shots fired by the Lithuanian policemen of the Ghetto guard. They did it because Grinberg, who is a Jewish police precinct commander, yesterday arrested a Lithuanian who had broken into a Jewish apartment and threatened its tenants. This Lithuanian was in fact a policeman. At the time of his arrest, he tried to run off and put his hand into his pocket. Grinberg thought the man intended to pull out a gun, so he chased after him, and wrested from him both a gun and a Finnish knife. On this occasion, Grinberg even "served" him some good blows. Then he contacted the German commandant of the Ghetto guard, asking him to come over and pick up the riotous Lithuanian.

The Lithuanian told the Ghetto guard that Jews had beaten him up and taken away his gun. His fellow Lithuanian policemen resolved to avenge their comrade. Already, yesterday, they began confiscating goods brought in through the Ghetto gate. Last night they fired shots along the perimeter fence and hit the main supply cable. As a result, some parts of the Ghetto were shrouded in darkness, and others were barely lit.

As the evening darkness enveloped the Ghetto, the door of my room in the council offices opened and the elderly Jew from Vilna entered, carrying a small bundle in his hand. He seated himself at the desk. All those present in my room then took their seats. Recently we have been burning with desire to hear some words from Vilna. Sitting at the desk, I could see him more clearly: his hair was white, his face a living testimonial to the troubles which had been his share in recent weeks. He seemed exhausted, but not crushed in spirit. His voice was clear, his eyes tired yet sparkling. He did not seem to be a man overcome by despair; on the contrary, the hardships he had gone through had hardened him. The old man laid his walking stick and his knapsack at his feet, and began to unfold a story straight from the *Thousand and One Arabian Nights.*

He comes from Vilna. His name is Melzer. He had been a businessman in Vilna. He knows traders from Kovno and from Siauliai. In the Vilna Ghetto he was not idle. He was a supervisor in a work camp in which everything was running as smoothly as clockwork. Needless to say, assistants were placed at his disposal; at the age of seventy he is not a young man anymore. He worked to everyone's satisfaction. Eleven days ago, when people were being abducted for hard labor and houses blown up, he did not go into hiding. His daughter was working as a clerk in the workshops. Gens gave her a paper releasing her father from the deportation to Estonia.

On that infamous Friday, Melzer left his house to buy some bread. He was seized on the street and thrown into a truck which took him to the railway station. From there, together with 3,000 people, he was taken to Estonia. They were locked inside the freightcars for three days without any food. Only a few people had taken food with them, since most of the deportees were recruited—or, like himself, seized—without any prior notice. Only on the third day did each of the deportees receive 200 grams of bread.

Upon arrival at the first train station in Estonia—Dzubchina—they were taken out of the cars and marched to a field. A German officer lined them up in rows: the able-bodied—those fit for work—on one side, and the elderly, the sick, women, and children on the other side. In Vilna, in the turmoil of the brutal recruitment for work in Estonia, even old people like him, as well as women and children, had been snatched from the streets and thrown into the cars.

In the field, the able-bodied (1,800 people) were ordered to go to the right, whereas those unfit for work (1,200 people) to the left—1500 of them all were men and the rest women and children.

Those on the left, together with this man, were loaded again on to the freightcars and sent on without any definite destination. They passed various villages and towns in Estonia, but no one was willing to take them, because they were incapable of working. Throughout this odyssey they lived in the freightcars, hungry and dejected. They even had to relieve themselves in the cars.

From Estonia the train crossed into Latvia. Here, too, no one wanted them. They passed dozens of stations, but the end of the journey was nowhere in sight.

Finally they were allowed to disembark at Tauroggen (in Lithuania). They were lined up in rows and told they were going to get washed.

Throughout this ordeal, Melzer thought about escape. Later, when the doors of the cars were opened unexpectedly in Siauliai, he was ready to jump off. He had to wait, however, for the Estonchiks—Estonian armed auxiliaries—who guarded the train to get away. When that happened, however, the doors were suddenly slammed shut. In Tauroggen, Melzer had told his companions in the wagon that everything was lost and that they must escape. They had already given all their belongings to the 1,800 Jews who had stayed behind in Estonia; now they were destitute. Most of them wore threadbare and worn-out clothing; only Melzer had decent clothes on. He went to the car supervisor complaining of a stomachache, and asked permission to go outside to relieve himself. Melzer went out and did not return. "And Jacob has run away," says Melzer with a touch of humor. He does not know what happened to the others.

Exhausted and hungry, Melzer entered a peasant cottage (before doing so he had torn off the yellow badge). He told the peasant that he was a Russian. The peasant served him a good meal. Afterward he decided to go on foot from Tauroggen to Siauliai, where several of his acquaintances—former merchants—lived. On the way he met a peasant who asked him where he was headed. "To Siauliai," Melzer replied. To this the peasant said that at the pace he was going he would never reach his destination. Thereupon he took Melzer to the railway station, where he persuaded the supervisor to let him on the morning train to Siauliai. That night, Melzer slept at the station, and in the morning waited for his train. Before it left for Kovno, he had to pay 200 marks for the ticket, but when it turned out that he was penniless, they let him travel free. At every station he said he was a Russian, to which everyone replied that everything was going to change for the better soon. Conductors on the train took pity on him and gave him food, even on one occasion a glass of vodka. To everyone he told the same story: he was a Russian, a native of Vilna; one daughter lived in Vilna and one in Kovno; he was on his way to see the daughter in Kovno. When asked what his daughters did, he replied that they worked for the government.

Exhausted by many sleepless nights, Melzer fell asleep. He woke up just before the train reached Kovno. He decided to get off at the station before Kovno, in order to avoid ticket inspection. As he was climbing off the train, a policeman asked him whether he had his identity card on him. "Of course I do," replied Melzer, "How could I set out on a journey without my identity card?"— and he kept on walking. He found himself in Kovno, but did not know the location of the Ghetto. By chance he came across a Jewish worker, who took him to his work brigade, where he was given food and drink. By five o'clock in the afternoon he was in the Ghetto.

Here, in the Kovno Ghetto, Melzer's daughter should be found; she was sent from Vilna to the Zezmer labor camp, and from there she was brought to Kovno. He is keen to find her. He has one more request: that we give him some clothing, as he has not changed clothes for twelve days and eleven nights. At the lice disinfection center, he had taken his first bath since his departure from Vilna.

Melzer recounted his wanderings clearly, and not without humor. At last he had reached a place where Jews live; Jews who gave him a loving reception. He asked for a cigarette and spoke very slowly. From his notebook he read out the names of the places through which the 1,200 Jews had passed. Who knows where they are now, and what befell them. Most of them were women and little children.

The news of the arrival of a Jew from Vilna spread quickly in the Ghetto. Dozens of people assembled at the Council offices. Among them there was a young woman who had arrived here from Zezmer and whose sister lives in Vilna. She wished to know whether her sister was still in Vilna, or had been sent to Estonia.

When the young woman saw her father, and father his daughter, a heart-rending spectacle unfolded. Father and daughter cried for joy in each other's arms. These were the tears of exile, the tears of wanderings on unknown and dangerous paths. We left the father and daughter alone for a moment. The father gazed closely into his daughter's face; she seemed exhausted and thin. Tears welled up in his eyes again, tears of grief and suffering.

This is how this odyssey ended. It reflected the sufferings of an old father who had perhaps escaped the jaws of death. It also reflected the breaking up of a Jewish family which had gone through the seven gates of hell. Two family members had come together in one place, in order to go through sufferings together.

1. This was Wilhelm Goecke, the last ruler of the Ghetto, who would turn it into a concentration camp and finally destroy it.

SEPTEMBER 25, 1943

Late in the evening I left my house, setting out in the direction of the hospital. The Ghetto was enveloped in autumnal darkness. Nothing could be seen; I was walking as if with my eyes closed. Once in a while, a tiny light, as if of a flashlight, glimmered in the darkness for a moment, illuminating the way of a single passerby in the narrow alley. Then everything was dark again.

This evening is unusually dark. Nothing can be seen. Here and there the sounds of steps in the sand on an unpaved street can be heard. People trudge along slowly. After the day's hard work, they labor under the weight of their own bodies. Everyone is absorbed in his own thoughts. The Ghetto is restless again. People talk about its liquidation, and the setting up of labor camps; about the separation of families—of parents from their children, of the healthy from the sick and elderly. They talk about the confiscation of belongings, and other such matters. No one knows what tomorrow will bring. Uneasy days have come upon the Ghetto again. The fog of uncertainty envelops everything.

In the evening darkness, I keep hearing fragments of sentences and single words spoken by the invisible passersby. "Tomorrow, at one o'clock at night, I must report for duty again at the police station of my precinct. It seems that we'll have to arrest people again," I hear the voice of a man. Shortly afterward, I hear the voice of a woman, accompanied by a sigh: "Oh, Jankele, you are off to catch people again. Woe is me!" This was a Ghetto policeman who had received orders to report for a special night assignment. He understands that people will be taken out of their houses and taken to the Ghetto detention center. From there they will be sent to do hard labor in labor camps.

Shortly afterward, I hear broken fragments of a conversation: "On Monday, who knows." Then silence. These people were probably speaking of some change in their work arrangements. On the coming Monday, several dozen labor brigades will be broken up and their members sent to large labor camps which hold 800 or even 1,000 inmates, situated near German Army units. They will no longer be able to return from there to the Ghetto.

Near the hospital, I hear the voice of an old Jew: "The Days of Awe[1] are coming upon us soon. We are on the eve of the New Year, the third Jewish New Year in the Ghetto. And the end is nowhere in sight. Will we have the strength to bear all this? Will they not put an end to our lives? Only a miracle can save us."

I reached the Ghetto hospital. It is a new two-story building, standing on the corner of a side street. Its wide windows and high gray-painted walls look on the Ghetto from three sides. The Ghetto fence, running along a narrow, sand-paved alley, forms a demarcation line between freedom and confinement.

Directly across from the large hospital building stands a smaller structure built in the same style and appearance; the same color, windows, and roof. The large building "gave birth" to the smaller one and they have remained linked to each other ever since. When the small building looks down on the old and squalid Ghetto houses, its heart fills up with pride. Human figures enveloped in white gowns keep moving from the large to the small building—to the kitchen, the laundry—and back. From a distance, one can sometimes see a white spot moving within a small space—to and fro.

In the courtyard, between the two buildings, there is a deep well. From here, water is drawn for the use of the hospital. For many months, buckets were used to draw up the water, which was then carried by hand to the hospital, until

Jewish skilled workers came and put an end to this laborious procedure. They installed a central water system by lowering pipes into the well. Now the water flows incessantly to the hospital in the large building, as well as to the kitchen and the laundry in the small building.

Like every other building in the Ghetto, the hospital building has its own history. Not long ago, a structure was put up to house the Ghetto elementary school. Soon it became a shelter for the homeless in the Ghetto, called the Reservat. After the "actions" during which scores of people were sent to places from which they will never return, the old hospital, the children's home, and the home for the elderly were destroyed. The large building was then turned into a hospital.

Like all other buildings in the Ghetto, the hospital is only half-lit. I climbed the unlit stairs cautiously, found the door, and entered.

In this hospital, the famous Professor Bieliatzkin is being treated for severe depression. One could count the Jewish professors in the prewar Lithuanian universities on the fingers of one hand. They were not allowed to keep their jobs for long, however, and Professor Bieliatzkin was the last of them. He was a brilliant, sharp, and erudite lawyer. He wrote several books on law and jurisprudence, and was one of the most prominent members of the legal profession in Lithuania. He was also very popular among the Lithuanian intelligentsia, and had befriended several heads of state. Now everyone has forgotten him or, at most, remembers him with an insincere sigh.

Professor Bieliatzkin lives alone in the Ghetto. One of his two sons was among the first 500 Jews murdered in the Ghetto. Two years of life in the Ghetto have taken their toll—both physical and mental—on the elderly professor. His strength has waned; now he is crushed and exhausted. For many months he has been prey to sad thoughts. His friends' efforts to cheer him up have proved futile. He gave himself up to depression and is now in bed in the hospital—in the clandestine psychiatric ward, which is located, not in the hospital building, but in Slobodka; the Germans do not know of it.

Professor Bieliatzkin is my admired teacher and patron. He is also a great friend of mine. My apprenticeship under his tutelage not only enriched my knowledge of the law but bound me to him with ties of spiritual affinity and friendship. I did my best, together with Dr. Elkes, Dr. Berman, and other members of our former Zionist student fraternity, to help him. When no recourse was left, with a heavy heart it was decided to admit him to this ward. For most of the time he is restless, even cantankerous; he speaks a great deal about putting an end to his life, and about the ignominy of existence.[2]

The other day Professor Bieliatzkin invited me to visit him. Today I came to see him. This isolated ward is situated in a small old house in the old Slobodka quarter. The house stands in a narrow alley, its walls crooked, its windows narrow, and its roof humped. One can enter it only from the courtyard. From the outside, it is impossible to tell that mentally ill patients are hospitalized here in complete isolation. Bars are made out of children's bed-frames, fixed to the walls behind the low windows; they do not attract any unwelcome attention. In this part of the Ghetto, people are used to this kind of "decoration."

In the kitchen I came across Gershonovitz.[3] We talked briefly about the good old days and then got down to business. "I must ask him whether he wishes to see you," said Gershonovitz. "But he invited me to come over for a talk," I said. "Well, the invitation was issued several days ago. Today things could be different," Gershonovitz explained.

He entered Professor Bieliatzkin's tiny ward and returned shortly afterward, telling me that I could go in. He led me to a door. Through the peephole I saw a strange scene: a small low room, its walls painted white. A half-naked old man, his hair all white, was lying on an iron bed next to a wall. Unshaven, his face and forehead furrowed with wrinkles, his protruding eyes looking on with concentration. Except for a ramshackle chair standing next to the bed, there was no furniture in the room. This was not the renowned Professor Bieliatzkin, but his shadow, a petulant creature. I closed my eyes in order to contain the overpowering emotions churning in my breast.

Gershonovitz opened the door and I entered the room. I walked up to the bed and extended my greetings to him in a loud voice: "Good morning, Professor! How are you? How do you feel?" Quickly he turned over to face me. He seemed to be about to cry. He extended his hand to me. Our meeting turned out to be tearfully moving.

Professor Bieliatzkin: "Oh, my Golubtchik, don't ask me how I feel. My life is expendable. I suffer. Save me. I am doomed to endless torments."

I tried to interject: "Professor, you are not in a good mood today. Every patient harbors pessimistic thoughts. You'll get better soon." His face assumed a stern expression and the look in his eyes grew even more penetrating.

Professor Bieliatzkin: "Oh, please, don't talk like this. It is not life I need, but its opposite. I will not get well; I cannot get well. Nor do I want to. My dear Golub: please, save me! Who needs me now? I am lonely and ill. Let them finish me off. The doctors keep saying that I will get well. This is their job, to say things like that. They are professionals. You are the only person able to put an end to my misery. Do it."

The old professor cried like a little child. Then he got angry again. I tried to calm him by saying that the bloody war would be over pretty soon. His eldest and beloved son Fedja would return home.[4] We will resume work together again. Professor Bieliatzkin: "Why do you do this to me? Why all this talk? This is not what I asked you to come here for."

The apple I had brought him (I had gone especially to the city and smuggled it back into the Ghetto) was hard for him to chew. I cut it into small pieces with my penknife. He snatched the pieces from my hand and swallowed them ravenously. As he was eating, he kept saying: "Don't give it to me. It's pointless."

He begged me to persuade the doctors to put an end to his life. He brought up various legal precedents which allegedly justified my doing so. No one will suffer as a result. No one will be held responsible for his death. He will take care of all the legal aspects. He will take upon himself all the responsibility. He asks me to do just one thing: to give him an injection or to administer a drug which will put an end to his sufferings.

I sat with him for about half an hour. He was adamant in insisting on getting a clear answer from me, but I resisted his pleas with all my strength. Then he tried to wrest from me a promise to do as he had asked. He knows, he said, what he wants.

Professor Bieliatzkin: "I suffer because I understand everything. I know the nature of my illness. I beg you: put an end to my sufferings."

I told him: "From the way you analyze things, I have no doubt that you'll recover soon. The doctors are of the same opinion." But he refused to yield.

Professor Bieliatzkin: "When you choke, you want to open a window, whereas I've been through this agony for a whole month now. This is going to last forever. No, Golub, no, my life is over."

After I left the white-painted room with its stifling atmosphere, the tragic figure of the elderly professor continued to appear before my eyes. For a long time afterward I was haunted by his thoughts, by his angry look, by the hurried way he was swallowing pieces of the apple I gave him, by his wrinkled face. I simply could not shake off the sad impression left on me by the old Professor Bieliatzkin.

There had not been any cases of mental illness in the Ghetto in the past for quite some time. Recently, however, according to the hospital management, the number of mentally ill Ghetto inmates has grown. People cannot withstand the pressure of events, of edicts, and of ominous rumors about the fate of the Ghetto.

After six days of unceasing agony, my friend from school days, Dr. Avraham Bruker,[5] died today in the Ghetto hospital. Large crowds turned up for his funeral.

1. The Days of Awe are between the Jewish New Year and the Day of Atonement; they are the ten days during which a Jew takes stock of his life and deeds.

2. Professor Simon Bieliatzkin was pessimistic not only about the fate of the Jews of the Ghetto but about the fate of those few Jews who would survive the war. There were many Jews in the Ghetto who believed, as Avraham Tory later recalled, that every Jew who survived would be feted throughout the world. In contrast to this view, Professor Bieliatzkin thought that the world would treat Jewish survivors with the same indifference it had shown toward the Jews

during the war. Shortly before the Ghetto was established in August 1941, Bieliatzkin had been offered a safe hideaway in Kovno by the former Lithuanian minister of justice, but he had refused it. He was killed in the "children's action" of March 27, 1944.

3. Nahum Gershonovitz, a former Maccabi activist, was superintendent of the isolation ward.

4. Professor Bieliatzkin's son Fedja had left Kovno before the war to study the herring industry in Iceland, hoping in due course to turn Lithuania into a center of salt herring production. After the war he remained in Iceland, where he died in 1984. Professor Bieliatzkin's younger son, Leon, had been killed in the "action" against the intellectuals on August 18, 1941.

5. Dr. Avraham Bruker had been a classmate of Avraham Tory's at the Hebrew high school in Marijampolé. A physician, he was sent by the Germans to work at the airport; later the Council succeeded in transferring him to the Ghetto hospital.

SEPTEMBER 28, 1943

The new authority in the Ghetto now is Captain Goecke. Since last Monday he has been coming to the Ghetto every day, even twice a day. His temporary headquarters are located at the German labor office.

Goecke's initial plan was to break up the Ghetto, dispersing those Ghetto residents who could still be exploited for their work among seven or eight labor camps.

Children and old people were to be left in the Ghetto, their fate undetermined. This plan was opposed by various economic and military bodies, including the city governor and the governor-general, as well as by factories and other enterprises which used Jewish labor to manufacture most of their products. As a result of this opposition, Goecke's plan was modified.

According to the new plan, the small labor brigades will gradually be broken up and joined to larger units. People will leave for work escorted by policemen from the Ghetto. They will return to the Ghetto at the end of the working day, marching in close formation. As a result, the Jews will disappear from the city streets, since they will no longer go to work before noon as part of small labor brigades. Thus they will not fill up the city streets; the feelings of the Aryan city residents will no longer be offended.

The large work-squads will march through side alleys in the more remote quarters of the city. They will be working in isolated camps where no one will be able to see them. As soon as the construction of huts is completed, the various necessary arrangements worked out, barbed-wire fences set up, and the guarding of the camps organized, the Jewish workers will be transferred to permanent living quarters in the camps. All the necessary preparations have already begun.

Goecke is a very energetic man with considerable experience in setting up military-style labor camps. He never used the word "Ghetto"; for him it is always a camp. He is a man of deeds. He gets an order and then carries it out. "I will not allow myself to be shot on account of your Jews," he replied to the Nazi

Party official who asked that the Jewish workers be allowed to remain in their places of work.

Hermann, who is in charge of the German labor office, gave another reason for Goecke's obstinacy: "He seeks to implement his plan under any conditions in order to get the Iron Cross. He is going to break up the Ghetto into a number of small camps; he will take away all the possessions of the Jews of the Ghetto and send the old people and the children to some unknown destination." Who will feed them for nothing then? Who will look after them? This is not a problem as far as Goecke is concerned. His main concern is that he will be able to report to his superiors in Estonia that he has carried out their orders, that the city of Kovno has been cleared of Jews and that the Ghetto has been broken up.

At first, more than thirty labor brigades were wound up. Since last Monday their workers have been going to work in Sanciai and Aleksotas, together with the military construction brigade. The workers are grumbling. Previously they were able to maintain contact with the city residents, and with former Lithuanian friends and acquaintances who helped them with money and various goods, and with whom they traded their old clothes for food. These small labor brigades were an important source of food for the Ghetto. Now this channel of food supply has been blocked. The "affluent" brigades have all been wound up. The new, larger units work outside the city under strict guard. The work is harder, too.

Goecke could not care less about "poor" or "affluent" labor brigades, about hard or easy work. He has introduced an iron work-discipline into the brigades. For four or five days, the Ghetto has been forced to send 150 workers to work in the brick factory at Palemonas (this in addition to the large brigades working at Sanciai and Aleksotas). The workers were put up there for the night, without any possibility of returning to the Ghetto.

Last night the Jewish police were hard at work all night trying to recruit the needed workers. Several days ago, Goecke ordered nine artisans to be sent to Riga. Four hundred Jews, who were working on the task of laying cable on the German-Lithuanian border, are due to be transferred to an army camp in the vicinity of Marijampolé, while an additional 150 will be sent to Koshedar. This is how Goecke has started implementing his new plan—step by step.

Goecke veils his true intentions by increasing the food rations. Thus, he announced that the food rations previously allotted to Jewish workers fell short of the standard rations, and that he intended to increase them. He gave orders for several trucks loaded with bread, carrots, jam, sugar, etc., to be brought in to the Ghetto. The food ration which he set for one worker, however, is no larger than the previous one. Only in exchange for greater output, he said, will he give the Jews better food. He will give them meat, fats, sugar, and other delicacies.

However, he will make sure that these commodities reach only those for whom they were intended.

Yesterday afternoon, Goecke invited Dr. Elkes for a discussion. It went as follows: "Excuse me, Doctor, for troubling you to come here. One does not trouble people of your age unless the matter is of the utmost importance, so I decided to speak to you personally. As you know, I am an SS man with a narrow outlook, yet hard and unbending as a rock. The Catholic religion tells us not to steal. But for us, this is not enough. We say, do not even touch any property that is not yours. It is sacred. You will find a willing ear in me if you turn to me in any matter. Sometimes I can even turn a blind eye to things. But if anyone should take food that is not intended for him, I will pump a bullet into his head in front of the whole Jewish community; no pleading will help."

"It goes without saying," the chairman of the Council answered, "that the food will reach only those for whom it is intended. We have a special staff for that purpose, and I have full confidence in my people."

"Don't talk to me about confidence, Herr Doctor," Goecke replied, raising his voice. "I have a sharp eye. I was once standing next to a cart while people were unloading sausages. Suddenly I saw one of them slip two sausages into his pockets."

Because food distribution is carried out by the Council's nutrition department, Goecke then called in Rapoport.[1] He repeated to him what he had said to Dr. Elkes and added: "I am capable of being very nasty, when occasion justifies it." Goecke even went on to express "concern" for the Jewish children: "Kindergartens should be set up for them so that their mothers can go out to work," he said, and ordered the council to submit to him a plan for child-care centers for 1,000 children.

Goecke's "concern" for the Jewish children caused the Council great anxiety, due to our tragic experience in the past and the heavy price we paid during the liquidation of the small Ghetto two years ago. We are not at all happy about the idea of concentrating 1,000 children in one place. We do not want to expose our children to the Germans. The Germans cast greedy glances in their direction. But Goecke was adamant.

Yesterday Goecke toured the workshops in the Ghetto. Here, too, he behaved like the master of the house. He inquired at every department as to the source of the raw materials, who had placed the order, where the finished products were being sent, and on whose orders. In the sewing shop he wanted to know for whom the ladies' coats being sewn there were intended. Who had ordered the children's cots that were being produced in the carpentry shop? How were the records of the sewing shop being kept? He kept asking questions like these endlessly.

Goecke was clearly intimating that until his arrival the internal affairs of the workshops had not been conducted properly, that there had been no proper supervision, and that from now on there will be changes in the way the work is done. Miller, who was present during Goecke's visit, was clearly uneasy at his investigations, but kept his mouth shut.

Every day new directives descend on the Ghetto. For example, the way the labor brigades march to work is not to Goecke's liking; the marching columns take up too much room in the street. Henceforth, the brigades must march in rows of five. Each labor brigade must be assigned a different place of exit from the Ghetto. Goecke also wants to know how supplies are distributed to the workers. Slowly, by degrees, he makes incursions everywhere.

Our arrangements in the Ghetto are intricate and complicated. They work, but only just. But if they are examined by someone from the outside—who knows? Here the work-detail quota is not filled according to the regulations; there are too many children and women, or, in places, too many people away on leave, and too many handicapped people. All in all, there are too many people and not enough workers. In Goecke's view, there are too many of us; nor do we produce enough for the Germans.

Several days ago, disturbing rumors reached us about twelve railway cars—packed with Jews—which had been seen passing through Keidan. Scraps of paper were thrown out, on which there were messages that the cars were filled with Jews from the Vilna Ghetto. Rumor has it that these Jews were murdered in the woods near Keidan.

We asked Rabbi Snieg to go to see Bishop Brizgys, and to ask him to try and find out where these miserable Jews in the train had disappeared to. The bishop promised to make enquiries about the matter, through priests in the district who were under his jurisdiction. If something turns up, he will inform us at once.

Today Rabbi Snieg set out once more for the bishop's residence. Each time he goes for a meeting with the bishop, we prepare a list of subjects which we ask him to raise with his host. We did the same thing on this occasion. The rabbi returned with answers to our queries.

What is the current situation in Lithuania? What do the Lithuanians think? What is their assessment of the situation?

It is important for us to know the mood among the Lithuanians and the subjects which currently engage their attention. They are in their own country, a place of their own. In case of a change of government, their influence cannot be underestimated. In any event, they can cause us serious trouble.

Bishop Brizgys complained that, recently, underworld figures have begun operating on Lithuanian soil. They have turned into German hirelings. Those of them who spent time in prison during the Soviet rule of Lithuania are sworn anti-Semites. There is no one to conduct serious negotiations within Lithuania at present. Kubiliunas[2] is not a wise man. Taryba (the Lithuanian council set up under German auspices) remains isolated and wavering. Criminal elements in the country are growing in strength. There is no security—not on the roads, not in the countryside, recently not even in the forest.

At present, a Lithuanian unit to fight criminals is being assembled. It will be commanded by Lithuanian officers. The Germans have promised that men belonging to this unit will be neither mobilized nor sent outside Lithuania. Up to the present, however, they have not been given arms. There is also a suspicion that the Germans may, after all, send this unit to the front.

The mobilization of 30,000 Lithuanian youths into the German Army is not proceeding well, the bishop told Rabbi Snieg. There are many cases of sabotage throughout the country. As reprisals, the SS and the Gestapo have erased whole villages from the face of the earth. Both the countryside and the urban areas remain insecure.

Soviet victories may bring significant changes in the countries occupied by the Germans. The German civilian administration will in all probability be replaced by a military one. If the German Army collapses within a very short time, the Germans will not have time to lay the country waste or seriously to hurt the population. If, on the other hand, the Germans retreat slowly, both the Lithuanians and the Jews will face great danger.

As far as the German treatment of Jews is concerned, the bishop says that there has been some change for the better. It is said that the Germans bring Jews from various countries to Germany to prove that there are still Jews left in those countries, and that the extermination of Jews in the occupied countries was carried out by local elements. In any event, the Germans no longer talk about the mass murder of the Jews. On the contrary, the Germans take pains to emphasize on every occasion that they will not allow the mass killing of Jews. In spite of this, both Lithuanians and Jews still face grave danger.

The bishop believes that the traditional fair treatment accorded to the Jews by the Lithuanians has not changed, especially in the countryside and in the professions. At the same time, however, there are still many opportunists and former convicts who do not conceal their anti-Semitic views.

The bishop also recounted an interesting conversation with General Rastikis,[3] the former chief of staff of the Lithuanian Army. His wife had been deported to Siberia by the Soviets. The general does not regard this as Jewish revenge. He does not swallow the propaganda according to which the Jews were the "real" rulers of the country during the Soviet occupation. At present, the general has distanced himself from any public activity; he has even refused to accept any post offered by the Germans, although he knows that the Germans could exact a heavy price from him for his refusal.

The bishop had also spoken to the general about the Jewish question. Rastikis revealed an interesting detail from the period of Lithuanian independence. It was at the time when Lithuania and Poland had established diplomatic relations, mainly because of the pressure exerted by the Poles. Chorwat, the first Polish ambassador to Kovno, suggested to the Lithuanian foreign minister, Urbsys, that Lithuania endorse the Polish policy of encouraging Jewish emigration from Poland—as well as from neighboring countries—to Palestine or other countries. The Polish government had a clear plan to enable Jews to emigrate from Poland and leave their property behind. For its part, the Polish government, in accordance with an agreement it sought to reach with the British government, was to pay—either to the British government or to other bodies—a certain sum of compensation for the Jewish property left behind. The Jews were to be allowed to take some of their property with them. In this way Poland sought to get rid of its Jewish population.[4]

In order to give this whole matter an international significance, Poland opened negotiations with Romania and with Latvia. These countries agreed to join the anti-Semitic bloc in order to get rid of their Jews. Polish efforts— through the Polish ambassador—to prevail on the Lithuanian government to join the anti-Jewish bloc, constituted the first Polish political initiative in Polish-Lithuanian relations after more than twenty years of lack of diplomatic relations between the two countries.

This subject was raised by Poland once again during the official visit paid by General Rastikis to the prewar commander-in-chief of the Polish Army, General Rydz-Śmigly. As this question was not on the official agenda of the meeting between the two generals, however, it made a very bad impression on the Lithuanian general.

This question was discussed in consultations held by the president of the Lithuanian Republic, Smetona.[5] The president announced at that time that Lithuania pursued an independent policy on various questions; on this question, too, Lithuania would maintain its traditional approach to the Jews. Rastikis had told the Poles that Jews were serving in the Lithuanian Army, and that he, as supreme commander, has no complaints whatsoever against them.

General Rastikis has remained firm in his prewar views of the Jewish question. It is difficult to say, however, how things will look after the war. The bishop is concerned about a future period of anarchy. He added that, personally, he always keeps us in his mind and in his prayers.

---

1. Rapoport, a respected merchant before the war, was not only head of the Council's nutrition department but custodian of the Council's store of materials.
2. General Petras Kubiliunas, a general in the prewar Lithuanian Army, had served since 1941 as a senior advisor to the German civil administration in Lithuania.
3. General Rastikis, at one time chief of staff of the prewar Lithuanian Army, had served as minister of defense in the temporary government established in Lithuania in July 1941.

4. In prewar Poland, out of a total population of just over 30 million, more than 3 million were Jews. From these 3 million came the largest single group of Jews murdered by the Germans between 1939 and 1945; fewer than 500,000 Polish Jews survived the war, most of them having escaped to the Soviet Union in 1939 and 1940.

5. Antanas Smetona had been president of Lithuania from 1926 until June 1940, when he fled during the Soviet annexation of Lithuania. He died in the United States after the war.

SEPTEMBER 30, 1943

Thick dew covered the ground, like a gray blanket, in the early morning of an autumn day. The first rays of the sun, rising far away, reached the earth but failed to penetrate the layer of dew on the ground.

The windows of some of the houses in the neighborhood were lit up by small lights. People were getting up to work. Here and there a Jewish policeman could be seen coming home after a night shift. Some zealous workers, who had gotten up early, could be seen making their way, lonely and absorbed in thought, to the Ghetto gate.

On Sunday, the first day of the Jewish New Year, I went home. Despite the dangers hanging over our heads, a festive atmosphere pervaded the Ghetto yesterday. Today the Jews prayed in a few *minyans*. Many religious houses of study and synagogues have been laid waste. Some of them have been turned into shelters for the homeless, into storage rooms, even into prisons. Provisional houses of prayer have been set up in their place in various public buildings, even in private apartments. They have their own cantors, Scrolls of the Law, prayer shawls, prayer books, and such like.

The Jews pray with great enthusiasm. They remember the holy-day spirit which reigned in Kovno during the High holy days before the war: the joy of a Jewish family after prayer. All this has disappeared as if it had never existed. Only a handful of survivors are left of once-large families. People now go to pray in small groups, to hear "a Jewish word," to heave a sigh, to shed a tear, and to plead with the Almighty to bring us a better year.

With great devotion, the Jews recite the blessing: "Blessed be he who has kept us alive and sustained us in order to reach the present time." Nowadays, this ancient blessing carries a special and tangible significance. The devil has held us in his clutches so many times and yet we have survived. This is why we say "Blessed be he who has kept us alive." This blessing also stirs sad thoughts in us about the loved ones who are not with us today: those who have perished in the Ghetto. It is difficult to decide which is more important: the blessing of "he who has kept us alive," or the memorial prayer for the dead.

According to the custom prevalent among Jewish communities, on the eve of the New Year the senior rabbi or the community leader delivers a sermon on some topical subject to the members of the community. This custom has also been observed in the Ghetto. A young man came in and addressed those at prayer.[1] Someone banged on the table, and the young man began to speak: "Jewish brothers, we are faced with grave danger, the danger of Jewish workers being concentrated in army camps, if we reject the demands of the authorities, if we fail to abide by the work-duty. In recent days many people have been missing from various workplaces. There is a fear that more people will be missing from work this holy New Year. Yet if more people do not turn up for work, this may bring a disaster on individuals and on the whole community. Notwithstanding our wish to celebrate the holy day as we are enjoined to do by our traditions, each one of us is duty bound to go out to work during the holy days, as on any other weekday."

This was an appeal from the Council to the Ghetto inmates.

A ruling issued by the Ghetto rabbis was also read: "The duty of saving lives overrides the Sabbath laws and the festival laws. Every Jew is not only allowed but required to work on the New Year holidays. By so doing, a year of redemption and salvation will come upon us, and upon all Jews. Amen."

Those praying in small groups scattered throughout the Ghetto heard these appeals with sorrow and fear. Again we are faced with peril. Again we are called upon to save ourselves and the whole community. For the last two years we have done everything to save ourselves, and we are still in great danger.

Today, the first day of the New Year, all the Jews who had work-duties were lined up in rows at the Ghetto gate, ready to go to work. Yesterday two Germans of the Waffen SS[2] were appointed to march thousands of Jews to work. These officers came this morning to the Ghetto gate. It was they who lined up the Jewish workers in rows. Like prisoners or slaves, the Jews stand, casting worried glances at the Germans in their gray uniforms—at the SS insignia sewn on their collars and sleeves.

These are our current rulers. It seems that the German civil administration was too lenient with us. The new rulers have reinforced the guards who stand over us and have imposed a much stricter regime. The SS men are military policemen. They are obedient servants of the wrathful authorities. Today, many people showed up for work; but sixty to seventy boys aged between twelve and fifteen were sent back home.

The Council has been in a somewhat more hopeful mood in recent days. But, as it happens, holy days keep bringing unpleasant surprises down on our heads and we therefore watch our step. Last night, in fact, an unpleasant surprise was visited upon us; the police informed us that Stasys Savickas, a watchman at the Ghetto's vegetable gardens, had been shot by a Lithuanian policeman beside the Ghetto fence.

Yesterday another tragic incident occurred: a Lithuanian patrol came upon two Jews walking along the bank of the Vilija river, near the Ghetto border. The Jews were carrying some bundles in their hands. The Lithuanian policemen ordered them to draw near. As the Jews approached, one of the Lithuanian policemen aimed his rifle and shot one of them to death. The name of the murdered Jew was Danishevski.

The man who was murdered on the banks of the Vilija was a native of Oszmiana in the Vilna district. From Oszmiana he had been sent to the Zezmer labor camp. In June he had been transferred to the Kovno Ghetto together with 600 other Jews from Zezmer. Here he worked in the sawmill by the Vilija river, near the Ghetto fence. It appears that at the time of the shooting incident he and his friend were on their way to buy some food. The Lithuanians shot him without giving much thought to the matter.

We spoke to the men of the Ghetto guard and to their commandant. Their verdict was: Jews are forbidden to walk outside the Ghetto perimeter. From the official point of view, the guard is right. But there are different sorts of people: one is incapable of hurting a fly, whereas another is capable of murdering people. The shots along the Ghetto fence do not look like a coincidence, particularly after we read the summary of the police investigation into the murder of Savickas.

Savickas was in charge of guarding the vegetable gardens along the Ghetto fence, not far from the shores of the Vilija river, inside the Ghetto. A Lithuanian policeman patrolled the perimeter fence from outside. When he saw Savickas from a distance, he asked him whether he was bored. Yes indeed, I am bored, replied Savickas. Thereupon the Lithuanian policeman asked him to draw near, so that they could patrol together. This Savickas did. As they started their patrol, his Lithuanian companion shot him.

Fatally wounded, Savickas lay on the ground near the barbed-wire fence on the shores of the Vilija. Jewish policemen hurried to the scene. The Jewish police inspector asked the Lithuanian policeman on the other side of the fence to allow him to rush the wounded man to the Ghetto hospital, as he was bleeding profusely. At first the Lithuanian refused, then changed his mind. The German Ghetto commandant, to whom the Jewish police reported the incident, refused to hear Savickas's version of the shooting. Accompanied by a translator, the commandant came to the hospital with one purpose only: to record the personal data of the victim.

Savickas was a Christian. His father was a Lithuanian diplomat and his country's ambassador in Stockholm and in Riga. His mother was Jewish. On frequent occasions before the war she brought her son to the synagogue. She was a religious woman. Stasys Savickas was a talented and upright young man. He had graduated from Kovno Art School and fallen in love with a Jewish girl. At first he lived in the city and she in the Ghetto. He used to sneak into the labor brigades returning from work to the Ghetto, put the yellow badge on his clothes, and visit his girlfriend in the Ghetto. In similar fashion he would return to the city. Finally he decided to come into the Ghetto in order to be with his beloved. He went through all the traumas and agonies of the Ghetto, but refused to go back to the city. He got a job as a watchman in the Ghetto's vegetable gardens.

About a week ago Savickas was dismissed from his job because of German orders to cut back the staff of all Jewish institutions in the Ghetto. He refused a job which was offered to him in the workshops. Every day last week he came to Goldberg and me, asking to be allowed to keep his job at the vegetable gardens for a few more weeks. Finally we agreed to his request. Last night he died while on duty.

The news of Savickas's death stunned the Council members and the Ghetto residents. Our earlier satisfaction at the positive response to our appeal that workers should show up for work on the New Year suddenly evaporated. New anguish enveloped the Ghetto. Our fears increased when the head of the contingent of the Jewish police in charge of the perimeter fence came to the Council offices. He brought with him detailed accounts of various acts of terror perpetrated by the Lithuanian patrols in recent nights along the perimeter fence. The Lithuanian policemen open fire incessantly, and without any justifiable reason. They force the Jewish policemen patrolling on the ghetto side of the perimeter fence to kneel before them and to give them valuables and money. They also fire at the rooftops of the Jewish houses near the Ghetto fence. Should these criminal acts continue, the Jewish policemen will be unable to discharge their duties along the fence. It is hard to believe that the Lithuanian policemen act on their own initiative. There must be some tacit consent coming from the top, and here the danger lies.

The head of the labor camp at Palemonas, to which 150 Jews were sent only a few days ago, arrived in the Ghetto. He brought the sad story of a young Jewess who was shot to death there. She tried to bribe a Ukrainian policeman to allow her to go to a nearby Lithuanian house to purchase food. Someone heard about her request to the Ukrainian and informed the head of the camp. At about the same time, Captain Goecke arrived at Palemonas in his car. When he learned what had occurred, he ordered the two of them—the Jewish woman and the Ukrainian policeman—to be shot. The Ukrainian begged for his life. Goecke pardoned him, on condition that he kill the Jewess with his own hands. "It is forbidden to maintain any contact with the Jews," Goecke said.

Having unsuccessfully tried to evade this devilish assignment, the Ukrainian finally accepted. The Jewish woman begged for her life, but Goecke spurned her.

For the first time, the mask has dropped from Goecke's face. He is just a cold-blooded murderer. In his conversations with Dr. Elkes and with Rabinovitz he had said that he could be "nasty." Now we know just how nasty Goecke can be.

On his return from Palemonas, Goecke summoned the commander of the Jewish police in the Ghetto and, after hearing a report about the excesses along the Ghetto fence on the part of the Lithuanian policemen, declared that he would not allow any untoward conduct on the part of anyone. He would talk to Captain Binger, the commander of the Lithuanian police in Kovno, and Binger would call the Lithuanian policemen to order. Should they attempt to oppose him, he would show them who Goecke is. The Jewish police are to continue their guard duties along the fence inside the Ghetto. He, Goecke, will take them under his protection, like all other policemen.

But what value can be attached to such a pronouncement, in view of Goecke's own heinous act of murder in the Palemonas camp? As for the Lithuanian policemen, true, there are many savages among them, but so far they had been held more or less in check. Now, however, that a new ruler of the Ghetto—Goecke—has arrived, they have lost all control and given free rein to their hatred of the Jews. We have become fair game again.

Goecke's reassuring pronouncement contrasts sharply with the events taking place in his "kingdom." Yesterday he issued an order that no one was to leave or enter the Ghetto without a written permit from himself. Neither the German civil administration in town, nor the German labor office in the Ghetto—not even the Gestapo—could now issue permits for individual Jews to leave the Ghetto for the city, as had been customary hitherto. Goecke alone had the authority to allow this.

Goecke's new order applied also to the workers in the large workshops in the Ghetto. None of them could go out to the city and no one from the city could come to them without his permission. The Ghetto was, therefore, hermetically sealed.

In the evening Segalson arrived, bringing fresh news. Hermann, the German director of the labor office, had revealed to him, in strictest confidence, that Goecke must not be believed. Goecke is bent on deceiving him, Hermann, too. His lips are not where his mind is. The Ghetto has entered its decisive stage; it will be broken up. This means that the younger and healthy residents will be taken away to concentration camps. The large workshops will be turned into military camps. The workshop workers will be housed in special blocks surrounded by barbed wire. The Council and its agencies will be disbanded. As for the fate of the remaining ghetto residents—Hermann is very pessimistic. He is not going to be present in the Ghetto on that day. He asked Segalson whether he had any children. When Segalson replied that he had a son aged ten, Hermann said that it would be better if the boy was twelve. Children twelve years and older will not be incarcerated in the camps. All this is going to happen within ten to fourteen days. At the conclusion of his revelations, Hermann made Segalson swear to keep them secret.[3]

Segalson revealed this information to the Council. He is beside himself with fear. What is going to happen? We are approaching the last stage. It seems that Goecke is going to exterminate us. He is also going to take over the workshops. Not for nothing did he order us to submit a plan for kindergartens to accommodate 1,000 children. Who knows what he plans for those children?

A Jewish inmate of the Zezmer labor camp arrived in the Ghetto. He passed on to us regards from Vilna: "When our camp learned that Jews are again being taken out from the Vilna Ghetto," he said, "we dispatched one of our people to Miligan, where they maintain direct contact with Vilna. It turned out that two of the Jews working at Miligan had been to Vilna two days earlier, together with the German head of the Miligan camp, in order to take back various materials. The gate of the Vilna Ghetto had been open. No policemen guarded it. They entered the Ghetto, but did not see anyone in the streets. The doors of the houses were ajar. It is said that the Jews were taken out of the Vilna Ghetto and transported to an unknown destination. Only two Jewish labor brigades were left: at the military transport depot and at the fur factory."

This information was confirmed by a number of notes which were brought by a labor brigade leader from Keidan. These notes—mere scraps of paper—had been thrown out of sealed railway cars at Keidan railway station. Jewish workers and Lithuanian peasants picked them up and brought them to us. On these papers was written that the Vilna Ghetto had been liquidated. Its residents had been sorted into age categories and dispersed among various locations. On September 23 and 24, young people—men and women—were loaded on to separate freight cars. The cars were then locked. No one knows their destination. Some say they were transported to work. The scraps of paper picked up at Keidan seemed like cries of S.O.S. thrown from a sinking ship.

The Jew from Zezmer confirmed the information on these scraps of paper. He also added that the looting of abandoned Jewish houses in the Vilna Ghetto had been going on for a week. "Memento"—this is how one could sum up the news reaching us from the abandoned Vilna Ghetto.

A new custom has been introduced in the minyan groups in the Kovno Ghetto: in order to enable all the Jews in the labor brigades to hear the blowing of the Ram's Horn on the New Year, the Ram's Horn will be blown twice during the two days of the festival: at six o'clock in the morning—before the workers leave for work—and again at six o'clock in the evening, after their return. The rabbis allowed this arrangement of blowing the Ram's Horn without prayer.

During these two days of the festival, the sounds of murder and destruction were heard in the Ghetto, intermingling with the sounds of the Ram's Horn.

These sounds herald the era of the new ruler, who will wage war on the Ram's Horn and usher in an era of death and destruction.

The New Year has opened with Job's tidings. The decisive battle has begun which, sooner or later, will bring the tidings of redemption.

1. The young man was Avraham Golub (Tory).
2. The Waffen SS was the military arm of the SS. Although Hitler accepted that the Wehrmacht, the traditional German Army, was indispensable, he was dubious about the loyalty of its leaders, and preferred to place his trust in the military arm of the SS, which, by the end of the war, numbered nearly a million men (in thirty-nine divisions). The Waffen SS were used both as front-line fighters and in operations against civilians. In the latter operations they were noted for their ruthlessness. At the Nuremberg Trials in 1946, both the SS and the Waffen SS were indicted as criminal organizations.
3. Both Segalson and his son survived the war; Moshe Segalson later lived in Israel, where he spent many years as head of administration of the Beilinson Hospital at Petah Tikvah.

OCTOBER 9, 1943

Since the liquidation of the Vilna Ghetto, breathing has become difficult here. Images of the decline and the destruction of the Vilna Ghetto keep appearing before our eyes. Reliable sources have revealed to us the circumstances of the liquidation. It turns out that after two weeks of wandering in the Vilna area, in the forests, and in the camps of the Vilna district, a young, emaciated young man, aged about thirty, has returned here to Kovno alive and unharmed.

I knew this young man some years ago, when he was a writer, and an employee of the Lovers of Knowledge Library.[1] We used to meet in the apartment of a common acquaintance of ours, Mrs. Sonia Bas. At that time, I did not notice anything particular about him. But during the Soviet occupation of Lithuania he emerged to prominence and climbed to a high position under the new social conditions which came into being at that time.

In the Ghetto I had run into this young man by chance on several occasions. His face told of suffering, of a life of poverty and squalor. For several months after his appearance in the Ghetto he did not dare to show his face on the street. He even refrained from meeting his friends from old times.

When I saw him next in the Ghetto, about a year ago, I asked him the usual questions one asks people whom one sees for the first time in the Ghetto: "How are you? What do you do? Who's been left of your family?" etc. It turned out that he was working in one of the labor brigades. The work was strenuous, but he had become used to it. He knew the brigade leader by then, and had acquired a sense of security in his surroundings. The food rations were not particularly good, but he made do with them. "One goes hungry on occasion," he said, "but I do not complain. The main thing is to survive."

We recalled Mrs. Bas, our common acquaintance from bygone times. She had been killed a while before in the Ghetto. She used to spend some time in the city, pretending to be a Christian, until her Jewishness was discovered and she was brought to the Ghetto. Here she learned that her parents, Grudnikov by name, lived in the Ghetto, and that her only son, aged six, was also here. She was executed on charges of concealing her Jewishness and posing as an Aryan. This was our common friend, Sonia Bas, who after her death was thrown into the pit in the Ninth Fort.

When we met for the second time, I invited the young man to join me at a gathering of a small group of devotees of literature which had been set up by a few friends. I wanted to know whether he still was writing. My offer was accepted with eagerness. "But this must be kept secret; I will not speak at the gathering."

Since then we had met quite often in the narrow circle of six to eight friends. One of them would read an essay or a chapter from a book; another would read a short story or an essay on a literary subject. After the reading we would hold a discussion. These meetings cemented our friendship.

The young man's name was Chaim Yellin.[2] When he failed to show up at one of those gatherings one day, his brother Meir[3] told us that his engagements prevented him from coming. Later I learned that he had left the Ghetto on an important and dangerous assignment.

Two weeks passed and Chaim did not return. We started worrying about his fate. Then my friend Dr. Volsonok,[4] who was also a participant in our literary gatherings, told me that Chaim would attend the next meeting; he had arrived in the Ghetto through the main gate two hours ago, he said. I was very glad to hear it. But, as it happened, the next gathering took place without him. His brother informed me that Chaim was still very tired, and also busy.

A few days later, Chaim and his brother came to visit me. He had not changed much, but his face radiated self-satisfaction; a smile played on his lips and his eyes sparkled. It turned out that he had passed the battle test successfully. Here in the Ghetto, according to him, everything is a trifle—the plans to concentrate the Jewish workers in army camps, the workshops where many Ghetto residents search for shelter, the new ruler in the person of Goecke. There is nothing new in the Ghetto and its institutions: there are nothing but favoritism and packets of food. The right place is there, in the woods. True, it is dangerous, but the chances of staying alive there are also greater. Here in the Ghetto the end is clear—death and destruction.

Three of us—Chaim, his brother Meir, and me—sat in my room while Chaim told his story. At times, the events he recounted resembled those in the *A Thousand and One Arabian Nights:* endless forests and desolate roads; robbers, shootings, and the grip of mortal fear; a camp in the middle of a deep swamp somewhere in the heart of the forest; ambushes; etc.

The story ran as follows: he had set out from the Ghetto for the city with a permit issued by the Council, ostensibly to take care of some important business on behalf of the Council. At a certain place where a labor brigade was at work, a truck—loaded with arms and headed for Vilna—was waiting for him. The truck belonged to the German police. It was taking arms from Kovno to Minsk, via Vilna. In exchange for money, the driver had agreed to take him as a helper, to unload the truck.

Chaim took off his yellow badge so that he would not be recognizable as a Jew. The truck was escorted by a car driven by a German police officer. Before the departure of the truck, the officer asked the driver about Chaim—who was he and what was his job? The officer wanted to see his papers. Chaim pretended that he did not understand the order. The driver then whispered a "secret" in the officer's ear: the mother of the worker lived in Vilna and he wanted to bring her to the Kovno Ghetto. The officer accepted the explanation.

At Vilkomir the officer again asked to see Chaim's papers; he intended to take him to a police station. The driver appeased him with a bottle of vodka. They drove on.

Thus Chaim reached Vilna in peace. There he learned that, on the previous day, Gens had been murdered. On reaching the city of Vilna, Chaim found that the Ghetto was surrounded. It was impossible to get in. He therefore went instead to see a woman friend. There he also met with other friends and acquaintances, who told him of the recent events in the Vilna Ghetto, culminating in the murder of Gens.

It turned out that many Jews were hiding in cellars, in caverns under the streets, in sewers, and in underground passages which connected the Ghetto with the city. The Ghetto abounded with weapons. The youth of various Jewish political parties were organized and armed. They were prepared to put up armed resistance when ordered to do so.

When the seizure of Ghetto inmates for work in Estonia began, the Ghetto was in uproar. The Jewish police, which carried out the first phase of the deportation, took people out of their underground hideouts and into the streets. Many people put up a strong resistance; gunfire was exchanged. In the second phase of the deportation, German policemen took part in the seizing of the Jews; they too encountered strong resistance. During the third phase, the underground hideouts were blown up with mines.

In some houses, members of the Zionist Revisionists barricaded themselves in and refused to let anyone enter. They had previously reached an agreement with Gens, according to which Gens would not lead the assault on their particular houses. Gens kept his part of the agreement. Moreover, when people started to flee to the forest in an organized fashion, Gens helped them. He let them leave the Ghetto through his own private alleyway. He had always kept the key to it in his pocket.

Since the Ponar massacre, Gens had changed considerably. His faith in German rule had been shaken. As a result, he had changed his regime in the Ghetto. He would linger near his private alleyway, which led from the Ghetto to the city, and let groups of Jews use it to escape to the forest. Thanks to Gens, the underground leader Glazman and 200 young Jews were able to escape. Many others also escaped; altogether 500 Jews reached the forest.

It is true that a group of forty Jews who had left the Ghetto in this way were denounced to the Gestapo. This was done by Desler and Lev, however; they not only informed the Gestapo about the escape, but also pointed out the direction the escapees had gone. This group was then surrounded by the Germans, and a battle ensued. Three of the escapees were killed. Ten escaped. In the clothes of those killed, the Gestapo found a list of the forty names of those who had made the escape attempt. Their families, as well as the labor brigade leaders where they had worked, were subsequently executed.

Gens carried on, until he himself became a victim, with the help of Desler and Lev. People in Vilna say that he died a hero's death. Others maintain that Gens refused to hand over to the Germans a certain number of Jews they had demanded. Allegedly, a sharp argument developed between Gens and the head of the Vilna Gestapo in the latter's room. The conversation was stormy and ended with a revolver shot. The head of the Gestapo killed Gens in his office. On the following day the family of Gens's brother was executed.

Desler was then appointed the new ruler of the Ghetto. Six days later he and Lev escaped from the Ghetto taking with them money and gold belonging to the Jewish community of the ghetto. Power in the Ghetto was transferred to the hands of Beniakonski. Several days later the Ghetto was liquidated.

According to Chaim Yellin, and to the information supplied to me by Lithuanian sources, the liquidation of the Vilna ghetto was carried out in great haste, owing to the rapid advance of the Red Army. The Germans have already begun evacuating Minsk, and a number of German military units passed through Vilna on their way from the front. Under such conditions, the continuing existence of the Ghetto, which at that time resembled a box of explosives, became intolerable for the Germans.

Hundreds of Jews found temporary shelter in the houses of Poles in Vilna itself and its vicinity. In some cases, the Jews had to pay for such shelter. There was even a fixed price for shelter until the end of the war: 250 gold rubles per person. Rich Jews availed themselves of this opportunity. But most Jews took to the forests, where they organized themselves in partisan units under the command of a local partisan command headquarters.

Chaim Yellin also told us how he and his girlfriend, for whose sake he had arrived in Vilna, together with six other people, escaped from Vilna to the forest. They traveled by night. The bridges were unpassable. Every bridge was guarded, and those asking to pass over it were required to show their papers. The guards were looking for deserters from work camps, army deserters, and people with no legal occupation, all of whom filled the roads leading from the cities to the countryside. Chaim's group was escorted by a guide who led them by side paths, through fields and marshland. After a night-long walk, they reached a forest fifty kilometers from Vilna.

There was no paved road in the forest. A good guide, however, can lead the escapees through byways to an appointed destination.

In the forest they entered a new world. Even people whom they had known earlier assumed a different appearance in the forest camp. There, even one's speech was different, the way one walked was different, one's thoughts were different. In the forest camp, Chaim met many friends among people who had escaped earlier from the Vilna Ghetto and from the labor camps in the Vilna district. These would laugh at the conduct of the newcomers to the forest. The forest veterans are "wolves" with combat experience. They are not afraid of danger. Some of them were commanders of units of fighters.

There are 400 Jews from Vilna in the forest. Glazman, together with 200 Jews, crossed into White Russia, where partisans rule over wide expanses of territory. The front line is nearer there, too. They did not want to have so many Jews close to Vilna. It is more dangerous there.

From time to time the Germans raid the forests. Not far away, 200 German soldiers and SS men were poised to surround the forest and destroy the camps of the Jewish refugees. When the partisans learned of this plan, they informed the Soviet partisan high command (they have radio sets at their disposal). Soon after, iron eagles swooped from the sky and drove the German enemy out of the forest. Now the refugee camps are peaceful. There have been scarcely any casualties recently.

The forest camp of the Vilna Jews has not yet been set up properly. They still lack deep pits, dug in the ground and covered with logs and soil. Inside such pits, people can be kept warm and the rain does not penetrate. There one can rest after a night of guard duty. The veteran camp commander—a man with nerves of steel, a penetrating gaze, a beard, and a moustache like that of a veteran Russian officer—has been in the forest for several years. He promised to find better accommodation for the Jewish refugees from Vilna.

The Vilna forest camp also shelters old women and small children, who pose a risk for the camp to some extent. The young people in the camp must provide food not just for themselves but for these women and children as well. This is the only camp in the forest with old women and children in it. In the forest, food supply is no easy matter. The nearest villages or townlets are twenty to thirty kilometers away. In addition, leaving the forest may have dangerous consequences. People going to any village outside the forest must take arms with them. Peasants in the villages are very much afraid of armed men. There is no other way, however, of getting any food from them; they do not even take money.

Because of the many wanderings necessary to survive in the forest, clothes are worn out quickly. When a sufficient quantity of supplies—purchased in a village—has accumulated, the fighters borrow a horse from a peasant, load it with the supplies, and lead it to the camp in the forest. When the horse has completed its "mission," the partisans take it to the edge of the wood and "order" it to return to its master. Needless to say, the horse does not always find the way. Sometimes another peasant takes such a horse to his stable. On occasion one can see peasants roaming the woods in search of their horses.

Apart from food, the partisans must supply themselves with oil, candles, soap, sugar, and such like. To do this, they leave the forest at night and get these products in the nearest village or townlet.

Once, a veteran forest camp leader went to a town at night to buy oil or candles, but, as it happened, these two products were simply not available on the shelves in the stores. What did the man do? He entered a church and took a large, fat candle from the altar. "The saints in the church will not suffer if the candle is missing," said the camp leader. "Tomorrow the faithful will bring another candle. We in the forest need this candle more than the church does." And so he took it away.

According to Chaim, the food in the forest is not bad. He even put on weight during his sojourn there. To prove it, he asks us to look at his face and his thick moustache. At first, he says, he did not feel well in the camp. The damp soil, sleeping under the open sky, no change of clothing for days on end, sores on hands and legs due to long marches, the fear and terror of life in the forest. The forest camp badly needs a doctor.

In other forest camps the situation is better. Airplanes drop medicine, fruit, canned food, and ammunition. They also parachute Red Army instructors. In the camps close to the front, airplanes land on the ground and unload various products—as well as Communist commissars and military instructors—and take off with wounded and sick partisans. One such airplane took a pregnant woman—who was about to give birth in a nearby forest camp—to a maternity ward in a hospital in Moscow.

The forest camp of the Jewish refugees from Vilna has not yet been recognized by the central bodies of Soviet partisans. To achieve this, the camp must prove itself for an extended period of time by its ability and willingness to fight the enemy. This particular forest camp is, for the time being, merely a candidate to join the family of partisan camps in the forest.

There are forest camps of Lithuanians and Russians. Each nation has a camp of its own. Each camp has its commander, its person in charge of guard duties, its liaison officer, etc. The fighters are divided into a number of units—for ambushes, for attacks, and for political activity. Each camp forms a separate fighting unit with its own theater of operations and its own special tasks. There are no idlers in the camps. Each fighter is assigned a job, according to his talents and abilities.

In one camp, Chaim Yellin heard Hebrew songs—the songs of the Land of Israel. The young people there are in a very good mood. If not now—when? How many tragedies and human ordeals are reflected in these songs, sung in this partisan camp under the indirect auspices of the Red Army?

The partisan camps make a contribution—each according to its strength—to the war against the Nazi enemy. The people in these camps are certain that not fighting means death. Only by fighting has one a chance to survive, or at least to die a hero's death.

From information exchanged among Jewish partisans, Chaim has learned that my brother-in-law, Benjamin Romanovski, is alive. This gave me the hope of seeing him sometime, together with his wife—my oldest sister, Batia—and their children.

On his way back to Kovno, Chaim traveled by foot. He joined a group of fighters who carried out operations in enemy territory: they mined railway lines, blew up a post office and German headquarters in Varenai, and carried out many other operations. Blowing up railway lines or killing a German sentry is an everyday occurrence. The partisans use Soviet-made guns, equipped with silencers. With such a gun, one can kill a German sentry here and there and keep on marching, without drawing attention to oneself.

Chaim's journey to the Kovno Ghetto took him through narrow byways, across fields, and through forests. Halfway to Kovno, he parted from the group of fighters. From this point on he walked around the villages, and even refrained from entering peasant cottages to ask for a glass of water. He preferred to quench his thirst from streams running through the fields. When they parted, the fighters filled his pockets with sugar. He did not understand the meaning of this at first; for what would he need such a large quantity of sugar? Would it not be better to take with him substantial amounts of bread and meat? As he trudged along, however, he understood that sugar suppresses hunger. It does increase one's thirst, but there was a lot of water to be had in the fields.

On his way, Chaim came across a man in uniform. Chaim was very frightened. What saved him was a badge he had, belonging to a railroad worker. He put this badge on his sleeve. The uniformed man looked at him and the badge, and went on his way.

After a march lasting three days and nights, Chaim reached Kovno. One thought had preoccupied him throughout: how would he get back to the Ghetto to tell his friends and acquaintances all that he had seen and heard in the forest camps of partisans fighting the enemy, to convey greetings to the prisoners of the Ghetto from those who had chosen a new life, a new way of self-preservation—by running away from slavery and from the German whip. His soul went out to his relatives and friends—until he reached the Ghetto alive and unharmed. He had completed his assignment. He had made contact with the Jews of Kovno.

1. A predominantly Yiddish library which had been established between the wars in both Kovno and Vilna.
2. Chaim Yellin, leader of the partisan movement in the Ghetto, a Communist, and a Yiddish writer; he brought together the Zionist and Communist factions of the underground. Later he organized a move from the Ghetto to the forests. He was caught by the Gestapo, and died—possibly by suicide.
3. Meir Yellin survived the war; today he lives in Tel Aviv, where he is (in 1988) a member of the board of the Association of Lithuanian Jews in Israel.
4. Dr. Rudolf Volsonok, who had come to Kovno from Memel before the war, was a gifted journalist, a member of the Jewish State Party in prewar Lithuania. In the Ghetto, he became one of the leaders of the Communist underground. He also gave a survey every two weeks, at the clandestine cultural circle in Pnina Sheinzon's room, on the war situation. Avraham Tory later recalled: "He was a genius at foreseeing what was happening on the war fronts." He survived the war, and died in 1946.

OCTOBER 13, 1943

Each morning, the square near the Ghetto gate was turned into a bustling and congested slave market. Confusion and turmoil pervaded the place, as thousands of Ghetto inmates ran feverishly to and fro, looking for a better labor brigade, a place of work where supplies for home could be purchased, or where work was not too hard. They also tried to avoid those labor brigades which would be going to the airfield or to work for Grün-Bielfinger or the Waffen SS. In such places, work is hard; on occasion one could be beaten up.

The Jewish police and the officials at the Ghetto labor office could barely discharge their duties in this confusion. The wish to join a better labor brigade was stronger than any efforts the Jewish police could make. Even the blows which rained down from the truncheons of the German policemen failed to produce the desired effect. Buses, trucks, and horse-drawn carts waited on the other side of the fence to take the workers to various places of work. Police sergeants confirmed with their signature that the required number of workers to a labor brigade had been reached.

This morning this arrangement came to an end. Acting on Goecke's order, two SS men appeared in the square in front of the Ghetto gate and began implementing a new arrangement. Each Jewish worker would be assigned permanently to a labor brigade and each labor brigade would be given its own specially designated place in the square. The brigades would then march from their designated places in the square to their workplaces. A special badge was affixed to the shirtsleeve of each worker from the large brigades, so as to prevent them from joining other labor brigades, and also to facilitate the quick detection of those who abandoned their designated brigades. In this fashion the congestion, the searches for a better brigade, and the turmoil at the Ghetto gate which had recurred every morning were brought to an end.

Goecke, the new Ghetto ruler, has abolished scores of labor brigades, particularly the good ones, by incorporating their workers into the large brigades working in army camps; these brigades have been set up as an intermediate stage in the plan to concentrate the Jewish workers in the army camps.

The Jewish workers do not like these new arrangements at all. They regard them as a sign of the deterioration of their situation. With knapsacks on their backs, people move like shadows toward the square at the Ghetto gate. The name of each brigade can be seen on a plank at the top of a wooden pole in a fixed place in the square. There the workers wait for the signal to leave for work. This is why they look so terrified and concerned.

It is a long way to Sanciai, Aleksotas, and Petrasun. The work there is hard. Two barbed-wire fences are in the process of being erected around the huts designated for workers' dwellings. These fences are two meters apart. On the other side of them, watchtowers, like those in prisons, are being constructed, so that armed guards can watch over the inmates. The entire area bristles with army camps containing German and Ukrainian soldiers who have recently been pressed into service with the German Army.

Goecke is a taciturn man. He issues orders quietly and serenely, dispatches people to work in remote places. If things do not run as he wishes, he can be—as he once said—"nasty." We know very well what this means. When killing a Jew, his hand does not shake. This is why a man shivers and does Goecke's will, when Goecke takes as much as one look at him.

This year, the New Year and the Day of Atonement were very sad days. One could even say fateful days. Before the Festival of Tabernacles, however, the mood in the Ghetto relaxed somewhat. The main reason for the change was a rumor that the concentration of Jewish workers in the army camps would be put off for some time, owing to difficulties in procuring building materials for the huts and in recruiting sufficient numbers of guards, etc. The Ghetto Jews have calmed down somewhat. To celebrate the Festival of Tabernacles some traditional booths were even erected, made from planks and covered in thatch. Even some citron and palm-branch decorations were found.

On my way to the Council offices in the morning I came across one such booth which had been erected near a large group of houses. This made me wonder about the Jewish will to live, which does not disappear, even in the Ghetto. It seems that a sharp knife is at our throat, yet we do not lose courage.

We do not cease being Jews. Today is the first day of the Festival of Tabernacles.

In the afternoon I was urgently summoned to the workshops. Germans from the city governor's office were waiting there. Walking quickly to the workshops, I again came across a festival booth. Its door was open. Inside, I could see an old Jew wearing a black hat on his head. He wore holiday clothes and his face radiated joy. Several other people were in the booth with him. They were singing a Chassidic song accompanied by the clapping of hands and the stomping of feet. They sang with devotion and enthusiasm, as if the Ghetto and the German rulers did not exist.

The old Jew noticed me and came out of the booth. He took me by the sleeve and asked innocently: "What are you doing in our neighborhood at Tabernacles? Peace be with you! A good and happy day to you!" He was in high spirits—even a bit tipsy. Probably he had drunk a glass of something to celebrate the festival. He did not listen to my reply, when I explained that I was hurrying to a meeting and was expected at the workshops.

"Have you sat in the booth this year?" the bearded Jew asked. "No," I replied. "I have not had the time. Excuse me, I am in a hurry." The Jew—incidentally, a former Kovno merchant by the name of Zusman and an acquaintance of mine—looked at me with uncomprehending eyes, as if I were a heretic. He grasped me by the arm and dragged me into the booth. "Please, come in!" he said in a resounding voice. I repeated my explanation: "I must hurry to a meeting affecting the whole community." But my replies failed to produce any effect on the bearded Jew. "Come in just for one moment," he said, and forcibly seated me on a bench inside the booth.

Being faced with a fait accompli, I sat down. I greeted the other Jews in the booth with "Peace be with you!" and looked around me. Zusman asked his guests: "Do you know this person? This is Golub. You know him from the Committee." The Jews answered in unison: "What kind of question is this, do we know him? Of course we do. He is one of our ministers." And each one of them gave me a hearty "Peace be with you!" I told them: "I am not a minister at all. I am a Jew like everyone else. A Jew from the Ghetto. And now, Jews, please excuse me, I really have to be on my way. I have been summoned to the workshops."

Zusman was not deterred. He signaled to his wife through the booth window; she responded instantly by coming in with vodka and cake in her hands. It turned out that the bearded Jew was celebrating the bar-mitzvah of his son. He asked me to drink a glass of vodka and to recite the benediction thanking God for making us holy by keeping his commandments, and who has commanded us to dwell in booths; also the blessing over wine and bread. Needless to say I was asked to taste the cake. As we were eating, the Jews burst into song again.

"If you say you are in trouble, the Lord's compassion will sustain you." These words carried a special and profound significance in this booth in the Ghetto. The Jews in the booth sang, with devotion and faith, of the compassion of God. I forgot myself and my mission, and joined the chorus and the faith.

I was on tenterhooks nonetheless. I could not leave the booth before I had fulfilled all Zusman's wishes and observed all the commandments. At long last Zusman said: "You have work to do on behalf of the community. We must not delay you." Seeing me off, he recited over me the traditional blessing: "The Lord will make you succeed; an errand of mercy is its own protection." He blessed me, wishing me to succeed in my errand and to bring good tidings, deliverance, and comfort, so that we might be saved.

I arrived at the workshop late. The Germans from the city governor's office were waiting for me impatiently. I settled some minor matter with them and returned to the Council.

There were many people gathered in the waiting room and the hallways of the Council building. They were seeking advice. Where should they go to work? Where should their wives be assigned? What should be done with their children? What did we think of the army camp threat? Countless such questions were flung at us, for which we have no answers.

Throughout the day I remained under the good impression of the festive atmosphere in the Chassidic booth. I admired those pious Jews and envied them their ability to set themselves free from the yoke of the Ghetto; from the everyday troubles which keep pressing on each individual and on the community as a whole.

Indeed, there is no one capable of replying to the questions asked by the Jews in the Ghetto. "The prophet Elijah will answer all questions and riddles." "If you say you are in trouble," sing the Jews filled with faith, "the Lord's compassion will sustain you." Happy is the one who believes.

OCTOBER 19, 1943

DOCUMENT:
Last Testament[1]
Letter from Dr. Elkes to his son and daughter in London[2]

My beloved son and daughter!

I am writing these lines, my dear children, in the vale of tears of Vilijampolé, Kovno Ghetto, where we have been for over two years. We have now heard that in a few days our fate is to be sealed. The Ghetto is to be crushed and torn asunder. Whether we are all to perish, or whether a few of us are to survive, is in God's hands. We fear that only those capable of slave labor will live; the rest, probably, are sentenced to death.

We are left, a few out of many. Out of the 35,000 Jews of Kovno, approximately 17,000 remain; out of a quarter of a million Jews in Lithuania (including the Vilna district), only 25,000 live plus 5,000 who, during the last few days, were deported to hard labor in Latvia, stripped of all their belongings. The rest were put to death in terrible ways by the followers of the greatest Haman of all times and of all generations. Some of those dear and close to us, too, are no longer with us. Your Aunt Hannah and Uncle Arieh were killed with 1,500 souls of the Ghetto on October 4, 1941. Uncle Zvi, who was lying in the hospital suffering from a broken leg, was saved by a miracle. All the patients, doctors, nurses, relatives, and visitors who happened to be there were burned to death, after soldiers had blocked all the doors and windows of the hospital and set fire to it. In the provinces, apart from Siauliai, no single Jew survives. Your Uncle Dov and his son Shmuel were taken out and killed with the rest of the Kalvaria community during the first months of the war, that is, about two years ago.

Due to outer forces and inner circumstance, only our own Ghetto has managed to survive and live out its diaspora life for the past two years, in slavery, hard labor, hunger, and deprivation. (Almost all our clothing, belongings, and books were taken from us by the authorities.)

The last massacre, when 10,000 victims were killed at one time, took place on October 28, 1941. Our total community had to go through the "selection" by our rulers: life or death. I am the man who, with my own eyes, saw those about to die. I was there early on the morning of October 29, in the camp that led to the slaughter at the Ninth Fort. With my own ears I heard the awe-inspiring and terrible symphony, the weeping and screaming of 10,000 people, old and young—a scream that tore at the heart of heaven. No ear had heard such cries through the ages and the generations. With many of our martyrs, I challenged my creator; and with them, from a heart torn in agony, I cried: "Who is like you in the universe, my Lord!" In my effort to save people here and there, I was beaten by soldiers. Wounded and bleeding, I fainted, and was carried in the arms of friends to a place outside the camp. There, a small group of about thirty or forty survived—witnesses to the fire.

We are, it appears, one of the staging centers in the East. Before our eyes, before the very windows of our houses, there have passed over the last two years many, many thousands of Jews from southern Germany and Vienna, to be taken, with their belongings, to the Ninth Fort, which is some kilometers from us. There they were killed with extreme cruelty. We learned later that they were misled—they were told they were coming to Kovno, to settle in our Ghetto.

From the day of the Ghetto's founding, I stood at its head. Our community chose me, and the authorities confirmed me as chairman of the Council of elders, together with my friend, the advocate Leib Garfunkel, a former member of the Lithuanian parliament, and a few other close and good people, concerned and caring for the fate of the surviving few. We are trying to steer our battered ship in furious seas, when waves of decrees and decisions threaten to drown it every day. Through my influence I succeeded, at times, in easing the verdict and in scattering some of the dark clouds that hung over our heads. I bore my duties with head high and an upright countenance. Never did I ask for pity; never did I doubt our rights. I argued our case with total confidence in the justice of our demands.

In these hardest moments of our life, you, my dear ones, are always before us. You are present in our deepest thoughts and in our hearts. In the darkest nights, your mother would sit beside me, and we would both dream of your life and your future. Our innermost desire is to see you again, to embrace you, and to tell you once again how close we are to you, and how our hearts beat as we remember you and see you before us. And is there any time, day or night, when your memory is not with us? As we stand here, at the very gates of hell, with a knife poised at our necks, only your images, dear ones, sustain us. And you, my children, how was your life these past five years, so hard and full of sorrow for the Jewry of Europe? I know that, far away from this place, you have shared our anguish and, in agony, listened to every slight rumor coming from this vale of tears; and that, deep down, you have felt with us this unparalleled tragedy of our people.

With regard to myself, I have little to report. Last year I suffered an acute and severe attack of rheumatoid arthritis, which kept me bedridden for nine months. However, even in the most difficult days of my illness, I carried on in my community, and from my bedside participated actively in the work of my friends. Now I am better; it has been about six months since I ceased being regarded as sick. I am not fully well, either, but I continue to work ceaselessly, without rest or respite.

About six months ago we received a message from Uncle Hans, transmitted to us by way of the Red Cross; it said that you were all right. The little note, written by a stranger, took nine months to reach us. We have written and written to you by way of the Red Cross and private persons. Have any of our words reached you? We are desolate that during our stay here we could not contact you and tell you that we are still among the living. We know full well how heavily the doubt of our survival weighs upon you, and what strength and confidence you would draw from the news that we are alive. This would certainly give you courage, and belief in work and life with a firm and clear goal. I deeply fear despair, and the kind of apathy which tends to drive a person out of this world. I pray that this may not happen to you. I doubt, my beloved children, whether I will ever be able to see you again, to hug you and press you to my heart. Before

I leave this world and you, my dear ones, I wish to tell you once again how dear you are to us, and how deeply our souls yearn for you.

Joel, my beloved! Be a faithful son to your people. Take care of your nation, and do not worry about the Gentiles. During our long exile, they have not given us an eighth of an eighth of what we have given them. Immerse yourself in this question, and return to it again and again.

Try to settle in the Land of Israel. Tie your destiny to the land of our future. Even if life there may be hard, it is a life full of content and meaning. Great and mighty is the power of faith and belief. Faith can move mountains. Do not look to the left or to the right as you pursue your path. If at times you see your people straying, do not let your heart lose courage, my son. It is not their fault—it is our bitter Exile which has made them so. Let truth be always before you and under your feet. Truth will guide you and show you the path of life.

And you, my dear daughter Sarah, read most carefully what I have just said to Joel. I trust your clear mind and sound judgment. Do not live for the moment; do not stray from your chosen path and pick flowers at the wayside. They soon wilt. Lead a life full of beauty, a pure life, full of content and meaning. For all your days, walk together: let no distance separate you, let no serious event come between you.

Remember, both of you, what Amalek has done to us. Remember and never forget it all your days; and pass this memory as a sacred testament to future generations. The Germans killed, slaughtered, and murdered us in complete equanimity. I was there with them. I saw them when they sent thousands of people—men, women, children, infants—to their death, while enjoying their breakfast, and while mocking our martyrs. I saw them coming back from their murderous missions—dirty, stained from head to foot with the blood of our dear ones. There they sat at their table—eating and drinking, listening to light music. They are professional executioners.

The soil of Lithuania is soaked with our blood, killed at the hands of the Lithuanians themselves; Lithuanians, with whom we have lived for hundreds of years, and whom, with all our strength, we helped to achieve their own national independence. Seven thousand of our brothers and sisters were killed by Lithuanians in terrible and barbarous ways during the last days of June 1941. They themselves, and no others, executed whole congregations, following German orders. They searched—with special pleasure—cellars and wells, fields and forests, for those in hiding, and turned them over to the "authorities." Never have anything to do with them; they and their children are accursed forever.

I am writing this in an hour when many desperate souls—widows and orphans, threadbare and hungry—are camping on my doorstep, imploring us for help. My strength is ebbing. There is a desert inside me. My soul is scorched. I am naked and empty. There are no words in my mouth. But you, my most dearly beloved, will know what I wanted to say to you at this hour.

And now, for a moment, I close my eyes and see you both standing before me. I embrace and kiss you both; and I say to you again that, until my last breath, I remain your loving father,

Elchanan

1. Dr. Elkes gave this testament, and the extra lines dated November 11, 1943, to Avraham Tory, who took them with him when he escaped from the Ghetto. After the war, Tory gave the testament and the letter to Dr. Elkes's widow, Miriam, in Israel. The original documents are now with the Elkes's son, Dr. Joel Elkes. This is the only testament of a Jewish Council chairman that has survived from those years.

2. Dr. Elkes's son and daughter had gone to Britain in 1938 to study medicine: his son Joel in London, his daughter Sarah in Birmingham. Joel Elkes subsequently emigrated to the United States, where he became head of the Faculty of Psychiatry at Johns Hopkins University. Sarah Elkes, who lives partly in England and partly in Israel, is a specialist in the problems of homeless children.

NOVEMBER 11, 1943

DOCUMENT: Postscript to letter from Dr. Elkes to his son and daughter in London

I add a few lines. It has been two weeks now since we passed from one authority to another. They have now changed our name; instead of being "the Ghetto," we are called "Concentration Camp no. 4, Kovno," with new officials and functionaries. Our share of misery is not over yet. On the twenty-sixth of last month they took 2,709 people out of our Ghetto. According to information we have received, they separated the children and the elderly—they are probably dead by now. Those who were able to work were sent to Estonia to hard labor. On the fifth of this month they took out of Siauliai all children under thirteen, as well as the elderly men and women. They were told that they were being brought to Kovno. They are probably all dead now.

As to our fate, we await it in the very near future. These lines, together with some other documents, I am putting in a safe place. I pray that they may reach your hands one day.

With love, affection and my blessing,
Your father

P.S. We have learned from a reliable source that the Germans are trying to erase any trace of their murders. The bones of our martyrs are to be burned in the Ninth Fort and in other places, by people who are experts in this kind of job (chemists).

JANUARY 9, 1944[1]

The Ninth Fort, a military fortress near Kovno, for a long time served as part of the Kovno prison for dangerous criminals. During the Nazi occupation it became a place of torture and mass executions. In secret, the Nazis called it *Vernichtungsstelle nr. 2*: Extermination place no. 2. Here were murdered some 25,000 of Kovno's Jews, as well as 10,000 Jews deported from Germany, Austria, and Czechoslovakia, thousands of Jewish prisoners-of-war who had served in the Red Army, and many other Jews.

Single and mass arrests, as well as "Actions" in the Ghetto, almost always ended with a "death march" to the Ninth Fort, which, in a way, completed the area of the Ghetto and became an integral part of it.

A road three to four kilometers long led uphill from the Ghetto to the Fort, a special road called by the Ghetto inmates the Via Dolorosa. The murderers called it the Way to Heaven (*Der Weg zum Himmel-Fahrt*).

Before their execution, the detainees were incarcerated in underground cells known as "casemates," in damp, darkness, and fear. There, people fought with one another for a brighter corner in the cells, for a piece of a straw mattress, for a scrap of food, or for a crumb of bread. There, Jews were shackled in iron chains, harnessed to ploughs in place of horses, forced to dig into peat-pits inside the Fort, and often whipped to death. There, one soon lost one's human image and one's own will; there, life turned into senseless pain, after which death came as redemption.

Keidan, a father of four children, who was incarcerated at the Fort and tortured there for five months, who with others stood naked in the pit awaiting execution, miraculously escaped from the Fort. He was the first to bring an authentic report from the Hell on Earth.[2]

In fifteen mass pits, some 45,000 innocent victims found their awful burial, 3,000 in each pit. Thousands of Red Army prisoners-of-war, all Jews, were separated from the other Soviet prisoners-of-war, and were systematically massacred at the Ninth Fort.

As long as German troops went on with their "March to the East," the digging of new mass graves at the Fort continued. When the German advance was blocked in July 1943, there was no more digging of mass graves. And when the Germans were forced to retreat, they hurried to erase all traces of their crimes.

In August 1943 the Kovno Gestapo received orders from Berlin to eradicate the mass graves: to exhume the corpses and to burn them. This was to be carried out by the end of January 1944, when the German retreat from the Baltic States was foreseen. The carrying out of this order was imposed upon seventy-five Jews who were already imprisoned at the Fort, among them Ghetto inmates who had been seized in the Ghetto and brought to the Fort, Red Army prisoners-of-war, and youngsters from the Ghetto who had been caught while on their way to join partisans in the forests. Eleven of the seventy-five declared at the outset that they were ill, and not capable of doing the "job." The Gestapo murdered them by injections of poison. The remaining sixty-four, sixty men and four women, formed a labor squad. All of them, apart from one Polish woman, were Jews.

The work started in September 1943. Fiery beacons started to rise from the Fort, crowned by clouds of smoke. The labor squad had begun to carry out the German order. The sixty-four were divided into four groups, each of which carried out a part of the "job." One group, the "diggers," had to dig out the dead corpses—to scrape off the upper layer of the earth from the pits, and then, with spades, remove the first layers of the corpses. This group then had to go down into the pit by ladder, and, using pitchforks, toss the remaining bodies up to the surface. The German supervisors used to make cynical remarks such as "stick the pitchfork in the belly of that disgusting Jew" or "toss up that Jewish woman—that Sarah—by digging your pitchfork into her hair," or similar pearls.

When the corpses were brought up, the gold teeth had to be extracted, all rings and bracelets removed, and searches made for gold and jewels in the rotting garments of the dead. Then all valuables had to be cleaned and polished and handed over to the German supervisors. Most of the corpses were half or totally decayed, but some were well preserved. More than once, the diggers recognized their own acquaintances. On one occasion, a digger recognized his own brother.

Once the belly of a woman in her last months of pregnancy cracked in the terrible heat of the pyre, and from inside her burst a small baby's body. The Jewish prisoners were stunned. Even the Nazi guards were astonished.

The corpses of the Lithuanian Jews were naked, and lying on one another lengthways and crossways. Only rarely were bullet holes to be found. From the expressions on the faces, and from the way they were lying, it could be seen that most of them had choked to death in the pits. The bodies of women with babies in their arms were also found. The corpses of German, Austrian, Czechoslovakian, and other Jews were found in separate graves. These were clothed and bore all the marks of a bitter struggle. This confirmed rumors which had spread in the Ghetto during the "Great Actions" of 1941, that these Jews had fought against their murderers and had not undressed before being murdered. At the time, some of the Gestapo men had returned from the Fort badly wounded and bleeding.[3]

After the corpses had been brought out of the pits by the diggers, the members of the second group, "porters," piled the bodies on special wooden pallets, counted them in the presence of a Nazi supervisor, and took them to the pyres.

There, the third group, the "firemen," were at work, headed by an expert on burning—the "Brandmeister." This group had to prepare the pyre once every twenty-four hours, as follows: In the courtyard of the Fort, not far from the pits, they would lay out a long row of logs, put a row of bodies on it, then lay another row of logs on top of the bodies, and another row of bodies on the second pile of logs. The daily quota was fixed at three hundred bodies. To make it easier to light the fire, kerosene was poured into holes dug in the ground, as well as over the corpses themselves. On either side were narrow trenches, into which ran the fat of the burning corpses. The firemen had to make sure the fire did not go out in the middle of burning the corpses. If as much as a hair was left unburned they were liable to pay for it with their own lives. After each fire there remained heaps of ashes and bones, which were pounded in huge mortars. This "flour" was flung into the air or dug into the soil.

The fourth group was engaged on various tasks in the courtyard, the kitchen, etc. One of this group was Dr. Portnoy. He had previously worked with a German pastor, by name of Pollet, in editing a German-Lithuanian dictionary. One day Portnoy disappeared without a trace. The pastor had considerable influence with the Kovno Gestapo, but not enough to bring back his Jewish assistant. Portnoy was supposed to be dead, but finally he turned up among the sixty-four and served as their doctor.

The SS men at the Fort carefully watched every move made by the Jewish workers, to make sure that not a single corpse was left in any of the pits. It was absolutely forbidden to fill in with earth any pit from which the bodies had been removed. The workers could expect to be beaten murderously if an unconsumed limb was found in the ashes when one of the pyres was put out. High Gestapo officers, and even Nazi generals, used to visit the Fort and watch the work. Some of them told the Jews that they were disposing of the victims of the Bolshevik terror; others claimed that the bodies were those of Communists, the blood-and-soul enemies of all humanity, and that it was a good deed to liberate the world from this peril. All of them tried to convince the Jews that no harm would be done to them; that after they had completed this work they would be transferred elsewhere, as there was more than enough work for them. This consoled the Jews very little—on the contrary, it made them nervous. During one such visit, one of the Jews blurted out a bitter remark: when his pitchfork lifted up, from the pit, the corpse of a child, he cried out, "This is a dangerous Bolshevik, a great threat to mankind! Take him to the pyre! Burn his bones!" The permanent SS supervisors at the Fort said more than once that the fate of the workers had already been decided, and that not one of them would ever leave the Fort. Witnesses of this kind cannot remain alive.

The four groups were ordered to speed up their work. The murderers had grown nervous all of a sudden. Their dead victims had begun to bother them, and they were in a hurry to destroy all traces of their crimes. In general, the life of the prisoners did not change. They were forced to work in chains and subjected to the whims and caprices of their torturers. However, to increase "productivity," SS Captain Gratt, the Fort commandant, ordered that the prisoners be allowed to eat their fill, and even supplied them with tobacco and alcohol occasionally, to help them withstand the dreadful stench from the pits. They were provided with pillows and blankets from the Ghetto, and three Jewish women were brought from the Ghetto to satisfy their sexual needs. But the prisoners did not delude themselves. They knew with absolute certainty that as soon as they had finished their dreadful task they would also be burned in the final conflagration. Every pit that was emptied, every pyre that was put out, brought them closer to their own extermination.

Before starting to burn the corpses, the Germans erected special walls of white sheeting, to prevent people from looking into the Fort from outside, and thus to conceal the digging up of the mass graves and the burning of the corpses.

It was impossible, however, to conceal the flames and the thick smoke that came from the Fort every twenty-four hours; it was impossible to suppress the terrible stench from the reopened pits, which was carried by the wind for many kilometers all around.

"Hell is burning"—so the peasants of the surrounding villages whispered to themselves while watching the glow of the flaming pyres.

"Our brothers are burning, our own blood is burning"—so observed the Jews, helpless and imprisoned in the Ghetto a few kilometers away, in the valley. The red strip in the sky, the new "crown" on the Fort, whispered quietly the word "revenge."

Not one of the sixty-four prisoners believed he would remain alive. Yet a spark of hope nevertheless flickered in their hearts. Only a few, however, dared to think of rescue. They were reminded morning and evening, day and night, that nobody had ever escaped from the Ninth Fort.

In October 1943 a new prisoner, Captain Kolia Vassilenko, was brought to the Fort from the Soviet prisoner-of-war camp near Kalvaria. At the camp, Vassilenko had been regarded as a Russian until he was compelled to go to the bathhouse, and was discovered to be a Jew. From the first day of his detention at the Fort he made up his mind to escape. While at work, he studied the internal and external arrangements of the Fort, observing the methods of guarding the place and the housing conditions of the guards. With the utmost secrecy, he gathered round him an initially small group, which he imbued with his own idea of escape and flight.

The original plan was to dig a tunnel that would be a kilometer long, and to go out to freedom through it. For several weeks the prisoners dug this tunnel with unskilled hands and without tools, digging beneath subterranean structures of the Fort. They carried the earth out in their pockets and threw it into the pits. They succeeded in hiding their excavations from the guards, and also from their fellow prisoners. It seemed as though their plan would be successful, until they reached a huge rock below the surface and had to give up, filling the tunnel once again with earth, after all the toil and effort with which they had dug it.

In spite of this setback, however, Vassilenko and his comrades did not despair and sought other methods of escape.

A second plan was to use gold and valuables taken from the corpses to bribe the SS guards, and to escape with them. At that time, however, not one of the SS men thought of deserting or of bribes. This plan could not be carried out because (1) the guards had already stolen so many valuables that more bribes would not induce them to take such a risk, and (2) the danger to the lives of the guards was not so near or so threatening as it was for the prisoners. Besides, according to this plan, only a few of the prisoners would be able to escape.

The third plan was to disarm the two supervisors who came every evening to confine the Jews for the night in the underground cells (from after work until seven o'clock they did not lock the individual cells), kill them quietly, steal their uniforms, kill the other two guards in the courtyard, infiltrate the guardroom, kill the guards on duty there, take gold and valuables from the safe, arm themselves, and then take the truck that always stood in the courtyard, kill the guards at the main tower, and drive away.

The main difficulty of this plan was to break into the guardroom, entrance to which required a password that no outsider knew. To break in by force was dangerous because there was a complicated signal system between the commander of the Fort, the central prison, the Gestapo headquarters, the police, and the military. Before someone could get into the guardroom the whole Fort would be flooded with reinforcements and surrounded by an impenetrable cordon of Gestapo and SS men. This plan was therefore rejected.

The plan finally decided on was this: the prisoners proposed to prepare a key to one of the storerooms above the underground cell in which the group was locked up at night. From this store, a door led to a tunnel in the courtyard of the Fort. From this tunnel it would be necessary to dig a second one to the outer wall of the citadel. Within the Fort there were small workshops which supplied the Fort's internal needs. A few Jews worked in these workshops; it was they who prepared the key. The hardest thing was to open the thick steel door to the tunnel. For this they had no tools.

It was a daring plan, but their situation was so desperate that they resolved to try to carry it out. A key was prepared, and the unused storeroom facing their quarters was opened. Every day, two men of the group remained behind, claiming to be ill; according to the rules, only two of the group were allowed to be ill and absent at any one time. One of them, equipped with a penknife which had been found in the rotting clothes of a corpse and with a small hand-drill removed from a workshop, drilled through the heavy steel door, while the other kept watch.

Gradually they made holes through the door and sawed through the steel between the holes. They also worked in the evenings, and used to sing songs and joke at the top of their voices to cover the sound of drilling. They were not discovered in their dangerous work, and were not interfered with even when they sang Soviet songs. After each drilling, they would conceal the door behind a pile of rags.

So as not to arouse the suspicion of the Gestapo, the Jews decided to work even harder at the pits, and raised the daily norm of three hundred corpses to five hundred. The Fort commandant was satisfied and believed that the Jews had come to accept their fate. Meanwhile, feverish preparations were being made; but the plotters hid the plan of escape from the majority of prisoners until the very last moment. They made keys to all the underground structures, and sawed the iron of one of the doors from within, leaving only a very thin layer on the outside facing the corridor. In the workshop they prepared a collapsible wooden ladder, and a second ladder of rope as well, ostensibly for fetching the corpses up from the pits.

After weeks of strenuous and unparalleled labor, the hole in the steel door was finally made. It was thirty by forty centimeters, which was just enough for a person to pass through. The day for the flight was finally fixed for December 25, 1943, Christmas day. All preparations were completed, and partial rehearsals were begun. The tunnels through which the escaping prisoners had to pass were still blocked, however, with wooden beams that had to be removed. What did they do? They complained that the wood they received for the pyres was wet and would not burn, either in the kitchen or on the pyres. They therefore asked for permission to take dry wood from the tunnels. The Fort commandant suspected nothing and gave permission, and so the last obstacle was eliminated. The experience the prisoners gained from the various rehearsals led them to recheck every detail of the plan.

As the agreed date approached, the prisoners rehearsed their flight again and again, and their tension also increased. The mere scale of the plan was enough to terrify them. They feared that a single incautious step would destroy all their preparations and put them in the hands of the murderers. They were also afraid that they would be replaced before December 25 by a different team of workers, and would thus be killed before they could carry out their plan. Each of the four groups had its own commander. Details were given to these leaders, who were provided with full and detailed instructions. They were warned that any incautious step might cause a catastrophe. Not a word was to be said. Not a step was to be taken without orders. Not the slightest sign of excitement was to be shown.

Finally the long-awaited 25th of December arrived.

Only half a day's work had to be done. In honor of Christmas day, SS Captain Gratt addressed the sixty-four prisoners, and expressed his satisfaction at the tempo of their work. Since the Jews were laboring so diligently, he said, he would try to improve the conditions under which they lived. Each of them would receive schnapps and cigarettes in honor of the holiday. They would not work for the two days of Christmas. Gratt wanted them to rest properly, so that they would return to their work the following Monday refreshed and with renewed strength. Once again, he promised that not a hair of their heads would fall to the ground, and that when this work was over they would be given more work somewhere else. One of the workers answered the captain on behalf of all of them, thanking him for his kind attitude and for the schnapps and tobacco. He wished the Fort commander "a quiet holiday." The Jews gave the drink and tobacco to the guards to make them get even more drunk, so they would not notice the excitement and nervousness of the prisoners.

Tension increased every moment. By 7 P.M. the workers were all in the underground structures, impatiently awaiting the arrival of the guards who would lock them in for the night and then go out on guard again as usual in the courtyard in front of the building. About half an hour after the door was locked, the lights would be put out, to be put on again only at 5 A.M. During those hours of darkness the prisoners hoped to carry out their plan. But the guards did not arrive at 7:00 as usual. They did not lock the workers in or put the lights out. Nobody understood what had happened; all feared the worst. A full hour passed in tense expectation. Precisely at 8:00, the two warders appeared and locked the doors. It turned out that in honor of Christmas they had wanted to give the Jewish prisoners some pleasure, and so had allowed their doors to remain unlocked. Half an hour later the lights were put out as usual, and the guards left the building.

The prisoners waited a little longer, and then began carrying out their plans. First they broke through the thin layer of iron over the steel door, which had been sawed through in advance. Then one of them climbed through the hole into the corridor and, using the keys that had been prepared, swiftly opened the doors of all the subterranean cells. The corridor floor and the iron stairs of the abandoned storeroom were immediately covered with blankets to deaden any noise of their movements. All the prisoners emerged into the corridor in absolute silence and assembled in their groups, two by two. The final instructions were given. Once more the leaders warned them that any hesitant or wrong step by a single one of them might cause the death of all. Any breach of discipline would be settled on the spot by a knifeblade in the heart.

And so they mounted the steps, group by group, one after the other. They opened the storeroom with a key and reached the entry through the steel door. Vassilenko and another of the first group stood on either side of the door, ensuring that everything was done properly. Without a word they all passed as planned through the hole and entered the tunnel. There the groups formed up again and slowly moved forward to the moat in the courtyard. Then they crossed the moat, entered the second tunnel, passed through that to another moat, and reached the outer wall of the Fort. Beside the wall they put up a screen of white sheets they had brought with them, thus concealing all movement around the ladders they were lowering over the wall, which was six meters high.

Each group was accompanied all the way by the leader of the next group, who then returned and led his own men and the leader of the following group. After they had all climbed over the wall and reached freedom, they were followed by Captain Vassilenko, the last of the sixty-four to leave the Fort.

It was night. All the roads and fields around the Fort were covered with a thick layer of snow. There was no sign of movement on the roadway or in the neighborhood. SS patrols moved lazily through the darkness, their heads withdrawn into their warm furs and their hands tucked away in their long, broad sleeves. They did not notice the march of the sixty-four because of their own increased ration of alcohol and the extra amounts given them by the Jews.

The prisoners were free. They were so carried away that they began to kiss one another. Then they formed up again, but this time each group took a different direction. The first group, of twenty men, moved north, directly to the partisan woods; the second moved to the west, to try and set up their own partisan base. The third group, including the four women and the doctor, ten in all, moved off across the fields and paths of the neighboring villages, each going where considered safest on his own responsibility. The fourth and last group, of thirteen men, headed by Captain Vassilenko, proceeded to the Kovno Ghetto.

Vassilenko had never yet been in any Ghetto. When his group approached the fence and he saw the sentry, he decided to kill him on the spot in order to clear the way. But his companions, who had been in the Ghetto themselves, prevented him from doing so. They knew that the death of a single German sentry was liable to bring down catastrophe on the entire Ghetto, in which some 17,000 Jews were still kept behind the barbed wire. So they all waited near the gate until the sentries had moved a little way off. Then they swiftly made a hole in the barbed wire, and crawled through without being noticed.

Not one went to his own family. They knocked at the doors of certain leaders of the underground, and soon all thirteen of them were concealed in hiding-places. Nobody in the Ghetto was to know of their arrival. It remained the secret of a handful of leaders of the joint underground. All of the escapees stank of corpses. It was hard to be near them. The dreadful smell itself was enough to give them away. They had to be bathed and dressed in other clothes, and their camp clothes had to be burned.

The inmates of the Ghetto could not understand why the guard around the walls and fences was so heavily increased on the day after Christmas Day. Larger patrols of sentries were placed all along the fence and at the gate.

The Ghetto began to whisper about Jews who had escaped. They did not know exactly what had happened, and that served to increase the tension. It was claimed that the Jews in the Ninth Fort had drugged the watchmen and had all escaped. Nobody knew how many were in hiding or where they were.

The Jews who worked in the Gestapo garage and workshops reported an exceptional series of searches in the city, and also in the provincial towns and villages. Gestapo and SS squads were patroling the vicinity of the Fort, searching in the peasants' huts, in every attic and cellar, thrusting their bayonets into every pile of hay, and turning searchlights into every sty and pen. They warned the inhabitants that very dangerous criminals had escaped from the Fort and were hiding among the peasants of the neighborhood, and that it would be to the advantage of the population to catch the criminals and hand them over to the authorities. Anyone daring to hide them or to conceal their hidingplaces would lose their lives and property.

Groups of Germans terrorized the population all around the Fort. Jews who had succeeded in hiding for months were taken from their hidingplaces and carried away to the Gestapo cellars, together with the peasants who had given them refuge in their homes. Many of the Jews had to leave their hidingplaces and escape into the fields by day or night in the piercing frost. The peasants hurriedly got rid of them, thrusting them into the claws of the Nazi monsters.

Day by day, the number of the Jews in the cells of the Gestapo increased. Among them were some of the fugitives from the Ninth Fort, who were interrogated and tortured with particular cruelty. From the hints they dropped while being led through the Gestapo corridors, and from the scraps of paper one or two of them succeeded in dropping on various occasions, it was clear that the Gestapo was determined to extort information from them as to who had planned the escape and what help they had received from the Ghetto. Yet not one of them uttered a word.

Four more of the fugitives fell into the hands of the Gestapo while trying to cross the barbed-wire fence into the Ghetto. Yet in spite of everything a number of them succeeded in making their way across. All in all, nineteen of them entered safely.

The Gestapo continued to say nothing about the escape from the Fort. The German labor office gave the Jewish Council instructions to provide fifty-two men for work outside the Ghetto for a period of two to three months. The workers were required to be young, healthy, and unmarried. It was obvious to the

Council that these workers would have to replace those who had escaped from the Ninth Fort. It was decided not to supply the workers. If the Gestapo itself were to try to recruit the workers, the latter would be told the nature of the work to which they were being sent. In the end the Ghetto did not provide workers, and it is worth noting that the Gestapo did not take any punitive steps. This time they found workers elsewhere, and left the Kovno Ghetto alone.

On one of the last nights of December, there was a secret meeting in a little wooden hut[4] in the Ghetto, at which were present Chaim Yellin, leader of the partisan movement in the Kovno Ghetto, Captain Kolia Vassilenko, and the writer of these lines. Vassilenko, a medium-sized man of about thirty-two with a round and open face, spoke fluent Yiddish. In simple words and without any embellishment, he told of the several plans for escape which had not succeeded, and of the final plan which had brought him and the rest of the prisoners to liberty. He described the proceedings of the escape with great ease, as though it all stood to reason. For this experienced soldier, who had served on various fronts and in several fortresses, the flight from the Ninth Fort was like a normal military operation which it was his duty to carry out. He smiled all the time he was describing these military measures. But his face grew grave and the smile vanished as he began to describe the tortures inside the Fort, the sufferings of his fellow prisoners—Jewish prisoners-of-war from the Red Army, who had been separated from the other prisoners-of-war during the earliest days of the war and imprisoned in the Fort. The prisoners were ordered to dig graves for the masses of murdered Jews and to pour quicklime over every row of corpses. Day and night they saw the earth moving over the pits in which the murdered masses had been thrown—many had been flung into the pits while they were still alive.

Vassilenko went on with his description. He told what he had seen with his own eyes, what he saw when he took corpses and burned them, and what he heard from his fellow prisoners who were veterans of long standing at the Fort. He also gave details about the murder of the family of Chief Rabbi Shapiro. Early in 1943 the rabbi's son, Dr. Chaim Nachman Shapiro—a university lecturer—had been taken to the fortress with his wife, their fifteen-year-old son, and his old mother, the rabbi's widow. They had all been shot that same day and their bodies flung into the flames.

The fugitives also brought with them evidence and materials they had collected in and around the graves during the excavations. "Let them be given to relatives in the Ghetto, to let them know for whom there is no point in waiting any longer," Vassilenko told us. The group had also brought with them the gold teeth of some of the slain—the gold weighed a quarter of a kilogram.[5] The other groups had also taken documents and valuables with them.

In spite of all the watchful care of their SS taskmasters, the Jewish diggers had even managed to hide a few of the corpses within the graves they were digging out, in order that some evidence of the mass murders would remain.

Vassilenko declared that he did not intend to remain in the Ghetto, which he considered only a temporary halt on his way to the forests and a life of partisan combat. He had not originally intended to enter the Ghetto at all, but his comrades had warned him that the population of the city was permeated with Jew-hatred and that any Christian or any Lithuanian youngster would be prepared to hand him over to the Germans. Vassilenko knew about the obstinate search for the sixty-four fugitives. He did not believe they would all be caught, but he did not wish to delay his escape from the Ghetto. It was true that the Jewish police, who had been sent to the evacuated area of the Small Ghetto to hunt for people in hiding, had not found anybody, in spite of all the fury of the Gestapo, and had merely alarmed Jews who were in hiding there. But it was obvious that the fugitives had to be transported from the Ghetto to the partisan woods near Vilna. There were many difficulties in the way. Suitable clothing and arms had to be provided, together with means of transportation. The departure from the Ghetto would have to be carefully prepared. Some of the fugitives had fallen ill, and this also delayed the departure. Gabriel Schustermann had frostbite in both his legs. He had wandered about for days in the snow after escaping from the Fort. He had to be operated on, but it was impossible to perform the operation in the Ghetto hospital. Another man's hand was perforated as a result of drilling through the steel door for weeks on end at the Fort, and there was a danger he would develop blood poisoning.

Before dawn on January 6, 1944, a truck bearing the insignia of the German police approached the main gate of the Ghetto as usual, in order to take a group of Jews to work in outlying places. The workers were waiting at the gate, inside the Ghetto. The guard opened the gate and twenty-eight Jews emerged, all dressed in rags, with the yellow patch on their chests and backs—apparently an ordinary labor group. They climbed onto the truck and it set off without delay. In the cabin next to the driver sat the "column leader" who accompanied the group. This time it was Chaim Yellin, the heroic leader of the Kovno Ghetto partisans. Yellin had a compass and a military map. There were also two Nagan pistols in the pockets of his military trousers, which he wore under his rags. He was conducting the Fort fugitives, and several other young members of the underground resistance, from the Ghetto to a partisan-held forest in the Vilna district. The others on the truck were also armed. Some had Nagans, others had hand grenades, and a few had automatic weapons. They had decided not to surrender, but to use their weapons if anything at all went wrong during their journey. The hired driver knew the way and knew what he had to do. He also knew that he must not stop even if he met Lithuanian or German police on the road.

After four days Chaim Yellin returned to the Ghetto, weary and exhausted, bringing greetings from those who had fled. They had all reached the partisan-held forest safely. The one fugitive remaining in the Ghetto was Gabriel Schustermann. His frostbitten legs were operated on, but he died a painful death. Meanwhile the Gestapo resumed the work of digging up the corpses from the pits at the Fort. Once again the dreadful stench of rotting corpses spread far and wide. Once again, the funeral pyres burned there.

1. Avraham Tory wrote this diary entry following a meeting with Captain Vassilenko, a Jew, an officer in the Red Army, a specialist in military fortifications, and a former prisoner-of-war, who had escaped from the Ninth Fort on December 25, 1943, together with sixty-three other prisoners. During their meeting, Vassilenko gave an account of life and death at the Ninth Fort, and of the escape itself. Tory noted down what he said, and then, on January 9, 1944, prepared a typed version of his notes, as translated here.
2. Avraham Tory later recalled: "Keidan was the first person to be released from the Ninth Fort. His release took place on June 11, 1942, after which he reported to Dr. Elkes, Garfunkel, Goldberg, and me as an eyewitness to the tortures and massacres at the Ninth Fort."
3. Avraham Tory later recalled that this fact had been reported at the time by Jews working at the Gestapo headquarters in Kovno.
4. This hut had been Pnina Sheinzon's tiny dwelling. She herself was already in hiding and only her cousin, Rachel Feinberg, lived in a corner of the kitchen of the hut. Outside it a young member of the Zionist underground, Sergey, stood on guard. Today (1989) Rachel Feinberg lives in Israel.
5. The equivalent of between fifty and sixty gold teeth.

EPILOGUE

The Ghetto after the Germans burned it down in July 1944. The Germans had searched for Jews in hiding, blowing up every stone house and setting fire to every wooden one. The Ghetto burned for several days, until it was completely destroyed.

In late March 1944, I unexpectedly had an opportunity to escape from the Ghetto and to join Pnina Sheinzon and her daughter, Shulamit, who had been hiding for several months with a Lithuanian peasant in the distant village of Virvigaliai. I was unable to decide whether to take advantage of this opportunity or to remain in the Ghetto, where the chances of survival were continually diminishing, especially once it had been formally declared a concentration camp, and its inmates transferred, group by group, to labor camps in various parts of Lithuania, under a strict SS regime.

Dr. Elkes and his noble wife, Miriam, strongly encouraged me to escape, in our dramatic last conversation in their tiny home, in the presence of his deputy, Leib Garfunkel, on the last night, a few hours before my escape. Dr. Elkes clasped my hands and, in a fatherly tone, said: "If you were my son, I would say to you without hesitation 'Go, go!' Who knows as well as you know the darkest happenings of the Ghetto? Your escape from the Ghetto is a mission of great importance."

From approximately the beginning of 1944—I do not recall the exact date— Dr. Elkes's Last Testament had been in the crate which had been buried last. About ten days before I left the Ghetto, he asked me to return it to him, which I did. On that night, at his home, he suddenly took it out, without our having mentioned it, and gave it to me, so that if I survived I could give it to his son Joel and his daughter Sarah, both of whom were then in London.

I gave Dr. Elkes and Garfunkel exact details of the hiding place of my diary and the other documents and told them of my conversation with the priest, V. Vaickus. We said our goodbyes before dawn, emotionally and tearfully. My close friends Jacob Verbovski, who had become famous among the Jews because of his help at the Ghetto gate, and Ika Grinberg, one of the central figures in the Kovno Ghetto underground, helped me to pass through the gate. The priest Bronius Paukstys, head of the Holy Trinity church on Rotuse Square, introduced me to Maria Jurjsaitiene, the woman owner of the farm where Pnina and Shulamit had been hiding, who had come to take me to the hiding place, responding to Pnina's urgent pleas.

With great risks and hardships, I reached Virvigaliai, and hid there for four months in constant tension and fear. Only Maria, her son Juozas, and her three daughters—apart from Pnina and little Shulamit—knew that I was in the hiding place, an isolated hut. I found release there in writing in my diary about our hideout and the happenings in the countryside, and I reconstructed from memory entire chapters of the diary I had kept in the Ghetto, since I feared that its hiding place would be discovered and that no trace of my writings would remain.

From an unidentified Jewish officer of the Red Army who had arrived at Virvigaliai with his front-line unit, I learned of a way of crossing the front lines to Kovno, which he told me had been liberated seven days before. The officer warned me to leave the farm as soon as possible, as it was in an area of heavy fighting between Soviet and German forces. I urged Maria Jurjsaitiene to come with me to Kovno until the hostilities were over. But she insisted on staying at the farm, where her husband was buried. Her children, respecting her feelings, likewise refused to leave. So at the beginning of August 1944, after the officer had told me which villages were still being held by stubbornly resisting German units, Pnina, Shulamit, and I took our leave with deep feelings of gratitude (we send them parcels of clothing to this very day) and made our way back to Kovno. There, in a building on Kestucio Street, Jews, survivors, destitute like us, had begun to assemble. Nobody had the mental strength even to try to return to their previous homes.

On reaching Kovno, we went to see the priest Paukstys at the Holy Trinity church, to express our gratitude to him. He was as moved as we were, and he embraced all three of us. Our feelings could not be described.

Lithuanians who had been entrusted with my furniture refused to return it. An exception in this matter, as well as in so much else, was the priest Bronius Paukstys, whose help to the Jews almost cost him his position in the church and endangered his life. (After many years, in 1982, upon my initiative and efforts, Yad Vashem, the Holocaust Memorial and Archive in Jerusalem, recognized him as a "Righteous Gentile.")

When we returned to Kovno and met other survivors, and compared memories, I heard from several friends that after my escape from the Ghetto the Germans had looked for me and my writings. The Gestapo thought that I had possessed the minutes of the Council, without knowing that no such minutes of the meetings were ever made. They interrogated and tortured people I had known, particularly my friend Ika Grinberg, my devoted secretary Lucia Elstein, and even the young secretariat messengers, but nobody revealed anything. Nothing can express my appreciation of those who were interrogated. My heart will always be heavy with sorrow for the torture they suffered.

I married Pnina Sheinzon in Kovno, on August 10, 1944. This was the first wedding which took place in Kovno after the liberation. It was conducted by Rabbi Ephraim Oshri, who had just taken up the post of rabbi of Kovno. There was no parchment or printed marriage certificate—the Ketubah—to be found. The rabbi wrote out the full text of the traditional religious certificate by hand, on a page taken from an exercise book, writing the traditional text from memory.

Soviet authority in the city had not yet been fully established. The war was not yet over. It was clear that this was the right time to escape, before the borders were defined, and while there was still a heavy traffic of refugees moving from country to country. First, however, I was faced with a mission which to me was of the utmost importance: locating the diary's hiding place in the ruined Ghetto, and removing the diary, in order to get it out of Lithuania. However, before I began, I was arrested by the NKVD in Kovno and was ordered, in the presence of a Jewish Communist who knew of the existence of my diary, to hand it over to them. I replied that I did not have any material, and that the place where I had hidden my diary was a complete ruin. Then I was warned not to dare to try approaching the hiding place without an NKVD escort, and was ordered by the NKVD to hand over immediately any material found. Should I fail to do so, I would be deported to Siberia forthwith.

Friends and acquaintances began to try to persuade me to do as I had been ordered, and to hand over the hidden material, thereby freeing myself from being followed by the NKVD. In any case, they said, nothing can be taken out of Soviet Lithuania, so what sense is there in taking such a risk. But their words served only to reinforce my determination to save my diary at any cost. On the night after I had been arrested by the NKVD, I approached my friend Feivchik Goldsmith, who had also survived and returned to Kovno, and together with Pnina, on that very night, we dug below the reinforced concrete foundations where the diary was hidden and removed three of the five crates. We were unable to reach the remaining two crates because of soil subsidence at the site. We emptied the contents of the three crates into three knapsacks and left in the darkness of the night, unseen, each as he had come. We all reached our destinations safely, long after midnight.

On the following day Pnina and I took the knapsacks to the home of one of Pnina's Lithuanian friends, the former city engineer of Kovno, whose wife agreed to hide them temporarily in a box underneath her child's cot. I nevertheless continued to be afraid of the long arm of the NKVD, and therefore made a special trip to Vilna, to consult with the poet and resistance fighter Avraham Sutzkever, who since the liberation had become the head of the Government Documentation Center there. Without hesitating, and in strictest confidence, he told me "Don't give!"—do not give the Soviets the material.

Encouraged, I returned to Kovno. My mind was set: I would not let my writings out of my possession, come what may. After a few months I learned that the NKVD officer who was keeping his eye on me had been transferred to Memel, which had just been liberated by the Red Army. So we left Kovno for Vilna, taking the material with us. This time we hid it in the cellar of the house where we were living, amid scrap and old household utensils.

During the months following the war, the Bricha movement, the "Escape," became more organized. At the same time, however, a series of arrests of Zionist activists began, and I was forced to escape before the date which had been set for Pnina, Shulamit, and me to leave.

I went to see Paukstys and suggested that he join me in my escape from Lithuania, warning him that, as a priest, he would not be able to carry on his humanitarian work or national traditions under Soviet rule, and that sooner or later he would be exiled to Siberia, as was already happening to other Lithuanian activists. That same day, February 22, 1945, I had been informed by a former Maccabi leader, Benjamin Friedman, that I myself was on a list of those to be exiled to Siberia, and that I must leave Pnina and Shulamit and escape immediately. I assured Paukstys that I would take him with me all the way to Palestine. But that noble man refused to leave, saying that he could not leave his community and that he would continue on his chosen path regardless of the peril or the threat of exile. He had not given in to the Nazis. He would not give in to the Bolsheviks either. (Some months later he was exiled to Siberia for ten years.) He and I embraced, and wept, when we parted.

I left for Poland on a military train, with a large knapsack containing the diary and the documents which had been hidden with it, except for a part—mainly labels, insignia, and many paintings—which I had given to my sister Batia Romanovski, who had returned from Russia to Vilna.[1] I reached Lublin, where some of the leaders of the underground had assembled after the war. A Jewish community organization had also been formed there after the war. The city had become one of the centers of the movement of Jews across Europe toward Palestine.

I was the first person from the Lithuanian underground to reach Lublin. I joined the Bricha and sent word back to Vilna that there was a way to proceed to Palestine. I also reported on the survivors in Lithuania, and visited the ruins of the Warsaw Ghetto with two former Warsaw Ghetto fighters, Antek Cukierman and Zivia Lubetkin.

After a few weeks, I was joined by Pnina and the little Shulamit. Then, at the end of March 1945, we left in a group of the Bricha, headed by myself, on foot, toward Czechoslovakia, I carrying the large knapsack of material. I was allowed to take it only after stormy arguments with the leaders of the Bricha in Lublin, who forbade us to take any documents and papers, with the exception of the forged identity papers which they themselves had given us. It was strictly forbidden to take children under the age of twelve. But I insisted on taking the seven-year-old Shulamit "at my own risk." When it was necessary to carry little Shulamit on our shoulders, one of us would take the knapsack and another knapsack containing our other belongings.

Dr. Elkes's Testament was carried by Pnina on her body, hidden in her underwear. We did not leave the material for a second. Nevertheless, during one of the many searches for documents conducted by the Red Army field police at one of the border crossings on our journey, Pnina, her brother Abram, and I miraculously and desperately succeeded in getting the better of the examiners, and got the knapsack and the Testament through without being caught. The leaders of the Escape told me that they refused to endanger the entire group again; I was therefore forced to give the material to them. I was promised that a trusted person of the Bricha would deliver it to Bucharest. When they took most of the material from me (I kept some of it in spite of everything) I felt as if one of my limbs had been amputated, but I could no longer refuse. Indeed, searches on the roads and at the borders became more frequent and thorough.

From Czechoslovakia, we went to Hungary and from there to Romania. In Bucharest, we were given 400 Palestine certificates, and visas for Palestine issued by the British Consulate. We were about to set sail for Haifa, but the Soviet secret police were informed that thirty-five people who had escaped from the Baltic countries were among the 400 about to set sail. The NKVD had warned the director of the Palestine Office in Bucharest that they would search the boat, and that if a single Jew of the thirty-five was on it he would send the boat eastward, not westward.

As a part of those thirty-five, we had once again to take up our wanderings, escaping the next day from Romania, where we had been for two and a half months.

We returned from Bucharest to Budapest. From there we went on to Austria, near the border with Italy. In mid-July 1945, a soldier from the Palestine Jewish brigade appeared, wearing a Star of David on his sleeve. After an emotional meeting, we crossed the border clandestinely into Italy, to a Jewish soldiers' camp at Tarvisio, where the soldiers of the Jewish Brigade received us like brothers, with open arms. That was the end of the Escape period, a period of exciting events, which are described here only very briefly.

We stayed in Italy for more than two years, during which I was asked to join the so-called illegal emigration committee as secretary. In Rome, our daughter was born. We named her Alina, thereby expressing our longing for reaching Palestine—*Aliya*. We finally reached Palestine on October 17, 1947, and there we learned that the diary and the documentary material had indeed been safely delivered to Bucharest by the organizers of the Escape. During the first years after the war, it was dangerous to smuggle the material from there; and it was only brought to Israel after my arrival with the help of Oscar Weiss and Shmuel (Muka) Eliashiv (Friedman). The former was one of the leaders of the Bricha from Hungary; the latter was Israel's ambassador to Romania. When the diary was finally handed to me, its long journey came to an end.

At first glance, I found that part of the material which I had given to the Bricha organizers had been lost. That part has never been found. Another part was burned by my sister Batia in Vilna, out of fear of the Soviet secret police. After a long and indirect correspondence, I also learned that the part which I had written from memory and hidden in the village of Virvigaliai had been burned during the last battles between the Russians and Germans. During the 1960s and 1970s, the Holocaust Memorial at Yad Vashem and the Ghetto Fighters Museum north of Haifa each received isolated pages, some of which were part of the material I had brought out of Lithuania and given to the organizers of the Bricha. It is hard to know exactly how those pages reached Israel. The pages have on them the Council stamp; some of them are signed by Garfunkel or me.

The material in my possession may not be complete, and this greatly distresses me. I am convinced, however, that the material which was rescued, about two-thirds of the total collection for which time and again Pnina and I risked our lives, gives an accurate picture of the history of the Kovno Ghetto from the time of the decree expelling Kovno's Jews to the Ghetto until it was liquidated.

1. Batia Romanovski's husband, Benjamin, decided not to risk joining the escape to Palestine; he and his wife remained in Vilna after the war, where he became the chief accountant of the ministry of light industry of the Lithuanian Soviet Socialist Republic. Benjamin Romanovski died in 1968 and his wife in 1960, both in Vilna.

MAPS

Europe on December 7, 1941

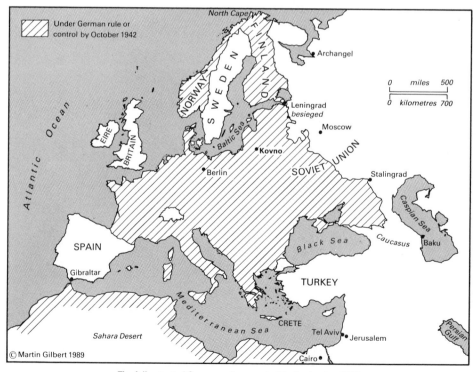

The full extent of German rule or control by September 1942

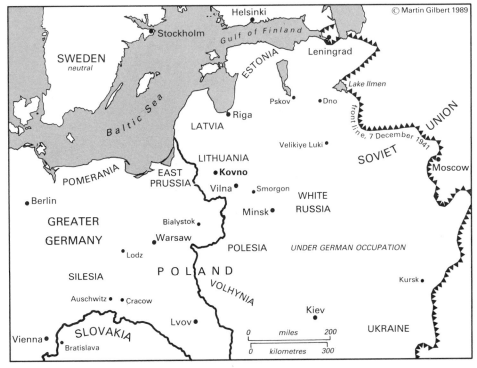

© Martin Gilbert 1989

Europe from Berlin to Moscow

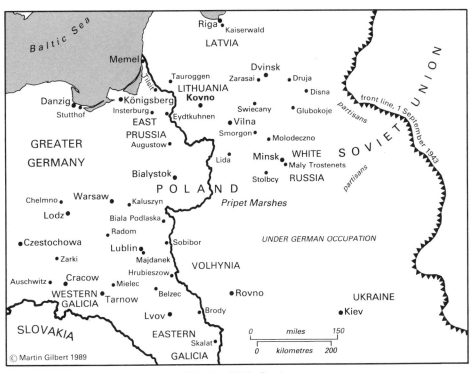

© Martin Gilbert 1989

Poland and White Russia

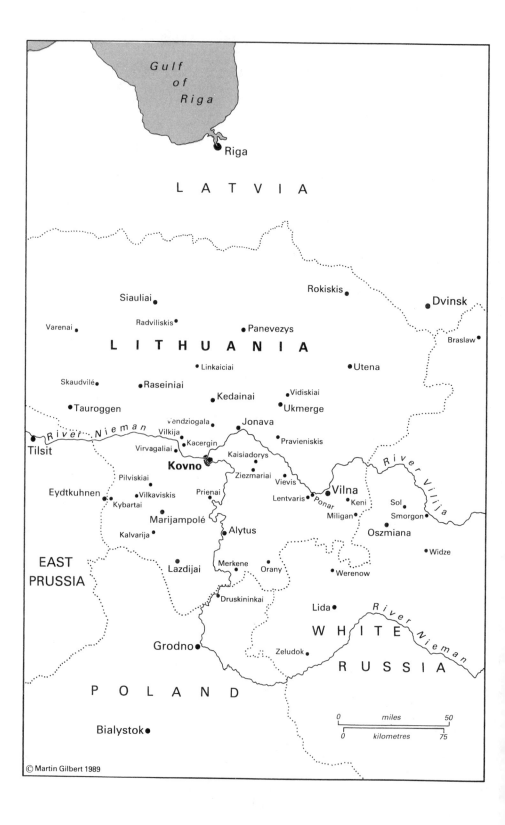

Gulf
of
Riga

Riga

L A T V I A

Rokiskis

Siauliai

Dvinsk

Varenai

Radviliskis

Panevezys

Braslaw

L I T H U A N I A

Linkaiciai

Utena

Skaudvilé

Raseiniai

Kedainai

Vidiskiai

Tauroggen

Vandziogala

Jonava

Ukmerge

Vilkija

River Nieman

Kacergin

Pravieniskis

Tilsit

Virvagaliai

Kaisiadorys

Kovno

Pilviskiai

Ziezmariai

Vievis

River Vilija

Eydtkuhnen

Vilkaviskis

Prienai

Lentvaris

Vilna

Keni

Sol

Kybartai

Ponar

Miligan

Smorgon

Marijampolé

Alytus

Oszmiana

Kalvarija

Widze

EAST
PRUSSIA

Lazdijai

Merkene

Orany

Werenow

Druskininkai

Lida

River Nieman

Grodno

Zeludok

W H I T E

R U S S I A

P O L A N D

0   miles   50
0   kilometres   75

Bialystok

© Martin Gilbert 1989

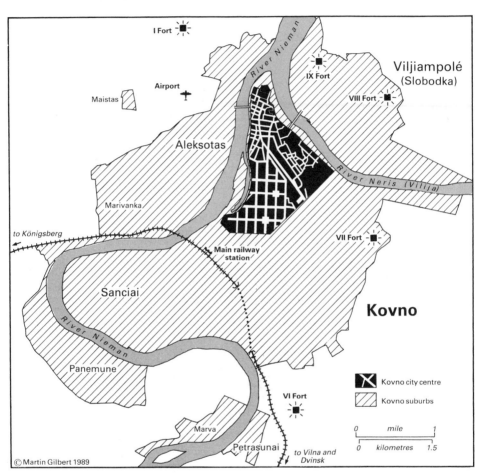

I Fort

River Nieman

IX Fort

Viljiampolé
(Slobodka)

Airport

VIII Fort

Maistas

Aleksotas

River Neris (Vilija)

Marivanka

to Königsberg

VII Fort

Main railway
station

Sanciai

Kovno

River Nieman

Panemune

Kovno city centre

Kovno suburbs

VI Fort

0   mile   1

Marva

0   kilometres   1.5

Petrasunai

to Vilna and
Dvinsk

© Martin Gilbert 1989

Kovno and its suburbs

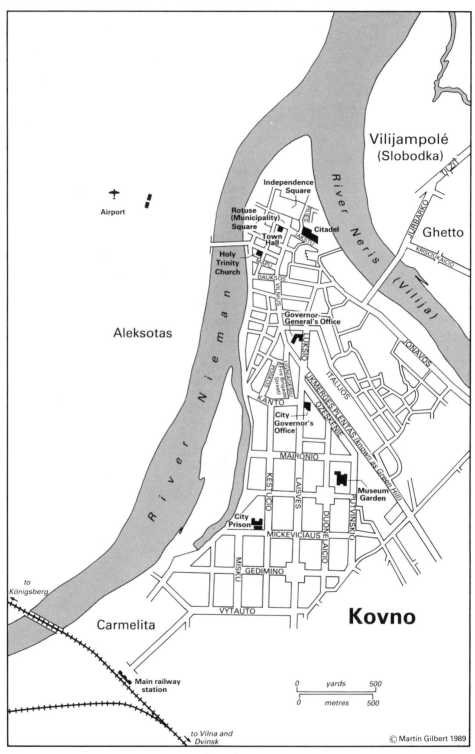

Vilijampolé
(Slobodka)

Independence
Square

Airport

Rotuse
(Municipality)
Square

Town
Hall

Citadel

River Neris

URBARKO

KRISCIUKAICIO

Ghetto

Holy
Trinity
Church

MAPU

PILES

AKSTU

DAUKSOS

VILNIUS

Governor-
General's Office

(Vilija)

Aleksotas

LUKSIO

UGNIAGESIU
(Fire Brigade)
Fire Street

POSKOS

KANTO

City
Governor's
Office

ITALIUS

UKMERGES PLENTAS (known as Green Hill)

OZESKIENE

JONAVOS

River Nieman

MAIRONIO

KESTUCIO

LAISVES

Museum
Garden

DUONELAICIO

PUTVINSKO

City
Prison

MICKEVICIAUS

MISKU

GEDIMINO

to
Königsberg

VYTAUTO

Carmelita

Kovno

Main railway
station

| 0 | yards | 500 |
| 0 | metres | 500 |

to Vilna and
Dvinsk

© Martin Gilbert 1989

Kovno city center

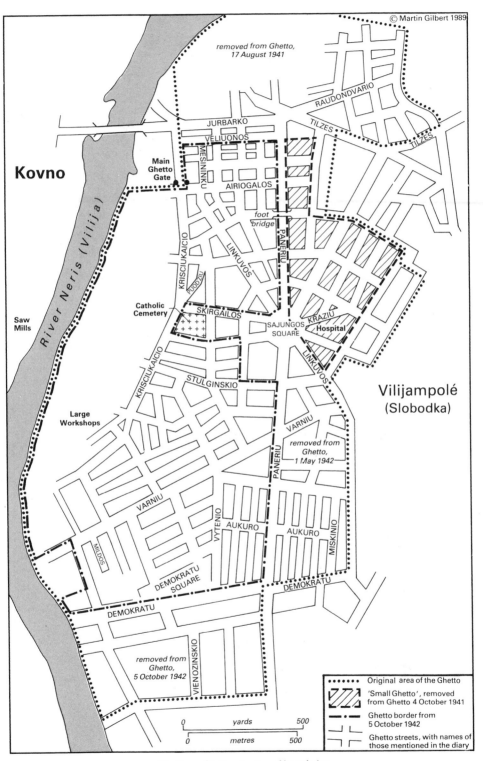

Kovno

River Neris (Vilija)

Saw
Mills

removed from Ghetto,
17 August 1941

© Martin Gilbert 1989

RAUDONDVARIO

JURBARKO

VELIUONOS

TILZES

TILZES

Main
Ghetto
Gate

MESININKU

AIRIOGALOS

foot
bridge

PANERIU

KRISCIUKAICIO

LINKUVOS

PUODZIU

Catholic
Cemetery

SKIRGAILOS

KRAZIU

SAJUNGOS
SQUARE

Hospital

LINKUVOS

KRISCIUKAICIO

STULGINSKIO

Vilijampolé
(Slobodka)

Large
Workshops

VARNIU

PANERIU

removed from
Ghetto,
1 May 1942

VARNIU

VYTENIO

AUKURO

AUKURO

MISKINIO

MILDOS

DEMOKRATU
SQUARE

DEMOKRATU

DEMOKRATU

VIENOZINSKIO

removed from
Ghetto,
5 October 1942

••••••	Original area of the Ghetto
▨	'Small Ghetto', removed from Ghetto 4 October 1941
—•—•—	Ghetto border from 5 October 1942
⊥⊤	Ghetto streets, with names of those mentioned in the diary

0 ——— yards ——— 500

0 ——— metres ——— 500

The Kovno Ghetto: streets and boundaries

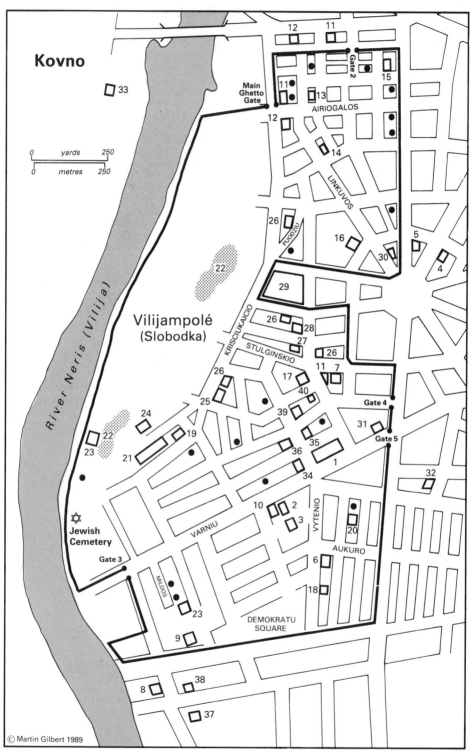

The Kovno Ghetto: places mentioned in the diary

KEY

1 Jewish Council building

2 Block A, in which Tory lived

3 Block C, under which Tory's diary was hidden

4 Hospital in the small Ghetto

5 Children's home in the small Ghetto, later the furniture workshop

6 German Labor Office

7 Ghetto pharmacy (clandestine radio in cellar below)

8 Vocational training school

9 Clandestine arms training

10 Ghetto Court

11 German Ghetto Guard

12 Jewish Labor Office

13 Soup kitchen

14 1st fire brigade; clandestine bakery

15 Beth Midrash

16 1st precinct of the Jewish police

17 2nd precinct of the Jewish police

18 3rd precinct of the Jewish police

19 Ghetto detention center

20 Ceramic workshop

21 Large workshops

22 Vegetable gardens

23 Clandestine meeting place

24 Public bathhouse

25 Stable; clandestine school

26 Clandestine arms training places

27 Chaim Yellin's hiding place

28 Ghetto hospital and health department

29 Catholic cemetery

30 Young Zionists meeting place

31 Ruined house: hiding place for those escaping to the forests

32 House of the Lithuanian woman Maria Leschinsky: hiding place on the way to the forests

33 House of the Russian Piotr Trofimov: hiding place for ammunition

34 Site of Meck's execution

35 Graphics workshop and criminal department of the Jewish Ghetto police

36 2nd fire brigade

37 3rd fire brigade

38 Hiding place for books

39 Jewish Council housing department and social aid department

40 Pnina Sheinzon's apartment

● "Malines": underground hiding places

INDEX

Library of Congress Cataloging-in-Publication Data

Tory, Avraham.
  Surviving the Holocaust : the Kovno Ghetto diary / Avraham Tory ;
edited with an introduction by Martin Gilbert ; textual and
historical notes by Dina Porat ; translated by Jerzy Michalowicz.
    p. cm.
  Translation of a diary originally written in Yiddish.
  Bibliography: p.
  Includes index.
  ISBN 0-674-85810-7 (alk. paper)
  1. Jews—Lithuania—Kaunas—Persecutions. 2. Holocaust, Jewish
(1939–1945)—Lithuania—Kaunas—Personal narratives. 3. Tory,
Avraham. 4. Kaunas (Lithuania)—Ethnic relations. I. Gilbert,
Martin, 1936–   . II. Porat, Dina. III. Title.
DS135.R93K288   1989   89-7496
940.53′18′09475—dc20   CIP